Theories of Human Communication

THIRD EDITION

Theories of Human Communication

THIRD EDITION

Stephen W. Littlejohn   Humboldt State University

Wadsworth Publishing Company

BELMONT, CALIFORNIA

A Division of Wadsworth, Inc.

Communications Editor: Kristine Clerkin
Editorial Assistant: Melissa Harris
Production Editor: Michael G. Oates
Managing Designer: Mary Ellen Podgorski
Print Buyer: Barbara Britton
Permissions Editor: Robert Kauser
Interior Design: Al Burkhardt
Copy Editor: Jennifer Gordon
Compositor: Thompson Type, San Diego, California
Cover: Mary Ellen Podgorski

© 1989 by Wadsworth, Inc.

Printed in the United States of America   85

1   2   3   4   5   6   7   8   9   10—93   92   91   90   89

LIBRARY OF CONGRESS CATALOGING IN PUBLICATION DATA

Littlejohn, Stephen W.
    Theories of human communication/Stephen W. Littlejohn.—3rd ed.
      p.   cm.
    Bibliography: p.
    Includes indexes.
    ISBN 0-534-09534-8
    1. Communication—Philosophy.   I. Title.
P90.L48 1988
001.51′01—dc19   88-14794
                CIP

Dedicated to my friend and colleague

DOUG LOSEE

Preface

Theories of Human Communication was first published eleven years ago. Those who have followed the text through to this third edition have seen substantial changes from one version to the next. These differences represent changes in the field, my own broadening interest and awareness, and what I hope has been perceived as natural improvements in the writing and content. The past decade has been a period of tremendous development in communication theory, and although no single text can pretend to present the state-of-the-art in communication theory, this third edition provides a good sense of what is happening in this field.

The general nature and level of this book remain the same. It provides a multi-disciplinary survey of many of the theories that have historical and contemporary value to communication scholars. The book remains appropriate as an advanced undergraduate and graduate text with theory-by-theory coverage. It includes a discussion of the nature of theory and inquiry in communication and a summary of general and contextual theories of communication. The introductory material on theory and inquiry has been updated and expanded, and the book as a whole includes many newer theories that were not covered in the previous edition. Sadly, economics forced the elimination of other theories from the text, and difficult judgments had to be made about what to add and delete to keep the book's length about the same.

Part II, which covers general theories of communication, has been completely recast. Instructors who have used previous editions may find some adjustment of course organization necessary. The new pattern emphasizes the natural philosophical divisions in the social sciences, and I am confident that it will give students a better sense of the similarities and differences among theories of language, meaning, information, and influence. Although the organization of individual chapters in the section on contexts (Part III) has been changed, the basic order of the contents remains the same. The capstone chapter is new and presents my thoughts on general trends in the field.

I wish to thank first and foremost my three consultants on this project. Stan Deetz of Rutgers University, James Fletcher of the University of Georgia, and Myron Lustig of San Diego State University provided advice and suggestions for improvement throughout the revision process. Although I assume ultimate responsibility for the writing and coverage, these individuals should receive a major part of the credit for the advances made in this edition.

I also wish to thank Janis Wright and Richard Rogers for their essential editorial assistance. Thanks also to Kris Clerkin of Wadsworth for her continued faith in the book and her patience with the revision process. I would also like to thank Michael Oates, production editor, Jennifer Gordon, copy editor, and Al Burkhardt, designer, for their support in the production of this book.

Finally, to Karen Foss, thanks for your loving support.

Stephen Littlejohn

Acknowledgments

Pp.15, 16, 22: From *The Conduct of Inquiry* by Abraham Kaplan. Copyright © 1964. Reprinted by permission of Harper & Row Publishers. **P.17:** From "Explaining Human Conduct: Form and Function," in *Explaining Human Behavior: Consciousness, Human Action and Social Structure*, pp. 127–154. Reprinted by permission of Sage Publications, Inc. **P.36:** From *The Ghost in the Machine* by Arthur Koestler. Copyright © 1968 by Arthur Koestler. Reprinted by permission of Macmillan Publishing Co. and A.D. Peters and Co., Ltd. **Pp.48–49, 127:** From *Communication Quarterly*, "Alternative Perspectives for the Study of Human Communication: Critique and Response," by Jesse Delia. Copyright © 1977. Reprinted by permission of *Communication Quarterly*. **Pp.63–64:** From *Kinesics and Context* by Ray Birdwhistell. Copyright © 1970 by the University of Pennsylvania Press. Reprinted by permission of the University of Pennsylvania Press. **P.70:** From *American Psychologist*, "On Understanding and Creating Sentences," by Charles Osgood. Copyright © 1963. Reprinted by permission of The American Psychological Association and the author. **Pp.97–98:** From *Symbolic Interactionism: Perspective and Method* by Herbert Blumer. Copyright © 1969. Reprinted by permission of Prentice-Hall, Inc. **P.103:** Adapted with permission from Bruce E. Gronbeck, "Dramaturgical Theory and Criticism: The State of the Art (or Science?)," *The Western Journal of Speech Communication*. Copyright © 1987 by the Western Speech Communication Association. **P.107:** From *Frame Analysis: An Essay on the Organization of Experience* by Erving Goffman. Copyright © 1959 by Erving Goffman. Reprinted by permission of Doubleday and Company. **P.108:** From *The Presentation of Self in Everyday Life* by Erving Goffman. Reprinted by permission of Doubleday and Company. **Pp.114–115:** From *Social Accountability and Selfhood* by John Shotter. Copyright © 1984. Reprinted by permission of Basil Blackwell. **Pp.120–121:** From *Communication Rules: Theory and Research* by Susan B. Shimanoff. Copyright © 1980 by Sage Publications. Reprinted by permission of Sage Publications. **P.126:** From *Communication Action and Meaning* by W. Barnett Pearce and Vernon Cronen. Copyright © 1980 by Praeger Publishers. Reprinted by permission of Praeger Publishers. **P.126:** From *Genetic Psychology Monographs*, "The Development of Listener Adapted Communication in Grade-School Children from Different Social-Class Backgrounds," by Kerby T. Alvy. Copyright © 1973. Reprinted by permission of the Helen Dwight Reid Educational Foundation. Published by Held-

ref Publications. **P.155:** From *The Psychology of Interpersonal Relations* by Fritz Heider. Copyright © 1958. Reprinted by permission of Grace M. Heider. **P.183:** From *The Acquaintance Process* by Theodore M. Newcomb. Copyright © 1961. Reprinted by permission of Holt, Rinehart and Winston, CBS College Publishing. **P.195:** From *Perspectives on Communication in Conflict*, "A Transactional Paradigm of Verbalized Social Conflict," by C. David Mortensen. Copyright © 1974. Reprinted by permission of Prentice-Hall, Inc. **Pp.196–197:** From *Communication Monographs*, "Attributions and Communication in Roommate Conflicts," by Alan L. Sillars. Copyright © 1980 by the Speech Communication Association. Reprinted by permission of *Communication Monographs*. **Pp.208, 210:** From *Groupthink: Psychological Studies of Policy Decisions and Fiascoes, Second Edition*, by Irving L. Janis. Copyright © 1982 by Houghton Mifflin Company. Used by permission. **Pp.210–211:** From "Communication in Faulty Group Decision-Making," by Randy Y. Hirokawa and Dirk R. Scheerhorn in *Communication and Group Decision-Making*. Copyright © 1986 by Sage Publications. Reprinted by permission of Sage Publications, Inc. **Pp.212–214:** From *SYMLOG: A System for the Multiple Level Observation of Groups* by Robert F. Bales, Stephen P. Cohen, and Stephen A. Williamson. Reprinted with permission of The Free Press, a Division of Macmillan, Inc. Copyright © 1979 by The Free Press. **Pp.228–229:** From *Communicating and Organizing* by Farace, Monge, and Russell. Copyright © 1977. Reprinted by permission of Random House, Inc. **P.246:** From "Communication and Organizational Climates," by Marshall Scott Poole in *Organizational Communication: Traditional Themes and New Directions*. Copyright © 1985 by Sage Publications. Reprinted by permission of Sage Publications, Inc. **Pp.247–249:** From *Communication Monographs*, "Organizational Communication as Cultural Performance," by Michael E. Pacanowsky and Nick O'Donnel-Trujillo. Copyright © 1983 by the Speech Communication Association. Reprinted with permission. **Pp.249–250:** From "Cultural Organization: Fragments of a Theory," by John Van Maanen and Stephen R. Barley in *Organizational Culture*. Copyright © 1985 by Sage Publications. Reprinted by permission of Sage Publications, Inc. **Pp.252, 270–271:** From *Perspectives on Media Effects*, "Living With Television: The Dynamics of the Cultivation Process," by George Gerbner, Larry Gross, Michael Morgan, and Nancy Signorielli. Copyright © 1986. Reprinted by permission of Lawrence Erlbaum Associates and the authors. **P.255:** From *The Medium is the Massage* by Marshall McLuhan and Quentin Fiore, produced by Jerome Agel. Copyright © 1967. Reprinted by permission of Bantam Books. **P.256:** From *Understanding Media* by Marshall McLuhan. Copyright © 1964. Reprinted by permission of McGraw-Hill Book Company. **Pp.257–258:** From "A Semiotic Model for the Study of Mass Communication," by Donald L. Fry and Virginia H. Fry in *Communication Yearbook 9*. Copyright © 1986 by Sage Publications. Reprinted by permission of Sage Publications, Inc. **Pp.260–261:** From *Critical Studies in Mass Communication*, "Marxist Approaches to Media Studies: The British Experience," by Samuel L. Becker. Copyright © 1984 by the Speech Communication Association. Reprinted by permission. **Pp.265–266:** From Noelle-Neumann, *The Spiral of Silence: Public Opinion—Our Social Skin*. Copyright © 1984 by The University of Chicago. All rights reserved. This book was first published in German under the title *Die Schweigespirale: Offentliche Meinungunsere soziale Houit* © R. Piper & Co. Verlag, Munchen 1980. **Pp.275–277:** From "Uses and Gratifications: A Theoretical Perspective," by Philip Palmgreen in *Communication Yearbook 8*. Copyright © 1984 by Sage Publications. Reprinted by permission of Sage Publications, Inc. **Pp.279–282:** From *Critical Studies in Mass Communication*, "The Uses and Dependency Model of Mass Communication," by Alan M. Rubin and Sven Windahl. Copyright © 1986 by the Speech Communication Association. Reprinted by permission.

Contents

PART II   General Theories   33

Chapter Three   System Theory   34

Chapter Four   Structural Theories of Signs and Meaning   52

Chapter Five   Cognitive and Behavioral Theories   68

Chapter Six   Symbolic Interactionist and Dramatistic Theories   95

Chapter Seven   Theories of Cultural and Social Reality   111

Chapter Eleven   Theories of Group Communication   202

Chapter Twelve   Theories of Organizational Communication   225

Theories of Human Communication

THIRD EDITION

I

Introduction

One

Communication Theory and Scholarship

As long as people have wondered about the world, they have been intrigued by the mysteries of their own nature. The most commonplace activities of our lives—those realms of human nature we take for granted—become puzzles of the largest magnitude when we try to conceptualize them.

Communication is intertwined with all of human life. Any study of human activity must touch on communication processes in one form or another. Some scholars treat communication as central, while others take communication for granted without making it the focus of their study. In this book we are concerned with the idea of communication as central to human life. Our guiding question is how scholars from various traditions have conceptualized, described, and explained human communication.

In a sense this book illustrates a part of our quest to understand ourselves. Specifically, it is a synthesis of many contemporary theories of communication. The book does not provide *the* answer to questions we ask about communication, but it does present several answers that have been proposed. In other words this book does not complete the puzzle of communication but illustrates how some of the pieces have been shaped and joined.

What Is Communication Theory?

Any attempt to explain or represent a phenomenon is a theory. As discussed in the next chapter, a theory is someone's conceptualization of an observed set of events. Communication professors often ask their students to devise explanations of certain aspects of communication. This theory-building exercise involves stating clearly what is believed to be happening in communication. Indeed, everybody operates by theory much of the time. Our theories consist of ideas that guide us in making decisions and taking actions. Sometimes our theories are flawed, and we may modify what we think the world is like.

Although the word *theory* can be used to describe the educated guesswork of laypersons, academics use the word somewhat differently. Scholars make it their work to study a particular kind of experience with a keen eye. A theory is the scholar's construction of what an experience is like, based on systematic observation. Thus, theory in this sense is the scholar's best representation of the state of affairs at any given time. As you will see in the next chapter, theory building is not an easy task. A great deal of focused observation, hypothesizing, and revision is required.

The term *communication theory* usually refers to the body of theories or understanding of the communication process. Much disagreement exists about what constitutes an adequate theory of communication. This text presents a wide variety of theories that are discussed in terms of their philosophical assumptions, their claims about what communication involves, and their strengths and weaknesses. You will find a basis for making your own decisions about which theories should and should not be included in our body of knowledge about communication.

Why Study Communication Theory?

Communication is one of our most pervasive, important, and complex clusters of behavior. The ability to communicate on a higher level separates human beings from other animals. Our daily lives are strongly affected by our own communication with others as well as by messages from distant and unknown persons. If there is a need to know about our world, that need extends to all aspects of human behavior, especially communication.

Specifically, understanding systematic theories of communication enables the individual to become more competent and adaptive. Teachers often provide students with a list of recipes when beginning the study of communication, but the communication process is too complex to be approached entirely on the level of simplistic guidelines. Students also need to learn about sending and receiving messages and relating to others through an understanding of what happens during communication and an ability to adapt to circumstances. The study of communication theory is a way to obtain this understanding.

Everybody tries to make sense out of their own experience. We assign meaning to what is going on in and around us. Sometimes the meaning is shared and sometimes idiosyncratic. Sometimes it is clear and other times vague or contradictory. Often, however, our interpretation of events reflects sensitivity and clear comprehension. When interpretation is difficult or when confusion results, people often make their theories of interpretation conscious. By developing an understanding of the variety of theories to explain communication, students can interpret communication experiences in more flexible, useful, and discriminating ways.

A colleague of mine used to say that the study of communication theory will cause the student to see things he or she has never seen before. N. R. Hanson writes: "The paradigm observer is not the man

who sees and reports what all normal observers see and report, but the man who sees in familiar objects what no one else has seen before."[1] This widening of perception, the unhitching of blinders, helps one transcend habits and become increasingly adaptable and flexible. To borrow some analogies from Thomas S. Kuhn: "Looking at a contour map, the student sees lines on paper, the cartographer a picture of a terrain. Looking at a bubble-chamber photograph, the student sees confused and broken lines, the physicist a record of familiar subnuclear events."[2] The basic justification for studying theories of communication is that they provide a set of useful conceptual tools.

The Academic Study of Communication

The diversity of communication theory reflects the complexity of communication itself. Looking for the best theory of communication is not particularly useful inasmuch as communication is not a single, unified act but a process consisting of numerous clusters of behavior. Each theory looks at the process from a different angle, and each theory provides insights of its own. Of course, all theories are not equally valid or useful, and any particular investigator may find a specific theory or theories more useful for the work to be undertaken. We should welcome rather than avoid a multitheoretical approach to the complex process of communication.[3]

An obstacle to a multitheoretical approach is the tendency to view communication from the narrow confines of specific academic disciplines. Because disciplines are somewhat arbitrary, disciplinary divisions do not necessarily provide the best method

1. N. R. Hanson, *Patterns of Discovery* (Cambridge, England: Cambridge University Press, 1961), p. 30.
2. Thomas S. Kuhn, *The Structure of Scientific Revolutions* (Chicago: University of Chicago Press, 1970), p. 111.
3. For an excellent case in favor of multiple approaches to communication, see John Waite Bowers and James J. Bradac, "Issues in Communication Theory: A Metatheoretical Analysis," in *Communication Yearbook 5*, ed. Michael Burgoon (New Brunswich, N.J.: Transaction Books, 1982), pp. 1–28.

of packaging knowledge. Interdisciplinary cooperation is essential for a useful understanding of communication. University courses related to communication are found in many departments, just as the theories described in this book represent a wide array of disciplines. As Dean Barnlund indicates: "While many disciplines have undoubtedly benefited from adopting a communication model, it is equally true that they, in turn, have added greatly to our understanding of human interaction."[4] Remember that when people tell you they are communication experts, they are saying little. Their primary interests may be in the sciences or the arts, mathematics or literature, biology or politics.[5]

Although scholars from a number of disciplines share an interest in communication, the scholar's first loyalty is usually to the general concepts of the discipline itself. Communication is generally considered subordinate. For example, psychologists study individual behavior and view communication as a particular kind of behavior. Sociologists focus on society and social process, seeing communication as one of several social factors. Anthropologists are interested primarily in culture, and if they investigate communication they treat it as an aspect of a broader theme. Do we conclude from this that communication is less significant as an academic study than behavior, society, and culture? Of course we do not.

In recent years scholars have recognized the centrality of communication and have emphasized it in their research and theory. Some of these scholars were trained in traditional disciplines. Others studied in academic departments called communication or speech communication. Regardless of their original academic homes, these scholars have come together in the new field of communication. They have shifted gears to make traditional themes support rather than dominate the study of communication. The field of communication is characterized not only by its focus on communication per se but also by its attention to the entire breadth of communication concerns. The work of such organizations as the International Communication Association and the Speech Communication Association, along with numerous journals devoted to the topic, typify what is happening in the field.

In this book we examine theories that relate directly to communication as a process as well as those that contribute less directly to our understanding of communication. The young communication field is now producing fresh theories, many of which are included in this text. As we discuss each theory, we examine the relevance of the theory to the broader study of human communication.

Defining Communication

Because of its complex, multidisciplinary nature, communciation is difficult to define. The word *communication* is abstract and, like all words, possesses multiple meanings.[6] Scholars have made many attempts to define communication, but seeking a single working definition may not be as fruitful as probing the various concepts behind the term. The term *communication* can be used legitimately in a number of ways. Frank Dance takes a major step toward clarifying this muddy concept.[7] He discovered fifteen distinct conceptual components in the various definitions. These components are the basic ideas used by the author to distinguish communication from other things. Table 1-1 summarizes the components and provides an example for each. In addition Dance found three points of

---

4. Dean Barnlund, *Interpersonal Communication: Survey and Studies* (New York: Houghton Mifflin, 1968), p. v.

5. The multidisciplinary nature of the study of communication is examined in Stephen W. Littlejohn, "An Overview of the Contributions to Human Communication Theory from Other Disciplines," in *Human Communication Theory: Comparative Essays*, ed. Frank E. X. Dance (New York: Harper & Row, 1982), pp. 243–85; and W. Barnett Pearce, "Scientific Research Methods in Communication Studies and Their Implications for Theory and Research," in *Speech Communication in the 20th Century*, ed. Thomas W. Benson (Carbondale: Southern Illinois University Press, 1985), pp. 255–81.

6. There are 126 different definitions of communication listed in Frank E. X. Dance and Carl E. Larson, *The Functions of Human Communication* (New York: Holt, Rinehart & Winston, 1976), Appendix A.

7. Frank E. X. Dance, "The 'Concept' of Communication," *Journal of Communication* 20 (1970): 201–10.

Table 1-1   Conceptual Components in Communication

1. Symbols/Verbal/Speech	"Communication is the verbal interchange of thought or idea."
2. Understanding	"Communication is the process by which we understand others and in turn endeavor to be understood by them. It is dynamic, constantly changing and shifting in response to the total situation."
3. Interaction/Relationship/ Social Process	"Interaction, even on the biological level, is a kind of communication; otherwise common acts could not occur."
4. Reduction of Uncertainty	"Communication arises out of the need to reduce uncertainty, to act effectively, to defend or strengthen the ego."
5. Process	"Communication: the transmission of information, idea, emotion, skills, etc., by the use of symbols—words, pictures, figures, graphs, etc. It is the act or process of transmission that is usually called communication."
6. Transfer/Transmission/ Interchange	"The connecting thread appears to be the idea of something's being transferred from one thing, or person, to another. We use the word 'communication' sometimes to refer to what is so transferred, sometimes to the means by which it is transferred, sometimes to the whole process. In many cases, what is transferred in this way continues to be shared; if I convey information to another person, it does not leave my own possession through coming into his. Accordingly, the word 'communication' acquires also the sense of participation. It is in this sense, for example, that religious worshipers are said to communicate."
7. Linking/Binding	"Communication is the process that links discontinuous parts of the living world to one another."
8. Commonality	"It (communication) is a process that makes common to two or several what was the monopoly of one or some."
9. Channel/Carrier/Means/ Route	"The means of sending military messages, orders, etc., as by telephone, telegraph, radio, couriers."
10. Replicating Memories	"Communication is the process of conducting the attention of another person for the purpose of replicating memories."
11. Discriminative Response/ Behavior Modifying Response	"Communication is the discriminatory response of an organism to a stimulus."
12. Stimuli	"Every communication act is viewed as a transmission of information, consisting of a discriminative stimuli, from a source to a recipient."
13. Intentional	"In the main, communication has as its central interest those behavioral situations in which a source transmits a message to a receiver (S) *with conscious intent to affect the latter's behaviors*."
14. Time/Situation	"The communication process is one of transition from one structured situation-as-a-whole to another, in preferred design."
15. Power	"Communication is the mechanism by which power is exerted."

NOTE: The sources of these definitions are cited in Dance, "The 'Concept' of Communication," *Journal of Communication* 20 (1970): 204, 208.

"critical conceptual differentiation," which form the basic dimensions along which the various definitions differ. The first is *level of observation*. Definitions vary in level of abstractness. Some definitions are broad and inclusive; others are restrictive. The second dimension is the inclusion or exclusion of *intentionality*. Some definitions include only intentional message sending and receiving; others preclude intention. Third is the factor of normative *judgment*. Some definitions include a statement of evaluation; other definitions do not contain such implicit judgments of quality.

The specific as well as the general conceptual discriminators listed above have more than passing significance. Theories of communication contain explicit or implicit definitions of communication, and the components of a definition in large measure set the boundaries and focus of the theory. For example, a theory adopting a very broad definition of communication, as, say, *linking and binding*, would have to take a sweeping approach and be limited in making substantive distinctions. Such a theory would probably focus on general relationships among elements in a system without identifying very specifically the nature of those relationships. In contrast, a theory using a more restrictive definition of communication, for example, *understanding*, would be able to identify particular kinds of acts without necessarily being able to relate those acts to broader concerns. One of the limitations of any single theory is its limited definition of communication. Consequently, no single definition of communication can suffice.

Dance's conclusion is important: "We are trying to make the concept of 'communication' do too much work for us."[8] He calls for a *family of concepts*. The theories included in the following chapters, seen collectively, represent a step in the direction of specifying the members of this family of concepts.

The Process of Inquiry in Communication

A Basic Model of Inquiry

Inquiry involves processes of systematic, disciplined ordering of experience that lead to the development of understanding and knowledge. Inquiry is what scholars do to "find out." Inquiry is not just one process, of course. Many modes are used, but all are distinguished from mundane or common experience. Inquiry is focused; it involves

8. Dance, "Concept," p. 210.

a planned means or method and it has an expected outcome. The investigator is never sure of the exact outcome of inquiry and can anticipate only the general form or nature of the results.

These scholars also share a general approach to inquiry that involves three stages.[9] The first and guiding stage of all inquiry is *asking questions*. Gerald Miller and Henry Nicholson, in fact, believe that inquiry is "nothing more . . . than the process of asking interesting, significant questions . . . and providing disciplined, systematic answers to them."[10] These authors outline common types of questions asked by the scholar. Questions of *definition* call for concepts as answers, seeking to identify what is observed or inferred (What is it? What shall we call it?). Questions of *fact* ask about properties and relations in what is observed (What does it consist of? How does it relate to other phenomena?). Questions of *value* probe aesthetic, pragmatic, and ethical qualities of the observed. Such questions result in value judgments about phenomena (Is it beautiful? Is it effective? Is it proper?).

The second stage of inquiry is *observation*. Here the scholar experiences the object of inquiry. Methods of observation vary significantly from one tradition to another. Some scholars observe by examining records and artifacts, others by personal involvement, others by using instruments and controlled experiment, others by taking testimony. Whatever form is used, the investigator employs some planned method for answering the questions.

The third stage of inquiry is *constructing answers*. Here the scholar attempts to define, to describe and explain, to make judgments. This stage, which is the focus of this book, is usually referred to as *theory*.

Students naturally tend to think of the stages of inquiry as linear, occurring one step at a time, but inquiry does not proceed in this fashion. Each stage affects and is affected by the others. Observations often stimulate new questions, and theories are challenged both by observations and questions.

9. The process of inquiry is described in Gerald E. Miller and Henry Nicholson, *Communication Inquiry* (Reading, Mass.: Addison-Wesley, 1976).

10. Ibid., p. ix.

Theories lead to new questions, and observations are structured in part by existing theories. Figure 1-1 illustrates the interaction among the stages of inquiry.

Types of Scholarship

The preceding section discusses inquiry in general terms, ignoring the distinctions between the many types of inquiry. These types stem from different methods of observation and lead to different forms of theory. Methods of inquiry often are grouped into three broad forms of scholarship: scientific, humanistic, and social scientific.[11] Although all of these forms of scholarship share the common elements discussed in the previous section, they also have major differences.[12]

Scientific scholarship. Science often is associated with objectivity. This association is valid or not, depending on how you view objectivity. If by objectivity you mean suspension of values, then science definitely is not objective. However, if by objectivity you mean standardization, then science is indeed objective; or, more accurately, it aims to be objective. The scientist attempts to look at the world in such a way that all other observers, using the same methods, will see the same thing in a given observation. Replications of a study will yield identical results. Remember that such objectivity is the goal-ideal of science but that it is not always achieved.

Science is consistent with the philosophical position that the world has form and structure apart from differences between individual observers. The world sits in wait of discovery. Where the scholar has reason to believe that a phenomenon exists in

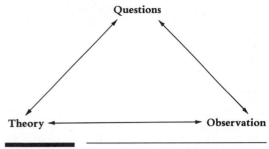

Figure 1-1   The stages of inquiry.

the world, the goal is to observe that phenomenon as accurately as possible. Since no divinely revealed way exists for knowing how accurate one's observations are, the scientist must rely on agreement among observers. This reliance is why objectivity or replicability is so important in science. If all trained observers report the same results, we can be assured that the phenomenon has been accurately observed. Because of the emphasis on discovering a knowable world, scientific methods are especially well suited to problems of nature.

Humanistic scholarship. While science is associated with objectivity, the humanities are associated with subjectivity. Science aims to standardize observation; the humanities seek creative individuality. If the aim of science is to reduce human differences in what is observed, the aim of the humanities is to understand individual subjective response.[13]

While science is an "out there" activity, humanities stress the "in here." Science focuses on the discovered world; humanities focus on the discovering person. Science seeks consensus; humanities seek alternative interpretations. Humanists often are suspicious of the claim that there is an immutable world to be discovered. The humanities scholar tends not to separate the knower from the known. The classical humanistic position is that who one is determines what one sees. Because of its emphasis on the subjective response, humanistic scholarship is especially well suited to problems of art, personal experience, and values.

11. An excellent discussion of scholarship can be found in Ernest G. Bormann, *Theory and Research in the Communicative Arts* (New York: Holt, Rinehart & Winston, 1965). See also Nathan Glazer, "The Social Sciences in Liberal Education," in *The Philosophy of the Curriculum*, ed. Sidney Hook (Buffalo: Prometheus Books, 1975), pp. 145–58; James L. Jarett, *The Humanities and Humanistic Education* (Reading, Mass.: Addison-Wesley, 1973); Gerald Holton, "Science, Science Teaching, and Rationality," in *The Philosophy of the Curriculum*, ed. Sidney Hook (Buffalo: Prometheus Books, 1975), pp. 101–8.

12. See C. P. Snow, *The Two Cultures and A Second Look* (Cambridge, England: Cambridge University Press, 1964).

13. James A. Diefenbeck, *A Celebration of Subjective Thought* (Carbondale: Southern Illinois University Press, 1984).

This discussion is not intended to lead you to believe that science and humanities are so far apart that they never come together. Almost any program of research and theory building includes some aspects of both scientific and humanistic scholarship. The differences mentioned relate to the primary thrust of the two groups of scholarship; points of cross-over also exist between them. At times the scientist is a humanist, using intuition, creativity, interpretation, and insight. Ironically, the scientist must be subjective in creating the mechanisms that will eventually lead to objective observation. Research design is a creative process. At times the humanist, in turn, must be scientific, seeking facts that enable scholars to understand the experiences to which ultimately they will respond subjectively. As we shall see in the next section, where science leaves off and humanities begin is not always clear.

The special case of the social sciences. A third form of scholarship is social science. Many social scientists would not separate this type of scholarship from science, seeing it instead as an extension of natural science. In fact, numerous methods used by social scientists are borrowed from physics. Social science, however, is a world apart. Paradoxically, it includes elements of both science and humanities, but it is different from both.[14]

Social scholars attempt to understand human beings as objects of study. They seek to observe and interpret patterns of human behavior. In practice scholars distinguish between behavioral science and social science, the former referring to individual behavior and the latter to human interaction. For our purposes these two branches are combined.

In order to understand human behavior, the scholar must observe it. If behavioral patterns do in fact exist, then observation must be as objective as possible. In other words, the behavioral scientist, like the natural scientist, must establish consensus

on what is observed. Once the behavioral phenomena are accurately observed, they must be explained or interpreted. Interpreting may be confounded by the fact that the object of observation, the human subject, is itself an active, knowing being. Unlike objects in the natural world, the human subject is capable of having knowledge, of possessing values and making interpretations. Can "scientific" explanation of human behavior take place without consideration of the "humanistic" knowledge of the observed person? This question is the central philosophical issue of social science.

Controversy about the nature of inquiry into human life is common in social science. In previous years the majority of social scientists believed that scientific methods alone would suffice to uncover the mysteries of human experience. Today most social scientists realize that while scientific methods are an important aspect of their scholarship, a strong humanistic element is present as well. Specifically, the individual subjective response must be considered in understanding how people think and evaluate.

The study of communication is a social science. It involves understanding how people behave in creating, exchanging, and interpreting messages. Consequently, communication inquiry combines both scientific and humanistic methods. The theories covered in this book, as examples of social science, vary significantly in their use of the languages of science and humanities. Traditionally in the field of speech communication, humanistic theories of communication have been referred to as *rhetorical theory* and scientific theories as *communication theory*. This distinction is not particularly useful. All of the theories we will discuss deal with human communication; both humanistic and scientific theories are worthy of inclusion in our body of knowledge about human communication.

In the field of communication there is no universal agreement on the limits of science and humanities. We are far from consensus on the questions that can and should be approached scientifically and those that should be the focus of humanistic methods. In the final analysis scholars defend the traditions in which they are trained and which they

14. See, for example, Hubert M. Blalock, *Basic Dilemmas in the Social Sciences* (Beverly Hills: Sage Publications, 1984), p. 15; Anthony Giddens, *Profiles and Critiques in Social Theory* (Berkeley: University of California Press, 1983), p. 133; Peter Winch, *The Idea of a Social Science and Its Relation to Philosophy* (London: Routledge & Kegan Paul, 1958).

enjoy the most. These issues of scholarship are taken up in more detail in Chapter 2 under the heading of philosophical issues in the study of communication.

The Creation of Knowledge

Inquiry is a process of creating knowledge. On the surface, the word *creating* may seem strange in this context. A closer look, however, reveals that knowledge is a product of human activity, a creation. A more exacting discussion of *reality* and the ways in which theory approximates it is taken up in Chapter 2. In this section we begin studying the general ways in which knowledge is created.

Each approach to knowledge makes certain assumptions about what is knowable and how knowledge arises. In brief, each posits a different set of relationships among questions, observations, and theory. Scholars typically make commitments to particular ways of knowing, although a given research project may, at different times, adopt different ways of knowing as appropriate.

In a sense, a way of knowing is like a game. It is selected because it is believed to be most appropriate in light of the problem being tackled. It comes with a set of rules that one is obliged to adopt during the course of the game. When playing a knowledge game, the scholar usually does not question the assumptions or rules, though on other occasions these assumptions and rules may be hotly debated. Although many variants can be found, scholars develop knowledge in three general ways—discovery, interpretation, and criticism.[15]

Knowledge by discovery. The discovery mode is so prevalent in natural and social sciences that it is often assumed to be the only appropriate route to knowledge, not just one possible avenue. This approach assumes that the world is outside the mind of the observer and lies in wait of discovery. Knowledge, in the discovery game, is something you "get" by "observing." The known is thus revealed to, or received by, the knower, leading to the label, "the

15. For a more complete discussion of these three, see Brian Fay, *Social Theory and Political Practice* (London: George Allen & Unwin, 1975).

received view." The standard of good knowledge in the discovery mode is objective and accurate observation, making *validity* the primary criterion of adequacy.

Clearly, the discovery mode is the typical approach of the natural sciences and has been widely adopted in the social sciences, too. Whether this is the best game in town for studying communication and other social processes is a matter of serious contention, as we will discuss in Chapter 2.

Knowledge by interpretation. For the interpretive scholar, knowledge cannot be discovered intact because reality is not independent from the human mind. Although a set of knowable events are assumed to exist, those events can be conceptualized in a variety of useful ways and can never be ascertained purely without the imposition of a set of concepts by the knower. Thus, knowledge is a transactional product of the knower and the known. Different observers will see different things in the stream of events because they assign different meanings to those events and conceptualize them in different ways. What mediates between knower and known, then, is a perspective, and knowledge is always colored by that perspective. Objectivity as defined in the classical sciences, therefore, is not a very useful construct for the interpretivist.

Since "reality" can be conceptualized in a variety of ways, no one way of seeing the world is believed to be best by the interpretive scholar. Although interpretations may be debated and criticized, the underlying assumption is that several theories may be good candidates for expressing what is known. If the discovery mode seeks to eliminate "incorrect" versions of reality, interpretive scholarship seeks to identify the powers and limits of various interpretations. What makes a good interpretation is not a question of validity in the traditional sense, but a question of utility. The question for interpretivists is this: Does the interpretation help us to talk about, understand, operate on, intervene in, teach, or fulfill some other cognitive or pragmatic goal? Further, interpretations that "make sense" to a community of scholars will prevail, at least for a time.

Knowledge by criticism. Many scholars are not satisfied to develop interpretations of events; instead they imagine ways in which change and improvement can be attained. Although there are numerous critical traditions, all share this common goal. Critical scholars adopt the basic interpretive stance, but carry it one step farther. In addition to a perspective, certain values are brought to bear on the interpretation. The knower's judgment is valued as a tool of knowledge, and the basic criterion of good knowledge in the critical mode is the potential for achieving desired change. Clearly, interpretive and critical approaches to knowledge are commonplace in the humanities and are becoming increasingly popular in the social sciences, including communication.

Two key questions are relevant to these three approaches: (1) What count as data? and (2) What do data count as?[16] In other words, what do we observe, and what are these observations taken to mean? In the discovery mode, objective observations, often made through instruments, are taken as data, and these observations count as instances of a structural reality in the world. In the interpretive mode, the scholar as a person is often treated as the "instrument," and data are the meanings and interpretations of the knowing scholar. Such data count as useful conceptualizations of events. In the critical approach, judgments are taken as data; these data then point to areas for social improvement and change.

Genres of Communication Theory

The theories discussed in this book are divided into two broad sections. The general theories (Part II) are relevant to the communication process in any context. The contextual theories (Part III) are designed to deal more specifically with communi-cation occurring in particular interpersonal, organizational, and mass communication settings.

The many distinguishing issues and dimensions of communication theory defy clear classification. No system of categories is perfectly appropriate for organizing this material, although several schemes could, with qualification, be used.

Four generic labels are used to classify theories in Part II:

1. structural and functional theories
2. cognitive and behavioral theories
3. interactional and conventional theories
4. interpretive and critical theories.

These genres are designed to capture some fairly important philosophical similarities and differences among the communication theories now in vogue. These genres also approximate the current divisions in the social sciences and as such constitute angles from which communication has been viewed. Although the theories within each of these genres share some philosophical assumptions, they are not mutually exclusive. There are numerous differences among the theories in each group, and you will detect similarities and overlaps among groups as well.[17]

Two general clusters seem to emerge: Structural and functional theories are akin to behavioral and cognitive ones, since both groups tend to be analytical and objectivist in orientation. Interactional and conventional theories overlap considerably with interpretive and critical theories; both groups tend to view meaning and knowledge as emerging from practice. The distinction between these two clusters of theory is fairly sharp, since each makes rather different assumptions about knowledge and reality. The theories in Part III could also be placed into these genres but are organized instead to accent contexts as currently conceived in the field.

---

16. W. Barnett Pearce, Vernon E. Cronen, and Linda M. Harris, "Methodological Considerations in Building Human Communication Theory," in *Human Communication Theory: Comparative Essays,* ed. Frank E. X. Dance (New York: Harper & Row, 1982), p. 5.

17. This analysis adapts material from Fred R. Dallmayr, *Language and Politics* (Notre Dame: University of Notre Dame Press, 1984); Lawrence Grossberg, "Does Communication Theory Need Intersubjectivity? Toward An Immanent Philosophy of Interpersonal Relations," in *Communication Yearbook 6,* ed. Michael Burgoon (Beverly Hills: Sage Publications, 1982), pp. 171–205; and Jon Stewart, "Speech and Human Being," *Quarterly Journal of Speech* 72 (1986): 55–73.

Structural and Functional Theories

This genre includes a broad group of loosely associated approaches to social science. Although the meanings for the terms *structuralism* and *functionalism* are imprecise, these approaches are generally characterized by a belief in real functioning structures outside the observing person.[18]

These approaches probably go back as far as Plato,[19] who believed that truth is ascertained through careful reflective thought, and Aristotle,[20] who believed in knowledge through observation and classification. System theory, as far back as Georg Hegel's idea of dialectical materialism, is firmly planted in the structural-functional tradition.[21] Modern structuralism generally recognizes Emile Durkheim, who promoted the idea of social structure, and Ferdinand de Saussure, the father of structural linguistics, as important seminal figures.[22]

Although structural and functional approaches are often considered in combination, they differ in emphasis. Structuralism, which is rooted in linguistics, stresses the organization of language and social systems. Functionalism, which is rooted in biology, stresses the ways in which organized systems work to sustain themselves. Putting these two approaches together results in a picture of a system as a functioning structure.

Structural and functional theories share certain characteristics. First, they stress synchrony over diachrony. *Synchrony* means stability over time, and *diachrony* means change over time. In other words, these approaches emphasize generalizations about structures believed to be invariant, or nearly so. In contrast, many theories not identified with this genre focus on change and situational contingencies.

Second, these approaches tend to focus on the unintended consequences of action rather than purposeful outcomes. Structuralists mistrust concepts like "subjectivity" and "consciousness" and look for factors that are beyond the control and awareness of human actors. For this reason, such theories are sometimes called antihumanist.

Third, such theorists share a belief in independent, objective reality. They therefore subscribe to the discovery method discussed earlier in the chapter, in which knowledge is discovered through careful observation. Fourth, the theories tend to be dualist because they separate language and symbols from the thoughts and objects being symbolized in communication. For these scholars, the world exists in and of itself, and language is just a tool for representing what already exists. This belief necessitates the fifth characteristic—the use of the correspondence theory of truth. The correspondence theory requires that language must correspond with reality; symbols must accurately represent things.

Structural and functional theories of communication apply these general philosophical commitments.[23] These theorists see communication as a process in which individuals use language to convey meanings to others. The language and symbol systems used in communication have a life of their own apart from the people who employ these tools. Predictably, then, structuralists judge good communication as accurate and clear, and they view communication competence as the accurate, precise, and skillful use of language and other symbol systems.

Such theories have been extremely influential in the field of communication and have probably determined in large measure how many, if not most, scholars in the United States view communication today. In recent years, however, communication theories of this genre have come under scrutiny, and other traditions have assumed parallel importance.

18. For an excellent discussion of structuralism and functionalism, see Anthony Giddens, *Central Problems in Social Theory* (Berkeley: University of California Press, 1979).

19. *Meno.*

20. *Prior Analytics; Posterior Analytics*

21. G. W. F. Hegel, *Phenomenology of Spirit*, trans. A. V. Miller (Oxford: Oxford University Press, 1977).

22. Emile Durkheim, *The Division of Labor in Society* (London: Collier-Macmillan, 1964); Ferdinand de Saussure, *Course in General Linguistics* (London: Peter Owen, 1960).

23. For a discussion of the effects of this tradition on communication theory, see Lawrence Grossberg, "Communication Theory"; George Lakoff and Mark Johnson, *Metaphors We Live By* (Chicago: University of Chicago Press, 1980).

Cognitive and Behavioral Theories

Like its structural-functional cousin, this genre is a fusion of two traditions that are not the same, but share many characteristics. These theories tend to espouse the same general assumptions about knowledge as do structural-functional theories, and they adopt almost exclusively discovery methods of generating knowledge. The primary difference between the two genres is in their focus and history. Structural and functional theories, which come out of sociology and other social sciences, tend to focus on social and cultural structures, while cognitive and behavioral theories, which come out of psychology and other behavioral sciences, tend to focus on the individual.

Psychology is the primary source of the cognitive and behavioral theories of human life. Psychological behaviorism throughout the twentieth century has dealt with the connection between stimuli or inputs and behavioral responses or outputs. Cognitivism recognizes the S–R link but deals mostly with the information processing that occurs between stimulus and response. Until the mid-1960s or so, *behaviorism* was the favored term. Today, psychologists of this tradition identify themselves as *cognitivists*. This change is a sign of increasing sophistication and the rise of information theory in the behavioral sciences. [24]

These theorists are "variable-analytic" in that they attempt to catalogue important cognitive variables and show ways in which these variables are correlated. They are also interested in the ways in which information and cognitive processing variables cause certain behavioral outputs. Some of these theories take a systems view, and others do not.

Communication is understood among such theories as a manifestation of individual behavior, individual thought processes, and bio-neural functioning. Consequently, the most important determining variables of one's cognitive equipment, including language, are usually beyond the awareness and control of the individual.

Interactional and Conventional Theories

In brief, the theories of this genre view social life as a process of *interaction*, which establishes, maintains, and changes certain *conventions*, including language and symbols. Communication is usually viewed by interactional theorists as the glue of society. This genre is an important part of communication theory because it upholds communication as the preeminent force of social life. This group of theories is primarily an outgrowth of symbolic interactionism in sociology[25] and ordinary language philosophy,[26] which are taken up in detail in Chapters 6 and 7. Theories in this genre tend to adopt discovery or interpretation modes of knowledge.

These theorists view social structure and function as products, not determinants, of interaction. While structuralism puts structure ahead of interaction, interactionism reverses this order. The focus here is not on structures that permit communication, but on how language is used to enact or create social structures and on how language and other symbol systems are reproduced, maintained, and changed through use. Meaning is not an objective entity to be transferred through communication, but emerges from and is created by interaction.

Structuralism imagines that organized and objective structures function to accomplish outcomes; *interactionism* imagines that those structures are themselves a product of the use of language and symbols in interaction. Interaction, therefore, leads to or reinforces shared meaning and establishes conventions like rules, roles, and norms that enable further interaction to take place.

Meanings themselves are conventions. They are arbitrary and are worked out through interaction; therefore, meanings change from time to time, from context to context, and from one social group to another. In the final analysis, then, interaction

24. For a good general discussion of cognitivism, see John O. Greene, "Evaluating Cognitive Explanations of Communicative Phenomena," *Quarterly Journal of Speech* 70 (1984): 241–54.

25. Jerome G. Manis and Bernard N. Meltzer, eds. *Symbolic Interaction* (Boston: Allyn & Bacon, 1978); Stephen W. Littlejohn, "Symbolic Interactionism as an Approach to the Study of Human Communication," *Quarterly Journal of Speech* 63 (1977): 84–91.

26. See, for example, John Searle, *Speech Acts: An Essay in the Philosophy of Language* (Cambridge, Mass.: Cambridge University Press, 1969).

within actual social groups is both the seat of tradition and the origin of change.

Interpretive and Critical Theories

This genre is a very loose confederation of ideas from a variety of traditions: interpretive sociology and the work of Max Weber, phenomenology and hermeneutics, Marxism and the Frankfurt school, and various text approaches, including rhetorical, Biblical, and literary theories.[27] Although cognitive and structural theories dominate in the United States, interpretive and critical approaches are more popular in Europe and elsewhere.

Although numerous differences exist among these traditions, they are linked by certain common characteristics. First, they all celebrate subjectivism, or the preeminence of individual experience, ascribing great importance to individuals' understandings of their experience. Second, meaning is highly significant in most of these theories. Experience is meaning-centered: By assigning meaning to experience, one becomes conscious of one's own being. Language is a central concept and is seen as the driving force of human experience. Language creates a world of meaning within which the person lives and through which all experience is interpreted.

Although these schools of thought share many ideas, there are also profound differences among the theories. Some of them, especially Marxist critical theories and some rhetorical theories, bear a strong resemblance to structuralist thought. Also, those theories primarily identified as "interpretive" tend to avoid prescriptive, absolutist judgments about observed phenomena; instead, observations are tentative and relative. Theories identified as "critical," on the other hand, are often highly judgmental and political. Such theories accent the limits of experience and prescribe ways of changing that experience. Although both interpretive and critical theories value reflective thought, critical theories place a special value on reflection as a means to overcome social and/or communication difficulties or weaknesses. In their more radical form, critical theories also prescribe political and sometimes revolutionary action.

Although these theories are substantially different from most cognitive and behavioral theories, they are not altogether different from conventional interactional approaches, and some of them also borrow from system theory, as does structuralism.

Contexts of Communication

Communication is frequently discussed in terms of the "levels" or "contexts" in which it occurs. In fact, handbooks, textbooks, and college curricula often are divided into sections corresponding to these levels. Because communication theories tend to cluster into context areas as well, Part III of this text is organized along these lines.

Although there is some variation in how contexts are labeled, four levels, which obviously range from narrow to very broad in focus, are commonly encountered in the literature and in curricular programs:

1. interpersonal communication
2. group communication
3. organizational communication
4. mass communication.

Interpersonal communication theories, presented in Chapters 9 and 10, deal with communication between people, usually in face-to-face, private settings. These chapters include theories relevant to characteristics of communicators, discourse, and relationships.

Group communication theories are presented in Chapter 11. These theories relate to the interaction of people in small groups, usually in decision-making settings. Group communication necessarily involves interpersonal interaction, and most of the

27. For a general source on interpretive sociology, see M. Truzzi, *Verstehen: Subjective Understanding in the Social Sciences* (Reading, Mass.: Addison-Wesley, 1974); for hermeneutics and phenomenology, see Stewart, "Speech and Human Being"; for the Frankfurt school, see Thomas B. Farrell and James A. Aune, "Critical Theory and Communication: A Selective Review," *Quarterly Journal of Speech* 65 (1979): 93–120; for rhetorical theory, see Sonja Foss, Karen Foss, and Robert Trapp, *Contemporary Perspectives on Rhetoric* (Prospect Heights, Ill.: Waveland Press, 1985).

theories of interpersonal communication apply also in the group context. Chapter 11 includes theories related to group dynamics, effectiveness, interaction, decision-making, and development. *Organizational communication theories*, discussed in Chapter 12, occur in large cooperative networks and include virtually all of the aspects of both interpersonal and group communication. In this text we discuss theories of the structure and function of organizations, human relations, communication and the process of organizing, and organizational culture.

Finally, Chapter 13 presents *mass communication theories*, which deal with public and mediated communication. Many of the aspects of interpersonal, group, and organizational communication enter into the process of mass communication. We address a wide variety of mass communication theories, including the general topics of (1) structure of media, (2) the media-society relationship, (3) the relationship between media and audiences, (4) cultural outcomes of mass communication, and (5) individual outcomes of mass communication.

The disadvantage of organizing theories of communication in this way is that it reinforces the already unfortunate tendency to think of these levels of communication as "types" that are different from one another. Although the contexts make a convenient way to organize theories, they should not be considered substantially different. Communication within each context will have some special characteristics, but all the contexts share important fundamental concepts and processes. Part II, which covers general theories of communication, addresses many of these basic concerns—language and coding, meaning, cognition, information, and social influence. The ideas encountered in Part II apply to the forms of communication in each of the four contexts discussed in Part III.

Two

Theory in the Process
of Inquiry

In the study of human communication, as in all branches of knowledge, it is appropriate, even compelling, to ask ourselves: How did we come to profess what we know or think we know? The question of truth, discovery, and inquiry is a particularly important place to begin this book because each of the chapters presents a kind of truth. Every theorist represented here has taken a stab at truth. This chapter discusses the special role of theory in the process of inquiry.

The Nature of Theory

What is theory? Uses of the term range from farmer Jones's theory about when his pullets will start laying eggs to Einstein's theory of relativity. People sometimes use the term *theory* to mean any unsubstantiated guess about something. Too, theory often is contrasted with "fact." Even among scientists, writers, and philosophers the term is used in a variety of ways. The purpose of this book is to represent a wide range of thought about the communication process. Therefore the term *theory* is used in its broadest sense as *any conceptual representation or explanation of a phenomenon*.[1] In their most general form communication theories are attempts of various scholars to represent what is conceived as important in the process of communication. Two generalizations can be made about theories.

First, all theories are abstractions. Theories of communication are not themselves the process being conceptualized. As a result every theory is partial; every theory leaves something out. Theories focus on certain aspects of the process at the expense of other aspects. This truism about theory is important because it reveals the basic inadequacy of theory. No single theory will ever reveal Truth.

Second, all theories must be viewed as constructions. Theories are created by people, not ordained by God. Theories represent various ways in which observers see their environments, but theories themselves are not reality.[2] Many readers and theorists forget this principle, and students often are trapped by the conception that reality can be seen in this or that theory. Abraham Kaplan writes: "The formation of a theory is not just the discovery of a hidden fact; the theory is a way of looking at the facts, of organizing and representing them. . . . A theory must somehow fit God's world, but in an important sense it creates a world of its own."[3]

1. For definitions of the terms *theory* and *model*, see Karl W. Deutsch, "On Communication Models in the Social Sciences," *Public Opinion Quarterly* 16 (1952): 357; Frank E. X. Dance and Carl E. Larson, *The Functions of Human Communication* (New York: Holt, Rinehart & Winston, 1976), p. 3; Leonard Hawes, *Pragmatics of Analoguing: Theory and Model Construction in Communication* (Reading, Mass.: Addison-Wesley, 1975), pp. 122–23. For a discussion of the several senses of the term *theory*, see Ernest G. Bormann, *Communication Theory* (New York: Holt, Rinehart & Winston), pp. 24–25.

2. See Max Black, *Models and Metaphors* (Ithaca, N.Y.: Cornell University Press, 1962).

3. Abraham Kaplan, *The Conduct of Inquiry* (San Francisco: Chandler, 1964), p. 309.

Let us take an analogy from biology. Two observers using microscopes may see different things in an amoeba, depending on their theoretical points of view. One observer sees a one-celled animal; the other sees an organism without cells. The first viewer stresses the properties of an amoeba that resemble properties of all other cells—the wall, the nucleus, the cytoplasm. The second observer concentrates on the analogy between the amoeba and other whole animals. This observer sees ingestion of food, excretion, reproduction, mobility. Neither observer is wrong. Their theoretical frameworks simply stress different aspects of the observed object.[4] We will see this point again and again in the following chapters. Because of the fact that theories and models are constructions, questioning a theory's *usefulness* is wiser than questioning its *truthfulness*. This statement is not intended to imply that theories do not represent reality, but that any given "truth" can be represented in a variety of ways, depending on the theorist's orientation. In this way, then, theories create reality.

Basic Elements of Theory

Concepts in Theories

The first and most basic aspect of a theory is its set of *concepts*. We as persons are by nature concept-processing beings. Our entire symbolic world—everything known—stems from concept formation. Kuhn writes: "Neither scientists nor laymen learn to see the world piecemeal or item by item; . . . both scientists and laymen sort out whole areas together from the flux of experience."[5] Although the process of conceptualizing is complex, basically it consists of grouping things and events into categories according to observed commonalities. The communication theorist observes many variables in communication and classifies and labels them according to perceived patterns. The

goal of theory is to increase the usefulness of its concepts. Kaplan describes the process:

> As knowledge of a particular subject-matter grows, our conception of that subject-matter changes; as our concepts become more fitting, we can learn more and more. Like all existential dilemmas in science, of which this is an instance, the paradox is resolved by a process of approximation: the better our concepts, the better the theory we can formulate with them, and in turn, the better the concepts for the next improved theory. . . . It is only through such successions that the scientist can hope ultimately to achieve success.[6]

An important part of conceptualizing is labeling. We mark our concepts by symbols, usually words. Hence, an integral part of any theory is the set of terms that captures the theory's concepts. Concepts and definitions cannot be separated. Together they tell us what the theorist is looking at and what is considered important.

Some theories stop at the concept level, providing only a list of concepts and definitions without explaining how the concepts interrelate or affect one another. Such theories are known as *taxonomies*. (Note that many scholars believe that taxonomies are not theories.) Introductory communication texts often include basic models that list the "parts" of the communication process, including such concepts as source, message, receiver, feedback, and so forth. The best theories, however, go beyond concepts to provide explanations, statements about how concepts interrelate. These explanations tell us why variables are connected. Theories that stop at the concept level are primitive at best, since the goal of theory building is to provide an understanding of how a phenomenon operates.

Explanation in Theories

The second element common to many theories is explanation. Explanation goes beyond naming and defining variables. It identifies regularities in the relationships among those variables. Explanations account for an event by referring to what is going on within that event or some other event. In

4. Examples from N. R. Hanson, *Patterns of Discovery* (Cambridge, Mass.: Cambridge University Press, 1961), pp. 4–5.
5. Thomas S. Kuhn, *The Structure of Scientific Revolutions* (Chicago: University of Chicago Press, 1970), p. 28.

6. Kaplan, *Conduct*, p. 53.

	Empowered Explanations	Enabling Explanations
Situation-centered (prior)	"He was required to . . ." "She was raised to . . ."	"She used certain information" "Someone suggested it."
Person-centered	"It is a habit." "It is a trait."	"He decided." "She felt like it."
Situation-centered (post)	"He is destined to . . ."	"He did it to reach a goal."

Figure 2-1   Forms of behavioral explanation.

simplest terms, explanation answers the question, Why? Explanation relies primarily on the principle of necessity.

The principle of necessity. An explanation designates some force among variables that makes particular outcomes *necessary*. If *x* occurs, then *y* is necessary or probable. Necessity is rarely taken as absolute, and a probablistic model is more appropriate. There are different kinds of necessity.[7]

One model outlines three types of necessity—causal, practical, and logical. We return to logical necessity later; for now, let us concentrate on the first two. *Causal necessity* explains events in terms of cause–effect. *Practical necessity* explains events in terms of act–consequent. In the former case, behavior is seen as an outcome of causal forces. In the latter case, behavior is seen as intentional action designed to achieve some goal or future state. Causal necessity explains behavior as response to

stimuli, while practical necessity attributes volition to the person or object. In causal necessity, the consequent event is a necessary outcome of the antecedent event. In practical necessity, however, behavior is "necessary" because the actor makes it so. (In fact, in practical explanation, the term *necessity* may be inappropriate.)

For the social sciences, a more useful model of theoretical explanation is that of Kenneth Gergen and Mary Gergen (see Figure 2-1).[8] In this scheme, explanations are *empowered* when they suggest that human behavior is determined or brought about by outside forces. Explanations are *enabling* when they attribute intention and volition to the acts of human beings.

Explanations can also be divided into two further categories. *Person-centered* explanations concentrate on factors inside the acting person, while *situation-centered* explanations involve primarily outside factors. Some situation-centered explanations focus on factors occurring before the action being explained, and some focus on those occurring after the target action. As Figure 2-1 illustrates, six types of explanation result.

7. Based on P. Achinstein, *Laws and Explanation* (New York: Oxford University Press, 1971); see also Donald P. Cushman and W. Barnett Pearce, "Generality and Necessity in Three Types of Theory About Human Communication, with Special Attention to Rules Theory," *Human Communication Research* 3 (1977): 344–53. For an excellent discussion of explanation in the social sciences, see Paul F. Secord, ed., *Explaining Human Behavior: Consciousness, Human Action, and Social Structure* (Beverly Hills: Sage Publications, 1982).

8. Kenneth J. Gergen and Mary M. Gergen, "Explaining Human Conduct: Form and Function," in *Explaining Human Behavior: Consciousness, Human Action and Social Structure* (Beverly Hills: Sage Publications, 1982), pp. 127–54.

Chaining explanations. Explanatory theories often seek to put together an elaborate explanatory framework. In such a framework, statements are linked by logical connection, so that by accepting certain statements, other statements become necessary. This kind of logical chaining makes use of the third kind of force mentioned earlier: *logical force.* This is the force of logical consistency. In the overall scheme of a theory, it is the glue that holds the various theoretical statements together. Logical necessity relies on a series of internally consistent definitions and a set of correspondences among events. Consider, for illustration, the example of relational communication theory (explained in Chapter 10). The following list is a set of propositions contained in that theory. As you read through these propositions, notice how each presents an explanation of its own, yet the explanatory power of the entire set of propositions is made complete by the logical necessity among them.

1. A complementary relationship exists when the behavior of one person follows naturally from the behavior of another. (prior situation-centered/enabling)

2. This condition exists when the relational rules are both understood and accepted by the partners. (person/centered/enabling)

3. Power is the ability to control relational rules. (person-centered/enabling)

4. One-up behavior asserts control over the relational rules. (post situation-centered/enabling)

5. One-down behavior accepts control by the other in a relationship. (prior situation/centered/enabling)

6. In a complementary relationship the person consistently behaving in a one-up fashion has the power. (person-centered/enabling)

Laws, rules, and systems. Traditionally in the field of communication, theories have been separated into three types, depending on their primary method of explanation. *Law theories* are believed to rely primarily on causal necessity, embodying the spirit of science. They make use of covering laws that specify universal causal relations among variables. *Rules theories*, which rely on practical neces-

sity, are believed to be more humanistic, claiming that people choose and change rules. Rules theorists are seen as doubting the viability of covering laws in communication. In between lies the *systems approach*, which purportedly relies on logical necessity. This type of theory is believed to center on the logical relations among elements of a system. Such theories stress the intercorrelations among events.

Doubt has been cast on the utility of this laws-rules-systems trichotomy.[9] Differences may not be as clear as suggested by its advocates. Although the covering law approach clearly embodies a scientific epistemology, the difference between systems and rules appears to be more a matter of generality or abstractness than method of explanation. Besides, there are important differences in explanation even among theories that are classed as systems or those classed as rules. For example, rules theorists disagree among themselves as to how much power rules exert over people's actions, and systems theorists equivocate about whether systems relations are causal, correlational, or both. Keep in mind that we are not discarding the terms *laws, rules,* and *systems.* (In fact, this book has chapters on both rules and systems.) The problem lies in using these labels together as a trichotomy to designate particular forms of explanation.

The Traditional Ideal of Theory

Traditional social science has been dominated by an approach to theory and research modeled on the experimental natural sciences.[10] Traditional social science methods are based on a fourfold approach:

9. This controversy is well summarized in Bormann, *Communication Theory,* chap. 7. See also Charles R. Berger, "The Covering Law Perspective as a Theoretical Basis for the Study of Human Communication," *Communication Quarterly* 25 (1977): 7–18; Donald P. Cushman, "The Rules Perspective as a Theoretical Basis for the Study of Human Communication," *Communication Quarterly* 25 (1977): 30–45; Peter R. Monge, "The Systems Perspective as a Theoretical Basis for the Study of Human Communication," *Communication Quarterly* 25 (1977): 19–29.

10. See, for example, Myron W. Lustig, "Theorizing About Human Communication," *Communication Quarterly* 34 (1986): 451–59; Fred N. Kerlinger, *Foundations of Behavioral Research* (New York: Holt, Rinehart & Winston, 1964), pp. 3–50; Robert J. Kibler, "Basic Communication Research Considerations," in *Methods of Research in Communication,* eds. Philip Emmert and William Brooks (Boston: Houghton Mifflin, 1970),

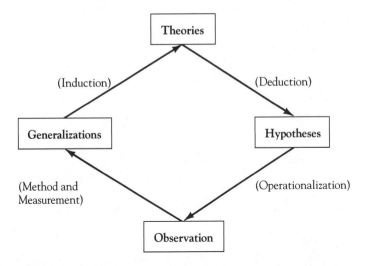

Figure 2-2   The classical ideal of science.

Reprinted with permission: Walter L. Wallace, ed., *Sociological Theory, An Introduction* (New York: Aldine de Gruyter). Copyright © 1969 by Walter L. Wallace.

(1) developing questions, (2) forming hypotheses, (3) testing the hypotheses, and (4) formulating theory. This approach constitutes the *hypothetico-deductive method*, in which relationships between variables are formulated and tested. A theory then becomes a codification of hypotheses and/or findings from a series of tests. This approach is based on the assumption that complex phenomena are best understood in terms of fine analysis of parts, giving rise to the alternate label, *the variable-analytic tradition*. It also assumes that social life consists of cause–effect relations.

Hypothesis testing is a painstakingly slow process, in which theories are developed and fine-tuned by numerous tests. The fourfold process is thus repeated to generate new questions and improved hypotheses in an incremental building-block process. Figures 2-2 and 2-3 illustrate the hypothetical deductive method.[11]

The hypothetico-deductive method is based on

pp. 9–50; Gerald Miller and Henry Nicholson, *Communication Inquiry* (Reading, Mass.: Addison-Wesley, 1976).

11. Figure 2-2 adapted from Walter L. Wallace, ed., *Sociological Theory: An Introduction* (Chicago: Aldine, 1967), p. ix.; Figure 2-3 from Irwin B. J. Bross, *Design for Decision* (New York: Macmillan), pp. 161–77.

five major concepts—hypothesis, operationism, control and manipulation, covering laws, and prediction. The first concept is *hypothesis*. A hypothesis is a well-formed guess about a relationship between variables. It is based on intuition, personal experience, or, most desirably, previous research and theory. In fact, hypothesis testing is often preceded by an *inductive* process of looking for generalizations. A hypothesis must be testable; in other words, the variables brought together must be carefully defined so that any trained researcher is able to observe them in precisely the same way. Further, the relationship posited by the hypothesis must be framed so that potential rejection is possible. If it is not, any test will yield either a positive result or an equivocal one, and it is impossible to discover whether the hypothesis is wrong. Hypothesis testing, then, is really a process of looking for exceptions.

Operationism states that all variables in a hypothesis should be stated in ways that provide means of observation. An operational definition answers the question, How do you know one when you see it? Operational definitions are the most precise possible definitions because they tell you how the concept is to be seen. An operational definition of

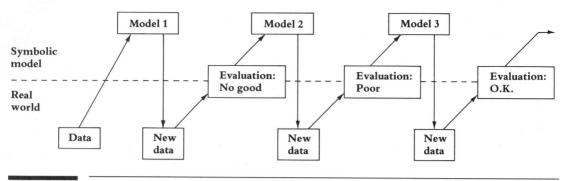

Figure 2-3   The decision-making process.

From *Design for Decision* by Irwin Bross. Copyright © 1953 by Macmillan Publishing Company. Reprinted with permission of the publisher. Copyright renewed 1981 by Irwin D. J. Bross.

intelligence, for example, is the Stanford-Binet intelligence test. An operational definition of dominance might be a particular set of observer ratings on dominant versus submissive messages.

Operationism relies on measurement, in which precise, usually numerical indices of observations are made. This measurement enables one to detect differences on an observed variable. Measurement is evaluated in terms of two criteria: validity and reliability. Validity is the degree to which an observation measures what it is intended to measure. How do we know, for example, that the observer's ratings really measure dominance in communication? Perhaps what is really influencing the ratings is some other hidden factor, or perhaps the ratings reflect nothing in particular. Researchers have methods of estimating whether such measures are valid.

Reliability is the degree to which the construct is measured accurately, and reliability is most often estimated by measuring consistency. If your bathroom scale gives you a different weight each day, even though you have not gained or lost, it is unreliable. And an intelligence test that yields a different result for the same person when administered on separate occasions is also unreliable. If all the items on a test are designed to measure the same thing, and they prove not to be very consistent with one another, the test is said to be unreliable. Clearly, validity and reliability are related to one

another. Reliability is a necessary but not sufficient condition for validity.

The third concept of traditional science is *control and manipulation* in observation. These factors are considered important because they are the only way in which causality can be ascertained. If one set of variables is held constant (control) and another set is systematically varied (manipulation), then the researcher can detect the effect of the manipulated variables without worrying about whether other variables were hidden causes. Control and manipulation can be exercised directly, as in experiments, or can be accomplished through particular kinds of measurement and statistical manipulation.

The fourth concept is the *covering law*. The covering law is a theoretical statement of cause and effect relevant to a particular set of variables across situations. In traditional science, the covering law is believed to be very significant because of its power in explaining events. Covering laws also enable the researcher to make predictions about future events. Theories in the classical tradition are statements of related covering laws, or more realistically, hypothesized laws.

Prediction is the final concept of classical social science inquiry. Prediction is an important outcome of inquiry; as an outcome, prediction gives people power over their environment. If, for example, I can predict that certain kinds of communication will lead to particular relationships, I may be able to control relationships by carefully designing communication messages. Prediction is also crucial in the process of inquiry. Often hypotheses are stated in the form of a prediction: If x and y, then z.

This classical approach to research and theory is firmly planted in the tradition of "knowledge as discovery," as explained in Chapter 1. As our previous discussion points out, however, the discovery method is often rejected by scholars in the interpretive and critical traditions. In general terms, these critics refer to the classical ideal as "old paradigm" social science and their own work as that of the "new paradigm."[12] A less biased designation is "traditional" and "alternative" paradigms. Later in this chapter, we will discuss the paradigms and the issues that divide these schools of thought. In brief, alternative paradigm scholars question two of the assumptions made by the older approach. First, they believe that reality does not have a singular, static structure to be discovered and represented by theory. Rather, reality itself changes and can be represented in a variety of useful ways. This shift questions the whole approach of hypothesis testing and validity in theory. Second, these researchers are suspicious of the view that human behavior can be broken down into a complex of variables that are determined by causal forces. These researchers therefore eschew covering laws and prediction in favor of interpretation.

The Functions of Theory

Nine important and overlapping functions of theory can be identified: (1) the organizing and summarizing function, (2) the focus function, (3) the clarifying function, (4) the observational function, (5) the predictive function, (6) the heuristic function, (7) the communicative function, and (8) the control function, and (9) the generative function.

12. See, for example, R. Harré and P. F. Secord, *The Explanation of Social Behavior* (Totowa, N.J.: Littlefield, Adams & Co., 1973), pp. 19–25.

The first function of theory is to organize and summarize knowledge. We do not see the world in bits of data. We need to organize and synthesize the world. Patterns must be sought and connections discovered. Theories and models are one way of accomplishing this organization of knowledge. An added benefit of this function is theory's contribution to accumulated knowledge. The student, practitioner, or scientist does not have to start anew with each investigation. Knowledge is organized into a body of theories, and the investigator begins a study with the organized knowledge of generations of previous scholars.

The second function is that of focusing. Theories, in addition to organizing data, focus attention on important variables and relationships, as a map depicts terrain. From the overall surface a map points out recreation spots, communities, picnic grounds, and shopping centers. To the persistent question of "What will I look at?" the theory points out areas for investigation.

Third, theories provide the advantage of clarifying what is observed. The clarification not only helps the observer to understand relationships in communication but to interpret specific events. Theories provide guideposts for interpreting, explaining, and understanding the complexity of human relations.

Fourth, theories offer an observational aid. Closely related to the focus function, the observational function points out not only what to observe but how to observe. Especially for those theories that provide operational definitions, the theorist gives the most precise indication possible about what is meant by a particular concept. Thus by following directions the reader is led to observe details elaborated by the theory.

The fifth function of theories, to predict, is one of the most widely discussed areas of scientific inquiry. Many theories allow the inquirer to make predictions about outcomes and effects in the data. This ability to predict is important in the applied communication areas such as persuasion and attitude change, psychotherapy, small group dynamics, organizational communication, advertising, public relations, and mass media. Teachers work toward

developing skills and abilities to improve communication competence. Various communication theories aid this process by enabling the student
to substitute well-founded predictions for good
guesses.

The sixth theoretical function, the heuristic
function, is also frequently discussed. A familiar
axiom is that a good theory generates research. The
speculation forwarded in theories of communication often provides a guide as to the direction the
research will take and thus aids in furthering the
investigation. This heuristic function of aiding discovery is vital to the growth of knowledge and is in
a sense an outgrowth of each of the other functions
of theory.

Seventh, theories serve an indispensable communicative function. Most investigators want and
need to publish their observations and speculations
for other interested persons. Theory provides a
framework for this communication and provides an
open forum for discussion, debate, and criticism.
Through the communication of numerous explanations of the phenomena we study, comparison
and theory improvement become possible.

The eighth function of theories is control. This
function grows out of value questions, in which the
theorist seeks to judge the effectiveness and propriety of certain behavior. Such theory is often referred to as *normative*, in that it seeks to establish
norms of performance. Much theory, of course,
does not seek to fulfill this function at all, remaining on the *descriptive* level.

The final function of theory is the generative
function. This is particularly relevant to the interpretive and critical traditions of alternative paradigm social science. In short, it means using
theory to challenge existing cultural life and to
generate new ways of living. It is, in other words,
the use of theory to achieve change. Gergen states
the generative function in these terms: "the capacity to challenge the guiding assumptions of the
culture, to raise fundamental questions regarding
contemporary social life, to foster reconsideration
of that which is 'taken for granted,' and thereby to
generate fresh alternatives for social action."[13]

13. Kenneth J. Gergen, *Toward Transformation in Social
Knowledge* (New York: Springer-Verlag, 1982), p. 109.

Theory Development and Change

Although it is important to understand that theory is an abstraction from reality, realizing the
relationship between the two is also necessary.
Theory is not purely abstract, without grounding
in actual experience. Experience affects theory,
and theory in turn affects one's conception of
experience.

From original experiences (including research),
we formulate theory. Good theory development,
then, is a constant process of testing and formulating. For the traditionalist, this testing is a process
of improving hypotheses about structures in the
"real" world. For the alternative paradigm theorist,
it is a process of fine-tuning interpretive frameworks
for understanding the flow of events.

This theory development process stresses the
need for research, which allows for:

1. specific investigation of facts that are considered significant
2. testing the theory's predictive power or interpretive utility
3. further developing and articulating the
theory.[14]

Theories may change in three ways. The first is
growth by extension. Here knowledge is expanded
piece by piece, moving from an understanding of
one bit of reality to an adjoining bit by adding
new concepts to the old. The second way, *growth
by intension*, is the process of developing an increasingly precise understanding of individual
concepts.[15]

The third way in which theories change is
through *revolution*.[16] In his well-known monograph
on scientific revolutions, Thomas Kuhn states that
"normal science" is a process of developing theory
through extension and intension with relative consensus on the basic nature of the reality being modeled. At some point an extraordinary case is

14. Kuhn, *Structure*, pp. 25–27.
15. Kaplan, *Conduct*, p. 305.
16. Kuhn, *Structure*. See also Ellen K. Coughlin, "Thomas
Kuhn's Ideas About Science," *Chronicle of Higher Education*,
September 22, 1982, pp. 21–23.

discovered that runs counter to prevailing assumptions of the theories in use. At this point a crisis develops, leading to the development of a new theoretical approach. The new theory (or set of theories) represents a different, competing way of looking at the world. Gradually, the revolutionary theory is accepted by more and more members of the field until it becomes the primary theoretical approach in a new normal science.

In a scientific revolution, two paradigms are pitted against one another. The old paradigm represents normal science, and the new represents the revised view. Paradigms are sets of concepts and variables that a group of scholars believe to be important to study, accompanied by a particular opinion of how these things operate. In normal science, most scholars agree that a certain set of phenomena, defined by a known set of concepts, are important and should be studied. These scholars also share a notion of the operations that explain the connections among these variables.

In a scientific revolution, the concepts and operations come to be conceptualized in a radically different fashion, requiring redefinition of an entire field of knowledge. Previous areas of study may die, others may be born, and new weddings may occur. "What were ducks in the scientist's world before the revolution are rabbits afterwards. The man who saw the exterior of the box from above later sees its interior from below."[17] We can now see why critics of traditional social science are quick to call their approach "new paradigm" and why traditionalists dislike this term.

Philosophical Issues in the Study of Communication

Communication Metatheory

Metatheory, as the prefix *meta-* suggests, is a body of speculation on the nature of inquiry that goes beyond the specific content of given theories. It addresses such questions as what should be observed, how observation should take place, and what form theory should take. Metatheoretical debates are a natural consequence of uncertainty over the status of knowledge in a field. In the last decade or so, metatheory has dominated the communication field. Communication scholars have come to question the adequacy of their methods, precisely because of the problems of social science summarized in Chapter 1.[18]

Philosophy as a discipline deals with problems of knowledge and reality. Philosophy questions the basic assumptions and methods of proof used in generating knowledge in all walks of life. Thus the kind of metatheoretical discussion that has occurred in communication in recent years constitutes an important philosophical analysis of communication research and theory. This philosophical examination is complex, yet it can be grouped into four major themes: epistemology (questions of knowledge), ontology (questions of existence), perspective (questions of focus), and axiology (questions of value).

Figure 2-4 identifies and briefly outlines the major issue areas of the field.[19] It is divided into three general levels—the metatheoretical, the hypothetical, and the descriptive. The metatheoretical level is the most general and includes one's basic assumptions. The hypothetical level is the level of theory in which one's picture of reality is painted and the framework for knowledge is established. The descriptive level includes actual statements of operations and findings closest to the thing observed. These three levels cannot be separated as distinct entities. When operating on one level, the scholar always examines the other two at the same time. The three levels within any knowledge tradition

---

17. Kuhn, *Structure*, p. 111.

18. For an excellent discussion of metatheoretical issues, see W. Barnett Pearce, Vernon E. Cronen, and Linda M. Harris, "Methodological Considerations in Building Human Communication Theory," in *Human Communication Theory: Comparative Approaches*, ed. Frank E. X. Dance (New York: Harper & Row, 1982), pp. 1–41. See also John Waite Bowers and James J. Bradac, "Issues in Communication Theory: A Metatheoretical Analysis," in *Communication Yearbook 5*, ed. Michael Burgoon (New Brunswick, N.J.: Transaction Books, 1982), pp. 1–28. For a thorough discussion of many of the issues in communication, see *Ferment in the Field*, a special issue of *Journal of Communication* 33 (Summer, 1983).

19. Adapted from Stanley Deetz, unpublished handout.

	Epistemological	Ontological	Perspectival	Axiological
Metatheory	Methodological questions	Metaphysical questions	Definitional questions	Aesthetic and value questions
Hypothetical	Methods and procedures	Theories, concepts, hypotheses, laws, and interpretive schemas	Definitions and metaphors	Ethical and moral premises and values
Descriptive	Instruments and techniques	Observational statements	Substantive focuses	Judgments
Things-in-Themselves	Flow of events			

Figure 2-4   Philosophical areas affecting theory.

reinforce one another. Let us now look more closely at some of the actual issues within each area.

Issues of Epistemology

Epistemology is the branch of philosophy that studies knowledge. Epistemologists ask how people know what they claim to know. These scholars question observations and claims as a way of understanding the nature of knowledge and the processes by which it is gained. Any good discussion of inquiry and theory will inevitably come back to epistemological issues.

Because of the diversity of disciplines involved in the study of communication and the resultant divergence of thought about research and theory, epistemological issues are important in this field. Some of the most basic of these issues can be expressed as questions.[20]

20. This analysis from Stephen W. Littlejohn, "Epistemology and the Study of Human Communication" (Paper delivered at the Speech Communication Association, New York City, November 1980). See also Stephen W. Littlejohn, "An Overview of Contributions to Human Communication Theory from Other Disciplines," in *Human Communication Theory: Comparative Essays*, ed. Frank E. X. Dance (New York: Harper & Row, 1982), pp. 247–49. For another approach, see W. Barnett Pearce, "Metatheoretical Concerns in Communication," *Communication Quarterly* 25 (1977): 3–6.

To what extent can knowledge exist before experience? Many theorists believe that all knowledge arises from experience. We observe the world and thereby come to know about it. Yet is there something in our basic nature that provides a kind of knowledge even before we experience the world? Many philosophers believe so. This kind of "knowledge" would consist of inherent mechanisms of thinking and perceiving. For example, strong evidence exists that children do not learn language entirely from hearing it spoken. Rather, they may acquire language by using innate models to test what they hear. (We will discuss this idea more in Chapter 5.)

To what extent is knowledge universal? Is knowledge certain, there for the taking by whoever is able to ascertain it? Or is knowledge relative and changing? The debate over this issue has persisted for hundreds of years. Communication theorists vary in terms of assumptions about the certainty of truth. Those who take a universal stance will admit to errors in their theories, but they believe that these errors are merely a result of not yet having discovered the complete truth. Relativists would have us believe that knowledge will never be certain because there is no universal reality that can be comprehended.

By what process does knowledge arise? This question is extremely complex, and the debate on the issue lies at the heart of epistemology. There are at least four positions on the issue. Mentalism or *rationalism* suggests that knowledge arises out of the sheer power of the human mind. This position places ultimate faith in human reasoning. *Empiricism* states that knowledge arises in perception. We experience the world and literally "see" what is going on. *Constructivism* holds that people create knowledge in order to function pragmatically in life. People project themselves into what they experience. Constructivists believe that phenomena in the world can be fruitfully conceptualized many different ways, knowledge being what the person has made of the world. Finally, taking constructivism one step further, *social constructionism* teaches that knowledge is a product of symbolic interaction within social groups. In other words, reality is socially constructed and a product of group and cultural life.

Is knowledge best conceived in parts or wholes? Gestaltists teach that true knowledge consists of general, indivisible understandings. They believe that phenomena are highly interrelated and operate as a system. Analysts, on the other hand, believe that knowledge consists of understanding how parts operate separately.

To what extent is knowledge explicit? Many philosophers and scholars believe that you cannot know something unless you can state it. Knowledge is thus seen as explicit. Others claim that much of knowledge is hidden, that people operate on the basis of sensibilities that are not conscious and that they may not even be able to express. Such knowledge is said to be tacit.[21]

The way in which scholars conduct inquiry and construct theories depends largely on their epistemological assumptions. Many basic positions arise from the issues just described. These positions can be called *world views*. Numerous fine distinctions can be made among these positions, but our discussion groups them into two broad opposing world views that affect thinking about communication.[22]

21. See Michael Polanyi, *Personal Knowledge* (London: Routledge & Kegan Paul, 1958).

World View I. This tradition is based on empiricist and rationalist ideas. It treats reality as distinct from the human being, something that people discover outside themselves. It assumes a physical, knowable reality that is self-evident to the trained observer.

Discovery is important in this position; the world is waiting for the scientist to find it. Since knowledge is viewed as something acquired from outside oneself, World View I is often called the *received view*. Objectivity is all important, with investigators being required to define the exact operations to be used in observing events. Most mainstream physical science is World View I, and much behavioral and social science follow suit.

World View I aims to make lawful statements about phenomena, developing generalizations that hold true across situations and over time. Scholars in this tradition try to reveal how phenomena appear and how they work. In so doing the scholar is highly analytical, attempting to define each part and subpart of the object of interest.

World View II. This tradition takes a different turn by relying heavily on constructivism, viewing the world in process. In this view people take an active role in creating knowledge. A world of things exists outside the person, but the individual can conceptualize these things in a variety of useful ways. Knowledge therefore arises not out of discovery but from interaction between knower and known. For this reason perceptual and interpretive

22. This particular analysis is supported in part by Georg H. von Wright, *Explanation and Understanding* (Ithaca, N.Y.: Cornell University Press, 1971), and Joseph Houna, "Two Ideals of Scientific Theorizing," in *Communication Yearbook 5*, ed. Michael Burgoon (New Brunswick, N.J.: Transaction Books, 1982), pp. 29–48. Many other schemes have been devised to classify epistemological approaches. See, for example, Stephen Pepper, *World Hypotheses* (Berkeley: University of California Press, 1942); B. Aubrey Fisher, *Perspectives on Human Communication* (New York: Macmillan, 1978); Kenneth Williams, "Reflections on a Human Science of Communication," *Journal of Communication* 23 (1973): 239–50; Barry Brummett, "Some Implications of 'Process' or 'Intersubjectivity': Postmodern Rhetoric," *Philosophy and Rhetoric* 9 (1976): 21–51; Gerald Miller, "The Current Status of Theory and Research in Interpersonal Communication," *Human Communication Research* 4 (1978): 175.

processes of the individuals are important objects for study.

World View II attempts not to uncover universal laws but to describe the rich context in which individuals operate. It is humanistic in that it stresses the individual subjective response. Knowing is interpreting, an activity everybody is believed to engage in. Many theories of communication take a World View II stance, being based on the assumption that communication itself is a vital vehicle in the social construction of reality.[23]

Issues of Ontology

While epistemology is the study of knowledge, ontology is the branch of philosophy that deals with the nature of being, or more narrowly, the nature of the phenomena we seek to know.[24] Actually, epistemology and ontology go hand in hand, since our conception of knowledge depends in part on our notions about the nature of the knowable. In the social sciences ontology deals largely with the nature of human existence. Thus ontological issues in the study of communication deal with the nature of human social interaction.

Ontological issues are important because the way a theorist conceptualizes communication depends in large measure on how the communicator is viewed. All communication theories begin with assumptions about being. Issues in this area reflect disagreements about the nature of human experience. Five issues are important.[25]

To what extent do humans make real choices? Although all investigators probably would agree that people perceive choice, there is a long-standing philosophical debate on whether real choice is possible. On one side of the issue are the determinists, who state that people's behavior is caused by a multitude of prior conditions and that humans are basically reactive and passive. On the other side of the debate are the teleologists, who claim that people plan their behavior to meet future goals. This school sees people as decision-making, active beings who affect their own destinies. Middle positions also exist, suggesting either that people make choices within a restricted range or that some behavior is determined while other behavior is a matter of free will.

To what extent are humans best understood in terms of states versus traits?[26] States are temporary conditions through which people pass. The state view believes that human beings change and go through numerous states in the course of a day, year, or lifetime. The state view characterizes human beings as dynamic. The trait view believes that people are mostly predictable because they display more or less constant characteristics. People may change because their traits have changed, but traits do not change easily. For the most part, human beings are static. Many social scientists, of course, believe that both traits and states characterize human behavior.

To what extent is human experience basically individual versus social? Many social scientists view human beings as individuals. Although these scholars understand that people are not in fact isolated from one another and that interaction is important, they interpret behavior as if it stems primarily from the individual. The unit of analysis for such scholars is the individual human life. Many other social scientists, however, focus on social life as the primary unit of analysis. These scholars believe that human beings cannot be understood apart from their relationships with others in groups and cultures. This issue is especially important to communication scholars because of our focus on interaction.[27]

23. See, for example, Peter Berger and Thomas Luckmann, *The Social Construction of Reality* (Garden City, N.Y.: Doubleday, 1966); Alfred Schutz, *The Phenomenology of the Social World*, trans. George Walsh and Frederick Lehnert (Evanston, Ill.: Northwestern University Press, 1967); Kenneth Gergen, "The Social Constructionist Movement in Modern Psychology," *American Psychologist* 40 (March 1985): 266–75; Harré and Secord, *Explanation.*

24. For a discussion of ontology, see Alasdair MacIntyre, "Ontology," in *The Encyclopedia of Philosophy*, ed. Paul Edwards (New York: Macmillan, 1967), vol. 5, pp. 542–43.

25. For an ontological discussion of communication theory, see Bowers and Bradac, "Issues."

26. This debate is summarized by Peter A. Andersen, "The Trait Debate: A Critical Examination of the Individual Differences Paradigm in the Communication Sciences," in *Progress in Communication Sciences*, eds. B. Dervin and M. J. Voigt (Norwood, N.J.: Ablex Publishing, 1986).

27. See, for example, Berger and Luckmann, *Social Construction*; Gergen, "Social Constructionist Movement."

To what extent is communication contextualized? The question is whether behavior is governed by universal principles or whether it depends on situational factors. Some philosophers believe that human life and action are best understood by looking at universal factors; others believe that behavior is richly contextual and cannot be generalized beyond the immediate situation. The middle ground on this issue is that behavior is affected by both general and situational factors.

To what extent are humans interpreting beings? This issue relates to problems of meaning. Some theorists believe that humans behave in accordance with stimulus–response principles, that people react strictly to pressures from the environment. Others believe that people are thinking interpreters. According to the second view, people create meanings and use these meanings to interpret and understand situations in which they find themselves.

Although numerous ontological positions can be seen in communication theory, this book groups them into two basic opposing positions: actional and nonactional. *Actional theory* assumes that individuals create meanings, they have intentions, they make real choices. The actional view rests on a teleological base, which says that people make decisions that are designed to achieve goals. Theorists of the actional tradition are reluctant to seek covering laws because they assume that individual behavior is not governed by universal prior events. Instead, they assume that people behave differently in different situations because rules change from one situation to another.

Nonactional theory assumes that behavior basically is determined by and is responsive to past pressures. Covering laws are usually viewed as appropriate in this tradition; active interpretation by the individual is downplayed.

Issues of Perspective

The perspective of a theory is its angle or focus. Perspectives to a large extent are correlated with epistemology and ontology because how the theorist views knowledge and being affects the perspective of the theory. Any theory of communication provides a particular perspective from which the process can be viewed. A perspective is a point of view, a way of conceptualizing an area of study.[28] Earlier in this chapter you learned that all theories are abstractions and constructions. The configuration of a theory depends on the perspective of the theorist. This perspective guides the theorist in choosing what to focus on and what to leave out, how to explain the process, and how to conceptualize what is observed. Aubrey Fisher states the idea: "Clearly, a concept that is trivial or irrelevant or even ignored in one perspective may suddenly leap into importance when one applies an alternative perspective."[29] In fact, a fuller, more complete picture of the process can be obtained by switching perspectives, which is certainly one of the methods of this book. Although theoretical perspectives can be conceptualized in a number of ways, the following four labels best describe the major divisions of the field.[30]

Behavioristic perspective. This perspective, which comes from the behavioral school of psychology, stresses stimulus and response. Communication theories that use this perspective tend to emphasize the ways that individuals are affected by messages. Such theories tend to conform to World View I assumptions, and they are usually nonactional.

Transmissional perspective. Transmissional theories view communication as the transfer of information from source to receiver. They use a linear model of movement from one location to another. This perspective stresses communication media, time, and sequential elements. Generally it is based on World View I and nonactional assumptions.

Interactional perspective. This perspective recognizes that communicators respond reciprocally to

28. For a discussion of perspective, see Fisher, *Perspectives,* pp. 57–85.
29. Ibid., p. 61.
30. Adapted from David M. Jabusch and Stephen Littlejohn, *Elements of Speech Communication* (Boston: Houghton Mifflin, 1981), pp. 12–24. Fisher's model (*Perspectives*) is somewhat different.

one another. While the metaphor of the transmissional perspective is the line, the circle captures the interactional approach. Feedback and mutual effects are key concepts. Such theories typically are World View II; they may be actional or nonactional, depending on the degree to which communicators are thought to be active choice-makers.

Transactional perspective. This perspective stresses sharing. It sees communication as something in which all participants actively engage. Theories of the transactional perspective stress context, process, and function. In other words communication is viewed as highly situational and as a dynamic process that fulfills individual and social functions. This perspective emphasizes holism, imagining communication to be a process of sharing meaning. Transactional theories tend to espouse World View II assumptions, and they use actional explanations.[31]

Axiological Issues

Axiology is the branch of philosophy studying values. For the communication scholar, three axiological issues are especially important:

Can theory be value-free? Classical science claims that theories and research are value-free; scholarship is neutral, attempting to get the facts as they are manifest in the real world. When a scientist's values impinge on his or her work, the result is bad science.[32] Another position on this issue is that scholarship is free of substantive values but that it embodies such metavalues as the pursuit of truth, the importance of ideas, objectivity, and the value of science itself. Here the contention is that science is not value-free because the researcher's work is guided by an interest in certain ways of conducting inquiry.[33]

Finally, some scholars contend that theory can never be value-free, in method or in substance. Scientists choose what to study, and those choices are affected by personal as well as institutional values. Governments and private organizations choose what research to fund; political and economic ideologies both feed and are fed by particular ways of viewing the world embodied by different forms of theory and research.[34]

There is a substantial political argument on values in science. Traditional scientists claim that they are not responsible for the ways scientific knowledge is used, that it can be used for good or ill. Critics object that scientific knowledge by its very nature is instrumentalist and control-oriented and that it necessarily promotes power domination in society. Traditional communication knowledge, especially as derived by media research, is believed by marxists to be a necessary administrative tool of the power elite. The critics of science do not themselves claim to be above power, but they see themselves as making a choice in favor of a set of values that challenges domination in society rather than perpetuates it. This debate is discussed in more detail in Chapter 13.

To what extent does the practice of inquiry influence that which is studied? This second major axiological issue centers on the question of whether scholars intrude upon and thereby affect the process being studied. The traditional scientific viewpoint is that scientists observe carefully, but without interference, such that observational fidelity is maintained. Critics doubt this is possible. Observation by its very nature distorts that which is being observed. Sometimes the distortion is great, sometimes small, but it is always there.

On a higher level, some critics maintain that theory and knowledge themselves affect the course of human life.[35] This presents two potential problems. First, the scholar, by virtue of scholarly work, becomes an agent of change. That role must be actively understood and reckoned with. At the very

---

31. Perhaps the most thorough discussion of this perspective can be found in C. David Mortensen, *Communication: The Study of Human Interaction* (New York: McGraw-Hill, 1972), p. 29.

32. See, for example, Kaplan, *Conduct*, p. 372.

33. See, for example, Juergen Habermas, *Knowledge and Human Interests*, trans. Jeremy J. Shapiro (Boston: Beacon Press, 1971), p. 302; Kaplan, pp. 370–97.

34. See, for example, Brian Fay, *Social Theory and Political Practice* (London: George Allen & Unwin, 1975).

35. See, for example, Fay, *Social Theory*; Gergen, *Transformation*, pp. 21–34.

least, the scholar must consider ethical issues involved. Second, studying human life changes that life, so that what you believe you know at one time may not be true at another time. This second point has particularly profound epistemological implications.

Finally, *To what extent should scholarship attempt to achieve social change?* Should scholars remain objective or should they make conscious efforts to help society change in positive ways? Many believe that the proper role of the scholar is to produce knowledge: Let the technicians and politicians do what they will with it. Other scholars vociferously disagree: Responsible scholarship involves an obligation to promote positive change. Obviously, this second view is consistent with the critical approach to the development of knowledge.[36]

Overall, then, two general positions reside in these axiological issues. First, *value-conscious* scholarship recognizes the importance of values to research and theory and makes a concerted effort to direct those values in positive directions. What those directions should be, of course, is a matter of debate. Second, *value-neutral* scholarship either believes that science is aloof from values or that good scholars control the effects of values.

How to Evaluate a Communication Theory

As you encounter theories of communication, you will need a basis for judging one against another. Here is a list of criteria that can be applied to the evaluation of any theory.[37] Remember that no theory is perfect; all can be faulted. Therefore the following criteria are goal-ideals.

Theoretical Scope

A theory's scope is its comprehensiveness or inclusiveness. Theoretical scope relies on the principle of generality.[38] This principle states that a theory's explanation must be sufficiently general to cover a range of events beyond a single observation. People continually provide explanations for events, but their explanations are not always theoretical. When an explanation is a mere speculation about a single event, it is not a theoretical explanation. However, when an explanation goes beyond a single instance to cover a range of events, it is theoretical. Normally, the more general a theory, the better it is.

Two types of generality exist. The first is the coverage of a broad domain. Theories that meet the test of generality in this way deal with many phenomena. A communication theory that meets this test would explain a variety of communication-related behaviors. A theory need not cover a large number of phenomena to be judged as good, however. Indeed, many fine theories are narrow in coverage. Such theories possess the second type of generality. Although they deal with a narrow range of events, their explanations of these events apply to a large number of situations. Such theories are said to be powerful.

Appropriateness

Is the theory's perspective appropriate for the theoretical questions the theory addresses? For example, the behavioristic perspective is not appropriate for questions related to meaning. Some theories of meaning, which are indeed behavioristic (see Chapter 6), can be faulted for lack of appropriateness. Their epistemological assumptions are inadequate for the domain they purport to cover.

Heuristic Value

Does the theory have potential for generating research and additional theory? One of the primary functions of theory is to help investigators decide what to observe and how to observe it. For example, a major contribution of Bales's interaction process theory (Chapter 11) is that it has spawned

36. See, for example, Cees. J. Hamelink, "Emancipation or Domestication: Toward a Utopian Science of Communication," *Journal of Communication* 33 (1983): 74–79.

37. Evaluation is discussed in greater depth in Bross, *Design*, pp. 161–77; Deutsch, "On Communication Models," 362–63; Calvin S. Hall and Gardner Lindzey, *Theories of Personality* (New York: John Wiley, 1970), chap. 1; Kaplan, *Conduct*, pp. 312–22; Kuhn, *Structure*, pp. 100–1, 152–56; Mortensen, pp. 30–34.

38. Achinstein, *Laws*; Cushman and Pearce, "Generality."

much research and further theorizing about group communication. Even Bales's critics find his ideas useful as springboards to develop new concepts.

Validity

Generally speaking, validity is the truth value of a theory. Of course, we must be careful to understand that "truth" is not intended to mean absolute, single-minded fact. Rather, there may be a variety of "truth values" to a theory. Consequently, validity as a criterion of theory has at least three meanings.[39]

One kind of validity is that of *value or worth*. This definition of validity concerns the question of importance or utility, whether the theory has conceptual or pragmatic value. This is the primary form of validity in interpretive and critical theories.

The second kind of validity is that of *correspondence or fit*. Here the question is whether the concepts and relations specified by the theory can be seen in observations of ongoing life. Both classical and interpretive-critical theories require fit as a form of validity, and one of the most important functions of research in both traditions is to establish that correspondence. Classical science assumes that one and only one representation will fit, while interpretive-critical sciences believe that a number of theories may simultaneously fit. When this is the case, we discriminate among those theories on the basis of the first kind of validity: value or worth.

The third kind of validity is *generalizability*, which refers to the extent to which the tenets of the theory apply across situations. This is the classical definition of validity and applies almost exclusively to traditional, discovery-oriented theories with covering laws.

Parsimony

The test of parsimony may be called logical simplicity. If two theories are equally valid, the theory with the simplest logical explanation is said to be the best. For example, although classical informa-

39. This analysis adapted from David Brinberg and Joseph E. McGrath, *Validity and the Research Process* (Beverly Hills: Sage Publications, 1985).

tion theory can be faulted on other grounds, it is highly parsimonious. A few core assumptions and premises lead logically to a variety of claims about channels, signals, messages, and transmission.

Integration

In summary, what can we say about communication theory? Theory is an integral part of the process of inquiry, which also includes asking questions and making observations. These three elements are strongly interconnected. Inquiry and theory vary depending on the type of scholarship with which they are associated. Scientific scholarship stresses objectivity. Humanistic scholarship stresses subjectivity. Social science attempts to understand the human being as an object of study; it includes elements of both science and humanities. The chief problem of social science inquiry is the degree to which scientific methods are appropriate for revealing human behavior.

What is a theory? We know that a theory is constructed by a human observer. A theory is always abstract and always leaves something out of its observations. Theories function to organize and summarize knowledge, to focus observation, to clarify what is seen, and to provide methods for observation. They also help to predict, to generate research, to communicate ideas, and to control. Theories are not immutable: Because of research, theories change and grow by intension, extension, and revolution.

Theories are based on concepts and explanations. Concepts are groups of observations sharing common elements and a common name. Explanations point out the relationships among concepts, relying on causal, practical, or logical necessity. Theories can be compared according to their levels of generality and methods of explanation.

Philosophical issues in the study of communication are reflected in metatheory. Metatheory deals with issues of epistemology, ontology, perspective, and axiology. Two general epistemological positions are apparent in communication literature.

World View I is basically scientific in orientation, stressing the ways in which knowledge about communication can be "received." World View II is basically humanistic, emphasizing the ways in which individuals create knowledge for personal and social use. The two basic ontological positions in communication are the actional and nonactional. Actional theories view humans as choice-making beings; nonactional theories present people as passive and reactive.

Four perspectives are apparent in communication theory:

1. the behavioristic perspective, which focuses on stimulus and response

2. the transmissional perspective, which stresses linear sending and receiving of messages

3. the interactional perspective, which includes feedback and mutual effect as central concepts

4. the transactional perspective, which centers on shared meaning.

Finally, value-conscious scholarship treats values as central to research issues; value-neutral scholarship believes that values are either outside of science or that good scholars do not allow values to affect their research.

As you proceed through this book, keep in mind the basic criteria for judging theories: scope or generality, appropriateness or suitability, heuristic value or research-generating ability, validity or consistency, and parsimony or logical simplicity. In the next chapter, we begin our survey of theories by examining system theory and cybernetics.

II

General Theories

Three

System Theory

This section of the text deals with theories of a general nature that apply to all forms and levels of communication. These theories are organized according to certain common philosophical tenets and include structural and functional approaches, cognitive and behavioral approaches, interactional and conventional approaches, and interpretive and critical approaches. These are defined in Chapter 1.

Structural and functional theories share the common premise that the world has a discernible structure and that the operations, behaviors, and actions (functions) accomplished in the world can be explained in terms of that structure. Perhaps the most general theoretical approach of this nature is system theory, the subject of this chapter. Chapter 3 deals with system theory and two related fields, cybernetics and information theory. These approaches offer broad perspectives on how to look at the world and have been useful in capturing the general nature of the communication process.[1] In general, system theory deals with the interrelatedness of the parts of an organization, cybernetics deals with control and regulation in the system, and information theory focuses on the nature of organizational patterns.

System theory, cybernetics, and information theory direct us to observe features of a wide variety of physical, biological, social, and behavioral phenomena. As such, they are not communication theories per se, but have had important applications in the study of communication and other sociocultural events. Many communication theories and related theories are based on the system concept, and we will address several of them later in the text. Some more focused structural-functional theories are discussed in the next chapter.

The roots of system thinking began at least as far back as the last century with the theory of Georg Hegel. For Hegel, the world is in process, and it is controlled by a dialectical tension between opposites. A state of affairs would be followed historically by an antithesis, and the tension would be resolved through a synthesis of the two poles. The synthesis itself becomes a new balanced position, only to be brought out of balance once again by a new antithesis, beginning the dialectical process again. Hegel explained historical development in terms of this dynamic process.[2] Karl Marx quickly applied Hegel's thinking to the distribution of power in society, using it as the basis for his goal of uniting labor in opposition to the power elite.[3]

1. For excellent discussions of general system theory and other systems approaches, see Peter Monge, "The Systems Perspective as a Theoretical Basis for the Study of Human Communication," *Communication Quarterly* 25 (1977): 19–29; and Brent D. Ruben and John Y. Kim (eds.), *General Systems Theory and Human Communication* (Rochelle Park, N.J.: Hayden Book Co., 1975). One of the foremost proponents of system theory in the communication field is B. Aubrey Fisher, *Perspectives on Human Communication* (New York: Macmillan, 1978), especially chap. 7.

2. See, for example, Walter Kaufmann (ed.), *Hegel: Texts and Commentary* (Garden City, N.Y.: Anchor Books, 1966).

3. See, for example, Anthony Giddens, *Profiles and Critiques in Social Theory* (Berkeley: University of California Press, 1982), especially chaps. 8 and 9.

Charles Darwin, too, relied on the idea that organisms evolve and adapt to pressures from outside. However, his explanatory mechanism was different from that of Hegel and Marx. For Darwin, change is brought about by adaptations and accommodations, and history, at least in the biological world, is governed by these processes.[4] Herbert Spencer, in a once popular but now disreputed theory, applied Darwinian thinking to differences in human class and race.[5]

Our own century has generated a great deal of system thinking. Alfred North Whitehead, for example, taught that things are always in process, so that to know a thing, one must tack back and forth among a variety of perspectives. This notion emphasizes the transactional nature of knowledge and the way in which things and observers constitute a knowledge system.[6] System theory as we known it today was probably best codified by Ludwig von Bertalanffy, whose ideas are summarized in more detail later in the chapter.

Fundamental System Concepts

What Is a System?

A system is a set of objects or entities that interrelate with one another to form a whole. One of the most common distinctions is between closed and open systems.[7] A *closed system* is one that has no interchange with its environment. It moves toward progressive internal chaos (entropy), disintegration, and death. The closed-system model most often applies to physical systems, which do not have life-sustaining qualities. An *open system* is one

that receives matter and energy from its environment and passes matter and energy to its environment. The open system is oriented toward life and growth. Biological, psychological, and social systems follow an open model. General system theory deals with systems primarily from this open perspective. When we speak of systems in this chapter, we are concerned only with the open model.

From the simplest perspective a system can be said to consist of four things.[8] The first is *objects*. The objects are the parts, elements, or members of the system. These objects may be physical or abstract or both, depending on the nature of the system. Second, a system consists of *attributes*, or the qualities or properties of the system and its objects. Third, a system must possess internal *relationships* among its objects. This characteristic is a crucial defining quality of systems and a primary theme in this chapter. A relationship among objects implies a mutual effect (interdependence) and constraint.[9] This idea will be elaborated in the following section. Fourth, systems also possess an *environment*. They do not exist in a vacuum but are affected by their surroundings.

The advocates of general system theory maintain that biological, psychological, and socio-cultural systems possess certain common characteristics. Collectively, these qualities are used to define the system concept; they are not separate, and to a large extent, they define one another.

Wholeness and interdependence. A system by definition constitutes a unique whole.[10] In order to understand this idea, examine for a moment the opposite view—physical summativity. In the summative model, a "whole" is merely a collection with no unique qualities apart from its components, like a box of stones. But in a system, the whole is more than the sum of its parts. It is a product of the forces or interactions among the parts.

We must view a system as a whole because its parts interrelate and cannot be understood separately. An object, person, concept, or other part of

4. Marjorie Grene, *The Knower and the Known* (Berkeley: University of California Press, 1974), chap. 7.

5. See, for example, Marvin Harris, *The Rise of Anthropological Theory* (New York: Thomas Y. Crowell, 1968), chap. 5.

6. See, for example, John Spiegel, *Transactions* (New York: Science House, 1971), chap. 1.

7. A. D. Hall and R. E. Fagen, "Definition of System," in *Modern Systems Research for the Behavioral Scientist*, ed. Walter Buckley (Chicago: Aldine, 1968), pp. 81–92; Anatol Rapoport, "Foreward," in Buckley, *Modern Systems Research*, pp. xiii–xxv. For an excellent short description of open versus closed systems, see Ludwig von Bertalanffy, *General System Theory: Foundations, Development, Applications* (New York: Braziller, 1968).

8. Hall and Fagen, "Definition."

9. Walter Buckley, "Society as a Complex Adaptive System," in Buckley, *Modern Systems Research*, pp. 490–513.

10. Rapoport, "Foreward"; Hall and Fagen, "Definition."

a system is always constrained by its dependence on other parts. This pattern of interdependence is what creates organization in the system. If you as an observer do not look at interrelationships, then you are missing what is important about the whole. Information theory, which is discussed later in the chapter, was developed largely to express the nature of the organization in a system. This theory deals with the amount of predictability in a system based on interdependence.

Interdependence is easily illustrated by families. A family is a system of interacting individuals, and each member is partially constrained by the actions of the other members. Although each person has some freedom, none has complete freedom because of their bonds with one another. Therefore the behaviors in a family are not independent, free, or random; instead, they are patterned and structured. What one family member does or says follows from or leads to an action of another.

Hierarchy. Systems tend to be embedded within one another. In other words, one system is a part of a higher system.[11] Arthur Koestler expresses this idea in the following tale:

> There were once two Swiss watchmakers named Bios and Mekhos, who made very fine and expensive watches. Their names may sound a little strange, but their fathers had a smattering of Greek and were fond of riddles. Although their watches were in equal demand, Bios prospered, while Mekhos just struggled along; in the end he had to close his shop and take a job as a mechanic with Bios. The people in the town argued for a long time over the reasons for this development and each had a different theory to offer, until the true explanation leaked out and proved to be both simple and surprising.
>
> The watches they made consisted of about one thousand parts each, but the two rivals had used dif-

ferent methods to put them together. Mekhos had assembled his watches bit by bit—rather like making a mosaic floor out of small coloured stones. Thus each time when he was disturbed in his work and had to put down a partly assembled watch, it fell to pieces and he had to start again from scratch.

> Bios, on the other hand, had designed a method of making watches by constructing, for a start, sub-assemblies of about ten components, each of which held together as an independent unit. Ten of these sub-assemblies could then be fitted together into a subsystem of a higher order; and ten of these sub-systems constituted the whole watch. . . .
>
> Now it is easy to show mathematically that if a watch consists of a thousand bits, and if some disturbance occurs at an average of once in every hundred assembling operations—then Mekhos will take four thousand times longer to assemble a watch than Bios. Instead of a single day, it will take him eleven years. And if for mechanical bits, we substitute amino acids, protein molecules, organelles, and so on, the ratio between time-scales becomes astronomical; some calculations indicate that the whole life-time of the earth would be insufficient for producing even an amoeba—unless he [Mekhos] becomes converted to Bios' method and proceeds hierarchically, from simple sub-assemblies to more complex ones.[12]

Every complex system consists of a number of subsystems. The system, therefore, is a series of levels of increasing complexity. The idea of system hierarchy is illustrated by the "tree" model in Figure 3-1.

Koestler calls system hierarchy the *Janus effect*:

> The members of a hierarchy, like the Roman god Janus, all have two faces looking in opposite directions: the face turned toward the subordinate levels is that of a self-contained whole; the face turned upward toward the apex, that of a dependent part. One is the face of the master, the other the face of the servant.[13]

The natural question at this point is where does a system end and its environment begin? Since systems are part of other systems, the boundary of the system may be quite arbitrary and can only be established by the observer. One can take a very

---

11. For excellent discussions of hierarchy, see Donna Wilson, "Forms of Hierarchy: A Selected Bibliography," *General Systems*, 14 (1969): 3–15; Arthur Koestler, *The Ghost in the Machine* (New York: Macmillan, 1967); W. Ross Ashby, "Principles of the Self-Organizing System," in *Principles of Self-Organization*, eds. Heinz von Foerster and George Zopf (New York: Pergamon Press, 1962), pp. 255–78.

12. Koestler, *Ghost*, pp. 45–47.
13. Ibid., p. 48.

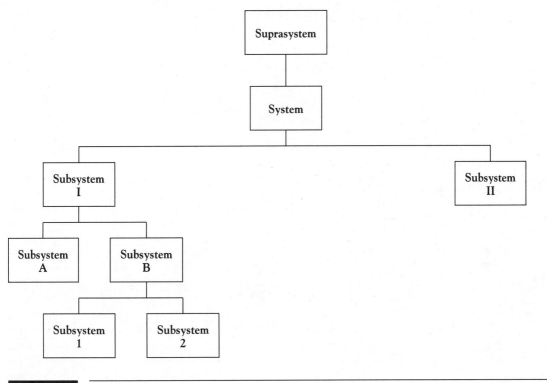

Figure 3-1   System hierarchy.

broad view—observing a number of interacting systems in a large suprasystem—or a narrower view—observing one or two smaller sub-systems interacting with the larger system as environment—as Figure 3-1 outlines.

Self-regulation and control. Systems are most often viewed as goal-oriented organisms. They are governed by their purposes. A system's activities are controlled by its aims, and the system regulates its behavior to achieve those aims. The parts of a system must behave according to guidelines and must adapt to the environment on the basis of feedback. This aspect of system functioning, known as cybernetics, is examined in detail in the next section.

Interchange with the environment. Remember that open systems interchange with their environment. They take in and let out matter and energy.

Thus, systems are said to have inputs and outputs. This concept follows logically from the ideas of hierarchy and cybernetics. Therefore, the system both affects and is affected by the environment.[14]

Balance. Balance, sometimes referred to as *homeostasis*, is self-maintenance.[15] One of the tasks of a system, if it is to remain "alive," is to stay in balance, or hold its own. It must work to do this by sensing deviations from the norm and correcting those "faults." The eventual consequence of failing to maintain balance is the fate of a closed system, increasing entropy (disorganization) and disintegration. (See the section on cybernetics for a detailed discussion of this aspect of systems.)

14. Gordon Allport, "The Open System in Personality Theory," in Buckley, *Modern Systems Research*, pp. 343–50; Hall and Fagen, "Definition."
15. Ashby, "Principles."

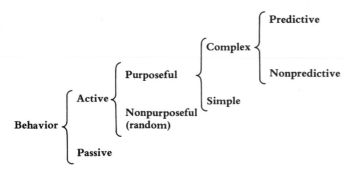

Figure 3-2   Model of cybernetic complexity.

From *Philosophy of Science*, "Behavior, Purpose, and Teleology," by Arturo Rosenblueth, Norbert Weiner, and Julian Bigelow. Copyright © 1943 by the Williams & Wilkins Co. Reprinted by permission of the publisher.

Change and adaptability. Because it exists in a dynamic environment, the system must be adaptable.[16] Paradoxically, adaptation often means homeostasis or counteracting outside forces. More than that, however, complex systems sometimes have to change structurally to adapt to the environment, and that kind of change means getting out of balance for a time. Advanced systems must be able to reorder themselves on the basis of environmental pressures. The technical term for system change is *morphogenesis.*

Equifinality. Finality is the goal achievement or task accomplishment of a system. Equifinality means that a particular final state may be accomplished in different ways and from different starting points. The adaptable system, which has a final state as a goal, can achieve that goal in a variety of environmental conditions. The system is capable of processing inputs in different ways to produce its output.[17] Business organizations are a good example. Businesses are set up to adjust to various governmental and economic conditions and to accomplish their goals.

Cybernetics

Cybernetics is the study of regulation and control in systems, with emphasis on feedback.[18] An important feature of open systems, as we have just

seen, is that they are regulated, that they seek goals, and that they therefore are purposeful.

Cybernetics deals with the ways systems (along with their subsystems) gauge their effect and make necessary adjustments. The simplest cybernetic device consists of a sensor, a comparator, and an activator. The sensor provides feedback to the comparator, which determines whether the machine is deviating from its established norm. The comparator then provides guidance to the activator, which produces an output that affects the environment in some way. This fundamental process of output-feedback-adjustment is the basis of cybernetics.

Obviously, feedback mechanisms vary in complexity. Figure 3-2 illustrates different levels of complexity in feedback and control.[19] The model demonstrates that the most basic distinction is between *active* and *passive* behavior. An organism dis-

17. Bertalanffy, *General System Theory*, chap. 3.

18. Rollo Handy and Paul Kurtz, "A Current Appraisal of the Behavioral Sciences: Communication Theory," *American Behavioral Scientist* 7, no. 6 (1964). Supplementary information is found in Gordon Pask, *An Approach to Cybernetics* (New York: Harper & Row, 1961); G. T. Guilbaud, *What Is Cybernetics?* (New York: Grove Press, 1959). For a historical review see Norbert Wiener, *Cybernetics or Control and Communication in the Animal and the Machine* (Cambridge, Mass.: MIT Press, 1961), pp. 1–29. For a cybernetic approach to communication, see D. J. Crowley, *Understanding Communication: The Signifying Web* (New York: Gordon and Breach, 1982), especially chap. 1.

19. Arturo Rosenblueth, Norbert Wiener, and Julian Bigelow, "Behavior, Purpose, and Teleology," *Philosophy of Science* 10 (1943): 18–24 (reprinted in Buckley, *Modern Systems Research*, pp. 221–25).

16. Hall and Fagen, "Definition"; Buckley, "Adaptive System"; Koestler, *Ghost.*

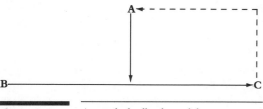

Figure 3-3   A simple feedback model.

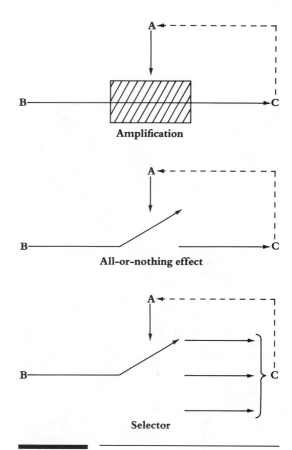

Figure 3-4   Illustrative control models.

playing active behavior is the primary source of energy initiating that behavior. Passive behavior is any response to outside stimulation. People have all kinds of bodily motions that are merely responses to stimulation, such as scratching an itch, although much bodily activity is active nervous energy. Within the category of active behavior, a further division can be made between *purposeless*, or random, and *purposeful* behavior. Purposeful behavior is directed toward an objective or aim, while random behavior is not. Rubbing one's face or moving a hand may be just a random action, but when done to express an idea or emphasize a point, the action is clearly achieving a purpose. All purposeful behavior requires feedback; the nature of that feedback may be more or less complex, as indicated in the model.

Purposeful behavior may be further subdivided into *complex* and *simple* feedback mechanisms.[20] In the simple condition, the organism responds to feedback only by turning on or off. A thermostat is a perfect example of a simple feedback mechanism. Complex systems, however, use positive and negative feedback to adjust and adapt during the action itself. This dynamic process of adjustment is explained in more detail below. Further, complex systems may be *predictive* or *nonpredictive*. Predictive behavior is based on anticipated position or response rather than actual position or response. A good quarterback passes the football to the spot where his receiver will be, not directly to the receiver. Usually, the quarterback releases the ball before the receiver turns to look for it.

A simple feedback model is represented in Figure 3-3. In the figure, B is an energy source directing outputs to C. A is the control mechanism responding to feedback from C. Depending on the complexity of the system and the nature of the output, the control mechanism itself is restricted in the kind of control it can exert. Figure 3-4 illustrates some possible situations.[21]

The first model in Figure 3-4 demonstrates a situation where the signal itself is modified (for example, amplified) by A. The high-pitched squeal in a loudspeaker system is an example. The next model illustrates a simple switch such as a thermostat or circuit breaker. The third model illustrates

20. I have changed the original nomenclature here to avoid confusion and inconsistency with previous word usage in this chapter. The authors' intent is unchanged.

21. Adapted from Guilbaud, *Cybernetics*.

selection control in which A chooses a channel or position on the basis of criteria. In a guided missile, for example, the guidance system may specify turning in one direction or another, based on feedback from the target.

The process of system regulation through feedback involves several facets. The regulated system must possess certain control guidelines. The control center must "know" what environmental conditions to respond to and how. It must possess a sensitivity to aspects of the environment that are critical to its goalseeking.[22]

Feedback may be classified as positive or negative, depending on the way the system responds to it. Negative feedback is an error message indicating deviation; the system adjusts by reducing or counteracting the deviation. Negative feedback is the most important type of feedback in homeostasis, for the principle of deviation-counteracting is the focus of traditional cybernetics. A system can also respond by amplifying or maintaining deviation. When this happens, the feedback is said to be positive. This kind of interaction is important in morphogenesis, or system growth (for example, learning). The inflationary cycle in economics is an example of positive feedback effects. The growth of a city is another. In communication when a speaker receives negative feedback from a listener, the speaker knows he or she is missing the aim. Negative feedback from a fellow communicator usually calls for a shift in strategy to close the gap between how the speaker wants the listener to respond and the actual response. Whether in mechanical or human systems, the response to negative feedback is "Cut back, slow down, discontinue." Response to positive feedback is "Increase, maintain, keep going."

Our discussion of feedback thus far has given the impression that a system responds as a unit to feedback from the outside. This impression is realistic only for the simplest systems such as a heater-thermostat arrangement. As a series of hierarchically ordered subsystems, advanced systems are more complex. A subsystem at any moment may be part of the larger system or part of the environment.[23] Further, we know that subsystems respond to one another in mutual interdependence. As a result the concept of feedback is expanded for complex systems. In a complex system a series of feedback loops exist within and among subsystems, forming networks. At some points the feedback loops are positive, at other points negative. But always, consistent with the basic feedback principle, system output returns as feedback input. No matter how complicated the network, one always comes back to the beginning.

A simple illustration of a system network is the example of urbanization in Figure 3-5.[24] In this figure the pluses represent positive relationships, the minuses negative relationships. In a positive relationship the variables increase or decrease together. In a negative relationship as one increases, the other decreases. For example, as the number of people in the city (P) increases, modernization also increases. With increased modernization comes increased migration, which in turn further increases the population. This relationship is an example of a positive feedback loop. A negative relationship is illustrated by the effect of the number of diseases (D) on population (P).

As our discussion up to this point indicates, cybernetics is a central concept in system theory. The cybernetic elements of control, regulation, and feedback provide a concrete explanation of such system qualities as *wholeness* (a portion of the system cannot be understood apart from its loops among subsystems); *interdependence* (subsystems are constrained by mutual feedbacks); *self-regulation* (a system maintains balance and changes by responding appropriately to positive and negative feedbacks); *interchange with the environment* (inputs and outputs can be largely explained in terms of feedback loops).

Although these cybernetic concepts originated in the fields of physiology, engineering, and mathematics, they have tremendous implications in the

22. Walter Buckley, *Sociology and Modern Systems Theory* (Englewood Cliffs, N.J.: Prentice-Hall, 1967), pp. 52–53.

23. Magoroh Maruyama, "The Second Cybernetics: Deviation-Amplifying Mutual Causal Processes," *American Scientist* 51 (1963): 164–79 (reprinted in Buckley, *Modern Systems Research*, pp. 304–16).

24. Maruyama, "Second Cybernetics."

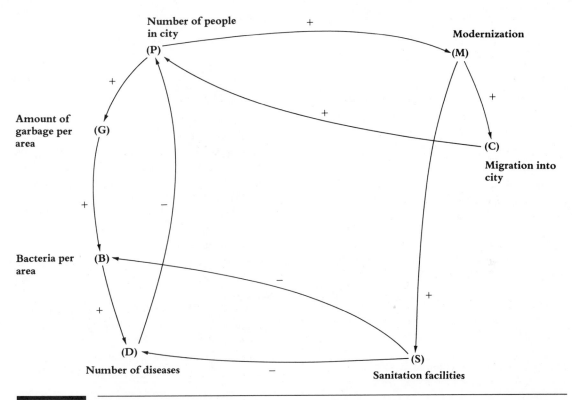

Figure 3-5   A simplified feedback network.

From *American Scientist*, "The Second Cybernetics," by Magoroh Maruyama. Copyright © 1963. Reprinted by permission of the publisher.

behavioral and social sciences as well.[25] As Norbert Wiener, the founder of cybernetics, states, "This principle [feedback] in control applies not merely to the Panama locks, but to states, armies, and individual human beings. . . . This matter of social feedback is of very great sociological and anthropological interest."[26]

Principles of cybernetics lead to one of the purported advantages of system theory; namely, that it is broad enough to allow various alternative explanatory logics.[27] As Peter Monge puts it, "Sys-

tems theory provides an explanatory framework that is capable of incorporating both behavioral and action positions."[28] He believes this incorporation is so because the basic teleology of systems, made possible by their cybernetic functions, may be of two types.

First, the system may achieve an end or goal by responding automatically to negative feedback, much as a heater responds to a thermostat. This off-on behavior displays causal necessity and follows nonactional ontology. Second, some systems or subsystems may behave with intention, actively choosing one of many possible courses of action to arrive at an end state. Human social systems, in contrast to physical systems such as the thermostat or guided missile, are viewed as purposeful in this way. This kind of explanation employs practical

25. See Karl Deutsch, "Toward a Cybernetic Model of Man and Society," in Buckley, *Modern Systems Research*, pp. 387–400.

26. Norbert Wiener, *The Human Use of Human Beings: Cybernetics and Society* (Boston: Houghton Mifflin, 1954), pp. 49–50.

27. For a listing of these logics, see Peter Monge, "The Systems Perspective as a Theoretical Basis for the Study of Human Communication," *Communication Quarterly* 25 (1977): 19–29.

28. Ibid., 28.

necessity and is highly actional in ontology. Hence, purpose may be explained by two alternative logics, and system theory is believed to accommodate either of these.

Therefore what distinguishes system theory from other approaches is its high level of generality and emphasis on interrelationships among elements, not on the type of necessity employed. This idea is controversial, as we shall see later in this chapter.

Information Theory

The area of study most concerned with communication in systems is information theory. Information theory grew out of the postwar boom in the telecommunications industry. A perspective that focuses on the *measurement* of information, it deals with the quantitative study of information in messages and the flow of information between senders and receivers. It has practical applications in the electronic sciences of communication that need to compute information quantities and design channels, transmitters, receivers, and codes that facilitate efficient handling of information. It has also been used widely in the behavioral and social sciences, often metaphorically. Before we get into the core concepts of information theory, let's discuss the development of the movement.[29]

Information theory developed out of investigations in physics, engineering, and mathematics, which were concerned with the organization among events. The primary work that drew all of this work together into a single theoretical approach was that of Claude Shannon, a telecommunications engineer at the Bell Telephone Laboratories. His classic book with Warren Weaver, *The Mathematical Theory of Communication*, is the basic source on information theory.[30]

29. Several brief histories of the movement are available. See, for example, Wendell R. Garner, *Uncertainty and Structure as Psychological Concepts* (New York: John Wiley, 1962), p. 8.

30. Claude Shannon and Warren Weaver, *The Mathematical Theory of Communication* (Urbana: University of Illinois Press, 1949). For a number of excellent brief secondary sources, see Bibliography. Two sources were particularly helpful in the preparation of this chapter: Allan R. Broadhurst and Donald K.

Basic Concepts

Information theory provides a precise definition of *information*. Perhaps it is easier to understand information by starting with a related concept, *entropy*, borrowed from thermodynamics. Entropy is randomness, or lack of organization in a situation. A totally entropic situation is unpredictable. Entropy is best thought of as variable. Most of the situations you are confronted with are partially predictable. If black clouds come over the sky, you might predict rain, and you would probably be right. Because weather is an organized system, certain probable relationships (for example, clouds and rain) exist. On the other hand, you cannot predict rain conclusively. The entropy existing in the situation causes some uncertainty. In short, the more entropy, the less organization and predictability.

What does this have to do with information? *Information is a measure of uncertainty, or entropy, in a situation.* The greater the uncertainty, the more the information. When a situation is completely predictable, no information is present. This is a condition known as *negentropy*. Most people associate information with certainty or knowledge; consequently, this definition from information theory can be confusing. As used by the information theorist, the concept does not refer to a message, facts, or meaning. It is a concept bound only to the quantification of stimuli or signals in a situation.

On closer examination, this idea of information is not as distant from common sense as it first appears. We have said that information is the amount of uncertainty in the situation. Another way of thinking of it is to consider information as the number of *messages* required to completely reduce the uncertainty in the situation. For example, your friend is about to flip a coin. Will it land heads up or tails up? You are uncertain, you cannot predict. This uncertainty, which results from the entropy in the situation, will be eliminated by seeing the result of the flip. Now let's suppose that you have received

Darnell, "An Introduction to Cybernetics and Information Theory," *Quarterly Journal of Speech* 51 (1965): 442–53; Klaus Krippendorf, "Information Theory," in *Communication and Behavior*, eds. G. Hanneman and W. McEwen (Reading, Mass.: Addison-Wesley, 1975), pp. 351–89.

a tip that your friend's coin is two headed. The flip is "fixed." There is no uncertainty and therefore no information. In other words, you could not receive any message that would make you predict any better than you already can. In short, a situation with which you are completely familiar has no information for you.

We have now related information to uncertainty and to the number of messages necessary to reduce uncertainty. There is yet a third way to view information. Information can be thought of as the number of *choices* or *alternatives* available to a person in predicting the outcome of a situation. In a complex situation of many possible outcomes, more information is available than in a simple situation with few outcomes. In other words, a person would need more messages to predict the outcome of a complex situation than to predict the outcome of a simple one. For example, there is more information in a two-dice toss than in the toss of a single die and more information in a single-die toss than in a coin flip. Since information is a function of the number of alternatives, it reflects the degree of freedom in making choices within a situation. The more information in a situation, the freer you are to choose alternatives within that situation.

The idea of information will become clearer after you understand the unit of information, the *bit*. Bit stands for *binary digit*. A bit is a unit used for counting alternatives. Technically, the number of bits in a situation of equally possible outcomes is equal to the number of times the outcomes would be halved in order to reduce the uncertainty to zero.

Consider the following family tree. One of the members of this family has committed a murder for a crime syndicate. As far as you can tell, all family members are equally suspect. How much information is in this situation?

First, you discover that Son (B) and his family (D and E) were on vacation on the other side of the world when the crime took place. They took Father (A) with them. This message provides one bit of information, since it eliminates half of the alternatives (A, B, D, and E). Further, you discover that Son (C) and Grandson (F) were at home, fighting, at the time of the murder. This alibi provides a second bit of information, halving the possibilities again. Then you find out that G died a year ago, providing a third bit of information. Thus you see that this situation has three bits of information.

This example is a *combinatorial* approach to counting bits. The approach, which assumes that each alternative is equally probable, is excellent for getting across the meaning of the information theorist's conception of information, but it is not realistic. Often some alternatives have a higher probability of occurring than others. When this happens, the *statistical* approach is necessary for computing bits.[31] The statistical approach recognizes that as certain alternatives increase in probability, entropy or uncertainty decreases. Thus the less equal the probability of occurrence, the less the information. In the example of the murder, suppose H were a more probable killer than any of the others, based on past record. Hypothetically, you might distribute the probabilities as follows: A = .05, B = .05, C = .05, D = .05, E = .05, F = .05, G = .05, H = .65. Plugging these values into a formula shows that the murder situation contains 1.88 bits of information or uncertainty.

Another important concept is *redundancy*. Redundancy is a function of its sister concept, *relative*

31. For a good distinction between these, see Krippendorf, "Information."

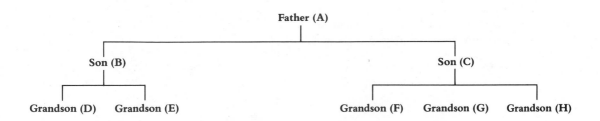

Father (A)

Son (B)   Son (C)

Grandson (D)   Grandson (E)   Grandson (F)   Grandson (G)   Grandson (H)

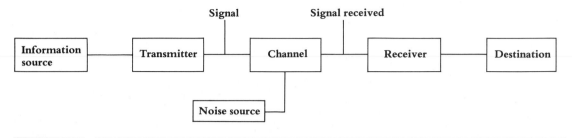

entropy. Relative entropy is the proportion of entropy present compared with the maximum amount possible. Entropy is maximum when all alternatives are equally probable. Let's look again at our example. The number of bits of uncertainty is 1.88. The maximum uncertainty possible is 3. Therefore, the relative entropy in this situation is

$$1.88/3 = .62 \text{ or } 62\%$$

The redundancy is

$$1 - .62 = .38 \text{ or } 38\%$$

In qualitative terms redundancy is the proportion of a situation that is predictable; it is a measure of certainty. If one alternative follows from another, it is predictable and therefore redundant. It should be apparent from this discussion that information theory is basically a tool for measuring and describing the pattern and structure of a system.

Information Transmission

Technical information theory is not concerned with the meaning of messages, only with their transmission and reception. This application is particularly important in electronic communication. The basic model of communication developed by Shannon and Weaver is shown in Figure 3-6.[32] In this model communication begins at the *source*. The source formulates or selects a message, consisting of signs to be transmitted. The *transmitter* converts the message into a set of signals that are sent over a *channel* to a receiver. The *receiver* converts

the signals into a message. This model can be applied to a variety of situations. In the electronic arena a television message is a good example. The producers, directors, and announcers constitute the source. The message is transmitted by air waves (channel) to the home receiver, which converts electromagnetic waves back into a visual impression for the viewer. In the interpersonal arena the speaker's brain is the source, the vocal system the transmitter, and the air medium the channel. The listener's ear is the receiver and the listener's brain the destination.

The final element in Shannon and Weaver's model is noise. *Noise* is any disturbance in the channel that distorts or otherwise masks the signal. The disturbance may be, literally, noise in auditory communication, but any kind of interference is included. We will return to this concept momentarily. First, let us integrate information into the model at this point.

In the last section information was defined as a measure of uncertainty in a situation. This is a general definition. In information transmission we are concerned with the special case in which the message itself is the "situation." Like any stimulus field, a message, consisting of symbols or signs arranged according to rules, has a degree of uncertainty or entropy. This uncertainty (information) is a result of the *code* or language into which the message is *encoded*. Normally, a message is a sequence of stimuli or signs that hit the receiver serially. Ordinary written language is an example. This idea of information can be applied to the predictability of a

32. Shannon and Weaver, *Mathematical Theory*, p. 5.

sequential arrangement such as a sentence. If the letters in the sentence were arranged randomly, there would be 100 percent entropy. *Decoding* would be difficult because of the great amount of information in the message. But letters (or sounds in speech) are not organized randomly. Various predictable patterns are found. These patterns make decoding easier because there is less information, lower relative entropy, and high redundancy. For example, an adjective has a high probability of being followed by a noun. A *q* is always followed by a *u* in English. Thus the overall arrangement of a sentence is patterned and partially predictable. On the other hand, a sentence does contain some information. Redundancy, predictability, is never 100 percent. If it were, there would be no freedom of choice. Once the first letter was written, all other letters would follow automatically. Language is blessed with moderate redundancy, allowing ease in decoding, with freedom of encoding.

Language information is an example of a *Markov process*, in which subsequent alternatives bear a probability relationship to antecedent occurrences in a chain. A Markov chain is a series of events, one happening after another in time, such that the occurrence of one element in the chain establishes a probability that another particular element will come next. In English, for example, there is a 100 percent probability that *u* will follow *q* in a string of letters. There is a much lower probability that *i* will follow *t*. Although language is an example of a Markov chain, many other phenomena follow the same pattern. One interesting application of Markov chains in communication research is in the study of communication control. Markov models have been used to study the likelihood that dominance will be followed by submission (see Chapter 10).

Markov chains like language must be discussed in terms of average relative entropy and average redundancy, since the actual amounts vary from point to point in the chain. For example, the average relative entropy-redundancy in English is about 50 percent.

Whether the message is coded into regular language, electronic signals, or some other verbal or nonverbal code, the problem of transmission is the same—to reconstruct the message accurately at the destination. Any television viewer with poor reception is painfully aware of the problem. Accurate transmission would be no problem were it not for certain factors such as noise.

Now you can begin to see the role of redundancy in a message. Redundancy compensates noise. As noise distorts, masks, or replaces signals, redundancy allows the receiver to correct or fill in missing or distorted stimuli. For example, suppose you receive from a friend a letter that has been smeared by rain. The first sentences might look like this: "How ——— yo—? I a——ine." Or perhaps because of static, a sentence of radio news comes across as, "The Pres——— ———ed States has —clared. . . ." You can make some sense out of these distorted sentences because of the predictability or redundancy in the language.

Another factor limiting accurate transmission is channel capacity. Channel capacity is usually defined in terms of the maximum amount of information that can be transmitted over a channel per second. The actual amount of information in the channel is *throughput*. If throughput exceeds channel capacity, distortion will occur.

What, then, is necessary for efficient transmission? Efficient transmission involves coding at a maximum rate that will not exceed channel capacity. It also means using a code with sufficient redundancy to compensate the amount of noise present in the channel. If there is too much redundancy, transmission will be inefficient; if too little, it will be inaccurate.

The major contribution of classical information theory to human sciences is that the latter have used the technical model as an analogue for modeling interpersonal communication. Witness the fact that Shannon and Weaver's model (Figure 3-6) is one of the most frequently reproduced depictions of communication in textbooks.

Except for this analogue function, information theory has little relevance to any domain outside information per se. It does relate to systems theory by suggesting that system parts are connected to one another through information transmission. It also speaks to the technical side of mass communication. However, as will be indicated in the criticism section, these incursions into other domains do not help us very much in understanding the human side of communication.

General System Theory as an Approach to Knowledge

General system theory (GST) is a broad, multidisciplinary approach to knowledge based on the system concept. GST was developed primarily by Ludwig von Bertalanffy, a well-known biologist.[33] Basically, GST postulates concepts governing systems in general and applies these generalizations to numerous phenomena.[34] Here is how Bertalanffy describes GST:

> It seems legitimate to ask for a theory, not of systems of a more or less special kind, but of universal principles applying to systems in general.
>
> In this way we postulate a new discipline called *General System Theory.* . . .
>
> General System Theory, therefore, is a general science of "wholeness" which up till now was considered a vague, hazy, and semi-metaphysical concept. In elaborate form it would be a logico-mathematical discipline, in itself purely formal but applicable to the various empirical sciences.[35]

Bertalanffy first conceived of GST in the early 1920s.[36] At that time he began to think about biology in organismic terms, but this proved an unpopular approach. Not until after World War II did he feel comfortable about publicizing his system ideas. After the war he promoted his view primarily

through lectures and symposia. Bertalanffy describes the criticism he faced:

> The proposal of system theory was received incredulously as fantastic or presumptuous. Either—it was argued—it was trivial because the so-called isomorphisms were merely examples of the truism that mathematics can be applied to all sorts of things . . . or it was *false* and *misleading* because superficial analogies . . . camouflage actual difference. . . . Or, again, it was philosophically and methodologically *unsound* because the alleged 'irreducibility' of higher levels to lower ones tended to impede analytical research.[37]

Bertalanffy persisted, however, and in 1954 the Society for General Systems Research was born.[38] Like most other movements, GST is not a singular theory developed by one person. While GST itself was promoted by Bertalanffy, others were doing similar work in other fields. The two most important cognate areas, which were developed almost simultaneously with Bertalanffy's work, were Norbert Wiener's cybernetics and Shannon and Weaver's information theory. In fact, these three approaches so completely support one another that they are like tributaries of the same river.

A primary aim of GST is to integrate accumulated knowledge into a clear and realistic framework. General system theorists attempt to do this through the principle of *isomorphism*. An isomorphism is a structural similarity between two models or between an abstract model and an observed phenomenon. Two systems that are widely different are said to be isomorphic if their behaviors are governed by the same principles. A generalized model such as GST attempts to elucidate these principles. The following is an example:

> An exponential law of growth applies to certain cells, to populations of bacteria, of animals or humans, and to progress of scientific research measured by the number of publications in genetics or science in general.

---

33. For a biographical sketch of Bertalanffy, see "Ludwig von Bertalanffy," *General Systems* 17 (1972): 219–28.

34. For an example of formalized GST, see Masanao Toda and Emir H. Shuford, "Logic of Systems: Introduction to a Formal Theory of Structure," *General Systems* 10 (1965): 3–27.

35. Bertalanffy, *General System Theory,* pp. 32–37.

36. For a brief survey of the history of GST, see Bertalanffy, *General System Theory,* chap. 1.

37. Ibid., p. 14. For a thorough review of GST criticism and rebuttal, see Ludwig Bertalanffy, "General System Theory—A Critical Review," *General Systems* 12 (1962): 1–20 (reprinted in Buckley, *Modern Systems Research,* pp. 11–30).

38. The Society's Yearbook, *General Systems,* has been published annually since 1956. It is an excellent compilation of theoretical and applied work in GST.

The entities in question . . . are completely different. . . . Nevertheless, the mathematical law is the same.[39]

There is a critical need to better integrate knowledge in many areas, such as communication. Kenneth Boulding provides a compelling argument for the use of GST as an integrator of knowledge:

> The need for general systems theory is accentuated by the present sociological situation in science. . . . The crisis of science today arises because of the increasing difficulty of such profitable talk among scientists as a whole. Specialization has outrun Trade. Communication between the disciplines becomes increasingly difficult, and the Republic of Learning is breaking up into isolated subcultures with only tenuous lines of communication between them. . . . One wonders sometimes if science will grind to a stop in an assemblage of walled-in hermits, each mumbling to himself words in a private language that only he can understand. . . . The spread of specialized deafness means that someone who ought to know something that someone else knows isn't able to find it out for lack of generalized ears.
>
> It is one of the main objectives of General System Theory to develop these generalized ears.[40]

A System Theory of Communication

System theory and information theory have been applied to communication in several ways. We will encounter system theories of various aspects of communication at different points in this book. Appropriate for this chapter, however, is a general theory of communication based on systems concepts. One such theory that serves to illustrate how communication can be seen as a system and an information-based process is that of Lawrence Kincaid.[41] Kincaid refers to his theory as *conver-*

gence theory for reasons that will become apparent below.[42]

Kincaid sees groups and cultures as open systems that sustain themselves by expending effort. The work required to sustain a human group is communication or the transfer of information among individuals, groups, and cultures. Without communication or information sharing, human society as we know it would disappear. Information sharing creates a network of relations among people that maintains structure or organization within the group or culture. Without communication, human groups would decay into a state of disorganization, or entropy. Communication is a process of providing other individuals with information about one's perspective, meaning, or opinion; it is also a means of receiving feedback from others regarding the ways in which their perspectives, meanings, and opinions are similar or different.

Imagine a group with no contact with the outside world, a completely isolated community. There is communication within the group, but no information enters from outside. Here we have a closed system, which, because of the communication within the group, will gradually come together, or *converge*, to the point of creating a common collective pattern of thought. Individual differences will disappear; there will be complete agreement, total organization, or negentropy, in the group. This is the pure case of convergence through communication.

Now imagine a group that is not only isolated from other groups, but has no communication within the group. There is no information shared among members of the group, no way in which group members can know how their perspectives,

39. Bertalanffy, *General System Theory*, p. 33.

40. Kenneth Boulding, "General Systems Theory—The Skeleton of Science," in Buckley, *Modern Systems Research*, p. 4.

41. D. Lawrence Kincaid, June Ock Yum, and Joseph Woelfel, "The Cultural Convergence of Korean Immigrants in Hawaii: An Empirical Test of a Mathematical Theory," *Quality*

and Quantity 18 (1983): 59–78; D. Lawrence Kincaid, "The Convergence Model of Communication," *East-West Communication Institute* (Honolulu), Paper No. 18; Everett M. Rogers and D. Lawrence Kincaid, *Communication Networks: Toward a New Paradigm for Research* (New York: The Free Press, 1981), pp. 31–78.

42. This label is used to identify two different theories, this one and the theory of Ernest Bormann discussed in Chapter 6. Both use the term *convergence* to designate the process of increased sharing or commonality among individuals and groups, but the explanatory bases for the two theories differ substantially.

meanings, and opinions are similar to or different from those of their companions. According to system theory, what will happen? *Divergence* will occur until a state of disarray, confusion, or entropy results.

Neither of these pure cases occurs in real life. Instead, groups have incomplete communication within themselves and varying amounts of contact with outside groups. Communication within and among groups leads to a degree of convergence or sharing and some divergence or difference. Kincaid uses information theory to explain how much convergence or divergence will occur. Generally speaking, the more communication within or among groups, the greater the expected convergence. The less information transfer, the more the divergence. This principle is the basis of culture. Cultures, which are nothing more than common ways of thinking and doing, develop because of relatively isolated in-group communication. Cultures differ from one another because of relative lack of contact with other cultures; they will share elements with other cultures as their inter-group contact increases. Cultural diversity within a society is caused by high levels of divergent information that keeps the level of entropy within the society somewhat high. Kincaid states that modern technology enables society to handle a high level of entropy or cultural diversity.

Criticism of System Theory

System theory has been attacked on several fronts, although its supporters remain undaunted.[43] Six major issues have emerged:

1. Does the breadth and generality of system theory provide the advantage of integration or the disadvantage of ambiguity?

2. Does the theory's openness provide flexibility in application or confusing equivocality?

3. Is system theory merely a philosophical perspective, or does it provide useful explanation?

4. Has system theory generated useful research?

5. Is the system paradigm an arbitrary convention, or does it reflect reality in nature?

6. Does system theory help to simplify, or does it make things more complicated than they really are?

The first issue clearly relates to theoretical scope. From the beginning supporters have claimed that system theory provides a common vocabulary to integrate the sciences. It establishes useful logics that can be fruitfully applied to a broad range of phenomena. Others, however, claim that system theory merely confuses. If it is everything, it is really nothing. If all phenomena follow the same system principles, we have no basis for understanding anything apart from anything else.

Along the same line, some critics point out that system theory cannot have its cake and eat it too. Either it must remain a general framework without explaining real-world events, or it must abandon general integration in favor of making substantive claims. Jesse Delia expresses this concern:

> General System Theory manifests a fundamental ambiguity in that at points it seems to present a substantive perspective making specific theoretical claims and at other points to present a general abstract language devoid of specific theoretical substance for the unification of alternative theoretical views.[44]

The second issue relates to the first. Does the theory's openness provide flexibility of thought or confusing equivocality? Detractors claim that the theory embodies what Delia calls "a fancy form of the fallacy of equivocation." In other words, by permitting a variety of substantive applications in different theoretical domains, it cannot prevent inconsistencies among these applications. Two theories using a system framework may even contradict

---

43. For arguments supporting system theory, see especially Bertalanffy, "A Critical Review"; Buckley, *Sociology*; Monge, "Systems Perspective"; Fisher, *Perspectives*.

44. Jesse Delia, "Alternative Perspectives for the Study of Human Communication: Critique and Response," *Communication Quarterly* 25 (1977): 51. See also Edgan Taschjan, "The Entropy of Complex Dynamic Systems," *Behavioral Science* 19 (1975): 3.

each other. Where, then, Delia asks, is the supposed unity brought about by system theory? This problem is exacerbated by the fact that system theories can employ various logics, which are not necessarily consistent with one another.[45] Supporters answer that this openness is one of the main advantages of system theory: It does not bias the researcher with an a priori notion of what to expect. Consequently, it promotes research that sees things as they are without imposing arbitrary theoretical categories.[46]

The third issue is also a matter of appropriateness. Some critics question whether the systems approach is a theory at all, claiming that it has no explanatory power. While it gives us a perspective or way of conceptualizing, it provides little basis for understanding why things occur as they do. Aubrey Fisher agrees:

> These principles are quite abstract (that is to say, general). Consequently, they can be applied in numerous ways by differing theorists with equally different results. In fact, system "theory" is probably a misnomer. . . . In short, system theory is a loosely organized and highly abstract set of principles, which serve to direct our thinking but which are subject to numerous interpretations.[47]

System advocates probably would agree with this assessment of general system theory but point out that any given system theory of communication could be highly explanatory.

The fourth issue relates to system theory's heuristic value, questioning its ability to generate research. According to Donald Cushman, "systems is a perspective which has produced more staunch advocates than theoretical empirical research."[48]

Again, critics return to the extreme generality of the approach as the basis of their criticism. They claim that the theory simply does not suggest substantive questions for investigation.

In contrast, advocates claim that the fresh perspective provided by system theory suggests new ways of looking at old problems and thus is highly heuristic. Wayne Beach points out, for example, that a great deal of fruitful research followed Aubrey Fisher and Leonard Hawes's 1971 article on small group systems.[49] Fisher himself has done research on small group interaction. This work is presented in Chapter 11.

The fifth issue relates to the validity of system theory. Critics question whether system theory was developed to reflect what really happens in nature or to represent a useful convention for conceptualizing complex processes. In fact, system advocates themselves differ in their views of the function of the approach in this regard. Critics place system theory in a dilemma. If the theory attempts to describe phenomena as they really are, it is invalid. It posits similarities among events that are not really there. If, on the other hand, the theory provides merely a useful vocabulary for ordering a complex world, attributed similarities among events are only semantic and are therefore useless for providing understanding of those events. As Delia points out: "[Events] have different referents; they require different explanations; calling them the same thing . . . does not make them the same."[50] Bertalanffy calls this objection the "so what?" argument: If we find an analogy between two events, it is meaningless.[51]

The final issue of system theory is parsimony. Adherents claim the world is so complex that a sensible framework such as system theory is necessary to sort out the elements of world processes. Critics generally doubt that events are that complex. They

45. Delia, "Alternative Perspectives," 51–52.

46. Wayne Beach, "Stocktaking Open-Systems Research and Theory: A Critique and Proposals for Action" (Paper delivered at the meeting of the Western Speech Communication Association, Phoenix, November 1977).

47. Fisher, *Perspectives*, p. 196. See also Bertalanffy, "Critical Review."

48. Donald Cushman, "The Rules Perspective as a Theoretical Basis for the Study of Human Communication," *Communication Quarterly* 25 (1977): 30–45.

49. B. Aubrey Fisher and Leonard Hawes, "An Interact System Model: Generating a Grounded Theory of Small Groups," *Quarterly Journal of Speech* 57 (1971): 444–53. See also Beach, "Stocktaking."

50. Delia, "Alternative Perspectives," 51.

51. Bertalanffy, "Critical Review."

claim that system theory overcomplicates events that are essentially simple. Charles Berger states the case against overcomplication:

> In the behavioral sciences . . . we may be the victims of what I call irrelevant variety. Irrelevant variety is generated by the presence of attributes in a situation which have little to do with the phenomenon we are studying but which give the impression that what we are studying is very complex. . . . Merely because persons differ along a larger number of physical, psychological, and social dimensions, does not mean that all of these differences will make a difference in terms of the phenomena we are studying. . . . It is probably the case that relatively few variables ultimately can account for most of the action.[52]

The criticism against system theory boils down to two basic problems. First, system theory is said to be so general as to be void of theoretical value. Second, there is disagreement and ambiguity about what the role of system theory is or should be in communication inquiry. This latter criticism is perhaps unfair, in that system theory in the general sense is not intended to represent the substance of particular objects of study. We should recognize system theory for what it is, a general approach to the world.

Information theory, too, has had its critics. Although it is indispensible for developing advanced electronic communication devices, some of the original information theorists, system theorists, and other scholars looked to information theory for answers it could not provide. Its original formulators, Shannon and Weaver, hoped to use the theory as a covering model for all human and machine communication. However, even Colin Cherry, whose famous 1957 treatise on communication was based largely on information theory, now argues in his 1978 third edition that "the language of physical science is inadequate for discussion of what is essentially human about human communication."[53]

Most criticism of information theory relates to the standard of *appropriateness*.[54] The philosophical assumptions of the theory are not considered appropriate for understanding many aspects of human communication. Roger Conant captures the essence of the argument:

> When Shannon's theory first appeared it provoked a lot of optimism, not only in the telephone company for which it had clear technical applications, but also among biologists, psychologists, and the like who hoped it would illuminate the ways in which cells, animals, people, and perhaps even societies use information. Although the theory has been put to use in these ways, the results have not been spectacular at all. . . . Shannon's theory provides practically no help in understanding everyday communication.[55]

Many critics have centered on the ill-advised use of the term *information* as a symptom of this problem. Because the usage of the term is at such odds with popular meanings for *information*, a great deal of confusion has resulted. Ironically, information theory is not at all about *information* as we commonly understand it. One critic has suggested that the approach be retitled the "theory of signal transmission."[56] Because the term *information* as used by these theorists is so difficult to apply to human communication, other scholars have developed new definitions of the term under the old rubric of *information theory* that have caused even more be-

---

52. Charles Berger, "The Covering Law Perspective as a Theoretical Basis for the Study of Human Communication," *Communication Quarterly* 75 (1977): 7–18. See also Gerald R. Miller, "The Pervasiveness and Marvelous Complexity of Human Communication: A Note of Skepticism" (Keynote address delivered at the Fourth Annual Conference in Communication, California State University, Fresno, May 1977). See also Beach, "Stocktaking."

53. Colin Cherry, *On Human Communication* (Cambridge: MIT Press, 1978), p. ix.

54. Criticism of information theory can be found in many sources, including the following, on which my summary relies: Anatol Rapoport, "The Promise and Pitfalls of Information Theory," *Behavioral Science* 1 (1956): 303–9; also reprinted in *Modern Systems Research for the Behavioral Scientist*, ed. Walter Buckley (Chicago: Aldine, 1968), pp. 137–42. See also Rollo Handy and Paul Kurtz, "Information Theory," in *American Behavioral Scientist* 7, no. 6 (1964): 99–104; Roger C. Conant, "A Vector Theory of Information," in *Communication Yearbook 3* ed. Dan Nimmo (New Brunswick, N.J.: Transaction Books, 1979), pp. 177–96.

55. Conant, "A Vector Theory," 178.

56. Yehoshua Bar-Hillel, "Concluding Review," in *Information Theory in Psychology*, ed. Henry Quastler (Glencoe, Ill.: Free Press, 1955), p. 3.

fuddlement.[57] Of course, terminological confusion is only a symptom of the problems involved in stretching the concept to fit alien domains. Three such problems have been cited frequently in the literature.

The first is that information theory is designed as a measurement tool based on statistical procedures. Human messages in their full complexity are not easily broken down into observable, measurable signals. Although the phonetic structure of language is amenable to analysis, when you add paralinguistic cues, not to mention kinesic and proxemic features, information theory becomes virtually useless. Also, many of the codes used in human communication are continuous, not discrete; that is, they do not consist of off-on signals. Such codes are difficult to fit into the mathematical paradigm.

A second problem of applying information theory to human communication is that the theory downplays meaning. Even if we were able to predict the amount of information received by a listener, we would know nothing of the degree of shared understanding among the communicators or the impact of the message on them.

Finally, information theory does not deal with the contextual or personal factors affecting an individual's channel capacity. For example, individual learning, which changes one's ability to comprehend certain types of messages and ultimately one's capacity to receive signals, is left untouched in classical theory.

Of greater significance in the social and behavioral sciences is the subject of how information, once received, is perceived and processed. This has great relevance to communication theory and is taken up in some detail in Chapter 7.

57. See, for example, Krippendorf, "Information Theory."

Integration

System theory has been an immensely useful tool in the study of communication. System theory and its relatives, information theory and cybernetics, are designed to capture the ways in which a variety of phenomena can be viewed holistically as a set of interacting forces. Systems—whether physical, biological, social, or individual—are organized into hierarchies of parts, and any system is therefore embedded in an environment from which it receives and to which it sends matter and energy.

The activities of an open system exert energy to maintain organization or structure, although changes are expected as the system adjusts to its environment. The adjustive process is largely a matter of self-regulation achieved through the use of feedback. Information, which is transferred through the channels of the system, links the system's parts with one another. Communication is the process of transmitting and receiving information. Information within a system is defined in terms of the amount of uncertainty, entropy, or variety in the system.

General system theory uses system principles to unify the sciences. The basic metaphor of the system is believed to provide a common vocabulary for specialists to understand and talk about one another's work. System principles also provide a set of common processes that may explain many different phenomena from a variety of fields. System theory is useful in the study of communication because it demonstrates how communication involves interaction of complex sets of variables. In the upcoming chapters of this book, we examine some of those variables in more detail.

Four

Structural Theories of Signs and Meaning

This chapter deals with one of the most important applications of the structural tradition in communication—theories of signs and meaning. Structural theories of language and other symbolic forms have been a mainstay in the communication literature. Although all of the genres of communication theory address the topics of language and symbols, structural approaches have enjoyed particular prominence.

There have been several variants on the structuralist theme, but the basic idea of all of these theories is that *persons* use *signs* to designate *objects*. The sign is taken to represent something other than itself, and that representation is the meaning of the sign. Meanings will vary as different people come to make different associations among signs or sign systems and the referents of those signs. One of the simplest models used to illustrate this structure is that of C. K. Ogden and I. A. Richards (Figure 4-1).[1]

All of the theories discussed in this chapter recognize that signification is more complicated than this simple diagram implies. All, for example, recognize the importance of the relationship of signs to other signs, or syntax. These theories emphasize the ways in which symbol systems are structured and how those systems operate. In the case of language, such theories identify the units of language and specify the rules by which those elements are related to one another. Although language has certainly been the central focus of structuralism, nonverbal systems have also received attention, and an entire literature has grown up around this theme. Some of the most popular structural approaches to nonverbal communication are covered in the final

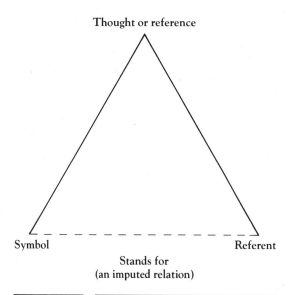

Figure 4-1 Ogden and Richards's meaning triangle.

From *The Meaning of Meaning*, by C. K. Ogden and I. A. Richards. Copyright ©1923. Reprinted by permission of Harcourt Brace Jovanovich and Routledge and Kegan Paul.

1. The triangle is attributed to various sources, including C. K. Ogden and I. A. Richards, *The Meaning of Meaning* (London: Kegan, Paul, Trench, Trubner, 1923).

section of this chapter. As a group, structural theories of signs are often referred to as *semiology.*

Semiology and Language

The term *semiology* was created by the founder of structural linguistics—Ferdinand de Saussure. Not only is Saussure the founder of modern linguistics, but he is considered to be a seminal figure in the development of contemporary structuralism in general.[2] We begin this section with a discussion of the general theory of signs.

A Theory of Signs

The general theory of signs, a branch of *semiology* known as *semiotics,* has a rich history in the twentieth century. The work of Charles Peirce and later the work of Charles Morris explored the ideas of how signs are used to represent meanings.[3] In this section, we describe the work of Italian semiotician Umberto Eco, who has produced perhaps the most comprehensive and contemporary theory of signs.[4] Eco's theory is important because it is highly developed and integrates so much earlier semiotic thinking; in addition, it incorporates a variety of structuralist ideas, being well implanted in the structuralist tradition. But the theory recognizes a much more intimate relationship between sign systems and practices than did earlier semiotic theories. Because the theory refuses to separate code structure from cultural practice, it overlaps substan-

tially with interactional-conventional theories, which are summarized in Chapters 6 and 7.

Eco believes that semiotics should include both a "theory of codes" and a "theory of sign production." The theory of codes must come to grips with structural and functional features of language and other coding systems; the complementary theory of sign production must explain the ways in which coding systems are both used and changed through communication in actual socio-cultural contexts. Thus Eco tacks back and forth between assumptions of stability in coding structure and rich variation in cultural practice. In so doing, he hopes to create a general theory that encompasses a number of symbolic and communicative concerns.

Eco's system of semiotics begins with the concept of a *sign.* A sign is anything taken by social convention to represent something else. The process of representing things by signs is *signification* or *semiosis.* Signification is best viewed as a four-part system:

1. conditions or objects in the world
2. signs
3. a repertoire of responses
4. a set of correspondence rules.

The correspondence rules pair the signs with objects (define what represents what), or they link signals with responses, thereby regulating a person's actions.

Eco uses the example of a dam in which a set of sensors activates a series of lights to tell an operator how high the water level is. The water levels are the worldly conditions, the lights are the signs, and the actions that an operator can take are the responses. Notice how these elements cannot function as a signification system without a set of correspondence rules. The rules tell the operator what water level each light represents and what he or she should do about it.

The system of objects, signs, and response possibilities constitutes an *s-code* or code system. The s-code is a structure in and of itself apart from its actual use and can be studied as such. (See section "The Structure of Language" on page 55.) A *code,* however, is a particular set of correspondence rules

---

2. Ferdinand de Saussure's primary work on this subject is *Course in General Linguistics* (London: Peter Owen, 1960). Excellent secondary sources include Anthony Giddens, *Central Problems in Social Theory: Action, Structure and Contradiction in Social Analysis* (Berkeley: University of California Press, 1979); and Fred Dallmayr, *Language and Politics* (Notre Dame: University of Notre Dame Press, 1984).

3. Charles Morris, *Signs, Language, and Behavior* (New York: George Braziller, 1946); and Charles Saunders Peirce, *Charles S. Peirce: Selected Writings,* ed. P. O. Wiener (New York: Dover, 1958).

4. Eco's primary semiotic works include *A Theory of Semiotics* (Bloomington: Indiana University Press, 1976); and *Semiotics and the Philosophy of Language* (Bloomington: Indiana University Press, 1984).

and cannot be studied apart from the person or group using it. Any s-code may be restructured time and time again because people can use and create a variety of codes or sets of rules for different purposes. We can better understand the difference between a *code* and an *s-code* by examining signs in more detail.

Eco discusses four modes of sign production, or ways in which people use signs. First, there is *recognition*, in which a person identifies or views an object or event as an expression of some content, through the application of an existing code or potential code. Recognizing symptoms and clues is an example. Second, there is *ostension*, the most elementary form of active signification. Here the person uses the object itself to signify a content. You might, for example, hold up a pack of cigarettes to demonstrate to a friend that you want the friend to buy you cigarettes at the store. Third, *replica* is the use of arbitrary signs in combination with other signs to signify. The use of language, certain gestures, emblems, musical notes, and so forth are examples of replica. Finally, there is *invention*, or proposing a new way to organize a field of stimuli to create a code. This involves positing signs in such a way as to make them acceptable to some group of code users. Art is a good example of invention. When you take something "symbolically," you are in an invention mode.

When a rule correlates a sign with something else, a *sign-function* is said to exist. The sign-function is the relationship between the sign and the signified, between an *expression* and a *content*. It is tempting to think of the content as an existing thing or a referent; however, Eco is careful to point out that the content is never the thing itself, but a cultural conception of the thing. He designates a sign with slashes, as in /dog/, and the actual object with double slashes, as in //dog//. The content of the sign function, however, is designated <<dog>>, which is a concept of "dogness." Sometimes the referent simply does not exist, as in the case of fantasies (for instance, mermaids), lies, and jokes. In the example of the dam, the real content of the sign-function is not the water level per se, but one's meanings for the water level, for

example, <<safe>>, <<danger>>, and <<flood>>.

Codes are organized sets of rules that relate to and define one another. Signs as expressions can be broken down into further expressions and contents, and contents, too, can be subdivided in this way. So the expression /red light/ has the subcode of /"flood"/, which means <<danger>>. The content <<high water>> can also be broken down into a subcode of /"open valve"/ with a meaning of <<let water out >>. In fact, code systems are completely defined in terms of their internal relations. All sign-functions are defined ultimately in terms of other sign-functions. Eco defines *denotations* as a simple sign-content relation. *Connotation* is a sign that is related to a content via one or more other sign-functions. For example, the sign-function /dog/ $\longrightarrow$ <<dog>> is a denotation; a connotation would be /dog/ $\longrightarrow$ <<stinky>>, which is derived from a more complicated linkage: /dog/ $\longrightarrow$ <<dog>> $\longrightarrow$ /hairy/ $\longrightarrow$ <<dirty>> $\longrightarrow$ /smells/ $\longrightarrow$ <<stinky>>.

Now we can see more clearly the difference between an s-code and a code. Any system of contents, signs, and responses can be related to one another in innumerable ways. Any sign can have many possible contents or sign-functions. Complex combinations of sign-functions are often used to elaborate an idea or feeling, which Eco calls *text*, *message*, or *discourse*. Because of the possibility of multiple meanings, then, communication always involves interpretation, which is the use of sign-functions to translate and explain other sign-functions.

An *interpretant* is the relationship between one sign-function and another; it is the means by which people understand and interpret texts. For example, I might ask you, "What is a /fire/?" You would then answer, "/Fire/ is <<burning>>." "What," I then ask, "is /burning/?" "/Burning/ is <<hot>>." Children in the process of learning codes drive parents crazy by their interminable quest for interpretants. Eco shows how dictionaries are simple catalogues of interpretants, one sign being related to another. Human interpretation, however, is more similar to the working of an encyclopedia because of the nearly infinite number of possible sign-functions that are related to one another in a complex web of actual and possible relations. Remember, interpretants are not facts or truths, but cultural conceptions that establish the representational meaning of signs.

Codes establish what correspondence rules are in force in a particular context. These codes are established by convention within cultural groups. Meanings are therefore cultural units. Not only is meaning cultural, but cultures are semiotic; as Eco describes:

> Perhaps we are, somewhere, the deep impulse which generates semiosis. And yet we recognize ourselves only as semiosis in process, signifying systems and communicational processes. The map of semiosis, as defined at a given stage of historical development (with the debris carried over from previous semiosis), tells us who we are and what (or how) we think.[5]

The Structure of Language

Saussure taught that signs, including the elements of language, are arbitrary.[6] He noted that different languages use different words for the same thing and that there is no physical connection between a word and its referent. Therefore, signs are conventions governed by rules. Not only does this axiom support the idea that language is a structure, but it reinforces the general assumption that language and reality are separate. Saussure himself referred to language as both a system and as a structure. As such, he believed that linguistic researchers must pay attention to language forms, such as sounds, word parts, and grammar.

The arbitrariness of language, however, is not absolute. First, Saussure pointed out that although language conventions are arbitrary, individual speakers are required to follow the conventions that are established, making those conventions not at all arbitrary. Further, since some words are based on other words, arbitrariness is a matter of degree.

Basic words like *his* and *story* are "radically arbitrary," while derived words like *history* are "relatively arbitrary."

Language described in these terms is strictly a system of formal relations without substance. The key to understanding the structure of the system is *difference*: The elements and relations embedded in language are distinguished by their differences. One sound differs from another (as *p* and *b*); one word differs from another (as *pat* and *bat*); one grammatical form differs from another (as *has run* and *will run*). This system of differences constitutes the structure of the language. Both in spoken and written language, distinctions among signified objects in the world are identified by corresponding distinctions among linguistic signs. No linguistic unit has significance in and of itself; only in conjunction with other linguistic units does a particular unit acquire meaning.

Saussure made an important distinction between formal language, which he called *langue*, and the use of language in communication, which he referred to as *parole*. These two terms correspond to *language* and *speech*. Language is a formal system with a life of its own apart from the people who use it. Speech is the use of language to accomplish purposes. Language is not created by users, but speech is. Indeed, speech makes use of language, but it is less regular and more variable than the formal system of language from which it derives. Linguistics, to Saussure, is the study of langue, not parole:

> Taken as a whole, speech is many-sided and heterogeneous; straddling several areas simultaneously . . . we cannot put it into any category of human facts, for we cannot discover its unity. Language, on the contrary, is a self-contained whole and a principle of classification.[7]

This distinction has had a significant impact on the study of language and communication to the present day.

One of the differences between langue and parole, according to Saussure, is stability. Language is characterized by *synchrony*, meaning that it

5. Eco, *Semiotics and the Philosophy of Language*, p. 45.
6. Saussure, *Course*.

7. Ibid., p. 9.

changes very little over time. Speech on the other hand, is characterized by *diachrony*, meaning that it changes constantly from situation to situation. Because of its constant flux, speech is not particularly suitable for scientific study, which is why linguistics must take a language-oriented, synchronic focus. The point here is not that language does not change; only that language form cannot be understood unless a synchronic focus is adopted. As we shall see in Chapters 6 and 7, however, the distinction between language and speech, and that between synchrony and diachrony, is sharply criticized by theorists from other traditions.

Saussure's ideas, which today may seem self-evident and simplistic laid the foundation for traditional linguistic thought in the twentieth century. Although these ideas may seem obvious on the surface, they have been criticized.[8] Most critics agree that language is certainly conventional, but its "arbitrariness" is more in question. Arbitrariness makes sense only if one accepts the tenet that language and speech are separate. Critics of the structuralist view posit that language and speech cannot be separated, that speech is the mechanism through which language itself is created, maintained, and changed, and that because of the social reality of language signs, those signs cannot be considered arbitrary. Saussure based his analysis on the relationship between the word and the thing, but critics insist that he missed the significance of the relationship between the word and the person who uses that word. This failure has been corrected by later structuralists and nonstructuralists alike. What most structuralists have been unable to surmount, however, is the requirement that language be studied as a formal, abstract system apart from its use. Answers to that problem are provided by nonstructuralist theories, some of which are presented in upcoming chapters.

Let us turn now to a more detailed discussion of language structure. Influenced by the work of Saussure, the standard model of sentence structure was developed between about 1930 and 1950 in the classical structural period.[9] Numerous linguists contributed to this model, but the most important included Leonard Bloomfield, Charles Fries, and Zellig Harris.[10] Basically, this model breaks down a sentence into component parts in hierarchical fashion. Sounds and sound groups combine to form word roots and word parts, which in turn combine to form words and phrases. Phrases are put together to make clauses or sentences. Thus language can be analyzed on various levels, roughly corresponding to sounds, words, and phrases.

The first level of sounds involves the study of phonetics. An isolatable speech sound is a *phone*. Phones of a particular type are grouped into a sound family called *phoneme*, which is the basic building block of any language. Any dialect of a language contains a number of phonemes. These phonemes are combined according to rules to produce *morphemes*, the smallest meaningful linguistic unit. Some morphemes are free—they can stand alone as a word in a sentence. Other morphemes are bound—they must be combined with other morphemes to form words. On the syntax level words are combined according to rules to form grammatical phrases, which are linked together into clauses and sentences. This structural approach provides an orderly classification of language parts. Actual observed segments are put into classes of a given type (phoneme, morpheme, and so forth), and these segments are sequenced in a sentence-building process. At each level of analysis is a finite set of classes (for example, phonemes or morphemes) that can be observed in the native language. Sentences are always built up from the bottom of the hierarchy, so that succeeding levels depend on the formation of lower levels. This scheme is known as phrase-structure grammar.

While this approach provides a useful descrip-

8. For a critique of structuralism, see Giddens, *Central Problems*.

9. An excellent summary and critique of this period can be found in J. A. Fodor, T. G. Bever, and M. F. Garrett, *The Psychology of Language: An Introduction to Psycholinguistics and Generative Grammar* (New York: McGraw-Hill, 1974).

10. Leonard Bloomfield, *Language* (New York: Holt, Rinehart & Winston, 1933); Charles Fries, *The Structure of English* (New York: Harcourt, Brace & World, 1952); Zellig Harris, *Structural Linguistics* (Chicago: University of Chicago Press, 1951).

tion of the structure of language, it fails to explain how people use language. This latter question, far more central to communication than language structure, has demanded the attention of psycholinguists since about 1950. We know that people must possess an intuitive knowledge of their language in order to produce meaningful, grammatical speech. What is the nature of this knowledge? How is it acquired? How is it used? The literature that has emerged from this work is extensive, controversial, and highly technical. Our purpose here is to provide only a general overview of this topic.

Phrase-structure grammar, a mainstay in grammar theory for many years, is no longer believed to be adequate by itself to explain the generation of sentences.[11] Phrase structure breaks down a given sentence into phrases. A sentence is a hierarchy of components, with each successively larger component being generated by a set of *rewrite rules*. For example, a sentence may be broken down according to the following rewrite rule:

sentence   ↔   noun phrase + verb phrase

Or, to use an actual example:

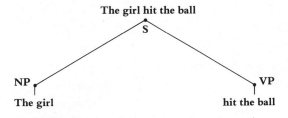

The verb phrase can be broken down further according to the following rewrite rule:

verb phrase   ↔   verb + noun phrase

Or, to continue the example:

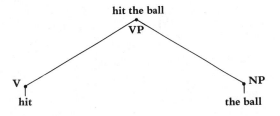

This process continues until all units of the sentence are accounted for, including small parts such as the articles *the* or *an*. These analyses are often illustrated by a tree diagram, as shown in Figure 4-2.

The primary objection to classical linguistics is that although it is useful as a taxonomic, or descriptive, approach, it is powerless to explain how language is generated. A simple example will suffice to illustrate this weakness. Phrase-structure grammar would analyze the following two sentences exactly the same way, even though the slightest inspection reveals that their syntactical origins must be different.[12]

- John is easy to please.
- John is eager to please.

These sentences have entirely different syntactical meanings. In the first sentence *John* is the object

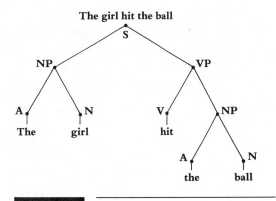

Figure 4-2   A simple tree diagram.

11. For an explanation and critique of finite-state and phrase-structure grammar, see Noam Chomsky, "Three Models for the Description of Language," *Transactions on Information Theory*, vol. IT-2 (1956), pp. 113–24; and Jerry Fodor, James Jenkins, and Sol Saporta, "Psycholinguistics and Communication Theory," in *Human Communication Theory*, ed. Frank E. X. Dance (New York: Holt, Rinehart & Winston, 1967), pp. 160–201.

12. Examples from Gilbert Harmon, *On Noam Chomsky: Critical Essays* (Garden City, N.Y.: Anchor Books, 1974), p. 5.

of the infinitive *to please*. In the second *John* is the noun phrase of the sentence. Regular phrase structure provides no easy way to explain these different grammatical meanings. Questions include the following:

- What constitutes a necessary and sufficient grammar, such that a speaker competent in the grammar of a language can produce an infinite number of novel sentences?
- By what cognitive process are sentences generated and understood?
- How is syntactical ambiguity to be accounted for?
- How is language acquired?

To answer questions such as these, generative grammar has been developed.

Noam Chomsky is the primary force behind generative grammar. As a young linguist in the 1950s, Chomsky parted company with the classical theorists to develop an approach that since has become the foundation of contemporary linguistics.[13] Like any theoretical tradition generative grammar now has several positions within it, although the tradition as a whole is built on a cluster of essential ideas.

Generative linguistics is both a theory of language and a theory of cognition. It is therefore taken up in greater detail in Chapter 5.

The Post-Structuralist Response

A fundamental assumption of the traditional structural theories of language is that, whatever else it may be, language functions primarily as an instrument of communication. Even strict formalists like Saussure recognize the ultimate function of language in parole. Communication is made possible by semiotic rules of correspondence *for people*, who then designate and interpret.

This assumption, however, is not universally adopted. The most striking departure from the traditional view is that of a group of theorists who see texts as completely independent from any use to which they may be put. Perhaps the most well known of these theorists are Jacques Derrida and Michel Foucault. Both of these scholars view texts, which are always written, as disembodied forces. Although they are produced by human beings, they are not possessed by writers and readers and are to be judged by their inherent structures rather than by any particular meanings they have for communicators. These theorists agree that the structures of texts give them a life of their own and that human use of a text is never the determining factor in establishing the text's meaning. For text theorists, then, interpretation of the meaning of texts is a central problem. For this reason, the post-structuralist tradition is closely allied with theories of hermeneutics. (We explore hermeneutics in Chapter 8, where we encounter the work of another important text theorist, Paul Ricoeur.) Although the theories of Derrida and Foucault share important post-structuralist assumptions, they differ substantially in several ways. Let us turn now to these two theorists.

Derrida's Grammatology

For Derrida, a text presents innumerable possible structures and meanings.[14] How a person uses a text—or the meaning assigned by a writer or reader—is only one possible meaning and rarely corresponds with alternative meanings in the text itself. Derrida's method is designed to uncover, through structural analysis, the various possible meanings of a text.

The structure of a text is determined at base by the ways in which signs delineate something from something else, a quality he calls *differance*, which is similar to Saussure's use of the same term. Thus

---

13. For a list of Chomsky's works, see Chapter 5 and Bibliography.

14. Derrida's primary work on this subject is *Of Grammatology*, trans. Gayatri Chakravorty Spivak (Baltimore: Johns Hopkins Press, 1974, 1976).

a sign always implies something excluded or absent. A sign makes the absent present, because every designation also presents a *trace* of that which is excluded. The word *tiger* designates a particular animal only insofar as it makes known what a tiger is not. Thus a trace is "sous rature," or *under erasure*, because at the same time that something is designated, it is negated by that which it is not. *Tiger* is understood by what it is and what it is not; it is therefore both present and absent. Derrida gets this idea across in his writings by crossing out words like tiger. This relationship between presence and absence is known as *archiecriture*.

Of particular importance to Derrida is the tension between speech and writing. Traditional structuralism is phonocentric, or speech-centered, which comes from the traditional notion of logocentrism or word-centeredness. For Derrida, the significance of writing is in its inherent structure because, unlike speech, writing is a form that transcends particular uses of language by authors and readers or hearers. Writing in this sense has a life of its own. Derrida uses the term *writing* generically, as text, not as the process of producing text (using a pen and paper).

Both the processes of writing (producing text) and speaking contain generic writing in them. That is, they consist of general structural features emanating from textual structures that are prior to any act of writing or speaking. A writer or speaker may make use of linguistic structures as a tool, but that usage is essentially irrelevant to the textual structure that made the speech and writing possible. Derrida refers to the independence of text as "writing before the letter."

Text, or the generic sense of writing, is an artifact—it lives on long after its creation. Such writing (text) demands structural analysis apart from the intensions of those who wrote it, rewrote it, read it, or interpreted it at any point in time. The study of the structural features of text is *grammatology*.

The way in which authors and readers use a text may belie or cover up the natural structure of writing. This is the risk of interpretation, which is a method designed to uncover personal and cultural meanings of texts. Instead of interpretation, Derrida calls for *deconstruction*, which is designed to get at possible alternative meanings in the text, apart from the temporal and untrue interpretations of individual users. By deconstruction you can reveal alternative meanings embedded in a text without being fooled by what people carry to the text in their heads.

Deconstruction, however, is not an objective procedure for revealing truth, but an attitude of reading (deconstructive reading) that lays open various alternative meanings. This technique of hypothesizing alternative conceptual structures is known in text theory as *bricolage*. The key to deconstruction is in the traces in the text, where various and indeterminate distinctions could be made. Deconstruction, then, is a heuristic process of bricolage, or positing a variety of alternative meanings by centering on unusual or surprising instances of difference. Derrida makes heavy use of the analysis of metaphors in this process. His writings lead the reader to a particular sense of a text's unified meaning; then he surprises the reader by finding an instance that contradicts this meaning, causing the reader to shift once again. Derrida does this to make the point that it is foolish to believe that good, clear writing somehow reflects truth.

Through this process of deconstruction, the critic continually reconstructs the text. Each reconstruction (deconstruction) reveals a new hidden picture. No one picture is protected; each is deconstructed. Therefore, deconstruction "produces rather than protects." The alternative readings, however, are not different ways in which the text's users might understand it, but alternative meanings structurally embedded in the text as independent entities.

The purpose of deconstruction is to demonstrate indeterminacy of knowledge and to debunk those who think they are using language to uncover truth. In his critiques, Derrida uses deconstruction to demonstrate the absurdity of the author's truth claims by showing the indeterminacy of the very language (writing) with which the author displays his or her certainty. Deconstruction is therefore inherently negative in that it denies meanings; it is also schizophrenic in that it always deconstructs itself.

Needless to say, deconstruction has been severely criticized, especially by the victims of Derrida's analyses. They see deconstruction as negative, indeterminate, counterproductive, antihumanist, even nihilistic. For Derrida, however, deconstruction is an important process to reveal the infinite openness of textual structure and the all-too-frequent close mindedness of speakers, writers, and readers.

Michel Foucault

Foucault is not a traditional structuralist and is, in fact, impossible to classify neatly.[15] Although he denies a structuralist bias in his work, he has a distinct structural-functional focus. Foucault, like Derrida, distances himself from that aspect of structuralism that juxtaposes language and "reality," yet he does point to certain structures and functions of discourse.

Foucault says that each period has a distinct world view or conceptual structure that determines the nature of knowledge in that period. The character of knowledge in a given epoch Foucault calls the *episteme* or *discursive formation*. The vision of each age is exclusive and incompatible with those of other ages, making it impossible for people in one period to think like those of another. The episteme, or way of thinking, is determined not by people, but by the predominant discursive structures of the day. These discursive structures are deeply embedded ways of practicing or expressing the episteme and are essentially expressions of faith and truism that reflect fundamental knowledge

structures. Consequently, you cannot separate what people "know" and the structure of discourse used to express that "knowledge."

The structure of discourse is a set of inherent rules that determines the form and substance of discursive practice. These rules control what can be talked or written about and who may talk or write (or whose talk is to be taken seriously). Finally, rules prescribe the conceptual form that discourse must take.

Contrary to popular belief, according to Foucault, people are not responsible for establishing the conditions of discourse. Rather, discursive formation itself determines the definition and place of the person in the scheme of the world. Our present discursive structure makes human beings the foundation and origin of knowledge, but people have never before achieved this status in any other period and will soon lose it. Foucault believes that the episteme will again shift, and human beings will once again disappear from their central place in the world: "It is comforting . . . and a source of profound relief to think that man is only a recent invention, a figure not yet two centuries old, a new wrinkle in our knowledge, and that he will disappear again as soon as that knowledge has discovered a new form."[16] This radical notion upholds that the human being is a product of discourse rather than the discourse being created by humans.

Discourse, then, does not require a knowing subject, a person who creates it, consumes it, understands it, and uses it. Rather, language itself prefigures personhood: Language creates the person. Indeed, people generate discourse, but in doing so they are merely fulfilling a function determined by the predominant discursive forms of the day.

Foucault's work centers on analyzing discourse in a way that reveals its rules and structure. This he calls *archaeology*, which is not unlike Derrida's de-

---

15. Foucault's primary works on this subject include *The Archaeology of Knowledge*, trans. A. M. Sheridan Smith (New York: Pantheon, 1972); *The Order of Things: An Archaeology of the Human Sciences* (New York: Pantheon, 1970); and *Power/Knowledge: Selected Interviews and Other Writings 1927–1977*, trans. Colin Gordon, et al., ed. Colin Gordon (New York: Pantheon, 1980). For an excellent short summary, see Sonja K. Foss, Karen A. Foss, and Robert Trapp, *Contemporary Perspectives on Rhetoric* (Prospect Heights, Ill.: Waveland Press, 1985). See also Carole Blair and Martha Cooper, "The Humanist Turn in Foucault's Rhetoric of Inquiry," *Quarterly Journal of Speech* 73

(1987): 151–172; Carole Blair, "The Statement: Foundation of Foucault's Historical Criticism," *Western Journal of Speech Communication* 51 (1987): 364–83; Sonja K. Foss and Ann Gill, "Michel Foucault's Theory of Rhetoric as Epistemic," *Western Journal of Speech Communcation* 51 (1987): 384–401.

16. Michel Foucault, *Order*, p. xxii.

construction. Archaeology seeks to uncover, through careful description, the regularities of discourse. It displays disparities or contradictions, rather than coherence, and reveals a succession of one form of discourse to another. For this reason, Foucault places emphasis on comparative descriptions of more than one piece of discourse.

Interpretation, or establishing the meaning of a text, cannot be avoided in text analysis, but it should be minimized because interpretation does not reveal discursive structure and, in fact, may obscure it. Foucault thinks that analysts should avoid associating discourse with authors, since authors are merely fulfilling the discourse's function and are not instrumental in any way in establishing the structure of the texts they produce. In short, the text is everything; the communicator is nothing.

Foucault's writings are preoccupied with the subject of power. He believes that power is an inherent part of all discursive formation. As such, power is a function of discourse or knowledge and not a human or institutional property. The episteme, as expressed in language, grants power. Thus power and knowledge cannot be divided. Power, however, is a good, creative force that finds its zenith in "disciplinary power" or the prescription of standards of correct behavior.

Criticism

Foucault and Derrida present a startlingly fresh and inventive approach to language and have been praised for their insights and originality.[17] Although their perspectives are unusual, they do contribute understanding to important traditional concepts like language, text, rhetoric, speech, interpretation, structure, and power.

They have been criticized, however, because of their radical departure from the traditions of philosophy, rhetoric, and linguistics and their blatant disregard for the labors of others in these fields. Derrida in particular makes a profession of deconstructing the work of others, a practice his victims

often find extremely irritating. Both Derrida and Foucault are hard to pin down on any one position, because of their basic stance that structure and truth are elusive. Derrida's practice of constantly shifting meaning makes his theory almost impossible to examine and critique.

What these theorists do for the communication scholar is to sensitize us to the centrality and significance of text in the historical and political processes of human life.

Structural Theories of Nonverbal Communication

Nonverbal communication is difficult to conceptualize. Scholars disagree about what nonverbal communication is, as Randall Harrison points out:

The term "nonverbal communication" has been applied to a broad range of phenomena: everything from facial expression and gesture to fashion and status symbol, from dance and drama to music and mime, from the flow of affect to the flow of traffic, from the territoriality of animals to the protocol of diplomats, from extrasensory perception to analog computers, and from the rhetoric of violence to the rhetoric of topless dancers.[18]

Because of the uncertainties about what counts as nonverbal communication, classifying and organizing this material is difficult. Judee Burgoon suggests a threefold scheme:

17. For a critique of Derrida, see Giddens, *Central Problems*, pp. 35–38. For a critique of Foucault, see Foss, Foss, and Trapp, *Contemporary*, pp. 208–11.

18. Randall Harrison, "Nonverbal Communcation," in *Handbook of Communcation*, eds. Ithiel de sola Pool, et al. (Chicago: Rand McNally, 1973). Conceptual issues are discussed in Judee K. Burgoon, "Nonverbal Communication Research in the 1970s: An Overview," in *Communication Yearbook 4* ed. Dan Nimmo (New Brunswick, N.J.: Transaction Books, 1980), p. 179; see also Mark Knapp, *Nonverbal Communciation in Human Interaction* (New York: Holt, Rinehart & Winston, 1978); Mark Knapp, John Wiemann, and Johy Daly, "Nonverbal Communication: Issues and Appraisal," *Human Communication Research* 4 (1978): 271–80; Robert G. Harper, Arthur Weiss, and Joseph Motarozzo, *Nonverbal Communcation: The State of the Art* (New York: John Wiley, 1978).

1. the structure of nonverbal code systems
2. cultural variation and patterns
3. social functions of nonverbal codes.[19]

Many of the topics relevant to the second and third categories are covered later in the book; for now, we concentrate on structural approaches to nonverbal coding.

Burgoon characterizes nonverbal code systems as possessing several structural properties. First, nonverbal codes tend to be *analogic* rather than *digital*. While digital signals are discrete, like numbers and letters, analogic signals are continuous, forming a spectrum or range, like sound volume and brightness. Therefore, nonverbal signals like facial expression and vocal intonation cannot simply be classed into one category or another.

A second feature found in some, but not all, nonverbal codes is *iconicity* or resemblance. Iconic codes resemble the thing being symbolized (like depicting the shape of something with your hands.) Third, certain nonverbal codes seem to elicit universal meaning. This is especially the case with such signals as threats and emotional displays, which may be biologically determined. Fourth, nonverbal codes enable the simultaneous transmission of several messages. With the face, body, voice, and other signals, several different messages can be sent at once. Fifth, nonverbal signals often evoke an automatic response without thinking. An example would be stepping on the brake at a red light. Sixth, nonverbal signals are often emitted quite spontaneously, as when you just let off nervous energy.

Finally, nonverbal code systems have several things in common with language, though Burgoon is careful to point out that there are also many differences. Both language and nonverbal code systems can be broken down into particular units, as we will see in the next section. Nonverbal and verbal codes have various dimenions: semantic, syntactic, and pragmatic. Semantics refers to the

meanings of a sign; syntactics refers to the ways in which signs are organized into systems with other signs; pragmatics refers to the effects or behaviors elicited by a sign or group of signs. The meanings attached to both verbal and nonverbal forms are context-bound, or determined in part by the context in which they are produced and read. Further, both language and nonverbal forms allow communicators to combine relatively few signs into an almost limitless variety of complex expressions of meaning.

Nonverbal code systems are often classed according to the type of activity used in the code. Burgoon suggests seven types:

1. kinesics or bodily activity
2. proxemics or use of space
3. physical appearance
4. haptics or use of touch
5. vocalics or use of voice
6. chronemics or use of time
7. artifacts or use of objects.[20]

In this chapter we will look at three prominent theories of the first two types of nonverbal coding—kinesics and proxemics.

Birdwhistell's Theory of Kinesics

Ray Birdwhistell is considered the originator of kinesics.[21] An anthropologist interested in language, Birdwhistell uses linguistics as a model for his kinesic work. In fact, kinesics is popularly referred to as *body language*, although critics doubt the validity of the language analogy. Let us look at the foundation ideas of Bidwhistell's theory.

Communication, as a complex process, is a multichannel phenomenon. It makes use of all sensory channels, and a complete analysis must encompass all channels in use. Birdwhistell describes the continuous process: "While no single channel is in constant use, one or more channels are always in operation. Communication is the term which I ap-

19. This analysis from Judee K. Burgoon, "Nonverbal Signals," in *Handbook of Interpersonal Communication*, eds. Mark L. Knapp and Gerald L. Miller (Beverly Hills: Sage Publications, 1985), pp. 350–53.

20. Burgoon, "Nonverbal Signals," pp. 349–50.

21. Birdwhistell's major works include *Introduction to Kinesics* (Louisville: University of Louisville Press, 1952); *Kinesics and Context* (Philadelphia: University of Pennsylvania Press, 1970).

ply to this continuous process."[22] Although developing methodologies for studying each channel is important, the theorist must always keep an eye on the whole. So, while Birdwhistell has concentrated his work on the visual channel, he has also attempted to relate his findings to the larger complex.

In *Kinesics and Context* Birdwhistell lists seven assumptions on which he bases his theory.

1. Like other events in nature, no body movement or expression is without meaning in the context in which it appears.

2. Like other aspects of human behavior, body posture, movement, and facial expression are patterned and, thus, subject to systematic analysis.

3. While the possible limitations imposed by particular biological substrata are recognized, until otherwise demonstrated, the systematic body motion of the members of a community is considered a function of the social system to which the group belongs.

4. Visible body activity, like audible acoustic activity, systematically influences the behavior of other members of any particular group.

5. Until otherwise demonstrated such behavior will be considered to have an investigable communicational function.

6. The meanings derived therefrom are functions both of the behavior and of the operations by which it is investigated.

7. The particular biological system and the special life experience of any individual will contribute idiosyncratic elements to his kinesic system, but the individual or symptomatic quality of these elements can only be assessed following the analysis of the larger system of which he is a part.[23]

One of the most important connections Birdwhistell found is the link between bodily activity and language, called the linguistic-kinesic analogy. This analogy extends classical linguistics into the realm of kinesics:

This original study of gestures gave the first indication that kinesic structure is parallel to language structure. By the study of gestures in context, it became clear that the kinesic system has forms which are astonishingly like words in language. The discovery in turn led to the investigation of the components of these forms and to the discovery of the larger complexes of which they were components. . . . It has become clear that there are body behaviors which function like significant sounds, that combine into simple or relatively complex units like words, which are combined into much longer stretches of structured behavior like sentences or even paragraphs.[24]

The similarity of hierarchical structure in kinesics to that of linguistics is striking. The problem of the kinesicist is similar to that of the linguist: "Kinesics is concerned with abstracting from the continuous muscular shifts which are characteristics of living physiological systems those groupings of movement which are of significance to the communicational process and thus to the interactional systems of particular social groups."[25]

Out of the thousands of perceptible bodily motions produced in a short period of time, certain of these emerge as functional in communication. Such movements are called *kines*: "A kine is an abstraction of that range of behavior produced by a member of a given social group which, for another member of that same group, stands in perceptual contrast to a different range of such behavior."[26] In other words, it is a range of motions or positions seen as a single motion or position. A perceptible movement of the eyelid or a turn of the hand are examples of kines. What is defined as a kine in one cultural group may not be in another. Kines are further grouped into *kinemes*, elements that display differential communicative function. Like the phoneme in linguistics, the kineme is a group of relatively interchangeable kines. For example, up to twenty-three different positions (kines) of the eyelids may be discerned, but they can be grouped into about four kinemes. Kinemes, like phonemes, occur in context. A complex combination of kinemes throughout the body may be called a *kinemorph*.

22. Ibid., p. 70.
23. Ibid., pp. 183–84.

24. Ibid., p. 80.
25. Ibid., p. 192.
26. Ibid., p. 193.

Hall's Theory of Proxemics

Edward Hall shares the view of his fellow anthropologist Birdwhistell that communication is a multichannel affair.[27] Hall believes that just as language varies from culture to culture, so do the other interacting media. Specifically, *proxemics* refers to the use of space in communication. "Proxemics is the term I have coined for the interrelated observations and theories of man's use of space as a specialized elaboration of culture."[28] A more specific definition is "the study of how man unconsciously structures microspace—the distance between men in conduct of daily transactions, the organization of space in his houses and buildings, and ultimately the layout of his towns."[29] Although this definition of proxemics is broad, most of the work in the area has been limited to the use of interpersonal space.

These definitions make clear that the way space is used in interaction is very much a cultural matter. In different cultures various sensory modalities assume importance. In some cultures, such as the American, sight and hearing predominate; in other cultures, such as the Arabian, smell is also important. Some cultures rely on touching more than do others. In any case, a necessary relation is present between the use of senses in interaction and interpersonal distances. Another reason that proxemic relations vary among cultures involves the definition of the self. People in most western cultures learn to identify the self through the skin and clothes. Arabs, however, place the self deeper in the middle of the body.

For these reasons, then, the people of a particular culture structure their space in particular ways. Hall defines three basic types of space. *Fixed-feature space* consists of the unmovable structural arrangements around us. Walls and rooms are examples.

Semifixed feature space is the way that movable obstacles, such as furniture, are arranged. *Informal space* is the personal territory around the body that travels with a person. Informal space determines the interpersonal distance among individuals. American culture utilizes four discernible distances: intimate (0 to 18 inches), personal (1½ to 4 feet), social (4 to 12 feet), and public (over 12 feet).

When people are engaged in conversation, eight possible factors are involved in the distance between them. Hall lists these factors as primary categories:

1. *Posture-sex factors*: These include the sex of the participant and the basic position (standing, sitting, lying).

2. *Sociofugal-sociopetal axis*: The word *sociofugal* implies discouragement of interaction; *sociopetal* implies the opposite. This dimension refers to the angle of the shoulders relative to the other person. The speakers may be facing each other, may be back to back, or may be positioned toward any other angle in the radius.

3. *Kinesthetic factors*: This is the closeness of the individuals in terms of touch-ability. Individuals may be in physical contact or within close distance, they may be outside body contact distance, or they may be positioned anywhere in between these extremes. This factor also includes the positioning of body parts as well as which parts are touching.

4. *Touching behavior*: People may be involved in any of the following tactile relations: caressing and holding, feeling, prolonged holding, pressing against, spot touching, accidental brushing, or no contact.

5. *Visual code*: This category includes the manner of eye contact ranging from direct (eye-to-eye) to no contact.

6. *Thermal code*: This element involves the perceived heat from the other communicator.

7. *Olfactory code*: This factor includes the kind and degree of odor perceived in the conversation.

8. *Voice loudness*: The loudness of speech relates directly to interpersonal space.

27. Edward Hall's major works include *Silent Language* (Greenwich, Conn.: Fawcett, 1959); "A System for the Notation of Proxemic Behavior," *American Anthropologist* 65 (1963): 1003–26: and *The Hidden Dimension* (New York: Random House, 1966).

28. Hall, *The Hidden Dimension*, p. 1.

29. Hall, "A System of Notation," 1003.

Ekman and Friesen

For many years Paul Ekman and Wallace Friesen have collaborated on nonverbal research that has led to an excellent general model of nonverbal signs.[30] They have concentrated their work on kinesic behavior (for example, face and hands). Their goal has been ambitious: "Our aim has been to increase understanding of the individual, his feelings, mood, personality, and attitudes, and to increase understanding of any given interpersonal interaction, the nature of the relationship, the status or quality of communicaton, what impressions are formed, and what is revealed about interpersonal style or skill."[31]

These authors have approached nonverbal activity from three perspectives: origin, coding, and usage. Origin is the source of an act. A nonverbal behavior may be innate (built into the nervous system), species constant (universal behavior required for survival), or variant across cultures, groups, and individuals. As examples, one could speculate that eyebrow raising as a response to surprise is innate, that territoriality is species constant, and that shaking the head back and forth to indicate no is culture specific.

Coding is the relationship of the act to its meaning. An act may be *arbitrary*; that is, no indication of meaning is inherent in the sign itself. Head nodding is a good example. By convention, in our culture we agree that nodding is an indication of yes, but this coding is purely arbitrary. Other nonverbal signs are *iconic*. Iconic signs resemble what is being signified. For instance, we often draw pictures in the air or position our hands to illustrate what we

are talking about. The third category of coding is *intrinsic*. Intrinsically coded cues contain their meaning within them; such cues are themselves part of what is being signified. Crying is an example of intrinsic coding. Crying is a sign of emotion, but it is also part of the emotion itself.

The third way to analyze a behavior is by usage, which is affected by such factors as external conditions around the behavior, awareness or nonawareness of the act, reactions from others, and the type of information conveyed. Usage also includes the degree to which a nonverbal behavior is intended to convey information. A *communicative* act is one used deliberately to convey meaning. *Interactive* acts are those that influence the behavior of the other participants. An act is both communicative and interactive if it is intentional and influential. For example, if you deliberately wave to a friend as a sign of greeting and the friend waves back, your cue is communicative and interactive. A third category of behaviors are those not intended to be communicative but that nevertheless provide information for the perceiver. Such acts are said to be *informative*. On a day when you are feeling less than friendly, you may duck into a hallway to avoid meeting an acquaintance coming your way. If the other person sees the avoidance, your behavior has been informative even though you did not intend to communicate.

All nonverbal behavior is one of five types, depending on origin, coding, and usage. The first type is the emblem. *Emblems* have a verbal translation of a rather precise meaning for a social group. They are normally used in a deliberate fashion to communicate a particular message. The victory "V" and the black power fist are examples. The origin of emblems is cultural learning; emblems may be either arbitrary or iconic in coding.

Illustrators are the second kind of nonverbal cues. Illustrators have a high relation to speech since they are used to illustrate what is being said verbally. They are intentional, though we may not always be directly aware of them. They include eight types: *batons* (movements that accent or emphasize), *ideographs* ("sketching" the direction of a thought),

30. Ekman and Friesen's major works include "Nonverbal Behavior in Psychotherapy Research," in *Research in Psychotherapy*, ed. J. Shlien, vol. III (Washington, D. C.: American Psychological Association, 1968); "The Repertoire of Nonverbal Behavior: Categories, Origins, Usage, and Coding," *Semiotica* 1 (1969): 49–98; *Emotion in the Human Face: Guidelines for Research and an Integration of Findings* (New York: Pergamon Press, 1972); *Unmasking the Face* (Englewood Cliffs, N.J.: Prentice-Hall, 1975).

31. Paul Ekman and Wallace Friesen, "Hand Movements," *Journal of Communication* 22 (1972): 353.

deictic movements (pointing), *spatial movements* (depicting or outlining space), *rhythmic movements* (pacing motions), *kinetographs* (depicting physical actions), *pictographs* (drawing a picture in the air), and *emblematic movements* (illustrating a verbal statement). These types are not mutually exclusive; some motions are combinations of types. Illustrators are informative or communicative in use and occasionally may be interactive. They are also learned.

The third type of nonverbal behavior is the *adaptor*, which serves to facilitate release of bodily tension. Such actions as hand wringing, head scratching, or foot jiggling are examples of adaptors. *Self-adaptors*, which usually occur in private, are directed to one's own body. They may include scratching, stroking, grooming, squeezing. *Alter-adaptors* are directed to another's body. *Object-adaptors* are directed at things. In any case, adaptors may be iconic or intrinsic. Rarely are they intentional, and one is usually not aware of one's own adaptive behaviors. They may occur when the individual is communicating with another, but they usually occur with greater frequency when the person is alone. Although they are rarely communicative, they are sometimes interactive and often informative.

Regulators, the fourth type of behavior, are used directly to regulate, control, or coordinate interaction. For example, we use eye contact to signal speaking and listening roles in a conversation. Regulators are primarily interactive. They are coded intrinsically or iconically, and their origin is cultural learning.

The final category of behavior is the *affect display*. These behaviors, which may be in part innate, involve the display of feelings and emotions. The face is a particularly rich source for affect display, although other parts of the body also may be involved. Affect displays are intrinsically coded. They are rarely communicative, often interactive, and always informative.

Criticism

Certainly the work of nonverbal coding has helped us realize the complexity and subtlety of communication codes. The various categories suggested by theory have been heuristic in producing an impressive quantity of research. The major problems of nonverbal communication theories lie in their appropriateness for explaining intricacies of the communication process and in their narrowness of scope.[32]

We can express the major criticism of these theories as a series of fallacies. The first is the *fallacy of the linguistic analogy*. Although some superficial similarities may be observed between language and kinesics, probably more differences than similarities exist. Language is presented sequentially and involves discrete signs; nonverbal codes are not presented solely in a sequential manner and rarely consist of discrete behaviors. Although language is organized hierarchically, no good evidence shows that nonverbal acts are organized in this way (despite Birdwhistell's linguisticlike categories). Language is always used consciously; nonverbal codes often are not. Thus we see that the assumptions of language may not be appropriate to the domain of nonverbal behavior.

The second problem is the *fallacy of analysis*. Most of the structural theorists admit that messages consist of inseparable complexes of verbal and nonverbal codes, yet these theories tend to approach a synthetic topic in an analytic way by focusing on particular behaviors to the exclusion of others. Again, this problem is one of appropriateness and scope.

Finally, there is the *fallacy of nonverbal preeminence*. Nonverbal communication is often assumed to be the most important aspect of any message. Language is reduced to a lesser role. Some writers on nonverbal communication have actually stated as much.[33] Most, however, imply undue impor-

---

32. For a more complete analysis and critique of several approaches to nonverbal communication, see Judee Burgoon and Thomas Saine, *The Unspoken Dialogue: An Introduction to Nonverbal Communication* (Boston: Houghton Mifflin, 1978), chap. 2. See also Knapp, Wiemann, and Daly, "Nonverbal Communication."

33. See, for example, Mark L. Knapp, *Nonverbal Communication*, p. 12.

tance by separating and concentrating on aspects of nonverbal codes apart from the entire coding complex. In most transactions language is absolutely central, but the relative importance of any part of the code varies from situation to situation.

These fallacies are especially apparent in structural theories of nonverbal communication, and they arise from the tendency of such theories to separate and classify bodily activity. The functional approaches tend to be less segmental in their treatment of verbal and nonverbal codes.

The attempt to move from finite description of nonverbal communication behavior to an explanation of how it functions in ongoing interaction is a necessary step. Yet this kind of work is fraught with difficulties. For example, accurate observation is a problem. How can we know what functions are being served by nonverbal behaviors? Indeed, at any given moment several functions may be involved.

Integration

Nothing is as central to all forms of communication as language and coding. This chapter has taken a look at one perspective on these topics—structuralism. Indeed, structural theories of language and signs have had a major impact on how we think about communication itself. The commonsense idea that communication is the use of signs to represent meanings lies at the heart of structuralism. Important also, however, is that the sign system, like a language, can be studied apart from any use to which it may be put. Language structure, as opposed to language use, is an important distinction in the structuralist tradition.

Signs, of course, are rarely treated as singular, independent units. Rather, organized or patterned systems of signs are required for communication as we know it. Even an isolated sign, like a powerful word or nonverbal gesture, can only be understood by virtue of its differences from other signs. In fact, signs acquire meaning from the ways in which they are different from other signs within the system.

Language is a highly complex system of verbal signs. Within the structuralist tradition, language is viewed as hierarchically organized, and it is governed by rules of grammar. The nature of the rules that determine how sentences are generated and understood has been a question of dispute for many years.

During the last two decades, nonverbal communication has become a topic of interest to communication scholars. Researchers have been intrigued with the ways in which nonverbal systems are similar to and different from language. We know that much meaning is communicated through the use of gesture, space, and other codes; and verbal and nonverbal codes go hand in hand, each enhancing the other.

Although language and nonverbal systems have been popularly understood as tools of human communication, post-structuralist critics have argued that writings and recordings as texts have a life of their own apart from any use to which they are put by human beings. Texts have numerous possible meanings, and any particular reading of a text will necessarily fall short of that text's potential.

We return to the subject of text later in the book. In the next chapter we turn to a group of theories that de-emphasize text and focus on the ways in which human beings process textual material.

Five

Cognitive and
Behavioral Theories

Cognitive and behavioral approaches to the study of communication share an interest in the ways in which stimuli lead to responses. Behaviorism has a long history in modern psychology, going back at least to the work of J. B. Watson and C. L. Hull early in this century.[1] Strict behaviorists strove to account for stimulus and response variables in a way that would make overt behavior predictable. These early behaviorists considered internal "thought" processes inaccessible and, therefore, uninteresting. Thinking and feeling were considered to be hidden in a "black box," and "mentalism" was discredited. Early behaviorism was therefore known as S–R (stimulus–response) psychology.

Today, strict behaviorism is out of favor among most behavioral and social scientists. In its place is "cognitivism," which attempts to crack the black box between stimulus and response. Old-style behaviorism is now believed to be too narrow to capture the truly essential variables of human action. Cognitive sciences arose, too, from the infusion of information theory (Chapter 3) in the behavioral sciences, and cognitivism, therefore, focuses on the ways in which human beings process information about their environment. Cognitivism, like behaviorism, remains interested in what is now termed *inputs* and *outputs*, but only in the context of the thought processes that bridge the two.

This chapter includes theories of communication emerging from the behavioral-cognitive tradition. All of the theories covered here emphasize behavior and its antecedents. Unlike the structural theories covered in Chapter 4, these viewpoints are relatively less concerned with the structure of language apart from the user; instead, the cognitive and behavioral approaches focus on the ways in which communicators' thought processes or behaviors form language patterns. And, unlike the interactional theories in Chapters 6 and 7, cognitive and behavioral scholars are less interested in what happens among people in communicative acts and more interested in what happens within individual persons. For this reason, most of the theories summarized in Chapter 5 are highly psychological in orientation.

The Tradition

The Behavioral Tradition

Behaviorism is a perspective that focuses on responses to external and internal stimuli. As such, it looks for predictable patterns between stimulus and response. There have been numerous ways of looking at the S–R relationship, but overall, two major traditions have emerged.[2] The first of these,

1. J. B. Watson, *Psychology from the Standpoint of the Behaviorist* (Philadelphia: J. B. Lippincott, 1919); C. L. Hull, *Principles of Behavior: An Introduction to Behavior Theory* (New York: Appleton, 1943).

2. J. W. Kling, "Learning: Introductory Survey," in *Woodward and Schlosberg's Experimental Psychology*, eds. J. W. Kling and Lorrin Riggs (New York: Holt, Rinehart & Winston, 1971), pp. 551–613.

classical conditioning, examines the way in which stimuli in the environment produce new responses in the organism. The common example of classical conditioning is Pavlov's early experiment, in which a bell was paired with a dog's food so that the dog came to respond by salivating to the sound of the bell.

Instrumental or *operant* theory concentrates not on the paired association of prior stimuli in the environment but on *reinforcement* elicited by behavior. While classical conditioning views behavior as dependent on prior stimulation, the operant school holds that the actual behavior of the organism is *instrumental* in causing consequences in the environment and is reinforced by those consequences. Animal training, in which behavior is shaped by administering rewards and punishments, is a good example of operant conditioning.

The behaviorist tradition has influenced three areas of communication theory—language, persuasion, and meaning. Because behaviorist theories of language and persuasion are no longer considered very important, we will discuss these only briefly. The subject of meaning will be discussed in more detail.

Language and behavior. The well-known behaviorist B. F. Skinner developed one of the simplest theories of language.[3] Skinner likens verbal behavior to all other behavior: It is emitted by the organism in accordance with the frequency with which it is reinforced. When a behavior is positively reinforced or rewarded, it will increase in frequency. When negatively reinforced, it will decrease. As a result, the actual language behavior of any person is a product of that person's history of reinforcement of verbal operants. Skinner's language theory is now discredited as simplistic and naive: Noting only the association between linguistic outputs and stimuli tells us nothing about what language is, how it is structured, how it functions, and what its potential is for information-processing. Consequently, most language theories today are cognitive, as we will see later in the chapter.

Persuasion and behavior. The second area of communication in which behaviorism has been influential is persuasion. Up through the 1960s, almost all persuasion research had a strong behaviorist bias. The most significant persuasion research program during this time was the Yale project.[4] This decade-long research program in the Psychology Department at Yale University, which is still influential today, was heavily behaviorist in orientation. It was devoted primarily to analyzing the complex interaction among variables in the communication situation, the predispositions of the communicators, and the observable effects. Although the Yale researchers certainly acknowledged the importance of "internal mediating processes," these were never very well defined or examined, and persuasion was viewed primarily as a stimulus–response operation.

The purest learning theory of persuasion was that of Robert Weiss, who likened attitude and behavior change to learning and attributed such change to classical and instrumental learning processes.[5] The problem with many early persuasion theories such as this one is that they failed to crack the black box and examine the cognitive processes involved in attitude and behavior change. Other theories, summarized later in the chapter, made rudimentary attempts to do so.

Meaning and behavior. The third area in which behaviorism has had an impact is in the theory of meaning. This influence is most evident in the work of Charles Osgood. As a behaviorist, Charles Osgood is especially interested in how meanings are learned and how they relate to internal and external behavior. His theory is one of the most elaborate of the behavioral theories of language and meaning, and it really does have a foot in both the

3. B. F. Skinner, *Verbal Behavior* (New York: Appleton-Century-Crofts, 1957).

4. For a brief summary of the findings of the Yale research, see Mary John Smith, *Persuasion and Human Action* (Belmont, Calif.: Wadsworth, 1982).

5. Robert Weiss, "An Extension of Hullian Learning Theory to Persuasive Communication," in *Psychological Foundations of Attitudes*, eds. Anthony Greenwald, Timothy Brock, and Thomas Ostrom (New York: Academic Press, 1968), p. 109; "Persuasion and the Acquisition of Attitudes: Models from Conditioning and Selective Learning," *Psychological Reports* 11 (1962): 709–32.

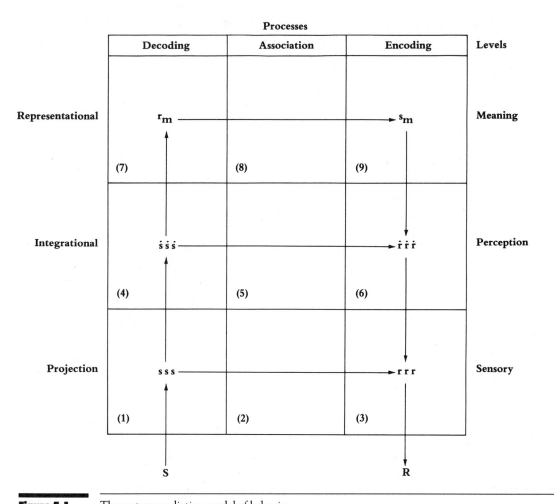

Figure 5-1   Three-stage mediation model of behavior.

The symbol s refers to internal stimuli, r to internal responses, both differentiated by level. S and R refer to external stimulus and response.

behavioral and cognitive traditions.[6] Osgood follows the classical learning tradition, which teaches that learning is a process of developing new internal and external behavioral associations. In this tradition learning theory begins with the assumption that individuals respond to stimuli in the environment. Osgood believes that the basic S–R association is responsible for the establishment of meaning. Although individuals can respond overt-ly to actual environmental stimuli, they also have a representation of the stimulus and response that is internal in the organism. While the symbols **S** and **R** are used to represent the overt stimulus and response, the lowercase letters **s** and **r** designate the internal representation. Meaning occurs on the internal (s–r) level. Osgood's model of this internal-external relationship is somewhat complex.

He proposes a three-stage behavioral model, illustrated in Figure 5-1.[7] This model can be used to

6. Charles Osgood, "On Understanding and Creating Sentences," *American Psychologist* 18 (1963): 735–51.

7. Osgood, "On Understanding," p. 740.

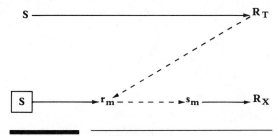

Figure 5-2　Development of a sign.

From *The Measurement of Meaning*, by Charles Osgood, George Suci, and Percy Tannenbaum. Copyright © 1957 by the Board of Trustees of the University of Illinois. Reprinted by permission of the University of Illinois Press.

analyze any behavior, but he applies it to language and meaning in particular. Three basic processes are involved: *encoding* (receiving stimuli), *association* (pairing stimuli and responses), and *decoding* (responding). These processes occur on one of three levels, depending on the complexity of the behavior involved. The *projection level* is the simple neural pathway system between sensor and effector organs. Behavior on this level is reflexive, such as knee jerks and eye blinks. Here the stimulus and response are linked automatically and directly. On the *integration level* the stimulus–response link is not automatic. Stimulus and response must be integrated by the brain through perceived association. An example is the routine greeting ritual: "How are you?" "I am fine."

The *representational level* is the level on which meaning occurs. The stimulus from the environment is projected onto the brain, where an internal response leads to an internal stimulus (meaning), which in turn leads to the individual's overt response. The internal response or meaning is a learned association between certain actual responses to the object and a sign of the object. Thus the sign (a word, perhaps) will elicit a particular meaning or set of meanings, which stem from the association of the sign and the object. To use a rather dramatic example, suppose you sit in a small fragile chair, and it collapses. In the immediate future a picture of the chair, the sight of another

similar chair, or the words "small fragile chair" will elicit an image (r_m) in your head that influences how you will respond. This internal response (fear or pain) is part of your meaning for the sign. In real life meanings are more complex than in this example, but they are formed, Osgood believes, through the same basic associational process. In summary, Osgood sees the first level as sensory, the second as perceptual, and the third as meaningful.

The development of meaning by associating a sign with an environmental stimulus is illustrated in Figure 5-2. This figure shows the development of a sign $\boxed{S}$ as the result of its association with a natural stimulus S. A portion of one's complex response to the natural stimulus R_T becomes represented in the form of an internal response r_m, which in turn becomes an internal stimulus to a new but related overt response R_x. Meaning is the internal mediating process represented in Figure 5-2 as $r_m \longrightarrow s_m$. Such meaning, since it is inside the person and unique to the person's own experience with the natural stimulus, is said to be *connotative*. Osgood presents a good example of this process. For a particular person a spider (S) elicits a complex response R_T. When the word *spider* is associated with the object as it might be in a small child, a portion of the response R_m (fear) becomes associated with the label. This internal meaning mediates the person's response to the word, even when the actual object is not present.[8]

Most meanings are not learned as a result of direct experience with the natural stimulus. In other words, they are learned by associations between one sign and another, a process that may occur in the abstract out of physical contact with the original stimulus. Figure 5-3 is Osgood's illustration of this more complex process.[9] This figure depicts a series of signs, $\boxed{S}$, each of which elicits meanings in the individual because of previous associations (r_m). These signs are associated with another new sign, /S/, and their internal responses (meanings) "rub

8. Charles Osgood, "The Nature of Measurement of Meaning," in *The Semantic Differential Technique*, eds. James Snider and Charles Osgood (Chicago: Aldine, 1969), pp. 9–10.

9. Osgood, "Nature," p. 11.

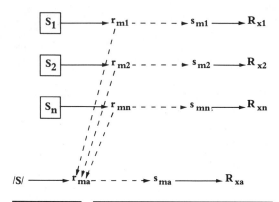

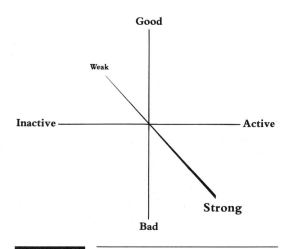

Figure 5-3 Development of an assign.

From *The Measurement of Meaning*, by Charles Osgood, George Suci, and Percy Tannenbaum. Copyright © 1957 by the Board of Trustees of the University of Illinois. Reprinted by permission of the University of Illinois Press.

Figure 5-4 Three-dimensional semantic space.

off" on the new sign (r_{ma}). To continue our example, imagine that the child who had already established internal responses to the words *spider, big,* and *hairy* listened to a story about a tarantula. In the story the tarantula was characterized as a "big, hairy spider." Through association the child will now have a meaning for the new word *tarantula.* This word may also carry some mixture of the connotations earlier attached to the other words because of its association with these words. If the child associated *spider* with fear, *big* with potentially dangerous, and *hairy* with feeling creepy, then the child might well react to a real or imagined tarantula by running away. In this example the words *spider, big,* and *hairy* are $\boxed{S_1}$, $\boxed{S_2}$, and $\boxed{S_3}$; r_{m1} is fear, r_{m2} is dangerous, and r_{m3} is creepy. The new word /S/ (tarantula), when associated with the other words, comes to elicit the internal response of avoidance (r_{ma}), which itself becomes a stimulus (s_{ma}) to cause the child to run away (R_{xa}) when threatened by a real or imagined tarantula.

Osgood is perhaps best known for the *semantic differential technique*, a method for measuring meaning.[10] This measurement technique assumes that one's meanings can be expressed by the use of words. The method begins by finding a set of adjectives that could be used to express individuals' connotations for some stimulus or sign. These adjectives are set against one another as opposites, such as good/bad, high/low, slow/fast. Individuals are given a topic, word, or other stimulus and are asked to indicate on a seven-point scale how they associate the stimulus with the adjective pairs. A sample scale looks like this:

good——:——:——:——:——:——:——bad

The subject places a check mark on any space between these adjectives to indicate the degree of good or bad associated with the stimulus. The subject may fill out as many as fifty such scales for each stimulus. Osgood then uses a statistical technique called factor analysis to find the basic dimensions of meaning that are operating in peoples' connotations of the stimulus. His findings in this research have led to the theory of semantic space.[11]

One's meaning for any sign is said to be located in a metaphorical space of three major dimensions: *evaluation, activity,* and *potency.* A given sign, per-

10. Osgood, "Nature."

11. More recently Osgood has hypothesized that bipolarity is the basic factor in all language and human thought. See Charles Osgood and Meredith Richards, "From Yang and Yin to *and* or *but,*" *Language* 49 (1973): 380–412.

haps a word or concept, elicits a reaction in the person consisting of a sense of evaluation (good or bad), activity (active or inactive), and potency or strength. The person's connotative meaning will lie somewhere in this hypothetical space, depending on the responses of the person on the three factors. Figure 5-4 illustrates semantic space.

Take the concept *mother*, for example. For any given person this sign will elicit an internal response embodying some combination of the three factors. One person might judge *mother* as good, passive, weak; another as good, active, and strong. In any case one's connotative meaning for *mother* will depend on learned associations in the individual's life. (Keep in mind that the three dimensions of meaning are not dichotomous but continuous variables.)

Osgood and others have done semantic differential research on a variety of sign types, including word concepts, music, art, and even sonar sounds.[12] In addition they have done research among a number of groups of people representing a wide range of cultures. Osgood believes that the three factors of meaning—evaluation, potency, and activity—apply across all people and all concepts.[13] If this is true, then Osgood has significantly advanced our understanding of meaning.

Although most behavioral researchers admit the usefulness of semantic differential technique for measuring a certain aspect of connotative meaning, they question the view that the factors of meaning—evaluation, potency, and activity—are invariant and universal across situations, concepts, and cultures. Although these factors have appeared in an amazingly diverse set of studies, they do not always appear; to suggest that they are universal is a gross overgeneralization. Problems of validity in

the use of semantic differential arise from at least two methodological problems.

First, somewhat similar responses may result from the use of a highly structured stimulus situation. The semantic differential always involves adjective scales, and subjects are often presented with many of the same scales in study after study. Subjects may respond more to the form of the instrument than to the real meanings of the concepts. Second, the semantic differential relies heavily on a statistical procedure called factor analysis. This technique shows how the several scales intercorrelate to form factors, but the researcher must subjectively interpret and name the factors. If a theorist such as Osgood believes that three factors are universal, a strong tendency may develop to interpret the factor structure in just that way. In short, the claim that factors of meaning are universal may be the result of a self-fulfilling prophecy.

The Cognitive Tradition

Like behaviorists, latter-day cognitivists are variable-analytic; in other words, they tend to see behavior as a complex of variables that can be directly or indirectly observed, measured, and analyzed. Cognitivists believe in the fruitfulness of examining stimulus–response patterns, but unlike strict behaviorists, they concentrate on the mental processes that mediate between the two.[14]

Behaviorism was almost completely deterministic, in that it aimed to predict behavior on the basis of antecedent conditions and afforded little power to the individual as a creative agent. Skinner stated this deterministic assumption in definite terms: "science insists that action is initiated by forces impinging upon the individual, and that caprice is only another name for behavior for which we have not yet found a cause."[15] Most cognitive theorists

12. A sampling of studies illustrating the applications can be found in Snider and Osgood, *Semantic Differential*. This work also includes an atlas of approximately 550 concepts and their semantic profiles.

13. This point of view is expressed in Charles Osgood, "Semantic Differential Technique in the Comparative Study of Cultures," in *The Semantic Differential Technique*, eds. James Snider and Charles Osgood (Chicago: Aldine, 1969), pp. 303–23; and *Cross Cultural Universals of Affective Meaning* (Urbana: University of Illinois Press, 1975).

14. Sally Planalp and Dean E. Hewes, "A Cognitive Approach to Communication Theory: Cogito Ergo Dico?" *Communication Yearbook 5*, ed. Michael Burgoon (New Brunswick, N.J.: Transaction Books, 1982), pp. 49–78; John O. Greene, "Evaluating Cognitive Explanations of Communicative Phenomena," *Quarterly Journal of Speech* 70 (1984): 241–54.

15. B. F. Skinner, *Cumulative Record: A Selection of Papers*, 3rd ed. (New York: Appleton-Century-Crofts, 1972), p. 8.

disagree with this assumption. Cognitive theories assume that individuals are purposeful and capable of creating action alternatives and choosing among them.

Given their emphasis on human powers, cognitive theories deal with mental processes that make action possible. Cognitivists usually posit a cognitive system that enables individuals to organize and understand information, to create possible behaviors, and to choose among behavioral options. Cognitive theories deal with (1) the structure of the cognitive system, or the manner in which information is organized in the system; (2) the processes by which that organization is achieved; and (3) the content of the cognitive system. The *content* is what is contained in the cognitive system—the information, thoughts, feelings, attitudes, and so forth. The *structure* is the pattern in which the content is organized. And the *process* is the operations by which content is handled and transformed. Typical topics of cognitive theories are meaning, memory, selection, plans of action, and inference making.

The cognitive approach is one of the most prominent perspectives in contemporary communication theory. Because information is the basic commodity of communication, the study of information processing becomes very important.[16] Many of the theories that follow in this text are cognitive in orientation. This chapter focuses on some of the most general of these, including cognitive theories of language, interpretation and action, and social influence.

Language and Cognition

One of the most important figures in contemporary cognitivism is linguist Noam Chomsky. Chomsky's theory of language has been so influential that it is considered to be a primary factor in the rise of cognitivism generally throughout

the behavioral sciences. Gilbert Harmon states, "Chomsky has let us see that there is a single subject of language and mind which crosses departmental boundaries."[17] This theory, which is called generative grammar, grew out of the field of linguistics but rapidly stimulated interest in other fields as well. It has become especially important in psycholinguistics, since it bears directly on problems of human cognition.

Yet, curiously, generative theory has had little impact on many scholars interested in communication. Chomsky prefers not to conceive of language primarily as a tool of communication, instead he views it as a natural phenomenon of import in and of itself. Needless to say, this claim is controversial, and we shall return to it at the end of this discussion.

Chomsky's work is philosophically interesting and complex. Its blend of philosophical views is provocative as Justin Leiber points out:

[Chomsky's ideas present] a peculiar, but explicable, paradox; . . . namely, that man has a kind of free creative nature that Chomsky believes depends on the highly constraining innateness, and derived mentalistic character, belonging to the human mind. The paradox is resolved by recalling that it is the infinite capacities of human thought, the infinistic and abstract character of man's linguistic competencies, that purport to establish that man is by nature beyond a behaviorist or determinist viewpoint. One needs a strong, built-in capacity, as it were, before full, free creativity can manifest itself as choice within this infinite, discrete range. . . . The freedom Chomsky wishes to emphasize is the freedom of a being with infinite and reasoned choices when so unrestrained by external force.[18]

In treating the study of mind as a natural science, Chomsky believes that elements of language and mind are universal and available for discovery. He is analytical in approach, seeking inherent mechanisms of mind. However, in fulfilling his view of the individual as distinctly human and creative, he

---

16. For a general overview of classical information processing theory, see C. David Mortensen, "Human Information Processing," in *Communication: The Study of Human Interaction* (New York: McGraw-Hill, 1972), pp. 69–124.

17. Gilbert Harmon, *On Noam Chomsky* (Garden City, N.Y.: Anchor Books, 1974), p. vii.

18. Justin Lieber, *Noam Chomsky: A Philosophical Overview* (Boston: Twayne Publishers, 1975), p. 182.

follows actional assumptions. He strongly believes in the a priori nature of knowledge and that much knowledge is tacit or implicit. He follows the notion that knowledge arises from an application of innate categories onto the world of experience.[19] In short, Chomsky is a champion of a point of view that has not been popular in this century—rationalism. He has revived the basic idea of René Descartes of the seventeenth century, that the mind is given its power by a priori qualities and that knowledge arises from the use of this power in understanding experience.

Let us now look more specifically at the ideas in Chomsky's theory, *generative grammar*. Original generative theory posits four basic components of grammar. *Deep structures* are believed to be underlying sentence models constructed by the use of base *phrase-structure rules*. The deep structure of any sentence is modified by *transformation rules*, resulting in an uttered (or utterable) *surface structure*. Sentence generation proceeds along the following lines.

Deep structure is created with base rules. The deep structure is a sentence model, a mental structure, not utterable as speech. It is a model of sentence parts resembling a simple declarative form. The rules used to generate the deep structure are rewrite rules that follow lines originally developed in phrase-structure grammar (see Chapter 4).

Next, a surface structure is generated by transformation rules, which are instructions of movement: Move component *x* to location *y*. For example, the active transformation moves components so that they appear in the order NP + VP (Sally hit the ball). The passive transformation prescribes NP + auxiliary + VP + NP (The ball is hit by Sally). A sufficient, but parsimoniously small, number of phrase-structure and transformation rules will permit the generation of any proper sentence.

Since this book is not a linguistics text, we will not cover the range of possible transformation rules of English. In order to understand the basics of the theory, however, we will look at an example. Our example uses two transformation rules: the passive transformation and the adjective transformation.[20] The passive transformation inverts the noun phrase and verb phrase, puts the verb in the passive form, and adds the preposition *by*:

- John loves Mary.
- Mary is loved by John. (passive)

The adjective transformation occurs by deleting the verb form *be* and placing the adjective in front of the noun:

- John loves Mary.
- Mary is pretty.
- John loves pretty Mary. (adjective)

Suppose you wish to generate the sentence, *Ripe mushrooms are loved by hobbits.*[21] You would do this in two stages. First, with the phrase-structure rules you would generate a deep tree, as shown in Figure 5-5. This deep tree provides the basic semantic interpretation of the sentence. All of the basic logical grammatical relations are present, and the meaning of the sentence is set. Don't worry that this deep structure does not resemble the intended surface structure. The deep structure is an abstract model from which the actual sentence will be generated in the next stage.

The surface tree—the actual sentence—is generated by applying the two transformations described above, passive and adjective. Figure 5-6 illustrates the surface tree.

With a relatively small number of phrase-structure rules and transformation rules, a speaker can generate any novel grammatical sentence. The basic semantic structure is generated on the deep or abstract level with phrase structure, and sentences are generated by subjecting the underlying structure to transformations. In essence this process is what a speaker intuitively "knows" about the language. The two-stage sentence-generation model is a parsimonious and descriptively adequate explanation of how the speaker uses this knowledge.

19. Chomsky discusses features of his epistemology in *Rules and Representations* (New York: Columbia University Press, 1980). Chomsky's other works are listed in the bibliography.

20. Several English transformations are explained in brief form by Peter Salus, *Linguistics* (Indianapolis: Bobbs-Merrill, 1969).

21. Example from Salus, *Linguistics*.

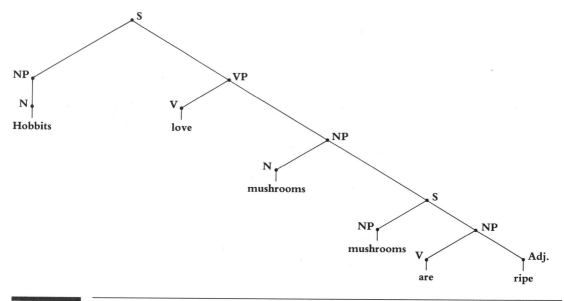

Figure 5-5   An example of deep structure.

From *Linguistics*, by Peter H. Salus. Copyright © 1969 by Macmillan Publishing Company. Reprinted by permission of the publisher.

An essential feature of standard theory is that a singular correspondence exists between a surface structure and its deep structure. Any meaningful sentence structure has one, and only one, deep structure. If an uttered sentence has more than one syntactical meaning, each meaning is derivable from a separate deep structure. For example, the sentence, *She is a dancing teacher*, has two possible meanings. No analysis of surface structure alone can explain this paradox. The two interpretations stem from separate deep structures with different configurations. One stems from a structure with the following components: NP (She) + VP (teaches dancing). The other is transformed from a deep structure of two clauses—(1) NP (She) + VP (dances), and (2) NP (She) + VP (teaches)—that have been combined into a single deep structure of the following form: NP (She) + S (who dances) + VP (teaches).

Obviously, this theory explains surface ambiguities, while the classical structure cannot. It also illustrates that in standard theory meaning must always be located at the deep level.

Chomskian linguistics has been described as a true Kuhnian revolution (see Chapter 2). It is generally praised as providing answers to questions that classical and behavioristic linguistics could not handle. Its major strengths are usually seen as its parsimony and explanatory power. However, language presents us with one of our most difficult intellectual puzzles, and even generative grammar has its weaknesses. Basically, generative grammar has been criticized on two fronts, its scope and its validity.

Two problems of scope warrant discussion here. First, generative grammar generally ignores or downplays semantics. Primarily it is a theory of grammar, of syntax; problems of individual lexical units and their meanings are ignored as unimportant.[22]

22. This criticism is discussed by John Searle, "Chomsky's Revolution in Linguistics," in Harmon, *Noam*, pp. 2–33.

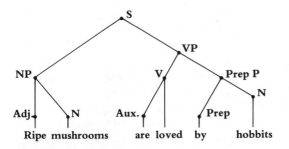

Figure 5-6   An example of a surface structure.

From *Linguistics*, by Peter H. Salus. Copyright © 1969 by Macmillan Publishing Company. Reprinted by permission of the publisher.

Second, critics are bothered by the failure of generative grammarians to consider problems of language as used in everyday life. Generative grammar treats language as an abstraction, claiming that an understanding of the anomalies of language use is unimportant to an understanding of language itself. This approach makes a sharp distinction between language *competence* and language *performance*. The former is knowledge of grammar; the latter is language use. Generative grammarians steadfastly have maintained that performance is not a linguistic concern. Consequently, they are not interested in how language is used in social interaction. The theory therefore does not account for local and cultural variations of language, nor does it account for the commonly observed phenomenon of ungrammatical speech.

Much of the criticism of generative grammar questions its validity. A good deal of disagreement exists within the generative movement itself about the locus of meaning. Where in the process of sentence generation is meaning established? Chomsky has shown that meaningfulness cannot reside strictly at the surface level, yet deep analysis by itself may not be adequate for the establishment of meaning.

Transformational theory's key problems result from the difficulty of observing generative processes. Linguists must rely on inferences made from observing spoken sentences. Classical linguistics

failed to make this inferential leap from observed behavior to hidden processes, and thus it fell short. As a result of its strong reliance on inference, generative theory operates primarily from logical force (see Chapter 2). Its explanations rest on the strength of the logical connections among inferences. It also relies heavily on reasoning from "residues." In other words, alternative explanations are attacked and shown to be inadequate. What cannot be disproved, the residue, is taken as the best explanation. Linguistic writings are filled with demonstrations of how this or that explanation will not work in explaining a particular construction. The use of inference, logical necessity, and residues in the development of generative theory is not inherently weak, and it is the only available method for developing theory in the absence of direct observation.

Cognition in Interpretation and Action

Many cognitive theories examine the ways in which individuals understand their experience. These theories study the processes by which people interpret and respond to information, a concern that is naturally significant in communication theory. Here we deal with three theories that probe communicative interpretation and action.

Social Judgment Theory

Social judgment theory is primarily a product of the work of the social psychologist Muzafer Sherif and his associates.[23] This theory finds its roots in the early psychophysical research in which persons

23. The first major work in this area was Muzafer Sherif and Carl Hovland, *Social Judgment* (New Haven: Yale University Press, 1959). See also Muzafer Sherif, Carolyn Sherif, and Roger Nebergall, *Attitude and Attitude Change: The Social Judgment-Involvement Approach* (Philadelphia: W. B. Saunders, 1965). For a brief overview of the theory, see Muzafer Sherif, *Social Interaction—Process and Products* (Chicago: Aldine, 1967), chaps. 16, 17, 18. Several secondary sources are also available; see, for example, Charles A. Kiesler, Barry E. Collins, and Norman Miller, *Attitude Change: A Critical Analysis of Theoretical Approaches* (New York: John Wiley, 1969), chap. 6.

were tested in their ability to judge physical stimuli. Using this work as an analogy, Sherif investigated the ways individuals judge nonphysical objects or social stimuli. He learned that many principles of psychophysics hold for social judgment as well.

Sherif and his colleagues found that individual judgments of things and people are highly situational and depend on one's initial orientation toward the world. The psychological literature shows that people make judgments about things based on anchors or reference points. Suppose that you are involved in an experimental situation in which you are asked to judge the relative weight of five objects. On what would you base your judgment? If the experimenter handed you a weight and told you it was 10 pounds, you would first feel the reference weight and then make judgments about the other objects based on the kinesthetic feeling you received from the known weight. In this case the known weight would act as an anchor, influencing your judgment of the others. In fact, with a different initial weight, you would judge the same objects differently. To demonstrate this idea of anchors, you could try a simple experiment. Take three bowls. Fill the first with hot water, the second with cold water, the third with tepid water. Put one hand in the hot water, the other in the cold water; and after a few moments, place both hands in the tepid water. Your perceptions of the tepid water will be different for each hand because each hand had a different anchor, or reference.

Sherif reasons that similar processes operate in judging communication messages. In social perception anchors are internal; they are based on past experience. The internal anchor or reference point is always present and influences the way a person responds in communication with others. The more important the issue is to one's ego, the stronger the anchor will influence what is understood.

The central concepts of social judgment theory include the *latitude of acceptance, rejection, and non-commitment*. In a social judgment experiment you would be given a large number of statements about some issue. You then would be asked to sort these messages into groups according to similarity of position. You could use as many groups as you wished.

Then you would order these groups in terms of position on a negative-positive scale, and you would indicate which groups are acceptable to you personally, which are not acceptable, and which are neutral. The first measures your latitude of acceptance, the second your latitude of rejection, and the third your latitude of noncommitment. We can see that an individual will approach real-life messages in the same way. While a person has a particular attitude about the issue, there will be a range of statements, pro or con, that the person can tolerate; there will also be a range that one cannot accept.

Another important concept from social judgment is *ego-involvement*. Previously, an attitude was thought to be measured primarily in terms of valence (direction, pro or con) and the degree of agreement or disagreement. But Sherif demonstrates that ego-involvement is significant apart from either of these other two dimensions of attitude. Ego-involvement is the degree to which one's attitude toward something affects the self-concept. It is a measure of how important the issue is to the individual. For example, you may have read a great deal of material supporting the viewpoint that marijuana should be legalized. You may feel strongly on the issue because of the literature you have read. Thus you would have a strong positive attitude toward legalization, but your ego-involvement might be very low if your life is relatively unaffected by the issue. But if you are a regular marijuana smoker and have been arrested for possessing the drug, no doubt you would be highly ego-involved. Ego-involvement makes a great deal of difference in how you respond to messages related to the issue. There is a relatively high correlation between involvement and extremity, but it is not a perfect correlation. In fact, it is possible for a person to be neutral on an issue, yet highly ego-involved.

Now let us consider what social judgment theory says about the communication process. The social judgment theory is a fine contribution to our understanding of communication because it explains two important behaviors of audiences in receiving messages. First, we know from Sherif's work that individuals judge the favorability of a message based on their own internal anchors of position and ego-involvement. On a given issue, such as legalization of marijuana, a person will distort the message by *contrast* or *assimilation*. The contrast effect occurs when individuals judge a message to be farther from their point of view than it actually is. The assimilation effect occurs when persons judge the message to be closer to their point of view than it actually is.

Basically, when a message is relatively close to one's own position, that message will be assimilated. In the case of relatively distant messages, contrast is likely to occur. These assimilation and contrast effects are heightened by ego-involvement. For example, if you were strongly in favor of the legalization of marijuana, a moderately favorable statement might seem like a strong positive statement because of your assimilation; while a slightly unfavorable statement might be perceived to be strongly opposed to one's view because of contrast. If you were highly ego-involved in the issue, this effect would be even greater. Suppose, for example, that someone told you that they thought possession and smoking of marijuana should be legal but that growing the plant on a commercial basis should be against the law. If you were highly ego-involved in your belief that the drug should be legalized, you might perceive this statement to be strongly against marijuana, even though it is a rather middle-of-the-road position.

The second area in which social judgment theory aids our understanding of communication is attitude change. The predictions made by social judgment theory are the following:

1. Messages falling within the latitude of acceptance facilitate attitude change.

2. If a message is judged by the person to lie within the latitude of rejection, attitude change will be reduced or nonexistent. In fact, a boomerang effect may occur in which the discrepant message actually reinforces one's own position on the issue.

3. Within the latitude of acceptance and noncommitment, the more discrepant the message from the person's own stand, the greater the expected attitude change. However, once the message

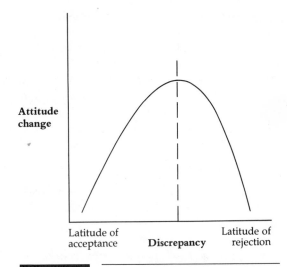

Figure 5-7   Theoretical relationship between discrepancy and change.

hits the latitude of rejection, change will not be expected.

4. The greater one's ego-involvement in the issue, the larger the latitude of rejection, the smaller the latitude of noncommitment, and thus the less the expected attitude change.

In summary, social judgment theory predicts a curvilinear relationship between discrepancy and attitude change, as Figure 5-7 illustrates.

The major strength of social judgment theory is its *parsimony*. It presents an intuitively believable set of claims based on just a few important constructs. Although this theory is no longer in vogue, its aesthetic elegance elicited great popularity in the 1960s, and it stimulated a good deal of research, which speaks well for its *heuristic* value. Ego-involvement, which the theory presented as a core construct, has since become a mainstay in persuasion literature.

The basic problem with social judgment theory is that it begs the question on some important claims. It fails to prove certain key assumptions. The theory assumes, for example, that there is a sequential, causal mechanism whereby judgment as a cognitive activity precedes attitude change. All of the claims of the theory follow from this assumption, which may not hold. For example, the theory claims that the judgment process may lead to distortion of a message, affecting latitudes of acceptance and thereby affecting the potential for attitude change. However, the same result could also be explained by other factors. This objection to social judgment theory casts doubt on its validity.

Constructivism

Constructivism, like social judgment theory, suggests that individuals interpret and act according to conceptual categories in the cognitive system. In other words, an event does not just present itself to the individual; rather, the person constructs experience according to the organization of the cognitive system. Unlike social judgment theory, however, constructivism posits that interpretation is far more complex than simple judgment of a position. The theory was developed by Jesse Delia and other colleagues and students at the University of Illinois, and it has had an immense impact on the field of communication.[24] The theory has also been highly heuristic in spawning a large body of research.[25]

Constructivism is based in part on George Kelly's theory of personal constructs.[26] Kelly proposes that persons create experience by grouping events according to similarities. *Constructs* are contrasting elements used to organize knowledge. A construct, which is the most basic element in the cognitive system, specifies a difference with which events can be classified. *Tall–short, hot–cold, black–white* are all simple constructs; an individual's cognitive system consists of numerous such distinctions. By classifying an experience into groupings along these construct distinctions, the individual gives meaning to the experience. So, for example, one may see mother as tall and father as short, coffee as hot and milk as cold, a favorite jacket as black and a favorite hat as white.

An organization of constructs used to interpret events is an *interpretive scheme*. Interpretive schemes both identify what something is and place the object in a category. With interpretive schemes, we make sense out of an event by placing it in a larger context of meanings. Interpretive schemes develop according to the *orthogenetic principle*, by moving from relative simplicity and generality to relative complexity and specificity.[27] Individuals with highly developed interpretive schemes make more discriminations in a given experience than those who see the world simplistically. In general, constructivist research shows that the construct system develops throughout childhood and adolescence, as the person matures cognitively; but even adults differ widely in their cognitive complexity. Also, within an individual, different parts of the construct system can differ in complexity.

Because *cognitive complexity* plays an important role in communication, this concept is a mainstay of constructivism. The idea of cognitive complexity is borrowed from a variety of theories, especially that of Walter Crockett.[28] Complexity or simplicity in the system is a function of the relative number of constructs and the degree of hierarchical construct organization. Individuals vary in their own cognitive complexity across topics and over time. The number of constructs used by an individual to or-

24. For a summary of the theory, see Jesse G. Delia, Barbara J. O'Keefe, and Daniel J. O'Keefe, "The Constructivist Approach to Communication," in *Human Communication Theory: Comparative Essays*, ed. Frank E. X. Dance (New York: Harper & Row, 1982), pp. 147–91. A rather complete bibliography of major constructive works to 1982 is included in this article.

25. Much of this literature is surveyed by Claudia Hale, "Cognitive Complexity-Simplicity as a Determinant of Communication Effectiveness," *Communication Monographs* 47 (1980): 304–11.

26. George Kelly, *The Psychology of Personal Constructs* (New York: North, 1955).

27. H. Werner, "The Concept of Development from a Comparative and Organismic Point of View," in *The Concept of Development*, ed. D. B. Harris (Minneapolis: University of Minnesota Press, 1957).

28. Walter H. Crockett, "Cognitive Complexity and Impression Formation," in *Progress in Experimental Personality Research* ed. Brendon A. Maher (New York: Academic Press, 1965), vol. 2, pp. 47–90. See also Harold M. Schroder, Michael S. Driver, and Siegfried Streufert, *Human Information Processing: Individuals and Groups Functioning in Complex Social Situations* (New York: Holt, Rinehart & Winston, 1967).

ganize a perceptual field is called cognitive differentiation. Cognitively sophisticated individuals are able to make more distinctions in a situation than cognitively uncomplicated people.

Constructivism has been included in this chapter because it is clearly a cognitive approach. At the same time, however, its roots in symbolic interactionism (Chapter 6) cannot be ignored. One's construct system is a direct result of a history of interaction in social groups and cannot be divorced from social life. Culture is therefore highly significant in determining the meanings of events. (For this reason, the theory is perhaps better labeled a theory of "social cognition.")

One's construct system enables interpretation, but it also directs action. Action is guided by intentions and goals as individuals develop strategies for organizing their own behavior. Often an action involves multiple intentions and may embody several strategies simultaneously. Individuals must coordinate their interpretive schemes in interaction. An *organizing scheme* is a type of interpretive scheme used to mesh one's interpretations and actions with those of others. This process of organizing becomes the means by which society and culture develop: "Thus, through social interaction individuals create and extend their shared interpretations of the world and the forms of social organization in which they participate. This ongoing process of defining reality and creating social order is the life of a sociocultural community."[29]

Communication is essential to this organizing process: "communication is a relation among persons that is characterized by the intention to express, the recognition of such intentions in others, and the organization of action and interaction around the reciprocal communicative intentions of participants."[30] Although interpretation by itself is not communication, communication cannot proceed without interpretation, making the construct system absolutely central to communicative behavior.

Interpersonal constructs are especially important because they guide how we understand other people. Individuals differ in the complexity with which they view others. Cognitive simplicity leads to stereotyping and nondifferentiation in one's perception of other people, while cognitive complexity allows a more subtle and sensitive discrimination among individuals.

The research of the Illinois team has shown that cognitive complexity in the interpersonal construct system generally leads to greater understanding of others' perspectives and better ability to frame messages in terms understandable to others. *Perspective taking*, therefore, seems to lead to more sophisticated arguments and appeals.[31]

Personal construct theory, cognitive complexity, and constructivism have several appealing features: They provide a basis for understanding information processing from an actional point of view, and they present a reasonable explanation, without falling into the mechanistic logic so typical of behaviorism. Although these theories take a step toward understanding the structure of cognition, they do not go far enough in relating cognitive complexity to other facets of information processing, nor do they uncover much detail about the structure and process of cognition in communication. More recent theories have attempted to fill this gap. We turn to one of those now.

Action-Assembly Theory

Action-assembly theory has been developed by John O. Greene as a first step toward elaborating possible structures and processes involved in the production of communicative behavior.[32] Constructivism notes the importance of cognitive processes and construct elaboration on communication, but action-assembly theory closely examines the actual organization and process by which constructs are ordered and used. The theory begins with the supposition that individuals have content

29. Delia, O'Keefe, and O'Keefe, "Constructivist," p. 158.
30. Ibid., p. 159.

31. This literature is reviewed in part by Hale, "Cognitive Complexity."
32. John O. Greene, "A Cognitive Approach to Human Communication: An Action Assembly Theory," *Communication Monographs* 51 (1984): 289–306.

knowledge and procedural knowledge: that is, they know about things and they know how to do things. Procedural knowledge consists of an awareness of the consequences of various actions in different situations. Storage of action-outcome contingencies in memory is a resource that enables effective behavior in a variety of different situations. Communication behavior, like any other, depends upon this procedural knowledge. How does one know how to act?

First, the person must "assemble" a set of appropriate action possibilities. An action sequence is brought out of memory when the conditions and desired outcome are similar to those encountered by the individual on a prior occasion. For example, you have some idea of how to introduce yourself to someone you would like to meet at a cocktail party based on your previous experience in this kind of situation. Most of the time, several action sequences will be suggested, and the person must then select a variety of these and integrate them into a coherent action plan. You know, for example, that you can approach a stranger at a party and introduce yourself in various ways. You combine the actions that you think would be desirable under these circumstances and make your move. In communication, a number of outcomes may be desired, including the achievement of a particular objective with another person, expressing information, managing conversation, producing linguistically intelligible speech, and other results. So, in the cocktail party illustration, you may want to meet the other person, make yourself look good, and have a good time, all in one set of actions.

Actions themselves are integrated within the cognitive system by bringing together a hierarchy of representations. The most abstract level is the *interactional representation*, or a sense of the overall objectives to be achieved by the action within the communication itself. One might, for example, wish to persuade another person to do something. Next is *ideational representation*, or a concept of the content or ideas to be expressed in the course of achieving the interactional objectives. To continue our example, if the persuasion is aimed at getting

another person to stop smoking, the ideational representation may include knowledge about smoking and health. The third level is the *utterance representation*, which is a depiction of the linguistic requirements necessary to express the idea or content of the message. In other words, one must know how to use language appropriately in a given situation. Finally, the *sensorimotor representation* enables one to activate the proper neural commands to produce the message, which may include use of the speech mechanism. Thus the cognitive system must coordinate very different levels of behavior in a single action sequence, requiring knowledge of how to speak (sensorimotor), language structures (utterances), appropriate content (knowledge), and the larger goal-oriented interactional behavior.

In the process of composing the above paragraph, for example, my cognitive system had to integrate into a coherent action at least four levels of representation: typing (sensorimotor), sentence structure (language), knowledge of action-assembly theory, and general strategy for communicating the theory clearly. All of the above were stored in my procedural memory; they were selected from a variety of possible representations.

In addition, the action-assembly theory deals with problems of memory or processing capacity, time required to assemble and select action sequences, the strength of association among various levels in the cognitive hierarchy, and other variables that need not concern us in this brief summary.

Greene's theory attempts to go deep into the black box to explain processes that are very difficult to observe. It is a simple theory, as are most cognitive theories at this point, but it does illustrate cognitive explanation very well. The chief problem of this theory and others like it is that they create a paradox: In attempting to uncover universal cognitive structures to allow the researcher to predict behavior, the theories re-establish on a different level the very behavioristic determinism that cognitivism is designed to overcome. This presents us with a basic puzzle of behavioral explanation: How can we explain the operations of human behavior without being deterministic? This question is answered by some of the theories discussed in upcoming chapters.

Communication Apprehension

A possible outcome of cognitive processing is fear of communication. Since about 1970, there has been quite a bit of research on the problem of communication apprehension and related concepts. Perhaps the most well developed of these programs is that of James McCroskey and his colleagues, who have discovered that fear of communicating is a serious practical problem for many people.[33]

Communication apprehension (CA) can be traitlike or situational. Traitlike CA is "a relatively enduring, personality-type orientation toward a given mode of communication across a wide variety of contexts."[34] Individuals who suffer from this kind of fear may avoid all sorts of oral communication. Some people are afraid of a certain kind of communication—like public speaking—but may exhibit very little fear of other types of communication. Such fear is called *generalized-context* CA. Still others are afraid of communicating with certain specific people or groups. This form of CA, *person-group* CA, is not a personality trait like those above, but is more situational. Almost everybody suffers from time to time from *situational* CA, which is the fear of communication in a particular context; this is a transitory fear and is definitely not a trait.

These forms of CA are variables. In other words, every person has some degree of apprehension ranging from low to high. Normal apprehension is not especially problematic. Of special concern, however, is pathological CA, in which an individual suffers high traitlike fear of communication. Abnormal CA creates serious personal problems, including most notably extreme discomfort and avoidance of communication, to the point of preventing productive and happy participation in society.

Communication apprehension, though it may have an hereditary base, is probably primarily a learned response. Although behavioristic learning theory and modeling may explain some CA, McCroskey believes that the best explanations of CA are cognitive. He suggests that people create expectations about how encounters with others will turn out. When one's expectations are accurate, the resulting confidence reduces apprehension because the individual experiences less uncertainty about future encounters; but when expectations turn out to be wrong, the individual loses confidence. CA may be the result of repeated inaccurate expectations about communication situations. This outcome is essentially a pattern of learned helplessness.

One of the bright spots in the research on CA is the discovery that the problem is treatable. Consequently, the practical application of this line of research has had a significant effect. However, the project does have some theoretical difficulties.[35] One problem is the uncertainty about the relationship among several similar constructs—including, for example, apprehension, shyness, reticence, and avoidance. There is little agreement on the overall dimensions that bind this cluster of variables. In addition, although McCroskey has offered an explanation of how apprehension is learned, there has been little explication of the cognitive processes involved in communication avoidance. In fact, the project has taken a rather behavioral track in defining, measuring, and treating CA, without a great deal of conceptual explanation of the phenomenon. To more fully address the issue, these researchers could relate communication apprehension to a

33. This work is summarized in James C. McCroskey, "The Communication Apprehension Perspective," in *Avoiding Communication: Shyness, Reticence, and Communication Apprehension*, eds. John A. Daly and James C. McCroskey (Beverly Hills: Sage Publications, 1984), pp. 13–38.

34. Ibid., p. 16

35. A critique of this line of work can be found in Gerald R. Miller, "Some (Moderately) Apprehensive Thoughts on Avoiding Communication," in *Avoiding Communication: Shyness, Reticence and Communication Apprehension*, eds. John A. Daly and James C. McCroskey (Beverly Hills: Sage Publications, 1984), pp. 237–46.

variety of general cognitive theories. For example, how does CA affect one's constructs of the communication situation? How are communication action plans and their assembly affected by apprehension, or, conversely, how is apprehension itself a cognitive definition within some larger action-assembly set? How does CA affect social judgment in communication situations?

Cognition in Social Influence

One of the most researched aspects of communication is social influence. This body of literature has been strongly affected by the cognitive approach. Here we summarize several theories of this tradition.

Information Integration Theory

The information integration approach centers on the ways people accumulate and organize information about some person, object, situation, or idea to form attitudes toward a concept. The construct *attitude* has been important in persuasion theory. An attitude usually is defined as a predisposition to act in a positive or negative way toward the attitude object. Much persuasion research has focused on *attitude change*. The information integration approach is one of the most credible models of the nature of attitudes and attitude change.[36]

According to this theory, an individual's attitude system can be affected by information that is received and integrated into the attitude information system. All information has the potential of affecting one's attitudes, but the degree to which it affects attitudes depends on two variables. The first is *valence*. Valence is an individual's judgment about the degree to which the information is good news or bad news. If it supports one's beliefs and attitudes, it generally will be viewed as good; if not,

it probably will be seen as bad. Of course any particular piece of information will be evaluated in terms of a scale from very bad to very good. The second variable that affects the importance of information to a person is the weight assigned to the information. *Weight* is a function of credibility. If the person thinks the information is probably true, a higher weight will be assigned to the information; if not, a lower weight will be given. Valence affects how information influences attitudes; weight affects the degree to which it does so. When the assigned weight is low, the information will have little effect, no matter what its valence.

For example, suppose that you have two friends, one who is strongly in favor of increasing the United States' nuclear strength and the other who is strongly in favor of unilateral arms reduction. Suppose further that you and your friends are told that the President is about to announce that the United States will initiate a good-faith arms reduction with the hope that the Soviet Union will respond likewise. How will this information affect your attitudes toward the President? If your two friends accept this information as true, they will assign a high weight to it, and it will affect their attitudes toward the President. One of your friends definitely will define the information as bad news, and his attitude toward the President will likely become more positive. You, on the other hand, don't believe this information is accurate and therefore you assign it little weight. Consequently, regardless of your initial attitude, the information probably will not affect your attitude toward the President one way or another.

An attitude is considered to be an accumulation of information about the attitude object, each piece of information having been evaluated as indicated. Thus attitude change occurs because of new information or changing judgments of truthfulness or value.

One of the best-known and respected information integration theorists is Martin Fishbein.[37]

36. Contributors include Norman H. Anderson, "Integration Theory and Attitude Change," *Psychological Review* 78 (1971): 171–206; Martin Fishbein and Icek Ajzen, *Belief, Attitude, Intention, and Behavior* (Reading, Mass.: Addison-Wesley, 1975); Robert S. Wyer, *Cognitive Organization and Change* (Hillsdale, N.J.: Erlbaum, 1974).

37. Fishbein has published several articles on this topic. See Bibliography. For an excellent secondary source see David T. Burhans, "The Attitude-Behavior Discrepancy Problem: Revisited," *Quarterly Journal of Speech* 51 (1971): 418–28. For a more recent treatment, see Fishbein and Ajzen, *Belief*.

Table 5-1   A Simplified Example of an Attitude Hierarchy According to the Fishbein Model

Attitude Object (o) → Jogging   N = 6 (Number of Beliefs in System)

Associated Concepts (x_i)	Probability of Association (B_i)	Evaluation (a_i)
x_1 Cardiovascular health	B_1 Jogging promotes cardiovascular vigor.	a_1 Cardiovascular vigor is good.
x_2 Disease	B_2 Jogging reduces the chance of disease.	a_2 Disease is bad.
x_3 Obesity	B_3 Jogging reduces weight.	a_3 Being overweight is bad.
x_4 Mental health	B_4 Jogging promotes peace of mind.	a_4 Letting off mental tensions is good.
x_5 Friendship	B_5 Jogging introduces a person to new friends.	a_5 Friendship is important.
x_6 Physique	B_6 Jogging builds better bodies.	a_6 A beautiful body is appealing.

Fishbein highlights the complex and interactive nature of attitudes in what is known as *expectancy-value theory*. According to Fishbein, there are two kinds of belief, both of which are probability statements. The first is what he terms *belief* in a thing. When one believes *in* something, he or she predicts a high probability of existence. The second kind of belief, *belief about*, is the predicted probability that a particular relationship exists between the belief object and some other quality or thing. Again, this is a probability situation, and one's belief is the predicted probability of the existence of a particular relationship. For example, one may believe *in* God, that God exists. One may also believe that God is omnipotent—a probability statement of a relationship between God and omnipotence.

Attitudes differ from beliefs in that they are *evaluative*. Attitudes are correlated with beliefs and predispose a person to behave a certain way toward the attitude object. Attitudes are learned as part of one's concept formation. They may change as new learnings occur throughout life. Furthermore, Fishbein sees attitudes as hierarchically organized. In other words, general attitudes are predicted from specific ones in a *summative* fashion. An attitude toward an object is the sum of the specific factors, including beliefs and evaluations, in the family hierarchy. This formula is represented algebraically as follows.[38]

$$A_o = \sum_{I}^{N} B_i a_i$$

where

A_o = the attitude toward object o
B_i = the strength of belief i about o; that is, the probability or improbability that o is associated with some other concept x_i
a_i = the evaluative aspect of B_i; that is, the evaluation of x_i
N = the number of beliefs about o

The distinctive feature of Fishbein's formula is that it stresses the interactive nature of attitudes. Attitudes are a function of a complex factor that involves both beliefs (probability predictions) and evaluations. The example in Table 5-1 will help to clarify this model. According to this conceptualization, attitude change can occur from any of three sources. First, information can alter the believability (weight) of particular beliefs. Second, information can change the value of a belief. Finally, information can add new beliefs to the attitude structure.

38. Martin Fishbein, "A Behavior Theory Approach to the Relations between Beliefs about an Object and the Attitude Toward the Object," in *Readings in Attitude Theory and Measurement*, ed. Martin Fishbein, (New York: John Wiley, 1967), p. 394.

Most of the negative criticism of information integration theory relates to the validity of measurement. Although the idea that attitudes consist of accumulated and weighted beliefs is generally accepted, there is quite a bit of doubt that one can measure the overall accumulated weight and value of a belief system with any degree of reliability. In the natural setting a researcher would first have to isolate beliefs contributing to an attitude, measure them accurately, and factor out the influence of other elements of the system. Since this process is difficult or impossible to do, most research in this tradition is artificial, hypothetical, and controlled. This problem thus casts doubt on the *external validity* of the claims.

The other serious problem among research studies in this area is that profound disagreement exists about the way one accumulates information to form an attitude. The research evidence is equivocal on this point. This controversy casts doubt on the *internal validity* of the approach.[39]

The difficulty with criticizing research methodology is that every method of observation, in the natural setting or in the laboratory, has weaknesses. One can always question the reliability and validity of data collection. The fact is that this theory has been widely acclaimed in the field. Methodological problems aside, this theory provides a useful model for understanding the nature of attitude and attitude change from an information processing point of view.

Information integration theory shows us how attitudes are affected by information. The following theory is useful in calling our attention to the routes through which this processing occurs.

Elaboration Likelihood Theory

Elaboration likelihood theory was developed by social psychologists Richard Petty and John Cacioppo as a general summation of insights from many other attitude change theories.[40] The basic thesis of their theory is that individuals process information from persuasive messages in one of two ways: through a central route or a peripheral route. Processing information through the *central route* means that the individual actively thinks about the information and weighs it against already existing knowledge. Processing through the *peripheral route* means that the individual does not think much about the message and is therefore more influenced by nonargumentative appeals. When one processes information centrally, arguments are carefully considered; and if attitude change results, it is apt to be relatively permanent. On the other hand, if the message is processed peripherally, arguments are less important, and personal impressions and other subsidiary concerns are more important; however, any resulting change is probably temporary.

The primary factor determining whether information is processed centrally or peripherally is the personal significance of the topic to the listener. If you judge a subject to be very important to you, you will consider the arguments more carefully and think more actively about the information received; if the subject is less important, you will not spend much time thinking about what you hear or read on the topic.

Personal relevance, however, is not the only factor determining whether a message will be processed centrally or peripherally. In order to use a central route, one must be both motivated and able to do so. Personal relevance determines motivation, but it does not necessarily mean that the individual is able to think carefully and critically about the information received. Ability includes hearing and understanding the message, attention without distraction, necessary time and energy, and sufficient background knowledge to comprehend the message. When both motivation and ability are high, elaboration of information is likely.

Figure 5-8 illustrates the two processing routes.[41] If the person is motivated and able to process centrally, the outcome will depend on the nature of the persuasion and the kinds of arguments used. If arguments seem strong to the listener, he or she will be persuaded; if not, a boomerang effect may occur. If the individual is not motivated or is unable to

39. For a review of the issues in this dispute, see Smith, *Persuasion*, pp. 245–48.

40. Richard E. Petty and John T. Cacioppo, *Attitudes and Persuasion: Classic and Contemporary Approaches* (Dubuque, Iowa: W. C. Brown Company, 1981), pp. 255–67.

41. Adapted from Petty and Cacioppo, *Attitudes*, p. 264.

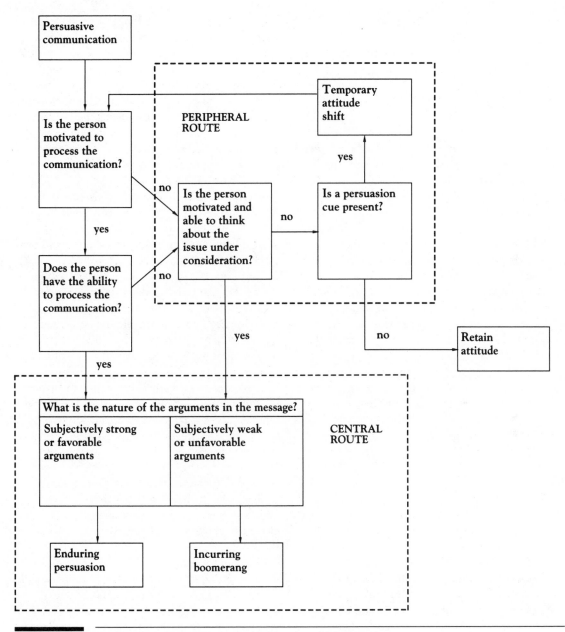

Figure 5-8   Simplified version of elaboration likelihood model.

process centrally, then various extrinsic cues, such as speaker image, will be taken into consideration and may lead to temporary attitude change.

This is an appealing theory. It is based on suggestions from several other approaches and seems to meet the test of research. Because of its simplicity, it consolidates a great deal of material in highly parsimonious fashion, leading to a sensible and useful insight. The failing of the theory is that it does not help us to understand much about what specific cognitive structures and processes are actually involved in central versus peripheral processing.

We turn now to a huge and highly influential body of theory relative to cognition and influence—consistency theories.

Consistency Theories

The largest portion of work in psychology related to attitude, attitude change, and persuasion is undoubtedly *consistency theory*. All consistency theories begin with the same premise: People are more comfortable with consistency than inconsistency. The vocabulary and concepts change from theory to theory, and the hypothesized relationships among variables differ, but the basic assumption of consistency remains. In system language, people seek *homeostasis*. In fact, this consistency theme can be related to the system view that the goal of an open system is self-maintenance and balance (Chapter 3). According to these theories, behavior change results from information that disrupts the balance of the cognitive system.

In the remainder of this section, two prominent theories of cognitive consistency are summarized. These were chosen because of their prominence in the field and their relative completeness of explanation. The first is the theory of cognitive dissonance by Leon Festinger and the second is the theory of attitudes, beliefs, and values of Milton Rokeach.

The theory of cognitive dissonance. Leon Festinger's theory of cognitive dissonance is the most significant and influential consistency theory. In fact, it is one of the most important theories in the history of social psychology. Over the years it has produced a prodigious quantity of research as well as volumes of criticism, interpretation, and extrapolation.[42] Festinger broadened the scope of consist-

ency theory to include a range of what he called cognitive elements, including attitudes, perceptions, knowledge, and behaviors. Two cognitive elements (an attitude and a behavior, perhaps) will have one of three kinds of relationships. The first of these is null or *irrelevant*, the second consistent or *consonant*, and the third inconsistent or *dissonant*. Dissonance is a relationship in which one element would not be expected to follow from the other. It is important to note that dissonance is a matter of psychological consistency, not of logical relationships. Dissonance and consonance therefore must be evaluated in terms of a single individual's psychological system. We must always ask what is consonant or dissonant for a person's own psychological system.

Two overriding premises are found in dissonance theory. The first is that dissonance produces tension or stress that pressures the individual to change so that the dissonance is thereby reduced. Second, when dissonance is present, the individual will not only attempt to reduce it but will avoid situations in which additional dissonance might be produced. These tendencies to reduce dissonance and to avoid dissonance-producing information are a direct function of the magnitude of dissonance present in the system; the greater the dissonance, the greater the need for change. Dissonance is a result of two antecedent variables, the importance of the cognitive elements and the number of elements involved in the dissonant relation. This latter variable is a matter of balance: The more equal the number of elements on the sides of the relation, the greater the dissonance.

Consider two examples of a low-dissonance prediction. On a particular day you may be faced with a decision of whether to eat breakfast. Suppose you are expected to meet a friend to go shopping, but your alarm didn't go off and you are late. You can skip breakfast and be on time, or you can eat toast

42. Leon Festinger, *A Theory of Cognitive Dissonance* (Stanford, Calif.: Stanford University Press, 1957). Many short reviews of dissonance theory are available, including Kiesler, Collins, and Miller, *Attitude Change*; Robert Zajonc, "The Concepts of Balance, Congruity, and Dissonance," *Public Opinion Quarterly* 24 (1960): 280–96; Roger Brown, "Models of Attitude Change," in *New Directions in Psychology* (New York: Holt, Rinehart & Winston, 1962), pp. 1–85; Roger Brown, *Social*

Psychology (New York: Free Press, 1965); chap. 11. For a readable exposition showing the practical applications of cognitive dissonance theory, see Elliot Aronson, *The Social Animal* (New York: Viking Press, 1972), chap. 4. For a detailed examination of the theory and related research, see J. W. Brehm and A. R. Cohen, *Explorations in Cognitive Dissonance* (New York: John Wiley, 1962).

and coffee and be a little late. You will quickly decide to do one or the other, but in any case some dissonance will result. This dissonance probably will be small because neither eating breakfast nor being on time is important. But if your situation involves being late for work, a different variable is operating. You probably would choose to skip breakfast and be on time. The prediction is the same (a small amount of dissonance), but the reason is different. The deck is stacked; a number of important cognitive elements lie on the "getting to work on time" side of the relation. Not only do you have a sense of obligation to your work, you also have a need to make a good impression on your boss, to get work done that is stacked up on your desk from the day before, and to avoid having your pay docked.

With these basic concepts in mind, we can now turn to the ways in which we deal with cognitive dissonance. Understanding that dissonance produces a tension for reduction, we can imagine a number of "methods" for reducing the dissonance. First, one might change one or more of the cognitive elements. Second, new elements might be added to one side of the tension or the other. Third, one might come to see the elements as less important than they used to be. Fourth, a person might seek consonant information. Fifth, the individual might reduce dissonance by distorting or misinterpreting the information involved. One of the most common examples of cognitive dissonance involves smoking. Suppose a smoker is reading and hearing a lot of facts about the health hazards of smoking. This occurrence is bound to produce dissonance, which might be very great, depending on the importance of the habit and the person's values on health and life. Here's what a smoker could do. The smoker might change the cognitive elements by stopping smoking or by rejecting the belief that smoking is unhealthy. Or the person might add new cognitive elements, such as smoking filters. The importance of the elements involved in dissonance might be reduced. For example, smokers sometimes say that they want a high quality of life, not a long life. The smoker might seek out consonant information supporting the view that smoking is not all

that bad. Finally, the smoker might decide to distort the information received, saying something like, "As I read the evidence, smoking is harmful only for people who are already sick anyway."

Much of the theory and research on cognitive dissonance has centered around the various situations in which dissonance is likely to result. These include decision making, forced compliance, initiation, social support, and effort. The first, decision making, has received a great deal of research attention. Salespeople call this kind of dissonance "buyer's remorse." The popular saying goes, "The grass is always greener on the other side." The amount of dissonance one experiences as a result of a decision depends on four variables, the first of which is the importance of the decision. Certain decisions, such as that to skip breakfast, may be unimportant and produce little dissonance. Buying a house, seeking a new job, or moving to a new community, however, might involve a great deal of dissonance. The second variable is the attractiveness of the chosen alternative. Other things being equal, the less attractive the chosen alternative, the greater the dissonance. Third, the greater the perceived attractiveness of the unchosen alternative, the more the felt dissonance. Fourth, the greater the degree of similarity or overlap between the alternatives, the less the dissonance. If one is making a decision between two similar cars, little dissonance potential exists.

The second situation in which dissonance is apt to result is forced compliance or being induced to do or say something contrary to one's beliefs or values. This situation usually occurs when a reward is involved for complying or a punishment for not complying. Dissonance theory predicts that the less the pressure to conform, the greater the dissonance. If you were asked to do something you didn't like doing but you were paid quite a bit for doing it, you would not feel as much dissonance as if you were paid very little. The less external justification (such as reward or punishment), the more one must focus on the internal inconsistency within the self. This is why, according to dissonance theorists, the "soft" social pressures one encounters may be powerful in inducing rationalization or change.

Other situational predictions are made by dissonance theory. The theory predicts that the more difficult one's initiation to a group, the greater commitment one will have to that group. The more social support one receives from friends on an idea or action, the greater the pressure to believe in that idea or action. The greater the amount of effort one puts into a task, the more one will rationalize the value of that task.

In short, the theory of cognitive dissonance has had a major impact in the field of persuasion. It has won an important place in communication theory because of what it says about messages, information, and persuasion.

Rokeach: attitudes, beliefs, and values. One of the finest recent theories on attitude and change is that of Milton Rokeach. He has developed an extensive explanation of human behavior based on beliefs, attitudes, and values.[43] His theory builds on the theories of the past and provides some pertinent extensions.

Rokeach conceives of a highly organized belief-attitude-value system, which guides the behavior of the individual and supports the person's self-regard. Briefly, he describes the system in the following way: "All these conceptually distinct components—the countless beliefs, their organizations into thousands of attitudes, the several dozens of hierarchically arranged terminal values—are organized to form a single, functionally interconnected belief system."[44]

Beliefs are the hundreds of thousands of statements (usually inferences) that we make about self and the world. Beliefs are general or specific, and they are arranged within the system in terms of their centrality or importance to the ego. At the center of the belief system are those well-established, relatively unchangeable beliefs that literally form the core view of self and world. At the periphery of the system lie the many unimportant, changeable beliefs. There are three hypotheses

about the belief system. First, beliefs vary in terms of centrality-peripherality. Second, the more central the belief, the more resistant it is to change. Third, a change in a central belief will produce more overall change in the system than will a change in a peripheral belief.

Groups of beliefs that are organized around a focal object and predispose a person to behave in a particular way toward that object are attitudes. If a belief system has hundreds of thousands of beliefs, it likewise will have perhaps thousands of attitudes, each consisting of a number of beliefs about the attitude object. Figure 5-9 illustrates, in overly simple form, the organization of an attitude.

Rokeach believes attitudes are of two important kinds that must always be viewed together. These are *attitude-toward-object* and *attitude-toward-situation*. One's behavior in a particular situation is a function of these two in combination. If a person does not behave in a given situation congruently with the attitude-toward-object, it is probably because the attitude-toward-situation does not facilitate a particular behavior at that time. A common example of this might be food preference. Your attitude toward red meat may say: Avoid. But your attitude toward eating red meat may say: It is not socially acceptable to refuse food served to you when you are a guest. Thus the vegetarian may eat meat, despite a private, negative attitude toward it. This idea is consistent with Fishbein's conception, summarized earlier. The main point of both models is that behavior is a complex function of sets of attitudes. In Rokeach's theory, then, the system consists of many beliefs ranging in centrality, which are clustered together to form attitudes that predispose the person to behave in certain ways. Attitudes are complex evaluations of objects and situations.

Rokeach believes that of the three concepts in explaining human behavior, value is the most important. Values are specific types of belief that are central in the system and act as life guides. Values are of two kinds: *instrumental* and *terminal*. Instrumental values are guidelines for living on which we base our daily behavior. Terminal values are the ultimate aims of life toward which we work.

43. Milton Rokeach, *Beliefs, Attitudes, and Values: A Theory of Organization and Change* (San Francisco: Jossey-Bass, 1969); *The Nature of Human Values* (New York: Free Press, 1973).

44. Rokeach, *Human Values,* p. 215.

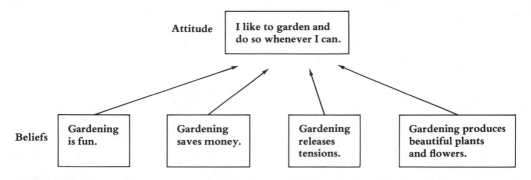

Figure 5-9   A simple example of the belief structure of an attitude.

One other component in the belief-attitude-value system that assumes great overall importance is the *self-concept*. Self-concept consists of one's beliefs about the self. It is the individual's answer to the question, Who am I? Self-concept is particularly important to the system because "the ultimate purpose of one's total belief system, which includes one's values, is to maintain and enhance . . . the sentiment of self-regard."[45] Thus while beliefs, attitudes, and values constitute the components of the system, the self-concept is its guiding goal or purpose. With these four concepts Rokeach has tied the theory into a cohesive package. At the heart lie one's self-conceptions, and the flesh is filled out by the other components.

Rokeach is basically a consistency theorist. He includes a number of significant hypotheses about attitudes, beliefs, and values, but in the final analysis, he believes that people are guided by a need for consistency and that inconsistency creates a pressure to change. Even in discussing consistency, Rokeach has broadened his base far beyond the other consistency theories. Taking the total system into consideration, he sees consistency as extremely complex. An individual may be inconsistent on several different levels. In all, ten areas in the psychological system interrelate and bear the potential for inconsistency. Table 5-2, reproduced from Rokeach's book, is a matrix of all the possible relations among elements in the belief-attitude-

value system.[46] In the cells of the matrix are indications of the areas of study that have focused on a variety of these relationships. One of the significant impressions we get from this matrix is the number of empty cells that have not been examined in any significant way, according to Rokeach. He criticizes consistency theory:

> None of the theories discussed can be regarded as a comprehensive theory of change. A comprehensive theory should ideally be able to address itself to the conditions that will lead to long-range as well as short-range change, behavioral change as well as cognitive change, personality change as well as cognitive and behavioral change, and a rising or lowering of self-conceptions as well as their maintenance. A major objective of this book is to build a theoretical framework that will, it is hoped, address itself to such issues, one that at least attempts to bridge the current gap between various personality, social-psychological, and behavior theories that for the most part do not speak to each other.[47]

Furthermore, Rokeach believes that the most important inconsistencies in a person's psychological system are those in row A involving cognitions about the self. Only when inconsistencies involve the self-conception will there be significant, lasting change. The reason for this is that such contradictions increase self-dissatisfaction. Since maintenance of the self-regard is the overall aim of the psychological system, it is natural that this should

45. Ibid., p. 216.

46. Ibid., pp. 220–21.
47. Ibid., p. 224.

Table 5-2   Matrix of Contradictory Relations Possible Within the Total Belief System

Organization of:	A	B	C	D	E	F	G	H	I	J
A. Cognitions about self	Psychoanalysis					Rational therapy Reality therapy Emotional role playing	Nondirective therapy	Encounter groups T-groups Psychodrama		
B. Terminal value system					Cognitive-affective consistency					
C. Instrumental value system						Achievement motivation				
D. Attitude system				Congruity theory Belief congruence			Balance theory			
E. Attitude					Syllogistic analysis of attitudes	Dissonance theory Attribution theory	Communication and persuasion Innoculation theory Assimilation-contrast theory			
F. Cognitions about own behavior									Modeling and observational learning	
G. Cognitions about significant others' attitudes										
H. Cognitions about significant others' values or needs										
I. Cognitions about significant others' behavior										
J. Cognitions about behavior of nonsocial objects										

be so. Rokeach's theory of the attitude-belief-value system is complex and lengthy. We have only been able to sketch it here.

Consistency theory has had a major impact on our thinking about attitude and attitude change. A mainstay of social psychology for many years, it is appealing because of its *parsimony* and *heuristic value*. For a twenty-year period it stimulated a great deal of research. The popularity of consistency theory is understandable, given the goal of this field to discover a few important variables that would predict social behavior. Consistency theories do just that. They isolate certain elements of cognition and show how manipulations among these variables can predict a person's feelings, thoughts, or actions. They also appeal to the social scientist's sense of logic, providing an explanation for behavior that makes intuitive sense. At one time consistency theories were so well accepted that debates centered not on whether people respond to dissonance but on ways to improve the precision of predictions based on these theories.

In recent years, however, consistency theory has become less popular. Several weaknesses have become apparent. These weaknesses revolve around three criteria: appropriateness, validity, and scope. The following comments about these failures center on dissonance theory.

The first objection to dissonance theory relates to its theoretical *appropriateness*. Basically, the dissonance hypothesis for change is overly simple. Natalia Chapanis and Alphonse Chapanis capture this objection in harsh terms: "To condense most complex social situations into two, and only two, simple dissonant statements represents so great an abstraction that the model no longer bears any reasonable resemblance to reality."[48] More recent research on cognition and information processing provides evidence that cognition is too complex to break down to simple consistencies and inconsistencies. For example, cognitive complexity theory posits that cognitions are organized in extensive hierarchies and that the individual's understanding of environment is variable and adaptive.

48. Natalia P. Chapanis and Alphonse Chapanis, "Cognitive Dissonance: Five Years Later," *Psychological Bulletin* 61 (1964): p. 21.

Another issue related to theoretical appropriateness is the question of whether people are passive in resonding to inconsistencies. Most research evidence of recent years indicates that they are not. Cognitions do not come prepackaged in consistent or inconsistent forms. Individuals actively define and redefine situations, depending on the needs of the moment.

The second basis for criticism of dissonance theory is *validity*. The basic standard for any predictive theory—and the theory of cognitive dissonance is precisely that—is to be stated in such a way that contradictory evidence could prove the theory wrong in its predictions. In other words, the theory must be falsifiable. The problem with dissonance theory is that it can be used to explain various, contradictory results and cannot be proved wrong, which creates a situation wherein the dissonance theorist wins no matter how an experiment comes out. If attitude change results from the manipulations, one can argue that the change was caused by dissonance; if attitude change does not occur, one can say that dissonance did not exist. Furthermore, dissonance is such a general concept that it can take any number of forms. Thus the experimenter can claim that a particular result was caused by one kind of dissonance but that an entirely different result was produced by another kind of dissonance. This circular reasoning results from the fact that dissonance researchers do not measure dissonance per se but infer dissonance from behavior. Indeed, there is some question as to whether dissonance is directly observable at all.

The third objection to dissonance theory relates to its *scope*. Originally thought to apply to a wide range of cognitive activity, dissonance theory is now seen as applying to a rather narrow area of behavior.

Rokeach's work has taken a giant step toward improving consistency theory. It overcomes virtually all of the weaknesses of the earlier models. First, it is broadly based, including a variety of cognitive concepts. It explains why cognitions do not always change and why some cognitions are more apt to change than others. The major contribution of Rokeach's theory is that it broadens our understanding of consistency and inconsistency.

Rokeach shows that what may appear consistent on one level may be entirely inconsistent on another (see Table 5-2).

The major problem of Rokeach's work is his attempt to operationalize constructs that are not amenable to measurement. His attempt to reduce all values to a standard list and to describe the value system in terms of a simple ranking is unrealistic at best and ludicrous at worst. Still, the power of this theory should not be underestimated. The time may be right to modify Rokeach's approach so that it is consistent with recent action-oriented, rules-based notions of human behavior.

Integration

Behavioral and cognitive approaches focus on the ways in which individuals think and act in communication situations. Although learning may be a factor in shaping individual responses in communication, we also know that active thought processes are involved. Some of the thought processes include internal associations among stimuli, meanings, and signs. As those associations change and as certain responses are reinforced in the environment, attitudes and behavior may change.

Processing communication involves more than simple association, reinforcement, and response. For example, it is believed that we have an innate sense of language and that we acquire a set of rules by which sentences can be generated and understood. In addition, statements and events are interpreted and actions are planned through elaborate cognitive mechanisms.

One aspect of cognitive processing involves weighing or judging the position of statements based on reference points or anchors in the mind. How we respond to messages may depend in large measure on these social judgments. We also interpret events in terms of constructs or categories of the mind; our understanding of events and our response to those events depend in part on the complexity of the construct system with which the events are interpreted. Over time, people develop a repertoire of knowledge and procedures for action in the world. When one encounters a new situation, he or she will draw upon that body of knowledge to "assemble" an action plan.

Social influence is largely a matter of cognitive processing. Our attitudes seem to be an organized set of orientations based on beliefs and values. New information received through communication may change those beliefs and values in such a way as to change attitudes and behaviors. However, we probably do not process information the same way in every situation. There is some evidence, for example, that when an individual is highly involved or interested in the communication, information is processed very carefully and consciously, while in less ego-involving situations, information processing may be much more peripheral.

One of the most popular ideas about social influence is that individuals strive to maintain consistency in the cognitive system. Awareness of inconsistency between various thoughts, values, attitudes, and actions may lead to personal change.

Six

Symbolic Interactionist and Dramatistic Theories

We turn now to the third of our four genres of communication theory—interactional and conventional approaches. These theories take quite a different direction than the functional, structural, and cognitive theories discussed in the previous three chapters. For the scholars in the interactional tradition, communication and meaning are unabashedly social. Unlike the theories discussed in the previous chapters, these approaches do not look for meaning in the structure of the language or intrinsic properties of the mind. Rather, meaning is created through and sustained by interaction in the social group. Interaction establishes, maintains, and changes certain conventions—roles, norms, rules, and meanings—within a social group or culture. Those conventions literally define the reality of the culture.

We discuss this group of theories in two chapters. Chapter 6 covers the foundational literature in symbolic interactionism and closely related ideas on dramatism. Chapter 7 examines theories of the social construction of reality, rules, and culture. There is also an affinity between this genre and the interactional and critical theories that are addressed in Chapter 8.

Symbolic Interactionism

Symbolic interactionism contains a core of common premises about communication and society. Jerome Manis and Bernard Meltzer published a compilation of articles in which they isolated seven basic theoretical and methodological propositions from symbolic interactionism, each identifying a central concept of the tradition:

1. The meaning component in human conduct: Distinctly human behavior and interaction are carried on through the medium of symbols and their meanings.

2. The social sources of humanness: The individual becomes humanized through interaction with other persons.

3. Society as process: Human society is most usefully conceived as consisting of people in interaction.

4. The voluntaristic component in human conduct: Human beings are active in shaping their own behavior.

5. A dialectical conception of mind: Consciousness, or thinking, involves interaction within oneself.

6. The constructive, emergent nature of human conduct: Human beings construct their behavior in the course of its execution.

7. The necessity of sympathetic introspection: An understanding of human conduct requires study of the actors' covert behavior.[1]

Manford Kuhn divides the time line of symbolic interactionism into two major portions. The first, which he calls the *oral tradition*, was the early period when the primary foundations of symbolic interaction developed. Following the posthumous publication of George Herbert Mead's *Mind, Self, and*

---

1. Jerome G. Manis and Bernard N. Meltzer (eds.), *Symbolic Interaction* (Boston: Allyn & Bacon, 1978), p. 437.

Society, the second period, which may be termed the *age of inquiry*, came to flower.[2] Of course, the ideas of symbolic interaction did not emerge overnight from the mind of a lone thinker. They can be traced to the early psychology of William James. The primary interactionists in the early tradition were Charles Cooley, John Dewey, I. A. Thomas, and George Herbert Mead. Before Mead's ideas on communication were published, the interactionist perspective found life and sustenance primarily through oral transmission, especially in Mead's classroom. Although Mead did not publish his ideas during his lifetime, he is considered the prime mover of symbolic interactionism.

During this early Meadian period, the important ideas of the theory were developed. Mead and other interactionists departed from earlier sociological perspectives that had distinguished between the person and the society. Mead viewed individuals and society as inseparable and interdependent. Early interactionism stressed both the importance of social development and innate biological factors as well. Further, the early symbolic interactionists were not as concerned with how people communicatd as they were with the impact of this communication on society and individuals. Above all, the early interactionists stressed the role of the shared meaning of symbols as the binding factor in society. The early theorists were strongly concerned with studying people in relation to their social situation. They maintained that a person's behavior could not be studied apart from the setting in which the behavior occurred or apart from the individual's perception of the environment. A result of this concern was that these early interactionists favored case histories as a research method.[3]

During the age of inquiry—the years that followed the publication of *Mind, Self, and Society*—

two divergent schools began to develop within the arena of symbolic interactionism. The original formulations of Mead were not altogether consistent, leaving room for divergent interpretation and extension. As a result the Chicago and Iowa schools developed. The Chicago School, led primarily by Herbert Blumer, continued the humanistic tradition begun by Mead. Blumer above all believes that the study of humans cannot be conducted in the same manner as the study of things. The goals of the researcher must be to empathize with the subject, to enter the subject's realm of experience, and to attempt to understand the value of the person as an individual. Blumer and his followers avoided quantitative and scientific approaches to studying human behavior. They stress life histories, autobiographies, case studies, diaries, letters, and nondirective interviews. Blumer particularly stresses the importance of participant observation in the study of communication. Further, the Chicago tradition sees people as creative, innovative, and free to define each situation in individual and unpredictable ways. Self and society are viewed as process, not structure; to freeze the process would be to lose the essence of person-society relationships.

The Iowa School takes a more scientific approach to studying interaction. Manford Kuhn, its leader, believes that interactionist concepts can be operationalized. While Kuhn admits the process nature of behavior, he advocates that the objective structural approach is more fruitful than the "soft" methods employed by Blumer. As we will see later in the chapter, Kuhn is responsible for one of the primary measurement techniques used in symbolic interaction research.[4]

Largely because of the basic split that grew out of the attempt to resolve ambiguities left by Mead, a number of tributaries have formed since about 1940. Kuhn lists six major subareas: role theory, reference group theory, social perception and person perception, self-theory, interpersonal theory, and language and culture.[5]

2. Manford H. Kuhn, "Major Trends in Symbolic Interaction Theory in the Past Twenty-Five Years," *The Sociological Quarterly* 5 (1964): 61–84.

3. Bernard N. Meltzer and John W. Petras, "The Chicago and Iowa Schools of Symbolic Interactionism," in *Human Nature and Collective Behavior*, ed. Tamotsu Shibutani (Englewood Cliffs, N.J.: Prentice-Hall, 1970).

4. Ibid.

5. Kuhn, "Major Trends."

The Chicago School

George Herbert Mead is usually viewed as the major source of the interactionist movement, and his work certainly forms the core of the Chicago School.[6] Herbert Blumer, Mead's foremost apostle, invented the term *symbolic interactionism*, an expression Mead himself never used. Blumer refers to this label as "a somewhat barbaric neologism that I coined in an offhand way. . . . The term somehow caught on."[7]

The three cardinal concepts in Mead's theory, captured in the title of his best-known work, are society, self, and mind. These categories are different aspects of the same general process, the social act. Basic to Mead's thought is the notion that people are *actors*, not *reactors*. The social act is an umbrella concept under which nearly all other psychological and social processes fall. The act is a complete unit of conduct, a gestalt, that cannot be analyzed into specific subparts. An act may be short, such as tying a shoe, or it may be the fulfillment of a life plan. Acts interrelate and are built upon one another in hierarchical form throughout a lifetime. Acts begin with an impulse; they involve perception and assignment of meaning, covert rehearsal, weighing of alternatives in one's head, and consummation.

In its most basic form a social act involves a three-part relationship: an initial gesture from one individual, a response to that gesture by another (covertly or overtly), and a result of the act, which is perceived or imagined by both parties. In a holdup, for example, the robber indicates to the victim what is intended. The victim responds by giving money or belongings, and in the initial gesture and response, the defined result (a holdup) has occurred. Even individual acts, like taking a solitary walk, are interactional in that they are based on gestures and responses that occurred many times in the past and continue in the mind of the individual. One never takes a walk by oneself, for example, without relying on meanings and actions learned in social interaction in the past. This capacity to act implies that the individual can deal with problem situations: "Instead of being merely an organism that responds to the play of factors on or through it, the human being is seen as an organism that has to deal with what it notes."[8]

Societal or group action is merely the extended process of many individuals accommodating their actions to one another. A joint action of a group of people consists of an *interlinkage* of their separate actions. Such institutions as marriage, trade, war, and church worship are joint actions. Group action is based in individual acts. Hence we must consider group conduct as the combined independent actions of the individual participants; Blumer states: "The participants still have to guide their respective acts by forming and using meanings."[9]

Blumer makes three basic observations about linkages. First, he notes that in an advanced society the largest portion of group action consists of highly recurrent and stable patterns. These group actions possess common and preestablished meanings in their social context. Because of the high frequency of such patterns, scholars have tended to treat the actions as structures or entities. Blumer warns us not to forget that new situations present problems requiring adjustment and redefinition. Even in highly repetitive group patterns nothing is permanent. Each case must begin anew with individual action. No matter how solid a group action appears to be, it is still rooted in individual human choices: "It is the social process in group life that creates and upholds the rules, not the rules that create and uphold group life."[10]

6. Mead's primary work in symbolic interactionism is *Mind, Self, and Society* (Chicago: University of Chicago Press, 1934). For outstanding secondary sources on Mead, see Bernard N. Meltzer, "Mead's Social Psychology," in *Symbolic Interaction*, eds. Jerome Manis and Bernard Meltzer (Boston: Allyn & Bacon, 1972), pp. 4–22; and Charles Morris, "George H. Mead as Social Psychologist and Social Philosopher," in *Mind, Self, and Society*, "Introduction"; and C. David Johnson and J. Stephen Picou, "The Foundations of Symbolic Interactionism Reconsidered," in *Micro-Sociological Theory: Perspectives on Sociological Theory*, vol. 2, eds. H. J. Helle and S. N. Eisenstadt (Beverly Hills: Sage Publications, 1985), pp. 54–70.

7. Herbert Blumer, *Symbolic Interactionism: Perspective and Method* (Englewood Cliffs: N.J.: Prentice-Hall, 1969), p. 1.

8. Ibid., p. 14.
9. Ibid., p. 17.
10. Ibid., p. 19.

Interlinkages may be pervasive and extended. Individual actions may be connected through complicated networks. Distant actors may be interlinked ultimately in diverse ways, but contrary to popular sociological thinking, "a network or an institution does not function automatically because of some inner dynamics or system requirements: it functions because people at different points do something, and what they do is a result of how they define the situation in which they are called on to act."[11]

With this outline in mind, then, let us look more closely at the first facet of Meadian analysis—*society*. Society, or group life, is a cluster of cooperative behaviors on the part of society's members. Lower animals have societies, too, but they are based on biological necessity and are physiologically determined. As a result an animal society behaves in predictable, stable, and unchanging ways. What is it, then, that distinguishes human cooperative behavior?

Human cooperation requires understanding the *intentions* of the other communicator. Since "minding" or thinking is a process of figuring out what actions one will undertake in the future, part of "feeling out" the other person is assessing what that person will do next. Thus, cooperation consists of "reading" the other person's actions and intentions and responding in an appropriate way. Such cooperation is the heart of interpersonal communication. The notion of mutual response with the use of language makes symbolic interactionism a vital approach to communication theory.

Human beings use *symbols* in their communication. People consciously conduct a process of mental manipulation, delaying of response, and assigning meaning to the gestures of others. The symbol is *interpreted* by the receiver, which makes *meaning* central to social life. Blumer develops three points about the centrality of meaning:

1. "Human beings act toward things on the basis of the meanings that the things have for them."

2. "The meaning of such things is derived from,

or arises out of, the social interaction that one has with one's fellows."

3. "These meanings are handled in, and modified through, an interpretive process used by the person in dealing with the things he encounters."[12]

Meaning is a product of social life. Whatever meaning a person possesses for a thing is the result of interaction with others about the object being defined. An object has no meaning for a person apart from the interaction with other human beings.

What is distinctive about the interactionist view of meaning is its stress on conscious interpretation. An object has meaning for the person at the point when the individual consciously thinks about or interprets the object. This process of handling meanings is basically an internal conversation: "The actor selects, checks, suspends, regroups, and transforms the meanings in light of the situation in which he is placed and the direction of his actions."[13]

Clearly, symbols must possess shared meaning in order for society to exist. Mead called a gesture with shared meaning a *significant symbol*. Society arises in the significant symbols of the group. Because of the ability to vocalize symbols, we literally can hear ourselves and thus can respond to the self, as others respond to us. We can imagine what it is like to receive our own messages, and we can empathize with the listener and take the listener's role, mentally completing the other's response.

This interplay between responding to others and responding to self is an important concept in Mead's theory, and it provides an excellent transition to the second member of the troika—the *self*. To state that a person has a self implies that the individual can act toward the self as toward others. A person may react favorably to the self and feel pride, happiness, encouragement; or one may become angry or disgusted with the self. The primary way that a person comes to see self as others see it (possess a self-concept) is through role taking. Of course, this act would not be possible without lan-

11. Ibid., p. 19.

12. Ibid., p. 2.
13. Ibid., p. 5.

guage (significant symbols), for through language the child learns the responses, intentions, and definitions of others.

The idea of the *generalized other* is central to Mead's notion of self. The generalized other is the unified role from which the individual sees the self. It is our individual perception of the overall way that others see us. The self-concept is unified and organized through internalization of this generalized other. Your generalized other is your concept of how others in general perceive you. You have learned this self-picture from years of symbolic interaction with other people in your life.

The self has two facets, each serving an essential function in the person's life. The *I* is the impulsive, unorganized, undirected, unpredictable part of the person. The *me* is the generalized other, made up of the organized and consistent patterns shared with others. Every act begins with an impulse from the I and quickly becomes controlled by the me. The I is the driving force in action, while the me provides direction and guidance. Mead uses the concept of me to explain socially acceptable and adaptive behavior and the I to explain creative, unpredictable impulses within the person.

The ability to use significant symbols to respond to oneself leads to the possibility of inner experience and thought that may or may not be consummated in overt conduct. This latter idea constitutes the third part of Mead's theory—the *mind*. The mind can be defined as the process of interacting with oneself. This ability, which develops along with the self, is crucial to human life, for it is part of every act. "Minding" involves hesitating (postponing overt action) while one consciously assigns meaning to the stimuli. Mind often arises around problem situations in which the individual must think through future actions. The person imagines various outcomes, selecting and testing possible alternative actions.

Because people possess significant symbols that allow them to name their concepts, the person can transform mere stimuli into real objects. Objects do not exist apart from people. The object is always defined by the individual in terms of the kinds of acts that a person might make toward the object.

A seascape is a seascape when I value looking at it. A glass of lemonade is a drink when I conceive of drinking it, or not drinking it. Objects become the objects they are through the individual's symbolic minding process; when the individual envisions new or different actions toward an object, the object is changed.

For Blumer, objects are of three types: physical (things), social (people), and abstract (ideas). Objects acquire meaning through symbolic interaction. Objects may hold different meanings for different people, depending on the nature of others' actions toward the person regarding the defined object. A police officer may mean one thing to the residents of an inner city ghetto while a police officer means something else to the inhabitants of a posh residential area; the different interactions among the residents of these two vastly different communities may determine different meanings.

The Iowa School

Manford Kuhn and his students, while maintaining basic interactionist principles, take two new steps not previously seen in the old-line interactionist theory. The first is to make the interactionist concept of self more concrete; the second, which makes the first possible, is the use of quantitative research. In this latter area the Iowa and Chicago schools part company. Blumer strongly criticizes the trend in the behavioral sciences to operationalize; Kuhn makes a point to do just that! As a result Kuhn's work moves more toward microscopic analysis than does the traditional Chicago approach.

Like many of the interactionists, Kuhn never published a truly unified work. The closest may be C. A. Hickman and Manford Kuhn's *Individuals, Groups, and Economic Behavior*, published in 1956.[14] (For an excellent short synthesis see Charles Tucker's critique.)[15]

Kuhn's theoretical premises are consistent with Mead's thought. Kuhn conceives of the basis of all

14. C. A. Hickman and Manford Kuhn, *Individuals, Groups, and Economic Behavior* (New York: Holt, Rinehart & Winston, 1956).
15. Charles Tucker, "Some Methodological Problems of Kuhn's Self Theory," *The Sociological Quarterly* 7 (1966): 345–58.

action as symbolic interaction. The child is socialized through interaction with others in the society into which he or she is born. The person has meaning for and thereby deals with objects in the environment through social interaction. To Kuhn the naming of an object is important, for naming is a way of conveying the object's meaning in communicable terms. Kuhn agrees with his colleagues that the individual is not a passive reactor but an active planner. He reinforces the view that individuals undertake self-conversations as part of the process of acting. Kuhn also stresses the importance of language in thinking and communicating.

Like Mead and Blumer, Kuhn discusses the importance of *objects* in the actor's world. The object can be any aspect of the person's reality: a thing, a quality, an event, or a state of affairs. The only requirement for something to become an object for a person is that the person name it, represent it symbolically. Reality for persons is the totality of their social objects. Kuhn agrees with other interactionists that meaning is socially derived. Meaning is assigned to an object from group norms regulating how people deal with the object in question.

A second concept important to Kuhn is the *plan of action*. A plan of action is a person's total behavior pattern toward a given object, including whether to seek or avoid it, how the object is thought to behave (since this determines how the person will behave toward the object), and feelings about the object as it is defined. Attitudes constitute a subset of the plan of action. Attitudes are verbal statements that act as blueprints for one's behavior. The attitude indicates the end toward which action will be directed as well as the evaluation of the object. Because attitudes are verbal statements, they can be observed and measured.

A third concept important to Kuhn is the *orientational other*. Orientational others are those who have been particularly influential in a person's life. They possess four qualities. First, they are people to whom the individual is emotionally and psychologically committed. Second, they are the ones who provide the person with general vocabulary, central concepts, and categories. Third, they provide the individual with the basic distinction between self and others, including one's perceived role differentiation. Fourth, the orientational others' communications continually sustain the individual's self-concept. Orientational others may be in the present or past, they may be present or absent. The important idea behind the concept is that the individual comes to see the world through interaction with *particular* other persons who have touched one's life in important ways.

Finally, we come to Kuhn's most important concept—the *self*. Kuhn's theory and method revolve around self, and it is in this area that Kuhn most dramatically extends symbolic interactionist thinking. Kuhn is primarily responsible for a technique known as the "twenty-statements" self-attitudes test. His rationale for developing this procedure is stated succinctly:

> If as we suppose, human behavior is *organized* and *directed*, and if, as we further suppose, the organization and direction are supplied by the individual's *attitudes toward himself*, it ought to be of crucial significance to social psychology to be able to identify and measure self-attitudes.[16]

A subject taking the "twenty-statements" test would be confronted with twenty blank spaces preceded by the following simple instructions:

> There are twenty numbered blanks on the page below. Please write twenty answers to the simple question, "Who am I?" in the blanks. Just give twenty different answers to this question. Answer as if you were giving the answers to yourself, not to somebody else. Write the answers in the order that they occur to you. Don't worry about logic or "importance." Go along fairly fast, for time is limited.[17]

There are a number of potential ways to analyze the responses from this test, with each method tapping a different aspect of self. Here are Kuhn's primary theoretical formulations. First, the self-conception is seen as the individual's plans of action toward the self as an object. This self-concept consists of the individual's identities (roles and statuses), interests and aversions, goals, ideologies,

16. Manford Kuhn and Thomas McPartland, "An Empirical Investigation of Self-Attitudes," *American Sociological Review* 19 (1954): 68.
17. Ibid., p. 69.

and self-evaluations. Such self-conceptions are anchoring attitudes, for they act as one's most common frame of reference for judging other objects. All subsequent plans of action stem primarily from the self-concept.

Two major aspects of the self may be termed the ordering variable and the locus variable. The *ordering variable* is the relative salience of identifications the individual possesses. It is observable in the order of statements listed by the subject in the "twenty-statements" task. For example, if the person lists "Baptist" a great deal higher than "father," the researcher may conclude that the person identifies more readily with religious affiliation than with family affiliation. The *locus variable* is the extent to which the subject in a general way tends to identify with consensual groupings rather than idiosyncratic, subjective qualities.

In scoring the self-attitude test, the analyst may place statements in one of two categories. A statement may be said to be *consensual* if it consists of a discrete group or class identification, such as student, girl, husband, Baptist, from Chicago, premed, daughter, oldest child, studying engineering. Other statements are not descriptions of commonly agreed-on categories. Examples of *subconsensual* responses are happy, bored, pretty, good student, too heavy, good wife, interesting. The number of statements in the consensual group is the individual's locus score.

The idea of locus is important to Kuhn:

Persons vary over a rather wide range in the relative volume of consensual and subconsensual components in their self-conceptions. It is in this finding that our empirical investigation has given the greatest advance over the purely deductive and more or less literary formulations of George Herbert Mead.[18]

The conflict between the Chicago and Iowa schools is apparent. In fact, the work of Kuhn and his associates has become so estranged from mainstream symbolic interactionism that it has lost its support among those who espouse the basic tenets of the movement. Kuhn's methods simply are not adequate for investigating *processual* behavior, an essential element of interaction. As a result a group

18. Ibid., p. 76.

of followers, who believe in both the central ideas of symbolic interactionism and the expressed need to examine social life in concrete ways, has emerged as the "new" Iowa School. One of its leaders, Carl Couch, describes the situation:

By the mid-1960s most of us affiliated with Kuhn had become disenchanted with the use of the TST [twenty-statements test] and allied instruments. There was an increasing awareness that this set of procedures was not generating the data required for serious testing, revision, and elaboration of the theory. Some turned to naturalistic observation. . . . Some gave up the search; others foundered.[19]

Couch and his associates began studying the structure of coordinated behavior by using videotaped sequences. They have produced research on how interaction begins (openings) and ends (closings), how disagreements are negotiated, and how unanticipated consequences that block achievement of interaction objectives are accounted for. By studying these areas, they attempt to isolate general principles of symbolic interaction. Such principles may form the basis for a grounded theory of symbolic interaction in the future.[20]

Criticism of Symbolic Interactionism

Although many specific objections have been raised against symbolic interactionism, for the most part they can be combined into three major criticisms.[21] First, symbolic interactionism is said to be nonempirical. That is, one cannot readily translate its concepts into observable, researchable units. Second, it is said to be overly restrictive in the

19. Carl J. Couch, "Symbolic Interaction and Generic Sociological Principles" (Paper presented at the Symposium on Symbolic Interaction, Boston, 1979), p. 9.

20. This work is summarized in Carl J. Couch and Robert Hintz (eds.), *Constructing Social Life* (Champaign, Ill.: Stipes Publishing Co., 1975); and Clark McPhail, "Toward a Theory of Collective Behavior," (Paper presented at the Symposium on Symbolic Interaction, Columbia, South Carolina, 1978). See also Carl Couch, "Studying Social Processes," (Videotaped presentation, University of Iowa Media Center, Iowa City, 1984).

21. For reviews of specific objections to symbolic interactionism, see Jerome G. Manis and Bernard N. Meltzer, "Appraisals of Symbolic Interactionism," in Manis and Meltzer, *Symbolic Interaction*, pt. IV, pp. 393–440; Bernard N. Meltzer, John Petras, and Larry Reynolds, *Symbolic Interactionism: Genesis, Varieties, and Criticism* (London: Routledge & Kegan Paul, 1975).

variables it takes into account. Critics have charged that it ignores crucial psychological variables on one end and societal variables on the other. Third, it uses concepts in an inexact, inconsistent way. Let us look at each of these objections more closely. In doing so, we will relate the objections to the categories for evaluating theory outlined in Chapter 2.

The first major criticism of symbolic interactionism has broad implications. Despite Blumer's protests to the contrary, critics maintain that in actual practice the researcher does not know what to look for in observing interactionist concepts in real life. This problem seems to stem from the vague, intuitive claims of early interactionists. What is mind, for example? How can this concept be observed? We already have noted Kuhn's failure to operationalize interactionist concepts without giving up its assumptions about the process nature of behavior. Most basically, this criticism questions the *appropriateness* of symbolic interactionism to lead to a more complete understanding of everyday behavior. As such, critics believe it to be more appropriately social philosophy, which may guide our thinking about events, but which provides little concrete conceptualization for explaining the events. John Lofland's criticism is especially biting. He claims that interactionists participate in three main activities: "doctrinaire reiteration of the master's teachings, . . . [making] slightly more specific the general imagery, . . . [and connecting] descriptive case studies and interactionism.[22]

As a result of this alleged failure, symbolic interactionism is not thought to be adequately *heuristic*. It has generated few testable hypotheses, and little research has been produced. Interactionist scholars thus have been unable to elaborate and expand their thinking. Carl Couch, a leading proponent (and house critic) of the movement, points out that interactionists do engage in research, but that their observations do not cast light on the theory's key concepts, making revision and elaboration diffi-

cult. Couch believes this circumstance need not be so, and the "new" Iowa tradition has emerged out of a need for interactionists to do "serious sociological work."[23]

The second major criticism is that interactionism has either ignored or downplayed important explanatory variables. Critics say it leaves out the emotions of the individual on one end and societal organization on the other. These arguments as a whole make clear that interactionism is overly restrictive in *scope*. To cover as much of social life as it pretends to do, interactionism must take into account social structures as well as individual feelings. The problem is not one merely of scope, of course; it casts doubt on the *validity* of the tradition as well.

The failure of symbolic interactionism to deal with social organization is a major concern for interactionists. Social organization or structure removes individual prerogative, a highly valued idea in old-style interactionism. Social structure is normally a matter of power, and interactionists have been loath to admit to power inequality. However, the concept of power can be investigated from an interactionist perspective, and since about 1965 several research programs have begun to look at power.[24]

Less attention has been paid to work in the area of emotions. Interactionists now generally agree that feelings have been neglected by symbolic interactionism, although they claim that interactionism is not antithetical to the study of feeling or affect.

The third general criticism of symbolic interactionism is that its concepts are not used consistently. As a result such concepts as *I, me, self, role*, and *others* are vague. However, we must keep in mind that symbolic interactionism is not a unified theory. Rather, it is a general framework, and as we have seen, it has different versions. Therefore, although this is a valid criticism of early interactionism, it is not a fair picture of the movement today.

---

22. John Lofland, "Interactionist Imagery and Analytic Interruptus," in *Human Nature and Collective Behavior*, ed. Tamotsu Shibutani (Englewood Cliffs, N.J.: Prentice-Hall, 1970), p. 37.

23. Couch, "Symbolic Interaction."
24. This line of work is discussed in Peter M. Hall, "Structuring Symbolic Interaction: Communcation and Power," in *Communciation Yearbook 4*, ed. Dan Nimmo (New Brunswick, N.J.: Transaction Books, 1980), pp. 49–60.

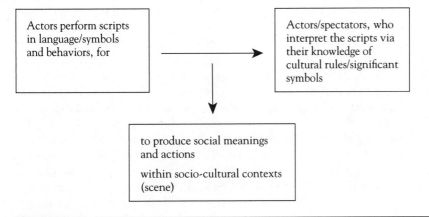

Figure 6-1   Dramaturgical model of society.

Interactionists have not been daunted by their critics. The movement has adjusted and matured. It is too early to tell what will happen to symbolic interactionism, although it appears that the grand movement will be replaced by a series of middle-range theories that provide concrete explanations of social behavior consistent with the general tenets of old-line symbolic interactionism. Rules theory (Chapter 7) shows promise for filling this gap.

Dramatism

The so-called dramaturgical movement is closely aligned with symbolic interactionism and has been heavily influenced by it. The dramaturgists see people as actors on a metaphorical stage playing out roles in interaction with others. Bruce Gronbeck sketches the basic idea of dramatism, as shown in Figure 6-1.[25] Here action is seen as performance, or the use of symbols to present a story or script to interpreters. In the process of performance, meanings and actions are produced within a scene or socio-cultural context.

In this sense, several theorists might be termed dramaturgical, but dramaturgical theory lacks the

unity required to be called a school. This section reviews the work of three very different dramaturgical theories. The first is the landmark theory of symbols by Kenneth Burke. The second is the influential role theory of Erving Goffman. The third is the convergence theory of Ernest Bormann.

The Dramatism of Burke

Kenneth Burke has written widely in many areas: from creative writing, to literary and rhetorical criticism, to social psychology, to linguistic analysis. Burke's concepts are not derived from the work of Mead and the other early sociologists. Some of his most important works, in fact, appeared concurrently with the publication of Mead's ideas. On the other hand, it would be incorrect to exclude Burke from the mainstream of symbolic interactionist thought, for while he has maintained his independence, his theory is highly consistent with the others presented in this chapter.

Kenneth Burke is no doubt a giant among symbol theorists. He has written profusely over a period of fifty years, and his theory is the most comprehensive of all the interactionists. Hugh Duncan wrote, "It may be said without exaggeration that anyone writing today on communication, however 'original' he may be, is echoing something said by Burke."[26] Burke has published eight major books,

25. Adapted from Bruce E. Gronbeck, "Dramaturgical Theory and Criticism: The State of the Art (or Science?)," *The Western Journal of Speech Communication* 44 (1980): 317.

26. Hugh Duncan, "Communication in Society," *Arts in Society* 3 (1964): 105.

spanning from 1931 to 1966.[27] A number of scholars have provided written interpretations of Burke's ideas.[28] In surveying Burke's communication theory, we will begin with a summary of his concept of dramatism; then we will turn to his central concepts of humanity, language, and communication; and finally we will sketch Burke's method.

Burke sees the act as the basic concept in dramatism. His view of human action is consistent with that of Mead, Blumer, and Kuhn. Specifically, Burke distinguishes between *action* and *motion*. All objects and animals in the universe can be said to possess motion, but only human beings have action. Action consists of purposeful, voluntary behaviors of individuals. *Dramatism* is the study of action in this sense; the study of motion is *mechanism*. Burke believes that a dramatistic view of people is needed in all of the "human" disciplines, for human behavior cannot be properly understood without it. With this perspective let us look at Burke's seminal ideas.

Burke views the individual as a biological and neurological being, who possesses all of the animalistic characteristics of lower species. Consistent with Mead, Burke distinguishes humans by their symbol-using behavior, the ability to act. People are symbol-creating, symbol-using, and symbol-misusing animals. They create symbols to name things and situations; they use symbols for communication; and they often abuse symbols—misuse them to their disadvantage. Burke's view of symbols is broad, including an array of linguistic and nonverbal elements as well. Especially intriguing for Burke is the notion that a person can symbolize symbols. One can talk about speech and can write about words. This second-level activity is a distinguishing characteristic of symbol use.

In addition Burke sees people as instrument creators. They create a variety of mechanical and social tools that, unlike lower animals, separate them

from their natural condition. People filter reality through the symbolic screen. For an animal reality just is, but for humans reality is mediated through symbols. Burke agrees with Mead that language functions as the vehicle for action. Because of the social need for people to cooperate in their actions, language arises and shapes behavior. Language, as seen by Burke, is always emotionally loaded. No word can be affectively neutral. As a result a person's attitudes, judgments, and feelings invariably are in that person's language. Language is by nature selective and abstract, focusing attention on particular aspects of reality at the expense of others. While language is economical, it is also ambiguous. Further, language is formal in that it tends to follow certain patterns or forms.

An overriding consideration for all of Burke's work is his concept of guilt. The term *guilt* is Burke's all-purpose word for any feeling of tension within a person: anxiety, embarrassment, self-hatred, disgust, and so forth. For Burke guilt is a condition caused only in humans by their symbol-using nature. He identifies three interrelated sources of guilt arising out of language. The first is *the negative*. Through language people moralize (animals do not). They construct a myriad of rules and proscriptions. Now, these rules are never entirely consistent. In following one rule, you necessarily are breaking another, creating guilt.

The second reason for guilt is the *principle of perfection*, or categorical guilt. People are sensitive to their failings. Human beings are able to imagine (through language) a state of perfection. Then, by their very nature, they spend their lives striving for whatever degree of this perfection they set for themselves. Guilt arises as a result of the discrepancy between the real and the ideal.

A third reason for guilt is the *principle of hierarchy*. In seeking order, people structure society in social pyramids or hierarchies (social ratings, social orderings). This ranking, of course, is a symbolic phenomenon. Competitions and divisions result among classes and groups in the hierarchy, and guilt results. For Burke guilt is the primary motive behind all action and communication: We communicate to purge our guilt.

27. See Bibliography for a listing of Burke's works.

28. For a comprehensive overview on Kenneth Burke, see William Rueckert (ed.), *Critical Responses to Kenneth Burke* (Minneapolis: University of Minnesota Press, 1969). For a brief and very clear summary, see Sonja K. Foss, Karen A. Foss, and Robert Trapp, *Contemporary Perspectives on Rhetoric* (Prospect Heights, Ill.: Waveland Press, 1985), pp. 153–88.

In discussing communication Burke uses several inseparable terms: persuasion, identification, consubstantiality, communication, and rhetoric. Let us see how these concepts are integrated in his theory. The underlying concept behind Burke's ideas on communication is that of *substance*, or in Burke's words the doctrine of substance. Substance is the general nature, fundamentals, or essence of any thing. Substance must be viewed in holistic terms; it is not a mere summation of the parts or aspects of the thing in consideration. Each person is distinct, possessing separate substance. Crucial to Burke's theory is the understanding that the substances of any two persons always overlap to some extent. The overlapping is not perfect, though, and thus prevents ideal communication. Whatever communication occurs between individuals is a direct function of their *consubstantiality* (sharing of common substance). Consubstantiality, or commonality, allows for communication because of the *shared meaning* it creates for the symbols used. When Barney and Joe are relaxing next to the swimming pool on a warm summer morning, they communicate with one another in a free and understanding manner because they share meanings for the language in use. They are, so to speak, consubstantial. On the other hand, when Mary and Bob ask a question of a harried bus boy in a Swiss restaurant, they may feel frustration because of their lack of shared meaning with this individual. To combine Mead and Burke, a significant symbol is one that allows for shared meaning through consubstantiality.

Another important concept of Burke is *identification*. As generally conceived, identification is the same as consubstantiality, or the sharing of substance. The opposite of identification is *division*. Division and the guilt it produces are the primary motives for communication. Through communication, identification is increased. In a spiraling fashion as identification increases, shared meaning increases, thereby improving understanding. Identification thus can be a means to persuasion or improved communication or an end in itself. Identification can be conscious or unconscious, planned or accidental. Three overlapping sources of identification exist among people. Material identification results from goods, possessions, and things. Idealistic identification results from ideas, attitudes, feelings, and values. Formal identification results from the form or arrangement of the act. If two people who are introduced shake hands, the conventional form of handshaking causes some identification to take place. Speakers can identify better with their audiences if they provide a form that is meaningful to the particular audience.

Before we proceed, let us look at a couple of cautions. First, identification is not an either-or occurrence but a matter of degree. Some consubstantiality will always be present merely by virtue of the shared humanness of any two persons. Identification can be great or small, and it can be increased or decreased by the actions of the communicators. Second, although identification and division exist side by side between any two persons, communication is more successful when identification is greater than division.

An interesting phenomenon that might seem to contradict Burke's view of identification is that people of lower strata in a hierarchy often identify with godlike persons at the top of the hierarchy, despite tremendous apparent division. This kind of identification can be seen, for example, in the mass following of a charismatic leader. Two overlapping factors explain its occurrence. First, individuals perceive in others an embodiment of the perfection they themselves strive for. Second, the mystery surrounding the charismatic person simultaneously tends to hide the division that exists. This phenomenon may be called identification through *mystification*.

In striving for happiness, each person adopts certain strategies of identification. Strategies are analogous to Kuhn's concept of plans of action. They are the tactics for living, the plans for communicating with another. Burke does not attempt to outline all available strategies for relating to others, because the list would be indefinitely long. One of the suggestions he makes for analyzing a rhetorical (communicative) act is to assess the strategies the communicators use to increase their identification. Burke provides a full-blown methodology for studying rhetorical acts. His method, in fact, has proved useful in areas such as rhetorical and literary criticism—the analysis of speeches, poems, books, and other rhetorical devices.

Burke's most basic methodological paradigm is the *dramatistic pentad*. Pentad, meaning a group of five, is in this sense an analytical framework for the most efficient study of any act. The first part is the *act*, what is done by the actor. It is a view of what the actor played, what was accomplished. The second part is the *scene*, the situation or setting in which the act was accomplished. It includes a view of the physical setting as well as the cultural and social milieu in which the act was carried out. The third component is the *agent*, the actor, including all that is known about the individual. The agent's substance reaches all aspects of his or her being, history, personality, demeanor, and any other contributing factors. The *agency*, the fourth component, is the means or vehicle the agent uses in carrying out the act. Agency may include channels of communication, devices, institutions, strategies, or messages. Fifth, the *purpose* is the reason for the act—the rhetorical goal, the hoped-for effect or result of the act.

For example, in writing a paper for your communication theory course, you, the agent, gather information and present it to the instructor (the act). Your course, your university, your library, your desk and room, the social atmosphere of your school, and more constitute the scene; the format of the paper itself is the agency. You have a variety of purposes, including, in all likelihood, getting a good grade.

Goffman's Social Approach

One of the most prolific sociologist of our day is Erving Goffman.[29] As a symbolic interactionist of the dramaturgical tradition, Goffman analyzes human behavior with a theatrical metaphor. The ordinary interaction setting is a stage. People are actors, structuring their performances to make impressions on audiences. According to Goffman, interpersonal communication is a pre

29. See Bibliography for a listing of Goffman's works.

sentation through which various aspects of the self are projected.

Goffman's observations of nearly twenty years are spread throughout his books, making synthesis difficult. Fortunately, Goffman provides a theoretical framework that outlines his general approach to human behavior.[30] He begins his reasoning with the assumption that the person faced with a situation must somehow make sense of or organize the events perceived. What emerges as an organized happening for the individual becomes that person's reality of the moment. This premise states that what is real for a person emerges in that person's *definition of the situation*.

A typical response of a person to a new situation is the question, What is going on here? The person's definition of the situation provides an answer. Often the first definition is not adequate and a rereading may be necessary, as in the case of a practical joke, a mistake, or a misunderstanding. The notion of a rereading is important for Goffman because he has observed that we are often deceived and deceive one another in our relations.

Several terms highlight Goffman's general approach. A *strip* is any arbitrary sequence of activity. A *frame* is a basic element of organization used in defining a situation. *Frame analysis* thus consists of examining the ways experience is organized for the individual. What the frame (or framework) does is allow the person to identify and understand otherwise meaningless events; it gives meaning to the ongoing activities of life. A *natural framework* is an unguided event of nature, with which the individual must cope. A *social framework*, on the other hand, is seen as controllable, guided by some intelligence. Thus humans have a sense of control when they enter the social frame. Of course, these two types of frameworks interrelate, since social beings act on and are in turn influenced by the natural

30. Erving Goffman, *Frame Analysis: An Essay on the Organization of Experience* (Cambridge: Harvard University Press, 1974). See also Jef Verhoeven, "Goffman's Frame Analysis and Modern Micro-Sociological Paradigms," in *Micro-Sociological Theory: Perspectives on Sociological Theory*, eds. H. J. Helle and S. N. Eisenstadt (Beverly Hills: Sage, 1985), pp. 71–100.

order. Goffman demonstrates the importance of frameworks for culture:

> Taken all together, the primary frameworks of a particular social group constitute a central element of its culture, especially insofar as understandings emerge concerning principal classes of schemata, the relations of these classes to one another, and the sum total of forces and agents that these interpretive designs acknowledge to be loose in the world.[31]

This view that a culture is defined in part by its definitions of situations is consistent not only with the central ideas of symbolic interactionism but with several theories of meaning presented in Chapter 6.

Primary framework is the basic unit of social life. Goffman points out in detail various ways that primary frames can be transformed or altered so that similar organizational principles are used to meet different ends. A game, for example, is modeled after a fight, but its purpose is different. A large portion of our frameworks are not primary at all, though they are modeled after primary events. Examples include games, drama, deceptions (both good and bad), experiments, and other fabrications. Indeed, what happens in ordinary interpersonal communication often involves this kind of secondary activity, including dramatic presentations, fabrications, and deceptions.

With this general theoretical approach as a base, we come to Goffman's central ideas on communication. Communication activities, like all activities, are viewed in the context of frame analysis. We will begin with the concept of *face engagement*.[32] A face engagement or *encounter* occurs when people engage in focused interaction. Persons in a face engagement have a single focus of attention and a perceived mutual activity. In unfocused interaction people in public places acknowledge the presence of one another without paying attention to one another. In such an unfocused situation the individual is normally accessible for encounter with others. Once an engagement begins, a mutual contract exists to continue the engagement to some kind of termination. During this time a relationship develops and is mutually sustained. Face engagements are both verbal and nonverbal, and the cues exhibited are important in signifying the nature of the relationship as well as a mutual definition of the situation.

People in face engagements of talk take turns presenting dramas to one another. Story telling— recounting past events—is a matter of impressing the listener by dramatic portrayal. This idea of presenting dramas is central to Goffman's overall theory.

> I am suggesting that often what talkers undertake to do is not to provide information to a recipient but to present dramas to an audience. Indeed, it seems that we spend most of our time not engaged in giving information but in giving shows. And observe, this theatricality is not based on mere displays of feelings or faked exhibitions of spontaneity or anything else by way of the huffing and puffing we might derogate by calling theatrical. The parallel between stage and conversation is much, much deeper than that. The point is that ordinarily when an individual says something, he is not saying it as a bold statement of fact on his own behalf. He is recounting. He is running through a strip of already determined events for the engagement of his listeners.[33]

In engaging others, the speaker presents a particular character to the audience. The person divides the self into a number of parts and like the stage actor presents this or that character in a particular engagement role. Thus in ordinary conversation we have the actor and the character, or the animator and the animation; the listener willingly is involved in the characterization being presented.

Of course, the individual has opportunities to present the self in situations other than conversation. Even in unfocused interactions, scenes are

31. Goffman, *Frame*, p. 27.
32. On the nature of face-to-face interaction, see Erving Goffman, *Encounters: Two Studies in the Sociology of Interaction* (Indianapolis: Bobbs-Merrill, 1961); *Behavior in Public Places* (New York: Free Press, 1963); *Interaction Ritual: Essays on Face-to-Face Behavior* (Garden City, N.Y.: Doubleday, 1967); and *Relations in Public* (New York: Basic Books, 1971).

33. Goffman, *Frame*, p. 508.

presented to others.[34] Goffman believes that the self is literally determined by these dramatizations. Here is how he explains the self:

> A correctly staged and performed scene leads the audience to impute a self to a performed character, but this imputation—this self—is a *product* of a scene that comes off, and is not a cause of it. The self, then, as a performed character, is not an organic thing that has a specific location, whose fundamental fate is to be born, to mature, and to die; it is a dramatic effect arising diffusely from a scene that is presented, and the characteristic issue, the crucial concern, is whether it will be credited or discredited.[35]

In attempting to define a situation, the person goes through a two-part process. First, the person needs information about the other people in the situation. Second, one needs to give information about oneself. This process of exchanging information enables people to know what is expected of them. Usually, this exchange occurs indirectly through observing the behavior of others and structuring one's own behavior to elicit impressions in others. Self-presentation is very much a matter of *impression management*. The person influences the definition of a situation by projecting a particular impression:

> He may wish them to think highly of him, or to think that he thinks highly of them, or to perceive how in fact he feels toward them or to obtain no clear-cut impression; he may wish to insure sufficient harmony so that the interaction can be sustained, or to defraud, get rid of, confuse, mislead, antagonize, or insult them.[36]

Since all participants in a situation project images, an overall definition of the situation emerges. This general definition is normally rather unified. Once the definition is set, moral pressure is created to maintain it by suppressing contradictions and doubts. A person may add to the projections but never contradict the image initially set. The very organization of society is based on this principle.

In consequence, when an individual projects a definition of the situation and thereby makes an implicit or explicit claim to be a person of a particular kind, he automatically exerts a moral demand upon the others, obliging them to value and treat him in the manner that persons of this kind have the right to expect. He also implicitly foregoes all claims to be things he does not appear to be and hence foregoes the treatment that would be appropriate for such individuals. The others find, then, that the individual has informed them as to what is and as to what they ought to see as the "is."[37]

If the presentation falters or is contradicted by later scenes, the consequence to the individual and to the social structure can be severe.

Bormann's Convergence Theory

Convergence theory, often known as fantasy theme analysis, is based on Robert Bales's research on small group communication.[38] Bales found that at moments of tension, groups will often become very *dramatic* and share stories or *fantasy themes*. Ernest Bormann applied this idea to rhetorical action in society at large.[39] Much of individuals' images of reality consists of narratives of how things are believed to be. These stories are created in symbolic interaction within small groups, and they are chained out from person to person and group to group.

Fantasy themes are part of larger dramas that are longer, more complicated stories called *rhetorical visions*. A rhetorical vision is essentially a view of how things have been, are, or will be. Rhetorical visions structure our sense of reality in areas that we cannot experience directly, but can only know by symbolic reproduction. Consequently, such vi-

34. The best sources on self-presentation are Erving Goffman, *The Presentation of Self in Everyday Life* (Garden City, N.Y.: Doubleday, 1959); and *Relations in Public.*
35. Goffman, *Presentation*, pp. 252–53.
36. Ibid., p. 3.

37. Ibid., p. 13.
38. Robert F. Bales, *Personality and Interpersonal Behavior* (New York: Holt, Rinehart & Winston, 1970).
39. Bormann's major works on fantasy theme analysis are *Communication Theory* (New York: Holt, Rinehart & Winston, 1980), pp. 184–90; *The Force of Fantasy: Restoring the American Dream* (Carbondale: Southern Illinois University Press, 1985); "Fantasy and Rhetorical Vision: The Rhetorical Criticism of Social Reality," *Quarterly Journal of Speech* 58 (1972): 396–407; and "Fantasy and Rhetorical Vision: Ten Years Later," *Quarterly Journal of Speech* 68 (1982): 288–305. See also John F. Cragan and Donald C. Shields, *Applied Communication Research: A Dramatistic Approach* (Prospect Heights, Ill.: Waveland Press, 1981).

sions give us an image of things in the past, in the future, or in faraway places; in large measure, these visions form a set of assumptions on which our knowledge is based.

Fantasy themes, and even the larger rhetorical visions, consist of *dramatis personae* (characters), a plotline, a scene, and sanctioning agents. The characters may be heroes, villains, and other supporting players. The plotline is the action or development of the story. The scene is the setting, including location, properties, and socio-cultural milieu. Finally, the sanctioning agent is a source that legitimizes the story. This source may be an authority who lends credibility to the story or authorizes its telling, a common belief in God or another sanctioning ideal like justice or democracy, or a situation or event that makes telling the story seem appropriate.

Rhetorical visions are never told in their entirety, but are built up by sharing associated fantasy themes. To grasp the entire vision, one must attend to the fantasy themes, since these comprise the content of conversation in groups of people when the vision is being created and chained out. Fantasy themes are recognizable by their quality of being repeated again and again. In fact, some themes are so frequently discussed and so well known within a particular group or community that the members no longer tell the whole episode. Instead, they abbreviate the telling of the fantasy theme by presenting just a "trigger" or *in-cue*. This is precisely what happens with an inside joke. Fantasy themes that develop to this point of familiarity are known as *fantasy types*—stock situations told over and over within a group.

As people come to share fantasy themes, the resulting rhetorical vision pulls them together and gives them a sense of identification with a shared reality. From the perspective of this theory, people *converge* or come to hold a common image as they share fantasy themes. In fact, shared rhetorical visions—and especially the use of fantasy types—can be taken as evidence that convergence has occurred.

Fantasy themes, therefore, constitute an important ingredient in persuasion. Public communica-

tors—in speeches, articles, books, films, and other media—often tap into or make use of the audience's predominant fantasy themes. Public communication can also add to or modify the rhetorical vision by amplifying, changing, or adding fantasy themes. The television film "The Day After," for example, effectively captured the public vision of nuclear war, including characters who were victims, a plot of destruction and mayhem, a scene of rubble and destruction, and a sanctioning agent of the undeniable threat of nuclear war.[40]

Criticism of Dramatism

The critical response to the three theorists summarized here has been copious and spirited, and it is not possible to review all of these viewpoints.[41] For a critique of dramaturgy in general, we will look at Bruce Gronbeck's summary statement.[42] First, dramatism is not a unified theory. It still remains basically an "interest group" or coalition of theories that share a metaphor rather than any particular set of theoretical terms or principles. The three theories chosen for this chapter illustrate this lack of coherence in the movement.

Burke's is the grandest and perhaps the most elaborate of the three theories covered here. This breadth and complexity has elicited both praise and blame. Some believe that it has opened vistas of great import; others believe that Burke's lack of focus has led to interminable confusion, if not exhaustion.

Goffman's ideas are perhaps least theoretical in that they are scattered and hard to assemble into a

40. For a sample fantasy theme analysis on the subject of nuclear war, see Karen A. Foss and Stephen W. Littlejohn, "*The Day After*: Rhetorical Vision in an Ironic Frame," *Critical Studies in Mass Communication* 3 (1986): 317–36.

41. For a summary of criticisms of Burke, see Foss, Foss, and Trapp, *Contemporary Perspectives*, pp. 183–88. For criticism of Goffman, see Stephen W. Littlejohn, *Theories of Human Communication*, 2nd ed. (Belmont, Calif.: Wadsworth, 1983), pp. 180–81; and Randall Collins, "Erving Goffman and the Development of Modern Social Theory," in *The View From Goffman*, ed. Jason Ditton (New York: St. Martin's Press, 1980), pp. 170–209. For criticism of Bormann, see Bormann, "Ten Years Later," and G. P. Mohrmann, "An Essay on Fantasy Theme Criticism," *Quarterly Journal of Speech* 68 (1982): 109–32.

42. Gronbeck, "Dramaturgical Theory."

single rubric. His numerous writings are insightful and interesting, but hard to integrate. He rarely uses the same vocabulary twice, and until the end of his career, seemed more interested in pointing out idiosyncratic observations than in making a general statement. Fortunately, his final work *Frame Analysis* provided an overall scheme with which to integrate a lifetime of work.

Bormann's theory is perhaps the most clearly focused of the three. It too has received both praise and blame. This theory is more recent than the other two, developing between about 1972 and 1982. During that period there was much terminological confusion, but Bormann and his associates also put a good deal of work into clarifying and elaborating the vocabulary of fantasy theme analysis. Bormann's work—and that of his critics and adherents—fulfills one of Gronbeck's suggestions: that the field of communication work to elaborate, clarify, and develop the concepts and terms of dramaturgy.

The second general critique of dramaturgy is its apparent confusion of the dramatic metaphor and reality. Some critics have been concerned about the confusion between the analogy and that being analogued. What are the real and central processes being modeled in the analogy? Since various dramatistic theories have borrowed from stage metaphors to represent different things, confusion remains. For example, Burke talks about the act, agent, scene, agency, and purpose of any rhetorical act, while Bormann talks about the same elements within the context of a rhetorical act (a fantasy theme). In Burke's case, the pentad seems to be a metaphor, while Bormann's use of drama seems to be an actual occurrence.

Third, the dramaturgical analysis is generally recognized as highly useful in understanding social processes. Some of the uses include:

1. describing reactions to public communications
2. clarifying the active role of audiences
3. understanding how messages appeal to and are used differently by various audiences
4. analyzing the deep meaning structures beneath surface enactments of the actors in rhetorical and social situations

The three theories reviewed here illustrate these advantages very well.

Integration

Communication is the thread with which the fabric of society is held together. A culture's reality is defined in terms of its meanings, which arise from interaction within social groups. Individuals' meanings for words and symbols, objects, and people are determined by the ways in which symbols are used to define objects and people in actual communication situations. Social institutions are nothing more than grand networks of interaction in which common meanings are generated. The self as an object is especially important; the self too is defined in terms of symbols and meanings derived from one's interaction with other people.

As people interact in society, they perform in ways that make social life very much like a drama. They act within scenes, they make presentations, they represent characters, and they tell stories. These communication activities create, sustain, and change the very nature of reality in a group or culture.

Seven

Theories of Cultural and Social Reality

Chapters 6 and 7 should be read as a unit: The theories discussed in this chapter are tightly intertwined with those of Chapter 6. Interactional approaches, represented most generally by symbolic interactionism, deal with the ways in which our understandings, meanings, norms, roles, and rules are worked out interactively in relationships. Chapter 6 explores some of the general concepts relevant to that process; here we take a look at theories that describe more exactly some of the conventions that emerge from interaction and the nature of the process in which those understandings are developed. As a group these conventions constitute the social reality of a group or culture.

People communicate to interpret events and to share those interpretations with others. Interactional theories claim that reality is constructed socially, that it is a product of communication. This idea of the social construction of reality comes from an important intellectual tradition of our century, a tradition that provides a conceptual backdrop for all of the theories to be covered in this chapter.

Communication and the Social Construction of Reality

The idea of the social construction of reality was expressed by philosopher Alfred Schutz in these words:

The world of my daily life is by no means my private world but is from the outset an intersubjective one,
shared with my fellow men, experienced and interpreted by others: in brief, it is a world common to all of us. The unique biographical situation in which I find myself within the world at any moment of my existence is only to a very small extent of my own making.[1]

Our meanings and understandings, in short, arise from our communication with others. This notion of reality is deeply embedded in sociological thought; its most well-known proponents are Peter Berger and Thomas Luckmann in their treatise *The Social Construction of Reality*.[2] With the impetus from symbolic interactionism and the foundations of the work of Schutz and Berger and Luckmann, the social construction of reality has become a respectable and popular idea in the social sciences. Kenneth Gergen has labeled it "the social constructionist movement."[3] According to Gergen, the movement is concerned with the processes by which individuals account for the world and their experience. It is based on four assumptions:

1. The world does not present itself objectively to the observer, but is known through human experience, which is largely influenced by language.

1. Alfred Schutz, *On Phenomenology and Social Relations* (Chicago: University of Chicago Press, 1970), p. 163.
2. Peter L. Berger and Thomas Luckmann, *The Social Construction of Reality: A Treatise in the Sociology of Knowledge* (New York: Doubleday, 1966).
3. Kenneth J. Gergen, "The Social Constructionist Movement in Modern Psychology," *American Psychologist*, 40 (1985): 266–75; see also *Toward Transformation in Social Knowledge* (New York: Springer-Verlag, 1982).

2. The linguistic categories through which reality is apprehended are situational in that they emerge from the social interaction within a group of people at a particular time and in a particular place.

3. How reality is understood at a given moment is determined by the conventions of communication in force at that time. The stability or instability of knowledge, therefore, depends more upon the vicissitudes of social life than on any objective reality outside of human experience.

4. Socially constructed understandings of reality shape many other important aspects of life. How we think and behave in ordinary life is largely a matter of how we understand our realities.[4]

Among the most important aspects of social life is the definition of self as it relates to other people. We turn now to two theories that emphasize the role of communication in self-definition.

Harré's Personal and Social Being

Among contemporary social scientists who have made constructionist assumptions central to their work is Rom Harré. Harré has developed a theory of how self is both a product and a precursor of communication. Recognizing that self is both individual and social, Harré places great emphasis on the ways in which individuals account for and explain their own behavior in particular episodes.

Harré and his colleague Paul Secord are responsible for *ethogeny*, which is the study of how people understand their actions *within specific episodes*.[5] An episode is a predictable sequence of acts that all parties define as an event with a beginning and an end. Having dinner, making a speech, a commencement ceremony, an argument, driving to work, and negotiating an agreement could all be defined as episodes. What the episode itself means to the participants and how they understand the various acts that comprise the episode are the focus of ethogeny. Further, the ordinary language that people use to describe and explain an episode reflects their meaning of that episode.

The social group or community, through interaction, creates "theories" to explain the experience of reality.[6] A group's theory conceptualizes the experience and includes a *scenario* of what the logical outcome of a particular action within an episode will be. Harré describes the scenario as a "structured template" of the course of action anticipated in the episode. For example, two people in a relationship may tell you that they are "in love." They have a theory of what love is and how it should be acted out. The theory becomes explicit when the communicators are required to describe, explain, or account for their actions.

The meanings attached to the events of an episode give rise to rules that guide the participants' actions within the episode. Participants know how to act because of the rules in force at a particular moment. (The concept of rules is especially important in constructionist thought and is explained in detail later in the chapter.) For example, our hypothetical couple may engage in the episode of "making love," which consists of a series of acts with a beginning and an end, which have meaning and an anticipated course. The episode of making love will be different for other couples, who have their own definitions of what it means to make love and the action sequence required.

Symbolic interactionism, as explained in Chapter 6, emphasizes the meaning of the self. It is precisely this problem with which Harré has been so centrally concerned in his theoretical work.[7] Like any other experience, the self too is structured by a personal theory. That is, the individual learns to understand the self by employing a theory, or cluster of theories, that conceptualizes who he or she is believed to be. Harré explains the self in these terms: "Everything that appears to each of us as the intimate structure of our personal being, I believe to have its source in a socially sustained and collectively imposed cluster of theories."[8]

One's notion of self as a person, then, is a theo-

4. Gergen, "Social Constructionist," 266–69.
5. Rom Harré and Paul Secord, *The Explanation of Social Behavior* (Totowa, N.J.: Littlefield, Adams & Co., 1972).

6. Rom Harré, *Social Being: A Theory for Social Psychology* (Totowa, N.J.: Rowman and Littlefield, 1979).
7. *Social Being*; see also *Personal Being: A Theory for Individual Psychology* (Cambridge: Harvard University Press, 1984).
8. *Personal Being*, p. 21.

retical concept, derived from the ideas of personhood embodied in the culture and expressed through communication. Here Harré distinguishes between person and self. The *person* is the publicly visible being and carries all of the attributes and characteristics of persons in general within the culture or social group. The *self* is one's private notion of his or her own unity as a person. Concepts of personhood are public, while concepts of selfhood, though they may be expressed to others, are ultimately private. The character of persons is governed by the group's theory of personhood; the self is governed by the individual's theory of his or her own being as one member of the culture. Personal being, thus, is two-sided, consisting of a social being (person) and a personal being (self). For example, many traditional cultures conceptualize the person as the embodiment of a role (for instance, mother, father, priest, worker). People in general are seen as manifestations of these roles. An individual within the culture, on the other hand, will assign a particular nature, feeling, and character to oneself, as an individual within the culture.

One's self theory, like a personhood theory, is learned through a history of interaction with other people. Throughout life people learn that individuals have different perspectives on the world, and the self is an autonomous actor with the power to do things. Harré shows how dimensions of the person that appear private and personal are actually socially derived. Our thoughts, intentions, and emotions are all cast in terms that are learned through social interaction. Precisely what perspectives individuals take, the nature of those perspectives, and the degree and character of personal powers depend upon one's self theory and are highly variable from one culture to another. For example, most western industrialized cultures stress theories of self that perceive individuals as whole, undivided, and independent entities. The Javanese, in contrast, see themselves as being divided into two rather independent parts—an inside of feelings and an outside of observed behaviors.[9]

The self consists of a set of elements that can be

9. Clifford Geertz, *Local Knowledge: Further Essays in Interpretive Anthropology* (New York: Basic Books, 1983), p. 60.

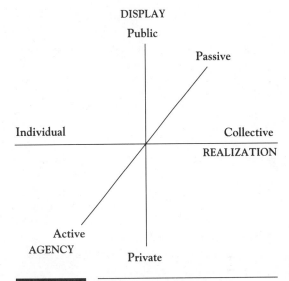

Figure 7-1   Dimensions of personhood.

Adapted from *Personal Being: A Theory for Individual Psychology*, by Rom Harré. Copyright © 1984 by Harvard University Press. Reprinted by permission of the publisher.

viewed spatially along three dimensions. These dimensions are illustrated in Figure 7-1.

The placement of an element in this grid depends upon one's theory of self. The first dimension is *display*, or whether an aspect of the self is displayed publicly or remains private. For example, with one theory of self, emotions may be kept relatively private, while personality may be public. The second dimension is *realization* or source. This dimension involves the degree to which some feature of the self is believed to come from within the individual, as opposed to evolving from a group. Elements of a self that are believed to come from the person are *individually realized*, while those elements believed to derive from the person's relationship to the group are *collectively realized*. For example, a self theory might treat "purpose" as individually realized because it seems to be something that individuals have on their own. On the other hand, "cooperation" may be collectively realized because it seems to be something that one can only do as a member of a group.

Agency is the degree of active power attributed to the self. Active elements (like "speaking" or "driving") are contrasted with passive elements (like "listening" or "riding"). Individual selves can be drastically different from one another—not only in the concepts used to define self, but also in the placement of these concepts in the three-dimensional scheme. For example, one theory might treat "emotions" as privately displayed, individually realized, and passive; another theory might treat emotions as public, collective, and active.

Although individuals have very different theories of self, all self theories have three elements in common. First, they all contain a sense of *self-consciousness*. This means that one thinks of oneself as an object. When I think about myself or talk about myself, I am displaying consciousness of myself as a person. There are, then, two senses of the word *I*—the self that knows and the self that is known about. Consider the following statement: "I_2 know that I_2 am afraid." I_1 reflects one's sense of being aware, and I_2 reflects one's sense of being the object of fear. The second element of all self theories is *agency*. The self is always seen as having certain powers to do things. One sees oneself as an agent, capable of having intentions and actions. Finally, the third element of the self is *autobiography*, or identity as a person with a history and a future. My *agency* is evident whenever I plan something, and my *autobiography* is apparent whenever I tell someone about myself.

Shotter's Social Accountability

John Shotter presents a theory of communication that is consistent with that of Harré; his theory also provides a useful extension of constructionist thinking into the subjects of responsibility and morality.[10] Shotter believes that human experience cannot be separated from communication. Our speech both reflects and creates our experience of reality. Central to this link between communication and experience is the process of making

accounts. Shotter's *social accountability thesis* is expressed as follows:

> . . . our understanding and our experience of our reality are constituted for us very largely by the ways in which we must talk in our attempts to account for the things and events within it . . . our ways of accounting for things have a coercive quality to them; only if we make sense of things in certain approved ways can we be accounted by others in our society as competent, responsible members of it.[11]

The communicator sees the self as having the power to act, yet feels constrained by rules of action. Rules may be followed or broken, but in any case, one is called upon to explain (account for) actions on the basis of rules and/or exceptions. Because of the presence of rules and our personal powers to follow them or to break them, we must think through and plan our actions, and these plans are largely framed in terms of potential accounts.

Consistent with the principles of constructionism, Shotter believes that people are constantly assigning meaning to and making sense of their experiences; they attempt to figure out "what the event means, what it is the means to, what it indicates, points to, specifies, etc."[12] The meanings assigned to an event are closely tied to the language used to account for the event in communication among participants. In short, "our understanding and our experience of our reality is constituted for us very largely by the ways in which we must talk in our attempts . . . to account for it."[13]

The relationship between communication (talking and making accounts) and the experience of reality constitutes a loop: Communication determines how reality is experienced, and the experience of reality affects communication. This relationship is illustrated in Figure 7-2.[14]

Shotter takes what he calls an *ecological approach*. Much like Harré, Shotter believes that the individual and the society are inseparable. Persons are not independent entities: "Attention is not concentrated upon the supposed relation between people's

---

10. John Shotter, *Social Accountability and Selfhood* (Oxford: Basil Blackwell, 1984).

11. Ibid., p. xi.
12. Ibid., p. 159.
13. Ibid., p. 173.
14. Ibid., p. 140.

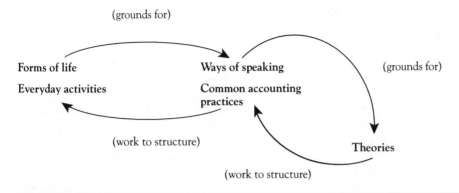

(grounds for)

Forms of life

Everyday activities

Ways of speaking

Common accounting
practices

(grounds for)

(work to structure)

Theories

(work to structure)

Figure 7-2   Communication–experience loop.

Adapted from *Social Accountability and Selfhood*, by John Shotter. Copyright © 1984 by Basil Blackwell Publishers. Reprinted by permission of the publisher.

'outer' behavior and their 'inner' workings, for it is not focused upon individuals at all, but upon the relations between people."[15] The overall milieu is an *Umwelt*, which is essentially a *moral world* of rights, duties, privileges, and obligations. The moral framework of human experience is expressed in and through communication: "To preserve their autonomy, people must be able to account, not only for their actions, but also for themselves, i.e. who and what they are."[16]

A Critical Response and Alternative Theory

Although the social construction of reality theory has become popular, it remains controversial because it conflicts with the commonsense notion that reality is objective and independent, an idea deeply rooted in western thought. Perhaps the most comprehensive critique of constructionism in recent communication literature is that of Richard Cherwitz and James Hikins.[17] These authors argue that although rhetoric is important in the communication and demonstration of truth, reality itself is independent from human subjectivity. Putting it bluntly, they remind us that nobody would test the social construction of reality by "venturing into the path of an oncoming locomotive on the assumption

that the mind could alter the unpleasant consequences of the ensuing collision."[18] The locomotive, in other words, is not socially constructed!

Cherwitz and Hikins put forth five arguments against the constructionist thesis. The first is the *naive argument*, which states simply that nobody really acts as though reality is socially constructed. We must assume in our daily actions that there is an independent reality. In other words, watch out for the train. Second, is the *evolutionary argument*: If one believes that human experience is evolving from prehistoric times to the present, an objective sense of reality is required as a baseline with which to measure this evolution. Third, Cherwitz and Hikins argue from *logical consistency*, stating that without an outside reality, there is no way to test the validity or quality of socially constructed knowledge. Fourth, the *anthropological argument* claims that despite human variability, there is in fact much commonality across cultures, to the point that "cross-cultural understanding can and does occur."[19] Finally, the *argument from persuasive discourse* advances the thesis that communication itself results in an undeniably objective world of discourse, speakers, audiences, and responses. In other words, the communication that supposedly "constructs" reality cannot be understood without reference to its own reality.

15. Ibid., p. 94.
16. Ibid., p. 152.
17. Richard A. Cherwitz and James W. Hikins, *Communication and Knowledge: An Investigation in Rhetorical Epistemology* (Columbia: University of South Carolina Press, 1986).

18. Ibid., p. 19.
19. Ibid., p. 121.

These authors do not deny the importance of communication and language to reality. In fact, they advance a theory of their own in which rhetoric takes a central role in the discovery, examination, and dissemination of truth. Truth claims describe reality, but these descriptions always occur through language. Communication is used to differentiate among things, to make inferences, to promote and preserve ideas, to evaluate claims, and to express perspectives on reality.

In Chapters 5 and 6, several references have been made to rules. Let us turn now to a more complete discussion of this topic.

The Rules Approach to Communication

In the history of ideas, two different strands of thought sometimes are found to be consistent with one another, converging to the benefit of both. Each tradition enhances or improves the other. Such is the case with symbolic interactionism and rules theory. Symbolic interactionism tells us of the importance of interaction and meaning in human experience; the rules approach gives form and substance to this interaction-meaning cycle. Susan Shimanoff discusses the importance of rules in symbolic interaction:

> In order for communication to exist, or continue, two or more interacting individuals must share rules for using symbols. Not only must they have rules for individual symbols, but they must also agree on such matters as how to take turns at speaking, how to be polite or how to insult, to greet, and so forth. If every symbol user manipulated symbols at random, the result would be chaos rather than communication.[20]

Despite its diversity the rules approach is held together by certain common assumptions.[21] Al-
though these are not identical to the premises of symbolic interactionism, they are consistent with and add to the latter framework. The action principle, which is central to symbolic interactionist thought, generally is considered to be a primary assumption of the rules approach. Although some human activity is mechanical and determined by uncontrollable factors, the most important behaviors are considered to be actively initiated by the individual. People are thought to choose courses of action within situations to accomplish their intentions. This action principle is opposed to the motion principle, in which human behavior is seen as determined by prior causes. Rules theorists agree that the motion principle, which gives rise to laws of nature, is appropriate in the science of objects but that it is not useful for understanding human social life. For this reason the rule-governed approach to communication theory often is set in opposition to the law-governed approach.

Another basic assumption of most rules theories is that social behavior is structured and organized. Certain behaviors recur in similar situations. Social interaction patterns, however, vary in different settings. Although these patterns are organized, they are not universal, but highly contextual. Thus most rules theories emphasize the relationship between the way people act and the culture and situation wherein the action occurs. In fact, rules scholars criticize law-governed theories precisely because of their failure to reflect such variation.

Rules are considered to be the mechanism through which social action is organized. The structure of interaction can be understood in terms of the rules governing it. Rules affect the options available in a given situation. Because rules are thought to be contextual, they explain why people behave similarly in similar situations but differently in different situations.

The rules approach began in the field of phi-

---

20. Susan B. Shimanoff, *Communication Rules: Theory and Research* (Beverly Hills: Sage Publications, 1980), pp. 31–32.

21. The similarities and differences among rules theories are discussed in such sources as Donald P. Cushman, "The Rules Perspective as a Theoretical Basis for the Study of Human Communication," *Communication Quarterly* 25 (1977): 30–45; W.

Barnett Pearce, "Rules Theories of Communication: Varieties, Limitations, and Potentials" (Paper presented at the Speech Communication Association, New York City, 1980); Stuart J. Sigman, "On Communication Rules from a Social Perspective," *Human Communication Research*, 7 (1980): 37–51; and Shimanoff, *Communication Rules*.

losophy in what has become known as ordinary language philosophy. That tradition, spirited by Wittgenstein, Austin, Searle, and others, is discussed later in the chapter. Other fields of study have taken up the banner, including speech communication, anthropology, linguistics, psychology, and sociology.[22] For now, we will examine several approaches to rules and the definitions they employ.

Approaches to Rules

The rules perspective includes several definitions.[23] Barnett Pearce outlines three main groups of rule conceptions.[24]

Rule-following approach. In this view rules are seen simply as observed behavioral regularities. A recurring pattern is said to happen "as a rule." Pearce calls such rules weak laws because they are cast in the form of a statement of what is expected to happen under certain circumstances. This approach is highly descriptive but does not explain why particular patterns recur; it aims only to catalogue predictable behaviors. Linguistic theories typically are of this type, suggesting that speakers follow rules of grammar with a high degree of regularity. Of all approaches to rules, this group least supports the basic assumptions of the rules tradition.

Rule-governed approach. Here rules are beliefs about what should or should not be done to achieve an objective in a given situation. The rule-governed approach attempts to uncover people's intentions and to define the socially acceptable ways in which people accomplish their intentions. For example, if a person wishes to engage another person in conversation at a party and the other person is talking with someone else, one would approach the two individuals and not speak until recognized nonverbally. To interrupt or to break in too quickly would be a rules violation that could prevent the desired conversation from occurring. This approach presumes that people know the rules and have the power to follow or to violate them. It also assumes that people usually act consciously, intentionally, and rationally.

Rule-using approach. This view is consistent with the rule-governed approach except that it posits a more complex social situation. The actor potentially is confronted with a variety of rules for accomplishing various intentions. The actor chooses which rules to follow (or more properly, to use) in carrying out an intention. As a rules critic the individual reflects on rules, following some and discarding others. This approach thereby provides a basis for evaluating what choices a person makes in a social situation and even allows for people to create new options. It also enables the theorist to discuss communication competence by observing how well a person sorts through the matrix of objectives and rules to plan an interaction strategy. In a highly homogeneous situation, such as breaking into a cocktail party conversation, the rules are few and simple. Here the rule-governed approach suffices to explain what occurs. The broader rule-using approach is better suited for understanding the preparation of a speech, the organization of a meeting, the writing of a letter, and other heterogeneous rule situations.

Now that we have discussed the general nature of the rules approach, let us turn to some specific treatments of rules. The following section deals with ordinary language philosophy, one of the seminal theoretical areas behind the rules approach. Later we discuss three rules theories—Shimanoff's rule-governing theory, Smith's contingency rules theory of persuasion, and Pearce and Cronen's theory of the coordinated management of meaning.

Ordinary Language Philosophy

Ludwig Wittgenstein, a German philosopher, was the originator of ordinary language philosophy. His early works were based strongly in the formal

22. Shimanoff, *Communication Rules,* pp. 33–34, lists some of the seminal figures in these fields.

23. See Shimanoff, *Communication Rules,* for comparison of various definitions as well as a discussion of the differences among rules and other similar concepts, such as norm.

24. Pearce, "Rules Theories." See also Joan Ganz, *Rules: A Systematic Study* (Paris: Mouton, 1971).

structural tradition, but he repudiated this approach in one of the most dramatic turnarounds in modern philosophy.[25] He later taught that the meaning of language depends on the context of use. Further, single words by themselves are rarely meaningful. Language, as used in ordinary life, constitutes a *language game*. In other words, people follow rules for accomplishing verbal acts. Giving and obeying orders, asking and answering questions, describing events are examples of ordinary uses of language that follow rules and hence constitute language games.

While the philosophical groundwork of ordinary language philosophy was laid by Wittgenstein, J. L. Austin developed the basic concepts of what his protégé, John Searle, later called speech acts.[26]

Searle's theory of speech acts. Building on the foundation laid by Wittgenstein and Austin, John Searle developed the well-known theory of speech acts.[27] Although Searle is not solely responsible for speech act theory, he is clearly the leader of the movement, and his name is most often associated with the theory.

25. Wittgenstein's best-known early work was *Tractus Logico-Philosophicus* (London: Routledge & Kegan Paul, 1922); his later work, which forms the foundation for ordinary language philosophy, is *Philosophical Investigations* (Oxford: Basil Blackwell, 1953). I have relied on the excellent summary by David Silverman and Brian Torode, *The Material Word: Some Theories of Language and Its Limits* (London: Routledge & Kegan Paul, 1980). See also Richard Buttney, "The Ascription of Meaning: A Wittgensteinian Perspective," *Quarterly Journal of Speech* 72 (1986): 261–73; and Allan Janik and Stephen Toulmin, *Wittgenstein's Vienna* (New York: Simon & Schuster, 1973).

26. J. L. Austin, *How To Do Things With Words* (Cambridge: Harvard University Press, 1962); Austin, *Philosophy of Language* (Englewood Cliffs, N.J.: Prentice-Hall, 1964).

27. John Searle, *Speech Acts: An Essay in the Philosophy of Language* (Cambridge, England: Cambridge University Press, 1969); Searle, "Human Communication Theory and the Philosophy of Language," in *Human Communcation Theory*, ed. Frank E. X. Dance (New York: Holt, Rinehart & Winston, 1967), pp. 116–29. Good secondary sources include John Stewart, "Concepts of Language and Meaning: A Comparative Study," *Quarterly Journal of Speech* 58 (1972): 123–33; Paul N. Campbell, "A Rhetorical View of Locutionary, Illocutionary, and Perlocutionary Acts," *Quarterly Journal of Speech* 59 (1973): 284–96; Robert Gaines, "Doing by Saying: Toward a Theory of Perlocution," *Quarterly Journal of Speech* 65 (1979): 207–17.

The *speech act* is the basic unit of language for expressing meaning. It is an utterance that expresses an intention. Normally the speech act is a sentence, but it can be a word or phrase, so long as it follows the rules necessary to accomplish the intention (or in Wittgenstein's terms, to play the language game). We will discuss rules in speech acts momentarily; for now let us turn our attention to the nature of speech acts. When one speaks, one performs an act. The act may involve stating, questioning, commanding, promising, or any of a number of other acts. Speech therefore is conceived of as a form of action or intentional behavior.

An important characteristic of a speech act is that the recipient understand the speaker's intention. Unlike the representational view of meaning, speech act theory does not stress the individual referents of symbols but the intent of the act as a whole. If you make a promise, you are communicating an intention about something you will do in the future; but more importantly, you are expecting the other communicator to realize from what you have said what your intention is.

Searle's classification divides speech acts into four types. The first is an *utterance act*. Such acts are the simple pronunciation of words, singly or in combination. Here the intention is to utter, nothing more. An example is an actor doing voice exercises. The *propositional act* is what Austin refers to as a locution. It is the utterance of a sentence with the intention of expressing a reference. In other words, the individual wishes to make an association between a subject and verb or to designate an object and refer this object to something else. An *illocutionary act* is designed to fulfill an intention vis-à-vis another person. Here one uses the speech act to elicit response in another. Finally, the *perlocutionary act* is one designed to have effects or consequences in other peoples' behavior. Since the difference between illocution and perlocution is sometimes hard to grasp, let's pursue it a little further.

An illocution is an act in which the speaker's primary concern is that the listener understand the speaker's intention. A perlocution is an act in which the speaker not only expects the listener to understand but to act in a particular way because of that understanding. If I say, "I am thirsty," with the intention of having you understand that I need a drink, I am performing an illocutionary act. If I make the same statement expecting you to bring me a glass of water, my act is perlocutionary. (The four kinds of acts are highly interrelated and often are uttered simultaneously.)

Now let us pursue propositional acts and illocutionary acts in more detail. The proposition can be understood as one aspect of the content of an illocution. It designates some quality or association of an object, situation, or event. *The cake is good, Salt is harmful to the body, Her name is Karen* are all examples of propositions. Propositions can be evaluated in terms of their truth value. In speech act theory, however, truth and logic are not considered important. Rather, the question is what a speaker intends to do by uttering a proposition. The meaning of an illocutionary act is determined in part by establishing how the speaker wishes others to take the stated proposition. Hence, for Searle, propositions must always be viewed as part of a larger context, the illocution. Searle would be interested in acts such as the following: I *ask* whether the cake is good; I *warn* you that salt is harmful to the body; I *state* that her name is Karen. What the speaker is doing with the proposition is the speech act, and how the proposition is to be taken by the audience is the *illocutionary force* of the statement. You could, for example, state the proposition *The cake is good* in such a way as to have the listener realize that you were speaking ironically, meaning to imply just the opposite: This cake is the worst I ever ate.

Searle states fundamentally that "speaking a language is engaging in a rule-governed form of behavior."[28] Two types of rules are important. *Constitutive rules* create new forms of behavior; that is, acts are created by the establishment of rules. For example, football as a game exists only by virtue of its rules. The rules constitute the game. When you observe people following a certain set of rules, you know the game of football is being played. These rules therefore tell you what to interpret as football.

28. Searle, *Speech Acts*, p. 22.

In speech acts, one's intention is largely understood by another person by virtue of constitutive rules, because these rules tell others what to count as a particular kind of act. An example is provided in the next paragraph. The second kind of rule is regulative. *Regulative rules* provide guidelines for acting out already established behavior. The behaviors are known and available before being used in the act, and the regulative rules tell one how to use the behaviors to accomplish a particular intention. For example, a host often opens the door for a guest who is leaving.

As an example of the use of constitutive rules, let us look at one of Searle's extended analyses of a speech act, the act of making a promise. Promising involves five basic rules. First, promising involves uttering a sentence that indicates the speaker will do some future act (*propositional content rule*). Second, the sentence is uttered only if the listener would rather that the speaker do the act than not do it (*preparatory rule*). Third, a statement is a promise only when it would not otherwise be obvious to the speaker and hearer that the act would be done in the normal course of events (*preparatory rule*). Fourth, the speaker must intend to do the act (*sincerity rule*). Finally, a promise involves the establishment of an obligation for the speaker to do the act (*essential rule*). These five rules "constitute" a sufficient set of conditions for an act to count as a promise.

Any illocutionary act must have the basic kinds of rules named in parentheses above. The propositional content rule specifies some condition of the referenced object. Preparatory rules involve the presumed preconditions in the speaker and hearer necessary for the act to take place. The sincerity rule requires the speaker to mean what is said. (In the case of insincere illocutions, the act is presented in such a way that the listener presumes the speaker actually intends what he or she says is intended.) The essential rule states that the act is indeed taken by the hearer and speaker to represent what it appears to be on the face. Of course, many acts are not successful in these ways, and speech acts can be evaluated in terms of the degree to which they meet these criteria. Searle believes that speech acts may be defective; Austin calls a defective act an infelic-ity. These constitutive rules are believed to apply to a wide variety of illocutionary acts, including at least requesting, asserting, questioning, thanking, advising, warning, greeting, and congratulating.

Although many speech acts are direct, involving the use of an explicit proposition that clearly states the intention, other speech acts are indirect. For example, in requesting that his family come to the table, a father might say, "Is anybody hungry?" On the face this appears to be a question, but in actual-ity it is a request.

Searle outlines five types of illocutionary acts. The first is called *assertives*. An assertive is a state-ment of a proposition that commits the speaker to advocate the truth of the proposition. In direct form such acts might contain such performative verbs as state, affirm, conclude, believe, and so forth. *Directives* are illocutions that attempt to get the listener to do something. They are commands, requests, pleadings, prayers, entreaties, invitations, and so forth. *Commissives* commit the speaker to a future act. They consist of such acts as promising, vowing, pledging, contracting, and guaranteeing. *Expressives* are acts that communicate some aspect of the speaker's psychological state. They include thanking, congratulating, apologizing, condoling, welcoming, and others. Finally, a *declaration* is de-signed to create a proposition that, by its very as-sertion, makes it so. Examples include appointing, marrying, firing, resigning, and so forth.

Shimanoff's Rule-Governing Approach

Susan Shimanoff's work is presented for several reasons.[29] Shimanoff surveyed the literature on rules and formulated an overview that incorporates what she judges to be the best thinking in the field. She added to rules theory in such a way as to make it particularly applicable to communication. Her work is integrative in that it critically considers and analyzes the divergent literature. Shimanoff does not, indeed could never, incorporate all notions of rules, but she explains her chosen position by com-paring and contrasting it with others. Finally, she

takes a first step toward developing a rules theory of communication that has the potential of clarifying and unifying the thought in this area.

Shimanoff defines a rule as "a followable pre-scription that indicates what behavior is obligated, preferred, or prohibited in certain contexts."[30] This definition incorporates the following four elements.

1. *Rules must be followable.* This criterion im-plies that actors can choose whether to follow or to violate a rule. If a person has no choice in a course of action, then a "rule" is not being followed. The laws of nature are not "followed" by the objects under their control; they are fulfilled. For example, you are not following a rule by running out of a burning building. On the other hand, rules must deal with the possible. One cannot follow an im-possible rule. This statement does not imply that people are indifferent to rules. Behavior is greatly affected by rules, as the following criterion indi-cates. (By the way, you perhaps have noticed that Shimanoff uses the word *follow* differently from Pearce's rule-following category described earlier.)

2. *Rules are prescriptive.* By this Shimanoff means that a course of action is called for and that the failure to abide by the rule can be criticized. Prescriptions may state what is obligated, preferred, or prohibited, but in any case negative evaluation may ensue if the rule is not followed. Thus rules cannot "prescribe" permitted behaviors because no criticism would follow if such behaviors were not chosen. For example, while telling a joke is permis-sible in certain situations, joke telling is not pre-scribed and therefore not rule following. One is obligated to apologize, however, after accidentally bumping another person, and the violation of this rule may result in criticism.

3. *Rules are contextual.* Shimanoff points out that theories vary in the degree of contextuality believed to exist in a rules situation. Some theories state that rules are idiosyncratic, that each situa-tion has its set of rules. Others seek broad, almost universal, rules that cover nearly all situations. Shi-manoff takes a position in the middle. Since rules

29. Shimanoff, *Communication Rules.*

30. Ibid., p. 57.

are a vehicle for understanding organized, recurring behavior, they must apply in at least two different occurrences; potentially they may be broad enough to cover many situations. Hence, rules can be understood in terms of their *range* or generalizability. The "apology rule" just mentioned applies in almost all situations and is therefore broad in scope. Still, it is contextual in that it applies only when one person bothers another in some way. In fact, you can probably think of situations in which apologizing is uncalled for and potentially annoying.

4. *Rules specify appropriate behavior.* They tell us what to *do* or *not do*. They do not specify how we must think, feel, or interpret. For example, a rule may require an apology, but it cannot require the apologizer to feel sorry.

In order to identify a rule properly, an observer must be able to specify its context and its obligated, preferred, or prohibited behavior. The rule also must be stated in a form that demonstrates that it is followable. Shimanoff believes that the if-then format allows the observer to identify rules by specifying four components: If . . ., then one (must, must not, should). . . . The if clause specifies the nature of the prescription and the prescribed behavior. Consider the following examples:

- If one is not the owner or guest of the owner, then one is prohibited from being in the land marked off by this sign.
- If one is playing bridge and is the dealer, then one must bid first.
- If one is wearing a hat and is entering a church, then one must remove his/her hat.
- If one is playing chess and one's chess pieces are white, then one must move his/her piece first.[31]

Notice that Shimanoff's use of if-then does not imply causal reasoning in which the antecedent causes a consequent. Rather, the antecedent serves as the context in which the rule applies.

31. Ibid., p. 79. Shimanoff adapted these rule examples from Gidon Gottlieb, *Logic of Choice: An Investigation of the Concepts of Rule and Rationality* (New York: Macmillan, 1968), p. 11; Max Black, *Models and Metaphors* (Ithaca: Cornell University Press, 1962), p. 106; Raymond D. Gumb, *Rule-Governed Linguistic Behavior* (Paris: Mouton, 1972), p. 21; and Ganz, *Rules*, p. 13.

To verify a rules theory, a researcher must be able to observe rules in operation in everyday interaction. If Shimanoff's rule model is accurate, one will be able to apply her rule criteria to any episode and thereby identify the rules in force. Some rules are easy to see in operation because they are *explicit*. Such rules are announced, for instance, on a sign or in a game rule book. Most rules are *implicit*, though, and must be inferred from the behavior of the participants. Behavior can be examined in terms of three criteria: (1) Is the behavior controllable (to assess the degree to which the underlying rule is followable)? (2) Is the behavior criticizable (to assess whether the underlying rule is prescriptive)? (3) Is the behavior contextual (to assess whether people behave differently in various situations)?

Applying these criteria is not necessarily easy. For example, consider how difficult it would be to determine whether an action is criticized. We know that rule behavior is open to evaluation and that compliance may be praised while violation may be punished. Overt sanctions are easiest to identify in observing interactions because they involve verbal or nonverbal rewards and punishments. Sanctions may range from simple frowns or smiles to a stern lecture about rule violation. In addition to noting sanctions, observers can also look for repairs. Here a rule violator will behave in a way that reveals that a rule was violated. Apologizing is an example. In the absence of overt sanctions or repairs, the observer can ask participants whether a given behavior was appropriate or not.

One of Shimanoff's most interesting contributions is her model of rule behavior, which indicates the ways people relate to rules in actual interaction (Figure 7-3).[32] This model identifies eight types of rule-related behavior. Four of these are rule conforming, and four are rule deviating. Let us look at these in pairs, beginning toward the center of the figure. *Rule-fulfilling* and *rule-ignorant* behaviors involve acting without knowing the rule. For example, a prevalent rule in some situations is for men to open doors for women. Imagine a little boy who

32. *Communication Rules*, p. 127.

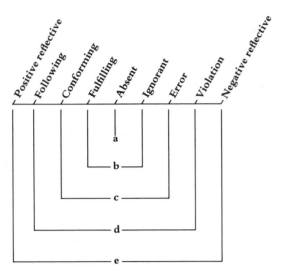

Key: a = noncontrollable, noncriti-
      cizable, or noncontextual
      b = rule-governed, but no
      knowledge of the rule
      c = tacit knowledge of a rule
      d = conscious knowledge of a rule
      e = conscious knowledge, plus
      evaluation of a rule

Figure 7-3   Rule-related behavior.

From *Communication Rules: Theory and
Research*, by Susan B. Shimanoff. Copyright
© 1980 by Sage Publications. Reprinted by
permission of the publisher.

naively opens a door for a woman. He is unaware
that he has followed a rule, but the woman might
respond by saying, "What a gentleman you are."
This behavior is rule fulfilling because the boy
didn't know he was following a prescription. On
the other hand, had the boy failed to open the door
in ignorance of the rule (rule-ignorant behavior),
the woman might whisper to the boy's parents,
"You need to teach your child good manners."

Conforming or *error* behaviors definitely are governed by rules, although the rule is not noted consciously by the individual at the time it is followed
or not followed. Men often unconsciously open
doors for women, and frequently they fail to do so,
not out of ignorance but because they are not thinking about it at the moment. The first instance is an

example of conforming behavior, the second of error behavior.

Rule-following behavior is conscious compliance
with the rule. To pursue our example, rule following would apply when a man intentionally steps
ahead of a woman and opens a door. *Rule violation*,
on the other hand, is intentional violation of
the rule. For instance, a man may be tired and
simply may not feel like opening the door for his
companion.

Reflective behavior involves *positive reflection* or
negative reflection (following or violating) of a rule
after evaluating it. The women's movement has
brought many social rules into question, such as
men opening doors for women. A feminist male
may consciously choose not to open the door for a
woman, precisely because of his evaluation of what
the gesture implies about sex roles. Or a woman
may take the initiative to open a door first. A man
who does not espouse feminist values may make a
point to open the door because, on reflection, he
believes that the rule is a good one.

Contingency Rules Theory

Contingency rules theory, originated by Mary
John Smith, applies the rule-using approach to
compliance-gaining situations.[33] There are three
assumptions to the theory: (1) People act with purpose and are influenced in their actions by what
they believe the outcome will be. (2) Persuasion is
controlled more by people's personal choices than
by the influence of others. (3) External threats and
rewards are meaningful only within the context of
one's personal goals and standards.

In persuasion situations, people select compliance-gaining message strategies and decide how to
respond to the messages of others. They make these
choices under the influence of rules that they believe apply in the situation. The individual will
normally perceive several choices. Given a goal, a
context, and a set of possible actions designed to
achieve the goal, the individual will perceive that

33. Mary John Smith, "Cognitive Schemata and Persuasive
Communication: Toward a Contingency Rules Theory," in
Communication Yearbook 6, ed. Michael Burgoon (Beverly Hills:
Sage Publications, 1982), pp. 330–63.

certain acts are more acceptable and/or more effective in the context than others.

The rules guiding a person's actions are of two types—self-evaluative and adaptive. *Self-evaluative rules* are tied to one's personal standards. Such standards are closely associated with the concept of the self, which was discussed earlier in the chapter. Some self-evaluative rules involve *self-identity* in that they are guided by what an individual believes to be his or her personal characteristics. If, for example, I perceive myself to be an honest person, I probably will have a rule against lying as a strategy for persuading people. Actions guided by self-identity rules serve to maintain the self-concept. Other self-evaluative rules are *image-maintaining* in that they are designed to present the self to others in a certain light. I don't want others to think I am dishonest, so my behavior is carefully planned to appear honest. While self-identity rules relate to one's private self-concept, image-maintaining rules have everything to do with one's public self-image.

The second class of contingency rules are *adaptive rules*. These rules tell one what actions will be effective or advantageous within a given situation. Some adaptive rules are *environmental contingency rules*: These help one select behavior that will lead to positive outcomes for oneself and others. I may, for example, have a rule that says, Never provoke a hostile person. Other adaptive rules are *interpersonal relationships rules*: These are created to help one behave in ways that maintain satisfying relationships with others. A person who is involved with a new lover may avoid bringing up negative feelings because these feelings may threaten the relationship at that stage. Finally, adaptive rules may be *social-normative*: These rules tell a communicator what is appropriate by standard social norms. In most situations, for example, one is obligated to reciprocate a greeting.

Rules are contingent, or context-specific: They depend upon the situation in which the compliance-gaining will take place. Many aspects of context are beyond the communicators' control; others, however, are created by the actions of the communicators themselves. These contextual factors include the nature of the relationship among the communciators, their intentions, and the degree to which they agree or disagree about the subject being discussed. Different rules will come into play in different relationships. When the communicators' intentions change, the rules also change. And rules that apply to situations in which communicators agree do not apply to situations in which they do not.

The contingency-rules theory provides an excellent sense of the rule-using approach, and it accents the ways in which rules theory departs from more traditional linear models of communication. With this introduction, we turn to the most comprehensive rule-using theory, the coordinated management of meaning.

Coordinated Management of Meaning

The theory of the coordinated management of meaning was developed by W. Barnett Pearce, Vernon Cronen, and their colleagues as a comprehensive theory of communication.[34] The theory integrates work from symbolic interactionism (Chapter 6), ethogeny (Chapter 7), system theory (Chapter 3), speech acts (Chapter 7), and relational communication (Chapter 10). The coordinated management of meaning (CMM) is interesting not only because it integrates and builds on a great deal of previous theoretical work, but also because it is broadly applicable to a variety of communication situations.

Pearce and Cronen borrow the concept of *constitutive* and *regulative* rules from speech act theory and make them a central part of their treatment. In CMM, constitutive rules are essentially *rules of meaning*, used by communicators to interpret or understand an event. Regulative rules are essentially

34. W. Barnett Pearce and Vernon Cronen, *Communication, Action, and Meaning* (New York: Praeger Publishers, 1980); Vernon Cronen, W. Barnett Pearce, and Linda Harris, "The Coordinated Management of Meaning," in *Comparative Human Communication Theory*, ed. Frank E. X. Dance (New York: Harper & Row, 1982); W. Barnett Pearce, "The Coordinated Management of Meaning: A Rules Based Theory of Interpersonal Communication," in *Explorations in Interpersonal Communication*, ed. Gerald R. Miller (Beverly Hills: Sage Publications, 1976), pp. 17–36; Vernon Cronen, W. Barnett Pearce, and Linda Harris, "The Logic of the Coordinated Management of Meaning," *Communication Education* 28 (1979): 22–38.

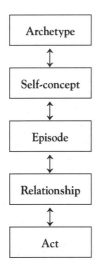

Figure 7-4   Hierarchy of contexts.

Adapted from *Communication, Action, and Meaning*, by W. Barnett Pearce and Vernon Cronen. Copyright © 1980 by Praeger Publishers. Reprinted by permission of the publisher.

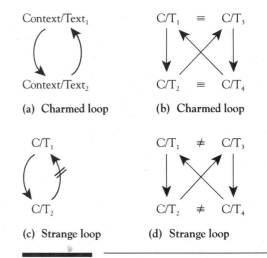

Figure 7-5   Text-context loop patterns.

Adapted from "Between Text and Context: Toward a Rhetoric of Contextual Reconstruction," by Robert J. Branham and W. Barnett Pearce, in *Quarterly Journal of Speech* 71 (1985): 23, 25. Reprinted by permission of the author and publisher.

rules of action, used to determine how to respond or behave. Rules of meaning and action are always chosen within a context. The context is the frame or reference point from which an action takes on meaning, and one's responses will differ from context to context. For example, Pearce and Cronen tell of a couple named Jan and Dave who have problems with their relationship. Jan understands her own actions within the context of her self-concept as a lazy person, believing that she requires others to motivate her to do necessary things. Dave understands his actions within his self-concept as a "laid back" guy, not a domineering person. The relationship pattern that troubles the couple goes like this: Jan would fail to do something important, and Dave would nag her to do it. Jan would then follow through and do what Dave asked. Within the context of the relationship, Jan defines Dave's actions as being dominant, but within the context of his self-concept, Dave sees his actions as submissive, since he is complying with Jan's manipulative desire to be pushed.

Pearce and Cronen see contexts as a nested hierarchy: One context is embedded within another. Figure 7-4 illustrates this idea. Here four typical contexts are depicted in a hierarchy. The *relationship* context includes mutual expectations among members of a group. The *episode* context involves defined events; it is modeled after Harré and Secord's episodic analysis outlined earlier in the chapter. The *self-concept* context is one's sense of personal definition. Finally the *archetype* context is an image of general truth.

Several qualifications can be added to clarify Figure 7-4. First, each context is part of a higher-level context, so that, for instance, one's relationship expectations might be framed within an episode, which in turn would be framed by self-concept. Second, the order of contexts shown in the figure is not by any means universal; in fact, it probably shifts constantly. Sometimes, for example, self is understood within the context of the relationship, while on other occasions relationships are understood in reference to self. Third, although the con-

Figure 7-6   The alcoholic's paradox.

Adapted from "Between Text and Context: Toward a Rhetoric of Contextual Reconstruction," by Robert J. Branham and W. Barnett Pearce, in *Quarterly Journal of Speech* 71 (1985):26. Reprinted by permission of the author and publisher.

texts listed in Figure 7-4 are representative and common, they by no means exhaust the possible contexts within which interpretations and actions are made.

People have a tendency to create new contexts in order to achieve change in their understandings and actions. An event or action being interpreted is known as a *text*; the reference from which the interpretation is made is *context*. Often text and context form a loop, such that each is used from time to time to interpret the other.[35] Jan, for example, uses the relationship as a context for interpreting her self as lazy, but she uses her self-concept as a lazy person to understand her relationship with Dave as one of dominance and submission. The text-context loop is shown in Figure 7-5. Where the interpretation rules are consistent throughout the loop, the loop is said to be *charmed*, or self-confirmatory. Jan's charmed loop, for example, goes like this: I am lazy and therefore Dave needs to push me; Dave pushes me so that I will do what needs to be done. Often, however, the rules of interpretation change from one point in the loop to another, causing a paradox. Pearce and Cronen refer to a paradoxical loop as a *strange loop*. The strange loop of the alcoholic is illustrated in Figure 7-6.

35. Loops are discussed in Vernon E. Cronen, Kenneth M. Johnson, and John W. Lannamann, "Paradoxes, Double Binds, and Reflexive Loops: An Alternative Theoretical Perspective," *Family Process* 20 (1982): 91–112; and Robert J. Branham and W. Barnett Pearce, "Between Text and Context: Toward A Rhetoric of Contextual Reconstruction," *Quarterly Journal of Speech* 71 (1985): 19–36.

In order to demonstrate the operation of rules, Pearce and Cronen developed a set of symbols denoting rule structures. Three are important here:

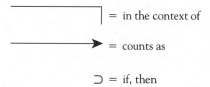

The first symbol denotes the context of an act, the second applies to a constitutive rule, and the third is used in regard to a regulative rule. Consider the following examples:

$$\frac{\text{play}}{\text{insult} \longrightarrow \text{joke}}$$

In the context of play, an insult is to be taken as a joke.

Constitutive rule: An insult counts as a joke.

$$\frac{\text{conflict}}{\text{insult} \longrightarrow \text{put-down}}$$

In the context of conflict, an insult is to be taken as a put-down.

Constitutive rule: An insult counts as a put-down.

episode of an argument

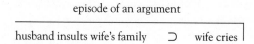

When arguing, the wife typically cries after the husband insults her family.

Regulative rule: When the husband insults, wife should cry.

episode of playful banter

[husband insults wife's family   ⊃
    wife playfully hits husband] ——————→ fun

In play it is considered fun for the wife to "hit" the husband after he insults her family.

Regulative rule: Wife should respond to husband's insult by "hitting" him.

Constitutive rule: This sequence of events is to be taken as fun.

These examples are simple, but complex acts may be diagrammed in the same fashion. Whereas simple examples are used here for clarity, most significant interactions are far more complex. Notice also that the bracketing of context is important for determining the rules in operation.

A rule system provides a *logical force* for acting in certain ways. One behaves in a manner consistent with one's rules. Two types of logical force operate in communication. *Prefigurative* or causal force is an antecedent-to-act linkage in which the individual is "pressured" to behave in certain ways *because of* prior conditions. *Practical* logical force is an act-to-consequent linkage in which one behaves in a certain way *in order to* achieve a future condition. In any communication encounter, an individual's rules present a series of "oughts" that guide interpretations, responses, and actions. These oughts are perceived logical forces in the interactional system.

In modern society a person is part of many systems, each with its own set of meaning and action rules. The rules are learned through interaction in social groups. Over time, individuals internalize some of these rules and draw on them to guide their actions. The basic problem of communication is that when an individual enters an interaction, that person has no way of knowing precisely what rules the other participants will be using. The primary task in all communication, then, is to achieve and then sustain some form of coordination. Coordination involves meshing one's actions with those of

another to the point of feeling that the sequence of actions is logical. The communicators in an exchange need not interpret the events the same way, but each must feel, from within his or her own system of rules, that what is happening makes sense—that is the essence of coordination.

The key problem of coordination is this: Each individual must use rules to interpret and respond to the actions of others. Figure 7-7 shows how coordination occurs.[36] (This model has been overly simplified in order to make the process clear.) Person A acts in a particular way in response to prior conditions or to achieve a consequence. The act is taken as a message by Person B, who uses meaning rules to interpret the message. Person A's act thus becomes an antecedent event to which Person B responds, based on B's action rules. B's act is in turn interpreted by A as a message from the standpoint of A's meaning rules, and B's act becomes the consequent to A's initial move. If A and B are operating with substantially different rule structures, they will quickly discover that one person's behavior does not represent the consequent intended, and they will readjust their rules until some level of coordination is achieved.

Consider the simple example of a child trying to get back a ball after accidentally having thrown it through a neighbor's window.[37] The adult begins with the following rule structure:

CONSTITUTIVE RULE: If I say, "Is this ball yours?" in a stern fashion, this act will be taken as anger, a demand for a confession, and a threat.

REGULATIVE RULE: My act, taken as anger, will elicit crying and apologies. I, in turn, will become less angry and will give back the ball.

The child, on the other hand, has a very different set of rules:

CONSTITUTIVE RULE: When the neighbor says, "Is this

36. Pearce and Cronen, *Communication*, p. 174.

37. The example is adapted from Pearce and Cronen, *Communication*, pp. 162–64. Originally, the example was developed in K. T. Alvy, "The Development of Listener Adapted Communication in Grade-School Children from Different Social Class Backgrounds," *Genetic Psychology Monographs* 87 (1973): 33–104.

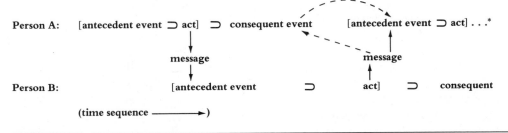

Figure 7-7   Enmeshment process.

*Solid arrows denote constitutive rules. Broken arrows denote the coorientational state of comparing the subsequent message to the anticipated consequent event in anticipation of the next act.
From *Communication, Action, and Meaning*, by W. Barnett Pearce and Vernon Cronen. Copyright © 1980 by Praeger Publishers. Reprinted by permission of the publisher.

your ball?" he is asking for information. My statement, "Give it back," will be taken as a request.

REGULATIVE RULE: When the neighbor requests information, I will respond with a factual answer, "Yes, it is." I will say, "Give it back," and he will give it back.

Now observe the actual conversation:

NEIGHBOR: "Is this your ball?"
CHILD: "Yes, it is. Give it back."

Obviously, the neighbor did not get the expected response and will interpret the child's remark as impudence rather than the simple request intended by the child. At this point the interaction is not coordinated. Now the neighbor must adjust the regulative rule by trying a different approach:

NEIGHBOR: "Give it back? This ball hit my window. Do you know that?"

If the child has a sufficiently complex rule structure to provide options, he may adjust so that a successful outcome can be achieved. If not, coordination may not be achieved. Consider:

Unsatisfactory outcome (no enmeshment):
CHILD: "Give my ball back. I'll tell Daddy if you don't give it back."
NEIGHBOR: "Get out of my yard, kid."

Successful outcome (coordination achieved):
CHILD: "I'm sorry. I didn't mean to do it, and I will be careful in the future."
NEIGHBOR: "Okay. Here's your ball."

Criticism of the Rules Approach

Criticism of rules theory typically has centered around two issues: conceptual coherence and explanatory power. Let us consider each of these in turn.

First, is rules theory conceptually coherent? The answer to this question is a resounding no. Even its adherents admit that the rules tradition lacks unity and coherence. Jesse Delia verbalizes this objection in strong terms:

> The terrain covered by notions of "rules," then, is broad, grossly diffuse, and imprecisely articulated. And the real problem for any position purporting to be a general rules perspective is that the meaning of "rule" does not remain constant either within or across these domains. The "rules" territory taken as a whole is, in fact, little short of chaotic. At the least, it is clear that there is no unifying conception of the rule construct, of the domain of phenomena to which the construct has reference, of whether rules have generative power in producing and directing behavior, . . . or of the proper way to give an account of some domain of phenomena utilizing the construct. The idea of "rules" as a general construct represents only a diffuse notion devoid of specific theoretical substance.[38]

The theories we have covered illustrate this lack of coherence. Shimanoff is firm in stating that a rule

38. Jesse Delia, "Alternative Perspectives for the Study of Human Communication: Critique and Response," *Communication Quarterly* 25 (1977): 54.

must deal with overt behavior. She believes that the concept should not apply to interpretation. Pearce and Cronen, however, place constitutive rules at the core of their approach. For them rules apply not only to overt behavior but to internal meanings as well.

Although some critics agree that intentions are an important aspect of meaning, that speech constitutes a form of action, and that speech acts are governed by rules, they argue that the conceptual categories of speech act theory are vague or meaningless. Austin's threefold distinction among locutionary, illocutionary, and perlocutionary acts has been severely criticized from this standpoint. One critic states: "And now Austin has, in my judgment, erected a structure that is in imminent danger of collapse.[39] His threefold analysis is criticized for being unclear. Critics question the utility of locution as a concept if the utterance of a locution automatically constitutes an illocution, as Austin claims it does. The distinction between illocutionary and perlocutionary acts is equally unclear to many readers, who point out that even if one could observe the difference between these concepts, it is doubtful that they constitute a useful conceptual framework for guiding our understanding of speech acts. It would perhaps be more fruitful to recognize that any given speech act may be fulfilling a variety of intents and may be taken in a variety of different ways by different listeners. Conceptually, the terms *illocution* and *perlocution* may apply more directly to types of force and effects than to types of acts per se.

The distinction between regulative and constitutive rules is equally fuzzy.[40] The problem here is that once any act becomes standardized, as in the case of almost all illocutionary acts, rules no longer are constitutive in the sense of creating new acts. Hence, rules that regulate can be taken as constitutive, and rules that constitute an act also regulate it.

The second question is, are rules theories suffi-

ciently explanatory? Critics generally believe that rules approaches cannot be explanatory as long as they fail to develop generic principles that cut across contexts. To identify the rules in operation within a particular context is not sufficient to explain communication processes. Charles Berger believes that "at some point one must go beyond the description of 'what the rules are' and ask why some rules are selected over others . . . [and] what social forces produced the kinds of conventions and appropriate modes of behavior we now observe."[41] Berger's view is that a covering law approach is ultimately necessary to provide explanation; attempts of rules theorists to provide generic principles are nothing more than covering laws in disguise.

Most rules advocates do not go along with this argument, of course. Shimanoff points out that most rules explanations, in contrast to laws explanations, are teleological or reason giving. Behaviors are explained in terms of their practical impact on creating desired outcomes. Such explanations can be generalized. While developing universal explanations would not be desirable, and perhaps not possible, rules theories should seek reason-giving explanations that cover relatively broad classes of situations, even to the point of allowing for prediction.[42]

The appropriate question here is not whether rules theories are explanatory but what kind of explanation the critic believes is necessary. Clearly, Berger and Shimanoff disagree on the level of generality necessary for adequate explanation. We must also keep in mind that different rules theories possess different levels of explanatory power.

Recall from Chapter 2 that explanation is made possible by principles of necessity and generality. Barnett Pearce discusses rules approach in terms of these criteria.[43] Rule-following approaches tend not to be explanatory because they merely describe recurring behavior without indicating any form of necessity. Rule-governed approaches explain in

39. Campbell, "A Rhetorical View," p. 287.
40. Shimanoff, *Communication Rules*, pp. 84–85. For additional critique, see Margaret L. McLaughlin, *Conversation: How Talk Is Organized* (Beverly Hills: Sage Publications, 1984), pp. 63–68.

41. Charles R. Berger, "The Covering Law Perspective as a Theoretical Basis for the Study of Human Communication," *Communication Quarterly* 25 (1977): 12.
42. Shimanoff, *Communication Rules*, pp. 217–34.
43. Pearce, "Rules Theories."

terms of practical necessity, although their generality is somewhat limited. Pearce believes that the rule-using approach, while presently limited, has the highest potential for explanatory power in terms of both practical and logical necessity and generality.

Shimanoff's theory is basically descriptive, providing detailed guidelines for identifying rules in a social situation. As such it is highly heuristic from a methodological standpoint. It is also strong in providing conceptual guidance in understanding rules. Shimanoff's theory, however, does not present much explanation. Little basis exists for understanding why particular kinds of communication behavior occur in various situations. Shimanoff's framework shows potential for developing explanation, but we shall have to see what theorists do with it in the future.

The power of the coordinated management of meaning is that it allows us to interpret a wide variety of events. It has tremendous scope of applicability and has been a fruitful framework for examining actual communication situations. The theory's credibility rests in large measure on the way in which it has integrated a variety of concepts from several different traditions. However, David Brenders has recently pointed out that this eclecticism has distorted several important concepts and led to confusion about the meaning of terms. [44] For example, the use of the concept of meaning in CMM buries important distinctions that have been made in the literature on meaning. Brenders believes that the theory confuses types of acts with the effects of those acts and that the distinction between constitutive and regulative rules from speech act theory has been distorted.

Language and Culture

In the final section of this chapter, we examine some prominent theories of culture and language. All of the theories presented in this chapter deal

with this subject in a sense because they all show ways in which communication patterns create and reflect the reality of a social group, society, or culture. Generally speaking, the study of the relationship between language and culture is known as *sociolinguistics*.

A Note on Sociolinguistics

Sociolinguistics is a very broad term covering any study of language that makes significant use of social data, or, conversely, any study of social life that makes use of linguistic data. [45] Although this label would not be adopted by all students of language and culture, it is certainly the most commonly understood term for this kind of research and theory.

Sociolinguistics contrasts sharply with the structural approaches covered in Chapter 4, which view language as essentially independent from the ways in which it is used. The rise of social constructionism in the 1960s and 1970s brought a renewed interest in language-culture relationships. Today most students of language believe that language is affected by both intrinsic structural properties and socio-cultural factors. [46]

We turn now to two important theoretical contributions to language and culture. The first, linguistic relativity, is a classic theory of this genre. The second, the ethnography of communication, is currently popular and influential.

Linguistic Relativity

The *Sapir-Whorf hypothesis*, otherwise known as the theory of *linguistic relativity*, is based on the work of Edward Sapir and his protégé Benjamin Lee Whorf. [47] Whorf is best known for his fieldwork in linguistics; his analysis of the Hopi is particularly

---

44. David A. Brenders, "Fallacies in the Coordinated Management of Meaning: A Philosophy of Language Critique of the Hierarchical Organization of Coherent Conversation and Related Theory," *Quarterly Journal of Speech* 73 (1987): 329–48.

45. Dell Hymes, *Foundations in Sociolinguistics: An Ethnographic Approach* (Philadelphia: University of Pennsylvania Press, 1974), p. vii.

46. Gillian Sankoff, *The Social Life of Language* (Philadelphia: University of Pennsylvania Press, 1980), p. xvii.

47. Edward Sapir, *Language: An Introduction to the Study of Speech* (New York: Harcourt, Brace & World, 1921); Benjamin Whorf, *Language, Thought, and Reality* (New York: John Wiley, 1956). In the Whorf, the following articles are most helpful: John B. Carroll, "Introduction," pp. 1–34; "The Relation of Habitual Thought and Behavior in Language," pp. 134–359; "Language, Mind, and Reality," pp. 246–69.

well known. In his research Whorf discovered that fundamental syntactical differences distinguish language groups. The Whorfian hypothesis of linguistic relativity simply states that *the structure of a culture's language determines the behavior and habits of thinking in that culture.* In the words of Edward Sapir:

> Human beings do not live in the objective world alone, nor alone in the world of social activity as ordinarily understood, but are very much at the mercy of the particular language which has become the medium of expression for their society. It is quite an illusion to imagine that one adjusts to reality essentially without the use of language and that language is merely an incidental means of solving specific problems of communication or reflection. The fact of the matter is that the "real world" is to a large extent unconsciously built up on the language habits of the group. . . . We see and hear and otherwise experience very largely as we do because the language habits of our community predispose certain choices of interpretation.[48]

This hypothesis suggests that our thought processes and the way we see the world are shaped by the grammatical structure of the language. As one reviewer reacted, "All one's life one has been tricked . . . by the structure of language into a certain way of perceiving reality."[49]

Whorf spent much of his life investigating the relationship of language and behavior. His work with the Hopi illustrates the relativity hypothesis. Like all cultural groups the Hopi possess a *thought-world microcosm,* which represents their view of the world at large or *macrocosm.* One area of Whorf's extensive analysis of Hopi thought is the analysis of time. While many cultures refer to points in time (for example, seasons) as nouns, the Hopi conceive of time as a passage or process. Thus the Hopi language never objectifies time. A Hopi would not refer to summer as "in the summer." Instead, the Hopi would refer to the passing or coming of a phase that is never here and now but always moving, accumulating. In our culture three tenses indicate locations or places in a spatial analogy: past, present, and future. Hopi verbs have no tense in the same sense. Instead, their verb forms relate to duration and order. In the Standard Average European languages (SAE), including English, we visualize time as a line. The Hopi conception is more complex, as illustrated in the following example.[50]

Suppose that a speaker reports to a hearer that a third person is running: "He is running." The Hopi would use the word *wari,* which is a statement of running as a fact. The same word would be used for a report of past running, "He ran." For the Hopi the statement of fact (validity) is what is important, not whether the event is presently occurring or happened in the past. If, however, the Hopi speaker wished to report a past event of running from memory (the hearer did not actually see it), a different form would be used, *era wari.* The English sentence, "He will run," would translate *warikni,* which communicates running as a statement of expectation. Again, it is not the location in past, present, or future that is important to the Hopi, but the nature of validity (observed fact, recalled fact, or expectation). Another English form, "He runs [on the track team]," would translate *warikngwe.* This latter Hopi form again refers to running, but in the sense of law or condition.

As a result of these linguistic differences, Hopi and SAE cultures will think about, perceive, and behave toward time differently. For example, the Hopi tend to engage in lengthy preparing activities. Experiences (getting prepared) tend to accumulate as time "gets later." The emphasis is on the accumulated experience during the course of time, not on time as a point or location. In SAE cultures, with their spatial treatment of time, experiences are not accumulated in the same sense. Elaborate and lengthy preparations are not often found. The custom in SAE cultures is to record events (space-time analogy) such that what happened in the past is objectified in space (recorded). Whorf summarizes this view: "Concepts of 'time' and 'matter' are not

---

48. Quoted in Whorf, *Language, Thought, and Reality,* p. 134.

49. Carroll (in Whorf's *Language, Thought, and Reality*), "Introduction," p. 27.

50. Adapted from Whorf, *Language, Thought, and Reality,* p. 213.

given in substantially the same form by experience to all men but depend upon the nature of the language or languages through the use of which they have been developed."[51]

Ethnography of Communication

Ethnography is a kind of cultural study in which an interpreter from outside the culture attempts to make sense of the actions of the group being studied.[52] As such, it brings two worlds together so that one can be understood from the other. The ethnographer not only describes the actions of a group, but attempts to construct an interpretive model that enables one to understand those actions. The interpretive process is one of relating observed acts to larger patterns of acts in order to figure out the meanings of the part and of the whole. (This approach also fits with the theories of the following chapter.) The ethnographer's account would not be the same as the native's, but the native would certainly be able to accept the ethnographer's view.

Ethnographic problems begin with a breakdown of understanding. Often the ethnographer conceives of the breakdown in order to expose problems for investigation. The researcher witnesses something that cannot be understood from his or her concepts and seeks to resolve the difficulty by creating an explanation that makes understanding possible. Ethnography attempts to achieve coherence by understanding practices that are otherwise foreign. How would you make sense of a cult's ceremony involving the fondling of rattlesnakes? Most of us have no frame for understanding such actions, but the ethnographer would—through careful examination, inference, and experience—create an explanation that would make such behavior sensible.

The ethnographic process is a gradual tacking back and forth between the concepts of the native, which are "experience-near," and those of the observer, which are "experience-distant." Eventually, a conceptualization is formed that enables the observer to make sense of the phenomena in a way that approximates the concepts of the participants themselves; yet the conceptualization of the ethnographer would be understandable to other outsiders.[53] Figure 7-8 illustrates the process. The figure shows how the observer goes through a series of schemas, or ways of understanding, which become increasingly refined and useful. One's first schema may not explain much, leading to a breakdown. After a series of breakdowns, a tentative resolution is achieved. The successful schema is then applied to other acts until further breakdowns occur, forcing the development of still further refined schemas.

The interpreter, of course, does not begin an ethnography empty-handed. Previous experience always provides some kind of schema for understanding an event, but ethnography is a process in which one's understandings become increasingly more refined and accurate.

The ethnography of communication is simply the application of ethnographic methods to the communication patterns of a group. Here, the interpreter attempts to make sense of the forms of communication employed by the members of the group or culture. The originator of this research tradition is anthropologist Dell Hymes.[54] Hymes suggests that formal linguistics is not sufficient by itself to uncover a complete understanding of language because it ignores the highly variable ways in which language is used in everyday communication. In Hymes's terms: "We deal here, in short, with the fact that the communicative event is the metaphor, or perspective, basic to rendering experience intelligible. . . . It is this fact that underlies the apparently central role of language in cultural life."[55] Communication is the use of language in context.

What counts as a communicative event within a culture cannot be predetermined. Cultures use different practices for communication. Whatever the communication practice may be, however, it constitutes a *message*—which requires a shared code,

51. *Language, Thought, and Reality*, p. 158.
52. See Michael Agar, *Speaking of Ethnography* (Beverly Hills: Sage Publications, 1986).

53. Geertz, *Local Knowledge*, p. 57.
54. Hymes, *Foundations*.
55. Ibid., p. 16.

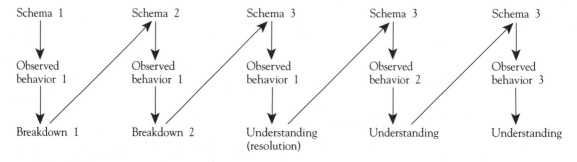

Figure 7-8   Ethnographic process of understanding.

Adapted from *Speaking of Ethnography*, by Michael Agar. Copyright © 1986 by Sage Publications. Reprinted by permission of the publisher.

communicators who know and use the code, a channel, a setting, a message form, a topic, and an event created by transmission of the message. An ethnographer's first schema for understanding communication within a group might well begin with this model of the message. However, this model by itself is insufficient, because it cannot tell you what specific practices meet these criteria. Anything may qualify as a message as long as it is construed as such by the natives. Is snake handling communication? Perhaps it is a shared code for expressing something among the members of the cult. We cannot know until further ethnographic study is undertaken.

Comparative ethnography involves the creation of a higher-level schema with which to understand and compare the practices of a variety of cultures. Hymes has been particularly emphatic about the need to establish comparative ethnography of communication: "What is needed, then, is a general theory and body of knowledge within which diversity of speech, repertoires, ways of speaking, and choosing among them find a natural place."[56] This statement calls for a movement between ethnographic description and generalized taxonomy. For Hymes, comparative ethnography is "a necessary part of the progress toward models . . . of sociolinguistic description, formulation of universal sets of features and relations, and explanatory theories."[57]

Hymes suggests a set of nine "fundamental notions" that might be included in such a theory:[58]

1. Ways of speaking: patterns of speech activity known by the competent speakers within a community.

2. Ideal of the fluent speaker: the image of a speaker exemplar.

3. Speech community: a group of people who share a coded set of communication practices. A "speech field" is the range of communities within which a person is communicatively competent.

4. Speech situation: a set of circumstances defined within the community as appropriate for communication.

5. Speech event: those practices or activities governed by communication rules.

6. Speech act: a practice defined as communicative by the speech community.

7. Components of speech acts: the dimensions or parts of a speech act, including such elements as message form, key (tone, manner), and so on.

8. The rules of speaking in the community.

9. The functions of speech in the community.

You can see from this brief outline that a comparative theory attempts to set out the general parameters of communication, while ethnographies themselves reveal the richly varying ways in which those parameters are defined within specific communities.

56. Ibid., p. 32.
57. Ibid., p. 35.

58. Ibid., pp. 29–66.

Critical Examination of Language and Culture

Although it seems patently obvious to constructionists and interactionists that human experience is formed largely in and through culture, many sociobehavioral scientists have not adopted this assumption at all. We have already reviewed, for instance, Cherwitz and Hikins' statement that cultures share large areas of commonality. Most scientifically oriented social science still rests on the assumption that the human experience is largely universal, owing to a common biological inheritance and common cognitive structures.

Noam Chomsky, for example, has taught that language structures are universal and that cultural differences in languages are merely superficial. Further, he believes that certain language universals are innate and that language is acquired by an interaction between experience and wired-in structures. Charles Osgood has done considerable cross-cultural research and has come to the conclusion that the dimensions of meaning are universal. (These two theories are explored in more depth in Chapters 5 and 6.)

If these structuralists are right, then cultural relativists are barking up the wrong tree. We should not be looking for richly different language and meaning experiences; instead we should discover the common universals that provide an explanatory basis for human behavior across the board. This is a debate that will not die, and we encounter it again at other points throughout this text.

The reality of a culture is reflected in the forms of speech produced by members of the culture. Accounts, or explanations, given by members of the culture for their behavior seem especially important in both expressing and reproducing the reality of the group.

Social reality is largely a matter of rules. Rules are guidelines for understanding events and for responding to situations. People speak and act to accomplish objectives, and these accomplishments are guided by socially derived rules. Social situations, however, are often complex, and there may be many appropriate meanings and actions associated with a situation. One of the chief problems of communication, therefore, is to mesh or coordinate rules with other individuals in a variety of situations.

Cultures are largely defined by their linguistically expressed meanings. Language, which develops over time through interaction in a culture, has much power to shape the reality of that culture. Further, cultures have rich speech forms consisting of ideals, manners, and types of speech performed within the culture. These speech forms also reflect and reproduce the reality of the culture.

Integration

The theories presented in this chapter all rest upon the assumption that reality is a social construction. Even ideas of what constitutes a person or a self depend upon "theories" that have evolved through communication, from one person to another in society. Cultures have distinct beliefs about what it means to be a person, and individuals characterize themselves as persons in accordance with socially derived theories of the self.

Eight

Interpretive and Critical Theories

art II of this book has covered several genres of communication theory, including the structural and functional approaches, interactional and conventional approaches, and behavioral and cognitive approaches. In this chapter we discuss the fourth genre—interpretive and critical approaches. The central assumptions of all of the theories discussed in this chapter are that human beings act in the world, that their actions are meaningful, and that interpretation is necessary for understanding human experience. As opposed to many behavioral and cognitive theories, which deal with the "objects" of human social life, the theories we are about to discuss here relate to the "works" of human experience.

Although interpretive and critical theories share a set of assumptions about human action, the theories differ in several important respects. In brief, interpretive theories aim to understand the lived experience of human beings, or to interpret the meanings of texts. Critical theories deal with ways in which the human condition is constrained and seek to create methods for improving human life.[1] We return to critical theories later in the chapter; for now, let us turn to interpretation.

Interpretive Approaches

Interpretation, sometimes known by the German term *Verstehen* or *understanding*, attempts to explain actions in terms of their meanings. Because an action may mean a number of things, meaning cannot be simply "discovered." Interpretation, by definition, is an active, inventive process. Although the actual meanings of the actors themselves are important in many types of interpretation, these theories generally recognize that meanings may surpass what any given actor can explain. Interpretation, then, is a creative act of ascertaining meaning possibilities.

Interpretive theories come in many varieties. Often social scientists are interested in understanding the ways in which members of a culture or social group understand their actions; or social scientists may wish to translate "local" meanings into terms understandable in a broader framework. Many interpretive theories center on messages or texts. Some of these attempt to determine what communicators mean by their discourse. Others are interested in the meanings of texts apart from any particular author or reader. Still other interpretivists explore the very meaning of interpretation itself and the ways in which human experience embodies understanding. This chapter includes theories from each of these schools.

The first section of this chapter deals with two converging lines of thought on interpretation— hermeneutics and phenomenology. Hermeneutics originally signified textual interpretation and in

1. Brian Fay, *Social Theory and Political Practice* (London: George Allen & Unwin, 1975).

many circles still retains that designation; however, to many people, hermeneutics has come to be almost synonymous with interpretation itself. Phenomenology is the study of the knowledge that arises in conscious experience. Today, phenomenology and hermeneutics are very closely associated.

Phenomenology

Phenomenology is the study of the ways in which human beings experience the world. It looks at objects and events from the perspective of the perceiver, the individual who experiences those things. Reality, in phenomenology, is always part of the conscious experience of the individual. This approach is a striking departure from objectivist methods that assume a reality apart from human consciousness or perception. Maurice Merleau-Ponty, a major phenomenologist, expresses this point of view as follows:

> All my knowledge of the world, even my scientific knowledge, is gained from my own particular point of view, or from some experience of the world without which the symbols of science would be meaningless. . . . To return to things themselves is to return to that world which precedes knowledge, of which knowledge always speaks.[2]

In other words, phenomenology makes actual lived experience the basic data of knowledge. It avoids the application of arbitrary theoretical categories: "phenomenology means letting things become manifest as what they are, without forcing our own categories on them."[3]

Stanley Deetz summarizes three basic principles of this movement.[4] First, knowledge is necessarily conscious. Knowledge is not inferred from experience, but is expressed in conscious experience itself. Second, meanings are assigned to things on the basis of the potential of those things for one's actions. How a person relates to an object determines its meaning. A set of keys, for example, becomes a paperweight when one considers its potential as a heavy object. Third, language is the vehicle through which meanings arise. We experience the world through the language used to define and express that world. We know keys because of the labels attached to the object: lock, open, metal, weight, and so forth.

Phenomenology is divided into two general camps. The modern originator of phenomenology, Edmund Husserl, taught that phenomenology could become a rigorous science—that by using clear consciousness, one could discover truth. In opposition, Martin Heidegger taught that precise knowledge is not possible and that human beings cannot separate themselves from their subjective experience. We return to these seminal figures later in the chapter.

Hermeneutics

Hermeneutics is the study of understanding, especially by interpreting action and text. There are several branches of hermeneutics, including interpretation of the Bible (exegesis), interpretation of ancient literary texts (philology), interpretation through the development and use of linguistic rules (technical hermeneutics), interpretation of human personal and social actions (social hermeneutics), the study of the process of understanding itself (philosophical hermeneutics), and discovering hidden meanings in any symbol system (for example, dream analysis).[5]

Although classical hermeneutics, designed as a technical method for interpreting texts, is still very much in use in those disciplines concerned with understanding ancient scriptures and literature, the social sciences today treat hermeneutics more generally as the interpretation of social life and expressive forms. Just about any interpretive activity can be labeled hermeneutic: "Throughout, the goal of

2. Maurice Merleau-Ponty, *The Phenomenology of Perception,* trans. Colin Smith (Routledge & Kegan Paul, 1974), pp. viii–ix. For an excellent general discussion of phenomenology, see also Michael J. Hyde, "Transcendental Philosophy and Human Communication," in *Interpersonal Communication,* ed. Joseph J. Pilotta (Washington, D.C.: Center for Advanced Research in Phenomenology, 1982), pp. 15–34.

3. Richard E. Palmer, *Hermeneutics: Interpretation Theory in Schleiermacher, Dilthey, Heidegger, and Gadamer* (Evanston, Ill.: Northwestern University Press, 1969), p. 128.

4. Stanley Deetz, "Words without Things: Toward a Social Phenomenology of Language," *Quarterly Journal of Speech* 59 (1973): 40–51.

5. Palmer, *Hermeneutics,* p. 43.

hermeneutic studies has been to develop understanding of human artifacts and actions by interpreting their nature and significance."[6] This may mean understanding another person's feelings and meanings, understanding the meaning of an episode or event, translating the actions of a group into terms understandable to outsiders, or uncovering the meaning of a written text. It also includes the general philosophical examination of understanding itself. One commentator put the matter succinctly: "The hermeneutical problem as a whole, I believe, is too important and too complex to become the property of a single school of thought."[7]

In general, hermeneutic scholars fall into three predominant groups: (1) those who use hermeneutics as a tool for interpreting actions in context; (2) those who use hermeneutics to understand texts apart from the contexts in which they were produced or consumed; (3) those who explore the very problem of understanding itself. The first type is perhaps best described as social or cultural hermeneutics, the second as textual hermeneutics, and the third as philosophical hermeneutics.[8] Most hermeneuticists of the textual tradition seek to understand written texts as texts, apart from what the original author may have intended and apart from what any particular audience may derive from the text. The assumption in contemporary textual hermeneutics is that any writing has intrinsic meanings in it, and the task is to bring that meaning out.

Although there is little agreement on specific techniques of interpretation, almost all schools of thought rely on a common notion of its general process. This process is called the *hermeneutic circle*. One interprets something by going from general to specific and from specific to general. An interpreter looks at a specific text in terms of a general idea of what that text may mean, then modifies the general idea based on the examination of the specifics of the text. Interpretation is ongoing, as one goes back and forth between specific and general. One may look at the composite meaning of a text and then examine the specific linguistic structures of that text. Then the interpreter returns to the overall meaning, only to go back to the specifics again.

Further, within the circle, one always relates what is seen in the object to what is already known. The interpreter then alternates between a familiar set of concepts and the unfamiliar until the two merge in a tentative interpretation. In interpreting the actions of a foreign culture, for example, the anthropologist first tries to understand what is happening in terms of concepts that are familiar to the observer; later the anthropologist discovers how the natives understand what they do in their own concepts, and he or she is able to modify the beginning categories. This process continues back and forth until an adequate account is generated. So, too, with the interpretation of a text: The interpreter begins by relating the text to what he or she already understands, looks for strange or unaccounted for details in the text, modifies the original interpretation, re-examines the text, and so on.

Another point on which virtually all hermeneutic scholars agree is that interpretation is a process that can never be divorced from language. The very experience of understanding is linguistic, which means that one's linguistic categories become a crucial part of any understanding. Further, language comes to us with meaning and discloses meaning to us. It is not something we use only as a tool of expression, but something that essentially forms reality for us. Here we see one of the important links between hermeneutics and phenomenology.

Classical Foundations of Hermeneutics and Phenomenology

Modern hermeneutics began in the early nineteenth century with Friedrich Schleiermacher.[9]

---

6. John Stewart, "Philosophy of Qualitative Inquiry: Hermeneutic Phenomenology and Communication Research," *Quarterly Journal of Speech* 67 (1981): 110.

7. Palmer, *Hermeneutics*, p. 67.

8. For an analysis of the different approaches to hermeneutics, see Zygmunt Bauman, *Hermeneutics and Social Science* (New York: Columbia University Press, 1978).

9. Friedrich Schleiermacher, *Hermeneutik*, ed. Heinz Kimmerle (Heidelberg: Carl Winter, Universitaetsverlag, 1959).

Schleiermacher attempted to establish a system for discovering what authors meant in their writings, which involved reconstructing the mental lives of the authors. Schleiermacher had a rather scientific approach to text analysis, which he believed would be the key to authors' original meanings and feelings. Later in the century, Schleiermacher's biographer, Wilhelm Dilthey, was strongly influenced by these ideas.[10] For Dilthey, however, hermeneutics is the key to all humanities and social sciences; he believed that we come to understand human life and works in all areas, not by reductionistic methods as in natural science, but through subjective interpretation. For Dilthey, the human world is social and historical and requires understanding in terms of the community in which human actors live and work. Human beings are not fixed and cannot be known objectively. Dilthey therefore promoted a kind of historical relativism common in social sciences today.

In sharp contrast with Dilthey is Edmund Husserl, the father of phenomenology.[11] Husserl, who wrote during the first half of the twentieth century, attempted to develop a method for ascertaining truth through focused human experience. For Husserl, no conceptual scheme is adequate for uncovering truth; rather, the conscious experience of the individual must be the route for discovering the reality of things in the world. Only through conscious attention can truth be known.

Husserl believed that in everyday life, human beings experience things in a kind of natural attitude. This natural way of experiencing the world is affected by all kinds of extraneous beliefs and perceptions that distract from true conscious experience. Husserl therefore advocated *phenomenological reduction* or *epoché*, which is the careful and systematic elimination of any subjective factors entering into one's pure experience of a thing. In reduction, one brackets a particular event or object, concentrates on that object, and eliminates any personal beliefs about it. When done effectively, one's consciousness of the object reveals its true essence. Once an event is successfully reduced in this way, a second *transcendental reduction* can be made. This reduction brackets consciousness itself, leading to a true understanding of what Husserl called the *transcendental ego* or pure state of consciousness. Social life (the *Lebenswelt*), which leads to one's beliefs, attitudes, and values, can, like any other object or event, be bracketed and reduced. Doing so reveals the true essence of social life.

Husserl's ideas are understandably controversial. His chief critic is the philosopher Martin Heidegger.[12] In Heidegger, phenomenology and hermeneutics become one in "hermeneutic phenomenology." Heidegger denies the ability to reach truth through any kind of reduction. Instead, what is most important in human life is the natural experience of merely being in the world. His philosophy has been called the "hermeneutic of Dasein," which means interpretation of being. In other words, Heidegger was interested in understanding as a mode of existence and as such was the originator of philosophical hermeneutics. For Heidegger, the reality of something is not known by careful analysis, but by natural experience, and that natural experience emerges from communication or the use of language in the world. In sum, what is real is what is experienced through the natural use of language in context: "words and language are not wrappings in which things are packed for the commerce of those who write and speak. It is in words and language that things first come into being and are."[13]

The following sections summarize the work of three interpretive theorists who have contributed to our understanding of communication. These

10. Wilhelm Dilthey, "The Rise of Hermeneutics," trans. Fredric Jameson, *New Literary History* 3 (1972): 229–44.

11. Edmund Husserl, *Ideas: General Introduction to Pure Phenomenology*, trans. W. R. Boyce Gibson (New York: Collier Books, 1962); *Phenomenology and the Crisis of Philosophy*, trans. Quentin Lauer (New York: Harper & Row, 1965). For a brief summary of Husserl's ideas, see Bauman, *Hermeneutics*, pp. 111–30.

12. Martin Heidegger, *Being and Time*, trans. John Macquarrie and Edward Robinson (New York: Harper & Row, 1962); *On the Way to Language*, trans. Peter Hertz (New York: Harper & Row, 1971); *An Introduction to Metaphysics*, trans. Ralph Manheim (New Haven: Yale University Press, 1959). For secondary treatments, see Bauman, *Hermeneutics*, pp. 148–71; Palmer, *Hermeneutics*, pp. 124–61; Deetz, "Words."

13. Heidegger, *Introduction*, p. 13.

works are deeply rooted in the tradition of phenomenology and hermeneutics, but they each provide a special perspective for our consideration.

The Social Interpretation of Alfred Schutz

Schutz was strongly influenced by both Dilthey and Heidegger.[14] He applies phenomenology to social life, believing that the natural attitude of *Lebenswelt* should be the focus. Schutz would investigate social events like communication from the perspective of those actually participating in it. When individuals operate in everyday life, they make three fundamental assumptions. First, they assume that the reality and structure of the world are constant—that the world will remain as it appears. Second, they assume that their own experience of the world is valid. Ultimately, individuals believe that their perception of events is accurate. Third, individuals see themselves as having the power to act and accomplish things, to affect the world.

The work of Schutz is important to communication theory because it makes communication central to the reality experienced by individuals. Our worlds depend on what we learn from others in our socio-cultural communities, which exist in an historical situation. People, in various times and places, experience the world differently, or as one commentator puts it: "The world, when filtered through my biographical situation, becomes 'my' world."[15]

What is real for us depends upon the categories we use to conceptualize experience. A category necessarily includes some observations and excludes others and is therefore a *typification*. People and things are understood and dealt with by being placed within a generalized category that "typifies" them. If people typify, and if their typifications differ, then how can we study social life at all? That is the central problem of the social sciences, and

Schutz's solution is to explore not universal categories of meaning, but the socially approved typifications of particular cultures and social groups. He also seeks to uncover the social structures that lead to those particular forms of knowledge. Thus, general truths about human behavior cannot be found, but specific truths of individual historical groups can be discovered.

For Schutz, social knowledge consists of formulas, or *social recipes*. These are typical, well-understood ways of doing things. They enable people to group things according to some kind of mutually understood logic, to solve problems, to take roles, to communicate, and to establish proper behavior in different situations. In short, one defines a situation in terms of the social recipes in force.

As social phenomenology, Schutz's philosophy provides backing for the social constructionist movement discussed in Chapter 7. It is an important part of the philosophy of social relativism prevalent in much communication theory today and sensitizes us to the many ways in which human communities differ. Schutz's ideas also focus the observer on the individual meanings that different people bring to a communication encounter. Schutz does not emphasize what is common in all humanity, nor does he help us to understand the meanings of human works that transcend individual historical lives, an issue that has been important in hermeneutics. We turn now to the work of a theorist who centers on the meaning-in-text that goes beyond the experience of any particular community of speakers or writers.

The Textual Interpretation of Paul Ricoeur

Paul Ricoeur is a current major interpretive theorist who relies heavily on both the phenomenological and hermeneutic traditions.[16] He also shares many ideas with the post-structuralists discussed in Chaper 4. Ricoeur notes that discourse, as the product of speech, can be understood both

14. Alfred Schutz, *The Phenomenology of the Social World*, trans. George Walsh and Frederick Lehnert (Evanston, Ill.: Northwestern University Press, 1967). For a clear summary of Schutz's ideas, see Robert A. Gorman, *The Dual Vision: Alfred Schutz and the Myth of Phenomenological Social Science* (London: Routledge & Kegan Paul, 1977).

15. Gorman, *Vision*, p. 38.

16. Paul Ricoeur, *Interpretation Theory: Discourse and the Surplus of Meaning* (Fort Worth: The Texas University Press, 1976); *Hermeneutics and the Human Sciences: Essays on Language, Action and Interpretation*, trans. and ed. John B. Thompson (Cambridge, England: Cambridge University Press, 1981).

linguistically, by analyzing the words, or personally, by seeking the author's own meanings for what was said. Because words have multiple meanings (*polysemy*), discourse demands interpretation.

Although he recognizes the importance of discourse in actual speech events, most important for Ricoeur is *text*. Once speech is recorded, it becomes divorced from the actual speaker and situation in which it was produced. Texts cannot be interpreted in the same fashion as discourse because they are not ephemeral; a text has an enduring life of its own. Textual interpretation is especially important when speakers and authors are not available, as is the case with historical documents. However, it need not be limited to these situations. Indeed, the text itself always speaks to us, and the job of the interpreter is to figure out what it is saying.

The separation of text from situation is *distanciation*. The text has meaning irrespective of the author's particular usage. In other words, you can read a message and get meaning from it despite the fact that you were not part of the original speech event. Thus, the author's intent does not prescribe what the text can subsequently be taken to mean, nor does any particular reader's meaning limit what the text itself says. Once written, discourse can be consumed by anybody who can read, providing a multitude of meaning possibilities, and multiple readings (meanings) are definitely probable. The shared reality that made communication possible between the original author and the original audience may no longer exist. For these reasons the interpretation of textual material is more complex and more interesting than that of spoken discourse. For Ricoeur, text interpretation is the central focus of hermeneutics.

This does not mean that hermeneutics should be limited to written material. In fact, any kind of action can be recorded. A text is essentially a recording, whether written, electronic, photographic, or preserved by some other means. The problem remains the same: How do we interpret a message that is no longer part of an actual played-out event?

The meaning of a text is always a pattern of the whole, never just a composite of individual elements. Ricoeur's version of the hermeneutic circle involves the fusion of "explanation" and "understanding." *Explanation* is empirical and analytic: It accounts for events in terms of observed patterns among parts. In studying a book of the Bible, for example, you would carefully examine the individual linguistic elements of each verse and note the ways in which they form patterns of meaning. *Understanding* is synthetic, accounting for events in terms of overall interpretation. So in continuing your study of the Bible, you would also look for a holistic or general meaning of the passage under consideration. In hermeneutics, one goes through both processes, breaking down a text into its parts and looking for patterns, then stepping back and judging subjectively the meaning of the whole. You move from understanding to explaining and back to understanding again in a complex dialectic. Explanation and understanding, then, are not separate, but are two poles in an interpretive process. That interpretation allows the text to speak to the interpreter. It becomes a way in which the interpreter's own experience can be changed. If the interpreter is open to the message of a text, its meaning can be appropriated, or made personal. Interpretation begins in distanciation, but ends in personalization. To interpret the sections of the Bible, you would remove your own interests from your study of the intrinsic meanings in the text, but then you would apply those meanings to your own situation.

Gadamer's Interpretation of Being

Hans-Georg Gadamer is today's leading proponent of philosophical hermeneutics.[17] A protégé of Heidegger, Gadamer is primarily interested in how understanding is possible in human experience. For Gadamer, individuals do not stand apart from texts in order to analyze and interpret them; rather, interpretation itself is part and parcel of being.

17. Gadamer's major work is *Truth and Method* (New York: The Seabury Press, 1975). An excellent secondary treatment can be found in Richard J. Bernstein, *Beyond Objectivism and Relativism: Science, Hermeneutics, and Praxis* (Philadelphia: University of Pennsylvania Press, 1983), pp. 107–69. See also Palmer, *Hermeneutics*, pp. 162–222.

The central tenet of Gadamer's theory is that one always understands experience from the perspective of presuppositions. Our tradition gives us a way of understanding things, and we cannot divorce ourselves from that tradition. Observation, reason, and understanding are never objectively pure; they are colored by history and community. Further, history is not to be separated from the present. We are always simultaneously part of the past, in the present, and anticipating the future. In other words, the past operates on us now in the present and affects our conceptions of what is yet to come. At the same time, our present notions of reality affect how we view the past. We cannot exist outside an historical tradition.

To say that one is part of a tradition is not to deny change. Indeed, over time one becomes distanced from events in the past. Our way of seeing things in the present creates a temporal distance from an object of the past such that artifacts have both a strangeness and a familiarity. We understand an artifact in terms of the categories provided by our tradition; then unessential features of an artifact drop away, leaving a residue of highly relevant meaning. Interpretation of historical events and objects, like texts, is enhanced by historical distance. Thus Gadamer would agree with Ricoeur that understanding a text involves looking at the enduring meanings of that text within a tradition and apart from the original communicators' intentions. Texts, therefore, become contemporaneous and speak to us in our own time. The Gettysburg Address was originally a piece of spoken discourse designed to achieve a certain effect during the Civil War. Once spoken, however, the text lived on as an object of its own, rife with internal meaning. Unessential details—that it was written on the back of an envelope on the train—drop away as the text itself reveals its meanings to us in our own time.

Hermeneutics is not only a dialogic process of questioning the text but also of allowing the text to question us. What questions does the text itself suggest, and when we ask those questions, what answers does the text offer? What questions does the text suggest for our own experience, and how do we respond to the questions of the text? This interpretive process is paradoxical: We let the text speak to us, yet we cannot understand it apart from our own prejudices and presuppositions. Change results from the dialogue between the prejudices of the present and the meanings of the text. Thus, prejudice is a positive force, to be acknowledged and used productively in our lives. As one observer has noted, "The problem for the study of communication is not the existence of prejudices but the unawareness of their presence and subsequent inability to separate appropriate from inappropriate ones."[18]

Like Heidegger, Gadamer believes that experience is inherently linguistic. We cannot separate our experience from language. The perspectives of tradition, from which we always view the world, are embodied in words. Gadamer says:

> The linguistic word is not a "sign" which one lays hold of; it is also no existing thing that one shapes and endows with a meaning, making a sign to render some other thing visible. Both possibilities are wrong; rather, the ideality of the meaning lies in the word itself. Word is always already meaningful.[19]

Note how this conception differs from the structural view of language summarized in Chapter 4, in which language is seen as a tool for expressing and referring to an objective reality. Gadamer's view is also different from the interactionist notion (even Schutz's), which suggests that language and meaning are created through social interaction. Gadamer's point is that language itself prefigures all experience. The world is presented to us through language. Thus, in communication, two people are not using language to interact with one another; rather, communication involves a triad of two individuals and a language.[20]

To get this idea across, Gadamer uses the analogy of the game. A game has its own nature and is independent from individual players. The game

18. Stanley Deetz, "Conceptualizing Human Understanding: Gadamer's Hermeneutics and American Communication Studies," *Communication Quarterly* 26 (1978): 14.

19. Gadamer, *Wahrheit und Methode [Truth and Method]* (Tuebingen: J.C.B. Mohr, 1960), p. 394.

20. John Angus Campbell, "Hans-Georg Gadamer's Truth and Method," *Quarterly Journal of Speech* 64 (1978): 101–22.

will exist and be the same whether it is being played or not and regardless of who is playing. Language and life are like games: We play them, just as we experience life, but they come to us preformed and remain intact after our particular playing is finished. One commentator explains it this way: "The world is already meaningful. That is, the world which comes to us in the only way that the human world can come to us, through language, is an already meaningful world.[21]

Critique of Interpretation

Two serious debates surround the interpretive approaches. On the right, these approaches conflict with traditional scientific perspectives similar to those summarized in Chapter 5. On the left, they conflict with critical theory. Traditional science accuses interpretive approaches of downplaying the causal effects of external structures, and critical theory accuses interpretive approaches of being too conservative and nonjudgmental.

Critique from the right. The structuralist critique is easily anticipated from ideas presented earlier in this text. It begins with the opposing assumption that things are real apart from the human experience of those things. In other words, discovery, rather than interpretation, is the correct route to knowledge. Although knowledge is personal, that which is known is impersonal, making the idea of social reality "monstrous."[22] People do construct knowledge, but reality itself puts a limit on what can legitimately be constructed.

Further, these structures are largely unintentional and unconscious. Cognition is a complex set of processes, many of which are hidden from the individual.[23] Although a lot of what we do is indeed conscious, many important structures governing social life are beyond awareness. One observer makes this point:

> Action theory is based upon a traditional conception of consciousness. It is increasingly difficult in contemporary theory to explain communication behavior while relying upon only the traditional conception of consciousness. The more a theory emphasizes "unconscious" or nontraditional dimensions of consciousness, the less possibility there is to explain communication behavior in terms of individual intention and action.[24]

Phenomenologists might agree with this summary but would suggest that what becomes conscious during cognitive processing is that which is essential and real about an experience.

Structuralists point out that social structures exist apart from any design or intention as people live their lives. Anthony Giddens calls these the "unintended consequences" of purposeful actions. As individuals go about their daily activities, certain outcomes that may not be intended nor even conscious come about, and these resultant structures have a serious impact on subsequent actions. Thus, structures are produced and reproduced in action. Interpretive approaches often ignore the unintended consequences of action. Giddens notes the importance of such structures:

> History is not an intentional project, and all intentional activity takes place in the context of institutions sedimented over long-term periods of time. The unintended consequences of action are of fundamental importance to social theory, especially insofar as they are systematically incorporated within the processes of the reproduction of institutions.[25]

To the structuralist, all of this means that people may not accurately understand, nor can they reliably report, their experience. If your intentions are elusive and important processes are hidden, then what is really going on in social life is not something a perceiver can tap into experientially. Instead, scientific methods of discovery are necessary.

21. Ibid., p. 107.

22. D. W. Hamlyn, "The Concept of Social Reality," in *Explaining Human Behavior: Consciousness, Human Action, and Social Structure*, ed. Paul F. Secord (Beverly Hills: Sage Publications, 1982), p. 194.

23. See, for example, Michael T. Motley, "Consciousness and Intentionality in Communication: A Preliminary Model and Methodological Approaches," *Western Journal of Speech Communication* 50 (1986): 3–23.

24. William Bailey, "Consciousness and Action/Motion Theories of Communication," *Western Journal of Speech Communication* 50 (1986): 74.

25. Anthony Giddens, "On the Relation of Sociology to Philosophy," in *Explaining Human Behavior: Consciousness, Human Action, and Social Structure*, ed. Paul F. Secord (Beverly Hills: Sage Publications, 1982), p. 180.

Research on attribution theory (Chapter 9) illustrates the difficulty of explaining one's own actions.[26] (Critics of attribution theory, however, are quick to point out that the findings in this line of research do not accurately reflect the everyday experience of people acting in context.[27] Indeed, this criticism has been leveled against all positivistic social science research.)

Critique from the left. Although interpretive and critical approaches to communication theory have certain common principles, there is also a substantial difference between the two, which has become the source of a debate.[28] Critical Theory accuses strictly interpretive approaches of being conservative and of failing to recognize their ideological character. In other words, understanding human action by itself does not go far enough. Scholars must study the ways in which individuals are oppressed so that people can rise up and change the circumstances of their lives. The failure of interpretive scholarship to do so merely legitimizes repressive power structures and perpetuates oppression in society.[29] (See this argument developed in the following section.)

Critical Approaches

In general, criticism implies the application of values to make judgments for the purpose of accomplishing positive change. Criticism has been applied to a variety of communication phenomena. Rhetorical criticism, for example, carefully examines and judges the effectiveness of discourse and other communication forms.[30] Aesthetic criticism focuses on the intrinsic artistic qualities of a message or other expressive medium.[31] Although important, these topics are not the concern of this chapter. Our subject here is with *critical social science*, which involves the critical examination of social structures.

Although there are several varieties of critical social science, all share three essential features.[32] First, they subscribe to the basic tenets of interpretive social science, as explained in the first part of this chapter. That is, the critical social scientists believe it necessary to *understand* the lived experience of real people in context. Specifically, critical approaches aim to interpret and thereby understand the ways in which various social groups are restrained and oppressed. Second, critical approaches examine social conditions in an attempt to bring these often hidden structures to light. Most critical theories teach that knowledge is power, for understanding the ways in which one is oppressed enables one to take action to change oppressive forces. Third, critical social science makes a conscious attempt to fuse theory and action. Such theories are clearly normative and act to accomplish change in the conditions that affect our lives.

Critical social science is often economic and political in nature, but much of it concerns communication and the communication order in society. However, critical theorists are usually reluctant to separate communication and other elements from the overall system. Thus, a critical theory of communication (or economics, or politics) necessarily involves a critique of society as a whole.

Critical communication theory deals with a variety of relevant topics, including language, organizational structures, interpersonal relationships, and media. Because of its increasingly prevalent role in mass communication theory, we return to

26. R. E. Nisbett and T. D. Wilson, "Telling More than We Can Know: Verbal Reports on Mental Processes," *Psychological Review* 84 (1977): 231–59. See also Palema J. Benoit and William L. Benoit, "Consciousness: The Mindlessness/Mindfulness and Verbal Report Controversies," *Western Journal of Speech Communication* 50 (1986): 41–63.

27. See, for example, John Shotter, *Social Accountability and Selfhood* (New York: Basil Blackwell, 1984), pp. 167–72; Kenneth Gergen, *Toward Transformation in Social Knowledge* (New York: Springer-Verlag, 1982), pp. 126–33.

28. This debate is summarized in Fay, *Social Theory*; and Ricoeur, *Hermeneutics.*

29. Fay, *Social Theory.*

30. See, for example, Bernard L. Brock and Robert L. Scott, *Methods of Rhetorical Criticism* (Detroit: Wayne State University Press, 1980).

31. See, for example, J. Stolnitz, *Aesthetics and Philosophy of Art Criticism: A Critical Introduction* (Boston: Houghton Mifflin, 1960).

32. Fay, *Social Theory*, p. 94.

critical theory again in Chapter 13. Here, we deal with two important examples of critical social science—feminist criticism and Marxist criticism.

Feminist Theory

Feminist theory is a generic label for a perspective or group of theories that explores the meaning of gender concepts.[33] Feminist theorists observe that many aspects of life apart from biological sex are understood in terms of gender qualities, including language, work, family roles, education, socialization, and others. Feminist critique aims to expose both the powers and limits of this division. Much feminist theory emphasizes the oppressive nature of gender relations.

Feminist theory begins with the assumption that gender is a pervasive category for understanding human experience. Gender is a social construction that, although useful, has been dominated by a male bias and is oppressive to women. Feminist theory aims to challenge the prevailing gender assumptions of society and to achieve more liberating ways for women and men to exist in the world. In these ways, feminist theory is by definition "radical"; it goes to the root of human experience and speaks out for change in the socio-cultural and linguistic structures that determine the relations between women and men.

Feminist criticism has become increasingly popular in the study of communication.[34] These critics examine the ways in which the male language bias affects the relations between the sexes, the ways in which male domination has constrained communication for females, the ways in which females have both accommodated and resisted male patterns of speech and language, the powers of feminine communication forms, and other similar concerns. The following section summarizes one

particular feminist theory of communication that embodies many of the themes prevalent in the literature on women and communication.

Muted Group Theory

Muted group theory originated with anthropologists Edwin Ardener and Shirley Ardener.[35] Edwin Ardener observed that anthropologists tend to characterize a culture in terms of the masculine: "The fact is that no one could come back from an ethnographic study of 'the X,' having talked only *to* women, and *about* men, without professional comment and some self-doubt, whereas the reverse can and does happen constantly."[36] In other words, ethnography seemed biased toward observation of males in a culture. Upon closer examination, however, it appeared to Ardener that the actual language of a culture had an inherent male bias, that men created the meanings for a group, and that the feminine voice was suppressed or "muted." This silencing of women, in Ardener's observation, leads to women's inability to eloquently express themselves in the male parlance.

Shirley Ardener added to the theory by suggesting that the silence of women has several manifestations and is especially evident in public discourse. Women are less comfortable and less expressive in public situations than are men, and they are less comfortable in public situations than they are in private. Consequently, women monitor their own communications more intensely than do men. Women watch what they say and translate what they are feeling and thinking into male terms. When masculine and feminine meanings and expressions conflict, the masculine tends to win out because of the dominance of males in society. So women are, and remain, muted.

Communication theorist Cheris Kramarae has expanded muted group theory by incorporating it

---

33. Karen A. Foss and Sonja K. Foss, "Incorporating the Feminist Perspective in Communication Scholarship: A Research Commentary," in *Doing Research on Women's Communication: Alternative Perspectives in Theory and Method*, eds. Carole Spitzack and Kathryn Carter (Norwood, N.J.), in press.

34. For a sampling of this work, see Fern L. Johnson, "Coming to Terms with Women's Language," *Quarterly Journal of Speech* 72 (1986): 318–52; Foss and Foss, "Incorporating."

35. Edwin Ardener, "Some Outstanding Problems in the Analysis of Events" (Paper presented at the Association of Social Anthropologists' Decennial Conference, 1973); "The 'Problem' Revisited," in *Perceiving Women*, ed. Shirley Ardener (London: Malaby Press, 1975); Shirley Ardener, *Defining Females: The Nature of Women in Society* (New York: John Wiley, 1978).

36. Ardener, "Problem," p. 3.

with thinking and research on women and communication.[37] She outlines the basic assumptions of muted group theory as follows:

1. Women perceive the world differently from men because of women's and men's different experiences and activities rooted in the division of labor.

2. Because of their political dominance, the men's system of perception is dominant, impeding the free expression of the women's alternative models of the world.

3. In order to participate in society women must transform their own models in terms of the received male system of expression.[38]

Kramarae suggests a number of hypotheses about women's communication based on research findings. First, females express themselves with more difficulty than do males. A common female experience is to lack a word for a feminine experience, apparently because males, who do not share that experience, have not developed a term for it. Second, women understand men's meanings more easily than men understand women's. The evidence of this generalization can be seen in a number of ways: Men may have distanced themselves from the expressions of women because they do not understand those expressions; women are subjected to experiences (for instance, lack of a word) that men have not had; men may suppress women and rationalize it on the grounds that women are not as rational or clear; women thus must learn the male system of communication, but men in return have isolated themselves from the female system.

This hypothesis leads to the third: Women have created their own means of expression outside the dominant male system. Letters, diaries, consciousness raising groups, and alternative art forms are examples. Women rely more on nonverbal expression and use different nonverbal forms than do men because they are verbally muted. Some research has shown, for example, that facial expressions, vocal pauses, and bodily gestures are more important in women's discussions than they are in men's.

37. Cheris Kramarae, *Women and Men Speaking: Frameworks for Analysis* (Rowley, Mass.: Newbury House, 1981), pp. 1–63.
38. Ibid., p. 3.

Women also seem to display a wider variability of expression in their speech.

Fourth, women tend to express more dissatisfaction about communication than do men. Women may talk more about their problems in using language or their difficulty in using standard male tools of communication. Women poets, for example, often express these concerns, and writers and public speakers sometimes state their feelings of being constrained by the customary practices in those fields. Thus—and this is the fifth hypothesis—women often make efforts to change the dominant rules of communication in order to get around or resist conventional rules. Advocates for women's liberation, for example, have created new words such as *Ms.* and *herstory* and have developed different communication forms that incorporate women's experiences. Consciousness raising groups are a good example of this.

Sixth, women are traditionally less likely to coin new words that become popular in society at large; consequently, they feel excluded from contributing to language. Finally, women find different things humorous than do men. Because they have different methods of conceptualization and expression, relations that appear funny to men may not be humorous at all to women.

Muted group theory is an excellent example of a critical communication theory. It focuses on the experience of particular groups in society, it exposes underlying structures causing oppression, and it suggests directions for positive change. We turn now to another kind of critical social theory.

Marxist Critique

An important strand of communication theory has emerged in this century in the tradition of the Frankfurt School. These theorists originally based their ideas on Marxist thought, although it has gone far afield from that origin in the past fifty years. The Frankfurt School has, in fact, developed a general social critique, but communication takes a central place in its tenets, and systems of mass communication have been an especially important focus in this work. The name normally given to this tradition is simply "Critical Theory."

Critical Theory began with the work of Max

Horkheimer, Theodor Adorno, Herbert Marcuse, and their colleagues at the Frankfurt Institute for Social Research in 1923.[39] The group was originally guided by Marxist principles, although they were never members of any political party, and their work was distinctly scholarly rather than activist. With the rise of National Socialism in Germany in the 1930s, essentially all of the Frankfurt scholars immigrated to the United States and there became intensely interested in mass communication and the media as structures of oppression in capitalistic societies, especially those structures in America.

Today, Critical Theory is thriving, although it has become more diffused and multitheoretical. Although not all adherents to Critical Theory are strictly Marxist, there is no question that Marx had an immense influence on this school of thought.

Marx taught that the means of production in society determines the very nature of that society.[40] In capitalistic systems, profit drives production and therefore dominates labor. Working class groups are oppressed by dominant groups that benefit from profit. Only when the working class rises up against dominant groups can new means of production and thereby the liberation of the worker be achieved. To win liberation (attain new means of production) would be to further the natural progress of history in which forces in opposition clash in a dialectic to result in a higher social order.

Critical Theorists view their task to be the uncovering of oppressive forces in society through dialectical analysis.[41] The population generally perceives a kind of surface order to things, and the

Critical Theorist's job is to point out an underlying struggle of opposing forces. Only by seeing the dialectic of opposing forces that creates a synthesis or order can individuals be liberated and free to change that existing order. Otherwise, they will remain alienated from one another and from society as a whole. This kind of analysis is also a form of action or, in the terms of Critical Theory, *praxis*, because it breaks down the status quo into a set of contradictions and distortions.

Critical Theory places great emphasis on the means of communication in society. Communication practices are an outcome of the tension between individual creativity in framing messages and the social constraints on that creativity. Only when individuals are truly free to express themselves with clarity and reason will liberation occur, and that condition cannot come about until a classless society arises. One of the chief constraints on individual expression is language itself. The dominant classes in society create a language of suppression and repression, which makes it very difficult for working class groups to understand their situation and to get out of it. (You can see the parallel here with both feminist theory and philosophical hermeneutics.) It is the job of the Critical Theorist to create new forms of language that will enable the predominant paradigm to be demythologized. The most important contemporary thinker in Critical Theory is Juergen Habermas, to whom we now turn.

Universal Pragmatics and the Transformation of Society

Juergen Habermas is clearly the most important spokesperson for the Frankfurt School today.[42] His theory draws from a wide range of thought and

39. For a brief historical perspective, see Thomas B. Farrell and James A. Aune, "Critical Theory and Communication: A Selective Literature Review," *Quarterly Journal of Speech* 65 (1979): 93–120.

40. Karl Marx, *The Communist Manifesto* (London: W. Reeves, 1888); *Capital* (Chicago: C. H. Kerr, 1909).

41. Robert Pryor, "On the Method of Critical Theory and its Implications for a Critical Theory of Communication," in *Phenomenology in Rhetoric and Communication*, ed. Stanley Deetz (Washington, D.C.: Center for Advanced Research in Phenomenology & University Press of America, 1981), pp. 25–35. See also Jennifer Daryl Slack and Martin Allor, "The Political and Epistemological Constituents of Critical Communication Research," *Journal of Communication* 33 (1983): 128–218; Dallas W. Smythe and Tran Van Dinh, "On Critical and Administrative Research: A New Critical Analysis," *Journal of Communication* 33 (1983): 117–27; Everett M. Rogers, "The Empirical and the Critical Schools of Communication Research," in *Com-

munication Yearbook 5*, ed. Michael Burgoon (New Brunswick, N.J.: Transaction Books, 1982), pp. 125–44.

42. The important works of Habermas include *Knowledge and Human Interests*, trans. Jeremy J. Shapiro (Boston: Beacon Press, 1971); *Legitimation Crisis*, trans. Thomas McCarthy (Boston: Beacon Press, 1975); *The Theory of Communicative Action, Volume I: Reason and the Rationalization of Society*, trans. Thomas McCarthy (Boston: Beacon Press, 1984). An excellent secondary summary can be found in Sonja K. Foss, Karen A. Foss, and Robert Trapp, *Contemporary Perspectives on Rhetoric* (Prospect Heights, Ill.: Waveland Press, 1985), pp. 213–40; see also Sue Curry Jansen, "Power and Knowledge: Toward a New Critical Synthesis," *Journal of Communication* 33 (1983): 342–54.

presents a coherent critical view of communication and society. Habermas teaches that society must be understood as a mix of three major interests: work, interaction, and power. All three interests are necessary and, in fact, inseparable from the human condition.

Work consists of the efforts to create necessary material resources. Because of its highly instrumental nature—achieving tangible tasks and accomplishing concrete objectives—this is basically a "technical interest." It involves an instrumental rationality and is represented in scholarship in the empirical/analytical sciences.

The second major interest is *interaction*, or the use of language and other symbol systems in relating to others. Since social cooperation is necessary to survive in life, Habermas names this the "practical interest." It involves practical reasoning and is represented in scholarship in history and hermeneutics.

The third major interest is *power*. Social order naturally leads to power distribution; yet, there is also a natural interest in being freed from the domination that comes from the application of power. Power leads to distorted communication, but by becoming aware of the ideologies that dominate in society, groups can themselves be empowered to transform society. Consequently, power is an "emancipatory interest." The rationality of power is self-reflection, and the branch of scholarship that deals with it is Critical Theory.

Human life cannot be properly understood within a single dimension or approach—work, interaction, or power. All three are necessary for a complete understanding of society. Further, no aspect of life is interest-free, even science. An emancipated society is free from unnecessary domination of any one interest, and everybody has equal opportunity to participate in decision making. A strong public sphere, apart from private interests, is necessary to insure this.

Habermas is especially concerned with the technical interest's domination in contemporary capitalistic societies.[43] In such societies, the public and private are intertwined to the degree that the public sector is unable to guard against the oppression of private, technical interests. Ideally, the public and private should be balanced, and the public sector should be strong enough to provide a climate for free expression of ideas and debate. With the rise of private technocracy, however, that climate is stifled.

It is clear from the foregoing discussion that Habermas values communication as essential to emancipation. Language itself is central to human life, and language becomes the means by which the emancipatory interest is fulfilled. Communicative competence, therefore, is necessary for effective participation in decision making. Competence involves knowing how to use speech appropriately to accomplish your purposes. This means communicating in such a way that one's propositions are compelling to an audience. It also means sufficient adaptation of one's speech so that the listeners understand the speaker's intention.

This perspective on communication is largely a reconstruction of speech act theory, which is summarized in Chapter 7. Habermas refers to his theory of speech acts as universal pragmatics, and he outlines three types of speech acts. *Constatives* are designed to get across a proposition as true. They are basically assertions. One might, for example, intend to state the truth of the claim that a union has engaged in unfair labor practices. *Regulatives* are intended to affect one's relationship with another person or party and include commands and promises. For example, a management statement on unfair labor practices might be intended to bring the union to the bargaining table. Finally, *avowals* are designed to express the speaker's internal condition, as a statement of labor practices might express the management's anger over union activities. Obviously, any single message could contain a combination of these types of acts.

The nature of a speech act determines the kind of *validity* that one must meet in a statement. In a constative speech act, one must demonstrate the truth of the claim. In a regulative speech act, one must meet standards of appropriateness. And an avoval speech act must be sincere or truthful. Since

---

43. See especially *Legitimation Crisis.*

a single speech act may fulfill any of the three types, various combinations of validity forms may also have to be met. For example, in order to meet all three of the validity requirements, the management's statement on union practices must be taken as true (that the union is indeed behaving in an unfair manner), as appropriate (that under the circumstances, bargaining is proper), and as sincere (that management is truly angry over the situation).

When one of the forms of validity is questioned, special work is required. Communicators may withdraw from the interaction, continue normal communication, or move to the level of "discourse." *Discourse* is special communicative action, in which one works to demonstrate the validity of the act. Unlike normal communication, discourse is systematic argumentation designed to bring special appeals to bear to demonstrate the validity of the statement.

When sincerity is challenged, regular communicative action, intended to express one's sincerity, is required; but when one of the other forms of validity is questioned, discursive action is necessary. One uses *theoretic discourse*, which emphasizes evidence, to argue the truth of one's proposition. One uses *practical discourse*, which centers on the norms of a given situation, in arguing appropriateness. Where communicators do not share the same standards or conceptual framework for evaluating the strength of an argument, the communicators must move to a higher level of discourse, which Habermas calls *meta-theoretical discourse*. And when the very nature of knowledge (epistemology) is under contention, *meta-ethical discourse* is required. Such discourse philosophically argues what constitutes proper knowledge. The last type of discourse is precisely what Critical Theory does, for it challenges the assumed procedures for generating knowledge in society.

Habermas believes that free speech is necessary for productive normal communication and higher levels of discourse to take place. Although impossible to achieve, Habermas describes the *ideal speech situation* on which society should be modeled. First, the ideal speech situation requires that speech be free; there must be no constraints on what can be expressed. Second, all individuals must have equal access to speaking. In other words, all speakers are recognized as legitimate. Finally, the norms and obligations of society are not one-sided, but distribute power equally to all strata in society. Only when these requirements are met, will completely emancipatory communication be able to take place.

Criticism of Critical Theory

The critique of critical approaches to communication theory comes from a variety of fronts.[44] Here we will look at criticisms of feminist theory and Critical Theory.

Feminist theory. While feminist theory revolves around the conceptual division of masculine and feminine genders, some question the very utility of this dualism.[45] Although the masculine-feminine distinction has been useful, it may have over simplified the situation and created a conceptualization that does not accurately reflect reality. Such labeling may, in fact, reify or reinforce distinctions that feminists themselves are trying to overcome. Linda Putnam states the point in these terms: "the problem of reification, the use of feminist labels has the double-edged effect of recognizing women while simultaneously isolating them."[46] And again, "Efforts to degenderize behaviors have the potential to liberate us from sex-role classifications that emanate from dualism."[47] The answer, according to Putnam, is not to abandon feminist theory or feminist ideals, but to look at the process of communication differently. Instead of simply assuming that

44. Several critical articles can be found in *Ferment in the Field*, a special issue of *Journal of Communication* 33 (Summer, 1983). A summary of this criticism can be found in Michael Real, "The Debate on Critical Theory and the Study of Communications," *Journal of Communication* 34 (Autumn, 1984): 72–80.

45. Linda L. Putnam, "In Search of Gender: A Critique of Communication and Sex-Roles Research," *Women's Studies in Communication* 5 (1982): 1–9.

46. Ibid., p. 4. See also, Julia T. Wood and W. Barnett Pearce, "Sexists, Racists, and Other Classes of Classifiers: Form and Function of 'ist' Accusation," *Quarterly Journal of Speech* 66 (1980): 239–50.

47. Putnam, "Search," p. 7.

gender is the cause of other effects, we should also examine the ways in which communication patterns have led to gender distinctions themselves.

Critical theory. The most significant criticism of critical approaches to communication theory come from interpretive scholars. As indicated above, the debate between critical and interpretive social science has produced objections to both interpretation and criticism. Just as critical scholars like Habermas criticize interpretive work for being conservative, interpretivists like Gadamer revere tradition and blame critical theory for trying to tear down the very history from which it can never escape. Interpretivists seek ways to uncover meanings and to overcome misunderstandings so that traditions can speak to us in positive ways, and they criticize critical theories for claiming that such misunderstandings are systematic distortions by powerful groups. Finally, from their position of dialogue, interpretivists object to critical theorists' call for ideal communication designed to rescue society from its iniquities.[48] Instead, they believe, language and communication as naturally given in everyday life constitute a positive voice that should be heard. Ricoeur crystallizes the perspectives of interpretive theory and critical theory in these terms:

> What is at stake can be expressed in terms of an alternative: either a hermeneutical consciousness or a critical consciousness. . . . In contrast to the positive assessment of hermeneutics, the theory of ideology adopts a suspicious approach, seeing tradition as merely the systematically distorted expression of communication under unacknowledged conditions of violence.[49]

Ricoeur himself argues for a "zone of intersection which . . . ought to become the point of departure for a new phase of hermeneutics."[50] Through distanciation, one is able to understand texts in a way that reveals the limits of context. Once it is freed

from situation and author, text provides insights into the problems of historical circumstances. In addition, when disembodied texts speak to us, they reveal our own limits and the limits of our own times. Such textual interpretation also opens up possibilities for new ways of being in the future. For Ricoeur, then, interpretive theory and critical theory are not very far apart.

Integration

Meaning can be found in both action and text. The expressions of individuals in actual historical situations communicate personal and cultural meanings, and once discourse is recorded, it lives on and becomes "disembodied" or distanced from those human beings whose original intentions and meanings guided its creation. Texts themselves have meanings within them that may not reflect the intentions of the originators of the discourse. Original discourse and timeless texts can be "read" in a variety of ways, making interpretation necessary.

Interpretation is the process of discovering the meaning in an action, an expression, or a text. Interpretation is a circular hermeneutic process of studying patterns in the action or text, determining what overall meanings are suggested by these patterns, then testing these meanings by examining the patterns once again and revising the interpretation as necessary.

Although the above summary suggests that individual speakers, writers, and interpreters are separate from their texts, many scholars believe that human experience is inseparable from the discourses and texts that are embedded in their lives. Experience itself is inherently linguistic. The language of our culture determines our experience and creates a bias or way of understanding. Texts do speak to us, but we always read texts from the standpoint of the historical milieu in which we live and think.

Often that milieu consists of powerful forces that subvert and oppress individual human beings.

48. The primary opponents in this debate have been Gadamer and Habermas. The debate is summarized by Ricoeur, *Hermeneutics*, pp. 64–80.
49. Ibid., p. 64.
50. Ibid., p. 79.

Dominant linguistic forms and communication media may prevent certain groups from full participation in the control structures of society. In our own times, some believe, this oppression is seen in economic structures, communication media, and gender relations.

This brings our discussion of general theories of communication to a close. In the following part of the book, we concentrate on specific theories applicable to the contexts of interpersonal, group, organizational, and mass communication.

III

Contextual Theories

Nine

Theories of Interpersonal Communication: Personal and Discourse Processes

Communication always occurs in context, and the nature of communication depends in large measure on this context. In Chapter 1 four main levels were described: interpersonal communication, group communication, organizational communication, and mass communication. These contexts form a hierarchy in which each higher level includes the lower levels but adds something new of its own. For example, mass communication is a distinctive context, but it includes many of the features of interpersonal, group, and organizational communication as well.

Although we all have an intuitive sense of what interpersonal communication is, defining it is more difficult. In Chapter 1 we saw that interpersonal communication is not fundamentally different from other forms of communication. Sarah Trenholm and Arthur Jensen's observation is valid: "Instead of thinking of interpersonal communication as separate from other forms of communication we prefer to think of all communication as having an interpersonal element."[1] These authors describe the pure case of interpersonal communication as two individuals interacting directly and personally. The communicators share the roles of sender and receiver, and in their interaction, they create understandings and meanings.

Any episode of interpersonal communication involves at least three elements—the communicators, their discourse, and their relationship. Chapters 9 and 10 are organized around this three-part division. Chapter 9 discusses theories relevant to *personal processes*, including the ways in which people reveal information about themselves and come to know other people through communication, and *discourse processes*, or the ways in which conversations are managed. Chapter 10 deals with the third element, *relational processes*, including the development, maintenance, and dissolution of relationships and other relevant topics.

Personal Processes

In this section we address a number of theories dealing with the ways in which individuals come to know themselves and others through communication. Specifically, these theories relate to people's orientations toward themselves and other people when they communicate. Five topics are included: interpersonal knowledge, attribution theory, self-disclosure, rhetorical sensitivity, and communicator style. As a group, these theories present a composite picture of personal processes in communication. The first theory provides an excellent general introduction.

Interpersonal Knowledge

The theory of interpersonal knowledge is the brainchild of Charles Berger and his colleagues.[2] It

---

1. Sarah Trenholm and Arthur Jensen, *Interpersonal Communication* (Belmont, Calif.: Wadsworth, 1988), p. 29.

2. The theory is clearly summarized in Charles R. Berger and James J. Bradac, *Language and Social Knowledge: Uncertainty in Interpersonal Relations* (London: Edward Arnold, 1982). See also C. R. Berger and R. J. Calabrese, "Some Explorations in Initial

deals primarily with the ways in which individuals know themselves and others in interaction.

The theory has two major concerns—self-awareness and knowledge of others. From research in social psychology, Berger observes that self-awareness varies from person to person and from situation to situation.[3] One's state of self-awareness is *objective* in the sense that one becomes an object in his or her own awareness. In objective self-awareness, the person centers on the self rather than other objects in the environment. *Subjective self-awareness*, on the other hand, puts the self in a peripheral position so that the self blends into the momentary stream of experience. Research indicates that objective self-awareness is not uncommon, as we are often made to concentrate on ourselves in various situations, but it tends to be an uncomfortable state. Although an individual's self-awareness will vary from moment to moment, each person has a relatively enduring norm of self-awareness. Some individuals are often or always self-aware, while others are rarely or never so.

The enduring trait of being self-aware is *self-consciousness*, and this characteristic is dominated by a tendency to *self-monitor*, or "watch yourself." High self-monitors are guarded and careful about the impression they give to others. They are highly sensitive to the feedback of other people and try to adapt their behaviors to suit others. Low self-monitors tend to be less sensitive to themselves or to others and are less concerned with making impressions. While high self-monitors tend to be actors, low self-monitors tend to "tell it like it is." A theory presented later in this section, rhetorical sensitivity, elaborates on this difference in some detail.

Berger and his colleagues believe that much of our social action is unconscious. Indeed, it would be laborious, if not impossible, to operate in a totally conscious state. An important adaptive mechanism is the use of scripts. A *script* is a routine action sequence or program used to respond to a particular situation.[4] By relying on scripts, communicators can reduce the uncertainty in a situation. Scripts alleviate the need to question and to create a plan of action for every situation. Adults have thousands of scripts available to them. The problem is whether an appropriate script exists for a given situation and, if so, how it should be enacted. Scripts are typically mindless because we go through a script without thinking about it. Actions become mindful when a novel situation is encountered, when the script becomes difficult to enact or is interrupted for some reason, when the outcome of the script is unexpected, or when the situation does not allow an entire script to be played out.

When we encounter a stranger, we have a strong desire to reduce uncertainty about that person by gaining information. Much of Berger's theory deals with this process. Indeed, uncertainty reduction is one of the primary dimensions of a developing relationship.[5] Often the normal behavior of the other person immediately reduces our uncertainty, greatly lessening the desire to get additional information. However, under certain circumstances, the need to know more about a person is heightened. Such circumstances include abnormal behavior on the part of the other person, the expectation that we will be communicating with the other person in the future, or the prospect that the encounter will be especially rewarding or costly. Under these conditions, we will probably take action to get more information about the other person.

How, then, do you go about getting such information? Berger suggests a variety of strategies, some

Interaction and Beyond: Toward a Developmental Theory of Interpersonal Communication," *Human Communication Research* 1 (1975): 99–112; C. R. Berger, R. R. Gardner, M. R. Parks, L. Schulman, and G. R. Miller, "Interpersonal Epistemology and Interpersonal Communication," in *Explorations in Interpersonal Communication*, ed. Gerald R. Miller (Beverly Hills: Sage Publications, 1976), pp. 149–71; and C. R. Berger and William Douglas, "Thought and Talk: 'Excuse Me, But Have I Been Talking to Myself,'" in *Human Communication Theory*, ed. Frank E. X. Dance (New York: Harper & Row, 1982), pp. 42–60.

3. See, for example, S. Duval and R. A. Wicklund, *A Theory of Objective Self-Awareness* (New York: Academic Press, 1972).

4. Script theory is explained in R. P. Abelson, "Script Processing in Attitude Formation and Decision Making," in *Cognition and Social Behavior*, eds. J. S. Carroll and J. W. Payne (Hillsdale, N.J.: Lawrence Erlbaum Associates, 1976), pp. 33–45.

5. This theory is in the tradition of relationship development and would also fit quite appropriately with the other theories in Chapter 10.

passive and others active. *Passive* strategies are observational, while *active* ones require the observer to do something to get the information. A third class of strategies are *interactive* in that they rely directly on communication with the other person.

The first passive strategy is *reactivity search* in which the individual is observed actually doing something—reacting in some situation. Observers generally prefer to see how people react when they are communicating with another person. *Disinhibition searching* is another passive strategy in which people are observed in informal situations where they are less likely to be self-monitoring and are therefore behaving in a more natural way. Active strategies of information involve *asking others about the target person* and *manipulating the environment* in ways that set up the target person for observation. Interactive strategies include *interrogation* and *self-disclosure*. Self-disclosure, which is discussed in more detail later in this chapter, is a significant strategy for obtaining information because if you disclose something about yourself, the other person is likely to disclose in return.

This theory alerts us to the importance of interpersonal knowledge and uncertainty reduction in communication. The theory is backed by a large body of research in the literature on cognition, communication, and relationships as well as a prodigious quantity of original research. The work of Berger and his colleagues is a good example of the systematic investigation of a rather narrow set of questions.

This strength, however, is also a weakness. The research has produced few insights that are not fairly obvious, at least about general behavior tendencies in Anglo-American culture. Some of the most interesting and difficult questions are left unanswered: How do people construe the information they receive in different social situations? In what ways is information seeking a cultural matter, and do different cultures and groups set different values on interpersonal information? How do people use the discourse and language of others in interaction to get information, and how do these methods change from situation to situation? Questions like these open interesting research possibilities for the future.

This theory, like all of the works covered in this section, is individualistic. And although the theory reminds us that we do act as individuals in communication, it ignores the largely social nature of interpersonal knowledge. In other words, what counts as interpersonal information and what that information means is largely a relational matter. Here we see a paradox in the theory: Relationships are a process of reducing uncertainty; yet, uncertainty reduction is a process undertaken by individual communicators. The question remains: How do different relationships value and treat interpersonal information in different ways? Perhaps one of the most important characteristics of a particular relationship is the idiosyncratic ways in which interpersonal knowledge is valued, generated, and treated.

Knowing that communicators engage in a process of interpersonal information gathering, let us turn now to the perceptual outcomes of that process. The following two theories deal with perceptions of the awareness of others and the ways in which we explain the behavior of self and others.

Attribution Theory

Attribution theory, also known as "naive psychology," deals with the ways people infer the causes of behavior. It explains the processes by which people come to understand their own behavior and that of others. Scientific psychology attempts to ascertain the actual causes of behavior; naive psychology centers on the perceived causes of behavior in ongoing interaction.

Attribution theory has three basic assumptions.[6] First, people attempt to determine the causes of behavior. When in doubt, they look for information that will help them answer the question, Why is she doing that? Harold Kelley puts it this way:

> In the course of my interaction with other people, I often wonder why they act as they do. I may wonder how to interpret a compliment a student makes of a lecture I recently gave, why my friend is so critical of a certain common acquaintance, or why my colleague has not done his share of work on our joint project.

6. The basic assumptions in attribution theory are outlined in Edward E. Jones, et. al., *Attribution: Perceiving the Causes of Behavior* (Morristown, N.J.: General Learning Press, 1972), p. xi.

These are questions about the attribution of the other people's behavior—what causes it, what is responsible for it, to what is it to be attributed?[7]

The second assumption of attribution theory is that people assign causes systematically. Kelley likens this occurrence to the scientific method: "The lay attributor . . . generally acts like a good scientist, examining the covariation between a given effect and various possible causes."[8] The third assumption is that the attributed cause has impact on the perceiver's own feelings and behavior. The communicator's attributions determine in large part the meaning for the situation.

Thus, attribution theory, while it relates directly to interpersonal communication, is supportive of several previous topics in this book, including symbolic interaction, meaning, and information processing.

Heider's attribution theory. Fritz Heider could easily be called the father of attribution theory. It was he who coined the term *naive psychology*. His early work has been extended by a number of later theorists. Heider summarizes the main points of his theory:

> According to naive psychology people have an awareness of their surroundings and the events in it (the *life space*), they attain this awareness through *perception* and other processes, they are *affected* by their personal and impersonal environment, they *cause* changes in the environment, they are able to (*can*) and *try* to cause these changes, they have wishes (*wants*) and *sentiments*, they stand in unit to other entities (belonging), and they are accountable according to certain standards (*ought*). All these characteristics determine what role the other person plays in our own life space and how we react to him.[9]

Thus in the major concepts of his theory, Heider presents the important attributes perceived in interpersonal communication. These are the commonly perceived causes of behavior: being affected by, causing, can, trying, wanting, sentiments, belonging, ought, and may.

Heider distinguishes between direct and indirect perception. Indirect perception occurs when one infers from overt behavior the causes of that behavior. Such causal perception is mediated by psychological variables in the perceiver. There is not a one-to-one relationship between the observed behavior and the cause. A variety of behaviors may be perceived as stemming from a single cause, or, conversely, one behavior may be thought to arise from multiple possible causes. One of the tasks of the perceiver is to resolve such ambiguities inherent in the situation. For example, a supervisor in a company may notice that one employee is particularly industrious. The supervisor must decide whether the employee's drive can be attributed to personal dedication or to a desire to seek personal favors, since either of these elements could be the cause.

Of course, every behavior is *embedded* in a situation, and the naive psychologist makes the most of the context in resolving ambiguities. For one thing, we usually have the benefit of exposure over time, as Heider points out:

> "It is probably fair to say that the stimulus fields basic for person perception are usually *more extended in time* than those relevant to thing perception. . . . In most cases we cognize a person's traits, and especially his wishes, sentiments, or intentions from what he does and says, and we know considerably less when we are limited to what we can see of him as a static object.[10]

The most important factor in resolving ambiguity is meaning. The attributor's meanings for stimuli are crucial in interpersonal perception, especially because of the use of language and speech, although Heider makes it clear that we have meanings for nonlinguistic acts as well. Basically, meanings are integrators in perception, organizing percepts into patterns that help us make sense of the world. From a need for consistency, the perceiver aligns meanings in such a way that causal attribution makes logical sense. In short, the total attribution process becomes integrated and consistent.

7. Harold H. Kelley, "Attribution in Social Interaction," in *Attribution: Perceiving the Causes of Behavior* (Morristown, N.J.: General Learning Press, 1972), p. 1.

8. Ibid., p. 2.

9. Fritz Heider, *The Psychology of Interpersonal Relations* (New York: John Wiley, 1958), p. 17.

10. Ibid., p. 39.

The lack of one-to-one correspondence between behavior and motive makes multiple interpretations of a given event possible. Thus it is reasonable to expect idiosyncratic patterns of perception, which Heider calls *perceptual styles*. This notion introduces another variable in perception, namely, individual manners of perception. (Because we are not dealing here with scientific or objective analysis, it is not appropriate to speak of accurate or erroneous perception.) Heider recognizes that any state of affairs may give rise to a number of interpretations, each of which seems true to the perceiver.

One of the most important attributions involves *purposive action*. When one perceives an action to be purposive, two underlying attributes are recognized: ability (*can*) and attempt (*try*). These causal agents are necessary and sufficient conditions to explain purposeful behavior. Trying means intention and exertion. Suppose, for example, that your friend fails to show up for a meeting. According to this theory, you will wonder why. Here are the possibilities as outlined by the naive analysis of action. Either your friend was not able to make it (couldn't), or she didn't try. If she wasn't able, something would have been wrong with her (for example, illness), or some environmental factor (for example, snowstorm) prevented her appearance. If she did not try, she either didn't want to (intention) or was too lazy (exertion). Now you can see what happens in interpersonal perception. In this instance you will infer the causes of your friend's behavior according to your overall experience, your meanings, the situational factors, as well as your own perceptual style.

This example of the naive analysis of action is included to illustrate Heider's conception of the perceptual process. In this case the realm of attribution is can and try. The same basic process is used in attributions dealing with desire and pleasure, sentiments, ought and value, benefit and harm, and others. Two of these attributional areas will be expanded further.

The *sentiments* we attribute to another person are consistent with our sentiments toward the other person and toward certain objects that we hold in common with the other. In interpersonal relationships we need to balance our various interrelated sentiments. In fact, Heider believes that people have a general tendency to balance the entire perceptual picture, a notion we will return to in a moment. First, let us look at the attributions of ought and value.

The *ought* attribution is particularly interesting because it departs from the normal patterns of attribution. The ought is seen by the person as a demand from some other nonpersonal source. The perceiver views the ought as an impersonal, objective demand, a truism. Further, the ought has interpersonal validity in that most people would agree that the demand is present. Thus a person says, "You ought to go to the dentist," or "I ought to report the theft."

But oughts do not necessarily correspond with *values*. I may dread going to the dentist even though I think I ought to. However, people seek congruity among attributions; especially they feel a need for balance between oughts and values:

> There exists a tendency to be in harmony with the requirements of the objective order. Thus the situation is balanced if one likes to do what one ought to do, if one likes and enjoys the entities one believes are valuable, if happiness and goodness go together, if *p* [perceiver] admires the person he likes and likes the person with whom he shares values, if what ought to be conforms with what really is, etc.[11]

Kelley's attribution theory. One of the most prominent theories of the process of attribution is that of Harold Kelley.[12] Kelley developed two postulates about causal attribution, which apply to both self-perception and perception of others.

The first postulate is the *covariation principle*: "An effect is attributed to the one of its possible causes with which, over time, it covaries."[13] This principle applies to situations in which the perceiver has information from more than one observation. The person sees which effects are associated (covary) with which causes. The second principle, which

11. Ibid., p. 233.
12. See Bibliography for a list of Kelley's works.
13. Harold Kelley, "The Processes of Causal Attribution," *American Psychologist* 28 (1973): 108.

applies in the case of single observations, is the *discounting effect:* "The role of a given cause in producing a given effect is discounted if other plausible causes are also present."[14] In other words, the perceiver tends to weigh possible causes in relation to one another. These two postulates describe attribution as a rational process in which the individual carefully examines the various causal possibilities and generalizes on the basis of the best available data.

The covariation principle applies when the person has multiple observations from which to generalize. The perceiver goes through a naive version of *analysis of variance.* Analysis of variance is a statistical procedure often used in experimental research. It allows the researcher to weigh the various sources of variation in such a way as to determine the causes in operation. Analogically, the perceiver uses the same basic pattern, treating possible causes as independent variables and effects as dependent variables. Figure 9-1 illustrates a three-way contingency model used in causal influence.[15] The three dimensions in this model include the several persons observed, the various times in which observation took place, and some other factors (entities) that enter the situation.

Suppose you learn that your friend likes a particular record. Why? A number of reasons are possible. Perhaps your friend generally likes recorded music and enjoys many records. This attribution is to the person, as illustrated in Figure 9-2(a). If this record is especially good and is enjoyed by most people, the attribution is to the entity, as in Figure 9-2(b). A third possibility is that something about the time is causing your friend's enjoyment of the music. Perhaps this is final exam week, and you have observed that most of your friends like music at this time of the semester since music tends to soothe anxieties. The attribution to time is illustrated in Figure 9-2(c). All of these attributions are *main effects.* In other words one of the three primary dimensions is inferred to be the cause.

Sometimes attribution is not so simple. In the

14. Ibid., p. 113.
15. Ibid., p. 110.

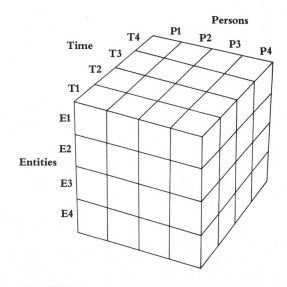

Figure 9-1   Analysis of variance model of attribution.

From *American Psychologist,* "The Process of Causal Attribution," by Harold Kelley. Copyright © 1973 by the American Psychological Association. Reprinted by permission of the publisher and the author.

parlance of analysis of variance, you may infer *interaction effects.* You might infer that the primary causal agents combine in certain ways to achieve effects. For example, you might have observed that your friend likes only one record, but that no one else likes that record. Thus you have attributed interaction between entity (record) and person (your friend), as illustrated in Figure 9-2(d). You are reasoning that peculiar aspects of the record interact with particular qualities in your friend to produce liking. A more complex three-way interaction, illustrated in Figure 9-2(e), is what you might call attribution to circumstances. In this attribution you believe that your friend is enjoying this particular record *at this time.* Your friend didn't enjoy it at any other time, and no one else enjoys it at this or another time.

In all of these cases the perceiver observes the covariation (association) of particular causes and effects in different situations over time. By putting

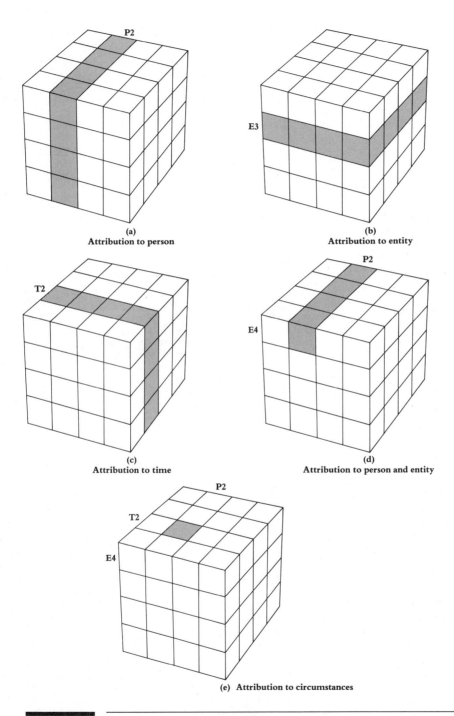

(a)
Attribution to person

(b)
Attribution to entity

(c)
Attribution to time

(d)
Attribution to person and entity

(e) **Attribution to circumstances**

Figure 9-2 Various attribution possibilities.

From *American Psychologist*, "The Process of Causal Attribution," by Harold Kelley. Copyright © 1973 by the American Psychological Association. Reprinted by permission of the publisher and the author.

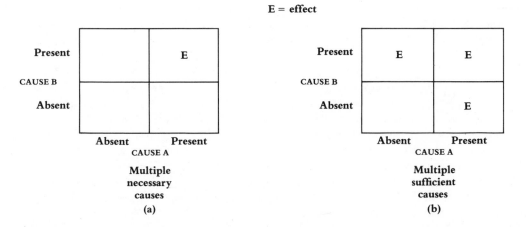

Figure 9-3   Causal schemata.

From *American Psychologist*, "The Process of Causal Attribution," by Harold Kelley. Copyright © 1973 by the American Psychological Association. Reprinted by permission of the publisher and the author.

these various observations together, the observer sees patterns emerge, and the causal inferences outlined above occur. Much of the time, however, we do not make multiple observations. We do not have the advantage of a complete data block such as that shown in Figure 9-1. At these times we use the discounting principle.

The discounting effect applies when the perceiver must rely on a single observation. The various possible causes of an observed effect are weighed against one another, and an inferred causal structure emerges. The process itself is no different from the analysis of variance paradigm above. What is different is the way the data block is filled in. In the discounting model most of the data (that is, causal patterns) are assumed, not observed. One makes assumptions about cause-effect relationships on the basis of past experience and learnings. As Kelley puts it:

> The mature individual . . . has a repertoire of abstract ideas about the operation and interaction of causal factors. These conceptions [enable one to make an] economical and fast attributional analysis, by providing a framework within which bits and pieces of relevant information can be fitted in order to draw reasonably good causal inferences.[16]

16. Harold Kelley, *Causal Schemata and the Attribution Process* (Morristown, N.J.: General Learning Press, 1972), p. 2.

By using experience and learning, the attributor brings various causal assumptions into play. The result is a *causal schema* in which assumed causes are placed in a contingent relation. A particularly good example of this occurs when you have both an assumed internal cause (in the person) and a competing external cause (in the situation). For example, your friend has just received an A on a term paper. You assume that this outcome occurred because of your friend's ability or because the assignment was easy. A couple of causal schemata are possible here. If you follow the schema of *multiple necessary causes*, you will reason that your friend got the A because she is able and the task was easy. This schema is illustrated in Figure 9-3(a). Or perhaps you will use the schema of *multiple sufficient causes*, in which you reason that either your friend is able or the task was easy or both. Figure 9-3(b) illustrates this possibility. Other more complex schemata have been studied by Kelley, but these simple ones provide sufficient illustration of the process for our purposes here. Kelley summarizes the importance of the attribution process:

> There is much evidence . . . that attributions do matter. Man's concern with the reasons for events does not leave him 'lost in thought' about those reasons. Rather, his causal explanations play an important role in providing his impetus to action and in his decisions

among alternative courses of action. When the attributions are appropriate, the person undoubtedly fares better in his decisions and actions than he would in the absence of the causal analysis.[17]

Criticism. Attribution theory provides an excellent set of operational concepts for describing and explaining a broad range of social perceptions. It has been immensely popular in social psychology because of its wide applicability in various social phenomena and its tremendous heuristic value.[18] On the other hand, attribution theory has been criticized for overreliance on the experimental setting, lack of generality of findings, and insensitivity to real social situations.[19]

The major weakness of attribution theory for the field of communication is one of scope. Ironically, this work is largely interpersonal, yet it has dealt little with interaction. The field is ripe for scholars to theorize and conduct research on the relation of messages to attribution. In addition, the theory is almost exclusively based on the model of the rational person, yet we know that much of our perception is affected by emotional factors. Edward E. Jones says these are "phenomena that I don't think attribution theory is well designed to handle."[20]

Self-Disclosure

Disclosure and understanding were important themes in communication theory in the 1960s and early 1970s. Largely as a consequence of the humanistic school in psychology, an ideology of "honest communication" arose, and much of our thinking about what makes good interpersonal communication was affected by this movement. Spurred by the work of Carl Rogers, the so-called "Third-Force" in psychology teaches that the goal

of communication is accurate understanding of self and others, and that understanding can only happen with genuine communication.[21] Interpersonal and personal understanding occur through self-disclosure, feedback, and sensitivity to the disclosures of others. Misunderstanding and dissatisfaction in relationships are promoted by dishonesty, lack of congruence between one's actions and feelings, poor feedback, and inhibited self-disclosure.

Much serious *self-disclosure* research has emerged from this humanistic movement. One theorist who has investigated this process of self-disclosure is Sidney Jourard.[22] Jourard's prescription for the human being is openness or *transparency*.

Transparency is a two-sided coin, involving the individual's willingness to let the world of things and other people disclose themselves. Jourard sees the world in its many forms as constantly disclosing itself, but the person as receiver may or may not be open to perceiving this multiple world view. Being transparent means, on one side, allowing the world to disclose itself freely. The other side of the coin is the person's willingness to disclose oneself to others. Thus ideal interpersonal relationships mean that people allow others to experience them fully and are open to experiencing others fully.

Jourard conceived this philosophical position after observing that his patients tended to be closed to the world. He found that they became healthy as a result of their willingness to disclose themselves to the therapist. Thus Jourard equates sickness with closedness and health with transparency.

Jourard sees growth, a person's moving toward new ways of behaving, as a direct result of openness

17. Kelley, "Processes," p. 127.

18. John K. Harvey, William J. Ickes, and Robert F. Kidd (eds.), *New Directions in Attribution Research*, vol. 2 (New York: John Wiley, 1978), pp. 376–77.

19. John K. Harvey, William J. Ickes, and Robert F. Kidd, "A Conversation with Edward E. Jones and Harold H. Kelley," in *New Directions in Attribution Research*, vol. 2, eds. John K. Harvey, William J. Ickes, and Robert F. Kidd (New York: John Wiley, 1978), p. 384.

20. See, for example, John Shotter, *Social Accountability and Selfhood* (Oxford: Basil Blackwell, 1984).

21. For a more complete summary of these theories, see the second edition of this book (Belmont, Calif.: Wadsworth, 1983), pp. 193–99. See also Carl Rogers, *Client-Centered Therapy* (Boston: Houghton Mifflin, 1951); Carl Rogers, "A Theory of Therapy, Personality, and Interpersonal Relationships, as Developed in the Client-Centered Framework," in *Psychology: A Study of Science*, vol. 3, ed. S. Koch (New York: McGraw-Hill, 1959), pp. 184–256; Abraham Maslow, *The Farther Reaches of Human Nature* (New York: Viking Press, 1971); Joseph R. Royce and Leendert P. Mos (eds.) *Humanistic Psychology: Concepts and Criticisms* (New York: Plenum, 1981); and Joseph Luft, *Of Human Interaction* (Palo Alto: National Press Books, 1969).

22. Sidney Jourard, *Disclosing Man to Himself* (New York: Van Nostrand, 1968); *Self-Disclosure: An Experimental Analysis of the Transparent Self* (New York: John Wiley, 1971); *The Transparent Self* (New York: Van Nostrand Reinhold, 1971).

to the world. The sick person is not willing to experience the world in various ways and is therefore fixed or stagnant. The growing person, being transparent, will come to new life positions. Such change is the essense of personal growth.

> The awareness that things are different is not growth, though it is a necessary condition of growth. A growth cycle calls for (a) an acknowledgement that the world has changed, (b) a shattering of the present experienced 'world structure,' and (c) a restructuring, retotalization, of the world-structure which encompasses the new disclosure of changed reality.[23]

Growth in this fashion relates closely to interpersonal communication, since the disclosing world is largely social. Ideally, growing communicators self-disclose to one another their many changing faces. To accept one's own changes requires verification via acceptance on the part of others. It is difficult to grow if others around you are not open to your disclosures of change.

> But if you suspend any preconceptions you may have of me and my being, and invite me simply to be and to disclose this being to you, you create an ambience, an area of 'low pressure' where I can let my being happen and be disclosed, to you and to be simultaneously—to me from the inside, and to you who receive the outside layer of my being.[24]

Jourard summarizes transparency in the following passage:

> Transparency, thus, is a multifaceted mode of being— it calls for a courage and a willingness to let the world be what it is, to let the other be who he is, and to let oneself be who one is. It calls as well for a commitment to truth, as it changeably presents itself. It calls for a readiness to suspend concepts and beliefs about self, others, and world, and to perceive what is. It calls for a willingness to suspend imagination, wish, and fantasy, a readiness to inform and revise concepts with fresh inputs of perception. That it calls for courage to disclose oneself *to* the world is self-evident.[25]

Since Jourard's ideas on self-disclosure were published, he and several others have conducted

research that elaborates on the rudimentary notions.[26] Here are some of these research findings in general form:

1. Disclosure increases with increased relational intimacy.

2. Disclosure increases when rewarded.

3. Disclosure increases with the need to reduce uncertainty in a relationship.

4. Disclosure tends to be reciprocal (dyadic effect).

5. Women tend to be higher disclosers than men.

6. Women disclose more with individuals they like; men disclose more with people they trust.

7. Disclosure is regulated by norms of appropriateness.

8. Attraction is related to positive disclosure but not to negative disclosure.

9. Positive disclosure is more likely in nonintimate or moderately intimate relationships.

10. Negative disclosure occurs with greater frequency in highly intimate settings than in less intimate ones.

11. Satisfaction and disclosure have a curvilinear relationship; that is, relational satisfaction is greatest at moderate levels of disclosure.[27]

The humanistic psychology movement presents a normative theory of communication. In other words, the theory tells us how we ought to communicate. Consequently, it embodies a very strong ideology of interpersonal relationships. As is always the case with normative theories, one may question the wisdom of the advice embedded in the ideology.[28]

23. Jourard, *Disclosing*, p. 154.
24. Ibid., p. 162.
25. Jourard, *Self-Disclosure*, p. 182.

26. I have relied on the excellent analysis and summary of Shirley J. Gilbert, "Empirical and Theoretical Extensions of Self-Disclosure," in *Explorations in Interpersonal Communication*, ed. Gerald R. Miller (Beverly Hills: Sage Publications, 1976), pp. 197–216. See also P. W. Cozby, "Self-Disclosure: A Literature Review," *Psychological Bulletin* 79 (1973): 73–91.
27. Adapted from Gilbert, "Empirical," p. 210.
28. A somewhat lengthy and penetrating critique of this ideology can be found in Malcom R. Parks, "Ideology in Interpersonal Communication: Off the Couch and Into the World," in *Communication Yearbook 5*, ed. Michael Burgoon (New Brunswick, N.J.: Transaction Books, 1982), pp. 79–108. See also Daniel E. Berlyne, "Humanistic Psychology as a Protest Movement," in *Humanistic Psychology: Concepts and Criticism*, eds. Joseph Royce and Leendert P. Mos (New York: Plenum, 1981), p. 261.

The self-disclosure research, despite its ideological leanings, has been a significant and important line of inquiry in communication; but the research has not always supported the values of the original humanistic proponents like Jourard. Arthur Bochner recently reviewed the literature on self-disclosure and made the following qualified conclusions: First, people think it is appropriate to disclose to others whom they like; but, second, they overestimate the extent to which they *in fact* self-disclose to those they like. Third, self-disclosure does not necessarily produce liking, and inappropriate disclosure can actually cause negative impressions. Fourth, liking may discourage self-disclosure because people do not want to risk damaging the relationship. The answer, in Bochner's reading, is not the lack of disclosure, but thoughtful disclosure, since discriminating disclosers seem more satisfied with their relationships than indiscriminating ones. Bochner summarizes his overall impression from this literature:

> Thus self-disclosure appears to be a highly overrated activity. Perhaps the time has come to lift the fog of ideology surrounding the concept. The fact that there has been only mild, if any opposition to the thesis that openness leads to better and more satisfying relationships suggests that some investigators have been lulled into an uncritical acceptance of an untenable proposition. There is no firm empirical basis for endorsing unconditional openness. A critical evaluation of the evidence suggests at most a restrained attitude toward the efficacy of self-disclosure. [29]

Shirley Gilbert suggests three conditions necessary for Jourard's ideal to occur in a relationship. First, the participants must have healthy self-concepts. Second, they must be willing to take relational risks. Third, they must be committed to unconditional positive regard in the relationship. Gilbert describes intimacy in these terms:

> There are interpersonal price tags attached to intimate relationships. Intimacy, as a dimension of affection,

may not be a unidimensional construct. It seems to be comprised of not only feelings (satisfaction) but also commitment (willingness to risk). Intimacy refers not only to the depth of exchange, both verbally and nonverbally, but also to the depth of acceptance or confirmation which characterizes a relationship. Thus, "intimate disclosure" and "intimate relationships" need to be clearly conceptualized and differentiated in future disclosure studies. While disclosure has been established as an index of communicative depth in human relationships, it does not guarantee an intimate relationship. [30]

One of the sharpest critiques of the self-disclosure ideology is that of Roderick Hart and his associates. [31] Hart's reaction to the humanistic psychology school spawned an interesting and significant alternative theory, to which we now turn.

Rhetorical Sensitivity

In criticizing humanistic approaches to understanding, Roderick Hart and his colleagues have created an alternative conceptualization. [32] For these theorists effective communication does not arise from congruence and disclosure but from *rhetorical sensitivity*. Relying on the categories of Donald Darnell and Wayne Brockriede, Hart contrasts three general types of communicators. [33] *Noble selves* conform to the humanistic image. These people stick to their personal ideals without variation and without adapting or adjusting to others. *Rhetorical reflectors* are individuals who, at the opposite extreme, are molding themselves to others' wishes, with no personal scruples to follow.

Rhetorically sensitive individuals, as a third type, moderate these extremes. Rhetorical sensitivity embodies concern for self, concern for others, and a situational attitude. The theorists outline five at-

29. Arthur P. Bochner, "The Functions of Human Communicating in Interpersonal Bonding," in *Handbook of Rhetorical and Communication Theory*, eds. Carroll C. Arnold and John Waite Bowers (Boston: Allyn & Bacon, 1984), p. 608.

30. Gilbert, "Empirical," pp. 212–13.

31. Roderick P. Hart and Don M. Burks, "Rhetorical Sensitivity and Social Interaction," *Speech Monographs* 39 (1972): 75–91.

32. Roderick P. Hart, Robert E. Carlson, and William F. Eadie, "Attitudes Toward Communication and the Assessment of Rhetorical Sensitivity," *Communication Monographs* 47 (1980): 1–22.

33. Donald Darnell and Wayne Brockriede, *Persons Communicating* (Englewood Cliffs, N.J.: Prentice-Hall, 1976).

tributes of rhetorical sensitivity. First, rhetorically sensitive people accept personal complexity; that is, they understand that each individual is a composite of many selves. Second, such individuals avoid rigidity in communicating with others. Third, the rhetorically sensitive person attempts to balance self-interests with the interests of others, a sensitivity called *interaction consciousness*. Fourth, rhetorically sensitive people are aware of the appropriateness of communicating or not communicating particular ideas in different situations. Fifth, such persons realize that an idea can be expressed in many ways, and they adapt their message to the audience in the particular situation.

In order to better understand the rhetorically sensitive person in contrast with the noble self and rhetorical reflector, Hart and his colleagues created a questionnaire called RHETSEN and administered it to over 3000 students at forty-nine universities and to other groups as well. They recognize that most people have varying degrees of all three types within themselves but that a given type predominates. They summarize their findings as follows:

> Our findings amount to at least this: (1) people vary greatly from one another in their attitudes toward encoding interpersonal messages; (2) some of these variances are partly a function of specific philosophical, economic, geographic, and cultural forces impinging upon people; (3) certain subcultural systems (families, ethnic groups, religious assemblages, etc.) reinforce and inhibit certain attitudes toward communication; (4) exceptionally "liberal" systems foster Noble Self predilections while especially "conservative" persons embrace Rhetorical Reflector attitudes; (5) rhetorical sensitivity seems to thrive in those middle-class environments which do not demand ideological zeal from members.[34]

The theory of rhetorical sensitivity is placed here because of its obvious and direct contrast with the theories of humanistic psychology. In addition Hart and Burks themselves apply their concept to interpersonal communication. However, their theory also applies to the domain of persuasion and, by

extension, to all communication contexts, including mass communication.

One of this theory's strengths is that it deals specifically with message sending, a central communication concern. Another strength is that it provides a set of sensible principles that can be used by the communicator to achieve more effective communication. The theory is also heuristic because of its involvement of the RHETSEN scale. A final advantage of the theory is its parsimony; it is elegant in the sense of presenting a small cluster of concepts from which much elaborative theorizing can follow in the future.

The theory's main weaknesses involve its epistemology. The theory has an interesting and not altogether consistent set of epistemological assumptions. It treats rhetorical sensitivity as a *trait*, implying that individuals may exercise little choice over whether they are noble selves, rhetorical reflectors, or rhetorically sensitive individuals, yet the very idea of rhetorical sensitivity implies change and choice. Another problem with the trait approach to rhetorical sensitivity is that it does not allow us to understand whether, or under what conditions, a single individual may act as noble self, rhetorical reflector, or rhetorically sensitive person.

Communicator Style

The idea of rhetorical sensitivity suggests that individuals may have a predominant manner or style in which they communicate. Communicator style has been investigated by Robert Norton and his colleagues.[35] The style construct is predicated on the idea that we communicate on two levels. Not only do we give others informational content, but we use words and actions to give form to the content of the primary message. This higher-order communication tells others how to understand and how to respond to a message. For example, on the content level, you might tell a friend about an experience; on a higher level, you might signal that your message is to be taken with authority, with levity, with disinterest, with humor, or with any

---

34. Hart, Carlson, and Eadie, "Attitudes," p. 19.

35. Robert Norton, *Communicator Style: Theory, Applications, and Measures* (Beverly Hills: Sage Publications, 1983).

number of different attitudes. The idea of a higher-order message is not new; it is often associated with communication in relationships, a topic examined in the following chapter. However, Norton believes that a speaker's higher-order communication functions as a "style message" by "signaling how a literal (primary) message should be taken, filtered, interpreted, or understood."[36] Style messages accompany content messages, but they may be delivered before, during, or after the primary message. Norton further believes that the tendency to expect style messages is so strong that if faced with ambiguous or contradictory messages, people look for style-level cues that will inform them of how the message is to be taken. For example, a comment that could be taken either seriously or jokingly will be interpreted in accordance with what the receiver believes to be the style of the speaker.

Over time, as an individual gains experience interacting with another person, various types of style messages will recur. For example, one might be viewed repeatedly as being gruff, laid-back, whimsical, serious, and so on. Norton's thesis is that a person's repeated associations form a dominant style. Styles, of course, are not totally individual. Cultures, for example, affect how people behave and how they perceive others, as in the case of the macho image of many western males. Although a person's style constitutes the individual's predominant way of communicating, it is not the only way in which the person communicates. Further, a person's style may be multifaceted; it may be complex and consist of several different aspects.

There are numerous possible styles. Each style is a combination of certain traits or variables. Norton has found nine variables that can enter into an individual's overall style. These variables are not independent from one another, and considerable overlap exists among them. They include dominance, dramatic behavior, contentiousness, animation, impression leaving, relaxation, attentiveness, openness, and friendliness. Of these, dramatic behavior and animation seem to go together,

as do attentiveness and friendliness, and as do dominance and contentiousness. Relaxation, openness, and impression leaving seem to be categories of their own.

This line of work is interesting and productive. Most people in our culture would agree that communicators possess particular styles; this theory is a step toward defining those styles and uncovering what constitutes them. Norton has also had some pragmatic success with the theory. In his study with teachers, for example, he found dramatic teachers to be more popular and successful than nondramatic ones. This finding suggests that different styles may be better or worse in different situations and that people may find it advisable to consider their style more carefully and to change it as necessary.

The problem with this theory is that it underplays the social nature of reality (Chapter 7). In other words, the ways in which people in general are perceived within a social group or culture may have much to do with the "theories" of personhood within the group itself. In certain cultures, it does not make sense to even speak of individual styles; in some cultures people are identified with roles or virtues rather than styles. Although Norton acknowledges the cultural aspect of style definitions, the theory may need to grow in the direction of exploring these cultural dimensions.

Discourse Processes

The second element in interpersonal communication is discourse. The study of message structure in communication goes by the general label *discourse analysis.*[37] This line of research and theory arose from the application of linguistics to texts,

---

36. Ibid., p. 31.

37. For a brief summary of the field, see Scott Jacobs, "Recent Advances in Discourse Analysis," *Quarterly Journal of Speech* 66 (1980): 450–72. For a more recent and detailed treatment, see Donald G. Ellis and William A. Donohue (eds.), *Contemporary Issues in Language and Discourse Processes* (Hillsdale, N.J.: Lawrence Erlbaum Associates, 1986).

which, in this case, are segments of language larger than a sentence. For the most part, such texts are naturally produced talk. This tradition is therefore quite different from much of hermeneutics, which treats texts as separate from the actual communication in which they might appear (Chapter 8).

Although there are many strands of discourse analysis, they share a common set of concerns. First, all are concerned with the ways in which discourse is organized. This means discovering abstract principles used by communicators to generate and understand talk. Second, discourse is viewed as action; it is a way of doing things, a means of communication. Discourse analysts assume that language users know not only the rules of sentence grammar, but also the rules for using larger segments of talk to accomplish pragmatic goals in social situations. This means that language is used strategically to achieve desired ends. Third, discourse analysis is a search for principles used by actual communicators *from their perspective*. As such, it is a phenomenological activity (Chapter 8). In this section we discuss two lines of discourse work—conversation analysis and compliance-gaining strategies.

Conversation Analysis

Not all discourse analysis deals with interpersonal communication per se, but conversation has certainly been one of the most important areas of this field. This section is therefore devoted to *conversation analysis*.[38] Conversation analysis has been concerned with a variety of issues.[39] First and foremost, the approach deals with what speakers need to know to have a conversation. This means, for the most part, knowledge of the rule structures of

conversations. Interactional features of conversation such as turn-taking, silences and gaps, and overlaps have been of special interest.[40] Conversation analysis has also been concerned with rule violation and the ways in which people prevent and repair errors in talk.

Certainly the most popular, and perhaps the most significant, aspect of conversation analysis deals with *conversational coherence*.[41] Simply defined, coherence is connectedness and meaningfulness in conversation. Coherent conversation seems well structured and sensible to the participants. It is a quality we normally take for granted; yet the production of coherence is highly complex and not altogether understood.

We cannot summarize here the large and growing literature in conversation analysis. This section, therefore, concentrates on two areas. We first discuss the highly recognized foundational work of H. Paul Grice and then take a look at three alternative theories of conversational coherence.

Conversational maxims. Perhaps the most important foundational theory of conversation is that of H. Paul Grice.[42] Grice proposed a set of very general assumptions to which all conversationalists must subscribe in order to be perceived as competent. The first is the most general principle of all conversation, the *cooperative principle*: One's contribution must be appropriate. Cooperation here does not necessarily mean expression of agreement, but it does mean that one is willing to contribute in a way that is in line with the purpose of the conversation. More specifically, cooperation is achieved by following four *maxims*. The first is the *quantity maxim*: One's contribution should provide sufficient, but not too much, information. The quantity maxim is violated when one's comments

38. This section deals with conversation in the discourse analysis tradition, emphasizing the verbal structure of conversational texts. There is also a tradition that studies the management of conversations in a broader sense, including the nonverbal elements. See Joseph N. Cappella, "The Management of Conversations," in *Handbook of Interpersonal Communication*, eds. Mark L. Knapp and Gerald R. Miller (Beverly Hills: Sage Publications, 1985), pp. 393–439.

39. These issues are outlined in Margaret L. McLaughlin, *Conversation: How Talk Is Organized* (Beverly Hills: Sage Publications, 1984).

40. See, for example, *Spoken Discourse: A Model for Analysis* (London: Longman, 1981).

41. See Robert T. Craig and Karen Tracy (eds.), *Conversational Coherence: Form, Structure, and Strategy* (Beverly Hills: Sage Publications, 1983).

42. H. Paul Grice, "Logic and Conversation," in *Syntax and Semantics*, vol. 3, eds. P. Cole and J. Morgan (New York: Academic Press, 1975), pp. 41–58.

are too brief or too verbose. The second is the *quality maxim:* One's contribution should be truthful. The quality maxim is violated when one deliberately lies or communicates in a way that does not reflect one's honest intention. The third is the *relevancy maxim:* One's comment must be pertinent to the context of the conversation at the moment. It is violated when one makes an "off the wall" or irrelevant comment in a conversation. The fourth maxim is the *manner maxim:* One should not be obscure, ambiguous, or disorganized.

On the surface, these maxims may seem absurdly simple and obvious, but the associated question of how speakers actually use these maxims and how they handle apparent violations is far more complicated. Grice's maxims constitute basic ideas that have provided structure for much research on these questions. Of course, the cooperative principle and attendant maxims are often violated, sometimes for strategic purposes; but what makes the maxims so important is that they are never violated without disrupting the flow of conversation or affecting the perceptions of others in the conversation.

When a maxim appears to be violated, communicators wonder about what is going on and make attributions that accommodate the apparent violation. These interpretations are called *conversational implicatures.* The question being considered through implicature is this: What is being implied or implicated by this apparent violation? In order to assume that the violator is living up to the cooperative principle, the listener must attribute some additional meaning that will make the speaker's contribution seem to conform to the principle. In fact, many deliberate violations are predicated on the assumption that the hearer will, through conversational implicature, understand that one indeed intends to be cooperative. If, for example, I say, "It is raining cats and dogs," I am literally violating the quality maxim; but I know that you will realize that I am speaking metaphorically. Conversational implicature allows communicators to use all kinds of strategically interesting, indirect statements to achieve their purposes, without risking the judgment of incompetence; in fact, competence itself requires the effective use of implicature.

One of the most common types of violation is to say something indirectly. Indirect communication is important for a variety of social and personal reasons such as politeness. If, for example, someone asks me how much my house cost, I might say, "Oh, quite a bit." Now, on the surface, that violates the maxim of quantity and appears uncooperative, but most competent conversationalists will realize that it is really an indirect statement of, "It's none of your business." Here one concludes that I am indeed not being cooperative, but that there is sufficient reason for me not to be. In fact, one of the important functions of talk is to justify rule violations. The study of conversational implicature is really the study of the rules people use to understand or to justify violations of other rules; and these implicatures are very important for the overall management of conversations.

Conversational coherence. Coherence involves the question of how communicators tell whether statements are meaningfully structured. How do communicators know what is appropriate and what is inappropriate for keeping a conversation well organized? A variety of theories have been proposed.[43] Some of these use *local* principles: They explain coherence in terms of the connectedness of adjacent statements. Local coherence assumes that communicators follow rules for what constitutes a permissible response to a statement. If I say, "Hi, how are you?" you are obligated to respond, "Fine." Other theories use *global* principles or rules that relate a given statement to the broad meaning of a larger segment of conversation. Communication scholars generally agree that coherence cannot be explained with strictly local rules; it is easy to identify sequences that are obviously coherent to the communicators, but have contiguous statements that by themselves do not appear consistent. We return to the local-global issue later.

Theories of coherence also differ in terms of the explanatory mechanism used. Three such approaches are common: the propositional, the

43. For a summary of some of the approaches, see Craig and Tracy, *Conversational Coherence.*

sequential, and the pragmatic.[44] *Propositional* theories explain coherence by referring to the meaning of statements. Here the rules state that the meaning of one's sentences must somehow relate to or be consistent with the meaning of other sentences or the meaning of the whole segment of conversation. The *sequence* approach looks for the rules governing the kinds of acts that are permissible after another act. The *pragmatic* approach relies on rules for accomplishing actual intentions. Thus, in propositional theories, coherence is a matter of the consistency of meaning; in sequencing theories, coherence is a matter of syntactical organization; and in pragmatic theories, coherence is a matter of appropriate practical action. Three representative theories are discussed below.

A propositional approach. An example of a propositional approach is the theory of Teun van Dijk.[45] Although this theory concentrates on single utterances rather than conversation, van Dijk believes the principles governing these utterances are also important for the overall coherence of a conversation. Van Dijk uses a global approach, relating each proposition to a larger proposition through the use of *macrorules*. A whole text has at least one thesis or general proposition, which is supported or elaborated by the various other statements. The structure of the text can be viewed as a hierarchy of propositions, such that each lower-level statement enters into a higher one until the general proposition of the text is reached. Macrorules are used to relate propositions to one another in the hierarchy. For example, the *deletion-insertion rule* states that propositions that are unnecessary for understanding another proposition are deleted, and those necessary as building blocks for a higher-order proposition are retained. There may be, for example, descriptions of an event that are not relevant to the overall point being made, and these are deleted when developing the general sense of the utterance.

44. These are summarized in McLaughlin, *Conversation*, pp. 35–90.

45. Teun A. van Dijk, *Macrostructures: An Interdisciplinary Study of Global Structures in Discourse, Interaction, and Cognition* (Hillsdale, N.J.: Lawrence Erlbaum Associates, 1980); *Studies in the Pragmatics of Discourse* (The Hague: Mouton, 1981).

The *generalization* rule requires that propositions be grouped into a more general proposition according to thematic commonalities. This rule is a method for finding the higher-order concept that holds individual propositions together. In describing one's garden, for example, there may be several descriptions of flowers and others of vegetables. The flower statements might consist of propositions about color and shape, while the vegetable statements are dominated by descriptions of taste. Higher-order propositions developed by the generalization rule might therefore be that flowers are judged by aesthetic qualities, while vegetables are judged by culinary ones.

Another macrorule is *construction*, or the principle that higher-order propositions should combine the elements of something that are stipulated by the lower-level propositions. In other words, the "facts" proposed in the lower propositions are integrated or combined in some way in the higher propositions. For example, if I say that (a) my gladiolus are colorful and make a good arrangement, (b) the sweet peas are abundant and stay fresh long after being picked, and (c) the carnations look especially pretty when mixed together in a vase, then a permissible higher-order proposition might be that flowers are valued as decoration.

Thus, with knowledge of macrorules, individuals are able to construct coherent discourse; the sentences in a lengthy utterance are ordered and make sense on a larger level by virtue of the hierarchical organization of the propositions contained in the discourse. If an utterance seems incoherent to a listener, either the speaker did not make proper use of macrorules, or the listener is unable to find the necessary rules to make sense of it. If such rules are not yet learned by a speaker, as in the case of child, or not retained, as in the case of a schizophrenic or brain-damaged person, then the discourse will seem incoherent in this propositional sense.

The propositional approach is useful when explaining the semantic sense of an utterance—what it means or refers to. The weakness of this approach, however, is that most utterances are part of a conversation and fulfill functions other than reference functions. Utterances are acts that are used to accomplish intentions, and the coherence of a conversation depends upon an organization of speech acts apart from logical propositional organization. Most theories of coherence, therefore, make use of speech act theory, which was explained in some detail in Chapter 7. These theories understand coherence as the organization of intentions and the rules by which those intentions are translated into actual conversational utterances. Both of the following theories are speech act approaches to conversational coherence.

A sequencing approach. The idea behind sequence-structure approaches to coherence is that a conversation consists of a series of speech acts, the order of which is governed by rules. As such, these approaches are strictly local theories of coherence. In other words, there are established kinds of speech acts that may follow a given utterance, and conversational competence depends on knowing these rules. For example, the greeting, "How are you?" is a question and demands an answer. Therefore, "How are you?" would not normally be answered by, "How are you?" More typically, the sequence would go like this: "How are you?" "Fine. How are you?" These approaches center on the *adjacency pair*, which are two speech act utterances in a row. The "first pair part" (or FPP) is the first utterance, and the "second pair part" (SPP) is the following utterance. By this approach, a conversation is coherent if proper rules of sequencing are consistently used between the FPP and the SPP.

Perhaps the most influential sequencing model is that of Harvey Sacks, Emanuel Schegloff, and Gail Jefferson.[46] This is basically a turn-taking theory, which stipulates that the next turn in a conversation must be a proper response to complete a particular adjacency-pair type. For instance, a question is to be followed by an answer, a greeting by another greeting, an offer by an acceptance, a request by an acceptance or a rejection. When one speech act is completed, that signals a next turn for another speaker, who is obligated to respond according to

46. Harvey Sacks, Emanuel Schegloff, and Gail Jefferson, "A Simplest Systematics for the Organization of Turn Taking for Conversation," *Language* 50 (1974): 696–735.

appropriate rules. The speaker may designate who that next speaker is to be, or another speaker can appropriately take a turn, so long as a proper response is given. Failing a response, the speaker may continue talking.

Further, adjacency pairs include a "structural preference for agreement." In other words, the second pair part is normally expected to agree with the first. For example, a statement is normally followed by an agreement ("Don't you just love the sun?" "Sure do.") and a request by an acceptance ("Can I borrow your pen?" "Sure.") This does not mean that people cannot or do not disagree, but disagreement calls for special action in the form of an account or excuse.

Of course, conversations are usually more complex than the simple adjacency-pair concept implies. This theory is adapted to more complex situations by recognizing presequences and insertions. A *presequence* is an adjacency pair whose meaning depends upon another series of acts that has not yet been uttered. They are prefatory to another set of acts. The initial FPP is an invitation for a subsequent one. Here is an example:

FPP: "Have you washed your hands?"
SPP: "No, why?"
FPP: "Cause dinner's ready."
SPP: "Okay, I'll do it."

The second sequence of acts is really a request, but it cannot be understood as such without the first set.

An *insertion* is an adjacency pair that is in between the two parts of another pair and is subordinate to the main pair. Such insertions are necessary to clarify the intention of the initial FPP. Here is an example:

FPP$_1$: "Would you like to go out sometime?"
FPP$_2$: "With you?"
SPP$_2$: "Yeah, me."
SPP$_1$: "Oh, okay."

Such a move is an example of an *expansion*, which means that a subsequent speaker expands the sequence to include additional or subsidiary intentions. Sequences of utterances can, by this system, be parsed, as one would diagram a sentence with rules of grammar. The conversation would therefore be analyzed into adjacency pairs and pair parts.

Unfortunately, this approach is vulnerable to criticism and now appears to be inadequate as an explanation of conversational coherence.[47] The problem with the theory is that it is not able to explain many conversational sequences. For example, some coherent sequences do not follow the sequencing rules stipulated by the theory. Further, some speech acts that could be first pair parts have no apparent structural preference for any particular other kind of act as a second pair part. What, for example, would be the preferred response to a promise or an accusation? This problem seems to result from the rather arbitrary system by which speech acts are classified: The system labels acts according to type without much sensitivity to their actual function in the conversation. The rational model explained below is designed to overcome this weakness.

A rational approach. Rational, or pragmatic, approaches assume practical action in conversation and predicate coherence on the reasoning process of the communicators. In other words, communicators make decisions about what to say and how to achieve their intentions, and coherence is really judged in accordance with this act-consequent link. If the sequence of acts appears rational vis-à-vis a set of goals, it is judged coherent. This theory is definitely a global approach. The rational approach is primarily the product of Sally Jackson and Scott Jacobs.[48]

Jackson and Jacobs use the game analogy to explain how conversation works (see also Chapter 7). A conversation is like a game. The game itself is controlled by a set of rules, which players must know. The players have objectives in the game, and they use the rules of the game to achieve those objectives. The game is coherent because of the appropriate use of rules to accomplish rational objectives. So players must have two kinds of knowledge: They must know the rules of the game, but they must also know what constitutes rational play within the parameters of the rules. Communication is complicated by the fact that conversation, like a game, is played in interaction with another, so that the moves of one person must mesh with those of the other, and this requires agreement on purpose and some reciprocity of perspective.

The rational model is also based on speech act theory. Utterances have a force that obliges a hearer to understand the speaker's intent, and the speaker must meet certain "felicity conditions" in order for understanding to occur. Communicators respond not to the speech acts of others, but to the intentions of others. The coherence of a conversation is judged, then, not by whether a particular act type is followed by some other permissible act, but by whether the unfolding sequence of acts is consistent with the perceived plan of goals.

Jackson and Jacobs stipulate two kinds of rules necessary for coherence. *Validity rules* establish the conditions necessary for an act to be judged as a sincere move in a plan of goals. For example, a promise must meet a variety of conditions: It must state that the speaker will do some future act; the future act must be something the hearer wants; the hearer has reason to believe that the future act would not otherwise be done in the normal course of events; and the speaker sincerely intends and feels obligated to do the act.

Reason rules require the speaker to adjust statements to the beliefs and perspectives of the other conversants. This does not mean that speakers say only what listeners want to hear, but that they frame their statements in a way that makes logical sense within the perspective of the other person. Reason rules do not prescribe agreement, but they set up a situation in which communicators are invited and somewhat pressured to agree. These rules require the use of a common set of concepts in which disagreement can be expressed, justified, and understood. For example, a statement of preference on the part of a speaker must be relevant to some

47. Scott Jacobs, "Language," in *Handbook of Interpersonal Communication*, eds. Mark L. Knapp and Gerald Miller (Beverly Hills: Sage Publications, 1985), pp. 330–35.

48. Jacobs, "Language;" also Scott Jacobs and Sally Jackson, "Speech Act Structure in Conversation: Rational Aspects of Pragmatic Coherence," in *Conversational Coherence: Form, Structure, and Strategy*, eds. Robert T. Craig and Karen Tracy (Beverly Hills: Sage Publications, 1983), pp. 47–66.

perspective of the listener, such that if the listener does not have a preference, he or she will come to agree with the speaker, or, if the listener already disagrees, he or she will consider agreeing or be able to express and justify the disagreement. The reason rule is an application of Grice's cooperative principle.

Basically, these rules enable communicators to set up a logical system within which utterances and utterance sequences can be judged as coherent or not. Remember that these rules may be violated, and coherence is not always achieved. Communicators may also disagree about whether a sequence meets the required conditions of validity and reason; such disagreement is often the basis for conflict in communication. Ultimately, since conversations are practical goal-oriented acts, communicators must constantly judge whether the interaction is leading toward the desired goal and, if not, whether and what kinds of adjustments must be made in the conversational moves. This fact makes conversation a dynamic process of practical reasoning.

This theory views adjacency pairs as a special case of a logical context for action. The first pair part invites the listener to join into a kind of microplan for achieving a goal. The second pair part is coherent with the first if it joins into that plan. For example, if the goal is social contact, a statement of greeting invites the listener to make contact, and a returned greeting fulfills the contract. Responses to a first pair part may simply and directly cooperate, they may indirectly cooperate, they may approximate agreement, or they may attempt to extend, change, or refuse the goal set up by the first utterance. Over a sequence of utterances, communicators may actually negotiate a goal-achievement plan. Jackson and Jacobs call this "the transformation of belief/want contexts." Communicators mentally ask, What do we want to accomplish here and what logical moves are required by each of us to accomplish this? If agreement is achieved on the goals, and the actions of the conversationalists seem appropriate for achieving these goals, then the conversation is coherent.

To see more concretely how these ideas can be applied, let us look at Jackson and Jacobs's appli-

cations of their theory to requests.[49] Actually, requests are among the most studied of all speech acts, and this theory provides an excellent extension and modification of a whole line of such research. Recall that coherent conversation consists of moves within a common goal-oriented frame negotiated by the communicators. A variety of request and response moves are possible. Such moves range on a continuum from very direct through indirect to irrelevant. The clearer and more direct a request, and the clearer and more direct a response, the more coherent the conversation. This is because directness supports clarity of goals and relevance of moves toward meeting those goals. Therefore, if I say, "Please pass the butter," my goal is quite clear and your response, "Sure," is obviously relevant. On the other hand, if I say, "My toast is dry," my goal of getting you to pass the butter is less clear; and if your response is, "You should turn the toaster down a little," this does not seem at all coherent with my desire to get butter.

Jackson and Jacobs provide a list of utterance types that may be taken as a request. These range from very direct to irrelevant. "Please pass the butter," is an absolutely direct request. An *indirect request* would be less clear: "My toast is dry." A *hint* is even less direct: "Some people at this table have something I sure would like." There is also an entire group of utterances commonly found in conversations that function as a *prerequest*. These set up the listener for a request in the future. An example might be, "Could I interrupt to ask for something?"

Once a request or prerequest is made, a listener can respond in a variety of direct or indirect ways. If the communicator recognizes the intent of a request, he or she can make the conversation coherent by responding quite directly. An example would be an *anticipatory move*, in which the listener recognizes the hidden or indirect request and grants it

49. Scott Jacobs and Sally Jackson, "Strategy and Structure in Conversational Influence Attempts," *Communication Monographs* 50 (1983): 285–304; Sally Jackson and Scott Jacobs, "Conversational Relevance: Three Experiments on Pragmatic Connectedness in Conversation," in *Communication Yearbook 10*, ed. Margaret McLaughlin (Newbury Park, Calif.: Sage Publications, 1987), pp. 323–47.

immediately. ("My toast is sure dry." "Here, have some butter.") Such moves provide coherence because they are oriented to the apparent goals of the other communicator. Less coherent would be responses that misinterpret the speaker's statement, as in the case of someone who takes an innocent statement to be a request that was never intended as such. A communicator may also make a move to avoid being influenced by a request, indirect request, or prerequest. Such responses create a problem in the conversation that results in frustration, avoidance, or readjustment of interactional goals.

This theory clearly overcomes many of the weaknesses of the sequence-structure approach. It explains adjacency-pair coherence and further solves the puzzles that the earlier theory left unanswered. On the other hand, the theory, which is still very much under development, remains abstract and as yet fails to specify more particularly the kinds of rules employed by conversants in judging the rationality of actual utterances. The work on requesting is just beginning in this direction.

Compliance-Gaining Discourse

The discourse used to gain the compliance of other people has been one of the most popular research topics in the past decade. The questions guiding this work have been as follows: What do people say to others when they want them to behave a certain way, and how are these messages chosen? A distinction is usually made between a specific message *tactic* or technique and a cluster or sequence of tactics known as a *strategy*.

One of the most comprehensive analyses of the compliance-gaining literature is that of Lawrence Wheeless, Robert Barraclough, and Robert Stewart, who review and integrate the variety of compliance-gaining schemes.[50] These researchers believe that compliance-gaining messages are best classified according to the kinds of power employed by communicators when attempting to gain the compliance of another individual. *Power* is access to influential resources, and it is a result of interpersonal perception: People have as much power as others perceive that they have.

Wheeless and his colleagues isolate three general types of power. The first is the perception that someone can manipulate behavior consequences or a person's expectation about the outcome of a certain course of action. Parents often use this kind of power in administering punishments and rewards. The second kind of power is the perception that a person is in an important relational position or is a source of identification with another individual. Here the powerful person can identify certain elements of the relationship that bring about compliance or can act as a model or example to others. For example, people in romantic relationships often attribute a great deal of power to their partners because they fear that if things don't go exactly right, the partner will leave them. The third type of power involves the perceived ability to define values and/or obligations. For example, one might be able to relate another person's behavior to something that should be done because of shared standards.

In a compliance-gaining situation, then, one assesses his or her power and chooses tactics that invoke that power. Wheeless lists a numer of tactics that are associated with the three classes of power. For example, the ability to affect another person's expectations and consequences will lead to such tactics as promises, threats, and warnings. The ability to affect the relationship with the other person may lead one to choose such tactics as expressing liking for the other person, attributing positive or negative esteem, making emotional appeals, flattering, and so on. The third category of power—defining values and obligations—will give rise to the use of moral appeals, debt, guilt, and other similar techniques.

Of course, one's choice of a compliance-gaining strategy may depend on a number of factors. One of the most important seems to be the communicators' perception of the situation in which compliance is being sought. Perhaps the most well-developed research and theory program on this

50. Lawrence R. Wheeless, Robert Barraclough, and Robert Stewart, "Compliance-Gaining and Power in Persuasion," in *Communication Yearbook 7*, ed. Robert N. Bostrom (Beverly Hills: Sage Publications, 1983), pp. 105–45.

topic is that of Michael Cody, Margaret Mc-Laughlin, and their colleagues.[51] Cody and Mc-Laughlin point out that situational perceptions are highly important, not only in compliance gaining, but in almost any communication situation. In other words, how you behave and what you choose to say depends in large measure on the situation in which you find yourself.

Two general principles seem to govern communication behavior. First, message strategies are chosen on the basis of how effective they are believed to be within a particular situation. Second, strategies are also evaluated in terms of their cost. In short, within any situation one will choose those messages that are believed to maximize gains and minimize costs.

Cody and his colleagues have identified six factors that enter into persons' definitions of the situation, and they believe that these factors affect the compliance-gaining strategies chosen by communicators. *Intimacy*, or perceived closeness between the communicators, seems especially important. Intimate communicators are more apt to use more emotional, less manipulative methods. Intimate communicators will tend to use appeals to love and empathic understanding. Intimates also may find that they are able to account for their behavior with one another more readily than strangers are able to do.

Dominance is the perception that one person has authority or control over another. Dominant communicators usually believe they have more options available for influencing the other person than do submissive communicators. Nondominant communicators may be limited to "reason-giving" or rational strategies, while dominant ones may be able to use pressure, assertiveness, sanctions, and other such tactics.

A third dimension of compliance-gaining situations is the perceived *right to persuade*. In some situations, you believe you have the right to influence other people; in others, you may think twice before trying to persuade another person. When people feel they have the right to persuade, they will use more direct pressure techniques than in situations where they do not.

Another factor is perceived *personal benefits* or self-interest. Here the question is, What do I have to gain from getting the other person to comply? If much is to be gained, one will probably use tactics designed to maximize that gain, even at the cost of the other person's welfare.

Still another factor is perceived *resistance*. If the resistance is expected to be high, evidence may be used to support one's claims. In such a situation one may also point out the benefits of compliance. If little resistance is expected, the participants may suggest trade-offs, or, if the speaker is dominant in the situation, tactics used to maximize his or her benefits may also be invoked.

Communicators will also perceive certain *relational consequences* to compliance-gaining attempts. Communicators will use trade-offs more frequently when their definition of the relationship is somewhat stable; and they will tend to bolster their argument with evidence when they think that the consequences of the compliance-gaining attempt will be short-term. More relational tactics, such as pointing out the benefits of compliance, are used when long-term consequences are expected. Direct and selfish tactics are the safest in stable relationships, especially if the consequence of compliance is minimal. Communicators seem much more cautious and indirect if the relationship is not very firm.

The final situational factor is *apprehension*. If the communicator expects to feel a lot of tension, he or she will probably use messages that are face-saving. High-pressure tactics are most likely not used when the communicator is apprehensive.

Compliance-gaining research is an especially fine example of a group of researchers building on one another's work. The research and theory in this area has been incremental and programmatic. However, it has not been as productive as many

51. Michael J. Cody and Margaret L. McLaughlin, "The Situation as a Construct in Interpersonal Communication Research," in *Handbook of Interpersonal Communication*, eds. Mark L. Knapp and Gerald R. Miller (Beverly Hills: Sage Publications, 1985), pp. 263–312; Michael J. Cody, et. al., "Situation Perception and Message Strategy Selection," in *Communication Yearbook 9*, ed. Margaret L. McLaughlin (Beverly Hills: Sage Publications, 1986), pp. 390–422.

hoped it would be. Much of the research is flawed in that it has failed to observe actual compliance-gaining communication in real situations. The problem is methodological: In order to study subjects systematically, very simple written compliance-gaining situations are presented to subjects, along with a list of pre-established strategies. The complexity of interacting factors that influence compliance-gaining behavior seems out of the reach of researchers.

The work of Cody and his associates has advanced our understanding of these situational complexities, but even they admit that many questions remain unanswered. Not only do we need to know about how people interact behaviorally with their environments, but we do not yet fully understand the cognitive mechanisms that operate in communication message selection.

Integration

In interpersonal communication people use discourse to achieve objectives within a relationship. An important goal of interpersonal communication is to get information about other people, and we often use information gathered through observation and interaction to attribute traits or to infer the causes of behavior. Disclosure of information about oneself is common in interpersonal communication, but the function and effect of such disclosure in a relationship are unclear.

People seem to have a particular style when they communicate with others. Style is a repeated pattern of verbal and nonverbal behaviors that affects how other people understand one's messages. Some people seem to be more adaptive to situational changes than others. Such individuals consciously adjust their messages to the situation and audience in order to maximize their effectiveness.

The medium of interpersonal communication is talk, or discourse. People have an intuitive sense of how to organize conversation so that it is coherent. They do so by following rules that enable them to structure information coherently, to take turns in an organized fashion, and to use speech rationally to accomplish objectives. A common goal is to seek the compliance of another person. People choose compliance-gaining strategies on the basis of their perceived power in the relationship, as well as a variety of situational factors.

In the following chapter, we look more closely at the ways in which communication enters into the definition, maintenance, and development of relationships.

Ten

Theories of Interpersonal Communication in Relationships

The previous chapter suggests that there are three types of interpersonal communication theories: those dealing with persons, discourse, and relationships. This chapter centers on the third group of theories. Unlike the theories outlined in the previous chapter, all the theories discussed here share a concern for a unit of analysis that encompasses at least two individuals and their relationship. This subject has been roughly labeled *relational communication*, and it dominates research and theory on interpersonal communication today.

This chapter examines the foundations of relational communication, theories of relational perception, theories of relational development, and theories of conflict.

Foundations of Relational Communication

At the core of relational communication is the assumption that interpersonal communication functions to establish, maintain, and change relationships, while the relationship itself determines the nature of interpersonal communication. In this section we discuss the contemporary origins of this idea.

Origins of Relational Theory

Anthropologist Gregory Bateson is founder of the line of theory that has come to be known as "relational communication."[1] Bateson's work led to the development of two foundational propositions on which most relational theories still rest. The first is the proposition of the dual nature of messages. Every interpersonal exchange bears two messages, a "report" message and a "command" message. The report message contains the substance or content of the communication, while the command message makes a statement about the relationship.[2] These two elements have come to be known as the content message and the relationship message, or communication and metacommunication, respectively. We will explore these concepts in greater detail in upcoming sections.

Bateson's second seminal proposition is that relationships can be characterized by complementarity or symmetry. In complementary relationships the dominant behavior of one participant elicits

1. Bateson began to formulate his ideas on relationships from his field observations of the Iatmul tribe of New Guinea in the 1930s. See, *Naven* (Stanford: Stanford University Press, 1958).

2. This proposition was first presented in the theory of communication by Juergen Ruesch and Gregory Bateson, *Communication: The Social Matrix of Society* (New York: Norton, 1951). For a summary of this theory, see the first edition of *Theories of Human Communication* (Columbus: Charles E. Merrill, 1978), pp. 43–47.

submissive behavior from the other. In symmetry, dominance is met by dominance, or submissiveness by submissiveness. We will return to these thoughts momentarily.

Although Bateson's ideas originated in anthropological research, they were quickly picked up in psychiatry and applied to pathological relationships. Bateson himself teamed with psychiatric colleagues to develop relational theory further. Perhaps Bateson's most famous contribution in this regard is the double bind theory of schizophrenia.[3] According to this theory, schizophrenia is caused by social factors, most notable of which is the double bind. Significant persons in the schizophrenic's life send contradictory messages, in which the command and report functions are inconsistent. This situation sets a no-win trap, such that the individual loses no matter what course of action is taken. For example, a parent may state on the report level that he or she wishes to comfort a hurt child, but nonverbally, on the command level, the parent tells the child to stay away. This double bind notion was revolutionary in psychiatry, for it suggested that mental illness may not be caused as much by internal personality factors as by interpersonal social factors.

The Palo Alto Group

In the 1950s and 1960s Bateson led an active group of researchers and clinicians in a program to further develop and apply ideas on relational communication. These scholars became known as the Palo Alto Group. Although their interests were primarily clinical, their work has had enormous impact on the study of interpersonal communication in general. About 1960 psychiatrist Paul Watzlawick joined the group and quickly became one of its leaders.

This group's work received wide publicity and popularity through the publication of *Pragmatics of Human Communication*.[4] Although this book does not express a complete picture of the Palo Alto Group, it is the most comprehensive single work of the group and has been treated as its basic statement of theory.

In the book Paul Watzlawick, Janet Beavin, and Don Jackson present a well-known analysis of communication based on system principles. (A system was defined in Chapter 3 as a set of objects that interrelate with one another to form a unique whole.) Part and parcel of a system is the notion of *relationship*, and in defining interaction, the authors stress this idea: "Interactional systems then, shall be *two or more communicants in the process of, or at the level of, defining the nature of their relationship*."[5]

Relationships emerge from the interaction between people. People set up for themselves interaction rules, which govern their communicative behaviors. By obeying the rules, behaving appropriately, the participants sanction the defined relationship. In a marriage, for example, a dominance-submission relationship may emerge and be reinforced by implicit rules. The husband may send messages of command, which are followed by compliance by the wife, or vice versa. A status relationship in an organization may be observed in a subordinate's nonverbal behavior. The subordinate, for example, may pause at the supervisor's door to await an invitation to enter. Such implicit rules are numerous in any ongoing relationship, be it a friendship, business relationship, love affair, family, or whatever.

In *Pragmatics of Communication* Watzlawick, Beavin, and Jackson present five basic axioms.[6] First, "one cannot *not* communicate."[7] This axiom has been quoted again and again in textbooks on communication. Its point is important, for the axiom emphasizes that the very attempt to avoid interaction is itself a kind of action. It also emphasizes that any perceivable behavior is potentially communicative. Second, the authors postulate that

3. Gregory Bateson, Donald J. Jacison, J. Haley, and J. Weaklund, "Toward a Theory of Schizophrenia," *Behavioral Science* 1 (1956): 251–64.

4. Paul Watzlawick, Janet Beavin, and Don Jackson, *Pragmatics of Human Communication: A Study of Interactional Patterns, Pathologies, and Paradoxes* (New York: Norton, 1967).

5. Ibid., pp. 120–21.

6. These axioms are summarized in Joseph DeVito, *The Interpersonal Communication Book* (New York: Harper & Row, 1976).

7. Watzlawick, Beavin, and Jackson, *Pragmatics*, p. 51.

"every communication has a content and a relationship aspect such that the latter classifies the former and is therefore metacommunication."[8] When two people are talking, each is relating information to the other, but simultaneously each is also "commenting" on the information at a higher level. This simultaneous relationship-talk (which often is nonverbal) is what is meant by *metacommunication*. For example, on the content level a teacher may tell you that a test will be given tomorrow. Many possible metamessages may accompany the content level. The instructor may be making any of the following impressions: I am the authority in this classroom; I teach, you learn; What I have lectured about is important; I need feedback on your progress; I have a need to judge you; I want you to think I am fulfilling my role as professor; and so on. This axiom further substantiates the theorists' idea that interaction is a constant process of defining relationships.

The third axiom of communication deals with the punctuation of communication sequences. Interaction sequences, like word sequences, cannot be understood as a string of isolated elements. To make sense, they must be punctuated or grouped syntactically. In raw form an interaction consists of a move by one individual followed by moves from others. The objective observer would see a series of behaviors. Like the series of sounds in a sentence, these behaviors are not simply a chain. Certain behaviors are responses to others. Behaviors are thus grouped or punctuated into larger units, which in the whole help to define the relationship. Of course, any given string of behaviors might be punctuated in various ways. One source of difficulty among communicators occurs when they punctuate differently. For example, consider a marriage involving nagging by the husband and withdrawing by the wife. This sequence can be punctuated in two ways. On the one hand, the wife's withdrawing may be a response to the husband's nagging: nag/withdraw, nag/withdraw. On the other hand, the opposite may be occurring: withdraw/nag, withdraw/nag. In the first case the punctuation of nag/

withdraw implies an attack/retreat relationship. But the husband's punctuation of withdraw/nag implies ignoring/imploring.

Fourth, "human beings communicate both digitally and analogically."[9] The authors describe two types of coding used in interpersonal communication. Each has two distinguishing characteristics. *Digital* coding is relatively arbitrary. In other words a digital sign is used to represent a referent that bears no intrinsic relation to the sign. The relationship between the sign and the referent is strictly imputed. Second, the digital signs are discrete; they are "on" or "off," uttered or not uttered. The most common digital code in human communication is language. Sounds, words, and phrases, arranged syntactically, communicate meanings.

The *analogic* code is quite different from digital signs. It also has two distinguishing characteristics. First, an analogic sign is not arbitrary. Either it resembles the significate (for example, photo) or is intrinsic to the thing being signified. Second, an analogue is often continuous rather than discrete; it has degrees of intensity or longevity. Most nonverbal signs are analogic. For example, a facial expression of surprise not only is a sign of a feeling or condition but is actually part of the surprise itself. Its meaning is intrinsic. Further, the facial expression is not an either-or sign. It is a continuous variable between no expression and extreme facial distortion.

While the digital and analogic codes are different from one another, they are used together and cannot be separated in ongoing communication. For example, a word (digital) can be uttered in a variety of paralinguistic ways (loud, soft; high, low; and so forth). The manner of utterance is analogic. Likewise, a written message consisting of letters and words (digital) is presented on paper using various layouts, styles of handwriting or print, and other analogic codes.

Within the stream of behaviors in interaction, both digital and analogic coding blend together. Watzlawick and the others believe that these two serve different functions. Digital signs, having rel-

8. Ibid., p. 54.

9. Ibid., p. 67.

atively precise meanings, communicate the content dimension; while the analogic code, which is rich in feeling and meaning, is the vehicle for the relationship (metacommunication) level. To relate this axiom to the content-relationship idea of the second axiom, we can say that while people are communicating digitally on the content level, they are commenting about their relationship analogically on the metalevel. For example, suppose a father at a playground sees his daughter fall and scrape her knee. Immediately, he says, "Don't cry. Daddy is coming." The content meaning is clear. The child receives a message stating that her father is going to come to her. Imagine the large number of relationship messages that might be sent analogically with body and voice. The father might communicate his own fear, worry, anger, boredom, or dominance. At the same time he might communicate a number of possible perceptions of his little girl, including "careless person," "attention getter," "injured child," "provoker," and so on. Truly this axiom captures the complexity of even the simplest interpersonal exchange.[10]

The final axiom of communication expresses a difference between *symmetrical* and *complementary* interaction. When two communicators in a relationship behave similarly, the relationship is said to be symmetrical; differences are minimized. When communicator differences are maximized, however, a complementary relationship is said to exist. In a marriage when two partners both vie for power, they are involved in a symmetrical relationship. Likewise, coworkers are communicating symmetrically when each abdicates responsibility for taking control of the job. A complementary marital relationship would exist when the wife behaves in ways that reinforce her submission, and the husband responds dominantly. In the work setting a complementary relationship would exist when one's feelings of superiority shape the way one responds to another's expressed low self-esteem. Ideally, an ongoing relationship includes an optimal blend of complementary and symmetrical interactions. Flexibility is the key.

10. For a more detailed discussion of coding, see Chapter 4.

The variable most often examined in regard to complementary and symmetrical relationships is *control.* To explore this idea, let us look at the work of Edna Rogers and Frank Millar and Malcolm Parks on the control dimension.

The Control Dimension

Frank Millar and L. Edna Rogers have been researching relational communication since the early 1970s. Their work remains one of the most cogent and heuristically valuable statements about relational communication, and it provides a concrete extension of the work of the Palo Alto Group.[11] Although Millar and Rogers have discussed various dimensions of relationships, most of their research has centered on control. Control is characterized by two variables. The first is the *rigid-flexible* continuum. The more flexible the relationship, the more control passes back and forth between the two parties. *Stability-instability* relates to the predictability of the control shifts. The more consistent the pattern of control over time, the more stable the control.

Let us take a closer look at how control operates in a relationship. Following from the work of early relationship theorists, Millar and Rogers define control in terms of complementarity and symmetry. Control cannot be defined by examining a single message. Rather, one must look at the pattern of messages and responses over time. Every message is a stimulus for the next message in the sequence. In other words when A makes a statement, B's response defines the nature of the relationship at that moment. If B responds in a way that asserts control, B's message is said to be *one-up.* If B responds in a way that accepts A's assertion of control, B's message is *one-down.* If B's response neither asserts control nor relinquishes it, the message is *one-across.* A complementary exchange occurs when one partner asserts a one-up message and the other responds

11. Although this work is explained in several sources, perhaps the most complete theoretical treatment is Frank E. Millar and L. Edna Rogers, "A Relational Approach to Interpersonal Communication," in *Explorations in Interpersonal Communication,* ed. Gerald Miller (Beverly Hills: Sage Publications, 1976), pp. 87–203.

Table 10-1 Control configurations

Control direction of speaker A's message	Control Direction of Speaker B's Message		
	One-up (↑)	One-down (↓)	One-across (→)
One-up (↑)	1. (↑↑) Competitive symmetry	4. (↑↓) Complementarity	7. (↑→) Transition
One-down (↓)	2. (↓↑) Complementarity	5. (↓↓) Submissive symmetry	8. (↓→) Transition
One-across (→)	3. (→↑) Transition	6. (→↓) Transition	9. (→→) Neutralized symmetry

Control Pattern Examples:

1. Competitive Symmetry (one-up/one-up):

   A: You know I want you to keep the house picked up during the day.

   B: I want you to help sometimes.

2. Complementarity (one-down/one-up):

   A: Please help. I need you.

   B: Sure, I know how.

3. Transition (one-across/one-up):

   A: Let's compromise.

   B: No, my way is best.

4. Complementarity (one-up/one-down):

   A: Let's get out of town this weekend.

   B: Okay.

5. Submissive Symmetry (one-down/one-down):

   A: I'm so tired. What should we do?

   B: I can't decide. You decide.

6. Transition (one-across/one-down):

   A: My Dad was pretty talkative tonight.

   B: You're right; he sure was.

7. Transition (one-up/one-across):

   A: I definitely think we should have more kids.

   B: Lots of people seem to be having kids these days.

8. Transition (one-down/one-across):

   A: Please help me. What can I do?

   B: I don't know.

9. Neutralized symmetry (one-across/one-across):

   A: The neighbor's house needs paint.

   B: The windows are dirty too.

one-down. In a complementary relationship this kind of transaction predominates. A symmetrical exchange involves both partners presenting one-up or one-down messages, and a symmetrical relationship is marked by a preponderance of such exchanges. A third state, *transition*, exists when the partners' responses are different (for example, one-up/one-across) but not opposite. Table 10-1 illus-trates nine control states generated by combinations of these types of control messages. [12]

The foregoing concepts of complementarity and symmetry are useful for understanding the configuration of relational patterns. Malcolm Parks has presented a set of axioms and theorems, based on

12. Ibid., p. 97.

research findings and clinical observations. These rely heavily on Millar and Rogers's taxonomy in Table 10-1 and can be viewed as an extension of this theory. Since the axioms and theorems are self-explanatory, they are listed without comment.[13]

Axioms

1. The greater the competitive symmetry, the greater the frequency of unilateral action in a relationship.

2. The greater the competitive symmetry, the lower the probability of relationship termination.

3. The greater the role discrepancy, the greater the competitive symmetry.

4. The greater the competitive symmetry, the greater the frequency of open conflict.

5. The greater the competitive symmetry, the greater the frequency of threat and intimidation messages.

6. The greater the competitive symmetry, the greater the frequency of messages of rejection.

7. The less competitive symmetry, the greater the satisfaction with communication.

8. The greater the external threat, the less the competitive symmetry.

9. The greater the role discrepancy, the less frequent is communication about feelings toward the other.

10. The greater the complementarity, the less empathy.

11. The greater the complementarity, the greater the role specialization.

12. The greater the complementarity, the greater the mutual envy.

13. The greater the rigidity, the greater the frequency of disconfirming messages.

14. The greater the rigidity, the greater the probability of psychopathology.

15. The greater the rigidity, the less frequent are attempts to explicitly define the relationship.

Theorems (derived from the above axioms)

1. The greater the role discrepancy, the greater the frequency of unilateral action in the relationship.

2. The greater the role discrepancy, the lower the probability of relational termination.

13. Malcolm Parks, "Relational Communication: Theory and Research," *Human Communication Research* 3 (1977): 372–81.

3. The greater the role discrepancy, the greater the frequency of open conflict.

4. The greater the role discrepancy, the greater the frequency of threat and intimidation messages.

5. The greater the role discrepancy, the greater the frequency of messages of rejection.

6. The greater the role discrepancy, the less satisfaction with communication.

7. The greater the external threat, the greater the frequency of mutual or joint action in a relationship.

8. The greater the external threat, the higher the probability of relationship termination.

9. The greater the external threat, the lower the frequency of open conflict within the relationship.

10. The greater the external threat, the lower the frequency of threat and intimidation messages within the relationship.

11. The greater the external threat, the lower the frequency of messages of rejection within the relationship.

12. The greater the external threat, the greater the satisfaction with communication within the relationship.

Relational Perception

The nature of a relationship and its corresponding communication patterns are largely a matter of perception. The key question for any relationship is how the partners perceive and understand their interaction. Several theories address this central concern. Here we look at three such theories—Laing's theory of metaperception, Burgoon's theory of relational dimensions, and Spitzberg and Cupach's theory of relational competence.

Perception and Metaperception

R. D. Laing, a British psychiatrist, has written a number of books related to the process of perception in communication.[14] Laing's thesis is that one's communicative behavior is largely shaped by one's

14. Laing's works most concerned with communication include *The Politics of Experience* (New York: Pantheon Books, 1967); *Self and Others* (London: Tavistock Publications, 1969); and R. D. Laing, H. Phillipson, and A. R. Lee, *Interpersonal Perception* (New York: Springer, 1966).

perception (experience) of the relationship with the other communicator.

Laing makes a distinction between experience and behavior. *Behavior*, which is the observable actions of another, is public; *experience* is private. Experience is the feeling that accompanies behavior or the perception of another's behavior. It consists of imagination, perception, and memory. We can imagine the future; we can perceive the present; we can recall the past. Such experiences are internal in the individual and not directly accessible to anyone else.

Behavior, on the other hand, can be observed, but another's experience cannot. Inferring experience from behavior is the heart of communication, but doing this is difficult, as Laing points out: "I see you, and you see me. I experience you, and you experience me. I see your behavior. You see my behavior. But I do not and never have and never will see your *experience* of me."[15] As implied in this quotation, experience is an intrapersonal matter, but one's experience is also affected largely by relations with others and how one perceives or experiences others. How we behave toward another person is a function of two related experiences, the experience of the other person and the experience of the relationship.

A person interacting with another has two levels of experience (perception), or *perspectives*.[16] The person experiences the other individual in a *direct perspective*. In a second or *metaperspective* the communicator imagines, or infers, what the other person is feeling, perceiving, or thinking. Laing describes the process:

> I cannot avoid trying to understand your experience, because although I do not experience your experience, which is invisible to me (and nontastable, nontouchable, nonsmellable, and inaudible), yet I experience you *as experiencing*. I do not experience your experience. But I experience you experiencing. I experience myself as experienced by you. And I experience you as experiencing yourself as experienced by me. And so on.[17]

15. Laing, *Politics*, p. 4.
16. Laing, Phillipson, and Lee, *Interpersonal*.
17. Laing, *Politics*, p. 5.

To use Laing's favorite characters, Jack perceives certain behaviors of Jill (direct perspective). He also infers or imagines Jill's perceptions (metaperspective).

A relationship then is defined by the communicator's direct perspectives and metaperspectives. Theoretically, metaperception can proceed indefinitely through higher levels. Jack loves Jill. Jack thinks Jill loves him. Jack thinks that Jill thinks that he loves her, and so on. Further, since experience affects behavior, one often behaves in accordance with his or her metaperspectives. If Jack thinks Jill thinks he does not love her, he may try to change Jill's imagined perception. The *metaidentity* is how the person believes others see one.

Of course, metaperspectives may or may not be accurate, and the health of a relationship is greatly determined by perceptual accuracy. Three concepts are pertinent at this point. *Understanding* is the agreement or conjunction between Jack's metaperspective and Jill's direct perspective. If Jack correctly infers that Jill loves him, understanding results. *Being understood* is the inverse. It is the conjunction of Jack's meta-metaperspective and Jill's metaperspective. If Jack correctly infers that Jill believes Jack loves her, he is understood. But being understood is not the same as *feeling understood*. The latter is defined as the conjunction between Jack's direct perspective and his own metaperspective. If Jack infers that Jill believes he loves her, and he does, then he feels understood.

Since communicators attempt to behave in ways that they believe will affect others, *spirals* can develop wherein each person acts toward the other in such a way that particular metaperspectives (for example, mistrust) become accentuated. This idea of spiral has been important for Laing as a psychiatrist because it explains various pathological relationships. For example, Jack, as a paranoid, mistrusts Jill. He does not believe she loves him. He then accuses her of having affairs with other men. Jill, in her metaperception of Jack's mistrust, attempts to prove her love. Jack sees this attempt as covering up her lack of love. Now he perceives Jill as a liar. The spiral will continue until the relationship is destroyed. This example is of a *unilateral spiral*. Jack's mistrust of Jill becomes more and more accentuated. A *bilateral spiral* occurs when both parties move toward increasingly extreme metaperceptions. For example, Jack believes Jill wants too much from him. He judges her as greedy. At the same time Jill sees Jack as selfish. Both feel the other is withholding what he or she needs. Since both parties feel misunderstood, they retaliate, causing their metaperceptions of greed and selfishness to increase. Such spirals need to be broken before the system (dyad or person) is destroyed.

Relational Dimensions

Recall that communication involves two parts—the content (or report) and relationship (or command) messages. We talk about a subject (content), but we also simultaneously communicate in a way that affects the relationship. The relationship message is largely nonverbal. Communicators' perceptions of the relationship therefore depend in large measure on the nonverbal elements of the interaction.

An important theoretical question remains: What relational perceptions typically arise from the messages in an interaction? Judee Burgoon and her colleagues have researched this question.[18] They conducted a huge survey of the interpersonal communication literature to find possible elements of relational communication and isolated twelve common aspects of relationships that seem to be communicated. Relying on Aristotle's term for basic *topics* of communication, the theorists labeled these *fundamental topoi of relational communication*. They include varying levels of the following:

1. dominance or submission (control)
2. intimacy or nonintimacy in the form of affection or hostility, intensity of involvement, and inclusion or exclusion, trust, and depth or superficiality
3. emotional arousal, including activation or responsiveness

4. composure or self-control
5. similarity
6. formality
7. orientation toward task or social elements of the relationship.

These topics were further narrowed into four basic, independent dimensions of relational communication:

1. emotional arousal, composure, and formality
2. intimacy and similarity
3. immediacy (liking)
4. dominance-submission.

Research showed that these four dimensions seem to characterize much relational communication. This important work tells us the kinds of perceptions that people get from the relationship messages of others.

Burgoon and her associates further studied the question of what nonverbal behaviors specifically affect these perceptions, and some interesting results emerged. Four behaviors seem especially important in the relationship message. *Proximity* can be significant in communicating intimacy, attraction, trust, caring, dominance, persuasiveness, and aggressiveness. *Smiling* seems especially important in communicating emotional arousal, composure, and formality, as well as intimacy and liking. *Touching*, too, communicates intimacy. *Eye contact* is like an exclamation point in intensifying the effect of other nonverbal behaviors.

Indeed, relational communication is complex and involves subtle, interacting behaviors. This theory moves toward unraveling that complexity and makes more concrete the axioms formulated in the early work on relational communication.

A major concern in the communication field is communication competence, or the question of what makes a good communicator. This subject is discussed in the following section.

Relational Competence

In this section we have dealt with theories related to the perception of relationships. Of particular interest in this regard is the perception of

18. Judee K. Burgoon and Jerold L. Hale, "The Fundamental Topoi of Relational Communication," *Communication Monographs* 51 (1984): 193–214; Judee K. Burgoon, David B. Buller, Jerold L. Hale, and Mark A. deTurck, "Relational Messages Associated with Nonverbal Behaviors," *Human Communication Research* 10 (1984): 351–78.

interpersonal competence. Brian Spitzberg and William Cupach have presented an integrative model of relational competence that addresses this concern.[19] Predicated on the assumption that interpersonal communication is a relational phenomenon, this model organizes numerous research findings on this subject into a coherent framework. Spitzberg and Cupach characterize competence with several principles.

First, competence is *perceived appropriateness and effectiveness*. Both appropriateness and effectiveness are important here, and these are always a question of perception. A person may be perceived as appropriate, but not effective, or vice versa, in which case the individual is not viewed as competent.

Second, competence is *contextual*. Competence is not a cross-situational trait; appropriateness and effectiveness are always judged in relation to some situation. For example, aggressiveness may be perceived as effective in one situation and not in another; and it may be perceived as appropriate in one situation and not in another. Only when aggressiveness is perceived both as appropriate and effective will such behavior be seen as competent. Competence is largely a function of the particular relationship; someone judged highly competent in one relationship may be incompetent in another. This is why flexibility and adaptability are so frequently associated with competence: People who understand situational contingencies and adapt well to them are more often perceived as competent than those who are not.

Third, competence is *variable*. An individual does not simply possess competence; rather, competence is a matter of degree. One is never entirely competent or incompetent, but one may be more or less so. Furthermore, individuals vary in their competence level from moment to moment and from situation to situation.

Fourth, perceptions of competence are based on both *molar and molecular assessments*. In other words, specific (molecular) behaviors may affect your perceived competence, yet competence is also an outcome of general impressions (molar). Again, the extent to which molar and molecular factors enter into the judgment of competence depends upon the context.

Fifth, competent communication is judged in part by its *function*. To be competent is to accomplish things with your communication. The perceived outcomes of an exchange are important elements in whether an individual is judged to be competent. Of course outcome is not objectively given, but is a function of the relational system. In other words, whether there is an outcome and what that outcome is seen to represent depends largely on the expectations established in the relationship itself. This idea gives rise to the sixth principle—relational competence is an outcome of an *interdependent process*. One's competence is never something that can be possessed; rather, it is always relative to the expectations of everyone involved in the system.

Finally—and this is strongly implied by all the other principles—competence is a matter of *interpersonal impressions*. It is neither a trait nor an enduring attribution. One is competent to the extent that others judge one to be so, and that judgment will wax and wane.

What, specifically, is judged in establishing an individual's relational competence? What impressions go into the perception that another person is competent? We have already indicated that the perception of effectiveness and appropriateness is important. In order for these qualities to emerge, however, other impressions are necessary. These include the perception of *motivation* to behave appropriately and effectively. Appropriate and effective behavior is intentional, and competent communicators are perceived to be motivated to behave in these ways. Further, competent communicators are seen as having *knowledge* and *skill*. Knowledge is the sense of how to accomplish an objective in an appropriate way, and skill is the ability to actually carry out planned actions.

The perceptions of motivation, knowledge, and skill are relative to the perceived outcomes of the

19. Brian H. Spitzberg and William R. Cupach, *Interpersonal Communication Competence* (Beverly Hills: Sage Publications, 1984).

interaction. Such outcomes may be feelings of satisfaction, interpersonal attraction, solidarity, trust, conflict resolution, or a number of others. When one is perceived to have participated in a positive outcome by being motivated, knowledgeable, and skilled, he or she is likely to be judged as competent.

Relational Development

A central assumption of most of the theories in this chapter is that relationships develop and change. This belief makes time and trajectory important. Unlike theories of personal and discourse processes, models of relational processes demand a view of change over time. In this section we look at three groups of theories in this tradition—theories of interpersonal attraction, theories of social penetration, and theories of relational dissolution—which roughly correspond with the three phases of relational development.

Interpersonal Attraction

Psychologists have long been interested in why people are or are not attracted to one another. The development of a relationship normally begins with some kind of initial impression, which can be graded along a continuum ranging from extreme liking to disgust. There are numerous theories on this subject. Here we examine only two of the most influential approaches—balance theory and social exchange theory.

Balance theory. Theodore Newcomb envisions a cognitive system in which various personal orientations interrelate.[20] An *orientation* is a relationship between a person and some aspect of the environ-

ment. Orientation involves directedness, selectivity, attitudes, and attention. If I am oriented toward something, I tend to be directed to it, attend to it in a selective way. One can be oriented to a number of personal, concrete, or abstract objects. A person has orientations toward other people, things, and concepts or ideas. An orientation has a number of qualities, including *sign* (positive or negative) and *intensity* (strong or weak). Orientations also possess what Newcomb calls *cognitive content*, or attributions made about the object of orientation. Newcomb offers the following example of cognitive content: "One parent's attraction toward a child may have strong cognitive components of pride and resemblance to himself, while for the other parent warmth of personal response may be a more important component."[21]

One's orientations interrelate to form a cognitive system. Specifically, three sorts of orientations interact. First, we have orientations of *attraction*. These are interpersonal orientations. Newcomb uses the term *attraction* generally here to imply both positive and negative orientations toward objects or concepts. Finally, there are one's *perceived orientations of others*. Here Newcomb also recognizes the concept of metaperception.

Basically, two kinds of systems exist within Newcomb's framework. The *individual* system is the person's own system of orientation toward another person and a relevant object. Such a system is viewed through the eyes of the perceiver. The second type of system is *collective* and is viewed from outside the individuals involved. In both cases three elements are present: person A, person B, and object X. In the individual system, illustrated in Figure 10-1(a), four orientations interact. These include A's attraction toward B, B's attraction toward A, A's attitude toward X, B's perceived attitude toward X. The collective system, illustrated in Figure 10-1(b), includes not only A's orientations, but B's orientations as well. The broad bands in Figure 10-1(b) indicate the interrelationships between the pairs of orientations.

---

20. Theodore Newcomb, *The Acquaintance Process* (New York: Holt, Rinehart & Winston, 1961). For a more complete discussion of the variety of theories of attraction, see Steve Duck (ed.), *Theory and Practice in Interpersonal Attraction* (New York: Academic Press, 1971).

21. Newcomb, *Acquaintance*, p. 6.

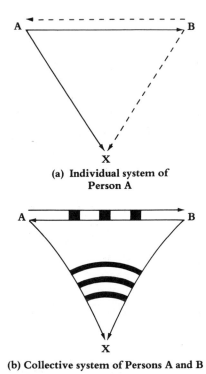

(a) Individual system of Person A

(b) Collective system of Persons A and B

Figure 10-1 Schematic representation of systems.*

*Arrows point from orienting person to person or object of orientation. Broken lines refer to orientations attributed by A to B; solid lines refer to own orientations of person from whom arrow stems. Broad bands refer to relationships between orientations connected by bands. From *The Acquaintance Process*, by Theodore M. Newcomb. Copyright © 1961 by Holt, Rinehart & Winston, Inc. Reprinted by permission of Holt, Rinehart & Winston, CBS College Publishing.

In the individual system certain conditions must be met. An individual system requires that the perceiver regard the object as relevant to the self as well as to the other person. The perceiver must attribute an attitude to B. In the individual system, whether A has an accurate perception does not matter. It is only necessary for the perceiver to believe that coorientation exists. If both parties see the coorientation, then the collective model may be used. The collective model usually presumes

communication, either verbal or nonverbal, between the persons in regard to X.

For example, suppose a man has recently met a woman in the library. He is attracted positively to her and admires her apparent interest in reading. In addition he believes she is positively attracted to him. Here we have an example of an individual system. This man has orientations toward the woman and toward reading. He also attributes orientations to his new acquaintance. If the woman shares the perception of attraction and coordination to reading, a collective system exists.

You will recall from Chapter 3 that one of the qualities of systems is that they tend to be homeostatic (balanced). Changes that cause imbalance create pressures for other changes that will return the system to balance. In this way a system maintains itself. Such is the case with the cognitive systems described by Newcomb. He explains this phenomenon:

> In propositional form, the stronger A's attraction toward B the greater the strength of the force upon A to maintain minimal discrepancy between his own and B's attitude, as he perceives the latter, toward the same X; and, if positive attraction remains constant, the greater the perceived discrepancy in attitude the stronger the force to reduce it. We shall refer to this force as strain.[22]

Thus strain toward symmetry is a function of the attraction of one person toward the other. Two other factors also relate. The *importance* of the object to the person is positively related to the amount of strain, as is the perceived *relevance* of the object to the relationship between the persons. To continue our example, if the man is highly attracted to the woman, if he values reading and sees it as important to his relationship with the woman, pressure is thus created for him to attribute interest in reading to the woman. If he finds out that the woman does not read—she was only visiting her friend the librarian—something will change in the system. The man may come to value reading less, changing his attitude toward X. He may distort his

22. Ibid., p. 12.

perception such that he continues to believe the woman likes to read. He may reduce the importance of his interest in reading. He may reduce the perceived relevance of reading to the relationship. Finally—and most important for the topic of this section—he may become less attracted to the woman. Attraction is thus explained in terms of the system dynamics involving the participants' various interrelated orientations.

This analysis suggests that new information has great impact on the system. New information, if congruent with one of a person's relevant and important orientations, will cause changes throughout the system. Newcomb calls such pressures *reality forces*. On the other hand are *balance forces* in the system that create pressure to minimize discrepancies. Thus the system is in a state of dynamic tension under which new information either will be distorted, or it will cause change.

Newcomb's primary contribution is that he places attraction in the context of the system of interrelated orientations. Attraction is, therefore, not an isolated attitude toward another person. It is part of a complex of elements that demand to be viewed as a whole. Further, Newcomb shows how the individual's orientational system is part of larger collective systems, in which interpersonal communication plays a major role.

Social exchange theory. There are several theories of social exchange.[23] Here we deal with the most popular view, that of John Thibaut and Harold Kelley. These theorists argue that interpersonal relationships, like other kinds of behavior, are evaluated by the person in terms of the value of the consequences.[24] The essence of relationship is interaction, which involves dyadic behavior: One's behaviors affect the other person.

If you could imagine all of the behaviors a person

is apt to produce, you could define the individuals' *behavior repertoire*. When people come together in a relationship, they choose various of these behaviors as part of their interaction. The extent to which a behavior is valued depends on the relative costs and rewards, or *outcomes*. Rewards include the pleasure and gratifications associated with the behavior; costs include such inhibitory factors as physical or mental effort, anxiety, or perhaps embarrassment. Such consequences follow all individual actions, but the situation is made more complex when interaction, which necessarily involves more than one person, takes place.

In dyadic interaction the behaviors of the participants are paired. Each person's action yields a particular *goodness of outcome*, based on rewards and costs, and each participant must value the mutual activity above a particular level in order for the relationship to be sustained. The consequences of the actions involved in a relationship may be endogenous or exogenous. *Exogenous* consequences are those external to the relationship. Such consequences, stemming from the person's individual needs and values, would accrue from the action whether another person were involved or not. *Endogenous* factors, however, stem from the unique pairing of actions of both individuals in interaction. For example, in studying this book, you might anticipate the reward of a high score on the test. If this were an exogenous reward, it would result whether you studied by yourself or with another person. However, an added reward of studying with others might be a sense of gratification received if the other person gave you positive feedback (such as stating that he learned from you). Since such a reward depends on the established relationship, it is endogenous.

Endogenous costs may result as well. One's behavior may inhibit the performance of the other person. In the study group, for example, the failure of one member to read the material ahead of time could slow down the entire group. This analysis leads to the thesis of Thibaut and Kelley's work: "Whatever the nature of the early exchanges between A and B, they will voluntarily continue their association only if the experienced outcomes (or

23. An excellent summary of this entire line of work is Michael E. Roloff, *Interpersonal Communication: The Social Exchange Approach* (Beverly Hills: Sage Publications, 1981).

24. J. W. Thibaut and H. H. Kelley, *The Social Psychology of Groups* (New York: John Wiley, 1959). For an extension and elaboration of their theory, see H. H. Kelley and J. W. Thibaut, *Interpersonal Relations: A Theory of Interdependence* (New York: John Wiley, 1978).

inferred but as yet unexperienced outcomes) are found to be adequate.[25]

But what determines adequacy? Here the theorists bring in two important concepts. The *comparison level* (CL) is the criterion or standard of attractiveness used to judge the group. However, even if the person does not like a group (the costs are judged too high relative to rewards), association with the group still may be more desirable than any of the alternatives. Therefore the second concept to be considered is the *comparison level of alternatives* (CLalt), which is the lowest level of outcomes tolerated considering other alternatives. Thus CL is the level above which the person is satisfied with the relationship. CLalt is the level of outcome above which the individual will remain in the relationship. CL is a measure of attraction: CLalt is a measure of dependency.

Outcomes vary over time, of course, and one's judgment of a relationship also varies depending on the salient outcomes. As the CL goes up and down, the individual changes standards of judgment:

> In other words, the person adapts to the presently experienced levels: after a shift upward to a new level, the once longed for outcomes gradually lose their attractiveness; after a downward shift to a new lower level, the disappointment gradually wears off and the once dreaded outcomes become accepted.[26]

As indicated above, endogenous rewards and costs result from the contingent relations between the behaviors of participants. A number of endogenous factors affect the outcome of the interaction. Some of those discussed by Thibaut and Kelley include power and dependence, norms and roles, tasks, and frustration and deprivation.

Social Penetration

Social penetration is the process of increasing intimacy in a relationship. Gerald Miller and his colleagues literally define interpersonal communication in terms of penetration.[27] The more communicators know each other as persons, the more of an *interpersonal* character their communication takes on. The less they know one another as persons, the more *impersonal* that communication. Interpersonal communication is therefore the very process of social penetration:

> If the communicators continue their relationship—that is, if they are sufficiently motivated to exert the effort to continue it, and if their interpersonal skills are tuned finely enough to permit its growth—their relationship may undergo certain qualitative changes. When such changes accompany relational development, communicative transactions become increasingly interpersonal.[28]

Miller states that human beings have a natural tendency to predict the outcomes of their actions. In communication, such predictions are largely based on the kinds of information they receive from and about other people. Three fundamental kinds of information are used. *Cultural information* is information about a person's most generally shared cultural attributes, including language, shared values, beliefs, and ideologies. If we know a person's culture, we have some information on which to predict how that person will respond in various situations like greetings and goodbyes; but cultural information by itself is rather shallow and impersonal. It assists communicators to perform acceptably in most general social situations, but is not very helpful in significant interpersonal encounters.

The second kind of information is *sociological*. Beyond cultural norms, sociological information tells us something about people's social groups and roles. You can be successful in communicating with your auto mechanic or dentist because you know something about that person's roles and affiliations, but you still know relatively little about the person as a person. Sociological information is more personal than cultural knowledge but is still rather abstract and general. Unless you know another per-

25. Thibaut and Kelley, *Social Psychology*, pp. 20–21.
26. Ibid., p. 98.
27. G. R. Miller and M. Steinberg, *Between People: A New Analysis of Interpersonal Communication* (Chicago: Science Research Associates, 1975); G. R. Miller and M. J. Sunnafrank,

"All Is for One But One Is Not for All: A Conceptual Perspective of Interpersonal Communication," in *Human Communication Theory: Comparative Essays*, ed. Frank E. X. Dance (New York: Harper & Row, 1982), pp. 220–42.
28. Miller and Sunnafrank, "All Is for One," pp. 222–23.

son fairly well, however, you must rely quite heavily on sociological knowledge.

Psychological information is the most specific and intimate of the three. To know a person psychologically is to know individual traits, feelings, attitudes, and other important personal data. It is the most useful type of information in making predictions about how an individual will respond in communication. When one gears communication to psychological information, that communication is truly *interpersonal.*

Social penetration, in these terms, is the process of moving from cultural interaction to psychological interaction. There are several theories of this process. The most well known is that of Irwin Altman and Donald Taylor, who coined the phrase "social penetration."[29] According to this theory, as relationships develop, communication moves from relatively shallow, nonintimate levels to deeper, more personal ones. Communicators' personalities can be represented by a circle with layers; it has both breadth and depth. Breadth is the array or variety of topics that have been incorporated into the individual's life. Depth is the amount of information available on each. On the outermost shell are highly visible levels of information, like dress and speech. Inside are increasingly private details about the individual's life, feelings, and thoughts. As the relationship develops, the partners share more aspects of the self (breadth), as well as deeper levels of each aspect. Such communication involves exchanging information, exchanging feelings, and sharing activities.

Communication thus proceeds by levels. Once a certain level is reached, under the right conditions the partners share increasing breadth at that level. For example, after dating a few times a couple may begin discussing previous partners, and more and more information about previous partners will be revealed before moving to a still deeper level of disclosure.

Social penetration theory is a social exchange theory; Altman and Taylor's version is modeled

29. Irwin Altman and Donald Taylor, *Social Penetration: The Development of Interpersonal Relationships* (New York: Holt, Rinehart & Winston, 1973).

largely on the work of Thibaut and Kelley, which was discussed earlier. During relational development, communicators not only assess the rewards and costs of the relationship at that moment, but they use the information they have to forecast the rewards and costs they think will occur down the road. If the partners judge that the rewards will be relatively greater than the costs, they will risk more disclosure, which has the potential of moving the participants to a deeper level of intimacy. Therefore, the greater the perceived rewards relative to cost, the more penetration will occur and the greater the rate of penetration. Altman and Taylor found that the most rapid penetration occurs in the early stages of development.

There are four stages of relational development. *Orientation* consists of impersonal communication, in which one only discloses very public information about oneself. If this stage is rewarding to the participants, they will move to the next stage, the *exploratory affective exchange*, or initial expansion of information and movement to a deeper level of disclosure on the topics chosen. The third stage, *affective exchange*, centers on more feelings at a deeper level. Such feelings may be evaluative and critical. The third stage will not be entered unless the partners have perceived substantial rewards relative to costs in earlier stages. Finally, *stable exchange* is highly intimate and allows the partners to predict one another's actions and responses very well. Although social penetration is a process of progressing through these stages, it may not happen in a strictly linear fashion; instead it may occur in a back-and-forth, cyclical fashion. A couple may go in and out of a stage as they test the rewards and costs; they may dwell at a stage for any length of time, or they may move on to the next one.

Relational Dissolution

Relational development does not mean only increasing social penetration. All too often it also involves decreased penetration, disengagement, and dissolution. Altman and Taylor suggest that as rewards are reduced and costs increased at the more intimate levels of communication, the social penetration process will be reversed. Several theories of this reverse process have been advanced.[30] We will discuss two of these here. The first, a dissolution "map," was developed by Steve Duck. It explains the process by which dissolution is accomplished. The second, based on the work of Leslie Baxter, discusses more directly the ways in which couples actually use communication to accomplish disengagement.

Mapping disengagement and dissolution. Steve Duck has proposed a general phase model of relational dissolution.[31] This model is predicated on the assumptions that dissolving a relationship involves complex decisions and that the relationship in the dyad, as well as the relationship with others outside, make such decision making difficult and nonlinear. In other words, the decision to break up occurs sporadically, inconsistently, and ambivalently over a period of time. There may be oscillation between attempts to reconcile and decisions to split. This rocky course is marked by certain thresholds or points of decision that define the boundaries of the stages. Figures 10-2 and 10-3 illustrate.[32]

In the *intra-psychic* phase, one focuses on his or her partner and assesses the dissatisfactions in the relationship. At this stage consideration of relationship problems remains pretty much on a private level with little intentional communication about the problems with the partner. In terms of social exchange, the disillusioned partner spends time weighing costs and rewards and, if the process continues, will decide to communicate explicitly about the relationship.

In the second, *dyadic* phase, the focus is on the relationship itself. In this phase communication is direct and explicit, and relational dynamics are discussed. One is forced to consider not only the partner's unsatisfying traits, but also the partner's perspective and the implications of perspective differences on the relationship itself. There is much talk about how to solve the problems, whether to

do so, or whether to split up. The dyadic phase may end with a decision to repair the relationship, but if this does not work, the process will continue to the next stage, which is coping socially with dissolution.

The *social phase* requires a focus on the larger social group—family, friends, associates, and acquaintances. Now the opinions and feelings of other people are taken into consideration; they may well affect what the couple decides to do. The final stage is called *grave dressing* because it occurs after the break-up has happened. Here the partners each give their own accounts and in their own ways cope with and recover from the termination of the relationship.

Accomplishing relationship disengagement. For several years, Leslie Baxter and her colleagues have conducted research on the disengagement process. These research results form the basic for a theory of the ways in which couples use communication to end relationships.[33] This program addresses three questions:

1. What communication strategies do couples use to break up a relationship?
2. Are the chosen strategies related to characteristics of the individual or the relationship?
3. What is the sequence of the disengagement process?

Baxter found that strategies of disengagement vary in directness and concern for the other person. Direct strategies involve the explicit statement of a desire to end the relationship, while indirect ones do not. Some people choose strategies that project concern for the other person, in an attempt to avoid hurt, while others choose strategies for their expediency. In addition, endings may be unilateral, in which only one member wishes to terminate the

30. See Steve Duck (ed.), *Personal Relationships 4: Dissolving Personal Relationships* (London: Academic Press, 1982).
31. Steve Duck, "A Topography of Relationship Disengagement and Dissolution," in *Personal Relationships 4: Dissolving Personal Relationships*, ed. Steve Duck (London: Academic Press, 1982), pp. 1–30.
32. Adapted from Duck, "Topography," pp. 16–25.

33. The most comprehensive statement of this work is Leslie A. Baxter, "Accomplishing Relationship Disengagement," in *Understanding Personal Relationships: An Interdisciplinary Approach*, eds. Steve Duck and Daniel Perlman (Beverly Hills: Sage, 1985), pp. 243–66. See also William W. Wilmot, Donal A. Carbaugh, and Leslie A. Baxter, "Communicative Strategies Used to Terminate Romantic Relationships," *Western Journal of Speech Communication* 49 (1985): 204–16; Leslie A. Baxter, "Strategies for Ending Relationships: Two Studies," *Western Journal of Speech Communication* 46 (1982): 223–41.

relationship, or bilateral, in which both parties feel that the relationship should end.

In unilateral disengagement, indirect strategies include withdrawal, pseudo de-escalation, and cost escalation. *Withdrawal*, of course, is just avoiding the other person or reducing the amount of contact one has with a partner. Here is an example from one of Baxter's interviews: "I took a stand that related too much homework for an excuse to avoid her. She then initiated notes to me which contained certain things that both of us didn't like about the relationship. I never answered the notes."[34]

Pseudo de-escalation is the lie that one just wishes to change the relationship to be a little less close. Here is an example: "I arranged to talk with her in a neutral location. . . . What I said basically was: 'Let's go back to being just friends' (knowing full well I meant I wanted to salvage my ego, and hers, by saying indirectly, the relationship was totally over.)" *Cost escalation* is behaving in a way that makes it more difficult for the other person to continue the relationship. In other words, one deliberately makes the relationship more costly to the other person so that he or she will be able to tolerate, or even initiate, a separation: "I thought I would be an 'asshole' for a while to make her like me less."

In bilateral disengagement, *fading away* is common. Here both parties acknowledge implicitly that the relationship is over: "My lover was a married man who was visiting overnight on his way through Portland. On the way to the airport the next day, we hardly spoke at all. When we did speak it wasn't concerning our relationship. We both knew that it was over." Mutual pseudo de-escalation is also common in bilateral disengagement.

Two common forms of direct communication in unilateral disengagement are the *fait accompli*, or a simple direct statement that the relationship is over, and *state of the relationship talk*, which is an attempt to analyze the relationship. In bilateral disengagement, direct communication may take the

---

34. All of the examples are from Baxter, "Accomplishing," p. 248.

BREAKDOWN: Dissatisfaction with relationship

↓

Threshold: I can't stand this any more

↓

Intra-Psychic Phase

Personal focus on partner's behavior
Assess adequacy of partner's role performance
Depict and evaluate negative aspects of being in the relationship
Consider costs of withdrawal
Assess positive aspects of alternative relationships
Face "express/repress dilemma"

↓

Threshold: I'd be justified in withdrawing

↓

Dyadic Phase

Face "confrontation/avoidance dilemma"
Confront partner
Negotiate in "Our Relationship Talks"
Attempt repair and reconciliation?
Assess joint costs of withdrawal or reduced intimacy

↓

Threshold: I mean it

↓

Social Phase

Negotiate postdissolution state with partner
Initiate gossip/discussion in social network
Create publicly negotiable face-saving/blame-placing stories and accounts
Consider and face up to implied social network effects, if any
Call in intervention teams?

↓

Threshold: It's now inevitable

↓

Grave Dressing Phase

"Getting over" activity
Retrospection: reformulative postmortem attribution
Public distribution of own version of break-up story

Figure 10-2   A sketch of the main phases of dissolving personal relationships.

From *Personal Relationships 4: Dissolving Personal Relationships*, "A Topography of Relationship Disagreement and Dissolution," by Steve Duck. Copyright © 1982. Reprinted by permission of Academic Press, Inc.

I   *Goals:* Identifying causes of dissatisfaction with partner
Identifying problems with present form of relationship
Adjusting partner's behavior
Increasing satisfaction with partner
Increasing satisfaction with relationship

Major specific concerns	*Researchable manifestations and consequences*
To weigh up partner's behavior	Hostility, vigilance, evaluation, increased personal attribution
To assess internal dynamics of relationship	Equity/exchange focus
To express discomfort (but not directly to partner)	Consultation with confidants; "leakage"
To question one's relationship judgements	Self-doubts; recrimination; negativity in personal descriptions of self and partner and "life"
To find ways to modify partner's behavior and to change relationship outcomes	Changes in communication style and communication focus within the relationship
To convince oneself that leaving could be better than staying	Anxiety, stress, guilt, indecision, brooding

Final outcome: The resolve to confront partner

II   *Goals:* Confronting partner
Gaining compliance from partner
Redefining relationship
Repairing/dissolving relationship

Major specific concerns	*Researchable manifestations and consequences*
To confront partner with person's dissatisfaction	Hostility; Negative communication style
To present own view of relationship	Guilt; anxiety
To express discomfort directly to partner	Stress
To assess costs (to partner) of own views	Increased private discussion with partner
To evaluate partner's view of relationship	Withdrawal from other contacts, temporarily
To cope with partner's rejoinders	Anger
To weigh up relationship together	Experimental withdrawal/experimental repair
To consider alternative or ideal forms of the relationship under review	Increased fantasizing about future form of the relationship
To choose between repair and dissolution	

Final outcome: Resolve to dissolve/repair the relationship

Figure 10-3   The dissolution process.

From *Personal Relationships 4: Dissolving Personal Relationships,* "A Topography of Relationship Disagreement and Dissolution," by Steve Duck. Copyright © 1982. Reprinted by permission of Academic Press, Inc.

III   *Goals:* To dissolve the relationship
To have the dissolution recognized and accredited by the relevant social network(s)
To come out of it all socially and psychologically intact

Major specific concerns	*Researchable manifestations and consequences*
To create agreed postdissolution state of relationship	Oscillation between reconciliation and withdrawal
To create acceptable postdissolution state for partners	Doubts and anxieties about own future
To consider implied status changes	Trial repair *vs* trial withdrawal
To evaluate consequences of dissolution	Stress, mourning, fear of "loss"
To place blame	Gossip
To save face	Scapegoating
To create and distribute public stories about the relationship dissolution	Attributing blame
	Seeking causal explanation for break
To obtain public sanction for the dissolution	Marketing versions and accounts of the break

Final outcomes: Publicly acknowledged dissolution of the relationship
Move to grave dressing

IV

Grave Dressing Phase:

Goal:	To get over it all and put it behind one
Concerns:	To create an acceptable personal story for the course of the relationship, its beginning, and its end
	To tidy up the memories associated with it.
Manifestations and consequences:	Reinterpretative attributional work concerned with "getting over it" (i.e. redressing and reconceptualizing the relationship path and significance: distinct from attributing blame for the break).

---

form of attributional conflict or negotiated farewell. *Attributional conflict* is basically a fight in which each party blames the other for the breakup. *Negotiated farewell* is a mutual parting of the ways without hostility.

Among these strategies, cost escalation, fait accompli, withdrawal, and attributional conflict embody little or no concern for the other person. The other strategies include at least some attempt to smooth the waters and save face.

Baxter's second question is whether one's strategy choice is related to any personal or relational variables. She has done quite a bit of research on this question, and her overall conclusion is that directness is most related to both individual and relational characteristics. This finding suggests that directness itself may be the primary issue in deciding how to end a relationship.

Some interesting findings related to strategies of disengagement are as follows. First, young children have fewer strategies for disengagement than adolescents, and adults seem to have more strategies than adolescents. Preadolescents' strategies tend to be direct, while adolescents and adults choose more indirect strategies. At all ages, however, people seem to have a larger repertoire of communication strategies for beginning relationships than for ending them.

Baxter found no differences between males and females in her studies, but she did find that androgynous individuals, who have a balance of masculine and feminine traits, are more apt to use direct strategies than are either masculine or feminine sex-typed subjects. Baxter speculates that masculine and feminine individuals have different reasons for avoiding directness. Masculine individuals may have less concern for relationships generally, and feminine sex-typed persons may find direct strategies too assertive. Communication apprehension is also related to the manner in which an individual will terminate a relationship. Predictably, apprehensive individuals are less likely to use direct strategies than are nonapprehensive ones.

When one is involved in a close relationship, the tendency is to use direct strategies that also embody concern for the other person. Predictably, individuals in a particularly close relationship seem to want to reduce the potential pain involved in the break-up process. Along the same line, romantic partners tend to use direct strategies more than friends.

The third question deals with the process of disengagement itself. Baxter found that disengagement is more complex than some other theorists believe. The dissolution of a relationship seems to be more than a mere backing out or reduction in the amount of intimacy of communication. Disengagement often involves repeated attempts to reduce or end the relationship in a cyclical fashion, with the use of several different strategies at different points in the process. However, no one pattern fits all relationship endings.

Social Conflict

This section of the chapter covers theories of social conflict. Like most topics in the chapter, conflict is rooted in interpersonal interaction, but it is also seen in other contexts.

Over the years many approaches to the study of conflict have emerged, and as in most theoretical areas, this work is not altogether consistent.[35] As a result defining conflict is difficult. Charles Watkins offers an analysis of the essential conditions of conflict, which form an operational definition.[36]

1. Conflict requires at least two parties capable of invoking sanctions on each other.

2. Conflicts arise due to the existence of a mutually desired but mutually unobtainable objective.

3. Each party in a conflict has four possible types of action alternatives:
   a. to obtain the mutually desired objective,
   b. to end the conflict,
   c. to invoke sanctions against the opponent,
   d. to communicate something to the opponent.

4. Parties in conflict may have different value or perceptual systems.

5. Each party has resources that may be increased or diminished by implementation of action alternatives.

6. Conflict terminates only when each party is satisfied that is has "won" or "lost" or believes that the probable costs of continuing the conflict outweigh the probable costs of ending the conflict.

35. A number of reviews are available. An excellent analysis of the diverse assumptions of conflict theories can be found in Leonard Hawes and David Smith, "A Critique of Assumptions Underlying the Study of Communication in Conflict," *Quarterly Journal of Speech* 59 (1973): 423–35. See also Thomas Steinfatt, "Communication and Conflict: A Review of New Material," *Human Communication Research* 1 (1974): 81–89; and David Johnson, "Communication and the Inducement of Cooperative Behavior in Conflicts: A Critical Review," *Speech Monographs* 41 (1974): 64–78. For a more recent general text on conflict, see Joyce Frost and William Wilmot, *Interpersonal Conflict* (Dubuque, Iowa: W. C. Brown, 1978).

36. Charles Watkins, "An Analytic Model of Conflict," *Speech Monographs* 41 (1974): 1–5.

One of the advantages of Watkins's definition is that it includes the possibility for communication. Ironically, many approaches to conflict have neglected the communication aspect. Three major approaches to communication and conflict are chosen for discussion. First, we talk about a game theory. Then we move to a theory based on persuasion in conflict, and finally to an attribution-based theory. These three approaches provide a fair representation of the ways communication in conflict can be conceptualized.

Game Theory

Game theory was developed many years ago by J. von Neumann and O. Morgenstern as a tool to study economic behavior.[37] Since its inception game theory has provided a base for popular research tools in several disciplines. For researchers studying the processes of decision making or choice making and goal competition or cooperation, game theory provides a possible paradigm. As a result it has been used extensively to study conflict.

Game theory includes several kinds of games. Two-person games, which are particularly useful in conflict research, consist of structured situations where two players take turns making choices that lead to payoffs. In all games the rational decision-making process is stressed. A key question is how players behave in order to gain rewards or goals. Types of games vary in several ways, including the amount of information provided to players, the amount of communication permitted among players, and the extent of cooperation versus competitive incentive built into the payoff matrix. Thomas Steinfatt and Gerald Miller show how game theory is useful in studying conflicts:

> Game theory is concerned with how to win a game, with strategies of move sequences that maximize the player's chance to gain and minimize his chance for loss. Because a major ingredient in conflict situations is the desire to gain something one does not possess

and to hold onto that which one does possess, certain games are analogous to particular conflict situations and game theory serves as a model to predict the behavior of persons in such conflict situations attempting to gain those ends.[38]

Since game theory stresses rational decision making, it involves games of strategy. In such games a player makes moves (choices) that lead to rewards or punishments based on the moves of others. The object is to maximize gains and minimize losses.

One of the most commonly used games is the Prisoner's Dilemma.[39] This simple game is useful because it illustrates a number of salient features of games in general. Also, it is interesting as a *mixed-motive game* since players may choose between cooperating or competing, and genuine reasons are present for choosing either. Here is the situation: Two people are arrested for a crime. After being separated, each must choose whether to confess. If one confesses and the other does not, the confessor will be allowed to go free, and this person's testimony will send the other to prison for twenty years. If both confess, both will be sent to prison for five years. If neither confesses, both will go to prison for one year on a lesser charge. Figure 10-4 illustrates the choices. With no communication between players, they will not know the choice of the other. Each is in a dilemma on whether to trust and cooperate by remaining silent or to compete by confessing. If both are willing to cooperate by not confessing, the long-term payoff is maximized for both. But if one does not behave cooperatively, the other cannot cooperate. Over several trials, most players will move ultimately toward the noncooperative strategy.

Steinfatt and Miller reviewed the literature in which games were used to investigate the process of communication in conflict. Their generalizations are a step toward a game theoretic analysis. Using

37. J. von Neumann and O. Morgenstern, *The Theory of Games and Economic Behavior* (Princeton: Princeton University Press, 1944). Numerous secondary sources are also available. See, for example, Morton Davis, *Game Theory: A Non-technical Introduction* (New York: Basic Books, 1970).

38. Thomas Steinfatt and Gerald Miller, "Communication in Game Theoretic Models of Conflict," in *Perspectives on Communication in Conflict*, eds. Gerald R. Miller and Herbert Simons (Englewood Cliffs, N.J.: Prentice-Hall, 1974), pp. 14–75.

39. This game is explained in Davis, *Game Theory*, pp. 93–107. This book is an excellent source of real-world analogues for many types of games.

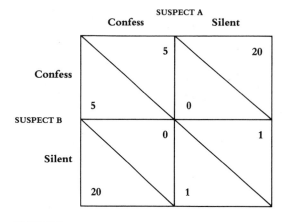

Figure 10-4 Prisoner's dilemma.

games as an analogue, Steinfatt and Miller list three ways in which parties in conflict come to assess each other's strategies. The first way is to observe the opponent's moves over several trials. In games such as the Prisoner's Dilemma, subjects play through a number of trials of the game. Typically a player will observe the opponent's moves and will thereby judge one's own subsequent moves. The second way of assessing strategy is to observe the total conflict situation. In so doing a player makes inferences from the situation to the opponent's strategy. In a game the player would study the matrix and try to figure out what the opponent's strategy is likely to be.

The third approach is direct communication. The authors point out:

> Ideally, communication makes it possible to conduct the entire conflict at the symbolic level, with each player stating how he would respond to the stated, rather than the actual, moves of the other. . . . Besides avoiding the hostility, disruption, and subsequent losses resulting from actual moves, negotiations allow the parties to move away from a winner-take-all position toward a solution that provides some rewards for everyone.[40]

If the players in the Prisoner's Dilemma game could communicate and agree to cooperate, both would receive lesser sentences.

40. Steinfatt and Miller, "Communication," pp. 32–33.

Steinfatt and Miller developd a three-point model of communication in conflict, as reflected in the following definition:

> We employ the word "communication" to indicate the use of mutually understood symbolic behavior such that the probability of engaging in a particular behavior (making a given move) is altered via the exchange of symbolic move sequences which carry no *necessary* consequences for the situation (the formal game matrix).[41]

The first point in this definition is that the communication is *symbolic* in the sense that the stated intention does not carry the actual consequence of the real move. Although real moves might "communicate" in the broader sense, it is necessary to limit the definition here to distinguish between a real move with payoff consequences and symbolic moves. Second, communication changes the probability of moves. If a player receives and understands a message from the other, this will change the likelihood that "rational" competitive moves will take place. If a change in probability does not occur, the message is said to constitute an *attempt to communicate*. The third aspect of the model is that communication may result in nonsituational consequences. We have already seen that symbolic exchanges do not affect the payoff matrix per se. What is affected by communication is the behavior of the person in the situation.

Thus people in conflict are in a situation that has the potential of providing mutually exclusive payoffs. By communicating the parties may reduce their own tendencies to behave chauvinistically. In fact studies have shown that this is what tends to happen. Pregame discussions increase cooperation. The greatest effect occurs when communication exists from the beginning of the conflict. Studies also show that the fuller the communication, the more open the channels, and the greater the resultant cooperation.

Now that we have examined the basic game theoretic concepts of communication and conflict,

41. Ibid., p. 37. This definition is based on the work of T. C. Schelling, *The Strategy of Conflict* (Cambridge: Harvard University Press, 1960). Schelling was one of the first to deal with communication in the game theoretic perspective.

we turn to two theories that attempt to explain the process of communication in real conflict situations.

Persuasion and Conflict

Herbert Simons has presented an analysis that adds greater depth to our understanding of conflict.[42] Simons believes that communication in conflict situations is marked by attempts to influence. Simons's analysis of strategies of influence includes interpersonal conflict, and it extends to the levels of intergroup and institutional conflict as well.

Behind Simons's theory lie four basic assumptions:

1. All human acts and artifacts constitute potential or actual messages. Thus, even physical acts such as riots, bombings, and political payoffs may have symbolic meaning, apart from whatever direct impact they may have.

2. All communicated messages have potential or actual suasive effects. Thus, there is a rhetorical dimension to all human behaviors.

3. Persuasive messages in social conflicts always take on meaning from their social contexts. Repeatedly . . . we have seen that acts such as confrontational protests made little sense apart from their contexts.

4. Influence in mixed-motive conflicts is neither a matter of the raw imposition of power nor of a friendly meeting of minds; instead, it is an inextricably intertwined combination of persuasive arguments backed up by constraints and inducements. In these social conflicts, once again, rhetoric serves power and power serves rhetoric.[43]

The last assumption is particularly important in that it reflects Simons's major thesis. In conflict situations the various types of influence strategies are used together and cannot be separated from one another. Traditionally, however, three types of influence are distinguished. *Inducements* are promised rewards used to bait one's counterpart into doing

what is desired. *Constraint* or *coercion* is used to force an opponent into a particular action. Simons calls these the carrot and the stick; commonly they are known as threats and promises. *Persuasion* traditionally has been defined as a different strategy in which genuine, voluntary choice is extended to the other party. Persuasive influence is most often conceived as relying on information and argumentation.

While this threefold distinction may be appropriate for various other communication situations, Simons believes it is inappropriate for conflict. As he says: "I shall argue here that in conflict situations, persuasion, broadly defined, is not so much an alternative to the power of constraints and inducements as it is an instrument of that power, an accompaniment to that power, or a consequence of that power."[44] Conflict occurs when the parties' interests are so incompatible that a struggle results. In such situations "power serves rhetoric and rhetoric serves power."[45] How is this so? Simons forwards two basic arguments. First, apparent acts of coercion or inducement must be supported by persuasion. At least, the receiver must be persuaded that the sender can and will institute sanctions. Second, apparent acts of persuasion are supported by an underlying power to constrain or induce. Influence in conflict situations is a two-sided coin. Persuasion supports power, and power supports persuasion. In practice the coin cannot be split.

Simons discusses a number of ways in which power and persuasion interact. An agent using coercion or inducement must establish one's own credibility; one must persuade the recipient that he or she has enough power to carry out the stated promise or threat and is willing to do so. On the other hand, coercion and inducement may be necessary to gain the authority or ethos necessary to persuade effectively. Also, the ends or consequences of power and of persuasion are often mutually supportive. Each may create obligations, pacify opponents, or create attitude change through dissonance reduction. A final area of overlap occurs when potential persuaders use coercive

---

42. Herbert Simons, "The Carrot and the Stick as Handmaidens of Persuasion in Conflict Situations," in *Perspectives on Communication in Conflict*, eds. Gerald R. Miller and Herbert Simons (Englewood Cliffs, N.J.: Prentice-Hall, 1974), pp. 172–205.

43. Ibid., p. 200.

44. Ibid., p. 177.

45. Ibid., p. 178.

and reward influence to "buy" valuable communication resources. For example, effective persuasion often requires money, access to decision centers, control of media, and other factors.

An Attribution Theory of Conflict

Alan Sillars has developed a theory of conflict and conflict resolution based on attribution theory.[46] (Attribution theory was discussed briefly in the previous chapter.) The premise of this approach is that when people are involved in conflicts, they develop their own "theories" to explain the conflict, and these theories are largely a product of the attributions made by the conflicting parties. Further, the attributions have an important effect on how the partners will deal with the conflict.

Sillars maintains that three general strategies of conflict resolution are seen in interpersonal relationships. These include *passive-indirect* methods, which are primarily avoidance strategies; *distributive* methods, which aim to win favorable outcomes for oneself and losses for the other person; and *integrative* strategies, which aim to achieve mutual positive outcomes for both parties and perhaps for the relationship itself. Passive methods employ no communication or at best indirect communication. Distributive methods involve negative messages. Integrative solutions entail more open and positive communication. Table 10-2 illustrates a variety of strategies found by Sillars in his research.[47]

Recall from the previous chapter that attributions are inferences made about the motives and causes of behavior. One may make inferences about the causes of some effect, a disposition or trait of another person or oneself, or a predicted outcome of a situation. Whenever people try to explain an event by making inferences, attribution is involved. Sillars believes that, in at least three ways, attributions are very important determiners of the definition and outcome of conflicts. First, people's

attributions in a conflict determine what sorts of strategies they will choose to deal with the conflict. This is true not only because one's reactions and feelings are colored by their attributions, but because future expectations are formed largely as a result of what has gone on in the past. If, for example, a partner in a relationship attributes cooperation to his or her partner, an integrative strategy will probably be chosen, while attribution of competition may lead to a distributive approach. One's attribution of responsibility for the conflict is also important: Attributing blame to oneself may lead to the use of integrative strategies; but when a person thinks the other communicator is responsible, a more distributive approach may be taken. Too, if one thinks his or her partner has certain personality traits that caused the conflict, he or she will be less likely to cooperate with integrative strategies.

Second, there are biases in the attribution process that discourage the use of integrative strategies. These include a tendency to see others as personally responsible for negative events and to see oneself as merely responding to circumstances. People believe that others cause conflict because of bad intentions, inconsideration, competitiveness, or inadequacy. Both partners in a conflict tend to believe that the other person caused it; people characterize their own behavior as merely responding to the provocations of others.

Third, the strategy chosen affects the outcome of the conflict. Integrative strategies encourage cooperative communication and information exchange. Distributive strategies escalate the conflict and may lead to less satisfying solutions.

Criticism

In this chapter we have taken a brief look at some of the most significant theorizing in contemporary communication. Many of the theories discussed here have been immensely popular and influential. For starters, most of these theories de-emphasize individual traits and focus instead on the interactive and relational dynamics of interpersonal communication. These theories are much more

46. Alan L. Sillars, "Attributions and Communication In Roommate Conflicts," *Communication Monographs* 47 (1980): 180–200; "The Sequential and Distributional Structure of Conflict Interaction as a Function of Attributions Concerning the Locus of Responsibility and Stability of Conflict," in *Communication Yearbook* 4, ed. Dan Nimmo (New Brunswick, N.J.: Transaction Books, 1980), pp. 217–36.

47. Sillars, "Attributions," p. 188.

Table 10-2 Types of Conflict Strategies Reported by Dormitory Roommates

I. **Passive and indirect strategies** (No direct discussion of the problem takes place.)

    A. *Nonstrategies* (Discussion is perceived to be unnecessary.)

        1. *Letting the issue resolve itself.* The problem either disappears or is expected to without any active attempt to resolve it.

        2. *Empathic adjustment.* Understanding develops between the parties and the problem is resolved without explicit attempts to communicate.

        3. *Disregarding the issue.* The problem is dismissed as unimportant.

    B. *Avoidance strategies* (Discussion is avoided to minimize negative reactions from the partner.)

        4. *Avoiding the issue.* The problem is tolerated to avoid negative reactions from the partner.

        5. *Avoiding the person.* The partner is avoided, communication is minimized, or the relationship is terminated to avoid conflict.

    C. *Indirect strategies* (The actor communicates indirectly. There is no explicit acknowledgment that a problem exists.)

        6. *Hinting.* Indicating perceptions and feelings through nonverbal communication and indirect comments only.

        7. *Setting an example.* The partner is expected to observe and imitate the actor's own behavior.

        8. *Joking.* The problem is discussed jokingly. The actor does not disclose actual feelings of concern or irritation. The problem is made to seem less serious than the actor perceives it to be.

    D. *Submissive strategies*

        9. *Yielding.* Passively complying without providing input to the solution of the problem.

       10. *Submissive emotion.* An emotional display that indicates weakness and passivity, such as crying or acting hurt or sick.

II. **Distributive strategies** (Explicit acknowledgment and discussion of conflict that seeks concessions from the partner.)

    A. *Noncoercive compliance gaining*

       11. *Requesting.* It is simply suggested or requested that the partner change his/her behavior. There is little elaboration or disclosure.

       12. *Demanding.* Same as requesting except that the request is assertive or aggressive. A negative evaluation of the partner is stated or implied.

       13. *Persuading.* The partner is given reasons for complying. The appeal attempts to change outlook, as well as behavior.

    B. *Coercive compliance gaining*

       14. *Aggressive emotion.* Emotional behavior is directed against the partner to gain compliance (e.g., insults, slurs, profanity, yelling, or anger).

       15. *Threat aversion.* Punishment is threatened or carried out for failure to comply.

III. **Integrative strategies** (Explicit acknowledgment and discussion of conflict that sustains a neutral evaluation of the partner and does not seek concessions.)

       16. *Disclosure.* The actor provides and elicits information to facilitate understanding of perceptions, feelings, and reasons for behavior. No attempt is made to explore alternative solutions to the problem. The problem may be viewed purely as a misunderstanding or the parties may "agree to disagree."

       17. *Problem solving.* Same as disclosure, except that the actor shows a willingness to consider alternative solutions to the problem that are mutually acceptable.

concerned about process factors like time and sequence than some of the other theories we have examined in this book.

The original work of the Palo Alto Group, for example, has had a major impact on our thinking. The notion that communication patterns define relationships has been and remains a central idea in communication theory. Social exchange theory, though it has not emphasized communication as much as some theorists would like, has a great deal to say to communication theorists, as its offshoot social penetration theory demonstrates. These theories are popular in part because of their intuitive appeal and explanatory power.[48] Part of the attractiveness of social exchange theory is its parsimony and ability to explain just about any aspect of social behavior. Most of the theories of relational perception, development, and conflict have been substantially influenced by the Palo Alto Group, social exchange theory, or both. These second generation theories adopt the best of the older theories, correct many of their faults, and add some new ideas of their own. Let us now take a closer critical look at these theories.

As a group relational theories display three key weaknesses. First, they tend to suffer from conceptual confusion. Second, although as a group they paint a fairly complete picture, the individual theories are quite myopic. Third, these theories tend to oversimplify what in everyday experience seems to be a complex process. Relational theories possess these faults in varying ways and to varying degrees, and the weaknesses of some of them are compensated by the strengths of others.

The first problem encountered in these theories is conceptual confusion.[49] The very term *communication* is fuzzy in much of the foundational work on relational communication. Watzlawick, Beavin, and Jackson's first axiom, that all behavior is communicative, places no limits on what communication is and essentially makes the concept meaningless. Carol Wilder discusses this problem with Paul Watzlawick in an interview:

WILDER: This first axiom in *Pragmatics*—"One cannot not communicate"—has a fine aesthetic ring to it and brings to mind some of the tacit dimensions of com-

munication, but some have argued that it expands the boundaries of what constitutes communication beyond any useful or meaningful grounds.

WATZLAWICK: Yes, this has been said. And it usually boils down to the question: "Is intentionality an essential ingredient of communication?" If you are interested in the exchange of information on what we would call a conscious or voluntary, deliberate level then, indeed, the answer is "yes." But, I would say, if you take our viewpoint and say that all behavior in the presence of another person is communication, I should think you have to extend it to the point of the axiom.[50]

Another area of conceptual confusion is the distinction between the report and command functions, or metacommunication.[51] One critical treatment calls the concept "muddled and confusing."[52] The problem is that the Palo Alto Group, at different points in their writing, imply as many as three different meanings for metacommunication. (The use of other labels, such as command message and relational message, does not help in this regard.) At points metacommunication refers to a verbal or nonverbal classification of the content message, in which one's partner guides the coding of the content. At other times metacommunication refers to nonverbal statements about the relationship itself, such as control. Or, metacommunication sometimes refers to explicit discussion by individuals about the nature of their relationship. To make matters worse, metacommunication has been treated alternatively as strictly analogic, analogic and digital, nonverbal, and both verbal and nonverbal.

The main confusion in social exchange theory is the definition of rewards and costs.[53] On the sur-

48. The prevalence of social exchange theory is discussed by Teru L. Morton and Mary Ann Douglas, "Growth of Relationships," in *Personal Relationships 2: Developing Personal Relationships*, eds. Steve Duck and Robin Gilmour (London: Academic Press, 1981); and Roloff, *Interpersonal*.

49. See, for example, Katherine L. Adams, "The Interactional View: Review and Critique" (Paper presented at the Western Speech Communication Association, Albuquerque, February 1983).

50. Carol Wilder, "From the Interactional View—A Conversation with Paul Watzlawick," *Journal of Communication* 28 (1978): 41–42.

51. This problem is discussed by William Wilmot, "Metacommunication: A Re-examination and Extension," in *Communication Yearbook 4*, ed. Dan Nimmo (New Brunswick, N.J.: Transaction Books, 1980), pp. 61–69.

52. Arthur Bochner and Dorothy Krueger, "Interpersonal Communication Theory and Research: An Overview of Inscrutable Epistemologies and Muddled Concepts," in *Communication Yearbook 3*, ed. Dan Nimmo (New Brunswick, N.J.: Transaction Books, 1979), p. 203.

53. Arthur Bochner, "The Functions of Human Communication in Interpersonal Bonding," in *Handbook of Rhetorical and*

face, what is rewarding and what is costly seems clear enough; but upon reflection, human rewards and punishments are not so clear. What is rewarding to one person may be punishing to another. What is punishing at one point in a relationship may be rewarding at another, and, in fact, people seem to be able to redefine or reframe a situation previously perceived as rewarding or punishing to its opposite. Also, social exchange theory ignores the ways in which couples actually use communication to define rewards and punishments within the relationship itself. The rewards-punishment problem is significant, and we return to it again below.

The second problem encountered in many of these theories is their limited focus. As a group the theories complete most of a rather intricate puzzle, but individually, each leaves out important elements. Despite all their talk about how communication is used to define the nature of a relationship within a system, original relational theorists from the Palo Alto Group and disciples like Millar and Rogers essentially ignore actual definitional processes of interpretation and cognition.[54] The research in this tradition deals with observable behavior, and the coding is done from the perspective of the outside observer, not from within the relationship.

Social exchange theory and social penetration theory put all their eggs in the cost-rewards basket and fail to deal with the relational and cognitive processes by which rewards and costs are defined. Because they center on how persons weigh rewards against costs, these theories are ironically individualistic, despite their purported emphasis on the relationship.[55] In fact, these theories say little about relationships per se, and *social* exchange theory, though it is useful to the communication scholar, essentially ignores communication. These

theories also underplay emotion and fail to explain such prosocial attitudes as altruism.[56] In short, they are individualistic and rationalistic.[57]

Social exchange theory and game theory are closely related: Both see relationships as a sequence of moves motivated by personal gain. Research in game theory and social exchange, often done in a laboratory, examines the choices people make in response to different reward and cost contingencies, using points or tokens as game outcomes. We are not at all sure whether social rewards work in this way.[58] These theories assume that people behave rationally in making decisions and that they always want to maximize positive outcomes. However, in actual social life it is not a simple matter to establish exactly what outcomes people are seeking. How people behave in real social conflict depends in part on their self-concept, motives, mental health, individual life goals, and an array of other complex factors. Steinfatt and Miller crystallize this objection: "In the daily political, economic, and social conflicts we all face, mutually advantageous solutions are seldom this sharply defined, and in seeking an acceptable solution, communication serves a myriad of cognitive and affective functions."[59]

Although game theory presents a limited view of conflict, the other theories compensate in important ways. The major strength of Simons's strategy approach is that it recognizes that conflict typically is marked by a great deal of communication designed to influence other people. In contrast to

Communication Theory, eds. Carroll C. Arnold and John Waite Bowers (Boston: Allyn & Bacon, 1984), pp. 575–82. See also Roloff, *Interpersonal*, p. 117.

54. Edna Rogers herself discusses this problem in "Analyzing Relational Communication: Implications of a Pragmatic Approach" (Paper presented at the Speech Communication Association, Washington, D.C., November 1983).

55. Morton and Douglas, "Growth," p. 19.

56. Roloff, *Interpersonal*, p. 127.

57. Ibid., p. 128; James L. Applegate and Gregory B. Leichty, "Managing Interpersonal Relationships: Social Cognitive and Strategic Determinants of Competence," in *Competence in Communication: A Multi-Disciplinary Approach*, ed. Robert N. Bostrom (Beverly Hills: Sage Publications, 1984), p. 38.

58. John L. LaGaipa, "Interpersonal Attraction and Social Exchange," in *Theory and Practice in Interpersonal Attraction*, ed. Steve Duck, (New York: Academic Press, 1971), pp. 129–64.

59. Steinfatt and Miller, "Communication," p. 70. For an excellent debate on the value of game theory in communication research, see Robert Bostrom, "Game Theory in Communication Research," *Journal of Communication* 18 (1968): 369–88; and Thomas Beisecker, "Game Theory in Communication Research: A Rejoinder and a Re-orientation," *Journal of Communication* 20 (1970): 107–20.

game theory, this theory actually centers on communication processes. Simons's theory takes a step away from oversimplification by recognizing that types of influence cannot be realistically separated from one another in a conflict situation. Sillars takes an additional step by suggesting that the strategies employed by participants in a conflict depends on their definition of the situation.

Balance theory also contrasts to theoretic approaches. It is relationship-centered and focuses on the cognitive processes involved in attraction and change; balance theory also takes communication into account. However, it suffers from all of the problems of consistency theory, outlined in Chapter 5, including a strong determinism. In its way, this theory is as narrow as is exchange theory.

The third problem encountered in this literature is that several of these theories tend to oversimplify the process of relational definition and development. They often assume a single trajectory or a single set of processes without discriminating among types of relationships or variability among relationships. Social penetration theory, for example, assumes that all relationships develop along the same line, which is really too orderly.[60] Different relationships may have different processes operating, and we cannot assume that cost-reward operates in each phase of a relationship.[61] Social penetration theory teaches that dissolution is merely penetration in reverse; yet relationships do not always follow this kind of simple backing-out, as Baxter's work illustrates. One of the advantages of Duck's model is that it recognizes the cyclical, back-and-forth nature of deteriorating relationships, and it does not try to predict the course of any one relationship. Duck's theory identifies certain threshold points, and he recognizes that within each stage, several courses and outcomes are possible.

Baxter has done an excellent job of filling in the details in the complex picture of relational dissolution. The major contribution of this theory is that it explicitly identifies many of the communication behaviors that other theories only indirectly and vaguely acknowledge.

Relational processes can be oversimplified in other ways as well. For instance, although her work takes relational theory a major step forward, Burgoon's theory assumes a standard set of dimensions of relational communication. What assurance do we have that these dimensions are relevant to all relationships? While they may work very well in certain communication situations, other situations may be framed in an entirely different set of dimensions.

Other theories assume a particular causal direction in relational development. Sillars, for example, speculates that conflict leads to attributions, which create a theory of the conflict and prefigure the strategy chosen to deal with the conflict. These strategies in turn are viewed as affecting the outcome of the conflict. In some situations the order of these processes may be different. Attributions may be a consequence, rather than a cause, of conflict-resolution strategies.[62]

Integration

Interpersonal communication is a process of defining the nature of a relationship. We communicate on two planes, a content level and a relationship level. The content message is always accompanied by comment—often nonverbal—on the relationship. Several dimensions of relationship messages have been explored, such as dominance, intimacy, arousal, self-control, similarity, and formality. One of the most important of these has been the control dimension. A control message asserts a particular definition of the relationship or situation at a moment in time. In interaction, patterns of control are evident, as control messages are greeted with other messages of control or of submission.

Interpersonal perception is an important deter-

---

60. Applegate and Leichty, "Managing," p. 39.
61. Bochner, "Functions," p. 579.

62. Sillars himself recognizes this problem; see "Attributions," p. 199.

minant of relationship patterns. We not only perceive others' behavior directly, but we also infer their perceptions of the relationship. Understanding and being understood is largely a matter of meshing these interpersonal perceptions, and communicators' competence is often judged in terms of how well individuals are perceived to operate within the confines of a relationship.

Relationships evolve. They develop as a function of interpersonal attraction and the costs and rewards associated with the relationship. As relationships grow, the communication becomes more intimate, and the partners disclose increasingly personal information about themselves. As relationships decline, complex patterns of disengagement emerge. The partners must deal with the dissolving relationship by communicating with one another, and accounts are made to others outside the relationship as well. The strategies used by individuals in getting out of a relationship vary in terms of their directness and the degree to which they embody concern for the partner.

Relational conflict involves communication in which differences are confronted. Sometimes conflict arises over competition for resources, and the struggle involves distribution of those resources in an attempt to maximize gains and minimize losses. Other times more integrative solutions are sought in which each party can gain something from the resolution of the conflict. Communication, especially persuasive communication, usually plays a crucial role in how the conflict is defined, expressed, and resolved.

In the next chapter, we discuss theories in which the interpersonal communication networks involve more than two persons.

Eleven

Theories of Group Communication

In the last two chapters we looked at a number of the theories related to face-to-face interaction. One important setting for interpersonal communication is the small group. A number of contemporary source books on small groups reflect the breadth of work in this area.[1] Theory and research related to small group communication is scattered and varied. Critics have singled out small group communication as a confusing area of study.[2] Yet several good theories of small group processes have emerged over the years. In this chapter we will look at some of the most interesting and insightful. There can be no doubt that the study of small group communication is important. For one thing the small group is a crucial part of society. As Clovis Shepherd points out, the group is "an essential mechanism of socialization and a primary source of social order." People derive their values and attitudes largely from the groups with which they identify. As a result "the small group serves an important mediating function between the individual and the larger society."[3]

What, then, distinguishes the group? After summarizing several other definitions stressing different aspects of groups, Marvin Shaw provides his own *interactional* definition:

> A group is defined as two or more persons who are interacting with one another in such a manner that each person influences and is influenced by each other person. A *small* group is a group having twenty or fewer members, although in most instances we will be concerned with groups having five or fewer members.[4]

This definition is a good one for our purposes because it includes communication as the essential characteristic of the group. Shaw points out that the most interesting groups are those that endure for a relatively long period of time, have a goal or goals, and have an interactional structure.

Foundations of Group Communication

The impetus for contemporary research and theory in group communication came from a variety of early twentieth century sources. One such source

1. See, for example, Randy Y. Hirokawa and Marshall Scott Poole (eds.), *Communication and Group Decision-Making* (Beverly Hills: Sage Publications, 1986); Gerald M. Phillips and Julia T. Wood (eds.), *Emergent Issues in Human Decision Making* (Carbondale: Southern Illinois University Press, 1984); Dennis S. Gouran and B. Aubrey Fisher, "The Functions of Human Communication in the Formation, Maintenance, and Performance of Small Groups," in *Handbook of Rhetorical and Communication Theory*, eds. Carroll C. Arnold and John Waite Bowers (Boston: Allyn & Bacon, 1984), pp. 622–59; Marvin E. Shaw, *Group Dynamics: The Psychology of Small Group Behavior* (New York: McGraw-Hill, 1981). For several other older sources, see Bibliography for this chapter.
2. For a summary of this criticism, see Marshall Scott Poole, David R. Seibold, and Robert D. McPhee, "Group Decision-Making as a Structurational Process," *Quarterly Journal of Speech* 71 (1985): 74.
3. Clovis R. Shepherd, *Small Groups: Some Sociological Perspectives* (San Francisco: Chandler, 1964), p. 1.
4. Shaw, *Group Dynamics*, p. 10.

was the work of Mary Parker Follett on integrative thinking.[5] Follett wrote in 1924 that group, organizational, and community problem solving is a creative threefold process of (a) gathering information from experts, (b) testing that information in everyday experience, and (c) developing integrative solutions that meet a variety of interests rather than competing among interests. Follett's notion reflects an idea that has gained much acceptance in twentieth century American thought—dealing with problems and conflicts through discussion.

Another major influence on current theories was the group discussion movement in the field of speech.[6] Here students were taught how to speak productively with others in a small group. Such education is still a big part of high school and college speech communication curricula. A third source of current group communication theory was the tremendous group dynamics research tradition in social psychology. Because of its influence on group communication theories, we will discuss this third influence in more detail below.

Group Dynamics

Most of what we know about groups and group communication today stems from empirical research in social psychology. Collectively this work is known as group dynamics. This section includes the work of the founder of psychological research on groups, Kurt Lewin, and a brief description of some of the research that has been generated in this field.

Lewin's field theory. Kurt Lewin was one of the most prominent psychologists of our century. Gardner Lindzey and Calvin Hall have written: "Lewin is considered by many of his peers to be one of the most brilliant figures in contemporary psychology. His theoretical writings and experimental work have left an indelible mark upon the development of psychology."[7] As a social psychologist interested in the nature of individual and group behavior, he is responsible for one of the most influential approaches to the study of behavior. Field theory is an organic approach that in its holistic orientation is consistent with the systems point of view.

We are interested in Lewin because of his work in group dynamics. Lewin was one of the first in the long line of researchers in this area. There can be no doubt that he was influential in shaping much of our thought about the nature of groups. In this section we first consider Lewin's orientation to the person; then we discuss how people relate to groups.

Lewin begins his thought with five assumptions about people. First, what is important to study is the perceptions of the person, or the individual's *psychological field* or *life space*. Second, the person at any moment occupies a position in the life space that can be best conceptualized in its distance from the other objects of the field. Third, the person has goals toward which one moves in the life space. Fourth, the person's behavior can be explained in terms of attempting to reach the goals. Fifth, the field also contains barriers to the goals, barriers that the individual must surpass.[8]

Lewin's theory leads us to see the person moving about in a psychological space, called the life space. This field is not an objective world, but the subjective world of the person. In this field are a number of objects that the individual wishes to approach or avoid, and in striving for goals, the person encounters various barriers. How the person behaves or moves within the life space is governed by *tensions* arising from the individual's needs and wants.

We must remember that the individual's life space includes groups. Individuals cannot be separated from the groups with which they identify.

5. Mary Parker Follett, *Creative Experience* (New York: Longmans, Green, 1924).

6. For a brief summary of this work, see Dennis S. Gouran, "The Paradigm of Unfulfilled Promise: A Critical Examination of the History of Research on Small Groups in Speech Communication," in *Speech Communication in the 20th Century*, ed. Thomas W. Benson (Carbondale: Southern Illinois University Press, 1985), p. 90.

7. Calvin S. Hall and Gardner Lindzey, "Lewin's Field Theory," in *Theories of Personality* (New York: John Wiley, 1970), p. 210. For an interesting biography of Lewin, see Alfred Marrow, *The Practical Theorist: The Life and Work of Kurt Lewin* (New York: Basic Books, 1969).

8. These assumptions are summarized by Shepherd, *Small Groups*.

Groups, too, have a kind of life space. Lewin developed a theory that can be applied to all kinds of groups ranging from families to work groups. His analysis includes large social groups such as communities or institutions. The term *group dynamics* implies that groups are products of various forces and tensions. Lewin studied groups from the perspective of their positive and negative forces, especially the ways in which these forces influence the person as a group member.

While a group is a set of people, it is more than the sum of its members. When people join together in a group, a resulting structure evolves with its own goals and life space. The group is an excellent example of a system as outlined in Chapter 3 of this book. As Lewin puts it:

> A group can be characterized as a "dynamical whole"; this means that a change in the state of any subpart changes the state of any other subpart. The degree of interdependence of the subparts of members of the group varies all the way from loose mass to a compact unit. It depends, among other factors, upon the size, organization, and intimacy of the group.[9]

Individuals are members of many groups at one time, which means that a person's groups are an important part of the life space. Consequently, one's groups will create tensions in the life space and therefore influence the movement of the person. Since the life space is fluid, the potency of a group for a particular person will vary from moment to moment. For example, when a person is at home, the family group generally exerts more influence than does the work group. Such may not be the case when the person is at work.

At this point we begin to see one of Lewin's most important themes—the impact of groups on individual life. This impact has four qualities. First, the group provides stability to the person's life. As Lewin states,

> The speed and determination with which a person proceeds, his readiness to fight or to submit, and other important characteristics of his behavior depend upon the firmness of the ground on which he stands and upon his general security. The group a person belongs

to is one of the most important constituents of this ground.[10]

Second, the group provides the person with a means for achieving valued goals. It is a vehicle for approaching or avoiding objects in the life space. Third, the person's values and attitudes are greatly influenced by the values and norms of the groups to which he or she belongs. Fourth, as part of the life space, the person moves about within the group; the person aims for various goals in the group itself.

While group pressures constrain the individual, the person also has some degree of freedom. Group values and norms never coincide completely with individual needs. Groups seem to have an optimal level of freedom. If the individual does not have enough freedom to pursue goals outside the group, dissatisfaction will result, and the individual may leave the group. On the other hand, if the influence of the group is too weak, it will be less functional in helping the individual achieve goals in the life space. Thus the person in face-to-face interaction with groups is constantly adjusting and adapting individual needs and group demands. As a result of this interaction between person and group, both personal needs and behavior and group norms and demands will change.

The most important attribute of groups is *cohesiveness*. Cohesiveness is the degree of mutual interest among members. In a highly cohesive group, a strong mutual identification is found among members. This quality is what keeps a group together. Without it the group will dissolve. Mutual identification is a function of the degree to which members are mutually attracted to certain goals or mutually repulsed by certain negative forces. Cohesiveness is a result of the degree to which all members perceive that their goals can be met within the group. This does not require that the members have similar attitudes, but that they are interdependent, that they must rely on one another to achieve certain mutually desired goals. The more cohesive a group, the more force it exerts on its members. The person is pressured by the group to conform to the group code. This theme has been

9. Kurt Lewin, *Resolving Social Conflicts: Selected Papers on Group Dynamics* (New York: Harper & Row, 1948), p. 94.

10. Ibid., p. 86.

elaborated over the years throughout small group research and theory.

Lewin is placed first in this chapter because his theory provides an excellent introductory approach to the study of groups. Field theory respects the needs of the individual, at the same time demonstrating how people and groups interact. The group is influenced by personal needs; the person is affected by group standards. While Lewin did not dwell on communication per se, he provides an excellent general orientation toward group and organizational behavior.

Lewin's work was just a beginning, and although he made significant contributions to our understanding of groups, most of these were general orientations and provided little substance about how groups actually operate. For a greater understanding of the variables of group dynamics, we must rely on more recent research.[11]

Ironically, the work of Kurt Lewin, which remains a foundation for contemporary research on group dynamics, is epistemologically and ontologically different from its latter-day counterparts. Lewin's theory is holistic, phenomenological, and field oriented. Social psychological research since Lewin for the most part has been analytic, scientific, and laboratory oriented. Lewin took a systems view of group life, noting the integrated and interdependent nature of group variables. Most group researchers today are from the variable-analytic tradition, in which distinct factors are isolated for close scrutiny. Therefore these two groups of theories must be criticized separately.

Research in group dynamics. The disadvantage of the work in group dynamics is that it consists largely of a vast, often unconnected body of research. Because of the quantity of this research and the fact that much of it does not directly address communication, we provide only a brief sketch here. (A more complete summary can be found in the second edition of this book.[12])

Much social psychological research in groups deals with the relationship between the individual and the group. For example, much of this research centers on the comparative effectiveness of group and individual problem solving, with the general finding that even though groups are less efficient, they usually make better decisions than do individuals. Groups have been shown to exert quite a bit of influence over members, but conformity seems to be mediated by other individual and group variables. (Conformity was one of the most heavily researched variables in group research.) All kinds of individual traits have been studied in relation to leadership emergence and communication patterns in groups. Leadership itself has become a very important topic of research in this tradition, with emphasis on leadership styles and traits.

Group structure also has been heavily researched. For example, research on group size indicates that medium-sized groups are more effective than large or very small groups, other things being equal, and that seating arrangements can be important in determining leadership and communication patterns. Role patterns and communication networks also have been researched. Centralized networks are found to be very efficient, but not very satisfying to members, while decentralized networks are more satisfying and capable of generating a variety of ideas for solving more complex problems.

Much of the research in groups centers on cohesiveness, with the general finding that highly cohesive groups are usually more compatible, satisfying, and effective than noncohesive groups. An important exception to this hypothesis is the condition of groupthink, which is discussed separately later in this chapter.

For the most part research on group dynamics follows an input-process-output model.[13] This model segments the group experience into the factors that affect the group (input), the happenings

11. For criticism of group dynamics, see Shaw, *Group Dynamics*, pp. 445–51.

12. Stephen W. Littlejohn, *Theories of Human Communication* (Belmont, Calif.: Wadsworth, 1983), pp. 222–26; see also, Shaw, *Group Dynamics*.

13. This model is discussed by Marshall Scott Poole, David R. Seibold, and Robert D. McPhee, "A Structurational Approach to Theory-Building in Group Decision-Making Research," in *Communication and Group Decision-Making*, eds. Randy Y. Hirokawa and Marshall Scott Poole (Beverly Hills: Sage Publications, 1986), pp. 238–40.

within the group (process), and the results (output). For example, a study might examine the effects of heterogeneity of group members (input) on the amount of talking in a group (process) or the effect of interaction patterns (process) on member satisfaction (output). Because of its impact on group communication theory, the input-process-output model is discussed in some detail below.

The Input-Process-Output Model

This section is divided into three parts. First, we present a simple descriptive model of group action in the input-process-output tradition. Second, we look at theories of group effectiveness. Finally, we discuss two highly influential theories of communication in groups—the work of Robert Bales and B. Aubrey Fisher.

A General Organizing Model

Most of the work on group dynamics centers on task groups. Figure 11-1 is the model of Barry Collins and Harold Guetzkow.[14] This simple model captures the major themes of task-group research in general terms, and it illustrates the input-process-output approach very well.

Any task group is confronted with two types of problems: task obstacles and interpersonal obstacles. *Task obstacles* are the difficulties encountered by the group in tackling the task or problem. Group members deal directly with the problem—analyzing it, suggesting possible solutions, and weighing alternatives. Such efforts are task-related group behaviors. However, whenever two or more people join together to handle a problem, *interpersonal obstacles* also arise. Such obstacles include the need to make one's ideas clear to others, to deal with conflict among participants, to handle individual member differences, and so forth. Thus in any

group discussion members will be dealing simultaneously with task and interpersonal obstacles.

The basic distinction between task work and interpersonal relations has been an overriding concern in the research and theory on small group communication. Both types of behavior are important in accomplishing the task or in achieving group productivity. Any analysis of group problem solving must deal with both task and interpersonal demands. The outputs of a group are affected by members' task and interpersonal efforts.

Interpersonal and task factors interrelate, and group productivity results from both. Interpersonal relations can inhibit problem solving as well as enhance it. The performance of a group depends primarily on its ability to integrate and organize the individual skills and resources of the members. When this integration is done effectively, an *assembly effect* occurs in which the group solution or product is superior to the individual work of even the best member. (We will return to this notion when we discuss ideas on syntality and the groupthink hypothesis later in the chapter.)

Group rewards can be positive or negative. Successful goal achievement is usually positively rewarding to group members. In addition the resolution of conflict and successful communication often reap interpersonal rewards. On the other hand, "rewards" may also be negative. In any case outcomes are evaluated by group members as positive or negative rewards, and these in turn affect future task and interpersonal efforts in the group, as indicated by the feedback arrows in Figure 11-1.

Theories of Group Effectiveness

We will now consider three theories that concentrate on the nature of interpersonal effects in groups. The first is Raymond Cattell's theory of group syntality, the second is Irving Janis's groupthink hypothesis, and the third is Randy Hirokawa's theory of faulty group decision making.

Cattell's theory of group syntality. Raymond Cattell's theory of group syntality (group personality) has been influential in the history of group

14. Barry Collins and Harold Guetzkow, *A Social Psychology of Group Processes for Decision-Making* (New York: John Wiley, 1964), p. 81.

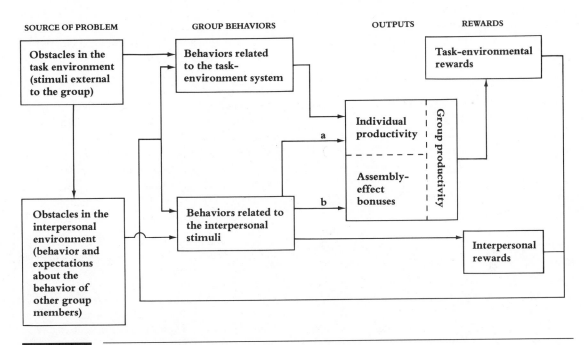

SOURCE OF PROBLEM   GROUP BEHAVIORS   OUTPUTS   REWARDS

Figure 11-1   A simple working model of decision-making groups.

From *A Social Psychology of Group Processes for Decision-Making*, by Barry Collins and Harold Guetzkow; John Wiley & Sons, publisher. Used by permission.

dynamics.[15] He suggests three defining aspects or *panels* for group description: syntality traits, internal structure, and population traits. While personality describes the predictable behavior of an individual, *syntality* is the predictable pattern of group behavior. Thus a group may appear aggressive, efficient, isolated, energetic, reliable. The second panel, *internal structure*, is defined in terms of the interpersonal relations among the group members. Such characteristics may deal with status structure, internal subgroupings, modes of government, and patterns of communication. The third panel is *population traits*, the traits of a group's individual members. In defining a group's population traits, you would discuss the modal or typical characteristics, including intelligence, attitudes, and so forth.

15. Raymond Cattell, "Concepts and Methods in the Measurement of Group Syntality," *Psychological Review* 55 (1948): 48–63.

These three panels are interrelated; syntality is a function of population traits and internal structure. This notion reinforces points made by Lewin about the relationships between the group and the individual. The theory as a whole can be summarized as follows: People with individual personalities and traits come together to achieve their goals more efficiently. In so doing, they commit their energies to achieving group tasks and to maintaining the group. What the group accomplishes is a direct function of the amount of energy invested by the separate members. The total group effect is a result of its energy input and output. Let us look more closely at these relationships.

The key concept in group effect is *synergy*. Group synergy is the total energy input of the members. However, much of the energy put into a group does not directly support its goals. Because of interpersonal demands, energy must be expended to maintain relationships and overcome interpersonal barriers. *Effective synergy* is the group energy remaining after *intrinsic* or *group maintenance synergy* is subtracted. While such intrinsic energy is productive in the sense that it works toward group cohesiveness, it does not contribute directly to task accomplishment.

The synergy of a group results from the attitudes of the members toward the group. To the extent that members have different attitudes toward the group and its operations, conflict will result, increasing the proportion of energy needed for group maintenance. Thus the more that individuals possess similar attitudes, the less the need for intrinsic investment, and the greater the effective synergy.

Let's use a simplified example to see how Cattell's theory explains real events. Suppose that in forming a study group, you discover that the members have varying attitudes toward the subject matter and differing manners of study. In your meetings you argue a lot about how to organize your efforts and how to learn the material. Much time and energy is spent working out these interpersonal problems. This is your intrinsic synergy. Now, after getting your test grade back, if you sense that the study group failed to achieve the goal of mutual benefit, you will withdraw your energy and join another group or study alone. In this case the effective synergy of the group was so low that it did not accomplish more than you could have accomplished yourself. Next suppose that you join another group. This group agrees immediately on how to proceed and gets down to work. Since there are few interpersonal barriers to overcome, the group is cohesive. The effective synergy is high, and everyone does better on the examination than they would have done had they studied alone.

Janis's groupthink theory. Cattell's theory gives us one answer to the question of interpersonal effects in groups. The groupthink hypothesis of Irving Janis is much different.[16] Janis examines in some detail the adequacy of decisions made by groups. He shows how certain conditions can lead to high group satisfaction but ineffective output. Janis's ideas give us a more concrete explanation of synergistic factors, and at the same time they demonstrate how actual practice may vary from predictions made by syntality theory.

Janis's theory is normative and applied. It is normative in that it provides a base for diagnosing problems and remediating weaknesses in group performance; it is applied to actual political groups. Janis has relied heavily on social-psychological research on group dynamics, integrating concepts such as cohesiveness in explaining actual observed group practices. Janis describes groupthink:

> I use the term groupthink as a quick and easy way to refer to a mode of thinking that people engage in when they are deeply involved in a cohesive in-group, when members' strivings for unanimity override their motivation to realistically appraise alternative courses of action. . . . The invidiousness is intentional: Groupthink refers to a deterioration of mental efficiency, reality testing, and moral judgment that results from in-group pressures.[17]

Janis's approach is intriguing. He uses historical data to support his theory by analyzing six political decision-making episodes in which outcomes were either good or bad, depending on the extent of groupthink.[18] These interesting historical analyses once again illustrate how communication theory may be generated in a variety of arenas. One of the finest qualities of Janis's approach is that his theory involves small group communication at the interface of psychology, political science, and history.

Groupthink can have six negative outcomes:

1. The group limits its discussion to only a few alternatives. It does not consider a full range of creative possibilities.

2. The position initially favored by most members is never restudied to seek out less obvious pitfalls.

16. Irving Janis, *Victims of Groupthink: A Psychological Study of Foreign Decisions and Fiascos* (Boston: Houghton Mifflin, 1982).

17. Ibid., p. 9.
18. The negative examples include the Bay of Pigs, the Korean War, Pearl Harbor, and the escalation of the Vietnam War. Positive examples include the Cuban Missile Crisis and the Marshall Plan.

3. The group fails to reexamine those alternatives originally disfavored by the majority.

4. Expert opinion is not sought.

5. The group is highly selective in gathering and attending to available information.

6. The group is so confident in its chosen alternative that it does not consider contingency plans.

Janis maintains that groupthink is marked by a number of symptoms. The first symptom of groupthink is an *illusion of invulnerability*, which creates an undue air of optimism. Second, the group creates *collective efforts to rationalize* the course of action decided on. Third, the group maintains an *unquestioned belief in the group's inherent morality*, leading to a soft pedaling of ethical or moral consequences. Out-group leaders are *stereotyped* as evil, weak, or stupid. In addition direct *pressure* is exerted on members not to express counteropinions. Dissent is quickly squelched. This leads to the sixth symptom, the *self-censorship* of disagreement. Thus there is a shared *illusion of unanimity* within the group. Finally, groupthink involves the emergence of *self-appointed mindguards* to protect the group and its leader from adverse opinion and unwanted information. The mindguard typically suppresses negative information by counseling participants not to "rock the boat."

Groupthink is a direct result of cohesiveness in groups. Most small group research and theory indicate that cohesiveness is functional in group performance. Lewin writes that cohesiveness is a reflection of the degree to which all group members share common goals and values. According to Cattell, the amount of effective synergy in groups results from cohesiveness, since cohesive groups need expend little intrinsic synergy. Although Janis does not deny the value of cohesiveness in decision-making groups, he shows how highly cohesive groups may still invest a lot of energy on maintaining goodwill in the group to the detriment of decision making.

The element that can make cohesiveness negative is the person's need to maintain self-esteem. Such rewards as friendship, prestige, and mutually

recognized competence are received in highly cohesive groups. With such rewards at stake, it is not surprising that group members invest intrinsic synergy to maintain solidarity. The doubts or uncertainties that arise may lead to an undermining of group confidence and hence of individual members' self-esteem.

Thus cohesiveness is a necessary but not sufficient condition for groupthink. Under conditions of low cohesiveness, factors may be present that prevent the illusion of unanimity. The natural conflict in noncohesive groups leads to much debate and consideration of all sides of an issue. Unfortunately such conflict is itself dysfunctional in decision making, as several theorists have pointed out. The amount of synergy absorbed by conflict significantly reduces group output.

What is the answer to this dilemma? Janis believes that decision-making groups need to recognize the dangers of groupthink. He suggests steps to prevent groupthink:

1. The leader of a policy-forming group should assign the role of critical evaluator to each member, encouraging the group to give high priority to airing objections and doubts.

2. The leaders in an organization's hierarchy, when assigning a policy-planning mission to a group, should be impartial instead of stating preferences and expectations at the outset.

3. The organization should routinely follow the administrative practice of setting up several independent policy-planning and evaluation groups to work on the same policy question, each carrying out its deliberations under a different leader.

4. Throughout the period when the feasibility and effectiveness of policy alternatives are being surveyed, the policy-making group should from time to time divide into two or more subgroups to meet separately, under different chairmen, and then come together to hammer out their differences.

5. Each member of the policy-making group should discuss periodically the group's deliberations with trusted associates in his own unit of the organization and report back their [sic] reactions.

6. One or more outside experts or qualified colleagues within the organization who are not core members of the policy-making group should be invited to each meeting on a staggered basis and should be encouraged to challenge the views of the core members.

7. At every meeting devoted to evaluating policy alternatives, at least one member should be assigned the role of devil's advocate.

8. Whenever the policy issue involves relations with a rival nation or organization, a sizable bloc [sic] of time (perhaps an entire session) should be spent surveying all warning signals from rivals and constructing alternative scenarios of the rivals' intentions.

9. After reaching a preliminary consensus about what seems to be the best policy alternative, the policy-making group should hold a "second-chance" meeting at which every member is expected to express as vividly as he can all his residual doubts and to rethink the entire issue before making a definitive choice.[19]

This groupthink theory involves in a practical setting some of the important concepts from previous research and theory. It demonstrates the viability of group dynamics. In addition, it provides new understandings in its own right. Janis's approach is valuable because, like Lewin's theory, it provides a multidisciplinary view.

Faulty group decision making. Janis emphasizes groupthink as one explanation for error in group decision making. This section examines a theory by Randy Hirokawa and his colleagues; this approach takes a more comprehensive look at a variety of error sources in group work with an eye toward identifying the kinds of things groups must address to become more effective.[20] The theory begins with a general description of the process used by groups to make decisions.

Groups normally begin by *identifying and assessing a problem.* At this point the group deals with a variety of questions: What happened? Why? Who was involved? What harm resulted? Who was hurt? Next, the group *gathers and evaluates information about the problem.* As the group discusses possible solutions to the problem, information continues to be gathered.

Next, the group *generates a variety of alternative proposals* for handling the problem and discusses the objectives it wishes to accomplish in solving the problem. These objectives and alternative proposals are evaluated, with the ultimate goal of reaching consensus on a course of action. This general sequence of problem solving is depicted in Figure 11-2.[21]

This sequence of activity largely mirrors Thomas Dewey's problem-solving sequence, which since the publication of *How We Think* in 1910, has greatly influenced twentieth century pragmatic thought.[22] Dewey's version of the problem-solving process has six steps:

1. expressing a difficulty
2. defining the problem
3. analyzing the problem
4. suggesting solutions
5. comparing alternatives and testing them against a set of objectives or criteria
6. implementing the best solution.

The factors contributing to faulty decisions are easily inferred from the decision-making process outlined in Hirokawa's theory. The first is *improper assessment of the problem.* This involves inadequate or inaccurate analysis of the problem or the situation in which the decision making occurs. The group may fail to see the problem, or it may not accurately identify the causes of the problem.

19. Janis, *Victims*, pp. 262–71.
20. Randy Y. Hirokawa and Dirk R. Scheerhorn, "Communication in Faulty Group Decision-Making," in *Communication and Group Decision-Making*, eds. Randy Y. Hirokawa and Marshall Scott Poole (Beverly Hills: Sage Publications, 1986), pp. 63–80; Dennis S. Gouran and Randy Y. Hirokawa, "Counteractive Functions of Communication in Effective Group Decision-Making," in *Communication and Group Decision-Making*, eds. Randy Y. Hirokawa and Marshall Scott Poole (Beverly Hills: Sage Publications, 1986), pp. 81–92; Randy Y. Hirokawa, "Group Communication and Problem-solving Effectiveness I: A Critical Review of Inconsistent Findings," *Communication*

Quarterly 30 (1982): 134–305; Randy Y. Hirokawa, "Group Communication and Problem-solving Effectiveness II," *Western Journal of Speech Communication* 47 (1983): 59–74; Randy Y. Hirokawa, "Group Communication and Problem-solving Effectiveness: An Investigation of Group Phases," *Human Communication Research* 9 (1983): 291–305.
21. Hirokawa and Scheerhorn, "Faulty Group," p. 66.
22. John Dewey, *How We Think* (Boston: Heath, 1910).

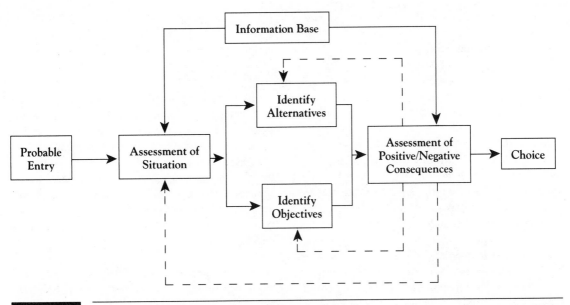

Figure 11-2   General model of the group decision-making process.

The second source of error in decision making is *inappropriate goals and objectives*. The group may neglect important objectives that ought to be achieved, or it may work toward unnecessary objectives. The third problem is *improper assessment of positive and negative qualities*. Here the group is unable to see the advantages and/or disadvantages of various proposals; or, conversely, the group may overestimate the positive or negative outcomes of a plan.

Fourth, the group may develop an *inadequate information base*. This can happen in several ways. Valid information may be rejected. Invalid information may be accepted. Too little information may be collected. Too much information may cause overload and confusion. Finally, the group may be guilty of *faulty reasoning from the information base*.

Why do groups fall into these traps? These theorists believe that the errors most often arise from the communicative influences of group members. In other words, the group is swayed by certain members who unwittingly mislead the group in some way. Therefore, the solution to these problems must also be in the hands of individual members. If

someone can misguide the group, someone can also influence the group positively.

Criticism

The value of Cattell's theory is that it presents a basic idea, synergy, that is useful in understanding groups. Although Cattell does not develop this idea of group energy to any appreciable degree, it has been applied repeatedly and developed in detail in the group dynamics literature summarized earlier. Janis's groupthink theory, in fact, is nothing more than application of the synergy notion. The problem with Cattell's representation of synergy is that it implies that intrinsic synergy is bad and that the more effective the synergy in a group, the better the group's output will be. Clearly Janis's work shows that this is not the case. The thrust of Janis's hypothesis is that in highly cohesive groups where intrinsic synergy is low, group output may in fact be inadequate. Groupthink occurs precisely because not enough conflict (intrinsic energy) is present in the group.

Janis's theory is appealing. It stems not only from laboratory research but from field application and historical case study as well.[23] It is a theory that demonstrates the utility of group dynamics ideas in understanding actual groups at work. As we have seen repeatedly in this book, one of the failings of most communication theories is that they are based on limited perspectives or on limited types of research. Theories such as Janis's are like a breath of fresh air in this regard.

Janis's theory is different also because of its applied nature. It is a normative, or prescriptive, theory, providing guidelines for improved group functioning. However, this aspect of the theory leads to one of its weaknesses, namely, that it does not take us very far in understanding or explaining how groups function. It suggests a way of guarding against one particular danger in groups, but it does not help us understand the nature of cohesiveness, conflict, roles, or communication. For this reason some scholars would be reluctant to call Janis's work a theory at all. Janis himself refers to this application merely as an hypothesis.

Hirokawa's theory is also highly normative. It is consistent with the everyday experience of groups in our society, and it seems to have practical potential in helping groups become more effective. This theory, however, adds little to our knowledge of communication processes. As a primarily descriptive theory, it does not provide an explanatory basis for its claims. What are the conditions or rules under which various forms of problem definition, information gathering, proposal development, objective evaluation, and choice occur? What factors lead to the uncritical acceptance of error-producing messages? The challenge to these researchers in the future will be to uncover causes or reasons for the rich variety of contingent outcomes in group decision making.

Hirokawa's theory also limits group functioning to a kind of rational task-only process. It fails to acknowledge the ways in which group successes and failures are a result of socioemotional or relational activity. In addition, the theory does not adequately integrate problems that are out of the con-

trol of the group, such as the vagaries of the situation or the pragmatic obstacles to information gathering.

The Interactional Tradition

Group outcome depends greatly on the nature of interaction in the group. Theories of group interaction are especially important in this book because of the central concern for communication as the base of group productivity. We will look at two theories of group interaction. The first, an old standard, is Robert Bale's interaction process analysis. The second modifies Bale's notion of interaction and takes interaction analysis in a different direction.

Interaction process analysis. One of the most prominent small group theories is Robert Bale's interaction process analysis.[24] Bale's theory concentrates on interaction or communication per se. Using his many years of research as a foundation, Bales has created a unified and well-developed theory of small group interaction. It is centered around the idea that people act and react in groups. As one person makes a comment, another person responds to the comment. Bales's aim, then, is to explain the pattern of responses in the small task group. Bales explains the value of his system:

> Interaction process analysis is built on a very simple common-sense base, and much that one intuitively believes about everyday conversation can be confirmed by it. The surprising thing, perhaps, is that it goes much further than one would suspect in revealing basic attitudes of people, their personalities, and their positions in a group.[25]

Figure 11-3 illustrates the categories of interactions.[26] These twelve categories are grouped into four broader sets, as outlined at the left of the fig-

23. For a laboratory test of the groupthink hypothesis, see John A. Courtright, "A Laboratory Investigation of Groupthink," *Communication Monographs* 45 (1978): 229–46.

24. Robert F. Bales, *Interaction Process Analysis: A Method for the Study of Small Groups* (Reading, Mass.: Addison-Wesley, 1950); *Personality and Interpersonal Behavior* (New York: Holt, Rinehart & Winston, 1970); Robert F. Bales and Stephen P. Cohen, *Symlog: A System for the Multiple Level Observation of Groups* (London: Collier, 1979).

25. Bales, *Personality*, p. 95.

26. Adapted from Bales, *Personality*, p. 92.

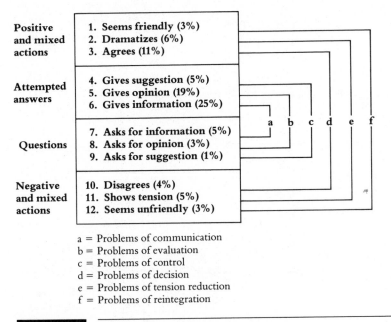

a = Problems of communication
b = Problems of evaluation
c = Problems of control
d = Problems of decision
e = Problems of tension reduction
f = Problems of reintegration

Figure 11-3   Categories for interaction process analysis.

ure. In addition, the behavior types are paired ac-cording to typical action-response expectations. Each of these pairs implies a particular problem area for groups, as labeled.

The four sets of behavior in the model can be further synthesized into two classes of group behav-ior. We have seen these in the earlier theories in this chapter. The first and fourth categories, posi-tive actions and negative actions, constitute the *socioemotional area*, which relates to the inter-personal relations in the group. In addition to accomplishing a task, the group must mesh psycho-logically, a goal that can be aided or impeded by socioemotional communication. The second and third classes can be considered the *task area*. The interactions in this section relate to the problem or task of the group. In investigating leadership, Bales has found that typically the same group will have two different kinds of leaders. The task leader, who facilitates and coordinates the task-related com-ments, directs energy toward getting the job done. The emergence of the task leadership role is impor-tant in group problem solving. Equally important is the emergence of a socioemotional leader. Usu-

ally a second leader takes this role. This individual works for improved relations in the group, concen-trating on interactions in the positive and negative sectors.

The way a person behaves in a group depends on the role the individual takes and the person's per-sonality. Role is situational. It depends on the de-mands of the interpersonal dynamics of the group, including the expectations of others. The way a person behaves will lead to certain perceptions by the other group members. "One might expect utter chaos with all this relativism of definition, but in many operating groups there is a surprising amount of consensus on the way in which most individual members are perceived and evaluated."[27]

Bales has shown how the perception of an in-dividual's position in a group is a function of three dimensions. These include (a) dominance–submission, (b) friendliness–unfriendliness, and (c) instrumental and controlled–emotional and ex-pressive. These factors are visualized in a three-dimensional space, as shown in Figure 11-4. The

27. Ibid., p. 4.

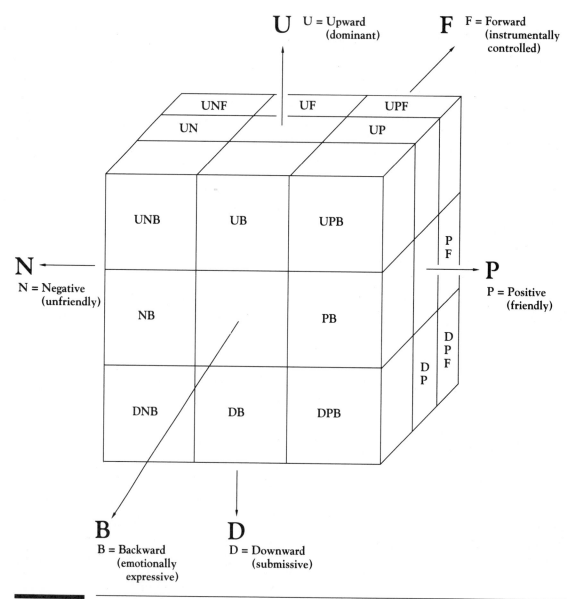

Figure 11-4   Three-dimensional space of interpersonal personality.

Adapted with permission of The Free Press, a Division of Macmillan, Inc. From *SYMLOG: A System for the Multiple Level Observation of Groups*, by Robert F. Bales, Stephen P. Cohen and Stephen A. Williamson. Copyright © 1979 by The Free Press.

axes of the space are labeled positive-negative, upward-downward, and forward-backward. Bales uses these spatial labels to name the various position types in his theory.

Within a particular group any member can be placed in this three-dimensional space, depending on how the individual's behavior relates to the factors. The direction of an individual's position de-

Table 11-1	Types of Group Roles and Associated Characteristics

U:	active, dominant, talks a lot
UP:	extroverted, outgoing, positive
UPF:	a purposeful democratic task leader
UF:	an assertive businesslike manager
UNF:	authoritarian, controlling, disapproving
UN:	domineering, tough-minded, powerful
UNB:	provocative, egocentric, shows off
UB:	jokes around, expressive, dramatic
UPB:	entertaining, sociable, smiling, warm
P:	friendly, equalitarian
PF:	works cooperatively with others
F:	analytical, task-oriented, problem solving
NF:	legalistic, has to be right
N:	unfriendly, negativistic
NB:	irritable, cynical, won't cooperate
B:	shows feelings and emotions
PB:	affectionate, likeable, fun to be with
DP:	looks up to others, appreciative, trustful
DPF:	gentle, willing to accept responsibility
DF:	obedient, works submissively
DNF:	self-punishing, works too hard
DN:	depressed, sad, resentful
DNB:	alienated, quits, withdraws
DB:	afraid to try, doubts own ability
DPB:	quietly happy just to be with others
D:	passive, introverted, says little

Adapted with permission of The Free Press, a Division of Macmillan, Inc. From *SYMLOG: A System for the Multiple Level Observation of Groups*, by Robert F. Bales, Stephen P. Cohen and Stephen A. Williamson. Copyright © 1979 by The Free Press.

pends on the quadrant in which that individual appears (for example, UPF); one's position within the quadrant is determined by the degree of each dimension represented. Thus, for example, a UPF

could appear at various points in the space, depending on the degree of U, of P, and of F. Table 11-1 lists the behavior types and their value directions. When all of the group's members are plotted on the spatial graph, their relationships and networks can be seen. The larger the group, the greater the tendency for subgroups of coalitions to develop. These subgroups consist of individuals with similar value dimensions. Obviously, affinity exists among individuals who are close in value dimension and direction, while distant individuals are not connected. Bales describes the typical pattern:

> No self-analytic group so far has shown a completely integrated network of all members. There are normally three or four networks in a group of about twenty-five members, the largest one in the group ranging from about seven to sixteen members, the second largest from five to ten members, the third from three to six members, and the fourth from two to four members. All groups have had some isolates, ranging in number from three to five per group. The isolates are more likely to appear on the thinly populated negative side of the space, but they may appear in any region.[28]

Not only can we predict the coalitions and networks of a group from a knowledge of the distribution of types, but Bales has shown that behavior type is related to the nature of interaction in groups. The interaction that a person initiates and receives depends in part on his or her behavior type. Keep in mind at this point that one's behavior in a group is determined by both personality and role. Table 11-2 shows how interaction is related to value directions.[29]

Bales's theory is valuable in studying small group *communication* because it stresses *interaction*. He emphasizes the ways people respond to one another verbally. We have seen how the character of interaction is manifest in social and task comments and in value statements. In the next section you will see that the way a group develops—the phases through which it passes—depends greatly on the interactional patterns within the group.

28. Ibid., p. 47.
29. Ibid., pp. 86–97.

Table 11-2   Relationship Between Interaction and Type

Category	Low initiation	High initiation	Low reception	High reception
Seems friendly	N	P	N	P
Dramatizes	DF	UB	NF	PB
Agrees	NB	PF	B	F
Gives suggestion	DB	UF	DN	UP
Gives opinion	B	F	NB	PF
Gives information	U	D	N	P
Asks for information	DN	UP	UF	DB
Asks for opinion	N	P	UP	DN
Asks for suggestion	UB	DF	B	F
Disagrees	P	N	DPB	UNF
Shows tension	UF	DB	DPF	UNB
Seems unfriendly	P	N	DPB	UNF

Fisher's interaction analysis. B. Aubrey Fisher and his associates have developed a theoretical perspective on group phases and decision emergence that stresses *interaction* and uses a system orientation. Since their theory is communication-oriented and incorporates much material of previous theories, we will study it in some detail. In preview we will look at the general orientation of the *interact system model*. Next, we will discuss Fisher's scheme for interaction analysis and the phases of decision emergence. We will conclude the section by recapping Fisher's notion of decision and modification. The thrust of this discussion is the process by which groups deal with decision-making tasks.

Often the unit of analysis in group research is the individual's behavior. Aubrey Fisher and Leonard Hawes refer to this as the *human system model*.[30] The human system approach has yielded a number

of analyses of individual behavior variables. Clearly Bales's method of analysis, though it is presented as "interaction" analysis, is really a human system approach. It focuses on single acts of individual group participants.

Fisher and Hawes believe that a more sensible approach for the study of group communication is the *interact system model*, in which the basic unit of analysis is not an individual act, but an *interact*. An interact is the verbal or nonverbal act of one person followed by a reaction from another. Here the unit for analysis is a contiguous pair of acts. Fisher and Hawes explore the nature of behavior-response sets. Particularly, they have observed that interacts seem to be organized over time in a hierarchical fashion. Three levels are defined.

The first level involves *interact categories*. These are the specific classes or types of interacts observed in groups. For example, an asserted interpretation of a proposal might be followed by a comment seeking clarification of the proposal. Over the entire discussion the frequency of such interact categories

30. B. Aubrey Fisher and Leonard Hawes, "An Interact System Model: Generating a Grounded Theory of Small Groups," *Quarterly Journal of Speech* 57 (1971): 444–53.

would be studied to determine how they tend to group into *interact phases*, the second level of analysis. A study of interact phases reveals the pattern of development in the group as it progresses toward task accomplishment. The third level of analysis is *cycles*. As the group proceeds through a number of tasks, the phases repeat themselves in cyclical fashion.

Let's take a closer look at Fisher's method of interaction analysis. Fisher concentrates on interacts in groups. In other words, he looks at pairs of contiguous acts. What his system classifies is an act and its response. Interacts can be classified on two dimensions, the content dimension and the relationship dimension. You recall from Chapter 10 that these theorists state that all communication messages have a content or information dimension and a relationship or metacommunication dimension. While a person is making a statement, the individual is also reflecting on the relationship in some way. The most common scheme for understanding relational messages is the threefold analysis of one-up, one-down, and one-across messages. In interaction analysis group members would be observed in terms of their complementary (for example, one-up, one-down), symmetrical (for example, one-up, one-up), and transitional (for example, one-up, one-across) responses. (You may find it useful at this point to review relational theory from Chapter 10.)

Despite the potential utility of an interaction analysis of the relational dimension in groups, Fisher has concentrated on the content dimension. Following the hypothesis that almost all comments in a task group are related in one way or another to a *decision proposal*, Fisher classifies statements in terms of how they respond to a decision proposal. The following outline is his classification scheme.[31]

1. Interpretation
   f. Favorable toward the decision proposal
   u. Unfavorable toward the decision proposal
   ab. Ambiguous toward the decision pro-

posal, containing a bivalued (both favorable and unfavorable) evaluation
   an. Ambiguous toward the decision proposal, containing a neutral evaluation
2. Substantiation
   f. Favorable toward the decision proposal
   u. Unfavorable toward the decision proposal
   ab. Ambiguous toward the decision proposal, containing a bivalued (both favorable and unfavorable) evaluation
   an. Ambiguous toward the decision proposal, containing a neutral evaluation
3. Clarification
4. Modification
5. Agreement
6. Disagreement

Two essential differences exist between the theories of Bales and Fisher. First, Bales classifies a given act strictly in terms of its task or socioemotional function. Fisher assumes that any given act may fulfill either or both functions simultaneously. (Actually, Fisher finds it more appropriate to look at the content and relational dimensions of acts, although these divisions may in some ways be close to Bales's task and socioemotional categories.) Second, Bales classifies only single acts, while Fisher classifies interacts. In observing a group, Fisher will create a matrix with twelve rows and twelve columns, corresponding to the twelve categories in his system. This matrix thus contains 144 cells, one for each potential type of interact. In other words the observer will classify the first act and the second act, placing a mark in the appropriate cell between the two. In this way the researcher can actually see the character and frequency of act pairs in a group discussion. Fisher believes this kind of data is useful for understanding how groups function, how decisions are made, and how groups pass through phases as decisions emerge. For our purposes this approach is exciting because it focuses directly and completely on *interpersonal communication* as no other group theory does.

In his theory of decision emergence, Fisher outlines four phases through which task groups tend to proceed: orientation, conflict, emergence, and

31. B. Aubrey Fisher, *Small Group Decision Making: Communication and the Group Process* (New York: McGraw-Hill, 1980), p. 117.

reinforcement.[32] In observing the distribution of interacts across these phases, Fisher notes the ways interaction changes as the group decision formulates and solidifies. The *orientation* phase involves getting acquainted, clarifying, and beginning to express points of view. A high level of agreement characterizes this stage, and comments are often designed to test the group. Thus positions expressed are both qualified and tentative. In this phase people grope for direction and interpersonal understanding.

The *conflict* phase includes a great deal of dissent. People in this second phase begin to solidify their attitudes, and much polarization results. The interacts in this phase tend to include more disagreement and unfavorable evaluation. As an observer you would notice that members argue and attempt to persuade at this point. Members also tend to form coalitions in the conflict phase. As people group together according to their common stands on the issues, polarization grows.

These coalitions tend to disappear in the third phase. In the *emergence* phase the first inklings of cooperation begin to show. People are less tenacious in defending their viewpoints. As they soften their positions and undergo attitude change, ambiguity becomes apparent in their interaction. Comments are more equivocal as ambiguity functions to mediate the attitude shifts the members are going through. The number of favorable comments increases until a group decision begins to emerge.

In the final phase, *reinforcement*, the group decision solidifies and receives reinforcement from group members. The group unifies, standing behind its solution. Comments are almost uniformly positive and favorable, and more interaction occurs on matters of interpretation. The ambiguity that marked the third phase tends to disappear.

Fisher shows us in the preceding analysis that groups go through phases of development in their decision-making interaction. These phases characterize the nature of interaction as it changes over time. An important related topic is that of *decision modification*.[33] Fisher finds that groups typically do not introduce a single solution and pursue that solution until all members agree. Nor do they introduce a single proposal and continue to modify it until consensus is reached. Rarely is parliamentary format the typical pattern in small group discussion. Fisher theorizes on the basis of his group observations that decision modification is cyclical; several proposals are made, each discussed briefly, and certain of them reintroduced at a later time. Discussion of proposals seems therefore to proceed in spurts of energy. Proposal A will be introduced and discussed. Suddenly the group will drop this idea and move to proposal B. After discussion this, the group may introduce and discuss other proposals. Then someone will revive proposal A, perhaps in modified form. The group finally will settle on a modified plan that was introduced earlier in the discussion in a different form.

Why does discussion usually proceed in such an erratic fashion? Probably because the interpersonal demands of discussion require "breaks" from task work. In effect group attention span is short because of the intense nature of group work. Such an explanation suggests that "flight" behavior helps manage tension and conflict. The group's need to work on interpersonal dynamics is supported by other theories as well, including Barry Collins and Harold Guetzkow's ideas on interpersonal barriers and Bales's notion of socioemotional (versus task) interaction.

Fisher finds that in modifying proposals, groups tend to follow one of two patterns. If conflict is low, the group will reintroduce proposals in less abstract, more specific language. For example, in a discussion of a public health nursing conference, an original idea to begin "with a non-threatening something" was modified to "begin with a history of the contributions which public health has made to the field of nursing."[34] A group, as it successively returns to a proposal, seems to follow the pattern of stating the problem, discussing criteria for solu-

32. B. Aubrey Fisher, "Decision Emergence: Phases in Group Decision Making," *Speech Monographs* 37 (1970): 53–60; Fisher, *Decision Making*.

33. Fisher, *Decision Making*; also B. Aubrey Fisher, "The Process of Decision Modification in Small Discussion Groups," *Journal of Communication* 20 (1970): 51–64.

34. Fisher, *Decision Making*, p. 155.

tion, introducing an abstract solution, and moving finally to a concrete solution. Keep in mind, however, that the group most likely will not move through these four steps with continuity. Rather, it will deal sporadically with these themes as members depart from and return to the proposal in a stop-and-start fashion.

The second typical pattern of modification occurs when conflict is higher. Here the group does not attempt to make a proposal more specific. Because disagreement exists on the very nature of the proposal, the group introduces substitute proposals of the same level of abstraction as the original. In the first pattern, which involves making proposals more specific, the group task seems to be one of mutual discovery of the best specific implementation of a general idea. In this social conflict pattern the task is more of debate and persuasion among various alternative proposals.

Criticism. In general Bales's and Fisher's theories share a common strength and a common weakness. The strength is that interaction analysis, whether of the Bales or Fisher type, allows us to look carefully at the communication behavior of groups, correlating interpersonal messages with other group factors. In other words interaction analysis provides a way to analyze group communication. Thus these theories are both appropriate and heuristic. These advantages, however, have been gained at the price of a trade-off, which leads to their common weakness. When individual acts (or interacts) are analyzed according to a classification scheme, rich idiosyncratic meanings are glossed over. The value of understanding general group trends is bought at the price of thorough understanding of particular events in groups.[35]

Bales's theory is an excellent beginning for understanding interaction in groups. His approach is highly parsimonious and internally consistent. It is built on a sensible and intuitively appealing conceptual base, from which a number of propositions about group interaction are derived. The theory's heuristic value is evidenced by the numerous stud-

ies based on the Bales categories, including Bales's own research over a twenty-year period at Harvard University.

Bales's system has been criticized for two weaknesses. First the theory is strictly act oriented. In other words it fails to describe interaction response. It presumes that any statement will stand on its own apart from contiguous statements by other people. Fisher, in contrast, shows how analyses that stop at the act level are not adequate. The second problem of Bales's system is that it separates the task and socioemotional areas of group discussion. Careful examination of groups in action shows that task and socioemotional functions are thoroughly mixed. One can fulfill both task and social functions in a single statement, and in classifying group behavior it is difficult to validly separate these functions. True, a given statement may be mostly task, or mostly social, but to separate them completely would be a mistake. Consequently Bales envisions the group as a body that swings between discussion of task matters to discussion of social matters, back and forth. Fisher, on the other hand, finds that groups do not operate in this way. Such criticism casts doubt on the validity of Bales's approach.

Fisher takes a major step toward correcting these problems, but his theory too has weaknesses. Although Fisher's theory admits to the existence of the relational dimension of interaction, it makes no attempt to correlate the content and relational aspects of group discussion. Its second weakness is related to the first: Fisher's method does not accommodate nonverbal elements of messages. Consequently many of the most central aspects of relational messages are ignored. Anyone who has participated in a group discussion knows that the nonverbal element is a powerful form of communication, both of content and relational dimensions. To be fair, of course, we must note how difficult it would be to accurately code nonverbal interaction, which undoubtedly is the reason Fisher has not attempted to do so.

Fisher's theory is an example of a phase model of group development. Phase models predict that groups go through a series of stages in dealing with a problem of set of tasks. There have been many

35. Ibid., p. 322.

such models in the history of small group theory; and the phase approach constitutes the dominant view of group development.[36] Recently, however, phase models have been criticized for being overly simple.[37] In the next section, we examine a theory that views group action and development in a more complex and potentially more useful way than have the approaches summarized above.

The Structurationist Perspective

The input-process-output model has contributed much to our understanding of small group phenomena. However, it has emphasized only one aspect of the group process by taking a fundamentally deterministic approach. Largely ignored is the way in which individuals in groups act to create their realities. Recently, a group of communication researchers have recognized this problem and proposed a new perspective—the structurational approach.[38] Before discussing this theory, let us briefly summarize the general theory of structuration.

Structuration theory is the brainchild of sociologist Anthony Giddens and his followers.[39] The thrust of the theory is that human action is a process of producing and reproducing various social systems. Groups act according to rules to achieve their goals and in so doing create structures that in turn affect future actions. Structures like relational expectations, group roles and norms, communication networks, and societal institutions both affect and are affected by social action. These structures provide individuals with rules that guide their actions, but their actions in turn create new rules and reproduce old ones.

Giddens overcomes the debate between those who hold that human action is caused by outside forces and those who advocate the intentionality of human action; instead, Giddens claims that both sides in this dispute are right, because social life is a two-sided coin. We do have intentions and act to accomplish these; at the same time, our actions have the unintended consequences of establishing or reinforcing structures that prefigure our future actions. Indeed, we do act to attain goals, and we monitor our actions and their outcomes; at the same time, however, we are unaware of many of the outcomes of action and their consequent structures.

Consider an example from group communication. A group member will talk to the group about certain concerns. In so doing, that individual is accomplishing specific objectives. At the same time, other group members come to see this person as one who has particular ideas and who can do special kinds of things. They will come to expect the person to behave in certain ways and to follow up on certain concerns. A role is thereby created for the person. Over time the person's role, which was very much an unintended consequence of his or her action, will become a kind of structure that constrains that individual's future behavior in the group. Giddens believes that this kind of "structuration" saturates all of human social life.

Giddens believes that structuration always involves three major modalities, or dimensions of structure, that affect and are affected by action. These are (a) interpreting or understanding, (b) a sense of morality or proper conduct, and (c) a sense of power in action. The rules we use to guide our actions, in other words, tell us how something should be understood (interpretation), what should

36. Some of the most prominent phase models are discussed in R. F. Bales and F. L. Strodbeck, "Phases in Group Problem-Solving," *Journal of Abnormal and Social Psychology* 46 (1951): 485–95; M. A. Bell, "Phases in Group Problem-Solving," *Small Group Behavior* 13 (1982): 475–95; W. G. Bennis and H. A. Shepard, "The Theory of Group Development," *Human Relations* 9 (1956): 415–37; R. Lacoursiere, *The Life Cycle of Groups* (New York: Human Sciences Press, 1980); Bruce Tuckman, "Developmental Sequence in Small Groups," *Psychological Bulletin* 63 (1965): 384–99.

37. These arguments are summarized in Marshall Scott Pole, "Decision Development in Small Groups, III: A Multiple Sequence Model of Group Decision Development," *Communication Monographs* 50 (1983): 321–42.

38. Poole, Seibold, and McPhee, "Group Decision-Making"; Poole, Seibold, and McPhee, "Structurational Approach."

39. See, for example, Anthony Giddens, *New Rules of Sociological Method* (New York: Basic Books, 1976); *Studies in Social and Political Theory* (New York: Basic Books, 1977). For a brief summary of the theory, see Anthony Giddens, *Profiles and Critiques in Social Theory* (Berkeley: University of California Press, 1982), pp. 8–11.

be done (morality), and how to get things accomplished (power). In turn, our actions reinforce those very structures of interpretation, morality, and power.

In actual practice, one's behavior is rarely affected by a single structure. Indeed, one's action of the moment is normally affected by and affects several different structural elements. Structures therefore relate to and affect one another. This can happen in two ways. The first is that one structure mediates another: In other words, the production of one structure is accomplished by producing another. For example, the group may produce a communication network, but it does so by establishing individual roles. Here the role structure mediates the communication structure.

The second way in which structures relate is through contradiction. Here the production of a structure requires the establishment of another structure that undermines the first one. This is the stuff of classical paradox. Contradictions lead to conflict, and through a dialectic or tension between contradictory elements, system change results. Several examples of contradictions in group communication are mentioned below.

A Structurational Theory of Group Communication

Relying on the ideas of Giddens and his followers, Scott Poole and his colleagues have begun work on a structurational theory of group decision making.[40] This theory teaches that group decision making is a process in which group members attempt to achieve convergence on a final decision. Individuals express their opinions and preferences and thereby produce and reproduce certain rules by which convergence can be achieved or blocked. In trying to achieve convergence, group members make use of Giddens's three elements of action—interpretation, morality, and power. Interpretation is made possible through language, morality is established through group norms, and power is achieved through the interpersonal power structures that have emerged in the group.

40. Poole, Seibold, and McPhee, "Group Decision-Making."

Suppose, for example, that a member of a group is interested in persuading other members to endorse a particular plan. He or she would express a shared understanding of the plan by using commonly understood language. The participant would behave in a way condoned by the group according to its norms. And the member would also attempt to persuade, to exert power, to be effective in meeting the objective. In order to do this, the speaker has to have some sources of power, like leadership ability or status. The speech delivered by this group member may or may not accomplish the objective, but it will certainly have the unintended consequence of reproducing the shared understandings and linguistic forms, the norms, and the power structure of the group.

This theory of group decision making recognizes the importance of outside factors in influencing the group's actions. However, consistent with structuration theory, outside factors have meaning only insofar as they are understood and interpreted by the group. Such interpretations are negotiated through interaction within the group. One of the most important outside factors is task type—what the group has been given to do. The group's task makes certain rules appropriate and others inappropriate. For example, a study group will behave in one way when preparing for an upcoming exam and in an entirely different way when designing a group project for the class.

This theory also recognizes that the definition of persons in the group is always an outcome of structuration. We act toward others in ways that reflect our views of their place in the group, and in time a "group" definition of each person and the group as a whole emerges. This group definition subsequently affects the interaction among the members of the group and is thereby reproduced again and again. The key concept to understanding the definition of the person is role. The expected behavior pattern in a group is a structure that emerges from the actions of the group in its ongoing work. This role-establishing work is "microstructuration."

Poole and his associates believe that task groups are rife with contradiction. Consistent with Giddens, they see group structuration as deeply imbedded in the process of producing and resolving these inherent tensions. For example, the group must meet certain time pressures, but they are also required to make good decisions, which may not be possible if done in a speedy fashion. They must attend to the requirements of the task, but in so doing they must also take care of their socioemotional needs, which by definition detract from task work. Members join the group to meet individual objectives, but they can only do so by attending to group objectives, which may undercut individual goals. Convergence can only come about through agreement, yet the group is told it must disagree in order to test ideas; by eliminating poor options, they can agree on the good options. In large measure, group structuration is a process of working through these contradictions.

A Multiple Sequence Theory of Group Development

The structuration theory of group decision making sets the stage for the more specific theory of group development. As we have seen, Poole has criticized the phase models of group development for being overly simple. He proposes a series of related tracks of development in a group. The group moves simultaneously along these tracks. Poole explains his theory as follows:

> The model developed here attempts to avoid the oversimplifications of the phasic conception, yet at the same time accounts for the observable unity of much group activity. Rather than picturing the group decision making as a series of phasic "blocks" dropped one after another into sequence, it portrays development as a set of parallel strands or tracks of activity which evolve simultaneously and interlock in different patterns over time. Each track represents a separate aspect or mode of group activity—for example, task process or topic focus—and the various tracks are assumed to develop unevenly. For this reason, coherent, unified phases do not exist at all points in a discussion. When the development of the tracks converges in a coherent pattern, phases similar to those in the classic research may be found. However, at other points there may be no relationship among the tracks and therefore no recognizable phases.[41]

The three main concepts of this theory are activity tracks, breakpoints, and task structure. The *activity tracks* are the courses along which the group develops or moves. There are probably many possible tracks, but three are elaborated in the theory— the task process track, the relational track, and the topic focus track. The *task track* consists of activities that directly deal with the problem or task. The *relational track* involves activities that establish and maintain interpersonal relationships in the group. These two correspond rather neatly with the task-maintenance duality encountered in several other theories presented in this chapter. The third track, the *topical focus track*, is the issue, topic, or concern of the group at a particular moment. The first two tracks are easier to define, based on previous research, as Table 11-3 illustrates.[42]

The multiple sequence model imagines that the group moves along the various tracks over time. At a given moment, the group may be at a particular "spot" in the development of each track. Figure 11-5 illustrates this idea.[43] The figure shows the three tracks, broken up into segments of activity. All three tracks are depicted as flowing along the same time line. Topic shifts are designated with the symbol T, and various kinds of breakpoints are designated with appropriate letters.

The second major concept in this theory is *breakpoint*. A breakpoint is a point of transition in a track from one topic or emphasis to another. Sometimes a breakpoint will mark a change in a single track, but often it will mark changes in several tracks. Breakpoints are important because they signal important points in the development of the group's decision-making activity. Three types of breakpoints are apparent. *Normal breakpoints* are expected, natural points of termination or transition. They include such things as adjournment, caucusing, or topic shifts. *Delays* are unexpected problems that cause a pause in normal group functioning. Delays often consist of re-discussion of issues necessary for the group to resolve conflicts or establish understanding. Delays may be a sign of impending difficulty, or they may be a more positive sign of careful thought or creative activity. *Disrup-*

41. Poole, "Decision Development," p. 326.

42. Ibid., p. 327.
43. Ibid., p. 329.

Table 11-3   Classifications for Two Activity Types

Task process activities	Relational activities
Problem Activity	*Work-Focused Relationships*
T1. Problem Analysis	R1. Focused Work (no criticism; extended idea development and analysis)
Executive Activity	R2. Critical Work (idea development through criticism and repartee)
T2a. Orientation	*Conflict*
T2b. Process Reflection	R3a. Opposition
Solution Activity	R3b. Resolution-Accommodation
	R3c. Resolution-Avoidance/Smoothing
T3a. Establish Solution Guidelines	R3d. Resolution-Integration (Bargaining/Consensus Building/Problem Solving)
T3b. Solution Design	
T3c. Solution Evaluation	*Integration*
T3d. Solution Confirmation and Selection	R4. Integration
	Ambiguous Relationships
	R5. Expression of Ambiguity

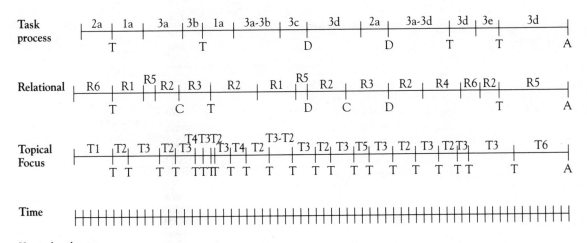

Key to breakpoints:

T: Topic shift (Topics are numbered—T1 is topic 1.)   C: Conflict
A: Adjournment/Breaks   F: Failure
D: Delays

Figure 11-5   A sample chart showing the three interrelated activity threads.

Table 11-3 and Figure 11-5 are both from *Communication Monographs*, "Decision Development in Small Groups III: A Multiple Sequence Model of Group Decision Development," by Marshall Scott Poole. Copyright © 1983 by the Speech Communication Association. Reprinted by permission of the author and publisher.

tions are more serious. These consist of major dis-agreements and group failures. These breakpoints are outlined in Figure 11-5; you can see in the figure how the flow of activity in each track is interrupted by various types of breakpoints.

The third element in group development is *structural requirements*. For the most part, these requirements are imposed by the nature of the task. Poole and his associates pointed out the importance of the task as an external constraint in the structurational theory outlined above. In summary, different tasks impose different requirements and constraints on the group.

Poole's multiple sequence model is a major advance in small group theory. Admittedly, however, it is just a beginning for a new set of ideas about how groups develop. Although the framework shows promise, much work remains to be done; we must still answer questions concerning how groups move along the pathways, what kinds of incidents bring the tracks together, what patterns of track development embody certain overall group phases, and especially what role various forms of communication have in multiple sequence development.

Integration

Groups are important to individuals and to society. As a person moves about in the life space, cooperation becomes essential in achieving goals. Human beings use communication to share resources in the solution of problems, and group communication thereby becomes not only an instrument for accomplishing tasks, but also a means of group maintenance and cohesion. Group communication can be viewed as a system of inputs, internal processes, and outputs. In decision making, the inputs include information and group resources, the process includes group interaction, and the outputs include completed tasks and solved problems.

The process of group interaction involves two kinds of group energy: task and socioemotional. Task energy is directed at problem solving, and socioemotional energy is directed at group maintenance and interpersonal relationships. Group effectiveness seems to depend on the balance between these two kinds of communication. Inadequate attention to these two factors can lead to dissatisfaction and poor decision making.

As group members communicate, they not only accomplish their intentions, but they also unintentionally structure future interactions. The interaction in groups is structured in at least three ways. First, individuals differ in the kinds of statements they make in a group. Second, a definite network or interaction pattern can be seen among the members of the group. Third, the interaction differs from one time period within a group to another.

Group problem solving is a developmental process. In other words, a group will go through different stages in its evolution. The character of the communication will vary from one stage to the next. Stages, however, are not easy to see in a group, because the group simultaneously operates on a variety of levels, and each level must be analyzed separately. The overall pattern of the group's development is tracked along its unique configuration of actions at each level.

Twelve

Theories of Organizational Communication

According to sociologist Amatai Etzioni:

> Our society is an organizational society. We are born in organizations, educated in organizations, and most of us spend much of our lives working for organizations. We spend much of our leisure time playing and praying in organizations. Most of us will die in an organization, and when the time comes for burial, the largest organization of all—the state—must grant official permission.[1]

We know that a great deal of communication takes place in the context of the organization. A large body of literature and theory has been written about human communication in organizations. In our search to understand the communication process, it is important for us to browse along the way in the area of organization theory.

Bernard Berelson and Gary Steiner outline four characteristics of an organization that distinguish it from other social groupings.[2] The first is *formality*. The typical organization has a set of goals, policies, procedures, and regulations that give it form. The second quality of organizations is *hierarchy*, typically expressed in terms of pyramidal structure. Third, organizations tend to consist of many people, "enough so that close personal relations among

all are impossible."[3] Fourth, organizations usually last longer than a human lifetime.

The second definition of organization is George Strother's. According to Strother, organizations consist of two or more people involved in a cooperative relationship, which implies that they have collective goals. The members of the organization differ in terms of function, and they maintain a stable hierarchical structure. Strother also recognizes that the organization exists within an environment or milieu.[4]

In this chapter we discuss four bodies of theory. The first deals with the structure and functions of organizations. These theories, which recount the ways in which organizations are structured to accomplish a variety of functions, have been a mainstay in the study of organizational communication. The second group of theories focuses on human relations. These theories constitute a counterpoint and critique of the structural-functional theories. The third group of theories concentrates not so much on the ways in which communication is *used* in organizations, but on the ways in which communication is the very process of organizing itself. The final group of theories takes a distinctly different turn by looking at organizations as cultures.

1. Amatai Etzioni, *Modern Organizations* (Englewood Cliffs, N.J.: Prentice-Hall, 1964), p. 1.
2. Bernard Berelson and Gary Steiner, *Human Behavior: An Inventory of Scientific Findings* (New York: Harcourt, Brace, 1964), p. 364.

3. Ibid.
4. George B. Strother, "Problems in the Development of A Social Science of Organizations," in *The Social Science of Organizations: Four Perspectives*, ed. H. J. Leavitt (Englewood Cliffs, N.J.: Prentice-Hall, 1963), p. 23.

225

Communication and Organizational Structure and Function

Classical Foundations: Max Weber

Certainly Max Weber was one of the most prominent social theorists of all time. In his lifetime, from 1864 to 1930, he produced a great quantity of work on the nature of human institutions. One of the areas for which he is best known is his theory of bureaucracy. This theory is part of a larger work found in *The Theory of Social and Economic Organization*, edited by Talcott Parsons.[5] These ideas, developed at the beginning of the century, form an important part of the early classical theory of organization.[6]

Weber defines organization as follows: "An 'organization' is a system of continuous, purposive activity of a specified kind. A 'corporate organization' is an associative social relationship characterized by an administrative staff devoted to such continuous purposive activity."[7] A central part of Weber's theory of bureaucracy is his concepts of power, authority, and legitimacy. For Weber power is the ability of a person in any social relationship to influence others and to overcome resistance. Power in this sense is fundamental to most social relationships. When power is legitimate, compliance is effective and complete. Etzioni summarizes this concept:

> Weber's study of legitimation introduces a whole new dimension to the study of organizational discipline. He used *power* to refer to the ability to induce acceptance or orders; *legitimation* to refer to the acceptance of the exercise of power because it is in line with values held by the subjects; and authority to refer to the combination of the two—i.e., to power that is viewed as legitimate.[8]

This idea of legitimate power is a central communication concern. Whether communications will be accepted in an organization hinges on the degree to which the superior has legitimate authority.

Weber outlines three types of authority.[9] The first is *traditional authority*. Traditional authority occurs when orders of the superior are perceived as justified by tradition. One's power is seen as legitimate because "it has always been legitimate." The second form of authority is *bureaucratic* or *rational-legal authority*. This form is most relevant in bureaucracies. The authorities in a bureaucracy derive their power from the bureaucracy's rules, which govern and are accepted by all organization members. Weber sees bureaucracy as the most efficient pattern for mass administration:

> Experience tends to show that the purely bureaucratic type of administrative organization—that is, the monocratic variety of bureaucracy—is, from a purely technical point of view, capable of attaining the highest degree of efficiency and is in this sense formally the most rational known means of carrying out imperative control over human beings. It is superior to any other form in precision, in stability, in the stringency of its discipline, and in its reliability.[10]

Weber's view of bureaucracy rests on a number of well-defined principles.[11] First, bureaucracy is based on rules. Such rules allow the solution of

5. Max Weber, *The Theory of Social and Economic Organizations*, trans. A. M. Henderson and Talcott Parsons (New York: Oxford University Press, 1947). A lengthy interpretation and discussion of Weber's theory can be found in Parson's introduction to the above book. Other secondary sources include: Strother, "Problems"; Dwight Waldo, "Organizational Theory: An Elephantine Problem," *General Systems* 7 (1962): 247–60; James March and Herbert Simon, *Organizations* (New York: John Wiley, 1958); Etzioni, *Modern Organizations*; Reinhard Bendix, *Max Weber: An Intellectual Portrait* (Garden City, N.Y.: Doubleday, 1962); Julien Freund, *The Sociology of Max Weber* (New York: Pantheon, 1968). For a more complete bibliography of primary and secondary sources on Weber, see S. N. Eisenstadt, *Max Weber on Charisma and Institution Building* (Chicago: University of Chicago Press, 1968).

6. The most important classical theories are those of Henri Fayol and Frederick Taylor. See Henri Fayol, *General and Industrial Management* (New York: Pitman, 1949) (originally published in 1925); and Frederick W. Taylor, *Principles of Scientific Management* (New York: Harper Brothers, 1947) (originally published in 1912).

7. Weber, *Social and Economic Organizations*, p. 151.

8. Etzioni, *Modern Organizations*, p. 51.

9. Weber, *Social and Economic Organizations*, pp. 330–32.

10. Ibid., p. 337.

11. Ibid., pp. 330–34. See also Etzioni, *Modern Organizations*, pp. 53–54.

problems, standardization, and equality in the organization. Second, bureaucracies are based on the concept of *sphere of competence*. Thus there is a systematic division of labor, each role having clearly defined rights and powers. Third, the essence of bureaucracy is hierarchy. Fourth, administrators are appointed on the basis of their knowledge and training. They are not generally elected, nor do they inherit their positions. Fifth, the members of the bureaucracy must not share in the ownership of the organization. Sixth, bureaucrats must be free to allocate resources within their realms of influence without fear of outside infringement. Seventh, a bureaucracy requires carefully maintained records. This final criterion is important in terms of communication:

> Administrative acts, decisions, and rules are formulated and recorded in writing, even in cases where oral discussion is the rule or is even mandatory. This applies to preliminary discussions and proposals, to final decisions, and to all sorts of orders and rules. The combination of written documents and a continuous organization of official functions constitutes the 'office' which is the central focus of all types of modern corporate action.[12]

Another feature of a bureaucracy is that it is usually headed by a nonbureaucrat. Nonbureaucratic heads are often elected or inherit their positions. They include presidents, cabinets, boards of trustees, and kings. Bureaucrats are dispensable; they may be replaced by similarly trained individuals, but the succession of the nonbureaucratic head may well be a crisis, precipitating innovation and change.

The first two types of authority are traditional and bureaucratic forms. The third is *charismatic authority*. Under this type of authority, power is justified through the charismatic nature of the superior individual's personality. Unlike bureaucratic authority charisma defies order and routine. The charismatic leader is revolutionary and establishes authority in opposition to the traditions of the day. One's leadership as a prophet or demagogue comes about through the demonstration of magical powers and heroism. Weber does not have much faith in this kind of mass persuasion.

Weber's theory is included here primarily as a general backdrop for the theories to come. In this regard it serves two functions. First, it provides a "classical" or standard picture with which the other theories can be contrasted. Second, it presents the common traditional view of organizations, relating the essence of the classical notion of organizations. Notice that communication and human behavior are downplayed in the theory; the thrust is structure and task factors. For our purposes this facet is the theory's greatest weakness. The theory gives implicit ideas of what communication is like in organizations, but communication is not treated as an explanatory variable, nor is it seen as the essence of organizational life. As the upcoming sections will indicate, this failure is significant.

The Systems Approach

While Weber's classical bureaucratic theory is a foundational work, recently, structural theories have been dominated by the so-called systems approach. (Chapter 3 discusses system theory in some detail.) This section describes the application of system theory to organizational communication. Indeed, system theory itself has been referred to as "structural-functionalism," as we noted in the earlier chapter.

Several system theories of organizations have been devised. One of the first was that of Chester Barnard. The work of Barnard was truly a phenomenon. As president of the New Jersey Bell Telephone Company, Barnard was not only a practicing executive but produced one of the most influential treatises on management and organization. Barnard provided two theories in one—a theory of organizations and of communication. His book, *The Functions of the Executive*, written in 1938, filled a theory void.[13] Barnard's thesis is that organizations can only exist through human cooperation and that cooperation is the medium through which individual capabilities can be combined to achieve superordinate tasks.

12. Weber, *Social and Economic Organizations*, p. 332.

13. Chester Barnard, *The Functions of the Executive* (Cambridge: Harvard University Press, 1938).

Charles Perrow writes the following of Barnard:

This enormously influential and remarkable book contains within it the seeds of three distinct trends in organizational theory that were to dominate the field for the next three decades. One was the institutional school; . . . another was the decision-making school as represented by Herbert Simon; . . . the third was the human relations school. . . . The leading theorists of these schools freely acknowledged their debt to Barnard.[14]

Calling him the last of the "practical theorists," Strother writes: "He draws on the work of the classical theorists, psychologists, sociologists, and institutional economists, as well as his own wealth of experience, to develop a closely reasoned, almost Euclidean treatment of industrial organization."[15]

One of the most influential theories of organization is that presented by James March and Herbert Simon in *Organizations*.[16] This technical treatise exemplifies theory in its purest form. Throughout their text March and Simon present hundreds of propositions related to decision making and organizational functioning. Charles Perrow recognizes this work as an important extension of human relations and classical theories. March and Simon themselves make it clear in the beginning of their book that their work was conducted for the purpose of providing a more complete conceptualization than that found in the "machine" models of the past. Perrow writes: "Herbert Simon and James March have provided . . . the muscle and flesh for the Weberian skeleton, giving it more substance, complexity, and believability without reducing organizational theory to propositions about individual behavior."[17] As a result of this fuller view, March and Simon's conceptualization provides a more complex picture of the person than does the human relations school and a more complex picture of organizations than does the classical school.

Another example of a systems approach to orga-

nizations is the work of Daniel Katz and Robert Kahn.[18] They present a clear and strong argument in favor of the open system model. Unlike a physical system the organization is social, created by people and bonded by psychological forces. Organizations as social systems are unique in their need for maintenance inputs or control mechanisms to keep human variability in check. Like Barnard, Katz and Kahn teach that the system involves overriding goals that necessitate the subordination of individual needs. Such is the nature of rule enforcement, accomplished through role behavior, norms, and values. These interrelated components provide a necessary integration within the system.

Although these early system theories of organizations are important, we have only been able to give them a cursory review here. In the following section, we take a closer look at one treatment that provides an excellent integration of system concepts.

An integrative theory. The work of Richard Farace, Peter Monge, and Hamish Russell constitutes an excellent overview of system concepts of the organization.[19] Their book *Communicating and Organizing* was actually written as a textbook, and the authors would probably not refer to their ideas as a theory; but the work does integrate an eclectic set of ideas in an internally consistent fashion, providing a fine synthesis of the systems view. In addition, it incorporates a substantial amount of original thinking based on the authors' research. In these ways, then, this work is indeed a theory, and it is a theory that makes communication central to organizational structure.

The authors define an organization as a system of at least two people (usually many more), with interdependence, input, throughput, and output. This group communicates and cooperates to produce some end product by using energy, information, and materials from the environment.

14. Charles Perrow, *Complex Organizations: A Critical Essay* (Glenview, Ill.: Scott, Foresman, 1972), p. 75.

15. Strother, "Problems," p. 16.

16. March and Simon, *Organizations*. A helpful secondary source is the interpretive work of Perrow, *Complex Organizations*.

17. Perrow, *Complex Organizations*, p. 146.

18. Daniel Katz and Robert Kahn, *The Social Psychology of Organizations* (New York: John Wiley, 1966).

19. Richard V. Farace, Peter R. Monge, and Hamish Russell, *Communicating and Organizing* (Reading, Mass.: Addison-Wesley, 1977).

One of the most important resources in organizations is *information*. Using information theory (Chapter 3) as a base, Farace and colleagues define information in terms of the reduction of uncertainty. As a person becomes able to predict which patterns will occur in the flow of matter and energy, uncertainty is reduced and information is gained. Communication is in part the reduction of uncertainty via information. Communication, however, also involves the use of common *symbolic forms* that refer to mutually understood referents.

The authors delineate two types of communication, which correspond to two types of information. *Absolute information* consists of all the pieces of knowledge present in the system. Thus the totality of communicated information in an organization is absolute communication. On the other hand, *distributed information* is that which has been diffused through the organization. The fact that information exists in an organization does not guarantee that it will be communicated adequately in the system. Questions of absolute information deal with what is known; questions of distribution deal with who knows it. The practical implication of this theoretical distinction is that "failures in distribution policies are due to failures by managers to identify which groups of personnel need to know certain things, or to establish where these groups are supposed to be able to obtain the information they need.[20]

The structural-functional framework for organizational communication rests on three analytic dimensions. The first of these is the *system level*, which is made up of four sublevels: individual, dyadic, group, and organizational. Here the principle of system hierarchy (as discussed in Chapter 3) is manifest. Individuals communicate with others in dyads; dyads cluster together into groups. The organization as a whole is a system of interconnected groups forming a macronetwork.

At each of these levels of analysis, we can examine the *functions* of communication, which is the second dimension. Among the variety of communication functions that exist, these authors stress

three: production, innovation, and maintenance. *Production* refers to the direction, coordination, and control of activities. *Innovation* generates change and new ideas in the system. *Maintenance* preserves individual values and interpersonal relations necessary to keep the system together.

The third dimension in the framework is *structure*. While function deals with the content of messages, structure deals with the emergent patterns or regularities in the transmission of messages. For every level in the organization—individual, dyadic, group, and organizational—we may investigate the way communication functions and how it is structured.

In their book Farace and colleagues address in some detail each of the four levels of organizing. We will go over the individual, dyad, and group briefly, highlighting some generalities. Since their discussion of the macronetwork is such an important contribution of this theory, we will spend more time on it.

The key concept related to individual communication is *load*. Communication load is the rate and complexity of information inputs to a person. Rate is the quantity of inputs such as messages or requests, while complexity is the number of factors that must be dealt with in processing the information. Two problem areas relate to load. *Underload* occurs when the flow of messages to a person falls below the person's ability to process them. *Overload* occurs when the load exceeds the person's capacity. While the notions of load, underload, and overload relate optimally to communication received by single individuals, these concepts also apply to all other levels, including dyadic, group, and organizational. Thus, for example, an entire organization might be underloaded or overloaded.

The key concept applicable to the dyad level of communication is *rules*. Members of dyads relate according to patterned expectations. Within organizations there are explicit and implicit rules for communicating. Such rules constitute the explicit or implicit communication policy of the organization. They tell one how to communicate, when to communicate, with whom to communicate, and what to communicate about. Some common rule

20. Ibid., p. 28.

topics include the following: who initiates interactions; how delays are treated; what topics are discussed and who selects them; how topic changes are handled; how outside interruptions are handled; how interactions are terminated; and how frequently communication occurs.

Through everyday contact among people in an organization, individuals in *groups* tend to work, interact, and communicate together. In fact, the structure of the overall organization depends on these groupings. Since people work together in different groups for different functions, different kinds of groups exist in an organization; a given individual simultaneously may be a member of several groups. Carrying this analysis one step further, we must realize that the organization consists of multiple structures. For example, structures may be built on task relations, power relations, liking, and others. We will return to this idea of organizational structure in a moment. First, let's look at some aspects of individual groups.

To begin with, we note that groups themselves tend to have internal structures. Farace and colleagues outline three types of structure. The first, the *communication structure* or *micronetwork*, is the pattern of interaction in the group. The question here is who communicates with whom within the group? The second kind of structure is the *power* structure. Here the question is who has what kind of power over whom? The third type of structure stressed in this theory is *leadership*. Leadership structure deals with role distribution in the group, specifically the distribution of roles related to interpersonal influence of group members.

We have outlined some key concepts related to the individual, dyad, and group levels of communication. We can move now to perhaps the most significant contribution of these authors, their notion of macronetwork.

A *macronetwork* is a repetitive pattern of information transmission among the groups in an organization. It represents the organization's overall structure. Several types of networks may be overlaid upon an organization, each providing a major function for the organization. Perhaps the most commonly understood network is the formal organization chart, which is the prescribed task network. In addition a number of informal networks may also exist. Any network consists of two fundamental parts: the members and their links.

Links are characterized by five properties. The first is *symmetry*, or the degree to which the members connected by a link interact on an equal basis. In a symmetrical relationship the members give and take information relatively equally. An asymmetric link is one way, with a distinct information sender and receiver. The second property of links is *strength*, which is a simple function of interaction frequency. Members who communicate more often have a stronger link, while those who communicate less often have a weaker link.

Reciprocity, the third property of links, is the extent to which members agree about their links. If one person believes that he or she often communicates with another, but the other denies it, the link is unreciprocated. The fourth property of links is the predominant *content* of the interaction. Is the communication primarily about work, social matters, or some other content area? By probing the content of links in a network, we can discern the network's overall function. The final property of links is *mode*. Here the question is: How is communication achieved? By what channel? Modes may be face-to-face conversations, group meetings, or communication via letter or telephone.

Thus a network consists of members linked together in various ways to share information. To adequately understand a network, we must look at additional factors. Organization members take different network roles. One role is the *isolate*. Before we get into the network itself, we are able to establish those who are not in the network. Isolates have no links with other network members. Of those who are linked to others, some cluster into *groups*. In network terminology a group is characterized by four criteria:

1. More than half of the group's communication is within the group.

2. Each person must be linked with all others in the group.

3. The group will not break apart with the exit of one person or the destruction of one link.

4. The group must have at least three members.

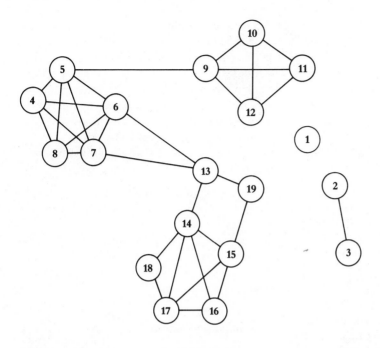

Groups:
Group 1—4, 5, 6, 7, 8
Group 2—9, 10, 11, 12
Group 3—14, 15, 16, 17, 18

Group Linkers:
Bridges—5, 9
Liaison—13
Other—19

Isolates:
True isolate—1
Isolated dyad—2, 3

Figure 12-1   Illustration of communication network roles.

From *Communicating and Organizing*, by Richard V. Farace, Peter R. Monge, and Hamish Russell (Figure 8-5). Copyright ©1977 by Addison-Wesley. Reprinted by permission of Random House, Inc.

These criteria, as you can see, make groups relatively stable structures.

A network thus is a series of groups and members who are interlinked. Two other roles are crucial in the network structure: liaison and bridge roles. *Bridges* are group members who also are linked to other groups. *Liaisons* are not members of any group, yet they link two or more groups. Figure 12-1 illustrates these aspects of the network structure.[21] This network concept provides a sensible way of looking at organizational structure and function *in terms of communication.*

21. Ibid., p. 192.
22. See, for example, Carl Weick, "Middle Range Theories of Social Systems," *Behavioral Science* 19 (1974): 358; Bengt Abrahamsson, *Bureaucracy or Participation: The Logic of Organization* (Beverly Hills: Sage Publications, 1977).

Criticism. The theory of Richard Farace and colleagues is valuable in showing the systemic nature of organizations and the role of communication as a structural and functional force. System theories, however, have been criticized.[22] (Chapter 3 summarizes some of the general objections to system theory.) The main complaint has been that system concepts are slippery and difficult to pin down when they are applied to particular events. System theory is so abstract that it can be used in numerous ways, making definition of actual systems very difficult. Two system theories may come up with quite different pictures of an organization. Even the theories presented above, though they share certain system principles, are rather inconsistent in what they outline as important in an organization.

System theories of organizations have been criticized specifically for their oversimplification of organizations. This objection is ironic because system theory is touted for its supposed ability to deal with a wide variety of variables in an organism. The problem is twofold. First, system theories tend to exaggerate the system claims in regard to an organization, ignoring aspects of the organization that are not systemlike. Second, along a similar vein, certain variables are downplayed because they do not fit well into the system paradigm. Carl Weick, himself a system theorist (see below), calls for a tempered approach that would address questions such as the following:

> When will a set of related entities—the standard definition of a system—act like a system and when will they not; what conditions tighten and loosen interdependencies; what conditions freeze or extend the range of values a variable will take; what conditions diffuse or intensify boundaries?[23]

The basic problem is that system approaches rarely are specific enough to explain or to predict individual variation. Consequently they are not often falsifiable. Most philosophers of science agree that the validity of a theory that is not falsifiable can never really be known and that such theories therefore should be rejected as inadequate. For example, both theories summarized in this section downplay the individual human as an important factor in organizational functioning. The interactional structure is emphasized over the needs of the individual. (This quality is in part a reaction against the hyperbole of the human relations school about the role of human needs.)

Another criticism is that these theories are ahistorical, ignoring the developmental course of organizations. The theories also de-emphasize the role of power in the organization, suggesting that system outcomes are a natural result of the mechanism of interactional structure and not of the influence of individuals and groups.

Unobtrusive Control and Identification

So far, Chapter 12 has dealt with theories that explain how organizations accomplish their goals. The theories discussed in the previous two sections illustrate ways in which the organization is struc-

tured to meet certain functions. Here we look at one specific function—control—and how it is accomplished subtly through communication. This theory is the product of a program by Phillip Tompkins and George Cheney.[24] It integrates important existing theory into a fresh conceptualization of decision making in organizations.

Control is exerted in organizations in a variety of ways. Tompkins and Cheney outline four processes by which control is accomplished:

1. *simple control* or use of direct, open power
2. *technical control* or use of machinery and technology
3. *bureaucratic control* or use of organizational structure
4. *concertive control* or use of interpersonal relationships and teamwork.[25]

Concertive control is a central concept in this theory, as the authors explain:

> In the concertive organization, the explicitly written rules and regulations are largely replaced by the common understanding of values, objectives, and means of achievement, along with a deep appreciation for the organization's "mission." This we call—to modify a phrase in current use—the "soul of the new organization." Concertive organizations display simultaneous "loose" and "tight" properties . . . because members can be depended upon to act within a range of alternatives tied to implicit but highly motivating core values.[26]

Although the four types of control are normally found in various combinations within an organiza-

23. Weick, "Middle Range," p. 357.

24. Phillip K. Tompkins and George Cheney, "Account Analysis of Organizations: Decision Making and Identification," in *Communication and Organizations: An Interpretive Approach*, eds. Linda L. Putnam and Michael E. Pacanowsky (Beverly Hills: Sage Publications, 1983), pp. 123–46; Phillip K. Tompkins and George Cheney, "Communication and Unobtrusive Control in Contemporary Organizations," in *Organizational Communication: Traditional Themes and New Directions*, eds. Robert D. McPhee and Phillip K. Tompkins (Beverly Hills: Sage Publications, 1985), pp. 179—210.

25. Tompkins and Cheney base this conceptualization on the work of R. Edwards, "The Social Relations of Production at the Point of Production," in *Complex Organizations: Critical Perspectives*, eds. M. Zey-Ferrell and M. Aiken (Glenview, Ill.: Scott, Foresman, 1981).

26. Tompkins and Cheney, "Communication and Unobtrusive Control," p. 184.

tion, there is a trend away from simple, direct control toward the more subtle and complex form described as concertive. The theory of unobtrusive control deals primarily with the ways in which control is managed within the concertive system.

Following the classical work of Herbert Simon, Tompkins and Cheney show how control is accomplished by shaping the decisions made by organization members.[27] Simon believes that organizational decision making follows a syllogistic pattern. In other words, decision makers reason deductively from general premises, and choices are based on those premises. Decisions are therefore shaped by organizational premises, and control is exerted by inducing workers to accept these general premises. The premises are accepted because of incentives like wages and the authority of people with legitimate power (see Weber above).

This acceptance does not come automatically, however. Often conflict results from differences between employees' personal beliefs and the premises of the organization. Indeed, a goodly amount of industrial strife results from such differences. How, then, do organizations achieve concertive control in the face of potential conflict? The answer lies in communication and the organizational enthymeme.

The *enthymeme* is a rhetorical device used to involve audiences actively in the advocate's reasoning process. It was discovered and described by Aristotle over two thousand years ago.[28] Aristotle wrote that the syllogism is a reasoning device for drawing conclusions, but that the enthymeme is a "rhetorical syllogism" used for persuading audiences. In an enthymeme, one or more premises in a reasoning chain are left out, to be supplied by the audience. The audience is then expected to imagine particular conclusions based on these implicit premises. Sometimes the suppressed premises are widely accepted cultural values; other times they are inculcated by the advocate as part of the persuasion process.

For example, a speaker advocating the prohibition of offshore drilling might reason privately like this: (a) Offshore drilling will endanger the fragile coastal ecology; (b) coastal ecology is valuable and should be protected; (c) therefore, offshore drilling should be prohibited. In addressing a group of environmentalists, this speaker relies on the audience's acceptance of the second premise and works only to demonstrate the truth of the first. Once the environmentalists come to believe that drilling will hurt the environment, they will reason that it should be prohibited.

Enthymemes are used in all kinds of persuasion, but Tompkins and Cheney are especially interested in how they are used in organizations for unobtrusive control of decision making. These authors point out that when organization members display loyalty and behave "organizationally," they are essentially accepting key organizational premises. Often organizations directly sell their premises to employees through house organs, training programs, and the like. Other times, organizations employ a variety of incentives to induce employees to become loyal. In any case, once employees accept certain premises, their conclusions and decisions are controlled.

For example, one of the premises of many industrial firms is that obsolescence is positive because it maintains progress, sustains the market, and protects jobs. Once engineers buy this idea, they will opt for designs that include "planned obsolescence." Engineering supervisors and executives do not have to order engineers to plan obsolescence into their designs; the engineers do so automatically because they accept the basic organizational premise. One could argue also that the scientists working on the Strategic Defense Initiative are able to proceed with the project because they have accepted the organizational premise that SDI will save the world from a nuclear holocaust.

The acceptance of organizational premises is part of a process of *organizational identification*.[29] The

27. Herbert Simon, *Administrative Behavior* (New York: Free Press, 1976). See also Perrow, *Complex Organizations*.

28. Lane Cooper, *The Rhetoric of Aristotle* (New York: Meredith, 1932). See also Lloyd Bitzer, "Aristotle's Enthymeme Revisited," *Quarterly Journal of Speech* 45 (1959): 399–408; Jesse Delia, "The Logic Fallacy, Cognitive Theory, and the Enthymeme: A Search for the Foundations of Reasoned Discourse," *Quarterly Journal of Speech* 56 (1970): 140–48.

29. George Cheney, "The Rhetoric of Identification and the Study of Organizational Communication," *Quarterly Journal of Speech* 69 (1983): 143–58.

theorists rely largely on the work of Kenneth Burke here. (See our previous discussion of identification in Chapter 6.) Identification occurs when individuals become aware of their common ground. We identify with individuals with whom we share something in common; and the more two parties share, the more the potential identification between them. When employees identify with the organization, they are more likely to accept the organization's premises and make decisions that are consistent with organizational objectives. In fact, Tompkins and Cheney define organizational identification in terms of decision making: "A decision maker identifies with an organization when he or she desires to choose the alternative that best promotes the perceived interests of that organization."[30]

Identification is achieved through communication, and communicators often choose strategies that encourage increased identification. For example, Cheney examined samples of ten corporate house organs and discovered a variety of strategies aimed at increasing organizational identification.[31] The most common strategy was the *common ground technique*, which points out important things that are shared between the organization and the individual employee. Some of the following tactics were used to create common ground:

1. expression of concern for the individual
2. recognition of individual contributions
3. espousal of shared values
4. discussion of benefits and activities
5. praise by outsiders
6. testimonials by employees.

Another strategy was *identification by antithesis*, which rallies employees to unite against some common adversity. An example of this is reference to government regulation as the enemy of the corporation. A third strategy is the *assumed we*. This strategy involves statements that distinguish the company (as a "we") from nonorganizational forces (the "they"). (This strategy was not used very fre-

quently in the material examined in this study.) Finally, *unifying symbols* involve the use of objects that identify the group as a group. Logos and trademarks are good examples.

This theory is fresh and valuable. While it is well integrated with important standard theories of organizational decision making, it still advances those ideas. In addition, it brings insights from rhetoric into a field that badly needs outside perspectives. This advantage not only provides significant new perspectives for organizational theory, but it helps to usefully combine divergent areas of the communication field. The theory is pragmatically helpful, and at the same time enables interpreters and critics to uncover implicit organizational values and premises not normally available for inspection. It thereby paves the way for a necessary and significant critique of organizational communication. The theory seems to have much heuristic value, and, in fact, has already generated a good deal of research.[32]

As a neophyte theory, this work remains at a fairly abstract level, presenting a major idea without specific insights into the processes and mechanisms by which organizational identification and enthymematic reason proceed within organizations. As these researchers examine more organizations with their scheme, lower-level understandings will emerge.

We turn now to a second category of organizational communication theory—human relations. The human relations movement in organizations constitutes a major critique of the entire structural-functional approach.

Communication and Human Relations

For the most part, structural and functional theories of organizations emphasize productivity and task accomplishment. Human factors are re-

---

30. Tompkins and Cheney, "Communication and Unobtrusive Control," p. 194.

31. Cheney, "Rhetoric."

32. Tompkins and Cheney summarize the research on the theory in "Communication and Unobtrusive Control," pp. 198–203.

garded as variables in a broader network of concerns. In large measure, the human relations movement was a reaction to and critique of the classical perspective.

One of the most vocal critics is Chris Argyris, who maintains that traditional organization theory and practice is dehumanizing.[33] The relationship between the person and the organization involves what Argyris calls "the basic dilemma between the needs of individuals aspiring for psychological success and self-esteem and the demand of the pyramidal structure."[34] The traditional organizational strategies to get the job done defeat individual growth. To make matters worse, the pattern is cyclical. As the individual self is suppressed, people are forced to take on organizational values, which deepens the problem. In Argyris's words, while technical competence is high, interpersonal competence is reduced.

Charles Perrow describes two general branches in the human relations movement.[35] The first deals primarily with leadership in organizations. The thesis of the leadership school is that leadership facilitates morale, which in turn leads to increased productivity. One of the most important manifestations of this branch is leadership training and T-groups (training groups). The second branch of the human relations movement is more general, dealing with organizational climate as a whole. Again, productivity and worker welfare are stressed. Etzioni points out that "above all, the Human Relations School . . . emphasized the role of communication, participation, and leadership."[36]

The basic tenets of human relations include the following: First, productivity is determined by social norms, not physiological factors. Second, noneconomic rewards are all important in motivating workers. Third, workers usually react as group members rather than individuals. Fourth, leadership is extremely important and involves both formal and informal aspects. Fifth, human relationists stress communication as the most important facilitator of shared decision making.[37]

Likert's Four Systems

Perhaps the most detailed theory of human relations, and surely the most explanatory, is that of Rensis Likert.[38] This rather elaborate theory can be found in *New Patterns of Management* and, more recently, in *The Human Organization*.[39] Likert outlines three broad groups of organizational variables. *Causal variables* are those that can be changed or altered. In this sense they may be considered as the independent variables in the model. *Intervening variables* are those that lead to the results of the causal manipulations. They reflect the general internal state and health of the organization. The *end-result variables*, the dependent variables or outputs, reflect organizational achievement.

An organization can function at any point along a continuum of four systems. System 1, at the extreme of the continuum, is the *exploitative-authoritative* system. Under this system the executive manages with an iron hand. Decisions are made by the executive, with no use of feedback. System 2, or *benevolent-authoritative* leadership, is similar to system 1, except that the manager is sensitive to the needs of the worker. Moving farther along the continuum, we come to system 3, which is *consultative* in nature. The authority figures still maintain control, but they seek consultation from below. At the other extreme of the spectrum, system 4 management or *participative* management, allows the worker to participate fully in decision making. System 4 leads to high performance and an increased sense of responsibility and motivation. These relationships are illustrated in Figures 12-2 and 12-3.[40]

Obviously communication is included throughout Likert's model. However, Likert especially

33. Chris Argyris, *Personality and Organization: The Conflict Between System and the Individual* (New York: Harper & Brothers, 1957); *Integrating the Individual and the Organization* (New York: John Wiley, 1964).

34. Argyris, *Integrating*, p. 58.

35. Perrow, *Complex Organizations*, p. 97.

36. Etzioni, *Modern Organizations*, p. 32.

37. Ibid., p. 38.

38. Perrow, *Complex Organizations*.

39. Rensis Likert, *New Patterns of Management* (New York: McGraw-Hill, 1961); Rensis Likert, *The Human Organization* (New York: McGraw-Hill, 1967).

40. Likert, *Human Organization*, pp. 76–137.

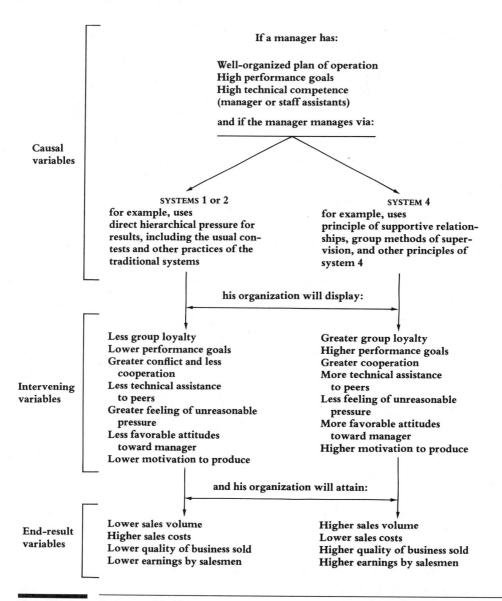

If a manager has:

Well-organized plan of operation
High performance goals
High technical competence
(manager or staff assistants)

and if the manager manages via:

Causal variables

SYSTEMS 1 or 2
for example, uses
direct hierarchical pressure for
results, including the usual con-
tests and other practices of the
traditional systems

SYSTEM 4
for example, uses
principle of supportive relationships, group methods of super-
vision, and other principles of
system 4

his organization will display:

Intervening variables

Less group loyalty
Lower performance goals
Greater conflict and less
  cooperation
Less technical assistance
  to peers
Greater feeling of unreasonable
  pressure
Less favorable attitudes
  toward manager
Lower motivation to produce

Greater group loyalty
Higher performance goals
Greater cooperation
More technical assistance
  to peers
Less feeling of unreasonable
  pressure
More favorable attitudes
  toward manager
Higher motivation to produce

and his organization will attain:

End-result variables

Lower sales volume
Higher sales costs
Lower quality of business sold
Lower earnings by salesmen

Higher sales volume
Lower sales costs
Higher quality of business sold
Higher earnings by salesmen

Figure 12-2   Sequence of developments in a well-organized enterprise, as affected by use of system 1 or 2 or system 4.

From "New Patterns in Sales Management," in *Changing Perspectives in Marketing Management*, ed. Martin Warshaw. Copyright © 1962 by The University of Michigan. Reprinted by permission of the publisher.

considers communication to be an intervening variable, related to the interaction-influence system and a subpart of the category of attitudinal, motivational, and perceptual variables. The rela-

tionship of communication variables with management systems is illustrated in Table 12-1.[41]

41. Ibid., pp. 16–19.

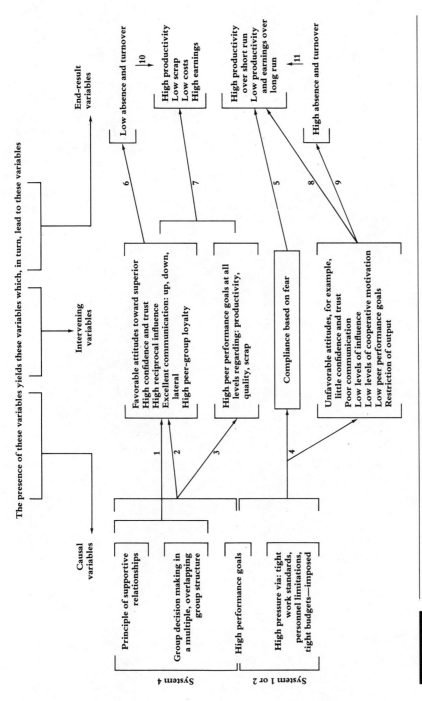

Figure 12-3 Simplified diagram of relationships among variables for system 1 or 2 and system 4 operations.

From *The Human Organization*, by Rensis Likert. Copyright © 1967 by McGraw-Hill. Reprinted by permission of the publisher.

Table 12-1   Organizational and Performance Characteristics of Different Management Systems Based on a Comparative Analysis

Operating characteristics	System of organization			
	Authoritative		Participative	
	Exploitative authoritative	Benevolent authoritative	Consultative	Participative group
a. Amount of interaction and communication aimed at achieving organization's objectives	Very little	Little	Quite a bit	Much with both individuals and groups
b. Direction of information flow	Downward	Mostly downward	Down and up	Down, up, and with peers
c. Downward communication				
1. Where initiated	At top of organization or to implement top directive	Primarily at top or patterned on communication from top	Patterned on communication from top but with some initiative at lower levels	Initiated at all levels
2. Extent to which communications are accepted by subordinates	Viewed with great suspicion	May or may not be viewed with suspicion	Often accepted but at times viewed with suspicion. May or may not be openly questioned	Generally accepted, but if not, openly and candidly questioned
d. Upward communication				
1. Adequacy of upward communication via line organization	Very little	Limited	Some	A great deal
2. Subordinates' feeling of responsibility for initiating accurate upward communication	None at all	Relatively little, usually communicates "filtered" information but only when requested. May "yes" the boss	Some to moderate degree of responsibility to initiate accurate upward communication	Considerable responsibility felt and much initiative. Group communicates all relevant information
3. Forces leading to accurate or distorted information	Powerful forces to distort information and deceive superiors	Occasionally forces to distort; also forces for honest communication	Some forces to distort along with many forces to communicate accurately	Virtually no forces to distort and powerful forces to communicate accurately

	System 1	System 2	System 3	System 4
4. Accuracy of upward communication via line	Tends to be inaccurate	Information that boss wants to hear flows; other information is restricted and filtered	Information that boss wants to hear flows, other information may be limited or cautiously given	Accurate
5. Need for supplementary upward communication system	Need to supplement upward communication by spy system, suggestion system, or some similar devices	Upward communication often supplemented by suggestion system and similar devices	Slight need for supplementary system; suggestion system may be used	No need for any supplementary system
e. Sideward communication, its adequacy and accuracy	Usually poor because of competition between peers and corresponding hostility	Fairly poor because of competition between peers	Fair to good	Good to excellent
f. Psychological closeness of superiors to subordinates (that is, how well does superior know and understand problems faced by subordinates?)	Far apart	Can be moderately close if proper roles are kept	Fairly close	Usually very close
1. Accuracy of perceptions by superiors and subordinates	Often in error	Often in error on some points	Moderately accurate	Usually quite accurate

From *The Human Organization*, by Rensis Likert. Copyright © 1967 by McGraw-Hill Book Company. Reprinted by permission of the publisher.

Criticism

The human relations movement became popular in the 1940s and 1950s, generating a great deal of both ideological support and research data. The movement helped practitioners and scholars understand that human beings have needs and values related to organizational functioning and that communication and group process are important aspects of organizational life. It has provided thought on the nature of organizational communication, group dynamics, and leadership, and it has produced a useful set of guidelines for improving interpersonal communication in organizations.

Human relations was severely criticized almost from its beginning.[42] Its problems are primarily attributable to its extreme position and simplistic view that high morale improves productivity. The correlations claimed to exist between human relations factors and organizational effectiveness have, for the most part, failed the test of empirical study. In many cases the correlations have not been found in research, and where they do appear, serious methodological objections have been raised. One of the biggest apparent weaknesses of human relations theories is that they ignore many nonhuman variables that affect the outcome of an organization. Such theories often fail to take into account the relationships among various structural and functional elements of organizational output.

Since much of human relations is based on the humanistic school of psychology, it shares many faults of the latter (see Chapter 9). For instance human relations envisions an organization in which conflict is minimal, suggesting that anything that might frustrate workers will stifle creativity and understanding. Yet we know that the natural conflict that occurs in groups and organizations can be functional, both for individual human growth and for organizational vigor, as Janis shows (Chapter 11).

Human relations, like its cousin humanistic psychology, is prescriptive in approach and does not provide much explanation of ongoing organizational processes as they occur in natural organizations. It has values for teaching and for developing certain practical strategies, but it has little theoretical value in the sense of helping us understand how and why individuals organize. Ironically, the ideology of the right, classical structural theory, and the ideology of the left, human relations, share this fault: Each calls for particular kinds of practices to improve organizational functioning without providing a basis for understanding how organizations operate.

Communication and the Process of Organizing

One of the most significant ideas in the organizational communication literature is that communication is not merely something that organization members do, nor is it a tool for accomplishing things. Rather, communication is itself the very process of organizing. We explore this idea in the following section. Two theories are apropos: the theory of organizing by Carl Weick and Marshall Scott Poole and Robert D. McPhee's theory of structuration in organizations.

Communication and Enactment

One of the most influential theories of organizational communication is that of Carl Weick.[43] Weick's theory of organizing is significant in the communication field because it uses communication as a basis for human organizing and because it provides a rationale for understanding how people organize. In short, Weick's theory is one of the few truly organizational *communication* theories. Since its inception in 1969, it has received wide acclaim and some criticism as well.

Weick sees organizations not as structures or entities but as activities. It is more proper to speak of *organizing* than of *organizations*, because organizations are something that people accomplish, via a process that must be constantly reenacted. Thus,

---

42. For a comprehensive critique, see Perrow, *Complex Organizations*.

43. Carl Weick, *The Social Psychology of Organizing* (Reading, Mass.: Addison-Wesley, 1969).

when people do what they do, their activities create organization, so that organizing is continual.

The essence of any organization is that people are acting in such a way that their behaviors are *interlocked*; one person's behavior is contingent on another's. All organizing activities consist of interlocked behaviors. A fundamental quality of interlocking is that communication takes place among the people in the organization. Thus organizing activities consist of *double interacts*. Remember from Chapter 11 that an *act* is a statement of communicative behavior of one individual, an *interact* involves an act followed by a response, and a *double interact* consists of an act followed by a response and then an adjustment or follow-up act by the first person. Weick believes that all organizing activities are double interacts. Consider an executive and a secretary as an example. The executive asks the secretary to undertake an activity (act); the secretary then asks for clarification (interact); and the executive explains (double interact). Or the executive asks the secretary a favor (act), and the secretary follows through (interact), after which the executive responds with a thank you (double interact). Simple? Yes, but these activities are exactly the kind that Weick believes organizations are built on.

Organizing activities fulfill the function of reducing the equivocality of information received from the environment. Equivocality is ambiguity or uncertainty. All information from the environment, according to Weick, is equivocal; organizing activities are instituted by members of the organization to make the information unequivocal. Of course equivocality is a matter of degree, and the organizing is done to reduce equivocality in the direction of unequivocality.

Let's return to the example of the executive again. Suppose the executive receives a directive from the firm's president to solve a problem of plant safety. What is the nature of this problem, and how should the executive go about solving it? The answers to these questions are not clear, inasmuch as the problem can be defined and solved in a number of ways. In other words the executive is faced with equivocal information.

Weick is saying that organizing activities, which consist of double interacts, interlocked behavior, or communication, are designed to make such situations clearer. Of course the importance of information and the degree of equivocality in the information vary. The executive's asking the secretary a favor is an example of an insignificant piece of information, whose equivocality is low; but the example of solving safety problems illustrates a more significant problem that has a great deal of equivocality. This difference is not important to Weick. What is important is that organizing is accomplished through processes that are developed to deal with equivocal information. The exact nature of that information is irrelevant to the fact that the organization members engage in the processes to maintain organization. Interaction serves to achieve common meanings among group members, which is the mechanism by which equivocality is reduced.

We have discussed how individuals interact to deal with equivocal information from the environment. But what is the environment? Traditional theories of organization imply that the environment is a known entity outside the organization. This dualistic notion pits the organization against the environment as if each were somehow preexistent. Weick has a substantially different idea of environment. Organizers are always surrounded by a mix of stimuli to which they must respond, but the "environment" has no meaning apart from what the individual makes of it. In other words the environment is a product of the person, not something outside the person. What makes the environment salient for the individual is the person's attention to particular aspects of the stimuli. People are selective in what they attend to in any situation, and what is attended to at any moment is the environment. Indeed, information from the environment is equivocal precisely because different people attend to different aspects of it. The interaction process (interlocking) is the mechanism by which the individuals in the group reduce this equivocality. Hence, environments are not preexistent; they are *enacted* by the people in the organization. People are continually reenacting their environments, depending on their attitudes, values, and experiences of the moment.

For example, the executive of our example is faced with a situation in which interpretation is necessary. Immediately, he or she will attend to certain aspects of the "safety problem." In enlisting the aid of others, for example the secretary, the executive is beginning processes that will enable the group to treat the safety problem as its environment of the moment. To deal with this equivocal environment, group members make proposals (acts) to which others respond (interacts) so that the proposers can refine their initial proposals (double interacts). For example, the executive may ask the secretary to check the files for accident records. This constitutes a proposal, an attempt to reduce the equivocality. The secretary may comply, pulling the appropriate file, so that the executive can be assured that the company knows the extent of the safety problem. Here the sequence of the double interact would be as follows: request file (act), provide file (interact), take file and review it (double interact). Notice how the participants' behaviors are interlocked. The secretary's activity of the moment depends on the executive's request, and the executive's subsequent behavior depends on the secretary's compliance.

Weick views organizing as an evolutionary process that relies on a series of three major processes: enactment, selection, and retention. *Enactment* is the definition of the situation or the registering of equivocal information from outside. Enactment is a process of attending to stimuli in such a way as to acknowledge that equivocality exists. The mere acceptance of certain aspects of the environment removes some equivocality. Accepting the task of dealing with safety problems narrows the field for the executive so that some uncertainty already is removed.

The second process is *selection*. Selection is a process that enables the group to admit certain aspects of information and reject others. It narrows the field, eliminating alternatives with which the organization does not wish to deal. This process therefore removes even more equivocality from the initial information. For example, in dealing with

the safety problem, the organization may decide to consider only the aspects of safety that management can control, eliminating all factors that relate to worker predispositions.

The third process of organizing is *retention*. Here further equivocality is removed by decision about what aspects of the initial information will be saved for future use. Retained information is integrated into the existing body of information on which the organization operates. To continue our example, the safety group may decide to deal with safety problems that are caused strictly by machinery, rejecting all other kinds of problems. As you can see, the problem has become much less ambiguous; it has, in Weick's parlance, moved from equivocality toward unequivocality.

After retention occurs, organization members face a choice point. They must make two kinds of decisions. The first is whether to reenact the environment in some way. Here they address the question: Should we (or I) attend to some aspect of the environment that was rejected before? The executive may decide, for example, to have the group go back and check out the rate of accidents that are not related to machinery. The second kind of choice is whether to modify one's behavior or actions. Here the question is: Should I take a different action than I did before? For example, the executive may decide that solutions for both machinery and nonmachinery accidents should be developed.

So far this summary may lead you to believe that organizations move from one process of organizing to another in lockstep fashion: enactment, selection, retention, choice. Such is not the case. Individual subgroups in the organization are continually working on activities in all of these processes for different aspects of the environment. Although certain segments of the organization may specialize in one or more of the organizing processes, nearly everybody undertakes all of them in one form or another most of the time. Such is the essence of organizing.

Knowing the evolutionary stages of organizing helps us see how organizing occurs on a general scale, but this knowledge does not provide an explanation for how equivocality is removed from the information. To address this problem, Weick outlines two elements that occur within each of the three organizing processes. These are assembly rules and interlocked behavior cycles. *Assembly rules* guide the choice of routines that will be used to accomplish the process being conducted (enactment, selection, or retention). Rules are sets of criteria on which organizers decide what to do to reduce equivocality. The question answered by assembly rules is this: Out of all the possible behavior cycles in this organization, which shall we use now? For example, in the selection process the executive might invoke the assembly rule that "two heads are better than one" and on this basis call a meeting of plant engineers. *Behavior cycles* are sets of interlocked behaviors that enable the group to come to an understanding about which meanings should be included and which rejected. Thus the safety meeting called by the executive would enable interested individuals to discuss the safety problem and decide how to proceed in defining and solving it. Assembly rules and behavior cycles are a natural part of each of the three processes of organizing. Remember that a behavior cycle consists of double interacts on the part of participating group members.

Now we have completed the basic elements of Weick's model. They are environment, equivocality, enactment, selection, retention, choices, assembly rules, behavior cycles, and equivocality removed. Weick envisions these elements working together in a system, each element related to the others.

As an abstract theory, Weick's model is not designed to explain the substance of activity that one might encounter in an organization; instead it presents a general way in which all organizing occurs. This theory is basically a system theory and shares all of the problems and benefits of system theories outlined in the previous section. We turn now to another theory of organizing that emphasizes the communication process.

Structuration in Organizations

In Chapter 11 we examined the theory of structuration and Poole and McPhee's application of this theory to group decision making. These researchers have also extended their application into the realm of organizational communication.[44]

Recall that the theory of structuration, which is attributable primarily to the work of sociologist Anthony Giddens, deals with the ways in which actions bring about unintended consequences, which in turn form social systems that affect future actions. The circle of actions and systems constitute a mechanism by which socio-cultural resources are produced and reproduced.[45] (You may wish to review this theory from Chapter 11 at this point.)

Organizations, like any social structure, are produced through the actions and interactions among individuals. As people rely on organizational resources such as roles, norms, and rules to guide their actions, they not only accomplish individual and organizational goals, but they also reproduce the organizational system itself. This process is what Weick calls enactment (see the above section). Poole and McPhee have applied this idea to two aspects of organizational communication—structure and climate.

In an essay on the subject, McPhee recognizes the importance of organizational structure: "I would say that Structure is a defining characteristic of an organization—it is what brings about or makes possible that quality of atmosphere, that sustained, routine purposiveness that distinguishes work in an organization from activities in a group, a mob, a society, and so forth."[46] As we saw in the

---

44. Marshall Scott Poole and Robert D. McPhee, "A Structural Analysis of Organizational Climate," in *Communication and Organizations: An Interpretive Approach*, eds. Linda L. Putnam and Michael E. Pacanowsky (Beverly Hills: Sage Publications, 1983), pp. 195–220; Marshall Scott Poole, "Communication and Organizational Climates: Review, Critique, and a New Perspective," in *Organizational Communication: Traditional Themes and New Directions*, eds. Robert D. McPhee and Phillip K. Tompkins (Beverly Hills: Sage Publications, 1985), pp. 79–108; Robert D. McPhee, "Formal Structure and Organizational Communication," in *Organizational Communication: Traditional Themes and New Directions*, eds. Robert D. McPhee and Phillip K. Tompkins (Beverly Hills: Sage Publications, 1985), pp. 149–78.

45. Anthony Giddens, *Central Problems in Social Theory* (Berkeley: University of California Press, 1979); *Profiles and Critiques in Social Theory* (Berkeley: University of California Press, 1982).

46. McPhee, "Formal Structure," p. 150.

first segment of this chapter, organizational structure provides the form necessary to accomplish a variety of functions. Structure is both a manifestation of and a product of communication in the organization. Consequently, McPhee refers to structure as "Structure-communication."

The formal structure of an organization as announced in employee manuals, organization charts, and policies and procedures, is really two types of communication. First, it is an *indirect* way of telling employees about the organization—its values, procedures, and methods. Second, it is a form of *metacommunication* (Chapter 10) in which the organization addresses its own communication patterns directly.

Organizational structure is created when individuals communicate with others through certain channels. Such communication occurs in three metaphorical *sites* or centers of structuration.[47] The first is the site of *conception*. This includes all of those episodes of organizational life in which people make decisions and choices that limit what can happen within the organization. For example, when the curriculum committee of a university decides that a new college of creative arts will be established, the future lines of communication within the college will be "structured" by this decision.

The second site of organizational structuration is *implementation*, which is the formal codification and announcement of decisions and choices. Once the decision is made to establish the new college, the provost may send out a formal memorandum to the faculty and staff announcing the change. That formal announcement itself will be instrumental in shaping the structure of the organization in the future.

Finally, structuration occurs in the site of *reception*, as organizational members act in accordance with the organizational decisions. Thus, after the decision to establish a new college, a dean will be recruited, certain department heads will meet with the new dean, and faculty lines of communication will change. In other words, the employees of the organization must live with the decision.

Although anyone in an organization may from time to time participate in communication at any or all of the three "sites," structuration tends to be specialized. Top management usually is involved in conceptual communication, various staff personnel perform the job of implementation, and the general workforce itself participates in reception. Of course, the communication activities at these three sites are often difficult and conflict-laden. Indeed, rarely is a new college established at a university without considerable disagreement and resistance at all three stages, and this is the case with major changes in any kind of organization. The communication patterns at the three sites may be complex and time consuming, and the outcome is very much affected by the skill of the people involved.

The second area in which Poole and McPhee have applied structurationist thinking is *organizational climate*.[48] Actually, climate has been a heavily researched topic in organizational communication.[49] Traditionally, climate has been viewed as one of the key variables affecting communication and the subsequent productivity and satisfaction of employees. Poole summarizes the research on climate in these terms:

1. Climate is a molar construct representing collective descriptions of an organization or subunit.

2. Climate serves as a frame of reference for member activity and therefore shapes members' expectancies, attitudes, and behaviors; through these effects it influences organizational outcomes such as performance, satisfaction, and morale.

3. Climates arise from and are sustained by

---

47. Robert D. McPhee, "Organizational Communication: A Structurational Exemplar," in *Re-thinking Communication: Vol. 2, Paradigm Exemplars*, eds. B. Dervin, L. Grossberg, B. O'Keefe, and E. Wartella (Beverly Hills: Sage Publications, in press).

48. Poole, "Communication and Organizational Climates"; Poole and McPhee, "Structurational Analysis."

49. This work is summarized in Poole, "Communication and Organizational Climates," pp. 79–97.

organizational or unit practices. Structural and contextual factors influence climates, but their effects are mediated by organizational practices and processes.

4. An organization may have several climates, corresponding to the major practices it exhibits. Because practices may vary from organization to organization, organizations are likely to have distinct and individualized climates.[50]

Poole and McPhee define climate structurationally as "a collective attitude, continually produced and reproduced by members' interaction."[51] In other words, a climate is not an objective "variable" that affects the organization; nor is it an individual's perception of the organization. Rather, climate is an *intersubjective phenomenon*; it arises out of the interaction among those who affiliate with the organization. Climate is a product of structuration: It is both a medium and an outcome of interaction.[52]

Poole sees climate as a hierarchy of three strata. The first is a *concept pool*, or a set of basic terms that members use to define and describe the organization. The second is a *kernel climate*, or basic, highly abstract shared conception of the atmosphere of the organization. Finally, the *particular climate* consists of groups' translations of the kernel climate into more concrete terms affecting their particular part of an organization. While the kernel climate permeates the entire organization, particular climates may vary from one segment of the organization to another.

The three layers in the hierarchy are linearly related. The concepts are the key to understanding what is going on in the organization. From these basic understandings, the kernel climate arises. Then subgroups translate these general principles into specific climate elements, which in turn affect the thinking, feeling, and behavior of the individuals. An example of this process is found in a study of a consulting firm.[53] The firm consisted of two generations of employees—a group that had been with the firm a relatively long time and a group of more recent employees. The two groups seemed to experience different climates. Both groups shared a common set of concepts, including, for example, profit, "first generation and second generation," specialist and generalist, commitment, creative routines, structure, bureaucracy, and "Renaissance Men." From these core concepts four key elements of a kernel climate emerged:

1. "The firm has a rigid formal structure that is often constraining."
2. "Contribution to profits is very important."
3. "Creative work is valued over routine work."
4. "Commitment of employees is important."

These four elements of the kernel climate were translated differently into the particular climates of the two groups. The first generation employees believed that "pressure is manageable, and that there is room for growth." The second generation employees, however, believed that "pressure hinders performance and that there is little room for growth." This example is illustrated in Figure 12-4.[54]

How do the elements of climate develop in an organization? We know already from a structurational perspective that the climate is produced by the practices of organizational members; and, in turn, climate affects and constrains those practices. Thus climate is not static, but constantly in the process of development. Three interacting factors enter into this developmental process.

The first is the structure of the organization itself. Since structure limits the kinds of interactions and practices that can be engaged in, it limits the kind of climate that can result from these interactions

50. Poole, "Communication and Organizational Climates," p. 96.

51. Poole and McPhee, "Structurational Analysis," p. 213.

52. For a contrast of the structurational approach to climate with traditional approaches, see Poole and McPhee, "Structurational Analysis."

53. This model of climate is based on a reinterpretation of a case study by H. Johnson. "A New Conceptualization of Source of Organizational Climate," *Administrative Science Quarterly* 3 (1976): 275–92.

54. Poole, "Communication and Organizational Climates," p. 98.

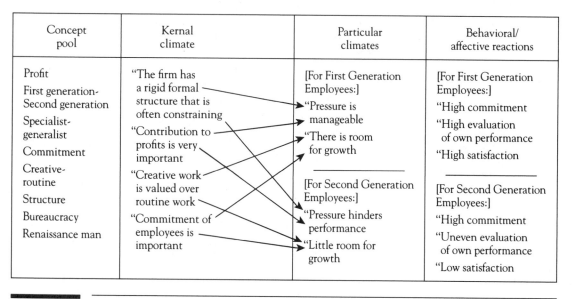

Concept pool	Kernal climate	Particular climates	Behavioral/ affective reactions
Profit First generation- Second generation Specialist- generalist Commitment Creative- routine Structure Bureaucracy Renaissance man	"The firm has a rigid formal structure that is often constraining "Contribution to profits is very important "Creative work is valued over routine work "Commitment of employees is important	[For First Generation Employees:] "Pressure is manageable "There is room for growth ――――――― [For Second Generation Employees:] "Pressure hinders performance "Little room for growth	[For First Generation Employees:] "High commitment "High evaluation of own performance "High satisfaction ――――――― [For Second Generation Employees:] "High commitment "Uneven evaluation of own performance "Low satisfaction

Figure 12-4   Schematic of climate structure.

and practices. For example, if the organization is highly segmented with strong differentiation among people and departments, individuals will have a limited pool of coworkers with whom they can communicate, which increases the chance of a "restrained" climate. The second factor affecting climate is various "climate-producing apparatuses." These are mechanisms designed to affect employee perceptions and performance, such as newsletters, training programs, and the like. The third factor is member characteristics, their skills and knowledge. For example, if employees are sufficiently intelligent and reflective, they may challenge existing authority and "see through" apparatuses. Member characteristics also include the degree of agreement or coordination within work groups.

Both organizational climate and structure, then, are a manifestation of the structuration process. This theory nicely extends Poole and McPhee's ideas about structuration in groups into the organizational climate. Like their group work, the theory shows much potential for providing a way of looking at group and organizational experience.

Structuration is especially useful in the theory of organizations because it can integrate the otherwise disparate explanations of human action in organizations. On the one hand, ideas of structural causation show the ways in which the resources of the system constrain and affect the behavior of participants. On the other hand, ideas of practical action show how individuals act to accomplish goals in organizations. Both of these views are appropriate within a structurational frame.

Communication and Organizational Culture

Most of the theories presented thus far in the chapter regard organizations as task structures. In this final section, we look at organizations in a rather different way: Organizations are cultures. Organizations not only enable the achievement of goals, but they are a way of life for their members. In other words, an organization has a shared reality that distinguishes it from other cultures. Gareth Morgan explains:

> Shared meaning, shared understanding, and shared sense making are all different ways of describing culture. In talking about culture we are really talking about a process of reality construction that allows people to see and understand particular events, actions, objects, utterances, or situations in distinctive ways. These patterns of understanding also provide a basis for making one's own behavior sensible and meaningful.[55]

The reality of the organizational culture is produced in the interactions and practices of the members. Task-oriented actions not only achieve immediate objectives, but they also create or reinforce certain ways of understanding experience within the organization. But culture is created in other ways in addition to the "official" task behaviors of employees. Indeed, even the most mundane activities in the organization enter into the culture-producing process. Let us take a closer look at the ways in which communication practices in an organization establish and reflect its culture.

Organizational Culture as Performance

Michael Pacanowsky and Nick O'Donnell-Trujillo are leaders in the organizational culture movement. These theorists ask an alternative set of questions about organizations, questions that reveal not their managerial, task-accomplishing functions, but their cultural elements. Pacanowsky and O'Donnell-Trujillo present a communication-centered theory of organizational culture, explaining the difference between their approach and traditional methods in these terms:

> We believe that an intriguing thing about communication is the way in which it creates and constitutes the taken-for-granted reality of the world. Social activity, as we see it, is primarily the communicative accomplishment of interrelated actions. So whereas the underlying motive of traditional research is coming to an understanding of how to make organizations work better, the underlying motive of the organiza-

tional culture approach is coming to understand how organizational life is accomplished communicatively. To understand how organizational life is brought into being, we cannot let ourselves be limited to asking questions that require some implicit or explicit link to organizational productivity for their legitimacy.[56]

Since culture is sense making, the organizational culture approach must look for indicators of meaning in an organization. What do organization members use to create and display their understanding of events within the organization? There are many indicators, including relevant constructs and related vocabulary, perceived facts, practices or activities, metaphors, stories, and rites and rituals. All of these are "performances" in that they "display" the lived experience of the group. However, performances, like stage plays, are not only displays, but accomplishments; they bring something about—the reality of the culture: ". . . performance brings the significance or meaning of some structural form—be it symbol, story, metaphor, ideology, or saga—into being."[57] Following the lead of Victor Turner, these authors note that "performances are those very actions by which members constitute and reveal their culture to themselves and others."[58]

Pacanowsky and O'Donnell-Trujillo outline four characteristics of communication performances. First, they are interactional, more like dialogues than soliloquies. They are social actions, not solitary ones. Organizational performances are something people participate in together. Second, performances are contextual. They cannot be viewed as independent acts, but are always embedded in a larger frame of activity. Context consists of the who, where, and when of the action. The performance both reflects and produces its context. Third, performances are episodes. They are events with a beginning and an end, and the performers

---

55. Gareth Morgan, *Images of Organization* (Beverly Hills: Sage Publications, 1986), p. 128.

56. Michael E. Pacanowsky and Nick O'Donnell-Trujillo, "Communication and Organizational Cultures," *Western Journal of Speech Communication* 46 (1982): 121.

57. Michael E. Pacanowsky and Nick O'Donnell-Trujillo, "Organizational Communication as Cultural Performance," *Communication Monographs* 50 (1983): 129.

58. Pacanowksy and O'Donnell-Trujillo, "Organizational Communication," 131. See also Victor Turner, *Dramas, Fields, and Metaphors* (Ithaca: Cornell University Press, 1974).

can identify the episode and distinguish it from other episodes. Finally, performances are improvised. There is flexibility in how a communication episode is played out, and although the same performances may be given again and again, they are never repeated exactly the same way.

From the many types of organizational communication performance, the authors present a suggestive list. The first is *ritual*. A ritual is a performance that is repeated regularly. It is an act that groups come to rely on as familiar and routine. Rituals are especially important because they constantly renew our understandings of our common experience, and they lend legitimacy to what we are thinking, feeling, and doing. Here is an example:

> Each and every day, Lou Polito, owner and general manager of Lou Polito Dodge, opens *all* the company mail. On those occasions when he is "free," he personally delivers this mail to the appropriate divisions in the company. This is just his way of letting his people know that he is keeping in touch with what they are doing.[59]

This is an example of a *personal ritual*. Another type is a *task ritual*, which is a repeated activity that helps members do their jobs:

> When a Valley View patrolman stops a driver for some traffic violation, he launches into a conversational routine that involves a question-answer sequence. "May I see your driver's license please?" "Is this your correct address?" "May I see your registration please?" "Do you know why I stopped you?" "Do you know what the speed limit is on this street?" "Do you know how fast you were going?" "Do you want to see the reading on the radar gun?" Although the officer has been taught this routine at the Police Academy as a way of being polite and professional, the Valley View police use it in order to see how the driver responds, to "size him up," and decide whether or not to give him any "breaks" in issuing a citation or warning.[60]

Social rituals are seen as distinctly not task-related, yet they are important performances within organizations. The after-work drink is a good example: "Every Friday afternoon, the foremen from Steele

Manufacturing go to the 'Pub,' one of the few places in their part of town that serves beer. The conversations are often filled with 'shop talk' but can range from sports . . . to politics . . ."[61] Finally, *organizational rituals* are those in which an entire work group participate with some regularity:

> Each year, the department of communication has its annual picnic, highlighted by the traditional softball game which pits the graduate students against the faculty. Competition is typically fierce; but alas for the graduate nine, they have had but one win in the last five years.[62]

The second category of performances is what the authors call *passion*. Here workers put on performances that make otherwise dull and routine duties interesting or passionate. Perhaps the most common way in which this is done is by *storytelling*. Almost everybody tells stories about their work, and the telling is often lively and dramatic. Further, these stories are told over and over, and people often enjoy telling each other the same stories again and again. We tell stories about ourselves (personal stories), about other people (collegial stories), or about the organization (corporate stories). Another way in which drama is created on the job is *passionate repartee*, which consists of dramatic interactions and the use of lively language: "The Valley View police, for example, do not deal with 'civilians,' but rather with 'assholes,' 'dirtbags,' 'creeps,' and 'maggots'—labels which serve as reminders that the 'negative element' is so much a part of the everyday experience of being a police officer."[63]

A third category of performances involves *sociality*. Such performances reinforce a common sense of propriety and make use of social rules within the organization. Courtesies and pleasantries are examples. *Sociabilities* are performances that create a group sense of identification and include things like joking, bitching, and "talking shop." Finally, *privacies* are sociality performances that communicate sensitivity and privacy. They include such things as confessing, consoling, and criticizing.

---

59. Pacanowsky and O'Donnell-Trujillo, "Organizational Communication," p. 135.
60. Ibid., p. 136.

61. Ibid., p. 137.
62. Ibid.
63. Ibid., p. 139.

A fourth category of performances involve *organizational politics*. These performances, which create and reinforce notions of power and influence, may include showing personal strength, cementing allies, and bargaining.

A fifth category is *enculturation*, or processes of "teaching" the culture to organizational members. We are always involved in enculturation throughout our careers in the organization, but certain performances are especially vital to this process. Orientation of newcomers is an example. On a less formal scale, "learning the ropes" consists of a series of performances in which individuals teach others how things are done. Although this can be accomplished by direct instruction ("That's how we do it here"), most often this kind of learning occurs when people metacommunicate or talk about things that happened in a way that helps other individuals learn how to interpret events. After dealing with a rowdy drunk, an older officer (Davis) helps a rookie (Benson) interpret what happened: Benson says he heard that Davis almost got in a fight with the drunk, and Davis replies, "Not really. I didn't give the guy a chance to get mad at me."

> We take Davis' interaction with Benson as a unique enculturation performance, a metacommunicative commentary that instructs Benson in how he should interpret the prior performance. This metacommunication informs the rookie that the prior exchange was not an endorsement of fighting but was backstage "play." And, as the rookie observes more instances of this backstage "tough" talk, he comes to understand it as "not real," but serious nonetheless.[64]

This list of cultural performances shows us how organizations are indeed cultures and some of the ways in which individuals create and display them. We turn now to a discussion of the processes by which culture is formed in organizations.

The Development of Culture and Conflict

John Van Maanen and Stephen Barley have presented a set of ideas on "the genesis, maintenance, and transmission" of organizational culture in what

they call "fragments of a theory."[65] The central question of this work is, Where do organizational cultures come from and how they are sustained? These theorists outline four "domains" that enter into the answer to this question.

The first domain is *ecological context*. This is the physical world, including location, the time and history, and social context within which the organization operates. This context constitutes "the primary catalyst for a culture's genesis."[66] The second domain affecting the development of culture is *differential interaction*. Individuals interact with one another in certain patterns, and as we saw earlier in the chapter, networks emerge. Networks determine in large measure what kind of culture will result. The third domain is *collective understanding* or common ways of interpreting events. This domain constitutes the "content" of the culture, as we saw above. The fourth domain consists of *individuals and their actions*. It is through the practices of individuals that the culture is sustained and changed.

These four domains constitute a model of organizational culture in which individuals interact with one another in certain patterns to create common meanings in a particular physical and social context. The outcome is a set of norms, rules, and codes that are used to understand and evaluate experience. The ecological context of the organization is its structure, which determines what people do, when they do these things, and where activities are performed. These structural constraints affect the second element—interaction patterns. Collective understandings are the direct outcome of patterned communication, and in turn, the collective understandings lead to certain organizational behaviors.

Of course it is unrealistic to think of a large organization as a single culture. In most cases, subcultures will emerge. Van Maanen and Barley define an organizational subculture as "a subset of an organization's members who interact regularly

---

64. Ibid., p. 145.

65. John Van Maanen and Stephen R. Barley, "Cultural Organization: Fragments of a Theory," in *Organizational Culture*, eds. Peter J. Frost, et al. (Beverly Hills: Sage Publications, 1985), pp. 31–54.
66. Ibid., p. 33.

with one another, identify themselves as a distinct group within the organization, share a set of problems commonly defined to be the problems of all, and routinely take action on the basis of collective understandings unique to the group."[67] (Imagine an organization as a complex set of Venn diagrams, or overlapping circles.) Several processes give rise to subcultures in organizations.

The first process is *segmentation* or the division of labor according to specialization. A company may have separate departments for engineering, manufacturing, and marketing. In addition, each of these divisions will break down into yet smaller subdivisions. Segmentation is a form of structure that largely determines who interacts with whom. *Importation* occurs when organizations bring in groups from outside, as is the case of a merger. Here at least two cultures are brought together, and the new cultures will contribute different ways of thinking and doing things. *Technological innovation* can also cause subcultures to form. New technologies demand new ways of interpreting and acting, making certain older subcultures obsolete and facilitating the establishment of new ones. An example is the advent of radiology machines in hospitals and laboratories. These innovations required new ways of interpreting the role of radiology in the medical establishment and new forms of behavior in radiology departments. Technicians had to become more specialized, and hospitals saw a regrouping of technicians into different patterns and subcultures.

Another factor in the development of subcultures is *ideological differentiation*. As organizations become more complex and job requirements more differentiated, people develop rather different ideas about what should be done and why. When this happens, new groupings occur around these ideological commitments. We often see this occurrence in academic departments at universities, when faculty members come to hold different perspectives on the field. Sometimes individuals who hold a particular point of view are shunned by the organization at large. When this happens a *contracultural movement* may occur. Here a new subculture of the

disaffected develops within the organization. For example, Van Maanen and Barley tell of a group of office workers who were not allowed to move from their work area. They eventually rebelled and retaliated by frustrating the efforts of others. Clearly, contracultural movements mark points of conflict, even strife, within the organization.

A final force in the development of subcultures is *career filters*. As people move up in the organization, or as they assume new career responsibilities, they filter out old norms, rules, and values in favor of new ones found within the new group with whom they work. In other words, the constant shifting around caused by career moves within an organization itself creates a variety of subcultures.

These forces behind the development of organizational cultures are obviously related. They are powerful forces that make multiple cultures within an organization almost inevitable, and they also lead to cultural clash. The authors explain:

> Many discussions have portrayed culture in organizations as a force for organizationwide solidarity. While we do not deny that normative unity is a distinct empirical possibility, our perspective on cultural organization intimates that cultures are just as likely, if not more likely, to act as centripetal forces that encourage the disintegration of that very unity for which commentators occasional pine. Whereas proponents of organizational culture sometimes argue that modern corporations suffer from a lack of culture, we submit that organizations often get more culture than they bargained for. From the perspective we have elaborated, the study of cultural organization is therefore closely bound to the study of organizational conflict.[68]

Critique

The cultural approach to organizational theory is a major advance. It refocuses our attention on a set of processes that are not examined carefully in the traditional management-oriented, variable-analytic tradition.[69] Traditionally, management is seen as a rational process of manipulating "things" for the benefit of the organization. The culture approach shows us that this is only partly true. In

---

67. Ibid., p. 38.

68. Ibid., p. 48.
69. Morgan, *Images*, pp. 134–140.

fact, a culture that is out of the conscious control of management is a major part of what characterizes that organization. The cultural approach refutes the idea that managers can somehow manipulate "objects" (like materials and machines) that are independent from the organization itself. The objects are only known through the meanings of the organizational culture, and those meanings will change from one organization, or even suborganization, to another. Organizations are not adapted to environments; rather organizations in a very real way create their own environments based on shared conceptions and interpretations.

The down side to the above observation is that the empirically minded manager may think of culture as just another variable to be manipulated, such that the culture can be managed. This idea can lead to the negative consequence of attempted ideological control. The theory of Van Maanen and Barley is an example of a cultural theory that could be used in this way. The answer to this criticism is that all forms of management exert some kind of ideological control; such cannot be escaped. Let us therefore create the most humane and productive cultures possible.

Another disadvantage of the culture approach is one that is true of many interpretive theories of communication generally: If you assume that the social reality of an organization comes from the interactions among members of the organization and that organizational cultures thereby differ, you put yourself into the very difficult theoretical position of not being able to make generalizations or predictions about organizational life. Each organization must be studied independently, and generalizations become difficult. The answer, of course, is standard: Theories should not attempt to be predictive, but should capture general categories of action, which we expect to be played out differently

in various organizations. Such middle-range theories, like that of Pacanowsky and O'Donnell-Trujillo, enable us to observe organizations with a sensitivity to their rich individuality.

Integration

Organizations are structures created through communication. People communicate to accomplish their individual and joint goals, and communication thereby serves to accomplish important functions. The process of communication also results in a variety of structural outcomes such as authority relations, roles, communication networks, and climate. All of these structural elements are results of the interaction between individuals and among groups within the organization, and all in turn affect future interactions within the organization.

In order for organizational functions to be accomplished, coordination and control are necessary. Although control can be exerted in a variety of ways, communication is one of the most important media through which organizational members are influenced to work toward certain goals. As members accept the assumptions of the organization, they identify with the organization itself and work on its behalf.

Organizations also meet human requirements. The manner in which the needs, wants, and ideas of employees are integrated into the organization determines the extent to which organizational life becomes an appropriate part of the human experience. Indeed, apart from achieving task-oriented goals, organizations are also human cultures, rich with tradition, shared meaning, and ritual. What people do in organizations creates and reflects the underlying culture of the organization.

Thirteen

Theories of Mass Communication

Whe are living in what Marshall McLuhan calls the "global village." Modern communication media make it possible for millions of people throughout the world to be in touch with nearly any spot on the globe. The omnipresent media present an important challenge to students in many disciplines.

Melvin DeFleur captures the importance of the study of communication:

> No student of human nature, whatever his disciplinary identification or theoretical orientation, can study human behavior without recognizing at the outset that man's communication processes are as vital to him as a human being as are his biological processes.[1]

George Gerbner adds the following:

> This broad "public-making" significance of mass media of communications—the ability to create publics, define issues, provide common terms of reference, and thus to allocate attention and power—has evoked a large number of theoretical contributions. Other theories of mass media have their origins in political thought, social-economic analysis, and historical-artistic-literary scholarship.[2]

Mass communication is the process whereby media organizations produce and transmit messages to large publics and the process by which those messages are sought, used, and consumed by audiences. Central to any study of mass communication are the media. Media are organizations that distribute cultural products or messages that affect and reflect the culture of society. Media provide information simultaneously to large heterogeneous audiences. Media systems are part of the larger societal context of political, economic, and other institutional forces.[3]

Because of its ubiquity and complexity, mass communication is difficult to study and conceptualize. Yet its importance has necessitated extensive investigation in this country and abroad. We can-

1. Melvin DeFleur, *Theories of Mass Communication* (New York: David McKay, 1966), p. xiv.
2. George Gerbner, "Mass Media and Human Communication Theory," in *Human Communication Theory*, ed. Frank Dance (New York: Holt, Rinehart & Winston, 1967), p. 45. There are numerous surveys of mass communication research and theory. See, for example, James A. Anderson, "Mass Communication Theory and Research: An Overview," in *Communication Yearbook I*, ed. Brent Ruben (New Brunswick, N.J.:

Transaction Books, 1977), pp. 279–90; Joseph M. Foley, "Mass Communication Theory and Research: An Overview," in *Communication Yearbook II*, ed. Brent Ruben (New Brunswick, N.J.: Transaction Books, 1978), pp. 209–14; Werner J. Severin and James W. Tankard, *Communication Theroies: Origins, Methods, Uses* (New York: Hastings House, 1979); Charles R. Wright, "Mass Communication Rediscovered: Its Past and Future in American Sociology," in *Media, Audience, and Social Structure*, eds. Sandra J. Ball-Rokeach and Muriel G. Cantor (Beverly Hills: Sage Publications, 1986), pp. 22–33; Denis McQuail, *Mass Communication Theory: An Introduction* (London: Sage Publications, 1984); Alexis S. Tan, *Mass Communication Theories and Research* (Columbus: Grid Publishing, 1981); Robert White, "Mass Communication and Culture: Transaction to a New Paradigm," *Journal of Communication* 33 (1983): 279–301.
3. Definitions of mass communication are discussed in Sandra J. Ball-Rokeach and Muriel G. Cantor (eds.), *Media, Audience, and Social Structure* (Beverly Hills: Sage Publications, 1986), pp. 10–11; McQuail, *Mass Communication*, pp. 33–34.

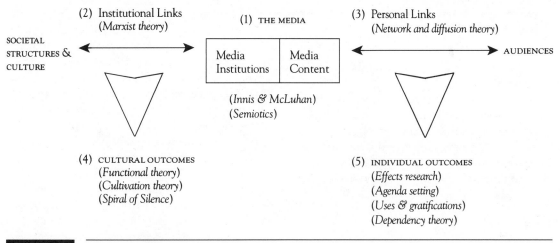

Figure 13-1   An organizing model.

not cover mass communication theory completely here due to its enormous scope. Therefore, the theories chosen for this chapter present a flavor for the history of mass communication theory as well as the current mainstream of thought on the topic.

An Organizing Model

Media scholars recognize two faces of mass communication. One face looks from the media to the larger society and its institutions. It displays the link between the media and other institutions such as politics, economics, education, and religion. Theorists interested in the media-society link are concerned with the ways in which media are embedded in a society and the mutual influence between larger social structures and the media. This we could call the macro side of mass communication theory. The second face looks toward people, in groups and as individuals. This face displays the link between the media and audiences. Theorists interested in the media-audience link focus on group and individual effects and outcomes of the media transaction. This is the micro side of mass communication theory.[4]

Figure 13-1 illustrates mass communication and its two faces. The model may imply that the institutional link is distinct from the personal one, that the media's relationship to institutions is somehow different from the link to persons. Yet, this cannot be true because institutions are people, groups, and cultures. The relationship between media and institutions is possible only through the media's transaction with audiences; and the audience-media relationship is impossible to separate from the institutions of the society in which those audiences reside. Thus, the model is not a map of the mass communication process, but is strictly intended to capture the different dimensions of media research and theory. This material defies tidy organization, and any ordering model would fail to characterize adequately the richness of the differences and similarities that abound in this field.

The chapter is divided into five sections, corresponding to the parts of the model. These are:

1. the media
2. the media-institutions link
3. the media-audience link
4. cultural outcomes
5. individual outcomes.

4. This conceptualization is adapted from a discussion of mass communication theory by McQuail, *Mass Communication*, pp. 53–57.

The Media

At the heart of mass communication are the media. Of course, media cannot be separated from the larger process of mass communication, nor can one examine media apart from their links with institutions and audiences as depicted in Figure 13-1. Yet certain theories have emphasized the structure of media over these other considerations. In this section we deal with two substantially different, yet central, theories of media.

Innis and McLuhan

Marshall McLuhan is perhaps the best-known writer on mass communication among the general public. In fact he may be the most popular communication "theorist" of our time. He has received acclaim primarily because of his interesting and bizarre style and his startling and impactful ideas. At the same time McLuhan has become one of the most controversial writers in the arena of pop culture. Whether one agrees with him or not, his ideas have received too much publicity to be ignored.[5]

McLuhan's early ideas on the media of communication stem from his mentor, Harold Adams Innis.[6] Both Innis and McLuhan treat communication media as the essence of civilization, and both see the course of history as a manifestation of the predominant media of the age.

Innis sees communication media as extensions of the human mind. He teaches that the primary interest of any historical period is a bias growing out of the predominant media in use. Heavy media such

as parchment, clay, or stone are *time-binding*, providing a bias toward tradition. Time-binding media facilitate communication from one generation to another. *Space-binding* media such as paper and papyrus, on the other hand, tend to foster empire building, large bureaucracy, and military interests. Space-binding media facilitate communication from one location to another. Speech as a medium encourages temporal thinking, which values knowledge and tradition and supports community involvement and interpersonal relationships. Written media produce different kinds of culture. The space-binding effect of writing produces interests in political authority and the growth of empires in a spatial sense. Innis teaches that the essence of western culture has been shaped by a strong print or spatial bias. His own viewpoint is expressed as follows:

> Mechanization has emphasized complexity and confusion; it has been responsible for monopolies in the field of knowledge. . . . The conditions of freedom of thought are in danger of being destroyed by science, technology, and the mechanization of knowledge, and with them, Western civilization. My bias is with the oral tradition, particularly as reflected in Greek civilization, and with the necessity of recapturing something of its spirit.[7]

One can easily see the connection between McLuhan's ideas and those of his predecessor, but McLuhan clearly has gone beyond the ideas of Innis in discussing the impact of media on society. In essence McLuhan's early theory can be broken down into a few basic propositions.[8]

McLuhan's most basic hypothesis is that people adapt to their environment through a certain balance or ratio of the senses, and the primary medium of the age brings out a particular sense ratio. McLuhan sees every medium as an extension of some human faculty, with the media of communication thus exaggerating this or that particular

5. McLuhan's most well-known works are *The Gutenberg Galaxy: The Making of Typographic Man* (Toronto: University of Toronto Press, 1962); *The Mechanical Bride* (New York: Vanguard Press, 1951); *Understanding Media* (New York: McGraw-Hill, 1964; Marshall McLuhan and Quentin Fiore, *The Medium is the Massage* (New York: Bantam, 1967). Other works by McLuhan are listed in the Bibliography. I have relied on the synthesis of Bruce Gronbeck, "McLuhan as Rhetorical Theorist," *Journal of Communication* 31 (1981): 117–28.

6. J. W. Carey, "Harold Adams Innis and Marshall McLuhan," *The Antioch Review* 27 (1967): 5–39. Innis's works include *The Bias of Communication* (Toronto: University of Toronto Press, 1951); *Empire and Communications* (Toronto: University of Toronto Press, 1950, 1972).

7. Innis, *Bias*, pp. 190–91.

8. Good brief summaries of McLuhan's theory can be found in the following: Kenneth Boulding, "The Medium is the Massage," in *McLuhan: Hot and Cool*, ed. Gerald E. Stearn (New York: Dial, 1967), pp. 56–64; Tom Wolfe, "The New Life Out There," in *McLuhan: Hot and Cool*, ed. Gerald E. Stearn (New York: Dial, 1957), pp. 34—56; Carey, "Innis and McLuhan."

sense. In his words, "The wheel . . . is an extension of the foot. The book is an extension of the eye. . . . Clothing, an extension of the skin. . . . Electric circuitry, an extension of the central nervous system."[9] Whatever media predominate will influence human beings by affecting the way they perceive the world.

Before printing was invented, tribal people were primarily hearing-oriented communicators. They were emotionally and interpersonally close. For the tribal person "hearing was believing." But the invention of the printing press changed this. The Gutenberg age brought a new sense ratio into being, in which sight predominated. McLuhan's basic premise about the development of western culture is that the nature of print forced people into a linear, logical, and categorial kind of perception. For McLuhan the use of the alphabet "fostered and encouraged the habit of perceiving all environment in visual and spatial terms—particularly in terms of a space and of a time that are uniform,

c,o,n,t,i,n,o,u,s and
c-o-n-n-e-c-t-e-d."[10]

We have entered a new age, though, according to McLuhan. Electronic technology has brought back an aural predominance. The Gutenberg technology created an explosion in society, separating and segmenting individual from individual; the electronic age has created an implosion, bringing the world back together in a "global village." As a result "it is forcing us to reconsider and reevaluate practically every thought, every action, and every institution formerly taken for granted.[11] McLuhan describes this impact:

> Electric circuitry profoundly involves men with one another. Information pours upon us, instantaneously and continuously. As soon as information is acquired, it is very rapidly replaced by still newer information. Our electrically configured world has forced us to move from the habit of data classification to the mode of pattern recognition. We can no longer build serially, block-by-block, step-by-step, because instant com-

munication insures that all factors of the environment and of experience coexist in a state of active interplay.[12]

Thus we come to the main thesis of McLuhan's work: "The medium is the message."[13] This catch phrase, at once curious and thought provoking, refers to the general influence that a medium has apart from its content. Tom Wolfe puts it this way: "It doesn't matter if the networks show twenty hours a day of sadistic cowboys caving in people's teeth or twenty hours of Pablo Casals droning away on his cello in a pure-culture white Spanish drawing room. It doesn't matter about the content."[14] And here, of course, is where McLuhan parts company from most contemporary researchers in mass communication. What really makes a difference in people's lives is the predominant media, not content, of the period: "They are so pervasive in their personal, political, economic, aesthetic, psychological, moral, ethical, and social consequences that they leave no part of us untouched, unaffected, unaltered."[15]

McLuhan makes a distinction between the *hot* and the *cool* media of communication. These concepts are the most confusing and probably the most controversial in his writing. McLuhan describes media in terms of the degree to which they involve people perceptually. Hot media are those that contain relatively complete sensory data, or high redundancy in the information-theory sense. With hot media the perceiver has less need to become involved by filling in missing data. McLuhan refers to hot media as low in participation. Hot media, because they give us everything, create a dulling or somnambulism in the population. Cool media, on the other hand, require the individual to participate perceptually by filling in missing data. This participation creates healthy involvement. It is important to realize that McLuhan's use of participation or involvement does not refer to the degree of interest or time spent attending to a particular medium of communication. Rather he refers to the

9. McLuhan and Fiore, *Massage*.
10. Ibid.
11. Ibid.

12. Ibid.
13. McLuhan, *Understanding Media*, p. 7.
14. Wolfe, "New Life," p. 19.
15. McLuhan and Fiore, *Massage*.

completeness (hot) or incompleteness (cool) of the stimulus. Film, for example, is considered to be a hot medium because the image projected on the screen is complete in every detail. The viewer of a film is not required perceptually to fill in anything. In an information-theory sense (Chapter 3) we could say that the film has high redundancy, low information. Television, on the other hand, provides the viewer with only a sketch through the illumination of tiny dots. Perceptually the viewer must fill in between these visual dots. In short the viewer must become involved perceptually with the stimulus. This distinction is crucial, for McLuhan sees it as a fundamental point of impact on society. As he puts it, "So the hotting-up of one sense tends to effect hypnosis, and the cooling of all senses tends to result in hallucination."[16]

Given his definition of cool media, you can see why McLuhan believes that television is changing the fabric of society. But the advent of television brings its own problems. McLuhan makes clear that a shift from one kind of medium to another creates tremendous stresses in society. For example, if a hot medium such as radio is introduced into tribal or nonliterate cultures, which are accustomed to cool media, a violent reaction may occur. Likewise, the reorientation required for hot societies such as our own to adapt to the introduction of cool media such as television has been upsetting.

In the 1970s McLuhan's teachings changed substantially. In his earlier works he strongly implies that the form of media in society *affects* or causes certain modes of perception on the part of society's members. In his later teaching he seems much less certain of this causal link. Instead, McLuhan says that media resonate with or reflect the perceptual categories of individuals. Instead of envisioning a causal link between media and personal perception, he later saw a simultaneous outpouring of certain kinds of thought on the part of the media and the person. Media forms do not cause but bring out modes of thought that are already present in the individual. The problem occurs when the individual is not familiar with the patterns of person-environment relationships depicted in media. The lack of consonance between the individual's perceptual categories and the depictions of the media creates stress in society.

McLuhan is in a world apart. His theory is not only unorthodox but is rarely classified with other theories of a certain genre. However, to the extent that McLuhan conceives of media as affecting society in a general way without discriminating various kinds of effects among different groups, he must be considered among the critics of mass society. His ideas are almost impossible to criticize using standard categories of theory criticism. The reason for this difficulty is that his work is mostly an artistic-historical-literary treatment and does not constitute a theory in the standard sense. Yet there has been no lack of criticism and commentary about the man.

McLuhan's ideas are useful for stimulating a fresh look at the subject matter, but they provide little guidance on how to understand the process of mass communication. They are valuable in that they point to the importance of media forms in society, but they do not give a realistic picture of the variables involved in the effects of media forms. In sum Kenneth Boulding points out: "It is perhaps typical of very creative minds that they hit very large nails not quite on the head."[17]

Semiotics

Semiotic theories of media are distinctly different in content and approach from those of Innis and McLuhan. While McLuhan teaches that the media forms themselves constitute the primary message of mass communication, semiotics makes a sharp separation between a medium and its content. For the semiotician, content matters a great deal, and that content depends upon the reading given to it by the audience member. Semiotics focuses on the ways in which producers create signs and the ways in which audiences understand those signs.

16. McLuhan, *Understanding Media*, p. 32.

17. Boulding, "The Medium," p. 68.

Semiotics was discussed in Chapter 4 as part of the general topic of language and meaning. Recall that semiotics goes back to the work of Charles Peirce and has a long history of development in the twentieth century.[18] Chapter 4 discusses in some detail the contemporary theory of signs by Umberto Eco. (You may wish to review that section at this point.) Here we rely on the work of Donald Fry and Virginia Fry, who apply the ideas of Peirce and Eco to the study of media.[19]

Semiotics is the study of signification, or the ways in which signs are used in the interpretation of events. Semiotics looks at the way in which messages are structured, the kinds of signs used, and the ways in which those structures are intended and understood by producers and consumers. Semiotics is a tool for analyzing what the content of media messages mean.

Fry and Fry organize their discussion into three major postulates. The first is that "mass media messages are textual resources capable of engendering multiple levels of potential meanings."[20] In other words, the text is understood by audiences through interpretion, and there are several possible interpretations of any given message. Media producers do intend to convey particular meanings in their works, but audiences may or may not understand these messages in the ways intended. Consider videos as an example:

> A music video is useful to illustrate that a particular expression can be correlated with a number of contents to produce different significations. For a teenager, video may be taken as a statement against the constraints that passing through adolescence seems to carry or as an image of the rebellious individual spurning social convention. A media researcher may study the video as a vehicle for the transmission of violent images to an audience. An executive of a record company may view the same video as an effective promotional device that is having a positive impact on sales of records. . . . In a cultural sense, the music video expression signifies different meanings for each because it is coded by each with different content planes.[21]

This discussion of individual interpretation does not mean that audience reaction is serendipitous. Indeed, producers go to some effort to predict the reactions of the audience and to use signs that will shape those reactions. Commercials are an excellent example. Although audience interpretations will vary, the advertiser certainly aims to elicit a predominant meaning and a particular response.

Denotation and connotation are central concepts in semiotics. *Denotation* refers to what a sign is believed to designate. Almost all literate consumers will get the denotation of a media message: You know a Preparation H commercial when you see one. If the actor says, "My mother-in-law is a doctor, and she likes Preparation H," you know what that means. What makes interpretations vary is not denotation, but connotation, or the feelings, judgments, and assessments that you make about the message content. ("Oh no, not another tacky hemorrhoid commercial.") While denotations are stable, connotations vary because they are based on *synthetic inferences* or extensions from the denotation. Media producers try not only to present a denotation, but to affect the subsequent connotation.

The second postulate is that "texts are made meaningful through a process of audience signification."[22] Here the authors use Peirce's concept of *interpretant*, which is the meaning of a sign in the mind of the perceiver. Communication is made possible by a consensual meaning in society. This Peirce calls the "final interpretant"; but the final interpretant is but one possible meaning for a sign. In media communication, then, any particular message will elicit a variety of meanings, and any one audience member may respond with a number

18. See, for example, C. Harshorne and P. Weiss (eds.), *Collected Papers of Charles Sanders Peirce*, vols. 1–6 (Cambridge: Harvard University Press, 1931–1934); Umberto Eco, *A Theory of Semiotics* (Bloomington: Indiana University Press, 1976).

19. Donald L. Fry and Virginia H. Fry, "A Semiotic Model for the Study of Mass Communication," in *Communication Yearbook 9*, ed. Margaret L. McLaughlin (Beverly Hills: Sage Publications, 1986), pp. 443–62.

20. Fry and Fry, "Semiotic," p. 445.

21. Ibid., p. 446.

22. Ibid., p. 448.

of levels of meaning. The audience member may have an *emotional interpretant* (a feeling associated with the content), an *energic interpretant* (an associated action such as compliance), and a *logical interpretant* (rationalization as to why a certain action is reasonable). For example, one of the most effective and interesting political spots in the 1984 presidential campaign was Ronald Reagan's "Morning in America" message. It was a series of beautiful photographic shots of morning in different places in the country. For many viewers, it left a feeling of warmth and contentment; it reinforced decisions to vote again for Reagan, and it provided a cognitive rationalization that "all is well in the country."

The third postulate is that "textual meaning is constituted by the interaction between textual and extra-textual factors."[23] The signs used in the text do play a role in shaping meaning; but numerous nontextual influences also bear upon the meaning that an individual will take from the text. The text will be influential to the extent that (a) the producer understands the kinds of content that will bring out certain meanings in the culture of the audience, and (b) the actual structure of the text emphasizes specific meanings over others. For example, a producer of a sitcom may wish to elicit a feeling of warmth and amusement from the characters. Knowing the kinds of situations that appeal to the general American audience helps writers to come up with situations that bring out those kinds of responses. Further, the writers and actors will concentrate on emphasizing a particular feeling for each character that will capture the attention of the audience.

How is this attention-gaining function accomplished? Eco says that it occurs through a process of *semantic disclosure*. This is the use of signs to emphasize certain properties and to make other properties neutral. Out of everything that a person could "see" in a message, some are highlighted and others are muted. Semantic disclosure in a sitcom might be accomplished by the character's costume, the character's use of certain expressions in dialogue, and the character's nonverbal demeanor. In

fact, stereotyping is an important kind of semantic disclosure in media messages, as can be seen in so many television commercials.

Once again, however, the audience response is not totally predictable. Indeed, there are many *extra-codes*, or outside factors, that can influence meaning. *Overcoding* occurs when meanings normally attached to one kind of message or situation are used to interpret another. For example, at Christmas time Hallmark releases "Christmas card" commercials that just depict a beautiful scene without directly mentioning the product (cards). Viewers will still get that the company is trying to sell its product because of the standard interpretation given to all other commercials. *Ideological overcoding* is especially important. This occurs when the viewer's ideology affects the interpretation of a message, even when the ideological interpretation is not intended. For example, a feminist may consider certain commercials objectionable because they depict women in subordinate roles, a Marxist may view network television news as an instrument of oppression, or a union leader might read *The Wall Street Journal* as a house organ for industrial management.

Semiotics has been an important strand of theory in the contemporary study of communication, and it has definite utility in understanding media. It is valuable, too, because it enables the observer to analyze the structure of media messages without ignoring the interpretive processes of the audience. The primary objection to semiotics is that it grants too much power to the individual in determining the meaning of a message. Interactional theorists (Chapters 6 and 7) would say that semiotics downplays the ways in which meanings arise from social interaction. These critics would contend that meaning is not something that individuals confer upon texts, but that meaning is a consensual product of communication in social groups. From this perspective, then, our meanings for texts are worked out in interaction among people, not by peculiar and individualistic interpretation of signs. On the other side, textual hermeneutics (Chapter 8) would claim that meanings are embedded in texts themselves. Textual meaning is distanciated

23. Ibid., p. 452.

from historical context and disembodied from human speakers and readers. Meanings come to us *in texts*; individuals bring a kind of cultural knowledge to bear in "reading" the meaning that is already in the text.

This criticism reflects an abiding conflict in the study of mass communication. How powerful are media depictions in the control of culture? Some, like McLuhan, argue that media are powerful forces in determining the character of culture and individual life. Other theories, some of which we will review later in this chapter, claim that individuals have much control over the outcomes of media transactions in their lives. Yet a third group believes that mass media are important, but that they are only part of a complex of factors involved in social domination, and that individuals are influenced by the entire system of dominating forces. We turn now to this particular school of thought.

Media as Social Institution

Although media institutions can be viewed in a variety of ways, we devote this section to a particular group of theories that can be generally labeled "Marxist critical theories." We concentrate on this approach here because of its prominence in the literature on media in the 1980s, its increasing popularity, and its insights into certain important macrotheoretical questions about the role of media in society.

Although Marxist approaches to communication theory are gaining in influence among American communication scholars, they are the predominant viewpoint on the subject in Europe. In fact, the study of mass communication in the two continents have quite a different flavor. Research in the United States tends to be heavily influenced by traditional social science methods and issues, questions of media effects and functions. With some exceptions, European research tends to be more globally concerned with ideology and domination and eschews traditional social science research.

The Marxist Tradition

We took a brief look at the Marxist critical tradition in Chapter 8. Because of its centrality in media theory, we return to it again here. There are several different approaches to Marxist communication theory. (Lawrence Grossberg discusses ten such theories.[24]) These different theories deal with two major problem areas, which Grossberg calls the "politics of textuality" and the "problematic of cultural studies." The politics of textuality has to do with the ways in which media producers encode messages, the ways in which audiences decode those messages, and the power domination apparent in these processes. The textual scholar, for example, might study the ways in which certain kinds of media content such as network news are produced, and how those depictions are understood by audiences so as to perpetuate the power of certain dominant economic institutions (such as government). The problem of cultural studies examines more closely the relation among media, other institutions in society, and the ideology of culture. Cultural theorists are interested in how the dominant ideology of a culture subverts other ideologies through social institutions such as schools, churches, and the media. Both of these traditions are centrally concerned with the evils of class society and the struggles that occur among the different social forces. Both emphasize the ways in which social structures are produced and reproduced again and again in the actual daily activities of individuals, groups, and institutions.

British Cultural Studies

An exemplar of both Marxist critique in general and cultural studies specifically is the British cultural studies tradition. This is a group of scholars associated with the Centre for Contemporary Cultural Studies at the University of Birmingham. The origins of this tradition are usually traced to the writings of Richard Hoggart and Raymond Williams in the 1950s, which examined the British

24. Lawrence Grossberg, "Strategies of Marxist Cultural Interpretation," *Critical Studies in Mass Communication* 1 (1984): 392–421.

working class after World War II.[25] Today, the leader of the movement is Stuart Hall.[26]

The British cultural studies tradition is distinctly reformist in orientation. These scholars want to see changes in western society, and they view their scholarship as an instrument of socialist cultural struggle. They believe that such change will occur in two ways—(a) by identifying contradictions in society, the resolution of which will lead to change, and (b) by providing interpretations that will help people understand domination and the kinds of change that would be desirable. Samuel Becker describes this goal as follows: ". . . these communication scholars want to keep jarring both the audience and the workers in the media back from becoming too accepting of their illusions or existing practices so they will question them and their conditions."[27]

The study of mass communication is central to this work, for the media are perceived as powerful tools of the dominant ideology. In addition, they have the potential of raising the consciousness of the population about issues of class, power, and domination. We must be cautious in interpreting cultural studies in this light, however, because media in this tradition are part of a much larger set of institutional forces: Media are important, but they are not the sole concern of these scholars. This is one of the reasons why they do not refer to their field as "media studies," but rather "cultural studies."

What is meant by *culture* here? There have been disagreements about the meaning of the term even within the cultural studies movement, but essentially two meanings, which go back to Williams's writings, are implied. The first meaning of *culture* is the common ideas on which a society or group within that society rest. It is collective ways in which the group understands its experience. The second meaning is the practices or the entire way of life of a group, what individuals do materially from day to day. These two senses of the word *culture* should not be separated. One of the contributions of the cultural studies program is to have us see how the ideology of a group is produced and reproduced in its practices. In fact, the general concern of cultural theorists is the link between the actions of societies' institutions such as the media and the culture. Indeed, texts as artifacts of a "culture" are not the culture itself, for practices and ideas must always be interpreted in light of the historical context in which they occur. For this reason, the cultural studies tradition is considered to be firmly *materialist*.

The theory posits that capitalistic societies are dominated by a particular ideology of the elite. According to Williams, an *ideology* is ". . . a relatively formal and articulated system of meanings, values, and beliefs, of a kind that can be abstracted as a 'world-view' or a 'class outlook.'"[28] It is thus a frame of reference by which individuals in a culture understand their experience. For the workers of society, the dominant ideology is a *false ideology* because it does not reflect their interests. Instead, the dominant ideology is involved in a *hegemony* against that of powerless groups. Hegemony is the process of one ideology subverting another. Hegemony, however, is always a fluid process, what Hall calls a temporary state in a "theatre of struggle." We must therefore "think of societies as complex formations, necessarily contradictory, always historically specific."[29]

Social institutions like education, religion, and government are interlinked in ways that support the dominant ideology, making resistance especially difficult. Especially important is the link between infrastructure and superstructure. *Infra-*

25. Richard Hoggart, *Uses of Literacy* (London: Chatto & Windus, 1957); Raymond Williams, *The Long Revolution* (New York: Columbia University Press, 1961).

26. For a good survey of the work of Hall and others at the Centre, see Stuart Hall, Dorothy Hobson, Andrew Lowe, and Paul Willis (eds.), *Culture, Media, Language* (London: Hutchinson, 1981). See also, Stuart Hall, "Cultural Studies: Two Paradigms," in *Media, Culture and Society: A Critical Reader* (London: Sage Publications, 1986). Two secondary treatments were especially helpful: Samuel L. Becker, "Marxist Approaches to Media Studies: The British Experience," *Critical Studies in Mass Communication* 1 (1984): 66–80; White, "Mass Communication."

27. Becker, "Marxist," p. 67.

28. Raymond Williams, *Marxism and Literature* (New York: Oxford University Press, 1977), p. 109.

29. Hall, "Cultural Studies," p. 36.

structure, sometimes referred to as the *base*, is the basic economic resources and systems of a society, including buildings, monetary system, capital, machinery, and so on. The *superstructure* consists of societal institutions. The exact relationship between infrastructure and superstructure is in dispute. Early Marxist theory taught that the infrastructure (economic resource base) determined superstructure.[30] Today, the relationship is viewed as more complex. The forces of society are considered to be *overdetermined* or caused by multiple sources. Infrastructure and superstructure may therefore be mutually interdependent. Because of the complexity of causation in society, no one set of conditions is required for a particular outcome to occur.

The media have a special role in affecting popular culture through the dissemination of information. The media are extremely important because they directly present a way of viewing reality. The media portray ideology explicitly and directly. This does not mean that opposing forces are silenced. Indeed, opposing voices will always be present as part of the dialectical struggle among forces in a society. But the media are dominated by the prevailing ideology, and they therefore treat opposing views from within the frame of the dominant ideology. This has the effect of discounting opposing groups as fringe elements. The irony of media, especially television, is that they present the illusion of diversity and objectivity, when in fact they are clear instruments of the dominant order.

Producers control the content of media by particular ways of encoding messages. As Becker describes the process, "events do not signify . . . to be intelligible events must be put into symbolic form . . . the communicator has a choice of codes or sets of symbols. The one chosen affects the meaning of the events for receivers. Since every language—every symbol—coincides with an ideology, the choice of a set of symbols is, whether conscious or not, the choice of an ideology."[31] At the same time, however, audiences may use their own categories to decode the message. Hall is especially interested in the following ideological situations: the decoding is consistent with the encoding (thereby reproducing ideology), the decoding is inconsistent with the encoding (thereby resisting ideology), and a negotiation between the decoding and encoding (thereby creating a new meaning).

Usually in capitalistic societies, the ideology is perpetuated in decoding because of the infusion of the ideology in all other realms of life. The audience is literally set up to read media texts in particular ways because of what they have learned in school, church, work, and so on. This may sound very much like a conspiracy, but Becker comments:

> As far as I can see, no British scholar perceives the role of the media in the reproduction of the conditions of capitalistic production to be the result of a plot by capitalists or by the ruling classes. . . . They perceive, rather, that the medium's reflection of that ideology is a natural consequence of the system by which the medium operates and the larger system in which that operation takes place.[32]

Criticism

Needless to say, the critical approach to media is highly controversial. There is a basic split between what had been termed "administrative" research—or research viewed by the Marxists as an instrument of ideological administration—and critical research—or an opposition to those ideological forces.[33] The primary critique of Marxist theory, therefore, comes from the "administrative" side. Jay Blumler summarizes some of these objections.[34]

First, even if media institutions should become more egalitarian, the critical approach does not provide sufficient guidance on how this is to be

30. This problem and other issues facing the cultural studies program are discussed in Stuart Hall, "Cultural Studies and the Centre: Some Problematics and Problems," in *Culture, Media, Language*, eds. Stuart Hall, Dorothy Hobson, Andrew Lowe, and Paul Willis (London: Hutchinson, 1981), pp. 15–47.

31. Becker, "Marxist," p. 72.
32. Ibid., p. 71.
33. This division is amply discussed in the special edition of *Journal of Communication* entitled *Ferment in the Field* 33 (Summer 1983).
34. Jay Blumler, "Communication and Democracy: The Crisis Beyond and the Ferment Within," *Journal of Communication* 33 (1983): 166–73.

done: "But the critical paradigm, as so far enunciated, lacks a clarity of ethic and realism of political diagnosis that, when drawn on and applied, could help communication institutions to realize a vision of human beings as active, choosing, purposeful subjects."[35]

Second, the movement has a "self-defeating tendency to utopianism."[36] In other words, these theories downplay the realities of political life that require democracy, and they ignore the fact that media are required for democracy to work. Indeed, Marxist approaches are inherently antidemocratic: ". . . the critical perspective tends to slam shut, instead of prying open, doors of possible improvement in the contributions of journalism to democracy."[37]

Finally, administrative researchers oppose Marxist antipathy toward behavioral and social research. The Marxist claims are believed to be unsupported by research. Marxists do research, of course, but it is of a very different sort. They are not interested in promoting the ideological values of social science methods. Let us turn now to theories of the administrative tradition by looking at the media-audience link.

Media and the Audience

The third part of our organizing model is the link between media and audience. Here we are concerned with the questions of how the media reach audiences. We now know that mass communication consists of both media information and interpersonal networks. Information and innovations are disseminated in the public in both manners. This finding has been the consistent result of mass communication research for many years.

In 1940 a classic voting study was conducted by Paul Lazarsfeld and his colleagues in Elmira, New York.[38] The researchers found an unexpected occurrence that, although unconfirmed, implied a possible strong involvement of interpersonal communication in the total mass communication process. This effect, which came to be known as the *two-step flow hypothesis*, was startling, and it had a major impact on the conception of mass communication.

Since the original Elmira study, much additional data have come in, and the hypothesis has received substantial support.[39] Lazarsfeld hypothesized that information flows from the mass media to certain *opinion leaders* in the community, who facilitate communication through discussions with peers. For example, Lazarsfeld found that voters seem to be more influenced by their friends during a campaign than by the media.

The two-step flow theory is best summarized in Elihu Katz and Paul Lazarsfeld's classic work, *Personal Influence*.[40] Central to the theory is the concept of opinion leaders—individuals in the community who receive information from the media and pass it to their peers. Opinion leaders are distributed in all groups: occupational, social, community, and others. The opinion leader typically is hard to distinguish from other group members, because opinion leadership is not a trait. Instead, it is conceived as a role taken within the process of interpersonal communication. An important aspect is that opinion leadership changes from time to time and from issue to issue. Katz and Lazarsfeld find that it differs in such areas as marketing, fashion, and public affairs. Interest in a particular issue is certainly an important determinant of opinion leadership, but leaders can be influential only when interest is shared by all members of the group.

Opinion leaders may be of two kinds: those influential on one topic and those influential on a variety of topics. These types have been called *monomorphic* and *polymorphic*. It has been hypothesized that monomorphism becomes more predominant as

---

35. Ibid., p. 168.
36. Ibid.
37. Ibid., p. 169.
38. Paul Lazarsfeld, Bernard Berelson, and H. Gaudet, *The People's Choice* (New York: Columbia University Press, 1948).

39. An excellent summary of this hypothesis is Elihu Katz, "The Two-Step Flow of Communication," *Public Opinion Quarterly* 21 (1957): 61–78.
40. Elihu Katz and Paul Lazarsfeld, *Personal Influence; The Part Played by People in the Flow of Mass Communications* (New York: Free Press, 1955).

systems become more modern. "As the technological base of a system becomes more complex, a division of labor and specialization of roles result, which in turn lead to different sets of opinion leaders for different issues."[41]

In any case the implication is that groups provide the key for mass communication influence. They do this by providing direction to the individual in terms of opinions, attitudes, values, and norms. Groups also give ready access to communication.

In recent years most theorists have moved to the newer multiple-step model of diffusion.[42] The multiple-step model is similar to the two-step hypothesis; it simply admits to more complex possibilities. Research has shown that the ultimate number of relays between the media and final receivers is variable. In the adoption of an innovation, for example, certain individuals will hear about the innovation directly from media sources, while others will be many steps removed.

The Diffusion of Innovations

One of the most fruitful theoretical areas contributing to our understanding of diffusion stems from the innovation research in rural agriculture, developing nations, and organizations. The diffusion of an innovation occurs when an idea spreads from a point of origin to surrounding geographical areas or from person to person within a single area.[43] Several prominent American and foreign researchers have been responsible for this line of research. The broadest and most communication-oriented theory is that of Everett Rogers and his colleagues.[44]

Rogers began his theory by relating it to the process of social change in general. Social change consists of invention, diffusion (or communication), and consequences. Such change can occur internally from within a group or externally through contact with outside change agents. In the latter case contact may occur spontaneously or accidentally, or it may result from planning on the part of outside agencies.

Diffusion of innovations is a time-consuming process. Many years may be required for an idea to spread. Rogers states, in fact, that one of the purposes of diffusion research is to discover the means to shorten this lag. Once established, an innovation will have consequences, be they functional or dysfunctional, direct or indirect, manifest or latent. Change agents normally expect their impact to be functional, direct, and manifest, although this outcome does not always occur.

The diffusion of innovations depends on four broad elements: the innovation, the communication, the channels, the time. An innovation is any new idea in a social system. The perceived newness of the idea is what counts, not its objective newness. Any idea perceived as new by the citizens of the community applies to this process.

Although mass communication channels may play significant roles in diffusion, interpersonal networks are most important.[45] Networks are more than a simple information linkage between opinion leader and follower, which is implied in the flow models just described. How individuals understand ideas and the degree to which ideas are accepted and modified depend in large measure on the *interaction* along the links in the network. Interaction is important, for diffusion appears to be a product of give and take rather than the simple sending and receiving of information. One new insight of this approach is that individuals modify innovations as part of adoption. Another insight is that innovations are often sought out or created in the system without the intrusion of a change agent. It is a

41. Everett M. Rogers and F. Floyd Shoemaker, *Communication of Innovations, A Cross-Cultural Approach* (New York: Free Press, 1971), p. 224.

42. One of the best summaries of this extension can be found in Rogers and Shoemaker, *Innovations*, chap. 6.

43. For a general summary, see Torsten Hagerstrand, "Diffusion II: The Diffusion of Innovations," in *International Encyclopedia of the Social Sciences*, vol. 4., ed. David Sills (New York: Macmillan, 1968).

44. Everett M. Rogers, *Diffusion of Innovations* (New York: Free Press, 1962); Rogers and Shoemaker, *Innovations*; Everett M. Rogers and Ronny Adhikarya, "Diffusion of Innovations: An Up-to-Date Review and Commentary," in *Communication

Yearbook III, ed. Dan Nimmo (New Brunswick, N.J.: Transaction Books, 1979), pp. 67–82; Everett M. Rogers and D. Lawrence Kincaid, *Communication Networks* (New York: Free Press, 1981).

45. Rogers and Kincaid, *Communication Networks*.

fallacy to think that an innovation is simply injected into a system and adopted or rejected. Communication is a *convergence* of meaning achieved by symbolic interaction.[46] The adoption, rejection, modification, or creation of an innovation is a product of this convergence process. Rogers obviously makes liberal use of symbolic interactionism, system theory, and network theory.

Beginning with the work of Paul Lazarsfeld, the research and theory of diffusion has been immensely successful. Dennis Davis and Stanley Baran remark of Lazarsfeld: "If one person deserves the title of founder of the field of mass communication research, that person is Paul Lazarsfeld. No one has done more to determine the way in which theory and research methods would be developed to aid our understanding of mass communication."[47] The work of Lazarsfeld and his successors has been influential in guiding our thinking about the process of mass communication. The parsimony of these theories has enabled observers to deal with a huge and complex phenomenon with relative ease. Additionally, these theories have been highly heuristic and have produced a large body of research. For many years the idea of the two-step flow (and later multiple-step flow) in the diffusion of information and innovation was a mainstay of mass communication theory, but diffusion theory is undergoing change and is quite unsettled at the present time.[48]

Much criticism of diffusion research and theory arose in the 1970s. Generally, this criticism relates to the simplicity and consequent lack of explanatory power of these theories. Critics now believe that these theories cannot adequately explain the complexities of diffusion processes.

We have realized for some time that diffusion does not follow a strictly two-step process, but the logic of the two-step flow is still a standard explanation. In this explanation diffusion is seen as a process of spreading information or innovation in a linear fashion from media to opinion leader to members of the public; the number of steps is considered irrelevant to the basic process. This logic does not explain enough, however. Research has not consistently supported this notion of how diffusion occurs. At times the media appear to inform the public directly, with little interpersonal involvement; at other times different forms of diffusion are revealed. Rogers believes that for the most part diffusion is a network-oriented process. The strict dichotomy between opinion leaders and followers is overly simple.

There are many problems of this linear model. It tends to be one-way, implying a unidirectional flow of information and one-way causation. The implication that information and influence flow neatly from one person to another is not supported by research, which indicates that a good deal of two-way interaction is involved in the spread of information. Further, the one-way model suggests that receivers are dependent on information sources, when in actuality individuals in the social group are interdependent. In the give and take of everyday conversation, people exchange information, question it, argue about it, and come to a shared understanding. Another problem with the linear model of diffusion is that it downplays context; the actual circumstances under which diffusion occurs may have a great deal to do with the pattern of dissemination used by individuals in sharing information and innovations. Since context creates variability in diffusion patterns, research based on the simplistic linear model will be inconsistent. Additionally, linear models tend to stress influence rather than interpersonal understanding. Yet, as Rogers points out, diffusion is more a matter of convergence or the achievement of shared meaning than of strict influence.

46. Lawrence Kincaid has been primarily responsible for the theory of convergence. See Rogers and Kincaid, *Communication Networks*, pp. 31–78; D. Lawrence Kincaid, "The Convergence Model of Communication," *East-West Institute Paper No. 18* (Honolulu, 1979); D. Lawrence Kincaid, June Ock Yum, and Joseph Woelfel, "The Cultural Convergence of Korean Immigrants in Hawaii: An Empirical Test of a Mathematical Theory," *Quality and Quantity* 18 (1983): 59–78.

47. Dennis K. Davis and Stanley J. Baran, *Mass Communication and Everyday Life: A Perspective on Theory and Effects* (Belmont, Calif.: Wadsworth, 1981), p. 27.

48. Rogers and Adhikarya, "Diffusion."

The Spiral of Silence

The previous section addressed the nature of the media-audience link. We saw there that individuals are not only exposed to media information but that they also talk among themselves, pass on information, and express opinions. Elisabeth Noelle-Neumann's theory of the "spiral of silence" continues this analysis by demonstrating how this interpersonal-media link operates in the development of public opinion.[49] As a political researcher in Germany, Noelle-Neumann observed in several studies that in elections certain views seemed to get more play than others; her idea of the spiral of silence accounts for this.

The spiral of silence occurs when individuals who perceive that their opinion is popular express it, while those who do not think their opinion is popular remain quiet. This process occurs in a spiral, so that one side of an issue ends up with much public expression, and the other side with little. In everyday life we express our opinions in a variety of ways: We talk about them, we wear buttons, and we put stickers on our car bumpers. According to this theory, people are more apt to do these kinds of things when they perceive that others share their opinion, and less apt to do so when they do not.

This thesis rests upon two assumptions. The first is that people know which opinions are prevalent and which are not. The second is that people adjust their expressions of opinion to these perceptions. Noelle-Neumann presents quite a bit of research evidence to support these assumptions. In political elections, for example, people usually perceive quite accurately the prevailing opinion about the candidates and issues, and they are more apt to express their preferences when these are shared by others.

Of course, other factors do enter into the decision to express one's opinion. People and groups vary in their tendency to express ideas, regardless of the prevailing opinion. Young people are more expressive than older people; educated individuals will speak up more than uneducated ones; men are generally more disclosive of their opinions than women. However, the spiral of silence is also a factor, and according to this research, a very powerful one.

The spiral of silence seems to be caused by the fear of isolation. As Noelle-Neumann puts it: "To run with the pack is a relatively happy state of affairs; but if you can't, because you won't share publicly in what seems to be a universally acclaimed conviction, you can at least remain silent, as a second choice, so that others can put up with you."[50] The spiral of silence is not just a matter of wanting to be on the winning side, but is an attempt to avoid being isolated from one's social group. Threats of criticism from others were found to be powerful forces in silencing individuals. For example, smokers who are repeatedly criticized for advocating "smokers' rights" were found to remain silent rather than state their views on this subject in the presence of vocal nonsmokers.

In some cases the threat of expressing an opinion is extreme:

> Slashed tires, defaced or torn posters, help refused to a lost stranger—questions of this kind demonstrate that people can be on uncomfortable or even dangerous ground when the climate of opinion runs counter to their views. When people attempt to avoid isolation, they are not responding hypersensitively to trivialities; these are existential issues that can involve real hazards.[51]

One can easily see how the spiral of silence affects public opinion. *Public opinion* has been defined in numerous ways. For Noelle-Neumann an operational definition is best: "Public opinions are attitudes or behaviors one must express in public if one is not to isolate oneself; in areas of controversy or change, public opinions are those attitudes one can express without running the danger of isolating oneself."[52] Stated differently, "public opinion is an

49. Elisabeth Noelle-Neumann, *The Spiral of Silence: Public Opinion—Our Social Skin* (Chicago: University of Chicago Press, 1984).

50. Ibid., p. 6.
51. Ibid., p. 56.
52. Ibid., p. 178.

understanding on the part of people in an ongoing community concerning some affect- or value-laden question which individuals as well as government have to respect at least by compromise in their overt behavior under the threat of being excluded or losing one's standing in society."[53]

There are, of course, exceptions to the spiral of silence. There are groups and individuals who do not fear isolation and who will express their opinions no matter what the consequences. This may be a characteristic of innovators, change agents, and the avant-garde.

The media are an important part of the spiral of silence. The media publicize which opinions are prevalent and which are not. When polled, individuals usually state that they feel powerless in the face of media. Two kinds of experience accentuate this feeling of helplessness. The first is the difficulty of getting publicity for a cause or point of view. The second is being scapegoated by the media in what Noelle-Neumann calls the "pillory" function of media. In each of these cases, the individual feels powerless in using or avoiding the media.

Although public opinion is formed by both personal observation and media, individuals mix the two and confuse what is learned through the media with what is learned through interpersonal channels. This tendency is especially true for television, with which so many people have a personal relationship. Noelle-Neumann addresses the complexity of media effects in the following excerpt:

> The longer one has studied the question, the clearer it becomes that fathoming the effects of the mass media is very hard. These effects do not come into being as a result of a single stimulus; they are as a rule cumulative, following the principle that "water dripping constantly wears away stone." Further discussions among people spread the media's messages further, and before long no difference can be perceived between the point of media reception and points far removed from it. The media's effects are predominantly unconscious; people cannot provide an account of what has happened. Rather, they mix their own direct perceptions and the perceptions filtered through the eyes of the

media into an indivisible whole that seems to derive from their own thoughts and experiences.[54]

It sometimes happens that journalists' opinions differ from that of the general public, and media depictions contradict the prevailing expressions of individuals. When this occurs, a *dual climate of opinion* results. Here two versions of reality operate. Noelle-Neumann likens this event to an unusual weather situation—interesting and seemingly bizarre.

The spiral of silence, then, is a phenomenon involving personal and media channels of communication. The media publicize public opinion, making evident which opinions predominate. Individuals express their opinions or not, depending upon the predominant points of view; and the media, in turn attend to the expressed opinion, and the spiral continues.

This is an interesting and useful theory. It is appealing because it acknowledges the powers of both media and interpersonal channels of expression, and it recognizes the fusion of the two. The idea has been under development for about twenty years and exemplifies careful theory development through research. Beginning with a mere hypothesis in the early 1970s, Noelle-Neumann undertook numerous studies designed to test the basic hypothesis, its assumptions, and ramifications. Not all theories of communication have been developed this systematically.

On the other hand, cultural scholars and Marxists would point to this line of research as an example of the kind of work they most distrust. First, they believe that it is false to assume that one can find an underlying structure to public opinion through surveys. Social science methods cannot be trusted to reveal any kind of reality beyond the meanings assigned by observers. Second, the failure to acknowledge the ideological nature of the public opinion is a major oversight. Third, these critics would object to the suggestion that the spiral of silence is a universal phenomenon. All social life must be viewed in the context of history; and the spiral of silence, like most traditional social science

53. Ibid., p. 179.

54. Ibid., p. 169.

findings, abstracts beyond the material world. Finally, this kind of research is truly "administrative" in the sense that it becomes a tool in which the dominant ideology can be managed, or promulgated.

Theories of Cultural Outcomes

We turn now to a study of the outcomes of the media transaction. Of all of the areas of mass communication research, outcome studies are the most prevalent, especially in the United States. A looming question throughout the history of media theory has been the effects of media on society and individuals. The theories included here are divided into two sections, those focusing on general cultural effects and outcomes of the media and those focusing on individual effects and outcomes.

The Functions of Mass Communication

One of the earliest and best-known theorists of mass communication is Harold Lasswell. Lasswell, a political scientist, wrote an article entitled "The Structure and Function of Communication in Society." This 1948 treatise presents the simple and often-quoted model of communication:[55]

- Who
- Says what
- In which channel
- To whom
- With what effect

The model outlines the basic elements of communication that have received the most research attention. Indeed, the last element in the model directs us to the entire outcome research tradition.

55. Harold Lasswell, "The Structure and Function of Communication in Society," in *The Communication of Ideas*, ed. Lyman Bryson (New York: Institute for Religious and Social Studies, 1948), p. 37. For information regarding Lasswell's contribution to political science, see Arnold A. Rogow (ed.), *Politics, Personality, and Social Science in the Twentieth Century: Essays in Honor of Harold D. Lasswell* (Chicago: University of Chicago Press, 1969), especially the following articles: Heinz Eulan, "The Maddening Methods of Harold D. Lasswell: Some Philosophical Underpinnings," pp. 15–40; Bruce Smith, "The Mystifying Intellectual History of Harold Lasswell," pp. 41–105.

Lasswell's work is paradoxical because it implies a linear process of mass communication, yet it also presents a set of functions fulfilled by mass communication, which are not easily classed as causal effects. Lasswell identifies three functions of the media of communication. These are "surveillance of the environment" (knowing what is going on), "correlation of the parts of society in responding to the environment" (having options or solutions for dealing with societal problems), and "the transmission of the social heritage of one generation to the next" (socialization and education).[56]

Charles Wright has expanded on Lasswell's model. Starting with Lasswell's three basic functions, he developed a twelve category model and a functional inventory for mass communication as shown in Table 13-1 and Figure 13-2.[57] The model is set up as a question, probing the various functions and dysfunctions of mass-communicated messages. Such functions are broken down according to social levels. The skeleton provided by the basic functional model is filled in, the questions answered, on the inventory. In Figure 13-2 we see a number of functions and dysfunctions of Lasswell's categories according to social level. Notice that Wright added a fourth function, entertainment, to Lasswell's list.

Lasswell's three functions and Wright's elaboration of this theory have been quoted frequently in the literature on mass communication. They provide an excellent simple outline of some functions and dysfunctions of mass communication. As such they are a useful pedagogical device. However, one must stretch to call this work theoretical in the standard sense because it does not help us understand when and how these various functions and dysfunctions operate. They constitute a good observational aid but are not powerful for explanation.

One of the criticisms of the functional approach in general is its inherent ambiguities in regard to explanation. Although the following two theories do not solve this problem, they take a step toward providing a different kind of explanation than that found in effects research.

56. Lasswell, "Structure and Function."
57. Charles R. Wright, "Functional Analysis and Mass Communication," *Public Opinion Quarterly* 24 (1960): 605–20.

Table 13-1 Partial Functional Inventory for Mass Communications

	System under consideration			
	Society	Individual	Specific subgroup (e.g. political elite)	Culture
1. Mass communicated activity: surveillance (news)				
Functions (manifest and latent)	Warning: Natural dangers; Attack; war Instrumental: News essential to the economy and other institutions Ethicizing	Warning Instrumental Adds prestige: Opinion leadership Status conferral	Instrumental: Information useful to power Detects: Knowledge of subversive and deviant behavior Manages public opinion: Monitors Controls Legitimizes power: Status conferral	Aids cultural contact Aids cultural growth
Dysfunctions (manifest and latent)	Threatens stability; News of "better" societies Fosters panic	Anxiety Privatization Apathy Narcotization	Threatens power: News of reality "Enemy" propaganda Exposés	Permits cultural invasion
2. Mass-communicated activity: correlation (editorial selection, interpretation, and prescription)				
Functions (manifest and latent)	Aids mobilization Impedes threats to social stability Impedes panic	Provides efficiency: Assimilating news Impedes: Overstimulation Anxiety Apathy Privatization	Helps preserve power	Impedes cultural invasion Maintains cultural consensus
Dysfunctions (manifest and latent)	Increases social conformism: Impedes social change if social criticism is avoided	Weakens critical faculties Increases passivity	Increases responsibility	Impedes cultural growth

3. Mass-communicated activity: cultural transmission

Functions (manifest and latent)	Increases social cohesion: Widens base of common norms, experiences, etc. Reduces anomie Continues socialization: Reaches adults even after they have left such institutions as school	Aids integration: Exposure to common norms Reduces idiosyncrasy Reduces anomie	Extends power: Another agency for socialization	Standardizes Maintains cultural consensus
Dysfunctions (manifest and latent)	Augments "mass" society	Depersonalizes acts of socialization		Reduces variety of sub-cultures

4. Mass-communicated activity: entertainment

Functions (manifest and latent)	Respite for masses	Respite	Extends power: Control over another area of life	
Dysfunctions (manifest and latent)	Diverts public: Avoids social action	Increases passivity Lowers "tastes" Permits escapism		Weakens aesthetics: "Popular culture"

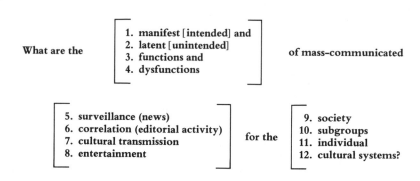

Figure 13-2   Wright's functional model.

From *Public Opinion Quarterly*, "Functional Analysis and Mass Communication," by Charles R. Wright. Copyright ©1960. Reprinted by permission of *The University of Chicago Press* and the author.

Cultivation Theory

A theoretical program dealing with the sociocultural outcomes of mass communication is that of George Gerbner and his colleagues.[58] This theory deals with an important effect of television, which the theorists call cultivation. In a nutshell, television is believed to be a homogenizing agent in culture. Because television is the great common experience of everyone, it has the effect of providing a shared way of viewing the world:

> Television is a centralized system of storytelling. It is part and parcel of our daily lives. Its drama, commercials, news, and other programs bring a relatively coherent world of common images and messages into every home. Television cultivates from infancy the very predispositions and preferences that used to be acquired from other primary sources. Transcending historic barriers of literacy and mobility, television has become the primary common source of socialization and everyday information (mostly in the form of entertainment) of an otherwise heterogeneous population. The repetitive pattern of television's mass-produced messages and images forms the mainstream of a common symbolic environment.[59]

Cultivation theory is concerned with the totality of the pattern communicated by television rather than any particular content or specific effect: "The pattern that counts is that of the total pattern of programming to which total communities are regularly exposed over long periods of time."[60] In other words, this is not a theory of media effects per se, but instead makes a statement about the culture as a whole. It is not concerned with what any particular strategy or campaign can do, but the total impact of numerous strategies and campaigns over time. Total immersion in television, not selective viewing, is important in cultivation of ways of knowing and images of reality. Indeed, subcultures may retain their separate values, but general overriding images depicted on television will cut across individual social groups and subcultures affecting them all.

The world of television does not necessarily reflect the world of reality. Gerbner's research on prime-time television, for example, has shown that there are three men to every woman on television, there are few Hispanics and those shown are typically minor characters, there are almost entirely middle class characters, and there are three times as many law enforcement officers as blue-collar workers. One of the most interesting outcomes of television cultivation is the "mean world syn-

58. George Gerbner, Larry Gross, Michael Morgan, and Nancy Signorielli, "Living with Television: The Dynamics of the Cultivation Process," in *Perspectives on Media Effects*, eds. Jennings Bryant and Dolf Zillmann (Hillsdale, N.J.: Lawrence Erlbaum Associates, 1986), pp. 17–40.

59. Ibid., p. 18.

60. Ibid., p. 19.

drome." Although less than one percent of the population are victims of violent crimes in any one-year period, "one lesson viewers derive from heavy exposure to the violence-saturated world of television is that in such a mean and dangerous world, most people 'cannot be trusted' and that most people are 'just looking out for themselves.'"[61]

Over time, culture is essentially homogenized and maintained by television. Television is not a force for change so much as it is a force for stability. Gerbner calls the homogenization effect of television *mainstreaming*: "Mainstreaming makes television the true 20th-century melting pot of the American people."[62]

Although cultivation is a general outcome of television viewing, it is not a universal phenomenon. In fact, different groups are affected differently by cultivation. Clearly, heavy viewers are more "cultivated" in this sense than are light viewers. The nature of one's personal interaction affects the tendency to accept the television reality. For example, adolescents who interact with their parents about television viewing are less likely to be affected by television images than are adolescents who do not talk with their parents about television. Interestingly, people who watch more cable television tend to manifest more mainstreaming than do people who watch less.

This theory, which is bolstered by a decade of research on cultural indicators, calls our attention to the important power of television; however, the cultivation hypothesis has not been without critique. In fact, television researcher Paul Hirsch has spoken out harshly against the cultivation effect. He reanalyzed Gerbner's data and failed to find evidence for cultivation. Hirsch concluded that "acceptance of the cultivation hypothesis as anything more than an interesting but unsupported speculation is premature and unwarranted at this time."[63]

Gerbner and his colleagues have responded to this critique by reaffirming the validity of their findings and concluding that "Hirsch's analysis is flawed, incomplete, and tendentious."[64]

The Agenda-Setting Function

Writing on the agenda-setting function is not new. Scholars have long known that media have the potential for structuring issues for the public. One of the first writers to formalize this idea was Walter Lippman, a foremost American journalist. Lippman is known for his journalistic writing, his speeches, and his social commentary.[65] Lippman takes the view that the public responds not to actual events in the environment but to a pseudoenvironment or, as he describes it, "the pictures in our heads."[66] Lippman's model interposes an image between the audience and the actual environment:

> For the real environment is altogether too big, too complex, and too fleeting for direct acquaintance. We are not equipped to deal with so much subtlety, so much variety, so many permutations and combinations. And altogether we have to act in that environment, we have to reconstruct it on a simpler model before we can manage with it.[67]

In recent years the agenda-setting function has been most completely described by Donald Shaw, Maxwell McCombs, and their colleagues.[68] In their major work on this subject, Shaw and McCombs write about the agenda-setting function:

> Considerable evidence has accumulated that editors and broadcasters play an important part in shaping our social reality as they go about their day-to-day task of choosing and displaying news. . . . This impact of the mass media—the ability to effect cognitive change among individuals, to structure their thinking—has been labeled the agenda-setting function of mass communication. Here may lie the most important effect of

61. Ibid., p. 28.

62. Ibid., p. 31.

63. Paul M. Hirsch, "The 'Scary World' of the Nonviewer and other Anomalies: A Reanalysis of Gerbner et al.'s Findings on Cultivation Analysis," *Communication Research* 7 (1980): 404. See also, Paul M. Hirsch, "On Not Learning from One's Own Mistakes: A Reanalysis of Gerbner et. al.'s Findings on Cultivation Analysis, Part II," *Communication Research* 8 (1981): 3–38.

64. George Gerbner, Larry Gross, Michael Morgan, Nancy Signorielli, "A Curious Journal into the Scary World of Paul Hirsch," *Communication Research* 8 (1981): 39.

65. See, for example, M. Childs and J. Reston (eds.), *Walter Lippmann and His Times* (New York: Harcourt Brace, 1959).

66. Walter Lippmann, *Public Opinion* (New York: Macmillan, 1921).

67. Ibid., p. 16.

68. Donald L. Shaw and Maxwell E. McCombs, *The Emergence of American Political Issues* (St. Paul: West, 1977).

mass communication, its ability to mentally order and organize our world for us. In short, the mass media may not be successful in telling us what to think, but they are stunningly successful in telling us what to think about.[69]

In other words agenda setting establishes the salient *issues* or *images* in the minds of the public. This theory obviously is applicable to political campaigns; consequently, nearly all research on agenda setting has used campaigns as case studies.

Agenda setting occurs because the press must be selective in reporting the news. The news outlets, as gatekeepers of information, make choices about what to report and how to report it. Therefore, what the public knows about the state of affairs at any given time is largely a product of media gatekeeping. Further, we know that how a person votes is determined mainly by what issues the individual believes to be important. For this reason some researchers have come to believe that the issues reported during a candidate's term in office may have more effect on the election than the campaign itself.

The agenda-setting theory is appealing for two reasons. First, it returns a degree of power to the media after an era in which media effects were thought to be minimal. Second, its focus on cognitive effects rather than attitude and opinion change adds a badly needed dimension to effects research. The idea of issue salience as a media effect is intriguing and important.

The basic problem with this line of work is that although the theory is clear in positing a causal link between media and issue salience, the research evidence on this point is not convincing.[70] Research has uncovered a strong correlation between audience and media views on the importance of issues, but it does not demonstrate that media choices cause audience salience. In fact one would argue that the emphasis given to issues in the media is a reflection, not a cause, of audience agendas. This is a chicken-egg issue. A more likely possibility is that

there is an interaction between media and public in terms of the issue agenda.

Theories of Individual Outcomes

The theories summarized in the previous section emphasize societal and cultural outcomes of mass communication. Much research has dealt also with the individual effects of mass communication. In this section we discuss several of the theories that have come out of this tradition. Let us begin with a general discussion of effects research.

The Effects Tradition

The theory of mass communication effects has undergone a curious evolution in this century. Early in the century researchers believed in the "magic bullet" theory of communication effects. Individuals were believed to be directly and heavily influenced by media messages. In other words media were considered to be extremely powerful in shaping public opinion. Then, during the 1950s when the two-step flow hypothesis was popular, media effects were considered to be minimal. Later, in the 1960s, we discovered that the media have effects on audience members but that these effects are mediated by audience variables and are therefore only moderate in strength. Now, after research in the 1970s and the 1980s, scholars have returned to the powerful-effects model, in which the public is considered to be heavily influenced by media. This later research centers on television as the powerful medium.[71]

The reinforcement approach. Early empirical research on the reinforcement approach was integrated most clearly by Joseph Klapper in *The Effects of Mass Communication*.[72] Klapper, in surveying the

69. Ibid., p. 5.

70. Criticism of this work can be found in Severin and Tankard, *Communication Theories*, pp. 253–54.

71. For information on the powerful-effects model, see Elisabeth Noelle-Neumann, "Return to the Concept of Powerful Mass Media," in *Studies of Broadcasting*, eds. H. Eguchi and K. Sata (Tokyo: The Nippon Hoso Kyokii, 1973), pp. 67–112.

72. Joseph T. Klapper, *The Effects of Mass Communication* (Glencoe, Ill.: Free Press, 1960).

literature on mass communication effects, develops the following propositions:

1. Mass communication *ordinarily* does not serve as a necessary and sufficient cause of audience effects, but rather functions among and through a nexus of mediating factors and influences.

2. These mediating factors are such that they typically render mass communication a contributory agent, but not the sole cause, in a process of reinforcing the existing conditions. . . .[73]

Raymond Bauer, in observing the failure of many attempts at persuasion, refers to this phenomenon as the *obstinate audience*.[74] He denies the idea that a direct hypodermic needle effect operates between communicator and audience. Instead, many variables involved in the audience interact to shape effects in various ways.[75] Two of the more important areas of audience mediation are group or interpersonal effects and selectivity. Studies have shown that audience members are selective in their exposure to information.[76] In its simplest form the hypothesis of selective exposure predicts that people in most circumstances will select information consistent with their attitudes and other frames of reference.

The reinforcement approach, which is often referred to as the limited-effects model, was a definite step in the right direction at the time it was in vogue. Compared with the bullet theory, the reinforcement approach viewed mass communication as more complicated than had previously been imagined. It envisioned an audience and situation ripe with mediating variables that would inhibit media effects. The research in this tradition did identify some important mediating variables, completing a more elaborate puzzle than had previously been constructed.

The problem of the limited-effects model is that it maintained a linear, cause-to-effect paradigm for research and theory.[77] It failed to take into account the social forces on the media or the ways that individuals might affect the process. The model remained one of active media and passive audience. In addition the limited-effects model concentrated almost exclusively on attitude and opinion effects, ignoring other kinds of effects and functions. Finally, true to tradition, such research focused on short-term effects of mass communication without questioning whether repeated exposure or time latency might affect the audience.

The work of Klapper and others on limited effects resulted in two general types of response. The first was a rejection of limited effects in favor of powerful effects, and the second was an attempt to explain limited effects in terms of the powers of individual audience members, not of media. These responses are covered in the following sections.

Powerful effects. Perhaps the most vocal spokesperson in favor of powerful effects is Elisabeth Noelle-Neumann.[78] She believes that limited-effects theory has "distorted the interpretation of research findings over the years," and "that the 'dogma of media powerlessness' is no longer tenable."[79] Noelle-Neumann claims that the pendulum, which began swinging the other direction after Klapper's famous work, has now reached its full extension and that most researchers believe that the media indeed have powerful effects.

This critic thinks that the limited-effects model was an ideological response on the part of professional journalists, who did not want to see themselves as manipulative. Most limited-effects researchers were either academic journalists or people who held the media in a free society in high

73. Ibid., p. 8.

74. Raymond Bauer, "The Obstinate Audience: The Influence Process from the Point of View of Social Communication," *American Psychologist* 19 (1964): 319–28.

75. Raymond Bauer, "The Audience," in *Handbook of Communication*, eds. Ithiel de sola Pool, et al. (Chicago: Rand McNally, 1973), pp. 141–52.

76. Studies on selectivity are well summarized in David O. Sears and Jonathan I. Freedman, "Selective Exposure to Information: A Critical Review," *Public Opinion Quarterly* 31 (1967), reprinted in Wilbur Schramm and Donald F. Roberts, *The Process and Effects of Mass Communication* (Urbana: University of Illinois Press, 1971).

77. Criticism of the limited-effects approach can be found in Severin and Tankard, *Communication Theories*, p. 249.

78. Elisabeth Noelle-Neumann, "The Effect of Media on Media Effects Research," *Journal of Communication* 33 (1983): 157–65; Noelle-Neumann, "Return."

79. Noelle-Neumann, "Effect of Media," p. 157.

regard. These individuals were interested in painting a picture of the media as disseminators of information, but not of influence. If they were viewed as important, but not as controlling, the media would continue to have the freedom to investigate and report whatever they felt to be important at a particular time. This interest led to the tendency to "see" limited rather than powerful effects in media research results. This Noelle-Neumann calls "the media's effect on media research."

There are still many who believe that this reaction to limited effects is extreme and oversimple. In the following sections, we review theories that take a more moderate stand than either the limited- or powerful-effects models.

Uses and Gratifications

One of the most popular theories of mass communication is the uses and gratifications approach. Until recently, uses and gratifications were considered to be a general approach to media with little theoretical coherence. In the 1980s, however, some important theoretical codification has taken place, making uses and gratifications a more acceptable theoretical area. We first examine the original idea of uses and gratifications and then take a look at a recent theory in this tradition.

The original idea. The uses and gratifications approach focuses on the consumer, the audience member, rather than the message. This approach begins with the person as an active selector of media communications, a viewpoint different from the one that sees the person as a passive receiver.[80] The basic stance is summarized as follows:

> Compared with classical effects studies, the uses and gratifications approach takes the media consumer rather than the media message as its starting point, and explores his communication behavior in terms of

his direct experience with the media. It views the members of the audience as actively utilizing media contents, rather than being passively acted upon by the media. Thus, it does not assume a direct relationship between messages and effects, but postulates instead that members of the audience put messages to use, and that such usages act as intervening variables in the process of effect.[81]

Thus the paradigm for this approach follows the order person–chosen messages–usage–effect.

The individuals most commonly associated with the uses and gratifications approach are Jay Blumler and Elihu Katz. These authors have outlined a number of basic theoretical and methodological assumptions. Three theoretical assumptions warrant discussion. The first is that the audience of mass communication is active and goal-directed. Unlike most effects theories, uses and gratifications theory assumes that audience members are not passive but take a proactive role in deciding how to use media in their lives. Second, the audience member is largely responsible for choosing media to meet needs. Audience members know their needs and seek out various ways to meet these needs. The third assumption, related to the other two, is that media compete with other sources of need gratification. In other words out of the options that media present, the individual chooses ways to gratify needs.

A theory of uses and gratifications. Philip Palmgreen has written the following of uses and gratifications: "Ten years ago critics argued with some success that such research was basically 'atheoretical.' Today, such an argument would be more difficult to defend . . . the last decade has been a period of rather vigorous theoretical growth for the uses and gratifications approach."[82] In this section we take a look at Palmgreen's own attempt to codify a theory of uses and gratifications. Actually, this summary includes the work of several media researchers, although Palmgreen has pulled it to-

---

80. Elihu Katz, Jay Blumler, and Michael Gurevitch, "Uses of Mass Communication by the Individual," in *Mass Communication Research: Major Issues and Future Directions*, eds. W. Phillips Davidson and Frederick Yu (New York: Praeger Publishers, 1974), pp. 11–35. See also Jay Blumler and Elihu Katz (eds.), *The Uses of Mass Communication* (Beverly Hills: Sage Publications, 1974). See also the entire issue of *Communication Research* 6 (January 1979).

81. Katz, Blumler, and Gurevitch, "Uses," p. 12.
82. Philip Palmgreen, "Uses and Gratifications: A Theoretical Perspective," in *Communication Yearbook 8*, ed. Robert N. Bostrom (Beverly Hills: Sage Publications, 1984), p. 20.

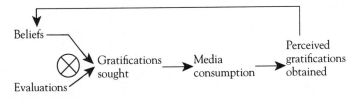

Figure 13-3   Expectancy-value model of gratifications sought and gratifications obtained.

gether, organized it, and enhanced it with his own original work.

Palmgreen bases his approach on expectancy-value theory, which was discussed in Chapter 5. Perhaps the most well-known expectancy-value theorist is Martin Fishbein. According to this theory, people orient themselves to the world according to their expectancies (beliefs) and evaluations. In Chapter 5 we noted that an *attitude* consists of a cluster of beliefs and evaluations. Viewing media gratifications as an application of the general expectancy-value phenomenon, Palmgreen and his colleagues have defined "gratifications sought" in terms of one's beliefs about what a medium can provide and one's evaluation of the medium's content. You might, for example, *believe* that sitcoms provide entertainment, and you *evaluate* entertainment as good. You would then seek gratification of your entertainment needs by watching sitcoms. Your friend, in contrast, might believe that sitcoms provide an unrealistic view of life and evaluate such content as bad. Your friend would avoid viewing sitcoms. More realistically, an individual will have a number of beliefs about a program type, each associated with a particular evaluation. To determine the extent to which the person would seek gratification from that type of program, one would need to take the entire cluster of beliefs and evaluations into account. Palmgreen's formula for this, which mirrors the general expectancy-value formula discussed in Chapter 5, is as follows:

$$GS_i = \sum_{1}^{n} b_i e_i,$$

where GS = gratification sought
b = belief
e = evaluation

The extent to which one would seek gratifications in any segment of the media (a program, a program type, a particular kind of content, an entire medium, and so forth) would be defined by the same formula. As one gains experience consuming this segment of the media, the perceived gratifications obtained will feed back to one's beliefs about that segment for future consideration. This process is therefore cyclical. Figure 13-3 illustrates.[83]

You can easily see that a particular combination of beliefs and evaluations about a media segment could be either positive (in which case one would use that segment) or negative (in which case one would avoid it). Figure 13-4 illustrates this idea.[84] A person who relies on television situation comedies to meet a cluster of needs would have a positive orientation toward that program type, while an individual who avoids sitcoms because of an overall negative cluster of beliefs and evaluations would not rely on this type of program and would, in fact, avoid it.

Although the idea of expectancy and value is used as the basic explanatory mechanism for uses and gratifications, several other causal factors must be taken into account. Palmgreen has put togther a complex model to depict the process of media use that he sees reflected in the research literature. It is clear from this model (Figure 13-5) that uses and gratifications are not a simple linear process.[85] Rather, they involve a multiple causal chain.

One's *beliefs* about what certain media segments can provide are affected by (a) one's culture and

83. Ibid., p. 36.
84. Ibid., p. 39.
85. Ibid., p. 47.

social institutions, including the media themselves, (b) social circumstances such as the availability of media, and (c) certain psychological variables (for example, introversion-extroversion or dogmatism). *Values* are affected by (a) cultural and social factors, (b) needs, and (c) psychological variables. Beliefs and values, as noted before, determine the *gratifications sought*, which in turn determine one's *media consumption behavior*. Depending upon what is consumed and what nonmedia alternatives are undertaken, certain *media effects* will be felt, and these in turn will feed back to one's beliefs about the media.

Criticism. The uses and gratifications approach was like a breath of fresh air in media research. For the first time scholars in this tradition focused on receivers as active participants in the communication process, rather than the traditional viewpoint of the passive, unthinking audience. Indeed, this approach is certainly one of the most popular frameworks for the study of mass communication. However, a good deal of criticism has been published.[86]

The criticism of the uses and gratifications approach can be divided into three major strands.[87] The first set of objections deals with the lack of coherence and theory in the tradition. Although this objection had merit until recently, we have just seen in the previous section that a more unified vision is emerging. In the following section, too, we will see that certain uses and gratifications researchers are developing a theory that connects this work with another important kindred program (see the section on dependency theory).

The second line of criticism focuses on social and political objections, and it comes primarily from Critical Theory. The problem is that uses and grat-

		Evaluation of attribute	
		negative	positive
Belief in possession of attribute	no	negative approach	seeking of alternatives
	yes	true avoidance	positive approach

Figure 13-4 Typology of media motivations.

ifications is so functional in orientation that it ignores the dysfunctions of media in society and culture. It is conservative at heart and sees media primarily as positive ways in which individuals meet their needs, without any attention to the overall negative cultural effects of media in society.

Finally, some critics have objected to the instrumental philosophy of uses and gratifications. Uses and gratifications makes media consumption terribly rational, behavioristic, and individualistic. Individuals are believed to control their media-consuming behavior according to conscious goals. No attention is paid to the ways in which media may be consumed mindlessly or ritualistically. The theory does not study the ways in which media content form and reflect cultural values or patterns of action. In other words, much of our consumption of mass media may not be easily traced to meeting individual needs, but is rather habits of the culture. Also, individuals may not be aware of many of the factors that enter into their consumption choices. Attribution theory, which was covered in greater detail in Chapter 9, suggests that people often misjudge the causes of their own behavior; some research indicates that this principle holds true for media consumption as well.[88]

A noted uses and gratifications researcher, Denis McQuail, takes this third point seriously and proposes that the traditional gratifications model is

86. See especially Philip Elliott, "Uses and Gratifications Research: A Critique and Sociological Alternative," in *The Uses of Mass Communication*, eds. Jay Blumler and Elihu Katz (Beverly Hills: Sage Publications, 1974), pp. 249–68; and David L. Swanson, "Political Communication Research and the Uses and Gratifications Model: A Critique," *Communication Research* 6 (1979): 36–53.

87. Denis McQuail, "With the Benefits of Hindsight: Reflections on Uses and Gratifications Research," *Critical Studies in Mass Communication* 1 (1984): 177–93.

88. See, for example, Dolf Zillmann, "Attribution and Misattribution of Excitatory Reactions," in *New Directions in Attribution Research*, vol. 2, eds. J. H. Harvey, W. J. Ickes, and R. F. Kidd (Hillsdale, N.J.: Lawrence Erlbaum Associates, 1978), pp. 335–68.

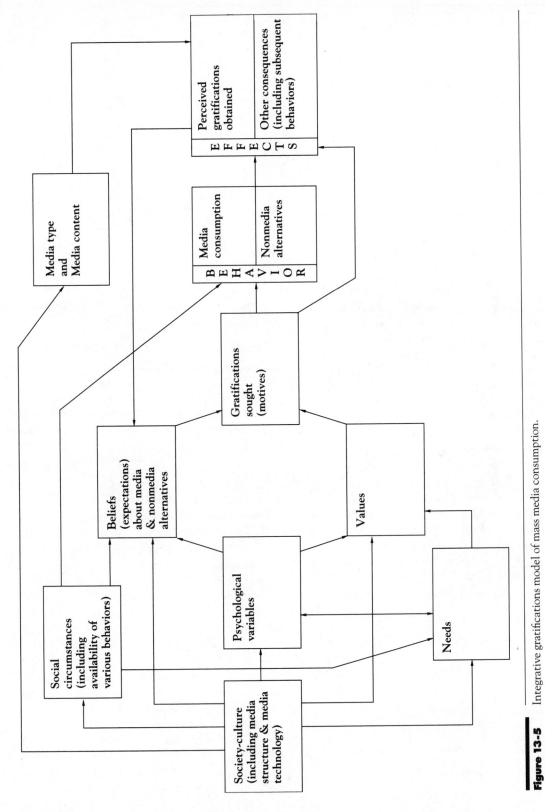

Figure 13-5 Integrative gratifications model of mass media consumption.

only part of what happens in media use.[89] He suggests that although individuals do use media for guidance, surveillance, and information, they also have a generalized arousal need that comes from and is informed by the culture. McQuail suggests that the uses and gratifications process is different between the first, more cognitive process of media use and the second, more cultural use. In the cultural model, individuals use media to achieve general arousal in the form of excitement, sadness, empathy, wonder, and so on.

Dependency Theory

Another recent formulation related to the effects of mass communication is the dependency model of Sandra J. Ball-Rokeach and Melvin L. DeFleur.[90] This model takes a step toward filling in the skeleton provided by the needs and gratifications approach. Like its predecessor this approach also rejects the causal assumptions of the early reinforcement hypothesis. To overcome this weakness, these authors take a broad system approach. In their model they propose an integral relationship among audiences, media, and the larger social system: "It is through taking these sets of variables into account individually, interactively, and systematically that a more adequate understanding of mass communications effects can be gained."[91]

At the center of this theory is the notion that audiences depend on media information to meet needs and attain goals. We see here that this approach is consistent with the basic ideas of the uses model, but unlike the latter, the dependency model assumes a three-way *interaction* among media, audiences, and society. This system interaction is illustrated in Figure 13-6.[92] This diagram indicates that the degree of audience dependency on media information varies. Two sources of variation are outlined. The first is the degree of *structural stability*

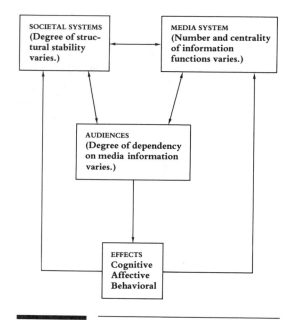

Figure 13-6   Society, media, audience: reciprocal relationships.

From *Communication Research*, "A Dependency Model of Mass-Media Effects," by S. J. Ball-Rokeach and M. L. DeFleur. Copyright © 1976 by Sage Publications. Reprinted by permission of the publisher.

in the societal system, and the second is the *number and centrality* of information functions being served.

We know that the media serve a gamut of functions such as monitoring governmental activities and providing entertainment. For any given group some of these functions are more central or important than others. A group's dependence on information from a medium increases as that medium supplies information that is more central to the group. Another source of dependency variation is social stability. When social change and conflict are high, established institutions, beliefs, and practices are challenged, forcing people to make reevaluations and choices. At such times reliance on the media for information increases.

The dependency theory includes three types of effects: cognitive, affective, and behavioral. Mass communication effects within these three areas are a function of the degree to which audiences are

89. McQuail, "Hindsight."

90. Sandra J. Ball-Rokeach and Melvin L. DeFleur, "A Dependency Model of Mass-Media Effects," *Communication Research* 3 (1976): 3–21. See also DeFleur and Ball-Rokeach, *Theories of Mass Communication* (New York: Longman, 1982), pp. 240–51.

91. Ball-Rokeach and DeFleur, "Dependency," p. 5.

92. Ibid., p. 8.

dependent on media information. Ball-Rokeach and DeFleur outline five types of cognitive effects. The first of these is *ambiguity resolution*. Events in the environment often create ambiguities, leading to a need for additional information. The media themselves often create ambiguity. When ambiguity is present, dependence on media increases. At such times the power of mediated messages to structure understanding or to define situations may be great. At other times when the ambiguity is lessened, this effect may be much reduced.

The second cognitive effect is *attitude formation*. The selectivity and other mediational processes outlined by Klapper and the diffusion theorists probably come into play in this effect. Third, media communications create *agenda setting*. At this point people use the media to decide what the important issues are, to decide what to be concerned about. Agenda setting is an interactional process. Topics are chosen by the media and disseminated through mass channels. From these topics people sort out information according to their individual interests and psychological and social characteristics.

The fourth cognitive effect is *expansion of the belief system*. Information may create a broadening of the number of beliefs within such categories as religion or politics, and it may also increase a person's number of categories or beliefs. The fifth cognitive effect, *value clarification*, may ocur, for example, when the media precipitate value conflict in such areas as civil rights. Faced with conflicts, audience members are motivated to clarify their own values.

Affective effects relate to feelings and emotional responses. Such states as fear, anxiety, morale, or alienation may be affected by mediated information. Effects may also occur in the *behavior* realm. *Activation*, initiating new behavior, and *deactivation*, ceasing old behaviors, may occur as a result of information received from the media.

The important point from dependency theory is that mediated messages affect people only to the degree that persons depend on media information. In a nutshell, "when people do not have social realities that provide adequate frameworks for understanding, acting, and escaping, and when audi-

ences are dependent in these ways on media information received, such messages may have a number of alteration effects."[93]

In their book *Theories of Mass Communication*, Ball-Rokeach and DeFleur present an integrated model of mass communication effects that incorporates many of the ideas of the effects and functions literature summarized in this section. (Figure 13-7).[94] For the most part it is self-explanatory. Notice that the model depicts media as a social system and denotes some of the ways in which aspects of the individual, media, and society interrelate.

The uses and dependency model. The uses and gratifications approach summarized earlier is a limited-effects theory. In other words, it grants individuals much control over how they employ media in their lives. The dependency theory discussed in the previous section takes a moderate stand, but essentially explains mass communication outcomes in terms of media influences. Some have argued that these two positions are not mutually exclusive, that individuals do have some choice, but that societal institutions, including media, also influence audiences. Alan Rubin and Sven Windahl have proposed a joint model called *uses and dependency*:

> Uses and gratifications, then, adds a voluntaristic element to dependency, just as dependency adds a more deterministic flavor to uses and gratifications. This makes a conceptualization of uses and gratifications more situational and context-bound . . . we propose that people's needs and motives vary as they evolve in interactions with societal and communication systems.[95]

In this section we take a closer look at the uses and dependency model. Figure 13-8 illustrates.[96]

This model shows that social institutions and media systems interact with audiences so as to create needs, interests, and motives in the individual.

93. Ibid., p. 19.
94. DeFleur and Ball-Rokeach, *Theories*, p. 252.
95. Alan M. Rubin and Sven Windahl, "The Uses and Dependency Model of Mass Communication," *Critical Studies in Mass Communication* 3 (1986): 186.
96. Ibid., p. 188.

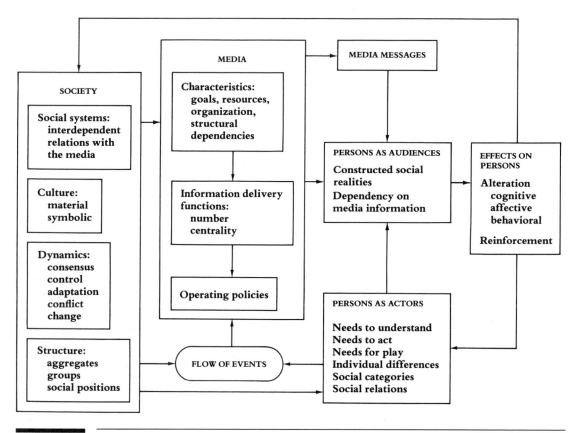

Figure 13-7 Mass media effects on individuals: an integrated model.

From *Theories of Mass Communication*, Fourth Edition, by Melvin L. DeFleur and Sandra Ball-Rokeach. Copyright ©1966, 1970, 1975, and 1982 by Longman, Inc. Reprinted by permission of Longman, Inc., New York.

These in turn influence the individual to choose various media and nonmedia sources of gratification, which may subsequently lead to various dependencies. Consistent with dependency theory, individuals who grow dependent upon a particular segment of the media will be affected cognitively, affectively, and behaviorally by that segment. Those dependencies, then, feed back to broader societal and media systems and institutions.

Dependency itself develops when certain kinds of media content are used to gratify specific needs or when certain media forms are consumed habitually as ritual, to fill time, or as an escape or distraction. People will fulfill their needs with media in different ways, and a single person may use media

differently in different contexts. Further, one's "needs" are not always strictly personal, but may be shaped by the culture or by various social conditions. In other words, individuals' needs, motives, and uses of media are contingent upon outside societal and cultural factors that may be out of the individuals' control. These outside factors act as constraints on what and how media can be used and on the availability of other nonmedia alternatives.

For example, an elderly person who does not drive and has few friends nearby may come to depend upon television in a way that other individuals, whose life situations are different, will not. A commuter may come to rely on radio for information and news. A teenager may become dependent

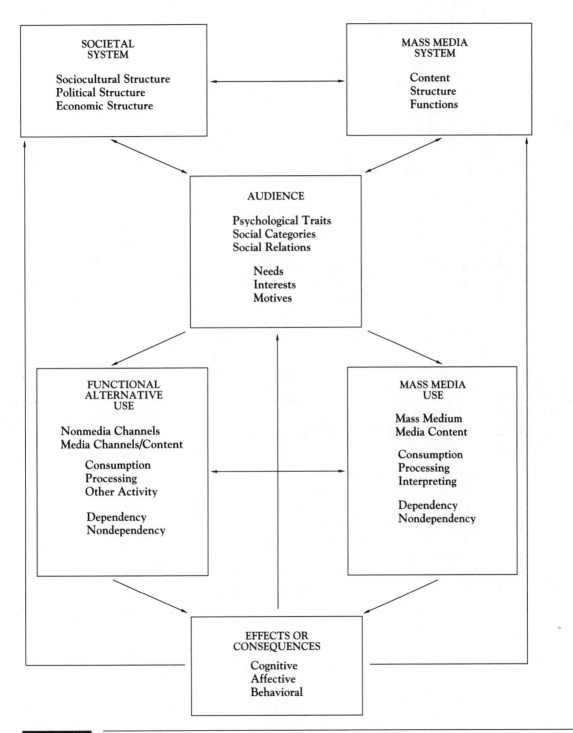

Figure 13-8   The uses and dependency model of mass communication.

From *Critical Studies in Mass Communication*, by Alan M. Rubin and Sven Windahl. Copyright ©1986 by the Speech Communication Association. Reprinted by permission of the author and publisher.

on music videos because of certain norms in the social group. In general, "The more readily available, the greater the perceived instrumentality, and the more socially and culturally acceptable the use of a medium is, the more probable that media use will be regarded as the most appropriate functional alternative."[97] Furthermore, the more alternatives an individual has for gratifying needs, the less dependent he or she will become on any single medium. The number of functional alternatives, however, is not just a matter of individual choice or even of psychological traits, but is limited also by sociocultural factors such as availability of certain media.

Critique. Dependency theory is a major advance in mass communication theory. It accounts for both individual differences in responses to media and general media effects. As a system theory, it shows the complexity of the interactions among the various aspects of the media transaction. The fusion of uses and gratifications and dependency theory provides an even more complete integration. The uses and dependency theory is a good place to end this chapter because it combines a variety of research and theory traditions into a sensible overview model.

Like most of the theories in the last half of this chapter, however, both dependency theory and uses and dependency clash with the Critical Theory school. The conflict of administrative and critical research has come up several times in this chapter. It hits a major stasis point in mass communication theory, indeed all communication theory: To what extent should theory describe and

explain, and to what extent should it reform? That remains an unanswered question.

Integration

Mass communication involves the dissemination of information and influence in society through media and interpersonal channels. It is an integral part of culture and is inseparable from other large-scale social institutions. Media forms like television, film, and print—as well as media content—affect our ways of thinking and seeing the world. Indeed, media participate in the very creation of culture itself, and many believe that media are instrumental in the dissemination of power and domination in society and are thereby instruments of ideology and hegemony.

Mass communication fulfills a variety of functions in society. It provides information, entertainment, and interpretation of events, and it is certainly an instrument of public opinion. The media also appear to set the agenda of what is important in society. The extent and nature of media influence is a matter of dispute. Mass communication reinforces attitudes and opinions, and evidence suggests that media effects are often much more profound than simple reinforcement. At the same time, however, people do make active use of media to gratify their own needs. In fact, as people become dependent on certain types of media and content, the impact of those outlets may increase.

The outcome of the media-influence process is complex. In the final analysis, the outcome of mass communication may be a product of the interaction among various societal structures and individual needs, desires, and dependencies.

97. Ibid., 193.

IV

Capstone

Fourteen

Trends in Communication Theory

The 1980s have proven to be a time of tremendous development and maturity in the field of communication. Along with expansion of curricular programs, increasing research and publication, and popular concern about the topic, this period has seen much growth and progress in communication theory. Neophyte research programs of the last decade have been more fully explicated, new projects have been established, and insights from a variety of traditions have been put together into more unified theories. The many changes in this edition of *Theories of Human Communication* reflect the last several years' advances in theory development.

This expanded theorizing has resulted in many new insights, but it has not resolved the pesky theoretical and philosophical issues that have troubled our field during the past twenty or thirty years. Nor has it led to a unified and accepted theory of communication. In short, we are still a field of many voices, and the concept of communication remains more a loose confederation of ideas than a cohesive perspective. This condition is not necessarily unsatisfactory: It makes ours a stimulating and fascinating field with endless possibilities for exploration and education. Thus, although communication scholarship is diverse and divided, it is not chaotic.

This final chapter reviews five major trends in communication theory in the past decade. The first is the rise of the new paradigm and the recognized legitimacy of both traditional and alternative ways of thinking about communication. The second is

the increasing prominence of mass communication. The third trend is the internationalization of communication theory, and the fourth is the recognition of the centrality of text in communication. Finally, there has been a healthy increase in theories produced within the field of communication and a corresponding independence from the theories of other fields.

The Rise of the New Paradigm

In Chapter 2 we discussed the classical ideal of social science, which we defined as an enterprise that relies on the hypothetico-deductive method for the purpose of discovering the structures of social life. For many years, there has been a set of alternative approaches to this classical idea. Rom Harré and Paul Secord, in their well-known work *The Explanation of Social Behavior*, were perhaps the first to label these "the new paradigm."[1] New paradigm thinking departs from the traditional mode in two primary ways. First, it denies that reality has a singular, static structure to be discovered by research and represented in theory. Second, it distrusts analytic scholarship that breaks complex experiences into causally determined variables. The new paradigm approaches attempt to interpret various episodes of social life and to produce useful concep-

1. Rom Harré and Paul F. Secord, *The Explanation of Social Behavior* (Totowa, N.J.: Littlefield, Adams & Co., 1979), p. 19.

tualizations for understanding and managing them. New paradigm theories strive to capture the intentions and actions of human beings, and they minimize deterministic relations.

To suggest that all communication scholarship fits neatly into these two categories is an oversimplification. The two paradigms should be thought of as families of thought with important similarities and differences within each family. At the same time, there are important differences between them; likening them to the Hatfields and the McCoys is not a strained metaphor. Actually, the term *new paradigm* is a misnomer; there is nothing terribly new about this challenge to traditional science. (Some would prefer the labels *traditional* and *alternative*.) However, in recent years the formal expression of the alternative approach has accentuated its differences from the traditional mode.

The struggle between these two ways of thinking about human social life came to a head in the so-called "metatheory debate" of the 1970s.[2] During this period the issues dividing the paradigms (Chapter 2) became clear. Some scholars believe that these issues are not real and that the differences are chimerical. In my view, however, the issues dividing the traditional and new paradigms are substantial, important, and difficult to resolve. One may adopt different modes of thinking at different points in an investigation for different functional purposes, but the two views cannot be assumed simultaneously, and I see no logical way to fuse them. We are left, then, with truly alternative approaches to the study of communication.

This condition reflects a general crisis in the social sciences. This crisis results from doubt about what the social sciences can and should do. Can social science produce knowledge akin to that in the natural sciences? Can human social experience be validly codified and explained? Has the record of research in the social sciences been effective and credible? Do social scientists, students, and the public have confidence in social science? Sociologist Hubert Blalock doubts the veracity of much current work in these fields:

I have become increasingly disturbed by a number of patterns and trends that characterize my own discipline of sociology. I have also become aware of similar patterns in political science and at least some fields of other social science disciplines as well. In the most general terms these patterns suggest that if we even possessed a sense of direction and the makings of an intellectual core in each of our disciplines, we appear to be moving increasingly in a haphazard fashion with little or no consensus—or even much concern—about the kind of intellectual products our aggregated actions are bringing about.[3]

Psychologist Kenneth Gergen voices a similar view:

In contrast to the mighty oaks of the natural sciences, one might describe the social sciences as a sprawling thicket. The oaks often bring forth widespread smiles of approval; they seem sturdy, powerful, and reliable. In contrast, the sociobehavioral sciences seem to have no clear and dependable product. One becomes perennially entangled in ambiguity.[4]

Interestingly, Blalock's solution is to retreat to and strengthen traditional social science methodology, while Gergen's tactic is to abandon the traditional view and adopt a distinctly new paradigm approach.

The rise of the new paradigm has been given further impetus from the ideological critique of the left. Critical scholars, who adopt a largely Marxist orientation, believe that traditional social science not only misses the opportunity to investigate the dysfunctions of power distribution, but in fact is a tool of the very system of domination itself.[5] Critical scholars often term traditional social science "administrative," implying that it aims to provide instruments for the administration of the power elite in society.[6] The critics have by and large adopted a new paradigm approach, though they have added an important critical dimension to it.

2. See, for example, the special issue of *Communication Quarterly*, vol. 25, no. 1 (1977).

3. Hubert M. Blalock, *Basic Dilemmas in the Social Sciences* (Beverly Hills: Sage Publications, 1984), p. 30.

4. Kenneth Gergen, Toward Transformation in Social Knowledge (New York: Springer-Verlag, 1982), p. 3.

5. See, for example, Brian Fay, *Social Theory and Political Practice* (London: George Allen & Unwin, 1975).

6. See, for example, William H. Melody and Robin E. Mansell, "The Debate over Critical vs. Administrative Research: Circularity or Challenge," *Journal of Communication* 33 (1983): 103–16.

Those who adopt the new paradigm imply in a Kuhnian sense (Chapter 2) that this approach will replace the older "normal science" of the traditional mode. I do not believe this will happen. Instead, the recent formal expression of the alternative paradigm and its clash with the traditional approach has resulted in the recognition of both scholarships as legitimate and beneficial. Because of the diversity of interest and background among scholars in the field, both schools of thought will remain popular and will continue to provide choices for ways in which to understand the communication process.

The Prevalence of Mass Communication Theory

Another trend in communication theory is the increasing popularity of mass communication. Although it would be an overstatement to say that mass communication dominates the field, there is no question that research and theory development in this area is on the rise. Our chapter on mass communication theory (Chapter 13) does not by itself adequately reflect the balance of mass communication work in relation to other areas of the field. Indeed, many of the theories presented in other chapters have also been applied to mass communication, and many of these originated in mass communication research.

The increasing popularity of mass communication scholarship is no surprise. Rapid growth of new technology makes work in this area especially interesting and important. The ubiquity of mass media in modern life necessitates questions of their nature and impact and demands research and theory development. In many cases these questions are associated with policy concerns relevant to public and commercial support for media and media regulation and control. Consequently, much of this work is of significant practical interest. The rise of cultural studies and institutional research in Europe and elsewhere has centered on the mass media as producers of culture and as instruments of domination and power. As these lines of research have become more popular, the interest in mass communication has spread correspondingly.

Another impetus to mass communication research and theory has been the expanding student interest. Today's students, whose lives have revolved around the electronic media, perceive the broadcast media to be important and to offer many career opportunities. As undergraduate programs in media studies have exploded, a corresponding need for larger graduate programs has also come about, leading to more and more theoretical interest in the mass media.

This trend does not mean that other communication concerns are declining. To the contrary, scholarly work and curricular programs in such areas as interpersonal and organizational communication is alive and thriving. In fact, an unfortunate aspect of the mass communication trend is that for many media scholars, *communication* means *mass communication*, with little or no acknowledgment of the important work being done in other areas of the field, or worse, inattention to the central processes that are common to all forms of communication. Indeed, more work needs to be done on the ways in which research and theory from a variety of areas support and inform one another.

The Internationalization of Communication Theory

Although for many years communication research has been conducted in countries other than the United States, until recently American communication scholars acted as though everything known about communication had been produced in North America. Indeed, the first edition of this book included almost no work outside the United States. One of the most important developments in the last decade has been the "discovery" of research and theory from Europe and Latin America.

As the name implies, the International Communication Association (ICA), which is admittedly dominated by scholars from the United States, acknowledges the importance of worldwide cooperation in communication research. Recently, the association has made greater attempts to integrate work done outside the United States into the field. Every fourth year the association sponsors a conference outside the U.S., and the association's newsletter now has a regular international column. ICA divisions are encouraged to include international panels as a regular feature of their convention programs. Another example of the growing interest in the communication work abroad is Sage Publications' sponsorship of a journal entitled *European Journal of Communication*.

The American "discovery" of European contributions has occurred on at least three fronts. The first is in the study of language. European structuralists like Saussure have had a significant impact on American communication thinking for many years, although we have not always been aware of these influences. The works of other scholars such as Eco, Derrida, Foucault, Habermas, and Ricoeur have been imported into the American communication field relatively recently.

The second area of internationalization has been in hermeneutics and phenomenology. Although European philosophy has been widely studied and applied in philosophical circles in this country for many years, this impact has not been felt much in communication until philosophy itself became more popular in the field in the mid-1970s. Hermeneutic and phenomenological views brought fresh insights to communication, as they challenged many old truisms.

Finally, Critical Theory and cultural studies in Europe have been increasingly explored by mass communication scholars in the United States. Although a basic United States-Europe split seems to exist among mass communication scholars, it is clear from the issue of *Journal of Communication* entitled "Ferment in the Field" that both sides have taken one another into account and are aware of their differences in this regard.

The Centrality of Text

A fourth trend in communication theory is increasing interest in language and text. Although nonverbal communication, which was immensely popular in the 1970s, is still an important area of investigation, the 1980s has been a time of renewed interest in language. This interest has centered on discourse and text. The study of texts has traditionally been an important part of humanistic scholarship, especially in such areas as literary criticism and Biblical studies. It is, however, a relatively recent addition to the communication literature.

The application of these ideas to communication has arisen from the basic belief that texts are the products of human communication, and as such, constitute a crucial element in the communication process. This emphasis has led to a movement away from person-centered theory to text-centered theory. The change does not mean that people are viewed as insignificant, only that the structure of human talk should also be an essential focus of our study.

We see this movement in several areas. First, conversation analysis focuses on the talk produced by people in interaction—its organization and management. Discourse studies recognize that human beings somehow manage their talk in conversation, and conversation analysts look at the actual structure of the talk for insights into how this is done.

Semiotics has been primarily interested in the ways in which signs are generated and understood by individuals; semiotic analyses focus on the ways in which elements of text are used to communicate particular meanings and the ways in which those signs are understood by audiences. While semiotics is interested in how people understand the content of communications in context, text hermeneutics centers on the intrinsic meanings of writings and other recorded communications, apart from any particular audience response. The poststructuralists have taken this view to an extreme; they essentially exclude human intentions from text interpretation and explore the multiple meanings inherent in texts themselves.

Cultural studies have questioned the ways in which texts are cultural productions. Here texts are viewed as instruments for inculcating values and worldviews in society at large. As we have seen, the content of media productions are especially important in this regard.

The Development of Disciplinary Theory

In the concluding chapter to the second edition of this book, I remarked that communication theory is basically multidisciplinary, but that more theory is being produced within the field of communication itself. Now the scale has tipped, and communication theory is primarily a product of those who identify with the field of communication. We once borrowed almost all our theories from fields tangentially concerned with communication; today, most important theories of communication are produced within the field.

This does not mean that we no longer rely on theories produced in psychology, sociology, anthropology, philosophy, and other fields. Indeed, this edition still includes many theories from such areas, and I expect that this multidisciplinary state will remain for many years to come. The difference between today's theory and that of previous times is twofold.

First, there is a substantially greater quantity of theories produced by individuals with doctorates in communication who teach in communication departments. There is simply no longer a need to borrow from other fields to the extent that we once had to. Second, the seminal ideas from other social sciences, which constituted the core of communication theory for many years, now have the status of historical support for more unified, direct theories of communication per se. For example, there are now important rules theories of communication produced by communication scholars. These theories rely on ideas developed out of philosophy and sociology, but they are not theories of rules so much as they are theories of communication that make use of rules concepts. The same is true in relational communication. Formerly, ideas from anthropology and psychiatry formed what we called relational communication theory. Today, we rely more on theories of communication in relationships, produced by communication scholars. These theories incorporate the earlier ideas, but they can be applied much more directly to communication. Similar examples can be found in almost every area of the field.

The increase in communication theory reflects maturity and growth within the field itself. Communication is still a young discipline, but it is no longer in its infancy. The number of university departments designated as some variant of "communication" is large and growing. The number of publication outlets for the field is also on the rise. For example, the Speech Communication Association, the Western Speech Communication Association, and the International Communication Association have recently added or will soon add new journals. Sage Publications has served the field very well by printing numerous monographs on a variety of research programs in communication. Indeed, Sage deserves special credit for the advancement of communication theory. In addition, many other specialized handbooks and other texts have been produced by professional associations, university presses, and other companies.

The growth and development of the field has also been spurred by the popularity of communication among students. Most university departments have experienced large growth in undergraduate majors, especially in mass communication and organizational communication. The emphasis of today's students on career orientation has had much to do with this trend. It is very difficult to predict the trajectory of the field at this point. I am confident, however, that the diversity of research and theory, and the consequent body of knowledge, provides a flexible and functional resource to support changes in almost any direction in the decade ahead.

Bibliography

Chapters One & Two
Communication Theory and Scholarship
Theory in the Process of Inquiry

Achinstein, P. *Laws and Explanation*. New York: Oxford University Press, 1971.

Andersen, Peter A. "The Trait Debate: A Critical Examination of the Individual Differences Paradigm in the Communication Sciences." In *Progress in Communication Sciences*. Edited by B. Dervin and M. J. Voight. Norwood, N.J.: Ablex Publishing, 1986.

Barnlund, Dean C. *Interpersonal Communication: Survey and Studies*. New York: Houghton Mifflin, 1968.

Berger, Charles R. "The Covering Law Perspective as a Theoretical Basis for the Study of Human Communication." *Communication Quarterly* 25 (1977):7–18.

Berger, Peter, and Luckmann, Thomas. *The Social Construction of Reality*. Garden City, N.Y.: Doubleday, 1966.

Black, Max. *Models and Metaphors*. Ithaca, N.Y.: Cornell University Press, 1962.

Blalock, Hubert M. *Basic Dilemmas in the Social Sciences*. Beverly Hills: Sage Publications, 1984.

Bormann, Ernest G. *Communication Theory*. New York: Holt, Rinehart & Winston, 1980.

———. *Theory and Research in the Communication Arts*. New York: Holt, Rinehart & Winston, 1965.

Bowers, John Waite, and Bradac, James J. "Issues in Communication Theory: A Metatheoretical Analysis." In *Communication Yearbook 5*. Edited by Michael Burgoon. New Brunswick, N.J.: Transaction Books, 1982, pp. 1–28.

Brinberg, David, and McGrath, Joseph E. *Validity and the Research Process*. Beverly Hills: Sage Publications, 1985.

Bross, Irwin B. J. *Design for Decision*. New York: Macmillan, 1953.

Brummett, Barry. "Some Implications of 'Process' or 'Intersubjectivity': Postmodern Rhetoric." *Philosophy and Rhetoric* 9 (1976):21–51.

Cronen, Vernon E., and Davis, Leslie K. "Alternative Approaches for the Communication Theorist: Problems in the Laws-Rules-Systems Trichotomy." *Human Communication Research* 4 (1978):120–28.

Cushman, Donald P. "The Rules Perspective as a Theoretical Basis for the Study of Human Communication." *Communication Quarterly* 25 (1977):30–45.

Cushman, Donald P., and Pearce, W. Barnett. "Generality and Necessity in Three Types of Theory about Human Communication, with Special Attention to Rules Theory." *Human Communication Research* 3 (1977):344–53.

Dance, Frank E. X. "The 'Concept' of Communication." *Journal of Communication* 20 (1970):201–10.

Dance, Frank E. X., and Larson, Carl E. *The Functions of Human Communication: A Theoretical Approach*. New York: Holt, Rinehart & Winston, 1976.

Deutsch, Karl W. "On Communication Models in the Social Sciences." *Public Opinion Quarterly* 16 (1952):356–80.

Diefenback, James A. *A Celebration of Subjective Thought*. Carbondale: Southern Illinois University Press, 1984.

Fay, Brian. *Social Theory and Political Practice*. London: George Allen & Unwin, 1975.

Fisher, Aubrey B. *Perspectives on Human Communication*. New York: Macmillan, 1978.

Gerbner, George, ed. *Ferment in the Field*: Special Issue of *Journal of Communication* 33 (Summer 1983).

Gergen, Kenneth J. "The Social Constructionist Movement in Modern Psychology." *American Psychologist* 40 (1985):266–75.

———. *Toward Transformation in Social Knowledge*. New York: Springer-Verlag, 1982.

Gergen, Kenneth J., and Gergen, Mary M. "Explaining Human Conduct: Form and Function." In *Explaining Human Behavior: Consciousness, Human Action and Social Structure*. Beverly Hills: Sage Publications, 1982, pp. 127–54.

Giddens, Anthony. *Profiles and Critiques in Social Theory*. Berkeley: University of California Press, 1983.

Glazer, Nathan. "The Social Sciences in Liberal Education." In *Philosophy of the Curriculum*. Edited by Sidney Hook. Buffalo: Prometheus Books, 1975, pp. 145–58.

Habermas, Juergen. *Knowledge and Human Interests*. Translated by Jeremy J. Shapiro. Boston: Beacon Press, 1971.

Hall, Calvin S., and Lindzey, Gardner. *Theories of Personality*. New York: John Wiley, 1970.

Hamelink, Cees J. "Emancipation or Domestication: Toward a Utopian Science of Communication." *Journal of Communication* 33 (1983):74–79.

Hanson, N. R. *Patterns of Discovery*. Cambridge: At the University Press, 1961.

Harré, R., and Secord, P. F. *The Explanation of Social Behavior*. Totowa, N.J.: Littlefield, Adams & Co., 1973.

Hawes, Leonard C. "Elements of a Model for Communication Processes." *Quarterly Journal of Speech* 59 (1973):11–21.

Holton, Gerald. "Science, Science Teaching, and Rationality." In *The Philosophy of the Curriculum*. Edited by Sidney Hook. Buffalo: Prometheus Books, 1975, pp. 101–18.

Houna, Joseph. "Two Ideals of Scientific Theorizing." In *Communication Yearbook 5*. Edited by Michael Burgoon. New Brunswick, N.J.: Transaction Books, 1982, pp. 29–48.

Jabusch, David M., and Littlejohn, Stephen. *Elements of Speech Communication*. Boston: Houghton Mifflin, 1981.

Jarrett, James L. *The Humanities and Humanistic Education*. Reading, Mass.: Addison-Wesley, 1973.

Kaplan, Abraham. *The Conduct of Inquiry*. San Francisco: Chandler, 1964.

Kerlinger, Fred N. *Foundations of Behavioral Research*. New York: Holt, Rinehart & Winston, 1964.

Kibler, Robert J. "Basic Communication Research Considerations." In *Methods of Research in Communication*. Edited by Philip Emert and William Brooks. Boston: Houghton Mifflin, 1970, pp. 9–50.

Kuhn, Thomas S. *The Structure of Scientific Revolutions*. Chicago: University of Chicago Press, 1970.

Littlejohn, Stephen W. "Epistemology and the Study of Human Communication." Speech Communication Association, New York City, 1980.

———. "An Overview of Contributions to Human Communication Theory from Other Disciplines." In *Human Communication Theory: Comparative Essays*. Edited by Frank E. X. Dance. New York: Harper & Row, 1982, pp. 247–82.

MacIntyre, Alasdair. "Ontology." In *The Encyclopedia of Philosophy*. Edited by Paul Edwards. New York: Macmillan, 1967, vol. 5, pp. 542–43.

Miller, Gerald. "The Current Status of Theory and Research in Interpersonal Communication." *Human Communication Research* 4 (1978):175.

Miller, Gerald E., and Nicholson, Henry. *Communication Inquiry*. Reading, Mass.: Addison-Wesley, 1976.

Monge, Peter R. "The Systems Perspective as a Theoretical Basis for the Study of Human Communication." *Communication Quarterly* 25 (1977):19–29.

Mortensen, C. David. *Communication: The Study of Human Interaction*. New York: McGraw-Hill, 1972.

Pearce, W. Barnett. "Metatheoretical Concerns in Communication." *Communication Quarterly* 25 (1977):3–6.

———. "Scientific Research Methods in Communication and Their Implications for Theory and Research." *Speech Communication in the 20th Century*. Edited by Thomas W. Benson. Carbondale: Southern Illinois University Press, 1985, pp. 255–81.

Pearce, W. Barnett; Cronen, Vernon E.; and Harris, Linda M. "Methodological Consideration in Building Human Communication Theory." In *Human Communication Theory: Comparative Essays*. Edited by Frank E. X. Dance. New York: Harper & Row, 1982, pp. 1–41.

Pepper, Stephen. *World Hypotheses*. Berkeley and Los Angeles: University of California Press, 1942.

Polyani, Michael. *Personal Knowledge*. London: Routledge & Kegan Paul, 1958.

Rorty, Richard. *Philosophy and the Mirror of Nature*. Princeton, N.J.: Princeton University Press, 1979.

Schutz, Alfred. *The Phenomenology of the Social World*. Translated by George Walsh and Frederick Lehnert. Evanston, Ill.: Northwestern University Press, 1967.

Secord, Paul F., ed. *Explaining Human Behavior: Consciousness, Human Action and Social Structure*. Beverly Hills: Sage Publications, 1982.

Snow, C. P. *The Two Cultures and a Second Look*. Cambridge, England: Cambridge University Press, 1964.

von Wright, Georg H. *Explanation and Understanding*. Ithaca, N.Y.: Cornell University Press, 1971.

Wallace, Walter L. *Sociological Theory: An Introduction*. Chicago: Aldine, 1969.

Williams, Kenneth R. "Reflections on a Human Science of Communication." *Journal of Communication* 23 (1973): 239–50.

Winch, Peter. *The Idea of a Social Science and Its Relation to Philosophy*. London: Routledge & Kegan Paul, 1958.

Chapter Three
System Theory

Allport, Gordon W. "The Open System in Personality Theory." In *Modern Systems Research for the Behavioral Scientist*. Edited by Walter Buckley. Chicago: Aldine, 1968, pp. 343–50.

Ashby, W. Ross. "Principles of the Self-Organizing System." In *Principles of Self-Organization*. Edited by Heinz von Foerster and George Zopf. New York: Pergamon Press, 1962, pp. 255–78.

Bar-Hillel, Yehoshua, and Carnap, R. "Semantic Information." *British Journal of the Philosophy of Science* 4 (1953):147–57.

Beach, Wayne. "Stocktaking Open-Systems Research and Theory: A Critique and Proposals for Action." Western Speech Communication Association, Phoenix, November 1977.

Berger, Charles. "The Covering Law Perspective as a Theoretical Basis for the Study of Human Communication." *Communication Quarterly* 75 (1977):7–18.

Bertalanffy, Ludwig. "General Systems Theory: A Critical Review." *General Systems* 7 (1962):1–20.

———. *General Systems Theory: Foundations, Development, Applications*. New York: Braziller, 1968.

Boulding, Kenneth. "General Systems Theory—The Skeleton of Science." *Management Science* 2 (1956):197–208.

Broadhurst, Allan R., and Darnell, Donald K. "An Introduction to Cybernetics and Information Theory." *Quarterly Journal of Speech* 51 (1965):442–53.

Buckley, Walter, ed. *Modern System Research for the Behavioral Scientist*. Chicago: Aldine, 1968.

Buckley, Walter. "Society as a Complex Adaptive System." In *Modern Systems Research for the Behavioral Scientist*. Edited by Walter Buckley. Chicago: Aldine, 1968, pp. 490–513.

———. *Sociology and Modern Systems Theory*. Englewood Cliffs, N.J.: Prentice-Hall, 1967.

Cherry, Colin. *On Human Communication*. New York: Science Editions, 1961, 1978.

Conant, Roger C. "A Vector Theory of Information." In *Communication Yearbook 3*. Edited by Dan Nimmo. New Brunswick, N.J.: Transaction Books, 1979, pp. 177–96.

Crowley, D. J. *Understanding Communication: The Signifying Web*. New York: Gordon and Breach, 1982.

Cushman, Donald. "The Rules Perspective as a Theoretical Basis for the Study of Human Communication." *Communication Quarterly* 25 (1977):30–45.

Delia, Jesse. "Alternative Perspectives for the Study of Human Communication: Critique and Response." *Communication Quarterly* 25 (1977):51–52.

Deutsch, Karl. "Toward a Cybernetic Model of Man and Society." In *Modern Systems Research for the Behavioral*

Scientist. Edited by Walter Buckley. Chicago: Aldine, 1968, pp. 387–400.

Fisher, B. Aubrey. *Perspectives on Human Communication.* New York: Macmillan, 1978.

Fisher, B. Aubrey, and Hawes, Leonard C. "An Interact System Model: Generating a Grounded Theory of Small Groups." *Quarterly Journal of Speech* 57 (1971):444–53.

Garner, Wendell R. *Uncertainty and Structure as Psychological Concepts.* New York: John Wiley, 1962.

General Systems: Yearbook of the Society for General Systems Research, 1956–present (annual).

Giddens, Anthony. *Profiles and Critiques in Social Theory.* Berkeley: University of California Press, 1982.

Grene, Marjorie. *The Knower and the Known.* Berkeley: University of California Press, 1974.

Guilbaud, G. T. *What Is Cybernetics?* New York: Grove Press, 1959.

Hall, A. D., and Fagen, R. E. "Definition of System." *General Systems* 1 (1956):18–28.

Handy, Rollo, and Kurtz, Paul. "A Current Appraisal of the Behavioral Sciences: Information Theory." *American Behavioral Scientist* 7 (1964):99–104.

———. "Information Theory." *American Behavioral Scientist* 7, (1964):99–104.

Harris, Marvin. *Rise of Anthropological Theory.* New York: Thomas Y. Crowell, 1968.

Kauffmann, Walter, ed. *Hegel: Texts and Commentary.* Garden City, N.Y.: Anchor Books, 1966.

Koestler, Arthur. *The Ghost in the Machine.* New York: Macmillan, 1967.

Kolmogoroff, A. N. "Three Approaches to the Quantitative Definition of Information." *Problemy Peredachi Informatisii* 1 (1965):3–11.

Krippendorf, Klaus. "Information Theory." In *Communication and Behavior.* Edited by Gerhard Hanneman and William McEwen. Reading, Mass.: Addison-Wesley, 1975, pp. 351–89.

La Rossa, Ralph. "Interpreting Hierarchical Message Structure." *Journal of Communication* 24 (1974):61–68.

"Ludwig von Bertalanffy." *General Systems* 17 (1972):219–28.

Miller, Gerald R. "The Pervasiveness and Marvelous Complexity of Human Communication: A Note of Skepticism." Keynote address, Fourth Annual Conference in Communication, California State University, Fresno, May 1977.

Monge, Peter. "The Systems Perspective as a Theoretical Basis for the Study of Human Communication." *Communication Quarterly* 25 (1977):19–29.

Pask, Gordon. *An Approach to Cybernetics.* New York: Harper, 1961.

Rapoport, Anatol. "Foreword." In *Modern System Research for the Behavioral Scientist.* Edited by Walter Buckley. Chicago: Aldine, 1968, pp. xiii–xxv.

———. "The Promises and Pitfalls of Information Theory." *Behavioral Science* 1 (1956):303–9.

Rosenbleuth, Arturo; Wiener, Norbert; and Bigelow, Julian. "Behavior, Purpose, and Teleology." *Philosophy of Science* 10 (1943):18–24.

Ruben, Brent D., and Kim, John Y., eds. *General Systems Theory and Human Communication.* Rochelle Park, N.J.: Hayden Book Co., 1975.

Shannon, Claude, and Weaver, Warren. *The Mathematical Theory of Communication.* Urbana: University of Illinois Press, 1949.

Spiegel, John. *Transactions.* New York: Science House, 1971.

Toda, Masanao, and Shuford, Emir H. "Logic of Systems: Introduction to a Formal Theory of Structure." *General Systems* 10 (1965):3–27.

Vickers, Geoffrey. "Is Adaptability Enough?" *Behavioral Science* 4 (1959):219–34.

Wiener, Norbert. *Cybernetics or Control and Communication in the Animal and the Machine.* New York: MIT Press, 1961.

———. *The Human Use of Human Beings: Cybernetics and Society.* Boston: Houghton Mifflin, 1954.

Wilson, Donna. "Forms of Hierarchy: A Selected Bibliography." *General Systems* 14 (1969):3–15.

Young, O. R. "A Survey of General Systems Theory." *General Systems* 9 (1964):61–80.

Chapter Four
Structural Theories of Signs and Meaning

Birdwhistell, Ray. *Introduction of Kinesics.* Louisville: University of Louisville Press, 1952.

———. *Kinesics and Context.* Philadelphia: University of Pennsylvania Press, 1970.

Bloomfield, Leonard. *Language.* New York: Holt, Rinehart & Winston, 1933.

Burgoon, Judee K. "Nonverbal Communication Research in the 1970s: An Overview." In *Communication Yearbook 4.* Edited by Dan Nimmo. New Brunswick, N.J.: Transaction Books, 1980, p. 179.

———. "Nonverbal Signals." In *Handbook of Interpersonal Communication.* Edited by Mark L. Knapp and Gerald R. Miller. Beverly Hills: Sage Publications, 1985, pp. 349–53.

Burgoon, Judee K., and Saine, Thomas. *The Unspoken Dialogue: An Introduction to Nonverbal Communication.* Boston: Houghton Mifflin, 1978.

Chomsky, Noam. "The Models for the Description of Language." *Transactions on Information Theory* vol. 1T-2 (1956):113–24.

Dallmayr, Fred. *Language and Politics.* Notre Dame: University of Notre Dame Press, 1984.

de Saussure, Ferdinand. *Course in General Linguistics.* London: Peter Owen, 1960.

Derrida, Jacques. *Of Grammatology.* Translated by Gayatri Chakravorty Spivak. Baltimore: Johns Hopkins Press, 1974, 1976.

Eco, Umberto. *A Theory of Semiotics.* Bloomington: Indiana University Press, 1976.

———. *Semiotics and the Philosophy of Language.* Bloomington: Indiana University Press, 1984.

Ekman, Paul, and Friesen, Wallace. *Emotion in the Human Face: Guidelines for Research and an Integration of Findings.* New York: Pergamon Press, 1972.

———. "Hand Movements." *Journal of Communication* 22 (1972):353–74.

———. "Nonverbal Behavior in Psychotherapy Research." In *Research in Psychotherapy.* Edited by J. Shlien, vol. III. Washington, D.C.: American Psychological Association, 1968, pp. 179–216.

————. "The Repertoire of Nonverbal Behavior: Categories, Origins, Usage, and Coding." *Semiotica* 1 (1969):49–98.

————. *Unmasking the Face.* Englewood Cliffs, N.J.:Prentice-Hall, 1975.

Fodor, J. A.; Bever, T. G.; and Garrett, M. F. *The Psychology of Language: An Introduction to Psycholinguistics and Generative Grammar.* New York: McGraw-Hill, 1974.

Fodor, J. A.; Jenkins, James; and Saporta, Sol. "Psycholinguistics and Communication Theory." In *Human Communication Theory.* Edited by Frank Dance. New York: Holt, Rinehart & Winston, 1967, pp. 160–201.

Foss, Sonja K.; Foss, Karen A.; and Trapp, Robert. *Contemporary Perspectives on Rhetoric.* Prospect Heights, Ill.: Waveland Press, 1985.

Foucault, Michel. *Power/Knowledge: Selected Interviews and Other Writings 1927–1977.* Translated by Colin Gordon, et al. Edited by Colin Gordon. New York: Pantheon, 1980.

————. *The Archeology of Knowledge.* Translated by A. M. Sheridan Smith. New York: Pantheon, 1972.

————. *The Order of Things: An Archeology of the Human Sciences.* New York: Pantheon, 1970.

Giddens, Anthony. *Central Problems in Social Theory: Action, Structure, and Contradiction in Social Analysis.* Berkeley: University of California Press, 1979.

Hall, Edward T. *The Hidden Dimension.* New York: Random House, 1966.

————. *The Silent Language.* Greenwich, Conn.: Fawcett, 1959.

————. "A System for the Notation of Proxemic Behavior." *American Anthropologist* 65 (1963):1003–26.

Harmon, Gilbert. *On Noam Chomsky: Critical Essays.* Garden City, N.Y.: Anchor Books, 1974.

Harper, Robert G.; Wiess, Arthur; and Motarozzo, Joseph. *Nonverbal Communication: The State of the Art.* New York: John Wiley, 1978.

Harris, Zellig. *Structural Linguistics.* Chicago: University of Chicago Press, 1951.

Harrison, Randall. "Nonverbal Communication." In *Handbook of Communication.* Edited by Ithiel de sola Pool et al. Chicago: Rand McNally, 1973.

Knapp, Mark. *Nonverbal Communication in Human Interaction.* New York: Holt, Rinehart & Winston, 1978.

Knapp, Mark; Wiemann, John; and Daly, John. "Nonverbal Communication: Issues and Appraisal." *Human Communication Research* 4 (1978):271–80.

Morris, Charles. *Signs, Language, and Behavior.* New York: Braziller, 1946.

Ogden, C. K., and Richards, I. A. *The Meaning of Meaning.* London: Kegan, Paul Trench, Trubner, 1923.

Ricoeur, Paul. *Interpretation Theory: Discourse and the Surplus of Meaning.* Fort Worth: Texas Christian University Press, 1976.

Wiener, P. O., ed. *Charles Peirce: Selected Writings.* New York: Dover, 1958.

Chapter Five
Cognitive and Behavioral Theories

Anderson, Norman H. "Integration Theory and Attitude Change." *Psychological Review* 78 (1971):171–206.

Aronson, Elliot. *The Social Animal.* New York: Viking Press, 1972.

Brehm, J. W., and Cohen, A. R. *Explorations in Cognitive Dissonance.* New York: John Wiley, 1962.

Brown, Roger. "Models of Attitude Change." In *New Directions in Psychology.* New York: Holt, Rinehart & Winston, 1962, pp. 1–85.

————. *Social Psychology.* New York: Free Press, 1965.

Burhans, David T. "The Attitude-Behavior Discrepancy Problems: Revisited." *Quarterly Journal of Speech* 57 (1971):418–28.

Carver, C. S., and Scheier, M. F. "Control Theory: A Useful Conceptual Framework for Personality." *Psychology Bulletin* 92 (1982):122–35.

Chapanis, Natalia P., and Chapanis, Alphonse. "Cognitive Dissonance: Five Years Later." *Psychological Bulletin* 61 (1964):21.

Chomsky, Noam. *The Acquisition of Syntax in Children from 5 to 10.* Cambridge: MIT Press, 1969.

————. *Aspects of the Theory of Syntax.* Cambridge: MIT Press, 1965.

————. *Cartesian Linguistics: A Chapter in the History of Rationalist Thought.* New York: Harper & Row, 1966.

————. *Current Issues in Linguistic Theory.* The Hague: Mouton, 1970.

————. *Essays on Form and Interpretation.* New York: North Holland, 1977.

————. *Language and Mind.* New York: Harcourt Brace Jovanovich, 1972.

————. *The Logical Structure of Linguistic Theory.* New York: Plenum Press, 1975.

————. *Problems of Knowledge and Freedom.* New York: Pantheon, 1971.

————. *Reflections on Language.* New York: Pantheon, 1975.

————. *Rules and Representations.* New York: Columbia University Press, 1980.

————. *The Sound Pattern of English.* New York: Harper & Row, 1968.

————. *Studies on Semantics in Generative Grammar.* The Hague: Mouton, 1972.

————. *Syntactic Structures.* The Hague: Mouton, 1957.

————. "Three Models for the Description of Language." *Transactions on Information Theory* vol. 1T-2 (1956):113–24.

————. *Topics in the Theory of Generative Grammar.* The Hague: Mouton, 1966.

Crockett, Walter H. "Cognitive Complexity and Impression Formation." In *Progress in Experimental Personality Research.* Edited by Brendon A. Maher. New York: Academic Press, 1965.

Delia, Jesse G.; O'Keefe, Barbara J.; and O'Keefe, Daniel J. "The Constructivist Approach to Communication." In *Human Communication Theory: Comparative Essays.* Edited by Frank E. X. Dance. New York: Harper & Row, 1982, pp. 147–91.

Festinger, Leon. *A Theory of Cognitive Dissonance.* Stanford: Stanford University Press, 1957.

Fishbein, Martin. "A Behavior Theory Approach to the Relations between Beliefs about an Object and the Attitude Toward the Object." In *Readings in Attitude Theory and Measurement.* Edited by Martin Fishbein. New York: John Wiley, 1967, pp. 389–400.

———. "A Consideration of Beliefs, and Their Role in Attitude Measurement." In *Readings in Attitude Theory and Measurement.* Edited by Martin Fishbein. New York: John Wiley, 1967, pp. 257–66.

———, ed. *Readings in Attitude Theory and Measurement.* New York: John Wiley, 1967.

Fishbein, Martin, and Ajzen, Icek. *Belief, Attitude, Intention, and Behavior.* Reading, Mass.: Addison-Wesley, 1975.

Fishbein, Martin, and Raven, Bertram H. "The AB Scales: An Operational Definition of Belief and Attitude." In *Readings in Attitude Theory and Measurement.* Edited by Martin Fishbein. New York: John Wiley, 1967, pp. 183–89.

Greene, John O. "A Cognitive Approach to Human Communication: An Action Assembly Theory." *Communication Monographs* 51 (1984):289–306.

———. "Evaluating Cognitive Explanations of Communicative Phenomena." *Quarterly Journal of Speech* 70 (1984):241–54.

Hale, Claudia. "Cognitive Complexity-Simplicity as a Determinant of Communication Effectiveness." *Communication Monographs* 47 (1980):304–11.

Harmon, Gilbert. *On Noam Chomsky: Critical Essays.* Garden City, N.Y.: Anchor Books, 1974.

Hull, C. L. *Principles of Behavior: An Introduction to Behavior Theory.* New York: Appleton, 1943.

Kelly, George. *The Psychology of Personal Constructs.* New York: North, 1955.

Kiesler, Charles A.; Collins, Barry E.; and Miller, Norman. *Attitude Change: A Critical Analysis of Theoretical Approaches.* New York: John Wiley, 1969.

Kling, J. W. "Learning: Introductory Survey." In *Woodworth and Schlossberg's Experimental Psychology.* Edited by J. W. Kling and Lorrin Riggs. New York: Holt, Rinehart & Winston, 1971, pp. 551–613.

Leiber, Justin. *Noam Chomsky: A Philosophical Overview.* Boston: Twayne Publishers, 1975.

McCroskey, James C. "The Communication Apprehension Perspective." In *Avoiding Communication: Shyness, Reticence, and Communication Apprehension.* Edited by John A. Daly and James C. McCroskey. Beverly Hills: Sage Publications, 1984, pp. 13–38.

Miller, Gerald R. "Some (Moderately) Apprehensive Thoughts on Avoiding Communication." In *Avoiding Communication: Shyness, Reticence, and Communication Apprehension.* Edited by John A. Daly and James C. McCroskey. Beverly Hills: Sage Publications, 1984, pp. 237–46.

Mortensen, David C. "Human Information Processing." In *Communication: The Study of Interaction.* New York: McGraw-Hill, 1972.

Osgood, Charles. "The Nature and Measurement of Meaning." In *The Semantic Differential Technique.* Edited by James Snider and Charles Osgood. Chicago: Aldine, 1969, pp. 9–10.

———. "On Understanding and Creating Sentences." *American Psychologist* 18 (1963):735–51.

———. "Semantic Differential Technique in the Comparative Study of Cultures." In *The Semantic Differential Technique.* Edited by James Snider and Charles Osgood. Chicago: Aldine, 1969, pp. 303–34.

Osgood, Charles, and Richards, Meredith. "From Yang and Yin to *and* or *but*." *Language* 49 (1973):380–412.

Parks, Malcolm. "Interpersonal Communication and the Quest for Personal Competence." In *Handbook of Interpersonal Communication.* Edited by Mark L. Knapp and Gerald R. Miller. Beverly Hills: Sage Publications, 1985, pp. 171–204.

Petty, Richard E., and Cacioppo, John T. *Attitudes and Persuasion: Classic and Contemporary Approaches.* Dubuque, Iowa: W. C. Brown, 1981.

Planalp, Sally, and Hewes, Dean E. "A Cognitive Approach to Communication Theory: Cogito Ergo Dico?" In *Communication Yearbook 5.* Edited by Michael Burgoon. New Brunswick, N.J.: Transaction Books, 1982, pp. 49–78.

Powers, W. T. *Behavior: The Control of Perception.* Chicago: Aldine, 1973.

Rokeach, Milton. *Beliefs, Attitudes, and Values: A Theory of Organization and Change.* San Francisco: Jossey-Bass, 1969.

———. *The Nature of Human Values.* New York: Free Press, 1973.

Salus, Peter H. *Linguistics.* Indianapolis: Bobbs-Merrill, 1969.

Schroder, Harold M.; Driver, Michael S.; and Streufert, Siegfried. *Human Information Processing: Individuals and Groups Functioning in Complex Social Situations.* New York: Holt, Rinehart & Winston, 1967.

Searles, John. "Chomsky's Revolution in Linguistics." In *On Noam Chomsky: Critical Essays.* Edited by Gilbert Harmon. Garden City, N.Y.: Anchor Books, 1974, pp. 2–33.

Sherif, Muzafer. *Social Interaction—Process and Products.* Chicago: Aldine, 1967.

Sherif, Muzafer, and Cantril, H. *The Psychology of Ego-Involvements.* New York: John Wiley, 1947.

Sherif, Muzafer, and Hovland, Carl I. *Social Judgment.* New Haven: Yale University Press, 1961.

Sherif, Muzafer; Sherif, Carolyn; and Nebergall, Roger. *Attitude and Attitude Change: The Social Judgment-Involvement Approach.* Philadelphia: W. B. Saunders, 1965.

Skinner, B. F. *Cumulative Record: A Selection of Papers*, 3rd edition. New York: Appleton-Century-Crofts, 1972.

———. *Verbal Behavior.* New York: Appleton-Century-Crofts, 1957.

Smith, Mary John. *Persuasion and Human Action.* Belmont, Calif.: Wadsworth, 1982.

Snider, James, and Osgood, Charles, eds. *The Semantic Differential Technique.* Chicago: Aldine, 1969.

Spitzberg, Brian H., and Cupach, William R. *Interpersonal Communication Competence.* Beverly Hills: Sage Publications, 1984.

Watson, J. B. *Psychology from the Standpoint of the Behaviorist.* Philadelphia: J. B. Lippincott, 1919.

Weiss, Robert. "An Extension of Hullian Learning Theory to Persuasive Communication." In *Psychological Foundations of Attitudes.* Edited by Anthony Greenwald, Timothy Brock, and Thomas Ostrom. New York: Academic Press, 1968, pp. 109–45.

———. "Persuasion and the Acquisition of Attitudes: Models from Conditioning and Selective Learning." *Psychological Reports* 11 (1962):709–32.

Werner, H. "The Concept of Development from a Comparative and Organismic Point of View." In *The Concept of Development.* Edited by D. B. Harris. Minneapolis: University of Minnesota Press, 1957.

Zajonc, Robert. "The Concepts of Balance, Congruity, and Dissonance." *Public Opinion Quarterly* 24 (1960):280–96.

Chapter Six
Symbolic Interactionist and Dramatistic Theories

Bales, Robert F. *Personality and Interpersonal Behavior.* New York: Holt, Rinehart & Winston, 1970.

Blumer, Herbert. *Symbolic Interactionism: Perspective and Method.* Englewood Cliffs, N.J.: Prentice-Hall, 1969.

Bormann, Ernest G. *Communication Theory.* New York: Holt, Rinehart & Winston, 1980.

————. "Fantasy and Rhetorical Vision: Ten Years Later." *Quarterly Journal of Speech* 68 (1982):288–305.

————. "Fantasy and Rhetorical Vision: The Rhetorical Criticism of Social Reality." *Quarterly Journal of Speech* 58 (1972):396–407.

————. *The Force of Fantasy: Restoring the American Dream.* Carbondale: Southern Illinois University Press, 1985.

Burke, Kenneth. *Attitudes toward History.* New York: New Republic, 1937.

————. *Counter-Statement.* New York: Harcourt, Brace, 1931.

————. *A Grammar of Motives.* Englewood Cliffs, N.J.: Prentice-Hall, 1945.

————. *Language as Symbolic Action.* Berkeley and Los Angeles: University of California Press, 1966.

————. *Permanence and Change.* New York: New Republic, 1935.

————. *The Philosophy of Literary Form.* Baton Rouge: Louisiana State University Press, 1941.

————. *A Rhetoric of Motives.* Englewood Cliffs, N.J.: Prentice-Hall, 1950.

————. *A Rhetoric of Religion.* Boston: Beacon Press, 1961.

Collins, Randall. "Erving Goffman and the Development of Modern Social Theory." In *The View from Goffman.* Edited by Jason Ditton. New York: St. Martin's Press, 1980, pp. 170–209.

Couch, Carl. "Studying Social Processes." Videotaped presentation, University of Iowa Media Center, Iowa City, 1984.

————. "Symbolic Interaction and Generic Sociological Principles." Paper presented at the Symposium on Symbolic Interaction, Boston, 1979.

Couch, Carl J., and Hintz, Robert, eds. *Constructing Social Life.* Champaign, Ill.: Stipes Publishing Co., 1975.

Cragan, John F., and Shields, Donald C. *Applied Communication Research: A Dramatistic Approach.* Prospect Heights, Ill.: Waveland Press, 1981.

Duncan, Hugh D. "Communication in Society." *Arts in Society* 3 (1964):105.

Foss, Karen A., and Littlejohn, Stephen W. "*The Day After*: Rhetorical Vision in an Ironic Frame." *Critical Studies in Mass Communication* 3 (1986):317–36.

Foss, Sonja K.; Foss, Karen A.; and Trapp, Robert. *Contemporary Perspectives on Rhetoric.* Prospect Heights, Ill.: Waveland Press, 1985.

Goffman, Erving. *Behavior in Public Places.* New York: Free Press, 1963.

————. *Encounters: Two Studies in the Sociology of Interaction.* Indianapolis: Bobbs-Merrill, 1961.

————. *Frame Analysis: An Essay on the Organization of Experience.* Cambridge: Harvard University Press, 1974.

————. *Interaction Ritual: Essays on Face-to-Face Behavior.* Garden City, N.Y.: Doubleday, 1967.

————. *The Presentation of Self in Everyday Life.* Garden City, N.Y.: Doubleday, 1959.

————. *Relations in Public.* New York: Basic Books, 1971.

Gronbeck, Bruce E. "Dramaturgical Theory and Criticism: The State of the Art (or Science?)." *The Western Journal of Speech Communication* 44 (1980):315–30

Hall, Peter M. "Structuring Symbolic Interaction: Communication and Power." In *Communication Yearbook 4.* Edited by Dan Nimmo. New Brunswick, N.J.: Transaction Books, 1980, pp. 49–60.

Hickman, C. A., and Kuhn, Manford. *Individuals, Groups, and Economic Behavior.* New York: Holt, Rinehart & Winston, 1956.

Johnson, C. David, and Picou, J. Stephen. "The Foundations of Symbolic Interactionism Reconsidered." In *Micro-Sociological Theory: Perspectives on Sociological Theory*, vol 2. Edited by H. J. Helle and S. H. Eisenstadt. Beverly Hills: Sage Publications, 1985, pp. 54–70.

Kuhn, Manford H. "Major Trends in Symbolic Interaction Theory in the Past Twenty-Five Years." *The Sociological Quarterly* 5 (1964):61–84.

Kuhn, Manford H., and McPartland, Thomas S. "An Empirical Investigation of Self-Attitudes." *American Sociological Review* 19 (1954):68–76.

Littlejohn, Stephen W. *Theories of Human Communication*, 2nd edition. Belmont, Calif.: Wadsworth, 1983.

Lofland, John. "Interactionist Imagery and Analytic Interruptus." In *Human Nature and Collective Behavior.* Edited by Tamotsu Shibutani. Englewood Cliffs, N.J.: Prentice-Hall, 1970, p. 37.

McPhail, Clark. "Toward a Theory of Collective Behavior." Paper presented at the Symposium on Symbolic Interaction. Columbia, South Carolina, 1978.

Manis, Jerome G., and Meltzer, Bernard N., eds. *Symbolic Interaction.* Boston: Allyn & Bacon, 1978.

Mead, George H. *Mind, Self, and Society.* Chicago: University of Chicago Press, 1934.

Meltzer, Bernard N. "Mead's Social Psychology." In *Symbolic Interaction.* Edited by Jerome Manis and Bernard Meltzer. Boston: Allyn & Bacon, 1972, pp. 4–22.

Meltzer, Bernard N., and Petras, John W. "The Chicago and Iowa Schools of Symbolic Interactionism." In *Human Nature and Collective Behavior.* Edited by Tamotsu Shibutani. Englewood Cliffs, N.J.: Prentice-Hall, 1970.

Meltzer, Bernard N.; Petras, John; and Reynolds, Larry. *Symbolic Interactionism: Genesis, Varieties, and Criticism.* London: Routledge & Kegan Paul, 1975.

Mohrmann, G. P. "An Essay on Fantasy Theme Criticism." *Quarterly Journal of Speech* 68 (1982):109–32.

Morris, Charles. "George H. Mead as Social Psychologist and Social Philosopher." In *Mind, Self, and Society* (Introduction). Chicago: University of Chicago Press, 1934, pp. ix–xxxv.

Rueckert, William, ed. *Critical Responses to Kenneth Burke.* Minneapolis: University of Minnesota Press, 1969.

Tucker, Charles W. "Some Methodological Problems of Kuhn's Self-Theory." *The Sociological Quarterly* 7 (1966):345–58.

Verhoeven, Jef. "Goffman's Frame Analysis and Modern Micro-Sociological Paradigms." In *Micro-Sociological Theory: Perspectives on Sociological Theory*, vol. 2. Edited by H. J. Helle and S. H. Eisenstadt. Beverly Hills: Sage Publications, 1985, pp. 71–100.

Chapter Seven
Theories of Cultural and Social Reality

Agar, Michael. *Speaking of Ethnography*. Beverly Hills: Sage Publications, 1986.

Alvy, K. T. "The Development of Listener Adapted Communication in Grade-School Children from Different Social Class Backgrounds." *Genetic Psychology Monographs* 87 (1973):33–104.

Austin, J. L. *How to Do Things with Words*. Cambridge: Harvard University Press, 1962.

———. *Philosophy of Language*. Englewood Cliffs, N.J.: Prentice-Hall, 1964.

Ayer, A. J. *Wittgenstein*. Chicago: University of Chicago Press, 1985.

Baker, G. P., and Hacker, P. M. S. *Wittgenstein: Meaning and Understanding*. Chicago: University of Chicago Press, 1983.

Berger, Charles R. "The Covering Law Perspective as a Theoretical Base for the Study of Human Communication." *Communication Quarterly* 25 (1977):7–18.

Berger, Peter L., and Luckmann, Thomas. *The Social Construction of Reality: A Treatise in the Sociology of Knowledge*. New York: Doubleday, 1966.

Black, Max. *Models and Metaphors*. Ithaca, N.Y.: Cornell University Press, 1962.

Branham, Robert J., and Pearce, W. Barnett. "Between Text and Context: Toward a Rhetoric of Contextual Reconstruction." *Quarterly Journal of Speech* 71 (1985):19–36.

Buttney, Richard. "The Ascription of Meaning: A Wittgensteinian Perspective." *Quarterly Journal of Speech* 72 (1986):261–73.

Campbell, Paul N. "A Rhetorical View of Locutionary, Illocutionary, and Perlocutionary Acts." *Quarterly Journal of Speech* 59 (1973):284–96.

Cherwitz, Richard A., and Hikins, James W. *Communication and Knowledge: An Investigation in Rhetorical Epistemology*. Columbia: University of South Carolina Press, 1986.

Cronen, Vernon E.; Johnson, Kenneth M.; and Lannamann, John W. "Paradoxes, Double Binds, and Reflexive Loops: An Alternative Theoretical Perspective." *Family Process* 20 (1982):91–112.

Cronen, Vernon; Pearce, W. Barnett; and Harris, Linda. "The Logic of the Coordinated Management of Meaning." *Communication Education* 28 (1979):22–38.

———. "The Coordinated Management of Meaning." In *Comparative Human Communication Theory*. Edited by Frank E. X. Dance. New York: Harper & Row, 1982.

Cushman, Donald P. "The Rules Perspective as a Theoretical Basis for the Study of Human Communication." *Communication Quarterly* 25 (1977):30–45.

Delia, Jesse. "Alternative Perspectives for the Study of Human Communication: Critique and Response." *Communication Quarterly* 25 (1977):54.

Gaines, Robert. "Doing by Saying: Toward a Theory of Perlocution." *Quarterly Journal of Speech* 65 (1979):207–17.

Ganz, Joan. *Rules: A Systematic Study*. The Hague: Mouton, 1971.

Geertz, Clifford. *Local Knowledge: Further Essays in Interpretive Anthropology*. New York: Basic Books, 1983.

Gergen, Kenneth J. "The Social Constructionist Movement in Modern Psychology." *American Psychologist* 49 (1985):266–75.

———. *Toward Transformation in Social Knowledge*. New York: Springer-Verlag, 1982.

Gottlieb, Gidon. *Logic of Choice: An Investigation of the Concepts of Rule and Rationality*. New York: Macmillan, 1968.

Gumb, Raymond D. *Rule-Governed Linguistic Behavior*. Paris: Mouton, 1972.

Harré, Rom. *Personal Being: A Theory for Individual Psychology*. Cambridge: Harvard University Press, 1984.

———. *Social Being: A Theory for Social Behavior*. Totowa, N.J.: Littlefield, Adams & Co., 1979.

Harré, Rom, and Secord, Paul. *The Explanation of Social Behavior*. Totowa, N.J.: Littlefield, Adams & Co., 1972.

Hymes, Dell. *Foundations in Sociolinguistics: An Ethnographic Approach*. Philadelphia: University of Pennsylvania Press, 1974.

Janik, Allan, and Toulmin, Stephen. *Wittgenstein's Vienna*. New York: Simon & Schuster, 1973.

McLaughlin, Margaret L. *Conversation: How Talk is Organized*. Beverly Hills: Sage Publications, 1984.

Pearce, W. Barnett. "The Coordinated Management of Meaning: A Rules Based Theory of Interpersonal Communication." In *Explorations in Interpersonal Communication*. Edited by Gerald R. Miller. Beverly Hills: Sage Publications, 1976, pp. 17–36.

———. "Rules Theories of Communication: Varieties, Limitations, and Potentials." Paper presented at the Speech Communication Association, New York City, 1980.

Pearce, W. Barnett, and Cronen, Vernon. *Communication Action and Meaning*. New York: Praeger Publishers, 1980.

Sankoff, Gillian. *The Social Life of Language*. Philadelphia: University of Pennsylvania Press, 1980.

Sapir, Edward. *Language: An Introduction to the Study of Speech*. New York: Harcourt, Brace & World, 1921.

Schutz, Alfred. *On Phenomenology and Social Relations*. Chicago: University of Chicago Press, 1970.

Searle, John. "Human Communication Theory and the Philosophy of Language: Some Remarks." In *Human Communication Theory*. Edited by Frank Dance. New York: Holt, Rinehart & Winston, 1967, pp. 116–29.

———. *Speech Acts: An Essay in the Philosophy of Language*. Cambridge: Cambridge University Press, 1969.

Shimanoff, Susan B. *Communication Rules: Theory and Research*. Beverly Hills: Sage Publications, 1980.

Shotter, John. *Social Accountability and Selfhood*. Oxford: Basil Blackwell, 1984.

Sigman, Stuart J. "On Communication Rules from a Social Perspective." *Human Communication Research* 7 (1980):37–51.

Silverman, David, and Torode, Brian. *The Material Word: Some Theories of Language and Its Limits*. London: Routledge & Kegan Paul, 1980.

Smith, Mary John. "Cognitive Schemata and Persuasive Communication: Toward a Contingency Rules Theory." In *Communication Yearbook 6*. Edited by Michael Burgoon. Beverly Hills: Sage Publications, 1982, pp. 330–63.

Stewart, John. "Concepts of Language and Meaning: A Comparative Study." *Quarterly Journal of Speech* 58 (1972):123–33.

Whorf, Benjamin L. *Language, Thought, and Reality*. New York: John Wiley, 1956.

Winch, Peter. *The Idea of a Social Science and its Relation to Philosophy*. London: Routledge & Kegan Paul, 1958.

Wittgenstein, Ludwig. *The Blue and Brown Books*. Oxford: Basil Blackwell, 1958.

———. *Philosophical Investigations*. Oxford: Basil Blackwell, 1953.

———. *Tractus Logico-Philosophicus*. London: Routledge & Kegan Paul, 1922.

Chapter Eight
Interpretive and Critical Theories

Ardener, Edwin. "Some Outstanding Problems in the Analysis of Events." Paper presented at the Association of Social Anthropologists' Decennial Conference, 1973.

———. "The 'Problem' Revisited." In *Perceiving Women*. Edited by Shirley Ardener. London: Malaby Press, 1975.

Ardener, Shirley. *Defining Females: The Nature of Women in Society*. New York: John Wiley, 1978.

Bailey, William. "Consciousness and Action/Motion Theories of Communication." *Western Journal of Speech Communication* 50 (1986):74–86.

Bauman, Zygmunt. *Hermeneutics and Social Science*. New York: Columbia University Press, 1978.

Benoit, Pamela J., and Benoit, William L. "Consciousness: The Mindlessness/Mindfulness and Verbal Report Controversies." *Western Journal of Speech Communication* 59 (1986):41–63.

Bernstein, Richard J. *Beyond Objectivism and Relativism: Science, Hermeneutics, and Praxis*. Philadelphia: University of Pennsylvania Press, 1983.

Brock, Bernard L., and Scott, Robert L. *Methods of Rhetorical Criticism*. Detroit: Wayne State University Press, 1980.

Campbell, John Angus. "Hans-Georg Gadamer's Truth and Method." *Quarterly Journal of Speech* 64 (1978):101–22.

Deetz, Stanley. "Conceptualizing Human Understanding: Gadamer's Hermeneutics and American Communication Studies." *Communication Quarterly* 26 (1978):12–23.

———. "Words Without Things: Toward a Social Phenomenology of Language." *Quarterly Journal of Speech* 59 (1973):40–51.

Dilthey, Wilhelm. "The Rise of Hermeneutics." Translated by Frederic Jameson. *New Literary History* 3 (1972):229–44.

Farrel, Thomas B., and Aune, James A. "Critical Theory and Communication: A Selective Literature Review." *Quarterly Journal of Speech* 65 (1979):93–120.

Fay, Brian. *Social Theory and Political Practice*. London: George Allen & Unwin, 1975.

Foss, Karen A., and Foss, Sonja K. "Incorporating the Feminist Perspective in Communication Scholarship: A Research Commentary." In *Doing Research on Women's Communication: Alternative Perspectives in Theory and Method*. Edited by Carole Spitzack and Kathryn Carter. Norwood, N.J.: Ablex, in press.

Foss, Sonja K.; Foss, Karen A.; and Trapp, Robert. *Contemporary Perspectives on Rhetoric*. Prospect Heights, Ill.: Waveland Press, 1985.

Gadamer, Hans-Georg. *Truth and Method*. New York: Herder and Herder, 1975.

Gerbner, George, ed. *Ferment in the Field*: Special Issue of *Journal of Communication* 33 (Summer 1983).

Gergen, Kenneth. *Toward Transformation in Social Knowledge*. New York: Springer-Verlag, 1982.

Giddens, Anthony. "On the Relation of Sociology to Philosophy." In *Explaining Human Behavior: Consciousness, Human Action, and Social Structure*. Edited by Paul F. Secord. Beverly Hills: Sage Publications, 1982.

Gorman, Robert A. *The Dual Vision: Alfred Schutz and the Myth of Phenomenological Social Science*. London: Routledge & Kegan Paul, 1977.

Habermas, Juergen. *Knowledge and Human Interests*. Translated by Jeremy J. Shapiro. Boston: Beacon Press, 1971.

———. *Legitimation Crisis*. Translated by Thomas McCarthy. Boston: Beacon Press, 1975.

———. *The Theory of Communication Action, Volume I: Reason and the Rationalization of Society*. Translated by Thomas McCarthy. Boston: Beacon Press, 1984.

Hamlyn, D. W. "The Concept of Social Reality." In *Explaining Human Behavior: Consciousness, Human Action, and Social Structure*. Edited by Paul F. Secord. Beverly Hills: Sage Publications, 1982, pp. 189–210.

Heidegger, Martin. *An Introduction to Metaphysics*. Translated by Ralph Manheim. New Haven: Yale University Press, 1959.

———. *Being and Time*. Translated by John Macquarrie and Edward Robinson. New York: Harper & Row, 1962.

———. *On the Way to Language*. Translated by Peter Hertz. New York: Harper & Row, 1971.

Husserl, Edmund. *Ideas: General Introduction to Pure Phenomenology*. Translated by W. R. Boyce Gibson. New York: Collier Books, 1962.

———. *Phenomenology and the Crisis of Philosophy*. Translated by Quent in Lauer. New York: Harper, 1965.

Hyde, Michael J. "Transcendental Philosophy and Human Communication." In *Interpersonal Communication*. Edited by Joseph J. Pilotta. Washington, D.C.: Center for Advanced Research in Phenomenology, 1982, pp. 15–34.

James, William. *The Principles of Psychology*, vol. 1. New York: Holt, 1890.

Janson, Sue Curry. "Power and Knowledge: Toward a New Critical Synthesis." *Journal of Communication* 33 (1983):342–54.

Johnson, Fern L. "Coming to Terms with Women's Language." *Quarterly Journal of Speech* 72 (1986):318–52.

Kramarae, Cheris. *Women and Men Speaking: Frameworks for Analysis*. Rowley, Mass.: Newbury House, 1981.

Marx, Karl. *Capital*. Chicago: C. H. Kerr, 1909.

———. *The Communist Manifesto*. London: W. Reeves, 1888.

Merleau-Ponty, Maurice. *The Phenomenology of Perception*. Translated by Colin Smith. London: Routledge & Kegan Paul, 1974.

Motely, Michael T. "Consciousness and Intentionality in Communication: A Preliminary Model and Methodological Approaches." *Western Journal of Speech Communication* 50 (1986):3–23.

Nisbett, R. E., and Wilson, T. D. "Telling More than We Can Know: Verbal Reports on Mental Processes." *Psychological Review* 84 (1977):231–59.

Palmer, Richard D. *Hermeneutics*. Evanston, Ill.: Northwestern University Press, 1969.

Pryor, Robert. "On the Method of Critical Theory and its Implications for a Critical Theory of Communication." In *Phenomenology in Rhetoric and Communication*. Edited by Stanley Deetz. Washington, D.C.: Center for Advanced Research in Phenomenology & University Press of America, 1981, pp. 25–35.

Putnam, Linda L. "In Search of Gender: A Critique of Communication and Sex-Roles Research." *Women's Studies in Communication* 5 (1982):1–9.

Real, Michael. "The Debate on Critical Theory and the Study of Communications." *Journal of Communication* 34 (1984):72–80.

Ricoeur, Paul. *Interpretation Theory: Discourse and the Surplus of Meaning.* Fort Worth: The Texas University Press, 1976.

Rogers, Everett M. "The Empirical and the Critical Schools of Communication Research." In *Communication Yearbook 5.* Edited by Michael Burgoon. New Brunswick, N.J.: Transaction Books, 1982.

Schleiermacher, Friedrich. *Hermeneutik.* Edited by Heinz Kimmerle. Heidelberg: Carl Winter, Universitaetsverlag, 1959.

Schutz, Alfred. *The Phenomenology of the Social World.* Translated by George Walsh and Frederick Lehnert. Evanston, Ill.: Northwestern University Press, 1967.

Shotter, John. *Social Accountability and Selfhood.* New York: Basil Blackwell, 1984.

Slack, Jennifer Daryl, and Allor, Martin. "The Political and Epistemological Constituents of Critical Communication Research." *Journal of Communication* 33 (1983):128–218.

Smythe, Dallas W., and Dinh, Tran Van. "On Critical and Administrative Research: A New Critical Analysis." *Journal of Communication* 33 (1983):117–27.

Stewart, John. "Philosophy of Qualitative Inquiry: Hermeneutic Phenomenology and Communication Research." *Quarterly Journal of Speech* 67 (1981):109–21.

Stolnitz, J. *Aesthetics and Philosophy of Art Criticism: A Critical Introduction.* Boston: Houghton Mifflin, 1960.

Wood, Julia T., and Pearce, W. Barnett. "Sexists, Racists, and Other Classes of Classifiers: Form and Function of '. . . ist' Accusations." *Quarterly Journal of Speech* 66 (1980):239–50.

Chapter Nine
Theories of Interpersonal Communication: Personal and Discourse Processes

Abelson, R. P. "Script Processing in Attitude Formation and Decision Making." In *Cognition and Social Behavior.* Edited by J. S. Carroll and J. W. Payne. Hillsdale, N.J.: Lawrence Erlbaum Associates, 1976, pp. 33–45.

Barnlund, Dean, ed. *Interpersonal Communication: Survey and Studies.* Boston: Houghton Mifflin, 1968.

Berger, C. R.; Gardner, R. R.; Parks, M. R.; Schulman, L.; and Miller, G. R. "Interpersonal Epistemology and Interpersonal Communication." In *Explorations in Interpersonal Communication.* Edited by Gerald R. Miller. Beverly Hills: Sage Publications, 1976, pp. 149–71.

Berger, Charles R., and Bradac, James J. *Language and Social Knowledge: Uncertainty in Interpersonal Relations.* London: Edward Arnold, 1982.

Berger, Charles R., and Calabrese, R. J. "Some Explorations in Initial Interaction and Beyond: Toward a Developmental Theory of Interpersonal Communication." *Human Communication Research* 1 (1975):99–112.

Berger, Charles R., and Douglas, William. "Thought and Talk: 'Excuse Me, But Have I Been Talking to Myself.'" In *Human Communication Theory.* Edited by Frank E. X. Dance. New York: Harper & Row, 1982, pp. 42–60.

Berlyne, Daniel E. "Humanistic Psychology as a Protest Movement." In *Humanistic Psychology: Concepts and Criticisms.*

Edited by Joseph Royce and Leendert P. Mos. New York: Plenum, 1981, p. 261.

Bochner, Arthur P. "The Functions of Human Communication in Interpersonal Bonding." In *Handbook of Rhetorical and Communication Theory.* Edited by Carroll C. Arnold and John Waite Bowers. Boston: Allyn & Bacon, 1984, pp. 544–621.

Cappella, Joseph N. "The Management of Conversations." In *Handbook of Interpersonal Communication.* Edited by Mark L. Knapp and Gerald R. Miller. Beverly Hills: Sage Publications, 1985, pp. 393–439.

Cozby, P. W. "Self-Disclosure: A Literature Review." *Psychological Bulletin* 79 (1973):73–91.

Craig, Robert T., and Tracy, Karen, eds. *Conversational Coherence: Form, Structure, and Strategy.* Beverly Hills: Sage Publications, 1983.

Darnell, Donald, and Brockriede, Wayne. *Persons Communicating.* Englewood Cliffs, N.J.: Prentice-Hall, 1976.

Duval, S., and Wicklund, R. A. *A Theory of Objective Self-Awareness.* New York: Academic Press, 1972.

Ellis, Donald G., and Donohue, William A., eds. *Contemporary Issues in Language and Discourse Processes.* Hillsdale, N.J.: Lawrence Erlbaum Associates, 1986.

Gilbert, Shirley J. "Empirical and Theoretical Extensions of Self-Disclosure." In *Explorations in Interpersonal Communication.* Edited by Gerald Miller. Beverly Hills: Sage Publications, 1976, pp. 197–216.

Grice, H. Paul. "Logic and Conversation." In *Syntax and Semantics,* vol. 3. Edited by P. Cole and J. Morgan. New York: Academic Press, 1975, pp. 41–58.

Hart, Roderick, P., and Burks, Don M. "Rhetorical Sensitivity and Social Interaction." *Speech Monographs* 39 (1972):75–91.

Hart, Roderick P.; Carlson, Robert E.; and Eadie, William F. "Attitudes toward Communication and the Assessment of Rhetorical Sensitivity." *Communication Monographs* 47 (1980):1–22.

Harvey, John K.; Ickes, William J.; and Kidd, Robert F., eds., *New Directions in Attribution Research.* 2 vols. New York: John Wiley, 1976, 1978.

Heider, Fritz. *The Psychology of Interpersonal Relations.* New York: John Wiley, 1958.

Jackson, Sally, and Jacobs, Scott. "Conversational Relevance: Three Experiments on Pragmatic Connectedness in Conversation." In *Communication Yearbook 10.* Newbury Park, Calif.: Sage Publications, 1987, pp. 323–47.

Jacobs, Scott. "Language." In *Handbook of Interpersonal Communication.* Edited by Mark L. Knapp and Gerald R. Miller. Beverly Hills: Sage Publications, 1985, pp. 330–35.

———. "Recent Advances in Discourse Analysis." *Quarterly Journal of Speech* 66 (1980):450–72.

Jacobs, Scott, and Jackson, Sally. "Speech Act Structure in Conversation: Rational Aspects of Pragmatic Coherence." In *Conversational Coherence: Form, Structure, and Strategy.* Edited by Robert T. Craig and Karen Tracy. Beverly Hills: Sage Publications, 1983, pp. 47–66.

———. "Strategy and Structure in Conversational Influence Attempts." *Communication Monographs* 59 (1983):285–304.

Jones, Edward E., et al. *Attribution: Perceiving the Causes of Behavior.* Morristown, N.J.: General Learning Press, 1972.

Jourard, Sidney. *Disclosing Man to Himself.* New York: Van Nostrand Reinhold, 1968.

———. *Self-Disclosure: An Experimental Analysis of the Transparent Self.* New York: John Wiley, 1971.

————. *The Transparent Self.* New York: Van Nostrand, 1971.

Kelley, Harold. *Attribution in Social Interaction.* Morristown, N.J.: General Learning Press, 1971.

————. "Attribution in Social Interaction." In *Attribution: Perceiving the Causes of Behavior.* Morristown, N.J.: General Learning Press, 1972, pp. 1–26.

————. "Attribution Theory in Social Psychology." In *Nebraska Symposium on Motivation,* vol. 15. Edited by David Levine. Lincoln: University of Nebraska Press, 1967, pp. 192–240.

————. *Causal Schemata and the Attribution Process.* Morristown, N.J.: General Learning Press, 1972.

————. "Causal Schemata and the Attribution Process." In *Attribution: Perceiving the Causes of Behavior.* Morristown, N.J.: General Learning Press, 1972, pp. 151–74.

————. "The Processes of Causal Attribution." *American Psychologist* 28 (1973):107–28.

Littlejohn, Stephen W. *Theories of Human Communication,* 2nd edition. Belmont, Calif.: Wadsworth, 1983.

Luft, Joseph. *Of Human Interaction.* Palo Alto: National Press Books, 1969.

McLaughlin, Margaret L. *Conversation: How Talk is Organized.* Beverly Hills: Sage Publications, 1984.

Maslow, Abraham. *The Farther Reaches of Human Nature.* New York: Viking Press, 1971.

Parks, Malcolm R. "Ideology in Interpersonal Communication: Off the Couch and Into the World." In *Communication Yearbook 5.* Edited by Michael Burgoon. New Brunswick, N.J.: Transaction Books, 1982, pp. 79–108.

Rogers, Carl. *On Becoming a Person.* Boston: Houghton Mifflin, 1961.

————. *Client-centered Therapy.* Boston: Houghton Mifflin, 1951, chap. 11.

————. *Counseling and Psychotherapy.* Boston: Houghton Mifflin, 1942.

————. "A Theory of Therapy, Personality, and Interpersonal Relationships, as Developed in the Client-centered Framework." In *Psychology: A Study of Science.* Edited by S. Koch. New York: McGraw-Hill, 1959, vol. 3, pp. 184–256.

Royce, Joseph R., and Mos, Leendert P., eds. *Humanistic Psychology: Concepts and Criticisms.* New York: Plenum, 1981.

Sacks, Harvey; Schegloff, Emanuel; and Jefferson, Gail. "A Simplest Systematics for the Organization of Turn Taking for Conversation." *Language* 50 (1974):696–735.

van Dijk, Teun A. *Macrostructures: An Interdisciplinary Study of Global Structures in Discourse, Interaction, and Cognition.* Hillsdale, N.J.: Lawrence Erlbaum Associates, 1980.

————. *Studies in the Pragmatics of Discourse.* The Hague: Mouton, 1981.

Chapter Ten
Theories of Interpersonal Communication in Relationships

Adams, Katherine L. "The Interactional View: Review and Critique." Paper presented at the convention of the Western Speech Communication Association, Albuquerque, 1983.

Altman, Irwin, and Taylor, Donald. *Social Penetration: The Development of Interpersonal Relationships.* New York: Holt, Rinehart & Winston, 1973.

Applegate, James L., and Leichty, Gregory B. "Managing Interpersonal Relationships: Social Cognitive and Strategic Determinants of Competence." In *Competence in Communication: A Multi-Disciplinary Approach.* Edited by Robert N. Bostrom. Beverly Hills: Sage Publications, 1984, pp. 33–56.

Bateson, Gregory. *Naven.* Stanford: Stanford University Press, 1958.

Bateson, Gregory; Jackson, Donald; Haley, J.; and Weaklund, J. "Toward a Theory of Schizophrenia." *Behavioral Science* 1 (1956):251–64.

Beisecker, Thomas. "Game Theory in Communication Research: A Rejoinder and a Reorientation." *Journal of Communication* 20 (1970):107–20.

Bochner, Arthur. "The Functions of Human Communication in Interpersonal Bonding." In *Handbook of Rhetorical and Communication Theory.* Edited by Carroll C. Arnold and John Waite Bowers. Boston: Allyn & Bacon, 1984, pp. 575–82.

Bochner, Arthur, and Kreuger, Dorothy. "Interpersonal Communication Theory and Research: An Overview of Inscrutable Epistemologies and Muddled Concepts." In *Communication Yearbook 3.* Edited by Dan Nimmo. New Brunswick, N.J.: Transaction Books, 1979, p. 203.

Bostrom, Robert N. "Game Theory in Communication Research." *Journal of Communication* 18 (1968):369–88.

Burgoon, Judee K.; Buller, David B.; Hale, Jerold L.; and deTurck, Mark A. "Relational Messages Associated with Nonverbal Behaviors." *Human Communication Research* 10 (1984):351–78.

Burgoon, Judee K., and Hale, Jerold L. "The Fundamental Topoi of Relational Communication." *Communication Monographs* 51 (1984):193–214.

Davis, Morton D. *Game Theory: A Nontechnical Introduction.* New York: Basic Books, 1970.

DeVito, Joseph. *The Interpersonal Communication Book.* New York: Harper & Row, 1976.

Duck, Steve. "A Topography of Relationship Disengagement and Dissolution." In *Personal Relationships 4: Dissolving Personal Relationships.* London: Academic Press, 1982, pp. 1–30.

————, ed. *Personal Relationships 4: Dissolving Personal Relationships.* London: Academic Press, 1982.

————. *Theory and Practice in Interpersonal Attraction.* New York: Academic Press, 1971.

Frost, Joyce, and Wilmot, William. *Interpersonal Conflict.* Dubuque, Iowa: W. C. Brown, 1978.

Hawes, Leonard C., and Smith, David H. "A Critique of Assumptions Underlying the Study of Communication in Conflict." *Quarterly Journal of Speech* 59 (1973):423–35.

Johnson, David W. "Communication and the Inducement of Cooperative Behavior in Conflicts: A Critical Review." *Speech Monographs* 41 (1974):64–78.

Kelley, Harold, and Thibaut, J. W. *Interpersonal Relations: A Theory of Interdependence.* New York: John Wiley, 1978.

La Gaipa, John J. "Interpersonal Attraction and Social Exchange." In *Theory and Practice in Interpersonal Attraction.* Edited by Steve Duck. New York: Academic Press, 1971, pp. 129–64.

Laing, R. D. *The Politics of Experience.* New York: Pantheon, 1967.

————. *Self and Others.* London: Tavistock, 1969.

Laing, R. D.; Phillipson, H.; and Lee, A. R. *Interpersonal Perception.* New York: Springer, 1966.

Littlejohn, Stephen W. *Theories in Human Communication*, 1st edition. Columbus: Charles E. Merrill, 1978.

Marwell, G., and Schmitt, D. R. "Dimensions of Compliance-Gaining Behavior: An Empirical Analysis." *Sociometry* 30 (1967):350–64.

Millar, Frank E., and Rogers, L. Edna. "A Relational Approach to Interpersonal Communication." In *Explorations in Interpersonal Communication*. Edited by Gerald Miller. Beverly Hills: Sage Publications, 1976, pp. 87–103.

Miller, Gerald R., and Parks, Malcolm R. "Communication in Dissolving Relationships." In *Personal Relationships 4: Dissolving Personal Relationships*. London: Academic Press, 1982, pp. 127–54.

Miller, G. R., and Steinberg, M. *Between People: A New Analysis of Interpersonal Communication*. Chicago: Science Research Associates, 1975.

Miller, G. R., and Sunnafrank, M. J. "All is for One But One is Not for All: A Conceptual Perspective of Interpersonal Communication." In *Human Communication Theory: Comparative Essays*. Edited by Frank E. X. Dance. New York: Harper & Row, 1982, pp. 220–42.

Morton, Teru L., and Douglas, Mary Ann. "Growth of Relationships." In *Personal Relationships 2: Developing Personal Relationships*. Edited by Steve Duck and Robin Gilmour. London: Academic Press, 1981, pp. 3–26.

Newcomb, Theodore. *The Acquaintance Process*. New York: Holt, Rinehart & Winston, 1961.

Parks, Malcolm. "Relational Communication: Theory and Research." *Human Communication Research* 3 (1977):372–81.

Ruesch, Juergen, and Bateson, Gregory. *Communication: The Social Matrix of Society*. New York: Norton, 1951.

Rogers, Edna. "Analyzing Relational Communication: Implications of a Pragmatic Approach." Paper presented at the convention of the Speech Communication Association, Washington, D.C., 1983.

Roloff, Michael E. *Interpersonal Communication: The Social Exchange Approach*. Beverly Hills: Sage Publications, 1981.

Schelling, T. C. *The Strategy of Conflict*. Cambridge: Harvard University Press, 1960.

Sillars, Alan L. "Attributions and Communication in Roommate Conflicts." *Communication Monographs* 47 (1980):180–200.

———. "The Sequential and Distributional Structure of Conflict Interaction as a Function of Attributions Concerning the Locus of Responsibility and Stability of Conflicts." In *Communication Yearbook 4*. Edited by Dan Nimmo. New Brunswick, N.J.: Transaction Books, 1980, pp. 14–75.

Simons, Herbert. "The Carrot and Stick as Handmaidens of Persuasion in Conflict Situations." In *Perspectives on Communication in Social Conflict*. Edited by Gerald Miller and Herbert Simons. Englewood Cliffs, N.J.: Prentice-Hall, 1974, pp. 172–205.

Spitzberg, Brian H., and Cupach, William R. *Interpersonal Communication Competence*. Beverly Hills: Sage Publications, 1984.

Steinfatt, Thomas M. "Communication and Conflict: A Review of New Material." *Human Communication Research* 1 (1974):81–89.

Steinfatt, Thomas M., and Miller, Gerald. "Communication in Game Theoretic Models of Conflict." In *Perspectives on Communication in Social Conflict*. Edited by Gerald Miller and

Herbert Simons. Englewood Cliffs, N.J.: Prentice-Hall, 1974, pp. 14–75.

Thibaut, J. W., and Kelley, H. H. *The Social Psychology of Groups*. New York: John Wiley, 1959.

Von Neumann, J., and Morgenstern, O. *The Theory of Games and Economic Behavior*. Princeton, N.J.: Princeton University Press, 1944.

Watkins, Charles. "An Analytic Model of Conflict." *Speech Monographs* 41 (1974):1–5.

Watzlawick, Paul; Beavin, Janet; and Jackson, Don. *Pragmatics of Human Communication: A Study of Interactional Patterns, Pathologies, and Paradoxes*. New York: Norton, 1967.

Wilder, Carol. "From the Interactional View—A Conversation with Paul Watzlawick." *Journal of Communication* 28 (1978):41–42.

Wilmot, William. "Meta-communication: A Re-examination and Extension." In *Communication Yearbook 4*. Edited by Dan Nimmo. New Brunswick, N.J.: Transaction Books, 1980, pp. 61–69.

Chapter Eleven
Theories of Group Communication

Allport, G. W. "The Genius of Kurt Lewin." *Journal of Personality* 16 (1947):1–10.

Bales, Robert F. *Interaction Process Analysis: A Method for the Study of Small Groups*. Reading, Mass.: Addison-Wesley, 1950.

———. *Personality and Interpersonal Behavior*. New York: Holt, Rinehart & Winston, 1970.

Bales, R. F., and Strodbeck, F. L. "Phases in Group Problem-Solving." *Journal of Abnormal and Social Psychology* 46 (1951):485–95.

Bell, M. A. "Phases in Group Problem-Solving." *Small Group Behavior* 13 (1982):475–95.

Bennis, W. G., and Shepard, H. A. "A Theory of Group Development." *Human Relations* 9 (1956):415–37.

Cattell, Raymond. "Concepts and Methods in the Measurement of Group Syntality." *Psychological Review* 55 (1948):48–63.

Collins, Barry, and Guetzkow, Harold. *A Social Psychology of Group Processes for Decision Making*. New York: John Wiley, 1964.

Courtright, John A. "A Laboratory Investigation of Groupthink." *Communication Monographs* 45 (1978):229–46.

Dewey, John. *How We Think*. Boston: Heath, 1910.

Fisher, B. Aubrey. "Decision Emergence: Phases in Group Decision Making." *Speech Monographs* 37 (1970):53–66.

———. "The Functions of Human Communication in the Formation, Maintenance, and Performance of Small Groups." In *Handbook of Rhetorical and Communication Theory*. Edited by Carroll C. Arnold and John Waite Bowers. Boston: Allyn & Bacon, 1984, pp. 622–59.

———. "The Process of Decision Modification in Small Discussion Groups." *Journal of Communication* 20 (1970):51–64.

———. *Small Group Decision Making: Communication and the Group Process*. New York: McGraw-Hill, 1980.

Fisher, B. Aubrey, and Hawes, Leonard. "An Interact System Model: Generating a Grounded Theory of Small Groups." *Quarterly Journal of Speech* 57 (1971):444–53.

Follet, Mary Parker. *Creative Experience*. New York: Longmans, Green, 1924.

Giddens, Anthony. *New Rules of Sociological Method.* New York: Basic Books, 1976.

———. *Profiles and Critiques in Social Theory.* Berkeley: University of California Press, 1982.

———. *Studies in Social and Political Theory.* New York: Basic Books, 1977.

Gouran, Dennis S. "The Paradigm of Unfulfilled Promise: A Critical Examination of the History of Research on Small Groups in Speech Communication." In *Speech Communication in the 20th Century.* Edited by Thomas W. Benson. Carbondale: Southern Illinois University Press, 1985, pp. 90–108.

Gouran, Dennis S., and Hirokawa, Randy Y. "Counteractive Functions of Communication in Effective Group Decision-Making." In *Communication and Group Decision-Making.* Edited by Randy Y. Hirokawa and Marshall Scott Poole. Beverly Hills: Sage Publications, 1986, pp. 81–92.

Hall, Calvin S., and Lindzey, Gardner. "Lewin's Field Theory." In *Theories of Personality.* New York: John Wiley, 1970, chap. 6.

Hirokawa, Randy Y. "Group Communication and Problem-solving Effectiveness: An Investigation of Group Phases." *Human Communication Research* 9 (1983):291–305.

———. "Group Communication and Problem-solving Effectiveness I: A Critical Review of Inconsistent Findings." *Communication Quarterly* 30 (1982):134–305.

———. "Group Communication and Problem-solving Effectiveness II." *Western Journal of Speech Communication* 47 (1983):59–74.

Hirokawa, Randy Y., and Poole, Marshall Scott, eds. *Communication and Group Decision-Making.* Beverly Hills: Sage Publications, 1986.

Hirokawa, Randy Y., and Scheerhorn, Dirk R. "Communication in Faulty Group Decision-Making." In *Communication and Group Decision-Making.* Edited by Randy Y. Hirokawa and Marshall Scott Poole. Beverly Hills: Sage Publications, 1986, pp. 63–80.

Janis, Irving. *Victims of Groupthink: A Psychological Study of Foreign Decisions and Fiascos.* Boston: Houghton Mifflin, 1967.

Lacoursiere, R. *The Life Cycle of Groups.* New York: Human Sciences Press, 1980.

Lewin, Kurt. *A Dynamic Theory of Personality.* New York: McGraw-Hill, 1935.

———. *Field Theory in Social Science.* New York: Harper & Row, 1951.

———. "Frontiers in Group Dynamics: Concept, Method and Reality in Social Science, Social Equilibria, and Social Change." *Human Relations* 1 (1947):5–41.

———. *Resolving Social Conflicts: Selected Papers on Group Dynamics.* New York: Harper & Row, 1948.

Littlejohn, Stephen W. *Theories of Human Communication,* 2nd edition. Belmont, Calif.: Wadsworth, 1983.

Marrow, Alfred. *The Practical Theorist: The Life and Work of Kurt Lewin.* New York: Basic Books, 1969.

Phillips, Gerald M., and Wood, Julia T., eds. *Emergent Issues in Human Decision Making.* Carbondale: Southern Illinois University Press, 1984.

Poole, Marshall Scott. "Decision Development in Small Groups III: A Multiple Sequence Model of Group Decision Development." *Communication Monographs* 50 (1983):321–42.

Poole, Marshall Scott; Seibold, David R.; and McPhee, Robert D. "Group Decision-Making as a Structurational Process." *Quarterly Journal of Speech* 71 (1985):74–102.

———. "A Structural Approach to Theory-Building in Group Decision-Making Research." In *Communication and Group Decision-Making.* Edited by Randy Y. Hirokawa and Marshall Scott Poole. Beverly Hills: Sage Publications, 1986, pp. 238–40.

Shaw, Marvin. *Group Dynamics: The Psychology of Small Group Behavior.* New York: McGraw-Hill, 1981.

Shepherd. Clovis. *Small Groups: Some Sociological Perspectives.* San Francisco: Chandler, 1964.

Tuckman, B. W. "Developmental Sequence in Small Groups." *Psychological Bulletin* 63 (1965):384–99.

Chapter Twelve
Theories of Organizational Communication

Abrahamsson, Bengt. *Bureaucracy or Participation: The Logic of Organization.* Beverly Hills: Sage Publications, 1977.

Argyris, Chris. *Integrating the Individual and the Organization.* New York: John Wiley, 1964.

———. *Interpersonal Competence and Organizational Effectiveness.* Homewood, Ill.: Irwin, 1962.

———. *Management and Organizational Development.* New York: McGraw-Hill, 1971.

———. *Personality and Organization: The Conflict between System and the Individual.* New York: Harper & Brothers, 1957.

———. "Understanding Human Behavior in Organizations." In *Modern Organization Theory.* Edited by Mason Haire. New York: John Wiley, 1959, pp. 115–54.

Barnard, Chester. *The Functions of the Executive.* Cambridge: Harvard University Press, 1938.

Bendix, Reinhard. *Max Weber: An Intellectual Portrait.* Garden City, N.Y.: Doubleday, 1962.

Berelson, Bernard, and Steiner, Gary A. *Human Behavior: An Inventory of Scientific Findings.* New York: Harcourt, Brace, 1964.

Bitzer, Lloyd. "Aristotle's Enthymeme Revisited." *Quarterly Journal of Speech* 45 (1959):399–408.

Cheney, George. "The Rhetoric of Identification and the Study of Organizational Communication." *Quarterly Journal of Speech* 69 (1983):143–58.

Cooper, Lane. *The Rhetoric of Aristotle.* New York: Meredith, 1932.

Delia, Jesse. "The Logic Fallacy, Cognitive Theory, and the Enthymeme: A Search for the Foundations of Reasoned Discourse." *Quarterly Journal of Speech* 56 (1970):140–48.

Edwards, R. "The Social Relations of Production at the Point of Production." In *Complex Organizations: Critical Perspectives.* Edited by M. Zey-Ferrell and M. Aiken. Glenview, Ill.: Scott, Foresman, 1981.

Eisenstadt, S. N. *Max Weber on Charisma and Institution Building.* Chicago: University of Chicago Press, 1968.

Etzioni, Amatai. *Complex Organizations.* New York: Free Press, 1961.

———. *Modern Organizations.* Englewood Cliffs, N.J.: Prentice-Hall, 1964.

Farace, Richard V.; Monge, Peter R.; and Russell, Hamish. *Communicating and Organizing.* Reading, Mass.: Addison-Wesley, 1977.

Fayol, Henri. *General and Industrial Management.* Translated by Constance Storrs. London: Sir Isaac Pitman & Sons, 1949.

Freund, Julien. *The Sociology of Max Weber.* New York: Pantheon, 1968.

Giddens, Anthony. *Central Problems in Social Theory.* Berkeley: University of California Press, 1979.

———. *Profiles and Critiques in Social Theory.* Berkeley: University of California Press, 1982.

Johnson, H. "A New Conceptualization of Source of Organizational Climate." *Administrative Science Quarterly* 3 (1976):275–92.

Katz, Daniel, and Kahn, Robert. *The Social Psychology of Organizations.* New York: John Wiley, 1966.

Likert, Rensis. *The Human Organization.* New York: McGraw-Hill, 1967.

———. *New Patterns of Management.* New York: McGraw-Hill, 1961.

McPhee, Robert D. "Formal Structure and Organizational Communication." In *Organizational Communication: Traditional Themes and New Directions.* Edited by Robert D. McPhee and Phillip K. Tompkins. Beverly Hills: Sage Publications, 1985, pp. 149–78.

March, James G., and Simon, Herbert. *Organizations.* New York: John Wiley, 1958.

Morgan, Gareth. *Images of Organization.* Beverly Hills: Sage Publications, 1986.

Pacanowsky, Michael E., and O'Donnell-Trujillo, Nick. "Organizational Communication as Cultural Performance." *Communication Monographs* 50 (1983):126–47.

Perrow, Charles. *Complex Organizations: A Critical Essay.* Glenview, Ill.: Scott, Foresman, 1972.

Poole, Marshall Scott. "Communication and Organizational Climates: Review, Critique, and a New Perspective." In *Organizational Communication: Traditional Themes and New Directions.* Edited by Robert D. McPhee and Phillip K. Tompkins. Beverly Hills: Sage Publications, 1985, pp. 79–108.

Poole, Marshall Scott, and McPhee, Robert D. "A Structurational Analysis of the Organizational Climate." In *Communication and Organizations: An Interpretive Approach.* Edited by Linda L. Putnam and Michael E. Pacanowsky. Beverly Hills: Sage Publications, 1983, pp. 195–220.

Simon, Herbert. *Administrative Behavior.* New York: Free Press, 1976.

Strother, George B. "Problems in the Development of a Social Science of Organization." In *The Social Science of Organizations: Four Perspectives.* Edited by H. J. Leavitt. Englewood Cliffs, N.J.: Prentice-Hall, 1963, pp. 1–38.

Taylor, F. *Principles of Scientific Management.* New York: Harper & Row, 1919.

Tompkins, Phillip K., and Cheney, George. "Account Analysis of Organizations: Decision Making and Identification." In *Communication and Organizations: An Interpretive Approach.* Edited by Linda L. Putnam and Michael E. Pacanowsky. Beverly Hills: Sage Publications, 1983, pp. 123–46.

———. "Communication and Unobtrusive Control in Contemporary Organizations." In *Organizational Communication: Traditional Themes and New Directions.* Edited by Robert D. McPhee and Phillip K. Tompkins. Beverly Hills: Sage Publications, 1985, pp. 179–210.

Turner, Victor. *Dramas, Fields, and Metaphors.* Ithaca, N.Y.: Cornell University Press, 1974.

Van Maanen, John, and Barley, Stephen R. "Cultural Organization: Fragments of a Theory." In *Organizational Culture.* Edited by Peter J. Frost, et al. Beverly Hills: Sage Publications, 1985, pp. 31–54.

Waldo, Dwight. "Organization Theory: An Elephantine Problem." *General Systems* 7 (1962):247–60.

Weber, Max. *The Theory of Social and Economic Organizations.* Translated by A. M. Henderson and Talcott Parsons. New York: Oxford University Press, 1947.

Weick, Carl. "Middle Range Theories of Social Systems." *Behavioral Science* 19 (1974):358.

———. *The Social Psychology of Organizing.* Reading, Mass.: Addison-Wesley, 1969.

Chapter Thirteen
Theories of Mass Communication

Anderson, James A. "Mass Communication Theory and Research: An Overview." In *Communication Yearbook I.* Edited by Brent Ruben. New Brunswick, N.J.: Transaction Books, 1977, pp. 279–90.

Ball-Rokeach, Sandra J., and Cantor, Muriel G., eds. *Media, Audience, and Social Structure.* Beverly Hills: Sage Publications, 1986.

Ball-Rokeach, S. J., and Defleur, M. L. "A Dependency Model of Mass-Media Effects." *Communication Research* 3 (1976):3–21.

Bauer, Raymond A. "The Audience." In *Handbook of Communication.* Edited by Ithiel de sola Pool, et al. Chicago: Rand McNally, 1963, pp. 141–52.

———. "The Obstinate Audience: The Influence Process from the Point of View of Social Communication." *American Psychologist* 19 (1964):319–28.

Bauer, Raymond A., and Bauer, Alice H. "America, Mass Society, and Mass Media." *Journal of Social Issues* 16 (1960):3–66.

Becker, Samuel L. "Marxist Approaches to Media Studies: The British Experience." *Critical Studies in Mass Communication* 1 (1984):66–80.

Bell, Daniel. "The Theory of Mass Society." *Commentary* July (1956):75–83.

Blumler, Jay. "Communication and Democracy: The Crisis Beyond and the Ferment Within." *Journal of Communication* 33 (1983):166–73.

———. "The Role of Theory in Uses and Gratifications Studies." *Communication Research* 6 (1979):9–34.

Blumler, Jay, and Katz, Elihu, eds. *The Uses of Mass Communication.* Beverly Hills: Sage Publications, 1974.

Boulding, Kenneth. "The Medium is the Message." In *McLuhan: Hot and Cool.* Edited by Gerald E. Stearn. New York: Dial, 1967, pp. 56–64.

Carey, J. W. "Harold Adams Innis and Marshall McLuhan." *The Antioch Review* 27 (1967):5–39.

Childs, M., and Reston, J., eds. *Walter Lippman and His Times*. New York: Harcourt, Brace, 1959.

Davidson, W. Phillips; Boylan, James; and Yu, Frederick. *Mass Media: Systems and Effects*. New York: Praeger Publishers, 1976.

Davis, Dennis K., and Baran, Stanley J. *Mass Communication and Everyday Life: A Perspective on Theory and Effects*. Belmont, Calif.: Wadsworth, 1981.

DeFleur, Melvin. *Theories of Mass Communication*. New York: McKay, 1966.

DeFleur, Melvin, and Ball-Rokeach, Sandra. *Theories of Mass Communication*. New York: Longman, 1982.

Eco, Umberto. *A Theory of Semiotics*. Bloomington: Indiana University Press, 1976.

Elliott, Philip. "Uses and Gratifications Research: A Critique and Sociological Alternative." In *The Uses of Mass Communication*. Edited by Jay Blumler and Elihu Katz. Beverly Hills: Sage Publications, 1974, pp. 249–68.

Elliott, Philip, and Swanson, David L. "Political Communication Research and the Uses and Gratifications Model: A Critique." *Communication Research* 6 (1979):37–53.

Foley, Joseph M. "Mass Communication Theory and Research: An Overview." In *Communication Yearbook II*. Edited by Brent Ruben. New Brunswick, N.J.: Transaction Books, 1978, pp. 209–14.

Fry, Donald L., and Fry, Virginia H. "A Semiotic Model for the Study of Mass Communication." In *Communication Yearbook 9*. Edited by Margaret L. McLaughlin. Beverly Hills: Sage Publications, 1986, pp. 443–62.

Gerbner, George. "Mass Media and Human Communication Theory." In *Human Communication Theory*. Edited by Frank Dance. New York: Holt, Rinehart & Winston, 1967, pp. 40–60.

Gerbner, George, ed. *Ferment in the Field*: Special Issue of *Journal of Communication* 33 (Summer 1983).

Gerbner, George; Gross, Larry; Morgan, Michael; and Signorielli, Nancy. "A Curious Journal into the Scary World of Paul Hirsch." *Communication Research* 8 (1981):39–72.

———. "Living With Television: The Dynamics of the Cultivation Process." In *Perspectives on Media Effects*. Edited by Jennings Bryant and Dolf Zillmann. Hillsdale, N.J.: Lawrence Erlbaum Associates, 1986, pp. 17–40.

Gronbeck, Bruce. "McLuhan as Rhetorical Theorist." *Journal of Communication* 31 (1981):117–28.

Grossberg, Lawrence. "Strategies of Marxist Cultural Interpretation." *Critical Studies in Mass Communication* 1 (1984):393–421.

Hagerstrand, Torsten. "Diffusion II: The Diffusion of Innovations." In *International Encyclopedia of the Social Sciences*. Vol. 4. Edited by David Sills. New York: Macmillan, 1968.

Hall, Stuart. "Cultural Studies and the Center: Some Problematics and Problems." In *Culture, Media, Language*. Edited by Stuart Hall, Dorothy Hobson, Andrew Lowe, and Paul Willis. London: Hutchinson, 1981. pp. 15–47.

———. "Cultural Studies: Two Paradigms." In *Media, Culture and Society: A Critical Reader*. London: Sage Publications, 1986, pp. 33–40.

Hall, Stuart; Hobson, Dorothy; Lowe, Andrew; and Willis, Paul, eds. *Culture, Media, Language*. London: Hutchinson, 1981.

Harshorne, C., and Weiss, P., eds. *Collected Papers of Charles Sanders Peirce*, vols. 1–6. Cambridge: Harvard University Press, 1931–1934.

Hirsch, Paul M. "The 'Scary World' of the Nonviewer and other Anomalies: A Reanalysis of Gerbner et al.'s Findings on Cultivation Analysis." *Communication Research* 7 (1980):403–56.

Innis, Harold A. *The Bias of Communications*. Toronto: University of Toronto Press, 1951.

———. *Empire and Communication*. Toronto: University of Toronto Press, 1972, 1950.

Katz, Elihu. "Diffusion III: Interpersonal Influence." In *International Encyclopedia of the Social Sciences*. Vol. 4. Edited by David Sills. New York: Macmillan, 1968.

———. "The Two-Step Flow of Communication." *Public Opinion Quarterly* 1957. Reprinted in *Mass Communications*. Wilbur Schramm. Urbana: University of Illinois Press, 1960, pp. 346–65.

Katz, Elihu; Blumler, Jay; and Gurevitch, Michael. "Uses of Mass Communication by the Individual." In *Mass Communication Research: Major Issues and Future Directions*. Edited by W. Phillips Davidson and Frederick Yu. New York: Praeger Publishers, 1974, pp. 11–35.

Katz, Elihu, and Lazarsfeld, Paul F. *Personal Influence: The Part Played by People in the Flow of Mass Communications*. New York: Free Press, 1955.

Kincaid, D. Lawrence. "The Convergence Model of Communication." *East-West Institute Paper No. 18*. Honolulu, 1979.

Kincaid, D. Lawrence; Yum, June Ock; and Woelfel, Joseph. "The Cultural Convergence of Korean Immigrants in Hawaii: An Empirical Test of a Mathematical Theory." *Quality and Quantity* 18 (1983):59–78.

Klapper, Joseph T. *The Effects of Mass Communication*. Glencoe, Ill.: Free Press, 1960.

Kornhauser, W. "Mass Society." In *International Encyclopedia of the Social Sciences*. Vol. 10. New York: Macmillan, 1968, pp. 58–64.

Lasswell, Harold D. "Propaganda." In *The Encyclopedia of the Social Sciences*. Vol. 12. New York: Macmillan, 1934.

———. "The Structure and Function of Communication in Society." In *The Communication of Ideas*. Edited by Lyman Bryson. New York: Institute for Religious and Social Studies, 1948.

"Laws of the Media." *Et Cetera* 34 (1977):173–79.

Lazarsfeld, Paul F. "Public Opinion and the Classical Tradition." In *Mass Media and Communication*. Edited by Charles S. Steinberg. New York: Hastings House, 1966, pp. 79–93.

Lazarsfeld, Paul F.; Berelson, Bernard; and Gaudet, H. *The People's Choice*. New York: Columbia University Press, 1948.

Lazarsfeld, Paul F., and Merton, Robert K. "Mass Communication, Popular Taste, and Organized Social Action." In *The Communication of Ideas*. Edited by Lyman Bryson. New York: Institute for Religious and Social Studies, 1948.

Lippman, Walter. *Public Opinion*. New York: Macmillan, 1921.

McLeod, J.; Becker, L.; and Byrnes, J. "Another Look at the Agenda-setting Function of the Press." *Communication Research* 1 (1974):131–66.

McLuhan, Marshall. "At the Flip Point of Time—The Point of More Return?" *Journal of Communication* 25 (1975):102–6.

———. "At the Moment of Sputnik the Planet Became a

Global Theatre in Which There Are No Spectators but Only Actors." *Journal of Communication* 24 (1974):48–58.

———. "The Brain and the Media: The 'Western' Hemisphere." *Journal of Communication* 28 (1978):54–60.

———. "Communication: McLuhan's Laws of the Media." *Technology and Culture* 16 (1975):74–78.

———. *The Gutenberg Galaxy: The Making of Typographic Man.* Toronto: University of Toronto Press, 1962.

———. "Implications of Cultural Uniformity." In *Superculture: American Popular Culture and Europe.* Edited by C. E. E. Bigsby. Bowling Green: Bowling Green University Popular Press, 1975.

———. "Laws of the Media." *Et Cetera* 34 (1977):173–79.

———. *The Mechanical Bride.* New York: Vanguard Press, 1951.

———. "Misunderstanding the Media's Laws." *Technology and Culture* 17 (1976):263.

———. "The Rise and Fall of Nature." *Journal of Communication* 27 (1977):80–81.

———. *Understanding Media.* New York: McGraw-Hill, 1964.

———. "The Violence of the Media." *The Canadian Forum,* September 1976, pp. 9–12.

McLuhan, Marshall, and Fiore, Quentin. *The Medium is the Massage.* New York: Bantam, 1967.

McQuail, Denis. *Mass Communication Theory: An Introduction.* London: Sage Publications, 1984.

———. *Toward a Sociology of Mass Communication.* London: Collier-Macmillan, 1969.

———. "With the Benefit of Hindsight: Reflections on Uses and Gratifications Research." *Critical Studies in Mass Communication* 1 (1984):177–93.

Noelle-Neumann, Elisabeth. "The Effect of Media on Media Effects Research." *Journal of Communication* 33 (1983):157–65.

———. "Return to the Concept of the Powerful Mass Media." In *Studies of Broadcasting.* Edited by H. Eguchi and K. Sata. Tokyo: Nippon Kyokii, 1973, pp. 67–112.

———. *The Spiral of Silence: Public Opinion—Our Social Skin.* Chicago: University of Chicago Press, 1984.

Palmgreen, Philip. "Uses and Gratifications: A Theoretical Perspective." In *Communication Yearbook 8.* Edited by Robert N. Bostrom. Beverly Hills: Sage Publications, 1984, pp. 20–55.

Rogers, Everett M. *Diffusion of Innovations.* New York: Free Press, 1962.

———. "Mass Media and Interpersonal Communication." In *Handbook of Communication.* Ed. Ithiel de sola Pool, et al. Chicago: Rand McNally, 1973, pp. 290–310.

Rogers, Everett M., and Adhikarya, Ronny. "Diffusion of Innovations: An Up-to-Date Review and Commentary." In *Communication Yearbook III.* Edited by Dan Nimmo. New Brunswick, N.J.: Transaction Books, 1979, pp. 67–82.

Rogers, Everett M., and Kincaid, D. Lawrence. *Communication Networks.* New York: Free Press, 1981.

Rogers, Everett M., and Shoemaker, F. Floyd. *Communication of Innovations, A Cross-Cultural Approach.* New York: Free Press, 1971.

Rogow, Arnold A., ed. *Politics, Personality, and Social Science in the Twentieth Century: Essays in Honor of Harold D. Lasswell.* Chicago: University of Chicago Press, 1969.

Rosengren, Karl E. "Uses and Gratifications: A Paradigm Outlines." In *The Uses of Mass Communication.* Edited by Jay Blumler and Elihu Katz. Beverly Hills: Sage Publications, 1974, pp. 270–71.

Rubin, Alan M., and Windahl, Sven. "The Uses and Dependency Model of Mass Communication." *Critical Studies in Mass Communication* 3 (1986):184–99.

Schramm, Wilbur. "Channels and Audiences." In *Handbook of Communication.* Edited by Ithiel de sola Pool, et al. Chicago: Rand McNally, 1973, pp. 116–40.

———. *Mass Communications.* Urbana: University of Illinois Press, 1960.

———. *Mass Media and National Development.* Stanford: Stanford University Press, 1964.

———. *Men, Messages, and Media: A Look at Human Communication.* New York: Harper & Row, 1973.

Schramm, Wilbur, and Roberts, Donald F. *The Process and Effects of Mass Communication.* Urbana: University of Illinois Press, 1971.

Sears, David O., and Freedman, Jonathan L. "Selective Exposure to Information: A Critical Review." *Public Opinion Quarterly* 1967. Reprinted in *The Process and Effects of Mass Communication.* Wilbur Schramm and Donald F. Roberts. Urbana: University of Illinois Press, 1971, pp. 209–34.

Severin, Werner J., and Tankard, James W. *Communication Theories: Origins, Methods, Uses.* New York: Hastings House, 1979.

Shaw, Donald L., and McCombs, Maxwell E. *The Emergence of American Political Issues.* St. Paul: West Publishing, 1977.

Siebert, Fred S.; Peterson, Theodore; and Schramm, Wilbur. *Four Theories of the Press.* Urbana: University of Illinois Press, 1956.

Stearn, Gerald E., ed. *McLuhan: Hot and Cool.* New York: Dial, 1967.

Swanson, David L. "Political Communication Research and the Uses and Gratifications Model: A Critique." *Communication Research* 6 (1979):37–53.

Tan, Alexis S. *Mass Communication Theories and Research.* Columbus: Grid Publishing, 1981.

Theall, Donald F. *The Medium Is the Rear View Mirror: Understanding McLuhan.* Montreal: McGill University Press, 1971.

Weiss, Walter. "Effects of the Mass Media of Communication." In *The Handbook of Social Psychology.* 2d ed. Edited by Gardner Lindzey and Elliot Aronson. Reading, Mass.: Addison-Wesley, 1969, pp. 77–195.

———. "Mass Communication." *Annual Review of Psychology,* Palo Alto: Annual Review Press, 1971.

Westley, Bruce, and MacLean, Malcolm. "A Conceptual Model for Communication Research." *Journalism Quarterly* 34 (1957):31–38.

White, David M. "The 'Gate Keeper': A Case Study in the Selection of News." *Journalism Quarterly* 27 (1950):383–90.

White, Robert. "Mass Communication and Culture: Transition to a New Paradigm." *Journal of Communication* 33 (1983):279–301.

Williams, Raymond. *Marxism and Literature.* New York: Oxford University Press, 1977.

Wolfe, Tom. "The New Life Out There." In *McLuhan: Hot and Cool.* Edited by Gerald Stearn. New York: Dial, 1967, pp. 15–34.

Wright, Charles R. "Functional Analysis and Mass Communication." *Public Opinion Quarterly* 24 (1960):605–20.

————. *Mass Communication: A Sociological Perspective*. New York: Random House, 1959.

————. "Mass Communication Rediscovered: Its Past and Future in American Sociology." In *Media, Audience, and Social Structure*. Edited by Sandra J. Ball-Rokeach and Muriel G. Cantor. Beverly Hills: Sage Publications, 1986, pp. 22–33.

Zillman, Dolf. "Attribution and Misattribution of Excitatory Reactions." In *New Directions in Attribution Research*, vol. 2. Edited by J. H. Harvey, W. J. Ickes, and R. F. Kidd. Hillsdale, N.J.: Lawrence Erlbaum Associates, 1978, pp. 335–68.

Author Index

Subject Index